Rebel Courts

Rebel Courts

The Administration of Justice by Armed Insurgents

RENÉ PROVOST
McGill University

OXFORD
UNIVERSITY PRESS

OXFORD
UNIVERSITY PRESS

Oxford University Press is a department of the University of Oxford. It furthers the University's objective of excellence in research, scholarship, and education by publishing worldwide. Oxford is a registered trade mark of Oxford University Press in the UK and certain other countries.

Published in the United States of America by Oxford University Press
198 Madison Avenue, New York, NY 10016, United States of America.

Library of Congress Cataloging-in-Publication Data
Names: Provost, René, 1965– author.
Title: Rebel courts : The administration of justice by armed insurgents / René Provost, McGill University.
Description: New York, NY : Oxford University Press, [2021] |
Includes index.
Identifiers: LCCN 2020056003 | ISBN 9780190912222 (hardback) |
ISBN 9780190912239 (Updf) | ISBN 9780190912246 (Epub) | ISBN 9780190912253 (digital-online)
Subjects: LCSH: Insurgency. | Justice, Administration of. | Legitimacy of governments. |
Recognition (International law)
Classification: LCC KZ4058 . P76 2021 | DDC 341.6/90268—dc23
LC record available at https://lccn.loc.gov/2020056003

DOI: 10.1093/oso/9780190912222.001.0001

1 3 5 7 9 8 6 4 2

Printed by Integrated Books International, United States of America

Note to Readers

This publication is designed to provide accurate and authoritative information in regard to the subject matter covered. It is based upon sources believed to be accurate and reliable and is intended to be current as of the time it was written. It is sold with the understanding that the publisher is not engaged in rendering legal, accounting, or other professional services. If legal advice or other expert assistance is required, the services of a competent professional person should be sought. Also, to confirm that the information has not been affected or changed by recent developments, traditional legal research techniques should be used, including checking primary sources where appropriate.

(Based on the Declaration of Principles jointly adopted by a Committee of the American Bar Association and a Committee of Publishers and Associations.)

For SVP,
who does
fieldwork
in the terrain
of legal
imagination

Contents

Acknowledgments xi

Introduction 1
- I. Rebel Governance: Can the Insurgent Rule? 4
- II. Legal Pluralism: Can the Insurgent Speak? 11
- III. Methodology: Talking to Insurgents 16
- IV. Overall Project: Insurgent Jurisprudence 24

1. Rebel Rule of Law and FARC Justice 29
   - I. Rebel Justice in Colombia 30
     - A. The Civil War in Colombia and FARC Governance 31
       - i. The Civil War in Colombia 31
       - ii. FARC Governance 34
     - B. FARC Justice 40
       - i. Evolution of FARC Justice 40
       - ii. FARC Military Justice 43
       - iii. FARC Civilian Justice 47
   - II. Rebel Rule of Law 56
     - A. Fragmented Rule of Law 57
     - B. Rule of Law in Armed Conflict 66
       - i. Human Rights: Derogation and Margin of Appreciation 66
       - ii. Humanitarian Law: Occupation as Hostile Relations 71
     - C. Elements of a Rebel Rule of Law 76
       - i. Broader System of Governance 77
       - ii. Stability and Predictability 81
       - iii. Minimal Fairness 82
       - iv. Narrative of Social Justice 84
   - III. Rebel Justice and Sovereignty 86
     - A. Basis of State Jurisdiction 89
     - B. Exercise of Jurisdiction by Others than the Territorial State 95

2. Legality of Rebel Courts—Islamic State and Taliban Justice 101
   - I. Introduction 101
   - II. Islamic State Justice: A Penchant for Paperwork 103
     - A. Islamic State Governance: "Fun, Food, and Services" 105
     - B. Islamic State Justice 107
   - III. Taliban Motorcycle Justice 118
     - A. Taliban Shadow Governance Post-2001 122
     - B. Taliban Justice 123

IV. Legality of Rebel Courts under International Law 140
A. Categories of Conflicts and Equality of Belligerents 141
i. Legal Categories of Armed Conflicts 141
ii. Equality of Belligerents 144
B. Rebel Courts in Legal Context 149
i. A Spectrum of Obligations 150
(a) From Prohibition to Obligation 151
(b) Duty to Prosecute War Crimes 154
(c) Respect and Ensure Respect of International Humanitarian Law 156
(d) Respect and Secure Human Rights 159
(e) Command Responsibility 164
ii. A Focus on Crimes and a Nexus with the Conflict 167
C. The Constitution of Rebel Courts 180
i. What Constitutes a "Court"? 180
(a) The Idea of a Court 181
(b) Oracles of the Law 184
(c) The Concept of Law 188
(d) Of Courts and Cathedrals 192
ii. "Regularly Constituted" Courts 195
(a) Regularly Constituted Courts in Humanitarian Law 195
(b) Courts Established by Law in Human Rights Law 200
iii. Judicial Guarantees of Independence and Impartiality 202
(a) Fairness as Rightness 203
(b) Institutional Requirements of Independence and Impartiality 206
V. Conclusion 215

3. Rebel Jurisdiction, Due Process, and Tamil Tiger Justice 219
I. Purr Curiam: Tiger Justice in Sri Lanka 220
A. Origins and Evolution of the LTTE 220
B. LTTE Governance 224
C. LTTE Justice 227
i. Evolution and Structure 229
(a) Evolution 229
(b) Structure 233
ii. Judicial Process 237
iii. Legal Practice 239
iv. Applicable Law 241
v. Overall Assessment of LTTE Justice 245
II. The Jurisdiction of Rebel Courts 248
A. The Idea of Rebel Jurisdiction 249
B. Territorial Jurisdiction of Armed Groups 253

C. Subject-Matter Jurisdiction of Armed Groups 257
i. Criminal Law Jurisdiction 260
(a) Applicable Law 260
(b) Treason and Participation in the Conflict 264
(c) Crimes against International Law 271
ii. Civil Law Jurisdiction 274
D. Personal Jurisdiction of Armed Groups 281
III. Due Process in Rebel Courts 289
A. Sources of Applicable Procedural Obligations for Non-State Armed Groups 290
B. Justice under Stress: Due Process in Conflict Zones 297
i. Due Process in War and Peace 298
ii. Due Process before Non-State Courts 303
C. Fair Trial Guarantees before Rebel Courts 308
i. Judicial Independence and Impartiality 310
ii. Right to Be Informed Promptly of the Charges 315
iii. Presumption of Innocence 318
iv. Necessary Rights and Means of Defence 321
(a) Right to Counsel 323
(b) Right to Present a Full Defence 329
(c) Right to a Public Trial 332
(d) *Ne Bis In Idem* 338
v. Individual Criminal Responsibility 341
vi. Principle of Legality 342
vii. Self-Incrimination 347
viii. Right to Judicial and Other Remedies 350

4. The Legal *Rayonnement* of Rebel Justice: Recognition, Complementarity, and Kurdish Courts 355
I. Kurdish Non-State Courts: A Spectrum of Extralegality 356
A. North Kurdistan: The PKK/KCK in Turkey and Iraq 357
i. PKK Governance 357
ii. PKK Justice 361
B. West Kurdistan: The PYD/YPG in Syria 364
i. PYD Governance 364
ii. PYD Justice 367
C. South Kurdistan: The KRG in Iraq 373
i. KRG Governance 373
ii. KRG Justice 376
II. International Recognition: Rebel Courts and International Tribunals 385
A. Insurgent Complementarity: Contextual Approach 388
B. Insurgent Complementarity: Textual Approach 392
i. Article 17(1)(a) and (b)—"A State Which Has Jurisdiction over It" 392
ii. Article 17(1)(c): *Ne Bis In Idem* 396

C. Insurgent Complementarity: Conceptual A
D. International Recognition in the ICC and F
III. Transnational Recognition by Third States
A. Third State Recognition of Rebel Justice
B. Legal Parameters of Recognition by Thir
IV. National Recognition by the Territorial St
V. Transversal Recognition by Other Armed
Conclusion
Index

virus-related closures, they remain a delight to work with. The Faculty of Law of McGill University provided the broader base for this research project. I am indebted to the many colleagues who over the years have made this place an ebullient cauldron of ideas, including our sorely missed colleagues Patrick Glenn and Rod Macdonald who did so much to expand our normative horizon.

The Pierre Elliott Trudeau Foundation in 2015 awarded me not only a generous prize but also a large research fellowship for me to use basically as I saw fit. It provided both the impetus for the idea of this project and the essential financial lifeblood to carry it out. Each year, the Foundation names four or five fellows from across the widely defined social sciences and humanities field. Having the chance to meet periodically with these brilliant scholars was an opportunity for the kind of intense intellectual exchange that academia should foster more systematically. A special word of thanks to one of these fabulous fellows, Myriam Denov, who tolerated me on her own project on children born of war and introduced me to the basics of ethnographic research. I acknowledge the U.C. Irvine Law Review, in which an early version of Chapter 1 was published in 2018.

Many people provided specific assistance in the realisation of this project. Several academic researchers were very generous in sharing ideas and materials with me as I set out to map the practice of various armed groups, including Zachariah Mampilly, Ana Arjona, Mara Revkin, Adam Baczko, Jonathan Somer, Kate Cronin-Furman, Nira Wickramasinghe, and Nimmi Gowrinathan. In the field, I became an expert at exploiting the most tenuous connection or introduction to talk to anyone and everyone who could have some insight into insurgent justice. Many people were generous beyond the call with their time and ideas. I have come to the conclusion that it is best to offer a blanket anonymous thank you, because the political landscape in war-afflicted countries can shift so unpredictably that it is difficult to predict who should not be named for their own safety. At McGill, I relied upon undergraduate and graduate law students to provide research assistance, including Mélissa Beaulieu Lussier, Fiona Cooke, Didem Dogar, Vincent Marquis, Lucas Mathieu, Anne-Sophie Ouellet, Dhananga Pathirana, Amy Preston-Samson, Tiran Rahimian, Isabelle Rémillard, and Jeffrey Smith. I was the happy beneficiary of their industry and intelligence, and the many long conversations with them about rebel courts were one of the pleasures of this project.

Throughout this project, I received words of encouragement like "haven't yo been working on that book for long enough?" or "isn't there a war you shou be going off to instead of bothering me?" from my three sons Daniel, Mic and Ari. *Vous voyez les gars, c'est fini; comme quoi tout arrive.* Their notic little sister, Pulga, was a quieter supportive presence for much of the writi the book. Finally, Shauna literally has been my partner-in-all-things for decades—I couldn't have done any of it without you.

Introduction

> When a country is being subverted it is not being outfought; it is being out-administered.
>
> — Bernard Fall, 'The Theory and Practice of Insurgency and Counterinsurgency' (1965) 18 *Naval War College Review* 21, 34

"It seemed the right thing to do at the time" may be what Haisam Omar Sakhanh is thinking from the relative comfort of the high-security prison in Sweden where he is serving a life sentence for war crimes. After completing the mandatory three-year military service in the Syrian army, he had worked as an electrician in Syria and abroad. When the regime of Bashar Al-Assad started killing children and committing other horrific crimes, he felt he had to do something, and he became active in the opposition movement.[1] After fleeing to Italy, Sakhanh participated in anti-Assad protests in Milan before deciding that he had to join the fight to free his country. He flew to Hatay airport in southern Turkey on 30 April 2012, crossing the border through the mountains to join the Suleiman Battle Company in the village of Kfar Kila. This rebel group had a reputation for being well armed and effective, operating independently of, but in collaboration with, the Free Syrian Army in the fight against the Assad regime. Sakhanh was immediately incorporated into the armed group, and his war experience took a turn only four days after joining the rebellion. On the night of 4 May, his unit was involved in an attack against a government outpost, leading to the capture of eleven soldiers of the Syrian armed forces. Two were freed immediately, but the other nine were detained on suspicion of mistreating passing refugees over previous weeks. The next day, Sakhanh was detailed to another village to participate in the funerals of one member of his unit killed in the attack. When he returned, he was told that a Free Syrian Army Judicial Council composed of judges who had defected from the regime had held a court-martial for the detained Syrian soldiers in a town a few kilometres away. The court had heard from numerous witnesses, and mobile

[1] Swedish Police Interview of Omar Sakhanh, 12 March 2016: Nationella Operativa Avdelningen, Förhör med Sakhanh, Haisam Omar, diarienr: 5000-K132600-16 (2016) 1057.

Rebel Courts. René Provost, Oxford University Press. © Oxford University Press 2021.
DOI: 10.1093/oso/9780190912222.003.0001

phones found on the accused contained videos of the soldiers raping women.[2] Two of the soldiers were acquitted, and seven were found guilty of the rape and murder of civilians. Applying the Syrian Penal Code, the rebel judges sentenced these seven men to capital punishment. When Sakhanh heard his name called to join the firing squad, he felt a bit nervous but not uncomfortable: he was a soldier, orders must be obeyed, and he had no reason to distrust the group that he had joined.[3] Fatefully, someone filmed the execution. After three months in Syria, Sakhanh decided that armed insurgency was not for him, and he made his way to Sweden. He claimed to be a refugee from Syria, affirmed that he had taken no part in armed hostilities, and was duly granted refugee status in October 2012. The video of the execution eventually made its way to the *New York Times*, which posted it online. Someone in Sweden recognised Sakhanh, and he was arrested in 2016 and accused of murder. At trial, Sakhanh acknowledged that it was him on the video, but argued that he had been carrying out a lawful punishment imposed by a regularly constituted court of an armed group in the context of a non-international armed conflict. In February 2017, the Stockholm District Court convicted Sakhanh of serious violations of Common Article 3 of the Geneva Conventions and sentenced him to life imprisonment, a decision confirmed by the Svea Court of Appeal.[4]

The story of Omar Sakhanh is emblematic of a widespread reality that until now has not been seriously documented nor analysed under public international law. There is a significant practice by non-state armed groups in zones of armed conflicts of establishing their own courts to administer justice. This has occurred in Sri Lanka, El Salvador, Nepal, Afghanistan, Sierra Leone, Colombia, Rwanda, Congo, Sudan, Kosovo, Syria, Iraq, Turkey, Western Sahara, India, Ethiopia, Russia, Indonesia, Eritrea, Ukraine, Philippines, Mali, Burma, and many other places. While the existence of rebel courts is a relatively well-known fact, very little is known as to the details of how such courts operate. A few works have been produced examining the operation of insurgent justice in a given conflict, and some broader works on insurgency have included a section on justice, but there is no full-length academic analysis of rebel justice that studies the practice across

[2] CJ Chivers, 'Brutality of Syrian Rebels Posing Dilemma in West' *New York Times* (5 September 2013).

[3] Swedish Police Interview of Omar Sakhanh, 27 May 2016: Nationella Operativa Avdelningen, Förhör med Sakhanh, Haisam Omar, diarienr: 5000-K132600-16 (2016) 1189.

[4] *Prosecutor v Haisam Omar Sakhanh*, Stockholms tingsrätt (Stockholm District Court), B 3787-16, Judgment of 16 February 2017, available in Swedish at <http://www.ejiltalk.org/wp-content/uploads/2017/03/Stockholms-TR-B-3787-16-Dom-2017-02-16.pdf> accessed 18 July 2018, with a partial English translation in (2018) 16 J. Int'l Crim. Just. 403–424; confirmed by *Prosecutor v Haisam Omar Sakhanh*, Svea hovrätt (Svea Court of Appeal), B 2259-17, Judgment of 31 May 2017; leave to appeal was denied by the Supreme Court of Sweden, B 3157-17, 20 July 2017.

different conflicts.[5] This book takes a first step in that direction, by offering a series of case studies detailing the operation of rebel courts in a range of conflicts involving very different non-state armed groups.

The very idea of a rebel court presided over by an outlaw judge applying non-state law may strike many jurists as a string of oxymorons. Irregular armed groups are typically represented as wholly permeated by illegality, from the very resort to armed force to the involuntary recruitment of fighters and the means and methods of warfare used. They are taken to be truly outside of law, and often are encompassed under a very wide understanding of "terrorism". International law broadly has refrained from declaring as illegal the use of force by or against the state in a national setting, limiting itself to extending to insurgents the same criminal sanctions for breaches of the laws of war as are applicable to governmental armed forces, and posing few limitations on a state's ability to criminalise insurgency under domestic law. The fact that by and large the domestic laws of states deem illegal the taking up of arms against the established government has coloured the general legal construction of insurgency even under public international law. While the fact that the actions of non-state armed groups are illegal under national law undeniably has considerable significance, it is nevertheless important to analyse the implications of armed and unarmed activities of such groups under international law for at least two reasons: first, international law may in fact impose some limits on a state's freedom to declare illegal what armed groups do; and second, as illustrated by Sakhanh's case, the actions of armed insurgents may well have legal consequences beyond the territory of the national state, in places that lie beyond the reach of the domestic law of that state.

The legality under international law of actions of non-state armed groups will necessarily depend on the specific nature of these actions. Even when embroiled in an armed conflict, armed groups do much more than fight. War is the continuation of politics partly by the very same means, *pace* Clausewitz. Like states, armed groups in conflict zones very often come to acquire authority over a population and territory and become involved in what can be broadly described as public administration. The rebel administration of justice thus can be situated within a larger notion of rebel governance, corresponding to an emerging field of enquiry which will provide some framing concepts for the analysis offered in this book (I). In another direction, the rebel administration of justice raises pointed and challenging questions with respect to the concept of law. Legal pluralism offers a vision of legal normativity that encompasses a wide range of actors and practices, and as such stands as an especially promising perspective from which

[5] The closest one gets is Frank Ledwidge's short book on the role of rebel law in counter-insurgency strategies, which does include some consideration of international law: Frank Ledwidge, *Rebel Law: Insurgents, Courts and Justice in Modern Conflict* (Hurst & Company 2017).

to consider insurgent justice (II). Any attempt to meaningfully consider the legality of a practice should be grounded in an understanding of the practice in question that is as precise as possible. For the rebel administration of justice, this implies an appraisal of the details of the structure and operation of insurgent courts. In that spirit, this book offers a legal analysis of rebel justice that relies on a series of case studies prepared for that purpose. Unsurprisingly, the preparation of case studies of the practice of armed groups in situations of armed conflict poses a number of methodological challenges (III). These elements provide the foundation for the presentation of the nature and objectives of the overall project of this book (IV).

I. Rebel Governance: Can the Insurgent Rule?

The very notion of civil war brings associations of the chaotic displacement of normal social structures, challenged by insurgent forces set on overcoming all resistance to their rise, whether this resistance corresponds to armed force or to the operation of other state institutions. When a rebel group is said to have taken control of a territory, the evocation is more often than not the imposition of absolute authority through raw, barely controlled violence, actual or threatened. Institutions that normally ensure stability in social relations are destroyed or disabled, leaving the civilian population in a position of acute vulnerability and powerlessness vis-à-vis the ruling non-state armed group. The image is of an all-powerful non-state actor unilaterally imposing its will through violence upon a civilian population cowering in fear. This vision corresponds to—and indeed is fuelled by—a characterisation of non-state armed groups as criminals or terrorists, typically conveyed in government narratives about non-international armed conflicts. More generally, as noted by Stathis Kalyvas, we tend to talk about civil war as manifestation of evil, disease, or madness, all expressions of the irrationality driving insurgency that results in situations of impenetrable mystery and chaos.[6]

This may be a common evocation of rebel control over a territory and population, one commonly pictured in Hollywood representations of civil wars, but it is a picture known for a very long time to be factually inaccurate. We can see, in classic works on insurgency by the likes of Mao and Che Guevara, the relation of dependence that is posited between a rebel group and the population on which it must necessarily rely if it is to survive and succeed.[7] Hannah Arendt in her essay

[6] Stathis N Kalyvas, *The Logic of Violence in Civil War* (Cambridge University Press 2006) 32–33; Zachariah Cherian Mampilly, *Rebel Rulers Insurgent Governance and Civilian Life during War* (Cornell University Press 2011) 241–242.

[7] See Mao Zedong, *Selected Military Writings of Mao Tse-Tung* (Foreign Languages Press 1966); Che Guevara, *Guerrilla Warfare: The Authorized Translation* (Vintage Books 1968).

On Violence noted that "No government exclusively based on means of violence has ever existed", drawing a link to guerrilla warfare and the limits of military domination from the Napoleonic invasion of Spain to the Vietnam War: violence can destroy power but, for Arendt, can never be politically productive in creating power.[8] This has been repeated and analysed often in relation to state power, but there seems to obtain what Zachariah Mampilly describes as a "Hobbesian conjecture" that only the state can wield power to bring about order in society.[9] It is assumed that if the state's power is challenged and undermined, then order is accordingly eroded, ultimately leading to chaos. This has been applied specifically to law, corresponding to the syllogism that if law is an emanation of the state, and the state comes to disappear, then there is no law.[10] In fact, sociological studies of non-international armed conflict indicate that life remains mostly orderly for most people, most of the time, in most places affected by war, which is not to say that war does not occasion profound social transformations that result in an order of war that is different than the order of peace.[11] How can this be so, if the state's power is partially or completely displaced by insurgency?

The emerging field of rebel governance suggests that war cannot be reduced to a straightforward struggle among belligerents for a monopoly on violence. As insightfully articulated by Paul Staniland, states and armed groups engaged in a non-international armed conflict have complex and variable relationships that stand determined not only by violent interaction but also by politics and bargains.[12] He suggests that a wartime typology of political order can be mapped using two key variables: territorial control, which can either be segmented (warring parties hold exclusive control over distinct areas) or fragmented (warring parties have overlapping, partial control over the same area); and levels of cooperation, which can be active (warring parties identify shared objective and coordinate strategies), passive (warring parties rely on informal but identifiable norms of acceptable practices), or non-existent (no shared understanding among warring parties, which pursue all-out aggressive hostilities).[13] In a given armed conflict, the same two belligerents can have different types of ongoing

[8] Hannah Arendt, *On Violence* (Houghton Mifflin Harcourt 1970) 56–57, 63; Béatrice Hibou, *The Political Anatomy of Domination* (Andrew Brown tr, Palgrave Macmillan 2017).

[9] Mampilly (n 6) 7.

[10] Adam Baczko, 'La guerre par le droit : justice, domination et violence en Afghanistan (2001–2018)' (PhD Thesis, EHESS 2018) 24.

[11] See: Laurent Gayer, 'La «normalité de l'anormal»: recomposer le quotidien en situation de guerre civile' [2018] Critique internationale 181; Stephen C Lubkemann, *Culture in Chaos: An Anthropology of the Social Condition in War* (University of Chicago Press 2010); Teresa Koloma Beck, *The Normality of Civil War: Armed Groups and Everyday Life in Angola* (Campus 2012); Ivana Maček, *Sarajevo Under Siege: Anthropology in Wartime* (University of Pennsylvania Press 2016).

[12] Paul Staniland, 'States, Insurgents, and Wartime Political Orders' [2012] Perspectives on Politics 243, 244.

[13] ibid 247–248; relying in part on Kalyvas (n 6) 88–89.

relationships depending on time and place. With respect to governance, it cannot be assumed that there is overall coherence in how authority is apportioned as between government and rebels in one conflict.[14] Belligerents may have active cooperation in one geographical area and fight all-out in a different area. Even in the same time and place, state and non-state actors may have active cooperation with respect to one type of activity and non-existent cooperation vis-à-vis another. For example, in areas under their authority, rebels not rarely will allow unimpeded delivery of education or health care by the state but entirely take over the maintenance of public security.

The spectrum of variable relationships just described is constituted not only by the conduct of armed hostilities but also by governance practices. Governance generally has been defined as "the various institutionalized modes of social coordination to produce and implement collectively binding rules, or to provide collective goods", covering both structure and process.[15] While governance traditionally was conceived as the imposition of order by the state, possibly through coercion, the reality of governance beyond or even without government has been acknowledged for several decades.[16] This broader vision of governance reflects the fact very few states have "consolidated statehood" or full domestic sovereignty: most states have areas of limited statehood in which other actors like civil society organisations, local communities, corporations, or third states can provide governance.[17] Governance is thus understood as corresponding to direct or indirect rule of varying degrees of hybridity.[18] Initially at least, actors producing public "bads" like criminals and terrorists were excluded from this approach because they were seen as fostering private or at least non-public goods.[19]

The study of rebel governance has emerged in the last decade to address the fact that non-state armed groups in some cases have filled a vacuum of public authority in zones of armed conflict.[20] Armed groups do so not merely or even mostly by way of violence, but rather by using a range of approaches

[14] Jeremy M Weinstein, *Inside Rebellion: The Politics of Insurgent Violence* (Cambridge University Press 2006) 17–18.

[15] Tanja A Börzel and Thomas Risse, 'Governance without a State: Can It Work?' (2010) 4 Regulation & Governance 113, 114.

[16] Shaun Breslin and Helen ES Nesadurai, 'Who Governs and How? Non-State Actors and Transnational Governance in Southeast Asia' (2018) 48 Journal of Contemporary Asia 187.

[17] See Thomas Risse (ed), *Governance without a State?: Policies and Politics in Areas of Limited Statehood* (Columbia University Press 2011); Stephen D Krasner, *Sovereignty: Organized Hypocrisy* (Princeton University Press 1999) 4; Heike Kreiger, 'International Legal Order' in Tanja Börzel and Thomas Risse (eds), *Oxford Handbook of Governance and Limited Statehood* (Oxford University Press 2018) 543, 545–546.

[18] Adnan Naseemullah and Paul Staniland, 'Indirect Rule and Varieties of Governance' (2016) 29 Governance 13, 16–17.

[19] Börzel and Risse (n 15) 115.

[20] See Ana Arjona, Nelson Kasfir, and Zachariah Mampilly (eds), *Rebel Governance in Civil War* (Cambridge University Press 2015).

that are not entirely dissimilar to governance by the state. In some but not all situations of non-international armed conflict, rebels do become providers of public goods. One fundamental public good that armed groups often provide is security, sometimes against violence at the hand of the government or other armed groups, and other times to suppress criminal or anti-social behaviour that may be unrelated to the conflict. The significance of this form of rebel governance is underscored by the fact that the vast majority of war-related deaths are not linked to combat but rather to the general breakdown of civil and political order in conflict zones.[21] In some non-international armed conflicts, the insurgents provided a wide array of public goods from health care to education, environmental protection, and trade regulation. Again, contrary to widely held assumptions, in some instances the provision of such public goods by rebels becomes institutionalised. In periods of civil war, state institutions can become weaker and disappear, but that does not mean that no institution can arise to replace them. Using a dataset covering all non-international armed conflicts between 1950 and 2006, Reyko Huang found that armed groups have established up to eleven distinct governance institutions covering, in order of prevalence, an executive branch, a legislature, courts, a tax system, a police force, an education system, a health care programme, humanitarian relief, media, and foreign affairs.[22] After all, armed conflict itself corresponds to a vision of violence that is institutionalised. It is a condition of applicability of international humanitarian law that hostilities take place between armed forces that either belong to a state (presumed institutionalised) or non-state armed groups "which, under responsible command, exercise such control over a part of its territory as to enable them to carry out sustained and concerted military operations and to implement this Protocol" (Art. 1, 1977 Additional Protocol II).[23] The requirements of "responsible command" and "sustained and concerted military operations" correspond to a group institutionalised to some degree. War, as a legal construct, is an activity that is organised and institutionalised to a significant degree, so it should not come as a radical suggestion that aspects of insurgency other than the conduct of armed hostilities should be institutionalised as well. Ana Arjona

[21] Mampilly (n 6) 231–232 (citing studies placing the number of military and civilian "battle deaths" at between 3% [in South Sudan] and 50% [in Sri Lanka] of the total number of war-related deaths).

[22] Reyko Huang, *The Wartime Origins of Democratization: Civil War, Rebel Governance, and Political Regimes* (Cambridge University Press 2016) 60. I list only ten, as the other one mentioned by Huang, a boycott of state taxation, does not seem to properly correspond to a form of governance institution fostering a public good.

[23] The requirement related to the organised nature of the armed groups is not stated but is implied in Common Article 3 of the 1949 Geneva Conventions. It is also echoed in the references to "organized resistance movements" and responsible command in the definition of prisoners of war in Article 4 of the 1949 Third Geneva Convention, and in the definition of armed forces in Article 43(1) of the 1977 Additional Protocol I.

offered one of the first institutional analysis of rebel governance and found that, in some non-international armed conflicts, armed opposition groups broadened their grasp on public governance so much that it came to correspond to what she terms "rebelocracy", that is the establishment of a government by the rebels that mirrors that of the official government of the state.[24] She contrasts this to "aliocracy", a more common situation in which there will be some degree of co-existence between the authority and institutions of non-state armed groups and those of the state and other agents.

The majority of non-state armed groups do not engage in widespread institutionalised governance approximating state-building, reflecting factors such as the length of the conflict and the degree of reliance on the civilian population for material and political support.[25] One factor that has particular resonance with international humanitarian law is the link between rebel governance and control of territory.[26] It is often assumed in writings about insurgency that non-state armed groups seek territorial control as a base of operation that can increase their strength and military effectiveness.[27] This reflects Mancur Olson's striking image of rebels as a type of "stationary bandits", reaping greater rewards from continuous interaction with a stable population, as contrasted with "roving bandits".[28] While that is indeed the case for many armed insurgents, others eschew territorial control in favour of transience for strategic or ideological reasons.[29] What is meant by "control of territory" in these discussions is far from self-evident. As noted by Lea Raible, "control", "power", and "authority" very often are used interchangeably both by academics and by institutions like the European Court of Human Rights.[30] While power is a means, an ability to bring about a state of affairs, control and authority characterise a certain type of relationship. Control, although at times

[24] Ana Arjona, *Rebelocracy: Social Order in the Colombian Civil War* (Cambridge University Press 2016) 170–192; Ana Arjona, 'Wartime Institutions: A Research Agenda' (2014) 58 Journal of Conflict Resolution 1360, 1375.

[25] Huang (n 22) 71; Weinstein (n 14) 186; Jori Breslawski, 'The Social Terrain of Rebel Held Territory' (2021) 65 Journal of Conflict Resolution 453; Megan A Stewart, 'Civil War as State-Making: Strategic Governance in Civil War' (2018) 72 International Organization 205.

[26] This refers to one of the conditions of applicability for Additional Protocol II, declared applicable only to armed conflicts between a state and armed groups which "exercise such control over part of its territory" (Art. 1(1), Protocol II). There is no requirement of territorial control for the application of Common Article 3.

[27] Arjona, *Rebelocracy* (n 24) 9; Didier Péclard and Delphine Mechoulan, 'Rebel Governance and the Politics of Civil War' (Swiss Peace Foundation 2015) 15.

[28] Mancur Olson, 'Dictatorship, Democracy, and Development' [1993] American Political Science Review 567.

[29] Nelson Kasfir, 'Rebel Governance—Constructing a Field of Inquiry: Definitions, Scope, Patterns, Order, Causes' in Ana Arjona, Nelson Kasfir, and Zachariah Mampilly (eds), *Rebel Governance in Civil War* (Cambridge University Press 2015) 26.

[30] Lea Raible, *Human Rights Unbound: A Theory of Extraterritoriality* (Oxford University Press 2020) 102.

said in international law to be "overall" as opposed to "effective", generally evokes a more absolute form of subservience. Authority speaks to a less fully asymmetrical relationship, one in which even the weaker party retains some measure of agency. Michel Foucault's notion of governmentality has been applied to non-state governance in conflict zone to further undermine an overly reductive understanding of the social distribution of power and the limits of an idea of control grounded in coercion.[31] Legal analysis, driven by the imperative of categories, tends to approach the question of territorial control as a zero-sum game: either there is control, or there is not. Such a Manichean outlook is challenged by rebel governance literature as unfounded in fact, finding that social control in conflict zones is frequently highly fragmented, resulting in "uneven, heterogenous landscapes of authority and control".[32] This speaks not only to the sharing of authority between government and rebels but also, very significantly for our purpose, to the persistent agency of the civilian population in conflict zones, able to protest, hinder, or even block actions of belligerents.[33] The second constitutive element of this notion, territory, also has been described as conceptually underexamined, suffering from a generalised assumption that its meaning is self-evident.[34] Human geography scholars like Stuart Elden and Saskia Sassen have offered that territory cannot be reduced to space, land, or terrain, but that it is a form of political technology combining elements of property, power, and geography.[35] If we say, as suggested by Paul Alliès, that administration produces territory, then it becomes obvious that the relationship between rebel governance and control of territory is unlikely to be a straightforward one.[36] That is indeed what many rebel governance scholars suggest, finding that it is unclear whether an ability to govern derives from territorial control, whether territorial control is made possible by rebel governance capabilities, or whether these are fluctuating variables that do not

[31] Karel Arnaut and Christian K Højbjerg, 'Gouvernance et ethnographie en temps de crise De l'étude des ordres émergents dans l'Afrique entre guerre et paix' (2008) 111 Politique africaine 5, 18–19.

[32] Staniland (n 12) 247.

[33] Ana Arjona, 'Civilian Resistance to Rebel Governance' in Ana Arjona, Nelson Kasfir, and Zachariah Mampilly (eds), *Rebel Governance in Civil War* (Cambridge University Press 2015) 191 ("As soon as one scratches below the surface of the official discourse that reigned where armed groups governed, it became evident that civilians found ways to express their views, complain about certain issues, negotiate with combatants, and even openly defy the new order"); Nimmi Gowrinathan and Zachariah Mampilly, 'Resistance and Repression under the Rule of Rebels: Women, Clergy, and Civilian Agency in LTTE Governed Sri Lanka' (2019) 52 Comparative Politics 1.

[34] Stuart Elden, 'Land, Terrain, Territory' (2010) 34 Progress in Human Geography 799, 800.

[35] Stuart Elden, *The Birth of Territory* (University of Chicago Press 2013) 322–323; Saskia Sassen, *Territory, Authority, Rights: From Medieval to Global Assemblages* (Princeton University Press 2006); Valérie November, *Les territoires du risque: le risque comme object de réflexion géographique* (P Lang 2002) 17; Jean Gottmann, *The Significance of Territory* (University Press of Virginia 1973) 2.

[36] Paul Alliès, *L'invention du territoire* (Presses universitaires de Grenoble 1980) 147.

conform to any neat systematisation: to some extent, jurisdiction is territorial and territory is jurisdictional.[37]

Rebel governance literature has examined the administration of justice by non-state armed groups in conflict zones as part of the array of governance institutions deployed by insurgents. Recent compilations of datasets suggest that about one-third of armed groups establish judicial institutions, amounting to 222 processes by sixty-seven different groups across fifty-seven armed conflicts since the end of the Second World War.[38] It is generally agreed that the involvement of armed groups in the administration of justice often acts as a foundation for broader rebel governance, because it can allow the group to penetrate a community very effectively in relation to both important and mundane aspects of civilian life.[39] Rebel governance literature particularly focusses on the conditions and circumstances that lead armed opposition groups to establish courts, whether strategic, transactional, or ideological, and on the impact of rebel justice on the effectiveness of both the insurgency and counter-insurgency measures.[40] One interesting insight from a segment of this literature is that civilians in conflict zones on the whole do not seem as concerned with whose justice is being applied as they are with the fairness of its rules and application.[41] In many remote parts of war-affected countries, ordinary people feel disenfranchised from public authority, whether it is wielded by the state or by armed opposition groups. What matters is how and why authority is used, and what impact it has on daily life. This suggests a vision of the rule of law "from below" that is strikingly at odds with a traditional approach that links the rule of law to state sovereignty. Even

[37] Ralf Michaels, 'Notes on Territory' in Jean D'Aspremont and John Haskell (eds), *Tipping Points in International Law—Commitment and Critique* (Cambridge University Press, forthcoming) 7; Arjona, 'Wartime Institutions: A Research Agenda' (n 24) 1381; Mariana Valverde, 'Deepening the Conversation between Socio-Legal Theory and Legal Scholarship about Jurisdiction' in Stephen Allen and others (eds), *The Oxford Handbook of Jurisdiction in International Law* (Oxford University Press 2019) 162.

[38] Huang (n 22) 72, 188; Cyanne E Loyle, 'Rebel Justice during Armed Conflict' (2021) 65 Journal of Conflict Resolution 108, 109; Cyanne E Loyle and Helga Malmin Binningsbø, 'Justice during Armed Conflict: A New Dataset on Government and Rebel Strategies' (2018) 62 Journal of Conflict Resolution 442, 443 (note that Loyle and Binningsbø adopt a wider concept of "during-conflict justice" that includes truth commissions, reparations, and amnesties).

[39] Arjona, *Rebelocracy* (n 24) 73.

[40] Tom Ginsburg, 'Rebel Use of Law and Courts' (2019) 15 Annual Review of Law and Social Science 495; Ledwidge (n 5) (with some analysis of international law); Joana Cook, Haid Haid, and Inga Trauthig, 'Jurisprudence Beyond the State: An Analysis of Jihadist "Justice" in Yemen, Syria and Libya' [2020] Studies in Conflict & Terrorism 1.

[41] Niels Terpstra, 'Rebel Governance, Rebel Legitimacy, and External Intervention: Assessing Three Phases of Taliban Rule in Afghanistan' (2020) 31 Small Wars & Insurgencies 1143, 1162; Florian Weigand, 'Afghanistan's Taliban—Legitimate Jihadists or Coercive Extremists?' (2017) 11 Journal of Intervention and Statebuilding 359, 376. One might label this the "Wi-Fi theory of justice governance": just like people connect to any available Wi-Fi network in cafés and shopping malls without being too concerned with the identity of the internet service provider, ordinary people do not care much whose justice is applied inasmuch as it is generally predictable and fair.

more broadly, it speaks to a wider construction of the concept of law consistent with that articulated by legal pluralism.

II. Legal Pluralism: Can the Insurgent Speak?

One of the most important public goods that the state provides is the administration of justice, both by way of adopting legal standards and by enforcing them through institutions like the police and the judiciary. Is it legally conceivable that, in the context of a non-international armed conflict, a non-state armed group would take it upon itself to enact its own "laws" and run its own "courts", properly so called? As we have just seen, the burgeoning field of rebel governance does include the administration of justice as an object of study, but so far the analysis largely has been carried out from the perspective of disciplines other than law. To what extent are the scare quotes around the words "laws" and "courts" justified, in view of *legal* concepts that correspond to these labels? The question is, in significant ways, definitional rather than ontological.

Most jurists today embrace a positivist concept of law that rests on four precepts: *monism* (the claim that law is a unified, coherent regime); *centralism* (associating the power to validly create legal standards with state sovereignty); *positivism* (viewing law as ontologically distinguished from fact, thus allowing the systematic delineation of the frontier of legality to reflect pre-existing legal standards); and *prescriptivism* (offering legal norms as external constraints descending upon legal agents to try to modify patterns of behaviour).[42] This is without doubt the concept of law that structures public international law. Adopting such a perspective, it becomes readily evident that norms adopted by non-state armed groups are not properly labelled as "law", and institutions that they create to interpret and enforce these norms are not "courts". This mainstream perspective on law and legal institutions is systematically adopted by governments confronted with armed opposition groups that claim to establish judicial bodies.[43] It corresponds to the radical silencing of insurgents, absolutely prevented from speaking law to power in the context of an armed conflict.

While the politics of a government objecting to any characterisation of insurgent courts that would endow legitimacy upon a rebel group are readily understandable, such a stance does correspond to an abdication by the legal profession

[42] Roderick A Macdonald and David Sandomierski, 'Against Nomopolies' (2006) 57 Northern Ireland Legal Quarterly 610, 615; Roderick A Macdonald, 'Here, There . . . and Everywhere. Theorizing Legal Pluralism; Theorizing Jacques Vanderlinden' in Lynne Castonguay and Nicholas Kasirer (eds), *Étudier et enseigner le droit: hier, aujourd'hui et demain. Études offertes à Jacques Vanderlinden* (Yvon Blais 2006).

[43] See, e.g., Case No 23438, Yesid Arteta Davila, 2 July 2008 (Penal Chamber, Supreme Court of Colombia).

of its capacity to use the conceptual tools of law to better understand the rebel administration of justice. A blanket declaration of illegality means that no distinction can be drawn between, on the one hand, non-state justice practices that are reasonable approximations of the legal requirements of fundamental justice and due process in the context of armed conflict and, on the other hand, arbitrary uses of authority masquerading as justice. Legal positivism relegates concerns about due process and international human rights generally to futile distinctions, like rearranging the deck chairs on the Titanic.

While positivism warrants a narrow focus on state-driven normativity, legal pluralism, on the contrary, explodes the limits of our conception of law to encompass forms of normativity beyond those connected to the state in any way. According to a pluralistic understanding, law is *fragmented* (with no necessary coherence across law as a whole), *decentralised* (where many centres and processes exist to create and interpret law), *contingent* (norms do not exist a priori but emerge from an engagement with the particular circumstances of their invocation, including agents and context), and *deliberative* (law is not so much a series of commands as a space in which meaning is collectively created in relation to social practices).[44] Detached from common institutional features linked to the state, legal normativity appears more malleable and variable according to particular contexts, cultural and other. Pluralism, when turning its gaze upon itself, calls for a rejection of any essentialist definition of law, and thus can accommodate state- and non-state-centred normativity. More than an acknowledgment that there are different normative regimes operating simultaneously in any given time and place, legal pluralism attempts to articulate the ways in which these different legal regimes intersect and interact. Seeing this, legal pluralism emerges as an especially promising perspective for the analysis of the administration of justice by insurgents. This is so both because such norms and practices do not derive any legitimacy from the state, quite the opposite, but also because in many if not most civil wars the official law of the state will cohabit with norms established by armed opposition groups. Viewed in this way, insurgent jurisprudence appears as legal pluralism incarnate.

The fact that multiple legal orders obtain in conflict zones over which non-state armed groups exercise a degree of authority can be seen as factually exceptional and normatively problematic, a perspective that stands challenged by legal pluralism. The systematic presence of multiple and interacting legal orders is a central claim of legal pluralism, carried over into legal analysis from its initial formulation by anthropologists in the colonial context.[45] Lon Fuller, many

[44] I have discussed the implications of legal pluralism for international law more fully in: René Provost, 'Interpretation in International Law as a Transcultural Project' in Andrea Bianchi, Daniel Peat, and Matthew Windsor (eds), *Interpretation in International Law* (Oxford University Press 2015).

[45] Sally Engle Merry, 'Law and Colonialism' (1991) 25 Law & Society Review 889.

years ago, insisted that formal legal rules found in statutes and caselaw could not be properly understood without considering what he referred to as "custom", the crystallised interacting expectations of an array of legal agents that invoke and apply these rules.[46] A variation of this idea is found in Sally Falk Moore's notion of the "semi-autonomous social field", based on ethnographic observation of the way in which formal legal standards are modulated by social practices to result in a regime that is more than just the difference between "law in the books" and "law in action", one that reflects a transformation of law resulting from the interaction of formal and informal normative orders.[47] Whether the wider ordering encompassed in this vision ought to be labelled law is something about which legal pluralists themselves have disagreed.[48] A central point that emerges from these debates is that the concept of law itself is subject to pluralistic understanding, rather than necessarily obeying to a positivist canon. If with Clifford Gertz we can say that law is "part of a distinctive manner of imagining the real", then the process through which that construction happens must be a central focus of any legal enquiry.[49] As offered by Boaventura de Sousa Santos in his brilliant essay on law as mapping:

> *Legal pluralism* is the key concept in a postmodern view of law. Not the legal pluralism of traditional legal anthropology in which the different legal orders are conceived as separate entities coexisting in the same political space, but rather the conception of different legal spaces superimposed, interpenetrated, and mixed in our minds as much as in our actions, in occasions of qualitative leaps or sweeping crises in our life trajectories as well as in the dull routine of eventless everyday life. We live in a time of porous legality or of legal porosity, of multiple networks of legal orders forcing us to constant transitions and trespassings. Our legal life is constituted by an intersection of different legal orders, that is, by *interlegality*. Interlegality is the phenomenological counterpart of legal pluralism and that is why it is the second key concept of a postmodern conception of law.[50]

46 Lon Fuller, 'Human Interaction and the Law' (1969) 14 American Journal of Jurisprudence 1.

47 Sally Falk Moore, 'Law and Social Change: The Semi-Autonomous Social Field as an Appropriate Subject of Study' (1973) 7 Law & Society Review 719; John Griffiths, 'What Is Legal Pluralism?' (1986) 18 The Journal of Legal Pluralism and Unofficial Law 1; Sally Engle Merry, 'Legal Pluralism' (1988) 22 Law & Society Review 869.

48 Brian Z Tamanaha, 'Understanding Legal Pluralism: Past to Present, Local to Global' (2008) 30 Sydney Law Review 375, 394–395; Emmanuel Melissaris, *Ubiquitous Law: Legal Theory and the Space for Legal Pluralism* (Ashgate 2013).

49 Clifford Geertz, 'Local Knowledge: Fact and Law in Comparative Perspective' in *Local Knowledge: Further Essays in Interpretive Anthropology* (Basic Books 1983) 173; Paul W Kahn, *The Cultural Study of Law: Reconstructing Legal Scholarship* (University of Chicago Press 2000).

50 Boaventura de Sousa Santos, 'Law: A Map of Misreading. Toward a Postmodern Conception of Law' [1987] Journal of Law and Society 279, 297–298 (emphasis in the original). As noted by Mariana Valverde, there are both spatial and temporal dimensions to the interactions described

Legal pluralism and interlegality have been brought to bear on public international law in recent years, to address the fragmentation of international law stemming from the pluralisation of legal regimes and their increasing institutionalisation as well as the emancipation of norm-creation processes from the monopoly of states.[51]

Widening the concept of law does not imply that everything is law, nor does it ineluctably lead to perpetual legal indeterminacy. The answer to normative plurality does not lie in claims of hierarchy, typically of state law over all other laws. Robert Cover has spoken eloquently of the limits of an approach that seeks to deal with the overlay of too many laws by "killing off" those laws not favoured by the state, corresponding to what he called the "jurispathic" function of courts.[52] Not only does this reduce law to a system of power, overlooking its function as a system of meaning, but it stands curtailed by the limits of the state's coercive power. This reflects not only the countervailing power of non-state armed groups in conflict zones from which state courts have been banned, but more mundanely the laws that people simply don't agree with, and refuse or neglect to obey. However great the coercive power of the state may be, it is limited, and can never provide a full explanation of the force of law.[53] Social life always breeds a multiplicity of legal orders interacting in relations of competition, coordination, or complementarity.[54] What legal pluralism seeks to offer is a legal, as opposed to a political, understanding of how such relations can be managed so that law remains a factor of social stability. Patterns of pluralism vary, even within the same country, so that, for example, official law may have more pull in urban centres, less so in poorer suburban areas, and least of all in isolated rural zones.[55] Legal geography is also gendered, in some communities more obviously than in others, corresponding to spaces that are regulated differently according to the gender identity of its members.[56] This is a significant insight for the study of armed

by Santos: Mariana Valverde, *Chronotopes of Law: Jurisdiction, Scale and Governance* (Routledge 2015) 48–51.

[51] Paul Schiff Berman, *Global Legal Pluralism: A Jurisprudence of Law Beyond Borders* (Cambridge University Press 2012); Jan Klabbers and Gianluigi Palombella (eds), *The Challenge of Inter-Legality* (Cambridge University Press 2019).

[52] Robert Cover, 'Foreword: Nomos and Narrative' (1983) 97 Harvard Law Review 4, 53 ("Judges are people of violence. Because of the violence they command, judges characteristically do not create law, but kill it. Theirs is the jurispathic office").

[53] Cover speaks of the need for interpretive commitments, public and private, by individuals and communities, to "determine what law means and what law shall be": ibid 7.

[54] Geoffrey Swenson, 'Legal Pluralism in Theory and Practice' (2018) 20 International Studies Review 438, 442–446.

[55] Brian Tamanaha, 'A Bifurcated Theory of Law in Hybrid Societies: The Rule of Law and Non-State Justice' in Matthias Kötter and others (eds), *Non-State Justice Institutions and the Law. Decision-Making at the Interface of Tradition, Religion and the State* (Palgrave Macmillan 2015).

[56] Sally Engle Merry, 'International Law and Sociolegal Scholarship: Toward a Spatial Global Legal Pluralism' in Michael Helfand (ed), *Negotiating State and Non-State Law: The Challenge of Global and Local Legal Pluralism* (Cambridge University Press 2015) 71.

conflicts in general, and rebel governance in particular, which tends to be much more prevalent in rural areas than in the cities, and usually male-dominated.[57]

The acknowledgment that many legal orders coexist and interact in all societies in variable patterns also reflects the legal agency of an array of actors. The state, non-state armed groups, civilian communities, down to individuals, are sites of internormativity in which these different legal orders converge and collide to permit, or more appropriately demand, the production of legal norms.[58] In this light, for example, the ability of the civilian population to sometimes resist the imposition of norms by an armed group documented by Arjona in Colombia and Gowrinathan and Mampilly in Sri Lanka is understood not merely as factual—a description of a degree of civilian political agency in war—but also legal: the norms formulated by rebels and civilians intersect to result in a hybrid legal order that will govern this relationship.[59] The dispersion of legal agency also challenges a unitary approach to these legal actors. Following Anne-Marie Slaughter's model of the disaggregated state, which documented the fact that a state speaks internationally in many voices corresponding to various branches and agencies of government, we must resist a unitary understanding of non-state actors.[60] There is no reason to believe that armed groups are more homogenous than states, especially those that are large enough to engage in rebel governance. Despite a pattern of state narratives on insurgency that tends to present armed groups as undifferentiated entities or, on the opposite, as reduced to the rebel leader, the study of rebel governance reveals that there are diverse constituencies within armed groups. For example, the LTTE and the Taliban are examples of non-state armed groups in which the administration of justice is carried out by a branch of the insurgency that is distinct from the fighting arm of the group. This suggests that, at least in some cases, legal norms established by non-state armed groups reflect specific constituencies within the group, which could prove privileged interlocutors for engagement in an international dialogue about the rule of law.[61]

Finally, the polyphonic and polycentric production, interpretation, and application of legal norms in conflict zones will necessarily have a cultural

57 Kalyvas (n 6) 38–39.

58 This is pushed to its furthest point in critical legal pluralism, as most fully expounded in the work of Rod Macdonald: Martha-Marie Kleinhans and Roderick A Macdonald, 'What Is a Critical Legal Pluralism?' (1997) 12 Canadian Journal of Law and Society 25.

59 Arjona, 'Civilian Resistance to Rebel Governance' (n 33); Gowrinathan and Mampilly (n 33).

60 Anne-Marie Slaughter, *A New World Order* (Princeton University Press 2004) 166; Paul Schiff Berman, 'Non-State Lawmaking through the Lens of Global Legal Pluralism' in Michael Helfand (ed), *Negotiating State and Non-State Law: The Challenge of Global and Local Legal Pluralism* (Cambridge University Press 2015) 20–22.

61 For an example of such a dialogue that targets the justice sector of several armed groups, see Geneva Call, Report from the 2017 Garance Talks—The Administration of Justice by Armed Non-State Actors (Geneva Call, 2018).

dimension. Cover insisted that the process of normative commitment necessary to give meaning to legal standards always takes place through an essentially cultural medium. Even for rules of international humanitarian law and human rights law, there must be a translation that Sally Engle Merry described as the vernacularisation of norms, corresponding to the transcription of legal standards into narratives reflecting the local dialect, accent, values, and practices, so that they become intelligible to local actors.[62] There are implications of cultural diversity for international humanitarian law that, as I have argued elsewhere, remain grievously undertheorised.[63] Be that as it may, suffice it to say for now that law, far from a tool that enables dominance of one culture over others, can allow for the mediation of cultural difference. Interpretation does not demand the erasure of the interpreter's own culture; on the contrary, a legal interpretation is valid only to the extent that it represents a maxim one is willing to live by. Interpretation thus must be one and the other: located in the culture of the interpreter but reflective of the fact of difference. The ethical stance of the interpreter is not one of dominance but of respect, not necessarily respect of the values embraced by other cultures but rather respect for the fact of difference and the fluidity of cultures.[64] As such, legal interpretation speaks to the nature of law not merely as a system of rules but also as a system of meaning, and to the interconnections that exist between different normative universes. In this deliberative sense, the law corresponds to an episteme, understood as an inter-subjective knowledge underpinning legal narratives that aim to organise differences rather than generate uniformity.[65]

III. Methodology: Talking to Insurgents

When I remark on the scorching heat, my guide-fixer-driver-translator retorts that we haven't yet hit 50 °C, so this isn't really a "hot day". It is late summer 2017, we are driving in Iraq on the road between Erbil and Mosul, and everything is stone and dust. About six weeks earlier, Mosul, the largest city held by the Islamic State, finally was won over, and we are heading to a camp to

[62] Sally Engle Merry and Peggy Levitt, 'The Vernacularization of Women's Human Rights' in Stephen Hopgood, Jack Snyder, and Leslie Vinjamuri (eds), *Human Rights Futures* (Cambridge University Press 2017).

[63] René Provost, 'The International Committee of the Red Widget? The Diversity Debate and International Humanitarian Law' (2007) 40 Israel Law Review 614.

[64] James Boyd White, *Justice as Translation: An Essay in Cultural and Legal Criticism* (University of Chicago Press 1994) 257.

[65] Emanuel Adler and Steven Bernstein, 'Knowledge in Power: The Epistemic Construction of Global Governance' in Michael Barnett and Raymond Duvall (eds), *Power in Global Governance*, vol 98 (Cambridge University Press 2005) 296. I have explored these ideas further in Provost (n 44).

interview people who have fled that region to the relative safety of Kurdish territory. The closest town still held by the Islamic State is 50 kilometres away, which seems quite close to me, but my guide maintains that this is a perfectly safe area, seeing all the Peshmerga light armoured vehicles sharing the road with us. After numerous checkpoints, crossing partially destroyed bridges, we veer off the main road and zigzag between ghost villages in which not a single house is left standing from the fighting. We arrive at a camp surrounded by barbed wire and guarded by the Asayish, the Kurdish security force. Access is tightly restricted, but thanks to my guide's *wasta* (connections) we have the necessary authorisation, and an interpreter and guide to the camp is provided. For several hours, we go from tent to tent to interview people, mostly women with their children, about life under the Islamic State and their encounter with the group's "justice" system. If it wasn't 50 °C outside, it is definitely much beyond that inside the tents, despite the cooling units that produce a deafening noise but nothing that could be called fresh or cool air. The oven-like heat and the slowness of translation (an Arabic dialect to Kurdish, then Kurdish to English) makes the gut-wrenching stories told by the refugees all the more overwhelming. In the first tent, after about fifteen minutes, the oldest boy of the family, about ten years old, comes in with a bottle of water and one glass. He carefully fills it and hands it to me so that I can drink first, as the honoured guest. Despite all the stories about people falling seriously ill—some for months—after drinking unsafe water in Iraq, I take the glass and empty it with a thanks to the boy; it is unthinkable to refuse the hospitality of people who have so little to share. The stories I hear about life under the Islamic State often have nothing to do with the group's court system, the focus of my research, but people clearly want *someone* to hear their story, and here I am, a Canadian academic stand-in for the absent and indifferent international community. Still, there are some who had been arrested and brought before Islamic State courts, and they describe how little justice there was to be had there, with systematic beatings and torture, blindfolding for court appearances, no right to counsel or to call witnesses, and not rarely ending in public executions. At the end of each interview, I ask the person if they know someone else in the camp who has had dealings with Islamic State courts. Each time, they walk me over to another tent, usually accompanied by the children, and they sit and listen to the next interview. This repeats itself for several hours, so that by the last tent, there are more than forty people listening, and I have drunk a considerable amount of water and tea. By then, I think we are nearly done, and I desperately need to go to the bathroom. But more people keep walking in wanting to tell their story. In the end, I have to ask the interpreter to explain my urgent need to the assembled crowd. They all seem to think it is quite amusing, and that mild embarrassment proves to be the only negative consequence of drinking all that water. Then we pack up and drive back to Erbil, to my air-conditioned hotel behind four-metre blast walls.[66]

This is a snippet of what fieldwork looks like or more accurately, as one anthropologist put it, the 1 percent of the time spent obtaining information, the other 99 percent being "spent on logistics, being ill, being sociable, arranging things, getting from place to place, and above all, waiting".[67] Law professors by and large do not do fieldwork, and research in law remains essentially doctrinal: venturing in the field for most legal academic means actually walking over to the law library to get a book unavailable electronically or, for the truly daring, going to consult archives in courthouses or official repositories. This is an evolving picture, however, and there are today more doctoral theses in law that do incorporate some element of fieldwork, especially for research that can be said to be "socio-legal".[68] Consideration of the rebel administration of justice by international law scholars has resulted in excellent doctrinal analysis of applicable legal standards on the basis of gossamer knowledge of the practice that it relates to.[69] To a large extent, jurists have applied legal standards to an imagined version of rebel justice derived from a limited number of documents produced by a few non-state armed groups themselves or described in stories in the media. This does allow meaningful and penetrating legal analysis of a range of fundamental questions, such as whether there is a general principle of international humanitarian law that proscribes, authorises, or requires armed groups to establish their own court systems. The very concept of the administration of justice, however, is bound up in notions of fairness that emanate from a constellation of small choices in the practice of establishing and operating a court system: How insulated are judges from the military leadership of the group? Can you freely choose your counsel? Do you have access to evidence before the trial? Do lawyers wear robes? Is the judgment written? . . . and countless other questions. The concept of "thick description"

[66] On the framing of this paragraph as a 'bridging narrative', see Teju Cole, 'The White-Savior Industrial Complex' (2012) *The Atlantic* (21 March 2012).

[67] Nigel Barley, *The Innocent Anthropologist: Notes from a Mud Hut* (Waveland Press 1983) 98.

[68] For a thoughtful reflection of the implications of fieldwork for legal scholarship based on her experience in preparing her doctoral dissertation, see Sarah MH Nouwen, 'As You Set out for Ithaka: Practical, Epistemological, Ethical, and Existential Questions about Socio-Legal Empirical Research in Conflict' (2014) 27 Leiden Journal of International Law 227; for a very good example of such research, see Rebecca Sutton, *The Humanitarian Civilian: How the Idea of Distinction Circulates Within and Beyond International Humanitarian Law* (Oxford University Press 2021). It goes without saying that scholars in other disciplines, and in particular anthropology, have been carrying out legal ethnographies for a very long time, and that these ethnographies have had an impact on legal scholarship. There are also some rare legal academics that have carried out true legal ethnographies, Karl Llewellyn being an early and important example.

[69] The landmark study was produced by Jonathan Somer, 'Jungle Justice: Passing Sentence on the Equality of Belligerents in Non-International Armed Conflict' (2007) 89 International Review of the Red Cross 655; this was followed by the excellent piece from Sandesh Sivakumaran, 'Courts of Armed Opposition Groups—Fair Trials or Summary Justice?' (2009) 7 Journal of International Criminal Justice 489.

that Clifford Geertz argued was necessary to meaningfully interrogate the concept of culture seems required to apprehend something like the rebel administration of justice.[70] Fieldwork not only generates more information that can provide better answers to the questions that applicable legal standards give rise to but, perhaps more importantly, it can lead to ask altogether different questions.[71] Legal analysis encourages a construction of the world that is unidimensional, corresponding to a normative dimension in which knowledge that is deemed objective and rational is valued above all else. In order to achieve a coherent vision of a practice that allows legal characterisation, much if not most of the messy reality of life is discarded as irrelevant to leave only a few factual markers of legality.[72] In stark contrast, Claude Lévi-Strauss noted that "research in the field . . . is the mother and nursemaid of doubt, the philosophical attitude par excellence".[73] This sort of doubt is anathema to most legal thinking, a problem to be dealt with instead of a virtue to celebrate, but it is precisely what Sarah Nouwen finds that "perhaps, that is what the field of international criminal law needs most—less certainty, less conviction, and more fundamental questions, inspired by the complex social, material, and political realities of situations of conflict".[74] We know precious little about the reality of the rebel administration of justice, and a description that aspires to "thickness" is needed to underpin a meaningful wide-ranging analysis under international law.

There are good reasons that explain why we don't know very much about how non-state armed groups administer justice. A first set of reasons has to do with attention, with the fact that the rebel administration of justice simply has not been a practice that has attracted the interest of scholars. Until the emergence of the field of rebel governance described earlier, insurgent courts were not studied except peripherally through the lens of counter-insurgency analyses like the US "Human Terrain System".[75] Even in the more recent rebel governance literature, relatively little attention has been paid to justice practices, and what limited research there is has been carried out by scholars from perspectives other than law,

[70] Clifford Geertz, 'Thick Description: Toward an Interpretive Theory of Culture' in Yvonna Lincoln and Norman Denzin (eds), *Turning Points in Qualitative Research: Tying Knots in a Handkerchief* (Altamira Press 2003).

[71] Mark Fathi Massoud, 'Field Research on Law in Conflict Zones and Authoritarian States' (2016) 12 Annual Review of Law and Social Science 85, 86.

[72] Anne Orford, 'In Praise of Description' (2012) 25 Leiden Journal of International Law 609, 622. In my teaching, I explain to my first-year students that this is the "pre-law blah blah blah", the mass of information that lawyers must sift through to get the "relevant" elements. This is put considerably more elegantly by Geertz, who remarks that "whatever it is that the law is after it is not the whole story . . . At base, it is not what happened, but what happens, that the law sees": Geertz, 'Local Knowledge' (n 49) 173.

[73] Claude Lévi-Strauss, 'The Problem of Invariance in Anthropology' (1960) 8 Diogenes 19, 24.

[74] Nouwen (n 68) 236.

[75] See, e.g., Montgomery McFate and Janice H Laurence (eds), *Social Science Goes to War: The Human Terrain System in Iraq and Afghanistan* (Oxford University Press 2015).

attentive to a set of concerns that do not match those demanded by legal analysis. A second set of reasons, more general in scope, relates to the fact that information on the practice of armed groups is very difficult to obtain. This reflects the nature of insurgency, often relying on concealment and movement as a parry against the overwhelming military superiority of the state. Any information about the actions of insurgents, even governance activities that do not relate directly to the conduct of armed hostilities, could prove a source of vulnerability for them. These reasons also reflect the nature of the environment, situations of armed conflict, which are broadly inimical to academic fieldwork. It is not altogether impossible to carry out ethnographic research in some war zones, despite the fact that it is undeniably risky, if it is done with flexible methodologies, a very solid knowledge of the environment, and a dense network of contacts.[76] Even where such fieldwork in conflict is possible, there are significant practical, methodological, emotional, and ethical challenges.[77] Violence shapes perceptions and identities, of both those who provide information and those who collect it, and any fact-finding enterprise in a conflict zone seems unlikely to be accepted as wholly neutral by those concerned.[78] Stathis Kalyvas identified a number of possible biases that might consciously or unconsciously colour the researcher's understanding of conflict, including urban bias (noting that studies of civil wars are typically produced by intellectuals in cities writing about violence in the countryside by peasant fighters) and partisan bias (feeling more sympathetic to one side or the other).[79] When studying governance practices of armed groups like the Islamic State or the Taliban, in Geertz's pithy formula, "we must learn to grasp what we cannot embrace".[80] That said, there are conflict zones in which fieldwork is simply not possible, and determining whether this is so at a given time and place is one of the most difficult and critical aspects of any such endeavour.[81]

For the facet of this project that aims at gathering more information on the practice of the rebel administration of justice, the challenges just described mandated a decidedly eclectic approach. This is not necessarily a problem because, as Laura Nader has suggested, resorting to a single fact-finding technique can

[76] Koen Vlassenroot, 'War and Social Research. The Limits of Empirical Methodologies in War-Torn Environments' [2006] Civilisations. Revue internationale d'anthropologie et de sciences humaines 191, 192.

[77] Jonathan Goodhand, 'Research in Conflict Zones: Ethics and Accountability' (2000) 8 Forced Migration Review 12, 12; Elisabeth Jean Wood, 'The Ethical Challenges of Field Research in Conflict Zones' (2006) 29 Qualitative Sociology 373; Meha Dixit, 'Field Research in Conflict Zones: Experience from India and Sierra Leone' (2012) 49 International Studies 133.

[78] Carolyn Nordstrom and Antonius Robben, 'The Anthropology and Ethnography of Violence and Sociopolitical Conflict' in Antonius Robben and Carolyn Nordstrom (eds), *Fieldwork under Fire: Contemporary Studies of Violence and Survival* (University of California Press Berkeley 1995) 4.

[79] Kalyvas (n 6) 36–38.

[80] Clifford Geertz, *Available Light: Anthropological Reflections on Philosophical Topics* (Princeton University Press 2001) 87.

[81] Wood (n 77) 374.

often stultify research, perhaps in law more than in most other fields.[82] An initial phase of the research, most intensely from 2015 to 2017, scoured existing academic literature in all disciplines (chiefly anthropology, history, international relations, political science, law), non-academic accounts from conflict zones (including from former guerrilla fighters, politicians, diplomats, international public servants, NGO workers, journalists, military personnel), media stories from established outlets and social media, and documents posted on the web by non-state armed groups themselves or by others who had come across them. This is archival work, broadly defined, and it can unearth fragments that must be approached as an archaeological project. What is found in these fragments can reveal a slice of the everyday exercise of power and resistance through law, but they can also mislead and hide other facets of rebel governance, intentionally or not. As with any archival work, sources can only make sense when situated within a broader scheme of social relations in which they are embedded.[83] On the basis of an initial search in an array of languages covering armed conflicts in every part of the world, a series of preliminary descriptions was prepared in relation to the justice practices of the following thirteen non-state armed groups: FARC (Colombia), Islamic State (Iraq-Syria), PKK (Turkey-Iraq-Syria), PYD (Syria), KRG (Iraq), CPN-M (Nepal), CPP/NPA (Philippines), MILF (Philippines), FMLN (El Salvador), SPLM/A (Sudan), Polisario (Western Sahara), LTTE (Sri Lanka), and Taliban (Afghanistan). In addition, some more limited information was collated and analysed with respect to a number of other insurgent justice practices.

On the basis of the findings of this initial round of research, I decided to attempt to arrive at thicker descriptions of a limited set of rebel courts systems that would offer a degree of diversity of contexts, approaches, and ideologies suitable to test the global aspirations of norms of public international law. Two armed groups that were always mentioned in the legal literature as having sophisticated involvement in the administration of justice were the LTTE in Sri Lanka and the FARC in Colombia. Movements inspired by a fundamentalist understanding of Islam seem likely to have distinct approaches to law and justice, leading to focus on the Islamic State in Iraq and Syria and the Taliban in Afghanistan. The three Kurdish entities exercising governance authority over different parts of Turkey, Iraq, and Syria, the PKK, PYD, and KRG, offered an interesting comparison of a spectrum of more or less hostile relations with the territorial state.

[82] Laura Nader, 'Moving On—Comprehending Anthropologies of Law' in June Starr and Mark Goodale (eds), *Practicing Ethnography in Law: New Dialogues, Enduring Methods* (Palgrave Macmillan US 2002) 198.

[83] Sally Engle Merry, 'Ethnography in the Archives' in June Starr and Mark Goodale (eds), *Practicing Ethnography in Law: New Dialogues, Enduring Methods* (Palgrave Macmillan US 2002) 128.

Finally, the SPLM/A was an insurgent movement that eventually became part of the official government of a new state, South Sudan. Taken together, they cover South America, Europe, Africa, the Middle East, and Asia. Most of these cases relate to situations of non-international armed conflict, although one includes a phase that was clearly an international armed conflict (Afghanistan) and another is arguably an internationalised non-international armed conflict (Syria).[84] The selected armed groups span a spectrum of formalism in their approach to the administration of justice, from highly institutionalised courts (LTTE) to instrumentalised community justice (FARC). Further documentary research was undertaken on these eight armed groups, in addition to in situ information gathering by collaborators and myself.

I carried out most of the fieldwork during a sabbatical leave in 2017–2018, going to Iraq (on the Islamic State, the PKK, PYD, and KRG), Sri Lanka (on the LTTE), and Colombia (on the FARC), in addition to interviews with members of diasporas in North America, Europe, and Asia. I came to the conclusion that, as far as I could tell, the situation in Afghanistan and Syria at that time was beyond the level of risk that I could manage, and I devised alternate strategies to supplement the information (by carrying out remote interviews, by finding local collaborators, or new sources of written materials). An initial plan to travel to South Sudan was derailed by the worsening security situation there in the window of time that I had available, and I was not successful at finding alternate sources of information, leading me to abandon the plan for a fuller description of the SPLM/A. I turned to the Polisario in Western Sahara instead, but an in-depth analysis revealed a very limited reliance on formal justice practices. Fieldwork took the form of semi-directed interviews arranged thanks to various gatekeepers in the relevant country, combined with a snowball approach.[85] As knowledge about insurgent justice is unlikely to be evenly distributed, I targeted concentric circles of individuals linked to rebel courts: rebel judges, court clerks, and administrators; lawyers or legal advisers; rebel commanders; individuals who had been prosecuted or had been parties to a civil case; clerics, community elders, and members of civil society organisations; and finally government officials, including state judges. Iraq was an active and fluid conflict zone when I was there, placing severe constraints on where I could go and how long I could stay. In Colombia, the FARC and the government signed a peace agreement in 2016 that saw the broad demobilisation of this rebel group. By the time I came to Colombia in early 2018, parts of the country had slipped back into insecurity

[84] Terry D Gill, 'Classifying the Conflict in Syria' (2016) 92 International Law Studies 11.

[85] Michael Kenney, 'Learning from the 'Dark Side'—Identifying, Accessing and Interviewing Illicit Non-State Actors' in Adam Dolnik (ed), *Conducting Terrorism Field Research* (Routledge 2013) 32–34. The methodology for the fieldwork component received approval from the McGill University Research Ethics Board.

because of dissident FARC units that refused to lay down their weapons, because other armed opposition groups like the ELN were jostling to take over areas that had been under stable FARC control, and because criminal bands and drug traffickers were reasserting their authority in places. It meant that sometimes, after travelling thousands of kilometres, I was not able to cover the last 100 kilometres to my target destination because the road was too dangerous. Finally, in Sri Lanka, the north-east remains heavily militarised and anyone who has connections to the LTTE is under constant surveillance by the State Intelligence Service. The result is that it is very challenging to find people willing to talk about the period when the LTTE governed this part of the country, although over time I did manage to find an interesting sample of informants. The Sri Lankan Tamil diaspora, the largest group of which is in Canada, proved largely hermetic to my attempt to collect information about LTTE justice, despite receiving generous words of support from community leaders and employing research assistants who were themselves Sri Lankan Tamils.

I do not claim the grand label of ethnography to characterise the case studies in this book. In seeking a factual foundation for an analysis of international legal standards that are universal in their aspiration and formal applicability, I was led to privilege diversity over depth. There is no doubt that more informed and insightful studies could be offered on the administration of justice by these or other non-state armed groups. A handful of in-depth single-group studies have already been carried out by non-legal scholars, and I have relied on these significantly.[86] Ethnographers differ on whether ethnography demands that the researcher be embedded in the local community for a period of several months, if not years, or whether multi-sited ethnography is possible to study the relationship between the local and global events.[87] Be that as it may, as recently put by two international law scholars, the aim is to chart "a path of inquiry . . . that navigates between the Scylla of legal formalism and the Charybdis of data-driven social science empiricism":[88] rather than an empirically driven project, this is a normative and conceptual analysis that relies on an examination of the practice of some non-state armed groups in administering justice to enrich the

[86] Two stellar examples are: Mario Aguilera Peña, *Contrapoder y Justicia Guerrillera: Fragmentación Política y Orden Insurgente En Colombia (1952–2003)* (IEPRI 2014) (for an approach grounded in history); Baczko (n 10) (for an approach grounded in sociology).

[87] Compare: Gearoid Millar, 'Engaging Ethnographic Peace Research: Exploring an Approach' (2018) 25 International Peacekeeping 597, 599; June Starr and Mark Goodale, 'Introduction: Legal Ethnography: New Dialogues, Enduring Methods' in June Starr and Mark Goodale (eds), *Practicing Ethnography in Law: New Dialogues, Enduring Methods* (Palgrave Macmillan US 2002) 3.

[88] Jens Meierhenrich and Richard Ashby Wilson, '"The Life of the Law Has Not Been Logic; It Has Been Experience." International Legal Ethnography and the New Legal Realism' in Shauhin Talesh, Elizabeth Mertz, and Heinz Klug (eds), *Handbook on New Legal Realism* (Edward Elgar, forthcoming) 21.

contextual understanding of this practice and prevent a tendency to normalise and normativise too eagerly what is observed in one place.[89]

A last methodological point must be made, regarding terminology. As will have been evident already, I use interchangeably the expressions non-state armed groups, armed opposition groups, armed groups, insurgents, rebels, irregulars, and (more rarely) armed non-state actors. Likewise, although I usually refer to international humanitarian law as the expression most commonly used in the academic literature, I also make use of other expressions such as the laws of war, the law of armed conflict, *jus in bello*, and the laws and customs of war. I am aware that some will see specific meaning and associations connected to one or the other of these expressions, but these reflect distinctions that are not germane to the analysis offered here.

IV. Overall Project: Insurgent Jurisprudence

This book presents an argument that it is possible for non-state armed groups in situations of armed conflict to legally establish and operate a system of courts to administer justice. Neither the concept of the rule of law nor the general principle of state sovereignty stands in the way of framing an understanding of the rule of law adapted to the reality of insurgent justice. Legal standards applicable to non-state armed groups in situations of international or non-international armed conflict, including international humanitarian law, international human rights law, and international criminal law, recognise their authority to regularly constitute or establish non-state courts. The lawful operation of such courts is of course subject to requirements of due process, corresponding to an array of guarantees that must be respected in all cases. Rebel courts that are regularly constituted and operate in a manner consistent with due process guarantees demand a certain degree of recognition by international institutions, by states not involved in the conflict, to some extent by the territorial state, and even by other non-state armed groups. These normative claims are grounded in a series of detailed case studies of the administration of justice by non-state armed groups in a diverse range of conflict situations. This project does not aim to explore the reasons that lead armed opposition groups to decide to become involved in the administration of justice in territory under their authority, nor whether there are identifiable social, economic, or political determinants of the success of rebel justice, nor whether the rebel administration of justice has an impact on perceptions of legitimacy of insurgents within the civilian population, nor whether armed groups operating courts are more likely to win a war, nor, finally, whether there

[89] Arnaut and Højbjerg (n 31) 16.

are counter-insurgency strategies that are particularly effective at countering rebel justice governance. Of course, rules of international humanitarian law and, to some extent, international human rights law are not wholly insulated from these concerns, and what is said here may have some relevance to these other lines of enquiry.

Chapter 1 considers the compatibility of the rebel administration of justice with the concept of the rule of law, using the FARC in Colombia as a case study. The *Fuerzas Armadas Revolucionarias de Colombia—Ejército del Pueblo* (FARC) was the largest non-state armed group during five decades of civil war in that country. At its peak, it wielded dominant territorial authority in more than half of Colombian municipalities. While it generally did not establish standing institutions to administer justice, it imposed legal norms, co-opted existing community justice mechanisms, and established informal and hybrid practices to settle legal disputes in the civil and criminal law fields. FARC justice practices are used to explore the concept of the rule of law, an essentially contested legal concept that cannot be exclusively attached to the modern state. The rule of law is shown to be a concept with a flexible content, modulated by circumstances such as the onset of armed conflict. Elements of a rebel rule of law adapted to the nature of non-state armed groups and context of armed conflict are articulated in the chapter. Finally, the principle of state sovereignty is analysed to show that it does not impart exclusive jurisdiction to the state over the administration of justice, but instead can accommodate justice practices by a diversity of actors, including non-state armed groups in conflict zones.

Chapter 2 assesses the legality of rebel courts pursuant to applicable rules of public international law, with the challenging if not provocative case studies of the rebel administration of justice by the Islamic State in Syria and Iraq and the Taliban in Afghanistan. The Islamic State is a Salafi-jihadist non-state armed group presenting itself as a caliphate, which at one point controlled a territory in Syria and Iraq as large as the United Kingdom. It had a highly developed institutional structure that was quite bureaucratic in nature, including a multi-tier court system that imposed harsh but undeniably effective justice. The Islamic State forcefully rejected notions such as the rule of law and judicial independence and impartiality. The Taliban started as an insurgent armed group, then acted as the government of Afghanistan from 1996 to 2001, and then again as non-state armed group after that date. Labelling itself the Islamic Emirate of Afghanistan, the Taliban has a hierarchical governance structure, in which courts are somewhat separate from other sections. Taliban judges are trained Islamic scholars that constantly rotate from province to province, and there are provincial appeal courts and central apex courts. The very concept of a "court" used in international law applicable to armed conflicts implies some basic attributes that will not be met by any and all adjudicative bodies. That said, the concept of a "regularly constituted court" in international humanitarian law and of a "court established by law" in human rights law corresponds to basic criteria that are not impossible to meet for an armed group. Likewise, the institutional requirement of independence and impartiality that define what is a court, once adapted to the reality of a non-state armed group operating in a conflict zone, can indeed be met by some armed insurgents.

Chapter 3 examines the implication of a broad requirement of due process for rebel courts, taking as a case study the judicial system put into place by the Liberation Tigers of Tamil Eelam (LTTE) in Sri Lanka. The LTTE launched an armed insurgency against the government of Sri Lanka in the early 1980s, eventually controlling nearly 40 percent of national territory. The LTTE developed an independent civil administration which included a state-like court structure with seventeen distinct courts at trial, appeal, and supreme court levels. The group also enacted comprehensive civil and criminal codes, as well as other important pieces of legislation. The chapter takes this exceptionally sophisticated insurgent court system to interrogate the concept of rebel jurisdiction, exploring the foundations in public international law of the extent and limits of territorial, subject-matter, and personal jurisdictions of rebel law and courts. The analysis then turns to the thorny issue of due process requirements that must be met under international humanitarian and human rights law to consider as fair a trial before a rebel court. The precise content of the requirement of a fair trial under international law does vary in situations of emergency like international and non-international armed conflicts. In addition, legal standards must be adjusted to reflect the nature of non-state courts and the particular contextual challenges faced by rebel governance in conflict zones. On that basis, each applicable due process guarantee is analysed to determine the precise requirements it imposes on rebel justice.

Chapter 4 analyses the possible legal recognition of insurgent justice by other actors, using the judicial practice of three independent Kurdish non-state armed groups in the Middle East as a case study. The Partiya Karkerên Kurdistan (PKK, Kurdistan Workers' Party) has been engaged in a bitter armed struggle with Turkey since 1984, with rear bases in northern Iraq and Syria. The Partiya Yekîtiya Demokrat (PYD, Democratic Union Party) is a Kurdish insurgent group that joined the anti-Assad uprising of 2011 and now controls parts of the northeast of Syria, in a precarious coexistence with the Syrian government. Finally, the Kurdish Regional Government (KRG) has governed independently since expelling Saddam Hussein's troops in 1991, and it remains in a military standoff with the central Iraqi government. All three Kurdish groups operate courts at trial and appellate levels, for civil and criminal matters. The chapter considers the possible application of the principle of complementarity under the Rome Statute in relation to a prosecution before the courts of a non-state armed groups. Likewise, the right or duty of third states under international law to give recognition to the operation of insurgent courts is examined. More radically perhaps, there is a possibility that even the territorial state might in some cases give legal effect to rebel court decisions. Finally, the Kurdish courts offer examples in which one non-state armed group is confronted with the need to determine the validity of the decisions of courts of other armed insurgents.

1

Rebel Rule of Law and FARC Justice

La guerrilla lo que tiene que hacer para vivir es ser la ley donde llega.
—Rebel Commander, Colombia

The rise of *jus in bello* as a part of public international law stands as at least a partial refutation of Cicero's aphorism that "*inter arma enim silent leges*". If it has come to be accepted that at least some laws do not fall silent during wars, it remains undeniable that armed conflicts are a deeply challenging environment for the administration of justice. Considerable attention has been devoted by academic commentators to the impact of armed hostilities on the substance of legal standards protecting individual and collective interests. Likewise, attention has been directed to the displacement of the sovereign authority of a state by the occupation of national territory by another state. Comparatively little has been said regarding the rise of non-state actors exercising public governance over territory and population in times of war. Some acts were deemed unlawful by international humanitarian law and, later, international criminal law, but again with little focus on the regulation of what fell short of the red lines drawn in these two fields of international law. There floats a haze, in international law, as to how governance by armed groups ought to be characterised. One central, framing question for jurists is whether any of what such groups do can be labelled as administering justice, for the administration of justice is one type of public governance that is thickly regulated by legal standards. This in turn begs the question of whether the concept of the rule of law ties the administration of justice to state sovereignty or whether that concept encompasses acts of legal governance carried out by non-state actors like armed groups in conflict zones.

In the more than half-century of civil strife in Colombia, there has been a constant ebb and flow in the sharing of power between the government and rebel groups, the largest of which was the *Fuerzas Armadas Revolucionarias de Colombia—Ejército del Pueblo* (FARC). The FARC was a highly structured group controlled by a designated hierarchy, said to have encompassed as much as 20,000 fighters at its peak in the early 2000s. While it exercised total control of part of national territory only during limited periods, it was a dominant presence in more

Rebel Courts. René Provost, Oxford University Press. © Oxford University Press 2021.
DOI: 10.1093/oso/9780190912222.003.0002

than half of Colombian municipalities over long periods of time. In those areas of mixed control, the population had to navigate between governance *de abajo* (from below, in the plains), emanating from state institutions, and governance *de arriba* (from above, in the hills), emanating from the FARC. The insurgents adopted a dual strategy of instrumentalisation and neutralisation, attempting to infiltrate official institutions to co-opt them to follow a line dictated by the rebels or, failing that, impeding the operations of these institutions. In a more limited set of circumstances, they replaced state organs altogether with their own institutions. As a result, the FARC was involved, for a period of time extending over several decades, in the management of a wide array of social issues, including labour relations, commerce, family life, taxation, environmental protection, and much more. One facet of this rebel governance was the administration of justice.

This chapter, relying on recent ethnographic research by anthropologists and sociologists in Colombia as well as my own field work, maps out the emergence and evolution of these FARC "courts" with a view to appraise the extent to which they correspond in any meaningful manner to the concept of the judicial function (Section I). This will in turn serve to interrogate, relying on the insights of legal pluralism, the concept of the rule of law. Unpacking the idea of the rule of law applicable in situations of armed conflict, I argue that a cogent concept of the rebel rule of law can be articulated to serve as yardstick to measure and guide insurgents in their legal governance (Section II), and that such a concept does not stand invalidated by the principle of state sovereignty (Section III).

I. Rebel Justice in Colombia

In the limited literature on rebel governance, when the administration of justice is examined, two cases are always mentioned as amounting to unusually developed insurgent legal regimes: Sri Lanka and Colombia.[1] Likewise, in the handful of international law studies that have discussed the creation of courts by non-state armed groups, the same two countries are brought up as vignettes of how far this practice can be developed.[2] In this chapter, I aim to go beyond the small vignette and delve deeper into the reality of rebel administration of justice by the FARC in Colombia, to tease out whether in such a practice we can discern legal norms and judicial institutions as understood using the insights of legal

[1] E.g., Zachariah Cherian Mampilly, *Rebel Rulers Insurgent Governance and Civilian Life during War* (Cornell University Press 2011) 2–6. Sri Lanka is analysed in detail in Chapter 3.

[2] Jonathan Somer, 'Jungle Justice: Passing Sentence on the Equality of Belligerents in Non-International Armed Conflict' (2007) 89 International Review of the Red Cross 655; Sandesh Sivakumaran, 'Courts of Armed Opposition Groups—Fair Trials or Summary Justice?' (2009) 7 Journal of International Criminal Justice 489; Sandesh Sivakumaran, *The Law of Non-International Armed Conflict* (Oxford University Press 2012) 549–562.

pluralism. I start by situating the conflict and presenting the governance structure of the FARC (A) before turning to its legal system per se (B).

A. The Civil War in Colombia and FARC Governance

After a brief sketch of the origins and evolution of the conflict in Colombia, the FARC's general governance structure and institutions are presented. Both provide context to the discussion of the administration of justice by the FARC in the following section.

i. The Civil War in Colombia

The Colombian armed conflict has its immediate roots in the period referred to as *La Violencia*, a period of chaotic domestic unrest that started with the assassination of the presidential candidate Jorge Eliécer Gaitán in 1948.[3] This era of Colombian history was marked by violence between the two traditional parties, the Liberals and the Conservatives, carried out by self-defence militias, guerrillas, and criminal organisations.[4] The conflict originated in competing political agendas and, more fundamentally, in deep-seated tensions around access to land that had marred Colombia for more than a century.[5] The disjointed orgy of violence that caused more than 200,000 deaths during *La Violencia* gradually gave way to a more structured civil war between a more cohesive Colombian government and several non-state armed groups. Although there have been several stages in this conflict, it never ceased completely. Early in the history of the conflict, several guerrilla groups came to emerge, including the FARC, the *Ejército de Liberación Nacional* (ELN), the *Ejército popular de Liberación* (EPL), and the April 19 Movement (M19). They were later joined by right-wing paramilitary groups, eventually federated as the *Autodefensas unidas de Colombia* (AUC). Throughout the civil war, but especially in more recent times, criminal groups referred to as *bandas criminals* (BACRIM), or drug lords, have operated across the conflict zones.[6]

[3] Catherine C LeGrand, 'The Colombian Crisis in Historical Perspective' (2003) 28 Canadian Journal of Latin American and Caribbean Studies 165; Human Rights Watch, *War without Quarter: Colombia and International Humanitarian Law* (Human Rights Watch 1998) 136; Mary Roldán, *Blood and Fire: La Violencia in Antioquia, Colombia, 1946–1953* (Duke University Press 2002); Germán Guzmán Campos, Orlando Fals-Borda, and Eduardo Umaña Luna, *La violencia en Colombia* (Taurus 2005).

[4] Norman Offstein, 'An Historical Review and Analysis of Colombian Guerrilla Movements: FARC, ELN and EPL' (2003) 52 Desarrollo y Sociedad 99, 101.

[5] Claire Metelits, *Inside Insurgency: Violence, Civilians, and Revolutionary Group Behavior* (New York University Press 2010) 88.

[6] Constantin von der Groeben, 'The Conflict in Colombia and the Relationship between Humanitarian Law and Human Rights Law in Practice: Analysis of the New Operational Law of the Colombian Armed Forces' (2011) 16 Journal of Conflict and Security Law 141, 142.

The FARC was involved in the Colombian conflict in its current form from 1966. Although the emergence of the FARC is commonly associated with the apparition of the Southern Bloc (*Bloque Sur*) in 1964, its roots can be traced to the period of *La Violencia* and resistance carried out by *Autodefensas campesinas* trying to shield peasant communities from other violent actors.[7] At its origins, proclaiming itself the revolutionary army of Colombia inspired by the Cuban revolution, the movement received support from the Colombian Communist Party and the USSR. Its stated goals were to fight poverty in agricultural regions of Colombia and improve peasants' quality of life.[8] The FARC, the longest-lasting guerrilla group in Latin America, was a unique insurgent movement in that it grew from peasant self-organisation, with a leadership that was entirely composed of lower-class peasants.[9] At least initially, it operated in areas that were largely cut off geographically and socially from the centres of power in Colombia and limited itself to defensive actions, with the result that it was not seen as a major threat.[10]

From the late 1960s to mid-1970s, the government carried out important investments in the rural agricultural sector, with a significant impact on peasant wellbeing. These investments combined with a changing international context significantly weakened support for the FARC and other guerrilla groups in some of the rural areas.[11] Partly as a result, starting in the mid-1970s, the FARC became involved in drug trafficking, a pattern which intensified in the 1980s when coca eradication campaigns in neighbouring Bolivia and Peru combined with economic hardship in Colombia to entice many peasants to turn to the culture of that leaf.[12] Reportedly, the FARC ensured their financial autonomy largely through the regulation and taxation of the production and trafficking of coca, supplemented by kidnapping and extortion.[13] Peace talks were initiated by the government in the early 1980s, leading to a ceasefire that was never fully respected. The FARC did branch out into the political arena with the *Union Patriotica* political party, but retreated to military action after several thousand *Union Patriotica* activists were assassinated by right-wing paramilitary groups.[14]

[7] Mario Aguilera Peña, *Contrapoder y Justicia Guerrillera: Fragmentación Política y Orden Insurgente En Colombia (1952–2003)* (IEPRI 2014) 241; Carlos Medina Gallego, 'FARC-EP: Notas Para Una Historia Política 1958–2006' (Universidad Nacional de Colombia Bogotá 2008); Offstein (n 4) 103.

[8] Offstein (n 4) 107.

[9] LeGrand (n 3) 176; Metelits (n 5) 94.

[10] Mario Aguilera Peña, *Guerrilla y Población Civil. La Trayectoria de Las FARC, 1949–2013* (3d edn, IEPRI 2014) 88.

[11] Offstein (n 4) 105.

[12] Metelits (n 5) 100–101.

[13] LeGrand (n 3) 181; Juridicción especial para la paz (JEP), Caso No. 01 Toma de rehenes y graves privaciones de la libertad cometidas por las FARC-EP, Auto No 19 de 2021, 26 January 2021, 90–137. Eventually, the decisions and archives of the JEP will offer a rich source of information on governance by the FARC.

[14] Metelits (n 5) 99.

After this failed attempt, some challenged the FARC's continued commitment to the best interest of the people and the revolution, as opposed to profiteering.[15] That said, despite internal dissensions, the membership of the FARC increased tremendously, from three to twenty-seven fronts between 1974 and 1984. The number of FARC fighters then grew from an estimated 3,600 in 1986 to about 20,000 around the year 2000, down again to about 7,000 in 2016.[16]

The 1990s was the bloodiest decade of the civil war in Colombia. Even though the government agreed to a new constitution in 1991, the FARC did not settle and demobilize. Negotiations did continue, and in 1998 the government agreed to "demilitarize" a remote swath of territory that was a FARC stronghold as a gesture to boost peace talks. This *zona de despeje* (demilitarized zone), the size of Switzerland, was abandoned for nearly four years by all institutions of the central government, leaving the FARC to take over many of the functions that had been performed by the government.[17] In 2001, the United States officially got involved in the Colombian conflict with "Plan Colombia": initiated by Colombian President Andrés Pastrana and US President Bill Clinton with an allocation of $1.3 billion from the United States, Plan Colombia was intended to stop drug trafficking. That said, the fight against the insurgency, especially against the FARC, was a key component, with US special operations units training the Colombian military in counter-insurgency tactics.[18] The new military capacities of the army, the coming to power of a hard-line government in Colombia, and the termination of the demilitarized zone all combined to push the FARC further in the Colombian jungle and to deny them the kind of stable geographic presence that they had enjoyed for several years in many areas. The government attempted another round of peace talks with the FARC, which failed in 2002.

Another important facet of the civil war in Colombia is the role played by paramilitary groups. The origins of these groups are tied to the rise in drug trafficking and the FARC's practice of kidnapping as a source of operating funds. With the growing wealth of drug lords, they became frequent targets of FARC kidnapping, leading them to form death squads called "Death to Kidnappers" (*Muerte a secuestradores*). These death squads eventually combined with private militias paid to protect large ranches to form the first paramilitaries.[19] Colombian law afforded a veneer of legality to such self-defence organisations, allowing them

15 Offstein (n 4) 110.

16 Aguilera Peña, *Contrapoder y Justicia Guerrillera* (n 7) 279; Jonathan D Rosen, *The Losing War: Plan Colombia and Beyond* (SUNY Press 2014). The estimated size of the troops from year to year is available at https://web.stanford.edu/group/mappingmilitants/cgi-bin/groups/view/89.

17 Lorena Carrillo, '"¡Juntos, Pero No Revueltos!" (O de Cómo Se Ha Concertado La Regulación Social En Medio de La Guerra) El Caso de La Región de El Pato. San Vicente Del Caguán, Colombia. 1956–2016' (Master's Thesis, Colegio de Michoacan 2016) 132; Aguilera Peña, *Guerrilla y Población Civil* (n 10) 251–252.

18 Rosen (n 16).

19 LeGrand (n 3) 181–182.

to cooperate with the army at the same time as they supported the drug trade. Over the decade of the 1990s, they grew to more than 10,000 in strength largely united under the banner of the *Autodefensas unidas de Colombia* (AUC), with a presence in 40 percent of municipalities.[20] The rise of paramilitaries transformed the conflict, leading to a spike in violence against civilians, mostly at the hands of the paramilitaries.[21] Colombia reached an agreement with paramilitary groups, which demobilized between 2003 and 2006 under an ironically named "Justice and Peace Law" that granted immunity to all paramilitaries.[22]

The final peace negotiations with the FARC began in August 2012, with the signing of the General Agreement for the Termination of the Conflict and Building of a Stable and Long-Lasting Peace ("Havana Accord"). The negotiations progressed steadily, and a general ceasefire agreement was reached in June 2016. The narrow rejection of a proposed accord by referendum in Colombia in October 2016 was one more hurdle before a final peace agreement between Colombia and the FARC could be approved by the legislature at the end of 2016.[23] The FARC, rebranded as "*la FARC*" (for "*Fuerza Alternativa Revolucionaria del Común*"), joined the electoral campaign as a political party in 2018. One section of the FARC, the Bloque oriental, never accepted the peace agreement and refused to lay down its weapons. In August 2019, Iván Márquez, one of the FARC leaders who had participated in the peace process, announced that he was relaunching the group's armed struggle, and there is much uncertainty as to whether this is a new phase of the conflict between the government and the FARC.[24]

ii. FARC Governance

From the formation of the FARC in 1964 until 2008, Manuel Marulanda Vélez (also known as "Tirofijo"—sure-shot) acted as supreme leader. The FARC was well organised, with a highly centralised command. Marulanda and his companions commanded the FARC from what they called the General Secretariat. This organ of the FARC was composed of seven individuals, each with a particular regional or substantive mandate. The FARC also had a High Command (*Estado Mayor*) responsible for military operations. Fighting forces were divided into blocks (*bloques*), which join several fronts as regional forces.[25]

[20] Metelits (n 5) 103–105.

[21] ibid 106.

[22] ibid 107.

[23] The peace process is described at http://colombiapeace.org. The text of the final agreement is available, in Spanish, at http://www.altocomisionadoparalapaz.gov.co/Paginas/inicio.aspx.

[24] 'Colombia Ex-Rebel Commander Issues Call to Arms' *BBC News* (29 August 2019), online: <https://www.bbc.com/news/world-latin-america-49508411> accessed 7 June 2020.

[25] Juan Guillermo Ferro Medina and Graciela Uribe Ramón, *El Orden de La Guerra: Las FARC-EP Entre La Organización y La Política* (CEJA 2002) 40–57. Fronts were themselves composed of any number of columns (of 110 fighters), each including two companies (of 55 fighters), which were further divided into guerrillas (of 26 fighters) and squads (of 13 fighters): ibid at 50.

In 1997, it was estimated that there were sixty-two rural fronts, three urban fronts, and nine elite units mirroring the army's specialised counter-insurgency brigade.[26] The FARC also established militias, a civilian component of the group that ensured a constant presence in a community, but whose members were not considered as full members of the group.[27] The Statutes of the group show very clearly that the organisation of the FARC is modelled after that of the military.[28] Although block commanders were dispersed throughout the country, often in remote regions far away from the reach of the central FARC administration, Marulanda and the General Secretariat are said to have maintained tight control over these units so as to determine the group's general strategy.[29] Marulanda died of natural causes in 2008 and was replaced at the helm of the FARC by Timoleon Jiménez, also known as Timochenko.

According to Timothy Wickham-Crowley, governance over a population by a non-state armed groups corresponds to three fundamental goals: "(1) defend the populace from foreign enemies, (2) maintain internal peace and order, and (3) make contributions to the material security of the population".[30] The FARC did not deviate from this model, adopting a dual strategy ("*doble poder o poder de dos caras*")[31] of instrumentalisation and marginalisation: they would try to infiltrate state institutions to gain legal protection and orient measures taken to improve the population's well-being, and at the same time try to impede the state's credibility by showing its lack of legitimacy and limited capacity.[32] Colombia in fact had quite strong state institutions, and government agencies often could still operate even where the rebels had territorial control.[33] The Colombian guerrillas rarely developed state structures as such. Indeed, Ana Arjona argues that

26 Human Rights Watch (n 3) 137.

27 Ferro Medina and Uribe Ramón (n 25) 55–57.

28 *Estatuto de las FARC-EP*, Chapter III, Article 3, p 8, online: http://farc-ep.co/wp-content/uploads/2013/10/Estatutos.pdf [FARC Statute]. The JEP issued a detailed analysis of the FARC governance structure, which it describes as a 'military-bureaucratic organization': JEP (n 13) 38–80.

29 Elena M Valencia, 'Theories of Compliance in International Conflict: The Place of the Third Geneva Convention in the Colombian Armed Conflict' (2007) 21 Temple International and Comparative Law Journal 445, 449.

30 Timothy Wickham-Crowley, 'Del Gobierno de Abajo al Gobierno de Arriba . . . And Back: Transitions to and from Rebel Governance in Latin America, 1956–1990' in Ana Arjona, Nelson Kasfir, and Zachariah Mampilly (eds), *Rebel Governance in Civil War* (Cambridge University Press 2015) 49. See also Ezequiel Heffes, 'From Words to Deeds: A Research Study of Armed Non-State Actors' Practice and Interpretation of International Humanitarian and Human Rights Norms—Fuerzas Armadas Revolucionarias de Colombia—Ejército del Pueblo' (Geneva Call 2021).

31 Aguilera Peña, *Contrapoder y Justicia Guerrillera* (n 7) 102.

32 ibid 108 ("Con sus ambigüedades o dualidades, los contrapoderes han significado un reto para el Estado, en tanto que estos pararon de ser únicos, marginales y muy locales [germinales o de Resistencia] a multiplicarse y formar verdaderas franjas de control compartido entre el Estado y la guerrilla, llegando a ofrecer una imagen creciente de fragmentación y de colapso del Estado").

33 Ana Arjona, 'Wartime Institutions: A Research Agenda' (2014) 58 Journal of Conflict Resolution 1360, 137.

> [i]n general, armed actors in Colombia do not directly engage in the creation of health or education systems as insurgents have done in other countries. Instead, they usually influence how local government officials provide those services, and sometimes fund certain projects. Armed groups frequently gave orders to mayors and council members directing expenditures of public funds for infrastructure, education, or health projects.[34]

Moreover, the same author posits that, "[w]ith a few exceptions, neither the guerrillas nor the paramilitaries sought to dismantle the formal local government altogether. Rather, they tried to control it by forcibly intervening in its decisions, capturing it through the appointment of their own members or allies, or both".[35] That said, in some rural community where the state was basically absent, such as in San Vicente del Caguán (Caquetá Department) during the 1970s and in the demilitarized zone in the late 1990s, the FARC became "the de facto ruler, intervening in social, political, and economic activities, and regulating many types of conducts".[36] The FARC went "to the locality peacefully, telling the community they were there to protect it".[37]

> *The FARC, in many parts of Colombian territory, replaced the state. It is not because an overthrow had occurred, I think it is rather that the state did not exist in many regions of the country, and then, when the FARC occupies these regions, in practice it becomes the state.*
>
> *Interview, FARC Commander Edoardo (July 2016)*

The degree to which the FARC and other armed opposition groups could exert authority over a population normally varied from place to place and over time. This political geography of power was translated into the FARC's own territorial organisation within what were called *zonas de retaguardia*. There were two types of *zonas de retaguardias*, the first was the area next to the battlefront, which served as a refuge or a place to regain forces, also called the *frente guerrilleros*; the second was the *retaguardia nacional*, chosen in light of the political and social capital that could be developed in an area or in view of the pre-existing influence of communist groups in the 1950s.[38] The latter areas were essential to propagate

[34] Ana Arjona, 'Civilian Resistance to Rebel Governance' in Ana Arjona, Nelson Kasfir, and Zachariah Mampilly (eds), *Rebel Governance in Civil War* (Cambridge University Press 2015) 190.

[35] ibid.

[36] ibid 192. In this community, "[m]ost interviewees agreed that civilians had little autonomy vis-à-vis the rebels. 'The control that the armed actor had when I arrived here was total', said a community leader who came in 1980. Nevertheless, locals found ways to communicate their preferences to FARC commanders and influence some of the ways in which things were done" (*id.*).

[37] ibid 193.

[38] Aguilera Peña, *Contrapoder y Justicia Guerrillera* (n 7) 93.

the revolution, secure FARC influence on the population, and militarily defend the movement. The demilitarized zone in the late 1990s certainly was an instance of such control. Once a zone is entirely controlled, it can be qualified as a liberated area (*zonas liberadas*). Such a qualification would be the achievement of the first step of the revolution. The next step would be for the population to take control of their land and, with the insurgents, carry out an offensive against the central government.[39] This stage in fact was never reached by any rebel group in Colombia—there were areas controlled by insurgents, but never completely liberated areas.[40] Although the FARC was never truly capable of developing *zonas liberadas*, it did develop *frentes guerrilleros*, and, more importantly, it developed *retarguardias nacionales* that were undoubtedly more stable and long-lasting than that of other guerrilla groups in the country.[41]

> *The FARC destroyed a cellular phone transmission tower during an attack near our village. In order to rebuild it, we had to obtain permission from the central government, from the military, and also from the same FARC unit that had destroyed it in the first place!*
>
> *Interview, JAC leader Marcelo (January 2018)*

FARC governance during the civil war was always intertwined with other sources of governance, both from the government and from local communities. In that respect, the *Juntas Acción Comunal* (JAC) are important local organisations when it comes to understanding what role the government was playing in contested zones or zones under the control of the FARC. The JAC are peasant organisations that were established by the state in order to give local communities representatives that could dialogue with the central government. In addition, the JAC normally run "conciliation committees", communal dispute-resolution mechanisms that are often the first place local people turn to when seeking justice. Although established by the state, the JAC remained independent of the government to some degree, and acted as interlocutors in communications with both the state and non-state armed groups.[42] Created by the state and imposed as a vehicle for

39 ibid.

40 ibid.

41 ibid 94–95. They were located in the departments of Meta, Guaviare, Putumayo, and Caquetá, and lasted broadly from 1980 to 2003.

42 Carrillo (n 17) 26; Aguilera Peña, *Contrapoder y Justicia Guerrillera* (n 7) 98 "[. . .] las juntas en esas condiciones no quedaron subordinadas a la insurgencia ni entraron a formar parte del organigrama político de los aparatos armados. Las JAC compartían los mimos espacios de las guerrillas, realizaban actividades complementarias de gobierno y de justicia, pero generalmente actuaban con independencia en la adopción de planes y programas para cubrir las necesidades de las veredas, en los desarrollos de sus comités de trabajo y en sus gestiones ante las autoridades regionales. Las JAC serían el Gobierno en algunas zonas controladas por las guerrillas y estas asumirían el papel coactivo. Las JAC eran el eje común entre la comunidad y la guerrilla, y estas no se atreverían por

official governance, the JAC were nevertheless also supported by the FARC.[43] The JAC remained mostly independent from the FARC, but in rural regions where the FARC have a strong influence, they typically maintained a close relationship. In some cases, the FARC infiltrated the JAC as a way of ensuring their collaboration. Conversely, FARC respect for the JAC enhanced its credentials in the eyes of the population.[44]

All forms of governance imply some element of power and repression, and governance by non-state armed groups is no exception.[45] The FARC, like all guerrilla groups, imposed rules not only on its own members to maintain discipline but also on civilians to direct their behaviours, regulating issues such as free speech, mobility, sexual conduct, personal appearance, labour standards, commercial trade, environmental protection, and so forth.[46] While there are a few reports that some units may have posted pamphlets to publicise what their rules were, mostly this was done through public statements by FARC commanders and word of mouth. In some areas the FARC simply decreed what the rules of behaviours were to be, while in others the local community was much more involved in shaping at least some of the norms applicable to daily life.[47] That being said, 90 percent of civilians interviewed by Arjona stated that, when living under the control of an armed group, they always knew how to behave and what rules to observe; they knew what to expect from the members of the guerrilla group.[48] What's more, the population often turned to the rebels when they encountered problems. Indeed, "in about two-thirds of the cases, civilians turned to combatants to solve problems related to public order".[49] The control over the population by the FARC also translated into tax collection. Even though some guerrillas in Latin America did not tax the population in order to avoid having to put a financial burden on the population, the FARC since the 1980s did selectively collect taxes from coca traders, cattle owners, and merchants.[50] In the

regla general a imponer sus puntos sin alterar las reglas de juego democráticas que predominan en la vida interna de dichos organismos".

[43] Nicolás Espinosa Menéndez, 'La Justicia Guerrillera En Colombia. Elementos de Análisis Para Los Retos de La Transición Política En Una Zona de Control Insurgente (El Caso Del Piedemonte Amazónico)' [2016] Estudios Latinoamericanos 87, 91 ("un modelo de organización social agenciado por el Estado, exigido por las instituciones oficiales para cualquier tipo de trabajo entre Estado y comunidad, y paradójicamente, promovido por la guerrilla en las zonas rurales").

[44] Aguilera Peña, *Contrapoder y Justicia Guerrillera* (n 7) 99, 103; Andrés Felipe Aponte González, *Grupos armados y construcción de orden social en la esquina sur del Tolima, 1948–2016* (Cinep 2019) 186.

[45] Wickham-Crowley (n 30) 48.

[46] Arjona, 'Wartime Institutions: A Research Agenda' (n 33) 1373; Aguilera Peña, *Contrapoder y Justicia Guerrillera* (n 7) 146.

[47] Carrillo (n 17) 155–156.

[48] Arjona, 'Wartime Institutions: A Research Agenda' (n 33) 1371.

[49] ibid 1372.

[50] Wickham-Crowley (n 30) 58; JEP (n 13) 67–71

1980s, this practice not only allowed the FARC to grow significantly because of its greater financial capacity, but it was also a process whereby some order was imposed on illegal activities that greatly contributed to violence and insecurity in Colombia.[51]

In closing on FARC governance, two reactive aspects bear mentioning: on the one hand, the operationalisation of rebel governance often triggered a backlash by the Colombian government against the population, in the hope that people could be intimidated into withdrawing any degree of support for, or acceptance of, rebel rule.[52] It is not clear that this succeeded in mitigating support for armed opposition groups, as sometimes the population would respond to terror tactics of the government or paramilitaries by seeking protection by insurgents.[53] On the other hand, rebel rule, like any other type of rule, can trigger its own resistance by the population. There is likely to be some degree of popular resistance to any attempt by a non-state armed group to impose its rule. The more significant and wide-ranging the rule by rebels, the more likely and significant the resistance by the population. This can take the form of spontaneous individual requests to rebel commanders, or collective, organised opposition to a perceived lack of respect by armed opposition groups. Arjona provides one example of civilian resistance to FARC rule in Colombia by an isolated and well-organised community:

> According to one of the community's leaders, "at the beginning [the FARC] tried to rule over everything. They came to our meetings. They told us what we could do, where we could go, and when. We could not let this happen. We had been our own rulers for years." To stop the FARC from taking control of their local cooperative, the community decided to talk to the commander: We told [him] very clearly that we did not want militiamen in the area. That it was not needed. "If what you need is some information, we will give it to you. But we do not need orientation or guidelines. We don't need any of that. We know very well what we need to do." And at the end, the commander agreed. After a long discussion that included threats and insults, the guerrillas agreed to respect the cooperative and avoid intervening in its affairs.[54]

[51] Aguilera Peña, *Contrapoder y Justicia Guerrillera* (n 7) 280 ("en esos lugares, por lo general de reciente colonización, la guerrilla aparecía como la única fuerza armada capaz de imponer un orden en el marco de economía ilegal y en donde tendían a operar diversos factores de violencia e inseguridad"); Aponte González (n 44) 151–153.

[52] Wickham-Crowley (n 30) 56–57.

[53] An example is narrated in Alfredo Molano, 'La Justicia Guerrillera' in Boaventura de Sousa Santos and Mauricio García (eds), *Caleidoscopio de las justicias en Colombia*, vol. 2 (2001) 338.

[54] Arjona, 'Civilian Resistance to Rebel Governance' (n 34) 198.

There are even examples of Indigenous communities resisting direct physical violence or death threats by the FARC and succeeding in effectively blocking its rule.[55] This illustrates the limits of insurgent governance grounded in violence alone. Rebel governance, indeed all forms of governance, must be grounded in some degree of symbiotic relation between those wielding power and those subject to it. One facet of governance in which this interactive dimension is especially apparent is in the administration of justice.

B. FARC Justice

Like many other non-state armed groups, the FARC started as a small group with a limited territorial basis, to later grow into a much more imposing movement with a heavier footprint in some parts of Colombia. As discussed in the previous section, rebel governance is evolving and transitory, a reflection of the group's military strength and relation with the civilian population. It is useful to trace the evolution of FARC justice over the course of the civil war (i) before turning to more specific analysis of its internal/military (ii) and external/civilian components (iii).

i. Evolution of FARC Justice

Mario Aguilera Peña, who has carried out the most extensive historical study of guerrilla justice in Colombia, claims that the FARC's perspective on the law is reflective of its origins as a rural peasant movement. At the beginning, in the 1950s, FARC rules were very basic: "do not steal, do not kill, do not rape, do not take someone else's woman".[56] For Aguilera Peña, despite the initial influence of the Communist Party, the FARC's perspective on law remained a fundamentally pragmatic one.[57] The FARC may have called it "*justicia revolucionaria*", but it is not revolutionary in the sense of being innovative since it incorporates large segments of *derecho burgués* (i.e. state law), albeit with simplified procedures and applied in a more arbitrary manner.[58] That said, FARC norms evolved significantly over the years, and the group became the guerrilla group with the most develop corpus of norms in Colombia.[59] Aguilera Peña divides the history of guerrilla justice in three phases, on the basis of the objective pursued: *exemplary*

[55] ibid 196–197.
[56] Mario Aguilera Peña, 'Las Guerrillas Marxistas y La Pena de Muerte a Combatientes. Un Examen de Los Delitos Capitales y Del "Juicio Revolucionario"' (2014) 41 Anuario Colombiano de Historia Social y de la Cultura 201, 209.
[57] ibid 204.
[58] Aguilera Peña, *Contrapoder y Justicia Guerrillera* (n 7) 115.
[59] Aguilera Peña, 'Las Guerrillas Marxistas y La Pena de Muerte a Combatientes' (n 56) 211.

justice (1964–1976), *retaliatory justice* (1976–1985), and *local empowerment justice* (1985–2003).[60] Each phase is briefly presented.

Exemplary justice (1964–1976). One of the prominent features of this era is described by Aguilera Peña as *expedicionaria*, which consists in an approach that directs attention towards small offences and ends with death penalty or forced exile for the offender, and was rather summary in its format. This approach aimed to gain sympathy from the population that was living in the conflict zone, but also to intimidate the people and deter criminality.[61] The demand for this justice against authors of crimes came from the peasant population itself, and the FARC wanted to answer the people's security concerns with exemplary justice. When someone was sentenced to death, the sentence was published in a pamphlet and distributed among the population. This corresponds to a time when the FARC was mostly nomadic. In order to keep their influence and power over the local population, they would use the *autodefensa campesina* or the *autodefensa agraria*, groups sharing common values with the FARC but not part of the guerrilla group or the military.[62] Thus in certain zones under the control of *autodefensa agraria*, where the state was absent or unwelcomed, these community organisations would self-govern to a great extent, controlling access to the region, regulating trade, and so forth. They would also deal with minor offences such as stealing or being intoxicated in public by imposing sanctions from small fines to expulsion. However, in cases of more serious crimes like murder or rape, and to deal with "sapos" (government informants), the FARC could intervene and possibly impose the death penalty.[63] In the zone where its headquarters were located, the FARC was completely in charge. Inhabitants within 3,000 square kilometres were completely subordinated to FARC governance, including penal repression of crimes such as murder, theft, rape, or use of cannabis, punishable by forced labour, exile, or execution.[64] It can be pointed out that the administration of justice by the FARC compared favourably in that period to that of the ELN, the second largest rebel group in Colombia, in which "justice" did not usually imply any form of trial and for which the outcome was usually execution.[65]

Retaliatory justice (1976–1985). This type of dissuasive and symbolic justice was popularised by the M-19 rebel group, but subsequently adopted by all guerrilla movements in Colombia to deal with two types of people: "enemies of the people" and "enemies of the revolution".[66] In common with other emerging

60 Aguilera Peña, *Contrapoder y Justicia Guerrillera* (n 7) 125.
61 ibid 126.
62 ibid 243–247.
63 ibid 251.
64 ibid 252.
65 Molano (n 53) 332.
66 Aguilera Peña, *Contrapoder y Justicia Guerrillera* (n 7) 128, 257, 315.

criminal law regimes, the death penalty was its climactic focal point, although the FARC used it less than other insurgent groups.[67] It was not a very transparent justice, with the indictment elaborated by the FARC regional commander and the trial and capital punishment sometimes pronounced unbeknownst to the individual in question.[68] The administration of justice is said to have corresponded to three distinct dynamics during that period: cases dealing with the security of the guerrilla group itself, often against informants, politicians, or state officials (*justicia defensiva*); cases dealing with felony or misdemeanour crimes within the civilian population (*justicia expedicionaria*); and cases dealing with disputes among members of the community, often delegated to community organisations (*justicia comunitaria*).[69]

Local empowerment justice (1985–2003). In this period, justice aimed at taking control of local and municipal power, most significantly in the *zonas de retarguardia nacional*. This local justice was largely criminal, dealing with local corruption, appropriation of public funds, mismanagement of public affairs, and collaboration with paramilitary militias. This justice took the form of trials of mayors and their advisors or also members of congress. The FARC carried out a true judicial offensive, acting as an *instancia extraordinaria* to deal with private law disputes, family matters, and criminal offences. Insurgent justice was also found in the *zonas de disputas*, but in a very sporadic manner, mostly aiming to protect the *frentes guerilleros*. There were attempts to exert greater centralised control on the way in which justice was run at the local level, especially in relation to the death penalty. There was a retreat from what was by then perceived as an excessive resort to capital punishment, by substituting it for forced labour or exile in many cases, and by requiring that any death sentence be confirmed by headquarters.[70]

After 2003, with the initiation of the Plan Colombia, the successful military offensive by the government against the FARC meant that it could no longer be as involved in the administration of justice as it had been in previous periods. Focussing its energies on armed action and survival, the FARC left a much greater degree of autonomy to the JAC in managing crime and private disputes. The exceptions were matters that affected the security of the insurgents, which were dealt with swiftly and harshly by the rebels.

[67] On the symbolic role of capital punishment in the criminal law, see generally Douglay Hay, 'Property, Authority and the Criminal Law' in Douglas Hay (ed), *Albion's Fatal Tree: Crime and Society in Eighteenth-Century England* (Verso 1975).

[68] Aguilera Peña, *Contrapoder y Justicia Guerrillera* (n 7) 315–319.

[69] ibid 350.

[70] ibid 129–131; JEP (n 13) 54.

ii. FARC Military Justice

Many non-state armed groups initially develop internal regulations and disciplinary mechanisms to ensure order within their ranks and increase the military effectiveness of their unit. As such, there is a pattern of insurgents having much more elaborate standards to deal with the administration of justice within their group than with respect to the civilian population. This is certainly the case for the FARC, whose code of conduct and internal processes are older, written, and more elaborate and consistent than the rules applicable to the general population.[71] For that reason, the analysis is best started with the internal administration of justice whereby the FARC apply a type of military justice to its own fighters.

The Statute and Regulations of the FARC provide combatants with guidelines on how to behave and their rights and duties as a member of the movement. The document (containing the Statute, the Disciplinary Regulations, and the Internal Norms of Commandment) was first approved in 1966, and revised in 1978, 1982, 1993, and 2007.[72] The last version, which was conveniently available online on the FARC's own website, appears to date from 2013.[73] The discipline regime is described as a new way of perceiving military discipline, which is not brutal and does not discriminate, and is referred to as a "proletarian-military".[74] Section 8 of the Regulation also provides that the members of the group must prevent the war from being a total war that will harm the people.[75] The Statute and Regulations are filled with revolutionary values, such as solidarity, equality, and complete devotion to the cause. The Regulation lists a number of prohibited acts, starting with a prohibition to kill fellow members of the FARC and men and women from the civilian population. Further in the list, the prohibition of sexual violence and looting can be found.[76]

Chapter I of the Regulation provides for sanctions applicable to all members of the movement found to have committed disciplinary breaches, regardless of rank.[77] The guerrilleros who fail to comply with the Statute or Regulation can permanently or definitively lose their rights to hold a position within the FARC or may have to perform forced labour or any other activity as a sanction that will be imposed through a decision of the appropriate body.[78] For the most

71 JEP (n 13) 53–56; Mario Aguilera Peña, 'Claves y Distorsiones Del Régimen Disciplinario Guerrillero' (2013) 26 Análisis Político (Colombia) 45, 52.

72 Aguilera Peña, 'Las Guerrillas Marxistas y La Pena de Muerte a Combatientes' (n 56) 211.

73 *Reglemento del Régimen Disciplinario de las FARC* [FARC Regulations], accessible at <https://web.archive.org/web/20200809090609/http://www.farc-ep.co/wp-content/uploads/2013/10/Estatutos.pdf>.

74 FARC Regulations, Introduction, Number 1, p 23.

75 FARC Regulations, Introduction, Number 8, p 25.

76 FARC Regulations, Chapter 1, Article 3a (a), (k), (l), p 28.

77 FARC Regulations, Chapter 1, Articles 4 & 11, p 31.

78 FARC Regulations, Chapter 1, Article 5, p 32.

serious crimes, including treason, spying, desertion, killing, sexual violence, and looting, there is a specific mechanism to determine the sanction: the revolutionary court-martial (*consejo revolucionario de guerra*). The court-martial is composed of a president, a secretariat, five "juries of conscience", and a prosecutor that are all elected by the general assembly of guerrilleros, composed of a minimum of twenty-five fighters. The defender is chosen by the accused from among those in the general assembly. The defender is given access to any relevant documents and will be allocated a reasonable time to confer with the accused. The FARC unit commander that convened the court-martial is not allowed to take part in the proceedings and must withdraw to another location, although there are reports of commanders often disregarding that rule and trying to influence the outcome.[79]

Informants indicate that the hearings were not tightly structured, and that various participants could intervene as many times as they thought useful. On the other hand, the accused was often tied to a tree during the proceedings. The defender would usually invoke the right to life as a fundamental natural right, the irreparable nature of the sanction, the involuntariness of the crime, the degree of seriousness of the allegations, and the youth of the accused. What is more, the Regulations provided an exemption from criminal responsibility where the order given could lead to a crime (meaning a violation of FARC Regulations).[80] The prosecutor would always invoke the specific section of the Regulations that had been violated, invoke the need to maintain discipline within the FARC, and invite the jurors to decide not based on their emotions but on their conscience.[81] The verdict was rendered by a majority of jurors, who could declare the accused guilty or discharged. The verdict had to be approved by the assembly. The participants in the assembly could comment on the verdict and provide the reasons why they agreed or disagreed with it. Witness accounts suggest that it would not have been rare for half of the assembly members to intervene during the discussions to speak their mind. For example, in one account of a court-martial, Graciela was a FARC fighter accused of desertion, having left her unit during the night to make her way to Bogota. After one month as a civilian, she had a change of heart and came back to the FARC, where she was charged with desertion and demoralising the troops, crimes punishable by death. In the court-martial, the assembly of sixty combatants did not hesitate to express their view that the fault in fact lay with the unit leader Ernesto, who had unfairly harassed Graciela for months, making her life in the unit unbearable. In the end, the jury condemned Graciela to six months without a weapon and extended firewood

[79] FARC Regulations, Chapter 1, Article 4 (b), p 31; Aguilera Peña, 'Claves y Distorsiones Del Régimen Disciplinario Guerrillero' (n 71) 55.
[80] FARC Regulations, Chapter II, Article 7, p 33.
[81] Aguilera Peña, 'Las Guerrillas Marxistas y La Pena de Muerte a Combatientes' (n 56) 228.

duty, a lenient sanction approved by the assembly that was largely seen as an implied rebuke of the unit leader Ernesto.[82] If a verdict was rejected by the assembly, the president had to read again the judgment, which was followed by a new vote.[83] It is also noteworthy that deserters could be judged *in absentia*, but otherwise the accused must be present and given a chance to participate. Aguilera Peña argues that although the FARC incorporated some basic principles of criminal law in their norms, several principles were left aside, such as different modes of participation, mitigating and aggravating circumstances, and criteria to define the appropriate sanctions.[84]

The course of a court-martial was established by the regulation and was quite ritualistic, composed of nine stages: (1) singing of the hymn of the FARC; (2) recording of the meeting and the attending members; (3) reading of the convocation; (4) election of court-martial members (prosecutor, defender, juries); (5) reading of the report (the allegations); (6) discussion by the assembly (the commanders were not in the room; the discussion started with the defender, followed by the prosecution and the members of the assembly, if they wanted to give their opinions); (7) deliberation of the jury; (8) reading and approval of the verdict; (9) conclusions (final reading of the judgment).[85] Within this structure, as mentioned, there was quite a bit of space for informality.

> *There was a case of a FARC leader that was convicted of being a government informant for many years. The court-martial not only ordered that he be executed, but also that his farm be confiscated and his family expelled from the area. Another battalion commander committed a grave breach of protocol that resulted in the death of many of his combatants; in addition, he had conducted a court-martial that did not comply with the FARC Regulations. The High Command sent in a replacement commander that convened a court-martial which ultimately ordered the execution of the battalion commander.*
>
> *Interview, FARC Commander German (January 2018)*

There was a range of sanctions that could be imposed by the court-martial, including physical labour, being disarmed for a period of time, having to study the Regulations, and so forth. Capital punishment was also a potential sanction, limited to the most serious crimes, such as murder and treason, desertion, disclosure of secret information, killing of a FARC member or a civilian, and "crimes of similar seriousness". Aguilera Peña suggests that "crimes of similar

82 Molano (n 53) 351–352.
83 Aguilera Peña, 'Las Guerrillas Marxistas y La Pena de Muerte a Combatientes' (n 56) 229.
84 ibid 212.
85 ibid 225–227.

seriousness" could include sexual violence and looting of civilians, depending on the circumstances.[86]

Notwithstanding the fact that execution was a sanction restricted for the most serious offences, it was the most controversial and the sanction that frequently raised attention in the media. *La Semana*, a Colombian newspaper, alleged in 2010 that the FARC executed more of their own troops than they killed enemies in combat. The journalist described the trials organised by the FARC and qualified those trials of "mock trial, fraud trial".[87] The newspaper *El Espectador* claimed that the FARC was sentencing guerrilleros to death by firing squad for ridiculous reasons, encompassed in the criminalisation of "any activities that could go against the revolutionary morale of the troops".[88] "They have been shooting their own troops for more than 30 years", said another newspaper, while former guerrilleros who fled from the FARC were quoted as saying that a minor offence or fault could be punished with a death sentence.[89] While there are reliable reports of insurgent groups in Colombia carrying out executions of their own members, such media reports often appear to owe more to anti-rebel propaganda than accurate depiction of the regular operation of military justice in groups like the FARC. On the opposite, there are some detailed accounts by FARC informants that convey the hesitations that commanders would often feel before meting out such a drastic punishment upon one of their own. In one case, a commander recalls how a fighter well liked in the unit was accused by a civilian women of sexual assault, with no other witness; confronted with a classic situation of "he says/she says", and suspecting that this might have been a romantic encounter gone wrong, the commander nevertheless felt pressured by the community to convene a court-martial to prosecute the fighter. The case was put to an assembly of villagers, with FARC fighters not entitled to vote, and a majority favoured execution. The verdict was challenged, a new assembly convened, and again the death penalty was approved. In the end, the fighter confessed and was duly executed. The commander remarked, "*el pueblo habla, el pueblo manda*", meaning that a guerrilla group that strays from the people cannot survive.[90]

[86] ibid 216; Ana Arjona, *Rebelocracy: Social Order in the Colombian Civil War* (Cambridge University Press 2016) 98.

[87] 'Los Fusilados de las FARC' *La Semana* (12 February 2010), online: <http://www.semana.com/nacion/Article/los-fusilados-farc/113072-3>.

[88] Juan David Laverde Palma, 'Un vistazo al régimen disciplinario de las Farc' *El Espectador* (23 May 2014), online: <http://www.elespectador.com/noticias/paz/un-vistazo-al-regimen-disciplinario-de-farc-Article-494178>.

[89] 'Consejos de Guerra y fusilamientos de las FARC, Los temas pendiente que buscan justicia' *Pulzo* (27 July 2015), online: <http://www.pulzo.com/nacion/consejos-de-guerra-y-fusilamientos-de-las-farc-los-temas-pendientes-que-buscan/381031>; Gonzalo Guillen, 'Las FARC fusilan a sus proprios guerrilleros' *El Nuevo Herald* (21 February 2010), online: <http://www.elnuevoherald.com/noticias/mundo/america-latina/colombia-es/article2003277.html>.

[90] Molano (n 53) 353–358; Heffes (n 30) 22–26. The sentiment expressed in the quote is roughly equivalent to "*vox populi, vox dei*".

According to the FARC Regulation, there was a possibility to appeal a verdict before a superior authority if the sanction could be considered unfair.[91] If the appeal was perceived to be inspired by malicious intention, a more severe sanction could be granted. Both the accused and the High Command and Secretariat could appeal the sanction.

iii. FARC Civilian Justice

As was suggested at the beginning of the previous section, the administration of justice for civilian matters was, for the FARC as much as for many other non-state armed groups in Colombia, an afterthought. Initial thinking about norms and practices occurred in relation to internal matters or, put differently, military justice. When the FARC came to wield some authority over certain civilian populations, one aspect of rebel governance that organically grew was a form of administration of justice. One FARC informant made a parallel to the Far West, where any figure of authority that appeared was solicited to help in the resolution of disputes and in the sanction of unacceptable behaviour. This was especially so in those parts of the country where the state was present in a very limited way or altogether absent. The FARC saw it as part of their revolutionary project to resolve these problems for the general population, but without necessarily on the basis of a central policy decision to take over the administration of justice.[92] The FARC was active both at the normative level, determining applicable law, and at the institutional level, providing structures to apply that law.

In the 1990s, the FARC was controlling or maintaining a strong presence in 40 to 50 percent of the 1,071 municipalities in Colombia. Again, it bears emphasising that the state had never been significantly present in large swaths of national territory where the FARC grew to be a powerful force. The government in Colombia is very centralised and very urban at every level. Many informants speak of the "state abandonment" of regions like the Caquetá Department, areas "of recent colonization" in which the state had provided very little in the form of public services until that point.[93] Where the state was absent or more tenuously present, the FARC would implement a state-like structure and apply what an American scholar described as "some primitive law".[94] Basically, the insurgents

[91] FARC Regulations, Chapter III, Article 9 and 10, p 34.

[92] Interview with FARC Commander Edoardo (July 2016); Aponte González (n 44) 155 ("las FARC no respondieron al problema de manera premeditada, sino que todo se debió a su capacidad de leer y abordar pragmáticamente las tensiones y problemas locales, mientras llevaban a cabe su plan de tomarse el poder"); Ariel Ávila, 'Así administran justicia las FARC en sus territorios' (2016), accessible at <https://pares.com.co/2016/04/23/asi-administran-justicia-las-farc-en-sus-territorios/>.

[93] Interview with FARC Commander German (January 2018); interview with Manuel, civilian in the Caqueta Department (February 2018).

[94] Arturo Carrillo-Suarez, 'Hors de Logique: Contemporary Issues in International Humanitarian Law as Applied to Internal Armed Conflict' (1999) 15 American University International Law Review 1, 94.

would invoke local customs, rooted in the values and traditions of peasant life, which happened to accord with those embraced by the FARC's own ideology.[95] This was especially so if the local community was unified and well-organised when the FARC emerged.[96] The law applied to the civilian population was often unwritten, which did not pose a problem when local norms were applied.[97]

The FARC in later years did make use of a more formal, written *Manual de Convivencia ciudadana*, literally a "manual for living together".[98] This manual, directed at the inhabitant of FARC-controlled territories, was a guide for the good functioning of the community, regulating any or all of the following: who could live and own property in the area, restrictions on movement of persons and goods, rules on the organisation of public events, a basic driving code, church activities, the prohibition of witchcraft, economic life (opening hours, price control, sanitary rules, etc.), the use of telephones, who could buy a car or motorcycle, penalties for assault, murder, or destruction of property, regulating fishing and hunting, the cutting of trees or controlled forest burns, the use of genetically modified seeds, and so on. The manual came about from a local experiment in El Caguan, where rules that had originally been devised by the JAC were revised through broad consultation and interaction between the community and FARC authorities over several months.[99] As one member of the FARC High Command described it:

> [Translation] In a region without state presence, a region abandoned, without any protection, the peasants were left to their own devices, to their own sacrifices, to the initiative of the guerrilla, to organize themselves, to lay down foundations, [. . .] to create norms. But these norms, how were they created? With the communities! And later with the approval of the guerrilla. Or the guerrilla suggested norms for living together without problems, to deal with problems of property lines, of animals escaping their paddock, of all sorts of issues that arise in the countryside, and the communities got to vote to approve them.[100]

95 Molano (n 53) 334.

96 Arjona, 'Civilian Resistance to Rebel Governance' (n 34).

97 Espinosa Menéndez (n 43) 100 ("Las FARC, como he mencionado antes, no tienen una normatividad establecida para trabajar la justicia local. Pero tomando en cuenta que las comunidades tienen definido el criterio de lo justo como factor que debe primar para solucionar un conflicto, las FARC trabajan sobre estos criterios").

98 The most extensive study, focussing on the manual in the El Pato area in Caqueta, is in Carrillo (n 17) 154–172. A copy of the FARC manual for Caqueta is accessible at <https://pares.com.co/2014/02/06/farc-dan-conocer-manual-de-convivencia-en-putumayo/>. The idea of a manual of rules for living together (*manual de convivencia*) is a commonly used notion in Colombian society in general, often adopted by cities and schools; see, e.g., Andrea Milena Burbano, 'La Convivencia Ciudadana: Su Análisis a Partir Del "Aprendizaje Por Reglas"' [2009] Revista colombiana de educación 28.

99 Carrillo (n 17) 155–157; Aponte González (n 44) 184–185.

100 Edison Romaña, interviewed in Carrillo (n 17) 160 (my translation).

Seeing the success of this approach, the manual was then exported to other parts of the country by the FARC, but without necessarily involving the same broad consultation with the local population.[101] In some zones like the Bajo Putumayo, the FARC simply decreed that such were the applicable rules, and there was no possibility for the civilian population to influence their content.[102] In the absence of a centralised imposition of a manual by the FARC, there were significant variations in the substance of the manual from region to region. In some respects, this reflected the social and geographic specificities of each region; in other respects, it reflected the approach taken by the local FARC leadership in the adoption of norms, related at least in part to the degree of territorial control by the guerrillas in a given area.[103] In 2013, when a journalist asked for official reactions to the use of this manual, the government of the department, the army, and the police all claimed to know nothing about it.[104] Beyond this relatively short and variable manual, the only attempt by the FARC to issue legislative texts that were more statutory in nature, formally proclaimed by the central authority and meant to apply to the entire country, were three "laws" adopted during the existence of the demilitarized zone mentioned earlier: "Law 001" on land reform, "Law 002" on taxation, and "Law 003" on corruption.[105] Other than these rules targeting specific issues, Aguilera Peña claims that norms used by the guerrilla to resolve interpersonal conflict among civilians were, at 95 percent, the official law of the state.[106] In one interesting example, a peasant went to the official court to complain that his land had been taken by a neighbour. The judge in this isolated zone with very significant guerrilla presence refused to hear the case because the neighbour in question was a member of the FARC, and he feared a violent reaction. The complainant then went to see the FARC area commander with his complaint. The commander resolved the title dispute by applying the provisions of the Civil Code of Colombia relating to property.[107] With regard to procedural rules and criminal sentencing, on the other hand, there were marked differences between FARC practices and official law.[108] The FARC was the one

101 Interview with FARC Commander Edoardo (March 2018).

102 Javier Alexander Macias, 'Así se vive bajo la ley de las Farc en el bajo Putumayo' *www.elcolombiano.com* (18 October 2013), online: <http://www.elcolombiano.com/historico/asi_se_vive_bajo_la_ley_de_las_farc_en_el_bajo_putumayo-AYEC_265713> accessed 23 February 2018.

103 Carrillo (n 17) 169; Nicolás Espinosa Menéndez, 'Entre La Justicia Guerrillera y La Justicia Campesina? Un Nuevo Modelo de Justicia Comunitaria?' [2003] Revista Colombiana de Sociología 117, 142.

104 Macias (n 102).

105 Aguilera Peña, *Guerrilla y Población Civil* (n 10) 353–354 (the statutes are reprinted at 353–358).

106 Aguilera Peña, *Contrapoder y Justicia Guerrillera* (n 7) 107.

107 Interview with Cesar Torres (February 2018).

108 Aguilera Peña, *Contrapoder y Justicia Guerrillera* (n 7) 107 ("las normas jurídicas que usan los insurgentes para resolver los conflictos interindividuales son en un 95% normas estatales, en lo que respecta a disposiciones o figuras sustantivas, mas no así en procedimientos y penas, en las que habría una involución respecto al derecho estatal. Las reglas sustantivas usadas pueden catalogarse

who interpreted the norms, decided what was fair and what was not, and ultimately imposed its view on what the law should be.

At an institutional level, there was again a diversity of approaches taken by the FARC in the administration of justice. On the whole, the FARC did not establish a judicial apparatus, but used an array of different mechanisms to resolve conflicts within the communities.[109] Oftentimes, there were community mechanisms that pre-existed the arrival of the FARC, and which continued to operate during the presence of the guerrillas in the area. Thus the JAC, as indicated earlier, had developed *Comités de conciliación* that attempted to settle disputes among members of the community.[110] Indigenous communities were often tightly knit and resistant to outside intervention, using their own *consejo de ancianos* to settle disputes and sanction crimes.[111] The 1991 Colombian constitution gave official recognition to Indigenous self-governance, including community justice, and that official recognition to some degree carried over into the realm of rebel governance.[112] In other less remote parts of the country where the state had had a more significant foothold, there were instances in which the state judge and prosecutor were allowed to continue to exercise at least some of their functions, within limits set by the FARC.[113] One judge described his experience in a remote village in Sur de Bolivar: "[Translation] Sure, of course, the guerrilla had a whole legal system. It was a much more effective justice than the one I stood for. [. . .] My role as a judge was limited to issuing summons. But nobody came. No cases were brought to me. The real judge was the FARC commander, not me". After several months, the judge managed to gain the trust of the villagers and, through them, the FARC:

como de domino público pues aparecer inscritas en los usos y costumbres campesinas, hacen parte del sentido común y del derecho consuetudinario, se inscriben en las prácticas de las relaciones entre individuos o comunidades con las instituciones y los representantes del Estado [. . .]".

[109] Espinosa Menéndez (n 43) 101 ("Esto implica que las FARC-EP no manejan una sola forma y una sola estrategia para solucionar problemas sino que hacen uso de varios mecanismos: se valen de los Comités, se apoyan en las comunidades, mantienen comandantes de área, envían comisiones con poderes, en ocasiones levantan actas, etcétera").

[110] Espinosa Menéndez (n 103) 128–131.

[111] Interview with Flor, Indigenous leader (January 2018).

[112] Arjona, *Rebelocracy* (n 86) 151–155. See more generally Daniel Bonilla Maldonado, *La constitución multicultural* (Siglo del Hombre Editores 2006).

[113] Mauricio García Villegas and others, *Jueces Sin Estado: La Justicia Colombiana En Zonas de Conflicto Armado* (Siglo del Hombre Editores 2008) 99. It should be made clear that in many places all state officials, including judges and prosecutors, were expelled or eliminated by the FARC, with the consequence that formal legal institutions were unavailable: Aguilera Peña, *Guerrilla y Población Civil* (n 10) 262.

[Translation] The sympathy I gained from the people finally helped me with the FARC commanders. When they saw that I got along with everyone, they called me in and told me:

FARC: Listen, judge, we want you to administer justice, but under our supervision.

JUDGE: I beg your pardon?

FARC: Look, it's simple: we'll send you some cases for you to deal with. If you're not sure, if you run into problems, you call us, and we'll help you out.

JUDGE: OK.

I was excited and scared but, what else could I do? It was better than nothing. At least I was going to be able to administer justice, even if it wasn't in the most ideal or the most legal way. So, for three years, I dealt with the cases that they sent me, mostly little things, domestic violence, alimony, debts, fights among friends, things like that. For some cases I issued formal judgments, others I managed in a more informal manner, and most of the time I acted as a mediator. That's how most disputes got resolved. Small things, but still disputes in the end.[114]

This is a striking example of the instrumentalisation of the official judicial system by the FARC, a phenomenon that was far from rare. At times, as suggested in the preceding passage, the FARC directly handled justice matters, if necessary ordering a judge to simply drop a case.[115] In all cases, the guerrilla group had a very significant impact on the administration of justice in the areas in which it was present, so that it can be said that justice mechanisms of the community, the state, and the non-state armed group were operating variably and interactively.[116]

For private law matters, the approach seemed to have been mostly minimalistic but nevertheless quite effective. The FARC tried to make an appearance in villages on market days, not only to stock up on essentials for their own needs but also to interact with the population for political and other matters.[117] The commander would set up a table in a public place, typically the school, and people would line up to present the problems that could not have been resolved through community mechanisms. This could cover the entire gamut of private law disputes, from neighbours fighting over property lines to abandoned wives seeking support from their ex-husbands, debt collection to injuries caused by animals. Often, both sides to the disputes came, or the commander would send

[114] Villegas and others (n 113) 119 (my translation).

[115] ibid 127. The judge noted that his predecessor had been killed by the FARC for ignoring such orders.

[116] Ariel Fernando Ávila Martínez and Juan Diego Castro León, 'Los Retos En Convivencia, Administración de Justicia y Seguridad Rural En El Posconflicto' [2015] Cuadernos de análisis Friedrich Ebert Stiftung 1, 20.

[117] This description was given to me by ex-FARC Commander Edoardo (July 2016).

word for the missing side to come immediately. The commander would listen to both sides and possibly hear from other witnesses as well. If some aspects remained unclear, he or she could ask around or go see the piece of land or damaged good.[118] In some types of cases, for example, a decision as to who had title to a piece of land, the commander would provide a written, signed decision to be kept by the parties should enforcement measures be needed. In some other cases, the decision was recorded in the official registry of decisions maintained by the local authority (the JAC).[119] The intimation in any case was that it would not be advisable to ignore or challenge a decision handed out by the FARC.

> *One day I arrived with my unit at a village named Puerto Camelia and saw a big black woman nicknamed "Tyson", who worked there as a prostitute, with a black eye and broken teeth. When I asked her what happened to her, she explained that a couple of weeks before she had gone with a client who was drunk and became violent when she refused to perform a specific act. The guy lived in the village, so I had him called, and he acknowledged what he had done. Violence against women had to be sanctioned, so he had to pay a fine into the community fund. Then he had to pay compensation to her for the cost of medical treatment and drugs, dental work, as well as lost income for the period during which her injuries prevented her from getting clients.*
>
> *Interview, FARC Commander Edoardo (March 2018)*

For disputes around illegal business, which could hardly be brought before the state courts, the civilians would turn to the guerrillas.[120] This was a very significant aspect of local justice in some regions in which the drug trade accounted for an enormous proportion of economic activities. In one case, a farmer named Leonardo kept his cows in a field that was not enclosed. One day, the cows went frolicking in his neighbour Saul's field where they devoured the coca leaves that were ready to be harvested after one year of hard work. In that case, the FARC

[118] Espinosa Menéndez (n 43) 100 ("Cuando la guerrilla interviene directamente en el arreglo de un problema, y si las condiciones de la zona se prestan (no hay presencia militar), el o la Comandante de área cita a las partes interesadas, pregunta por testigos que puedan confirmar versiones e inspecciona—si es necesario—los sitios en disputa o donde se lleva a cabo el litigio (verificar el trazado de un camino, ubicar los linderos, mirar daños causados por ganado, fuego, etcétera). En problemas complicados, comisiona milicianos o colaboradores para que le averigüen datos, lo acompañen en las inspecciones o las hagan ellos mismos. En problemas sencillos (por ejemplo, de convivencia entre vecinos), con sólo leer un acta el o la comandante toma la decisión. Se ha sabido de casos en donde los o las comandantes reciben a la gente únicamente con un acta firmada por el Comité de Conciliación").

[119] ibid 101.

[120] ibid 95 ("cuando habitantes del casco urbano tienen conflictos en situaciones ilegales—como puede ser una transacción fallida con pasta base de coca, concerniente a la venta ilegal de combustibles o al comercio de maderas protegidas—buscan en la zona rural a la guerrilla para tramitar allí, y con ellos, sus conflictos").

decided that Leonardo's liability for the independent acts of his animals was tempered by the contributory negligence of both farmers for failing to enclose their field as was required under local custom.[121] Other matters were brought to rebel justice as opposed to official courts not because of the illegality of the acts but because it reflected local norms not recognised in formal law. Thus, in zones of recent colonisation in which peasants had fled *La Violencia* to settle remote parts of the country, land had been apportioned through a largely organic and informal process. Who owned which precise plots of land was common knowledge in the community, despite the fact that there were no formal legal property titles. If a dispute arose in relation to property, which was not rare, the owner could not turn to the regular courts, as the absence of a formal title would prevent the formulation of a valid claim. Informal justice, whether run by the community or by the guerrilla, did not turn on the availability of a formal property deed.

There was one phase of the civil war in Colombia during which the FARC did move to institutionalise its administration of justice. Between 1998 and 2002, when the government agreed to take all its troops out of the *zona de despeje* (demilitarized zone), the entire law enforcement apparatus from the state departed as well. That left the FARC as the *de facto* government of this enormous territory, with greater control over the population and territory than in any other phase of the conflict. As the sole source of authority, the FARC became solicited more than ever to settle all manner of disputes in the community. The burden on the fighting force became so great that the FARC decided to establish standing complaint offices (*oficinas de quejas y reclamos*) throughout the demilitarized zones.[122] Manned by people in authority who were usually not the rebel area commander but rather either a second-in-command or an older combatant who was passed the age of active service, the complaint offices could handle all the problems of life in the countryside and provide a resolution in a matter of hours, as opposed to the months that the official legal system would have taken. Standing as the visible face of the rebel law and order, they reportedly had a caseload between 100 and 700 cases a week.[123] One FARC commander reported that he resolved 2,745 cases over a period of eight months.[124] Some people came from outside the demilitarized zone, even from urban centres like Bogota and Cali, to submit their complaints to rebel justice; sometimes people turned to rebel justice out of frustration that the official court system was simply not delivering effective or timely decisions.[125] The complaint offices had an impact that varied from

[121] Espinosa Menéndez (n 103) 121–124.
[122] Carrillo (n 17) 148–150. For mention of a similar office in a different part of the country despite the continued presence of the police, see Aponte González (n 44) 152.
[123] Inés Miranda, 'Justicia Guerrillera En Colombia' *El Mundo (Spain)* (6 July 2000); Aguilera Peña, *Guerrilla y Población Civil* (n 10) 254–255.
[124] Miranda (n 123).
[125] ibid; Carrillo (n 17) 152.

place to place in the demilitarized zones. They were gradually closed, with the task of conflict resolution going back to the JAC *comité de conciliación*.[126] The strategy behind this was to return the resolution of conflict to their stakeholder, in order for the FARC to strengthen their authority and focus on combat.[127] However, when the local institutions were weak or ineffective, the FARC was always there to intervene.[128]

For criminal matters, the FARC would hold popular trials in rural areas for civilians who were accused of misdemeanours or felony. The range of misdeeds would go from murder, rape, domestic violence, theft, or failing to pay a "war tax".[129] The popular trial, according to civilians from the region of Guaviare interviewed by Human Rights Watch, worked as follows: the trial was announced by the FARC, then, the civilian population converged to the community meeting, and the FARC heard what people had to say. The civilians testified and then the FARC decided and executed the decision. According to another civilian, the FARC could decide on the guilt of someone without consulting anyone, and they could take drastic decisions. In 1997, Human Rights Watch reported that approximately thirty people were killed for being suspected of having links with right-wing paramilitary groups. The Human Rights Watch report also alleged that the FARC, while conducting those popular trials, rarely informed the accused of the charges that were held against them and did not allow them to present a suitable defence. For Human Rights Watch, fundamental rights such as the presumption of innocence were not being respected.[130]

> *There was a case of a man who was accused of sexually abusing a child. A popular assembly was called by the guerrilla to deal with this matter. There was a heated debate, with some wanting to castrate the man, others to execute him, and still others to expel him from the area. In the end, the majority agreed to sentence him to many months of hard labour on community projects. The guerrilla felt that it*

[126] Espinosa Menéndez (n 43) 96–97 ("La decisión de traspasar a las Juntas la responsabilidad de la resolución de conflictos comunitarios significó una nueva etapa para el proyecto insurgente de control territorial, en donde el poder local de carácter comunitario ha sido una prioridad, y su movilización, en función de reivindicaciones regionales ante el Estado, parte fundamental de la plataforma insurreccional").

[127] Interview with Cesar Torres (February 2018), quoting a FARC commander "no podemos seguir arreglando problemas de borrachos"; Molano (n 53) 333–334 ("la guerrilla tuvo que crear un sistema jurídico y organizar la justicia. El comandante ya no podía seguir juzgando como durante mucho tiempo lo hizo, por lo que comenzó a crear y fortalecer aparatos de justicia como los tribunales elementales y las asambleas").

[128] Espinosa Menéndez (n 43) 98; JEP (n 13) 214.

[129] Human Rights Watch (n 3) 142.

[130] ibid 142–143. Sivakumaran challenges the HRW critique of the FARC as overbroad, for including violations such as the denial or a right to appeal when this is in fact not protected by international humanitarian law: Sivakumaran, 'Courts of Armed Opposition Groups—Fair Trials or Summary Justice?' (n 2) 508.

was better to let the community decide rather than impose its own decision. On the other hand, the government considered that anyone who participated in such an assembly was guilty of an act of rebellion.

Interview, FARC Commander German (January 2018)

The rather strident critique of FARC justice offered by Human Rights Watch seems certainly justified if its description of insurgent administration of justice is accurate. Indeed, what they describe are extrajudicial executions, pure and simple. Significant ethnographic work carried out since then suggests that the picture painted by the human rights organisation may have validly represented some events, in particular the treatment of those thought to be government spies or paramilitaries (referred to as *sapos*). Recent fieldwork indicates that crimes committed against the security of the guerrilla group, like informing or spying on behalf of the government, were considered as a separate class by the FARC, leading to execution with very little due process of any kind.[131] In relation to other, "ordinary" crimes committed against person or property in the community, the FARC did adopt practices that come closer to what could be called administering justice. There are many narratives of proceedings dealing with crimes committed by civilians which approximately follow the rules for courts-martial of FARC fighters, with popular assemblies of villagers called upon to determine guilt and choose a sanction. It appears that the due process aspects were more limited, however, or not consistently applied. Thus, there was no systematic practice of naming a defender or counsel for the accused.[132] Not rarely, the FARC in fact played a calming role, when mob lynching appeared as the most likely alternative to FARC justice.[133]

Sometimes, the trial was closer to a restorative justice model. For example, in one case in which some men were accused of not contributing to the community and of harassing women, the FARC commander asked if the accused acknowledged the harm they had caused and estimated an amount of money that corresponded in his view to the injury, money that would go to the community.[134] If the community did not agree, they could suggest another amount or another sentence.

The sanctions applied to civilians by FARC justice were, more often than not, financial penalties and community service.[135] If there was a specific victim, that

131 Interview with FARC commander German (January 2018). The January 2021 decision by the JEP seems to confirm that mistreatment of civilians most often was linked to a suspicion of being an informant for the government: JEP (n 13) 80–247.

132 Interview with FARC commander Edoardo (July 2016).

133 Interview with FARC commander Edoardo (July 2016); Aponte González (n 44) 151–153.

134 Molano (n 53) 345.

135 Interview with FARC commander Edoardo (July 2016). In zones in which their presence was more permanent, the FARC imposed mandatory community service for everyone on a scheduled basis, for example, to clean public areas or maintain roads. The group occasionally forced some

person would be entitled to receive compensation for the harm done, including moral damages. There was often a community fine as well, money that would be paid into a community fund used to cover expenses benefitting the community as a whole, such as building a school or repairing a road or dam. Finally, the FARC would also collect the equivalent of court fees for its troubles. Repeat offenders or authors of more serious crimes could be ordered to leave the region and never come back. Exile was considered a harsh penalty for local offenders, because in times of war people are distrustful of strangers. To send a local person away was to put him or her at risk of being taken for a spy, a criminal, or any other type of undesirable, with unpredictable consequences.[136] Finally, when the crimes were of extreme gravity, such as murder or rape, the FARC felt pressured to impose the death penalty. To fail to do so would be taken as a sign of weakness, a failure to fulfil the rebel's role in the community's governance, and lead to a loss of legitimacy and thus of authority.[137]

It appears that the civilian population often trusted the FARC, and not only out of fear. Civilians navigated the administration of justice, using various actors and practices that served them best. Court records show that in zones where the guerrilla group was present, there was a precipitous drop in the number of new legal actions initiated, despite the fact that the FARC did not have a policy of prohibiting people from using the state's courts if they were available.[138] That said, it would not be fair to argue that the legitimacy enjoyed by the FARC did not sometime come from fear of the arbitrary use of their power.[139]

II. Rebel Rule of Law

The picture that emerges from this more extensive survey of FARC governance related to matters of justice begs the question of how it should be characterised. As we see with the FARC, and indeed in the operation of other armed opposition groups in armed conflicts around the world, rebel governance does not necessarily emerge as a proto-state, mimicking the structure and practices of the government, although there is no questioning the fact that the latter can indeed be a model that is followed by rebels in significant ways. This is certainly so

individuals to spend a few hours or a few days to work on a special project like opening a new road or building a bridge. As people rarely will admit to having been 'condemned' for misbehaviour, narratives from civilians tend to lump everything together as 'forced labour'. See JEP (n 13) 182–183, 214.

[136] Interview with FARC commander Edoardo (July 2016).
[137] Molano (n 53) 360–361.
[138] See Villegas and others (n 113) ch 4.
[139] Espinosa Menéndez (n 43) 103, 106.

for the FARC, which grew nearer to a form of governance guided by liberalism than some other insurgents such as, for example, ISIS in Syria and Iraq. With respect to governance touching on matters of justice, this raises the question of whether it should appropriately be described as a form of administration of justice. Is rebel justice a valid challenge to the uniqueness of the model embraced by all states, as a reflection of the concept of sovereignty, under the guise of the rule of law? Is there a legitimate concept of a rebel rule of law that can provide a benchmark and an ideal against which judicial practices such as the FARC's can be measured?

In the rest of this section, I argue that the exclusive association of the rule of law with the state is conceptually both recent and unjustified, as there are accepted non-state institutions and practices corresponding to the rule of law (A). Within formal law applicable during armed conflicts, there are adjustments to the rule of law to reflect the unique constraints on the administration of justice during war (B). From that recognition and in consideration of the insights gleaned from the closer study of the practice of non-state armed groups like the FARC in Colombia, the basic components of a rebel rule of law can be suggested (C).

A. Fragmented Rule of Law

The idea of the rule of law is one that seems to attract support from every corner, whether it be national governments or international organisations, whether they be democratic or authoritarian, whether they embody Western traditions or those of other parts of the world, whether they speak for the necessity of public authority or the defence of individual liberty: everyone seems in favour of the rule of law.[140] A rare exception to viewing the rule of law as common sense is ISIS, whose embrace of divine law leads it to reject positive law and the doctrine of the rule of law (in addition to democracy, human rights, and separation of powers).[141]

The rhetorical popularity of the rule of law can be explained in at least two ways. First, as evocatively put by Mark Massoud, the rule of law is "a construct of desire", so that it occupies a space that can never entirely correspond to reality

140 Brian Z Tamanaha, *On the Rule of Law: History, Politics, Theory* (Cambridge University Press 2004) 1–5.

141 Mara Revkin, *The Legal Foundations of the Islamic State* (Center for Middle East Policy at Brookings 2016) 12; Islamic State Committee of Research and Fatwas, *Clarifying Statement on the Ruling on the Educational System of the Nusayri [Alawite] Government [of Syria]*, November 2014, online: http://drsc-sy.org/wp-content/uploads/2015/06/ALRAQA1.pdf; Christopher May and Adam Winchester, 'Introduction to the Handbook on the Rule of Law' in Christopher May and Adam Winchester (eds), *Handbook on the Rule of Law* (Edward Elgar 2018) 1.

save in the tangible presence of a yearning.[142] As such, it has something to offer to any society, no matter how accomplished it is. Put differently by Philip Allott, the idea of the rule of law is "an absurd but necessary fiction".[143] It is ineluctable that there will be rule of law issues in any given place and time because these can and will arise in every place and at all times. When everyone fails, to some degree, to comply with the aspirational objectives that correspond to the rule of law, then to stand accused of the same does not amount to the most damning indictment: the answer will always be that this is a work in progress. Second, the popularity of the concept of the rule of law is a reflection of the malleability of its content. It is a label so broad and fuzzy that it answers many aspirations and hides many sins. The lack of a fixed content is not an accident nor the failure to bring to fruition a diplomatic negotiation or theoretical conversation; rather, the ambiguity of the rule of law is one of the concept's defining features. The range of actors invoking the rule of law madly off in all directions actually sustains the demand for conceptual obscurity.[144] This is compounded at the international level by the challenges of translating the concept, from *État de droit* to *pravovoe gosudarstvo* to *fahzi* (法规), with every language offering a label that orients its substance in one direction or another.[145]

The fact that the rule of law is an essentially contested concept does not mean that it is wholly impossible to explore its content. The possible content of the rule of law has been the subject of numerous studies that catalogue its component parts, although none attracts anything like a wide consensus. Generally speaking, descriptions of the rule of law range on a spectrum from "thin" to "thick" versions, or procedural to substantive, progressively locating more and more content within the concept.[146] The 2004 definition included in the UN Secretary-General report on the rule of law and transitional justice is often given as a starting point:

> [The rule of law] refers to a principle of governance in which all persons, institutions, and entities, public and private, including the State itself, are

[142] Mark Fathi Massoud, 'Ideals and Practices in the Rule of Law: An Essay on Legal Politics' (2016) 41 Law & Social Inquiry 489, 494.

[143] Philip Allott, 'The Rule of Law' in Jean D'Aspremont (ed), *Concepts for International Law: Contributions to Disciplinary Thought* (Edward Elgar Publishing Limited 2019) 804.

[144] Peer Zumbansen, 'The Rule of Law, Legal Pluralism, and Challenges to a Western-Centric View: Some Very Preliminary Observations' in Christopher May and Adam Winchester (eds), *Handbook on the Rule of Law* (Edward Elgar 2018) 61.

[145] Robert McCorquodale, 'Defining the International Rule of Law: Defying Gravity?' (2016) 65 International and Comparative Law Quarterly 277, 279; Randall Peerenboom, *Asian Discourses of Rule of Law* (Routledge 2003).

[146] For a discussion of the evolution of the concept, see Pietro Costa, 'The Rule of Law, an Outline of Its Historical Foundations' in Christopher May and Adam Winchester (eds), *Handbook on the Rule of Law* (Edward Elgar 2018); Allott (n 143).

> accountable to laws that are publicly promulgated, equally enforced and independently adjudicated, and which are consistent with international human rights norms and standards. It requires, as well, measures to ensure adherence to the principles of the supremacy of law, equality before the law, separation of powers, participation in decision-making, legal certainty, avoidance of arbitrariness and procedural and legal transparency.[147]

This corresponds to a "thick" version of the rule of law, also endorsed by the EU Venice Commission and by scholars like Lord Bingham.[148] As can be seen from the definition quoted here, there is in this view a considerably overlap between the rule of law and other notions like human rights, democracy, good governance, and constitutionalisation. At this end of the spectrum, perhaps most clearly embodied in Bingham's writing, the debate corresponds to the extent to which the rule of law incorporates all "fundamental" human rights standards. It stands for an affirmation that a legal regime issued from a non-democratic authority that fails to respect basic principles of equality under the law or judicial independence cannot be described as corresponding to the rule of law.[149] This is meant as a rejection, at times in emphatic terms, of a "thin" version of the rule of law according to which the concept is a looser guide to the ways in which governmental authority must be bounded by rules that are fixed and knowable prior to their application. Advocates of this approach make the point that if all our aspirations are rolled into the concept of the rule of law, then it loses much of its usefulness because it will add little to the sum of its component parts. Lon Fuller proposed a set of eight attributes, largely procedural, that can be taken as defining the rule of law: laws must be general, publicly announced, prospective, clear, internally consistent, realistic, stable, and consistently enforced.[150] In this view, the rule of law speaks more to a set of values and meta-principles that must guide how governments behave, and as such amounts to "speaking law to power". For Joseph Raz, this is an important virtue that we seek to develop in any legal regime, but only one among many virtues, not co-extensive with the aggregate of human rights, democracy, or justice. As a result, he concludes, it is not impossible that an undemocratic government that persecutes some of its citizens on the basis of discriminatory policies could nevertheless be compliant with the rule of law.[151] At the same time, the concept cannot be diluted to the

147 United Nations Secretary-General, *Rule of Law and Transitional Justice in Conflict and Post-Conflict Societies*, UN Doc S/2004/616 (2004) para 6.

148 Tom Bingham, *The Rule of Law* (Penguin UK 2010).

149 ibid 66–67; Jeremy Waldron, 'Are Sovereigns Entitled to the Benefit of the International Rule of Law?' (2011) 22 European Journal of International Law 315.

150 Lon Fuller, *The Morality of Law* (Yale University Press 1969) 39.

151 Joseph Raz, *The Authority of Law: Essays on Law and Morality* (Clarendon Press; Oxford University Press 1979) 211. Arguably, one example could have been South Africa during the

point at which it merely becomes a validation of state sovereignty. Even in its thin version, there is some identifiable content to the rule of law, including the need for laws to be prospective, clear, and stable, and that there be an independent and accessible mechanism to oversee the application of these laws.[152] Whether defined as thicker or thinner version of the rule of law, it is agreed that the concept embodies aspirational values that remain unlikely to be fully achieved in any state. As such, the invocation of the rule of law in any context does not lead to all-or-nothing conclusions, but rather to situating the government under consideration along a spectrum of compliance with its tenets, however defined.[153]

The analysis of the rule of law in legal commentary largely has taken the state as a focus, a reflection of the fact that it originates in constitutional doctrine like that of A.V. Dicey in English law.[154] The link to the state is even more immediately evident in the continental concepts of *État de droit* and *Rechtsstaat*.[155] Even in its thin version, a central ambition of the concept is to subject the exercise of governmental authority to legal regulation. There is here a certain circularity in that we seek to control the state by way of laws emanating from the state. This approach also raises the question of whether the exercise of authority by entities other than the state ought to be subject to the rule of law, as well as the question of whether the rules that regulate nongovernmental authority can only emanate from the state, or whether they could find their basis in non-state actors. The fact that rule of law scholarship—with a few exceptions—focusses on the state is a reflection of the attribution to the state of a monopoly on law. As put by Laura Grenfell, "[t]he modern concept of the rule of law is based on two assumptions: first, the existence of a modern state and, second, that within this modern state paradigm the state is sufficiently strong and organized to enjoy a monopoly of law. In this sense the rule of law is shorthand for the rule of state law".[156] Law is both a product of and a justification for the sovereignty of the state, leading the UN Secretary-General to remark that "[t]he rule of law is at the heart of State sovereignty".[157]

It is worthwhile to be reminded of the relative novelty of the association of law and the state. Until a few centuries ago, law was an aspect of life that in a

apartheid regime. See David Dyzenhaus, *Hard Cases in Wicked Legal Systems: Pathologies of Legality* (2d edn, Oxford University Press 2010) 223–257.

[152] Raz, *The Authority of Law* (n 151) 214–219.
[153] McCorquodale (n 145) 291.
[154] Judith N Shklar, 'Political Theory and the Rule of Law' in Allan Hutchsinson and Patrick Monahan (eds), *The Rule of Law: Ideal or Ideology* (Carswell 1987) 5–6.
[155] Matthias Kötter and Gunnar Folke Schuppert, 'Applying the Rule of Law to Contexts beyond the State', *The Legal Doctrines of the Rule of Law and the Legal State (Rechtsstaat)* (Springer 2014) 72.
[156] Laura Grenfell, *Promoting the Rule of Law in Post-Conflict States* (Cambridge University Press 2013) 4.
[157] UN Secretary-General (n 147) para 48.

significant manner reflected social structures other than the state. Going back even further, to the Middle Ages, we see that law was not considered an instrument of earthly power to be wielded by the prince. Quite the opposite, the law was essentially customary, "an unwritten and unchanging eternal norm" that evolved slowly and invisibly rather than by the fiat of a ruler.[158] The capture of law by the state was a slow and progressive process, extending over many centuries and following patterns that differed from country to country. For very long periods, in Europe, multiple legal regimes overlapped in any given place. Some were applied only to certain classes of society, the nobility with its *leges feudorum*, the merchants with the *lex mercatoria*, city dwellers with municipal law; some laws followed geography, with each village and valley having its own custom, often expressed in a distinctive local dialect; some laws followed blood rather than land, on the model of the Ottoman millet system; other laws still attached to religious identity, with canon law acting as a transnational *ius commune* for Christians across Europe, but also Islamic law and Talmudic law in parallel; the rediscovery of Roman legal texts in the twelfth and then again in the sixteenth century, thanks to the rise of the university, overlaid "scientific" legal norms that weren't linked to any segment of the population nor to the state but that played an important role in private law matters, especially property law.[159] In many cases, there were courts that corresponded to particular communities or legal regimes, from manorial courts and royal courts to merchant courts and religious courts. There was no neat division between court and law, such that a given court could be called to apply norms from a range of regimes depending on the identity of the parties and the nature of the issue in dispute.[160]

In France, the state appeared in the picture in a push to force the writing down of customary laws, ordered by Charles VII in 1454, to bring some order to the more than 300 distinct customs applied in the kingdom at the time. During the same period, a small number of ordinances (*Ordonnances Colbert*) were issued by the king, to impose rules touching on some discrete fields like commerce or gifts. This started a process of appropriation that combined with the intellectual dominance of the *Coutume de Paris* to make possible the revolutionary codification of French law in the Napoleon Code of 1804, replacing in one fell swoop the myriad non-state customs with a single state law.[161] In England, the state's

158 Raoul Charles Caenegem, *Legal History: A European Perspective* (Bloomsbury Publishing 1990) 123; Costa (n 146) 138.

159 Jean-Louis Gazzaniga, *Introduction historique au droit des obligations* (Presses Universitaires de France 1992) 51–53; Caenegem (n 158) 115–116; Paul R Hyams, 'What Did Edwardian Villagers Understand by "Law"' [1996] Medieval Society and the Manor Court 69; Paolo Grossi, *L'ordine giuridico medievale* (Ed Laterza 2017).

160 Brian Z Tamanaha, 'Understanding Legal Pluralism: Past to Present, Local to Global' (2008) 30 Sydney Law Review 375, 377–378.

161 Gazzaniga (n 159) 56–60.

capture of law was more significantly institutional, with royal courts travelling on periodic circuits around the country to bring the king's justice to the people, in a manner that was initially complementary to other courts but that gradually came to assume a prominence that reflected the centralisation of law in the state.[162] Similar patterns have been mapped in colonial contexts with the writing down of Indigenous custom by colonial officials and the parcelling of jurisdiction to various types of bodies, resulting not only in a profound transformation of local law but also the progressive appropriation of what had been decentralised popular law into institutionalised state law.[163] It was famously said by Martin Chanock that "law was the cutting edge of colonialism", not merely as a governance tool but fundamentally as a gift of civilisation.[164] Indeed, the pervasive reliance of legalisation in colonial governance brought with it the myth of the ineluctable centrality of the state to the administration of justice. While it may be admitted that law was not only the handmaiden of colonial domination but also a site of resistance for colonised peoples, all these dynamics operated on a matrix reflecting Western notions of the rule of law.[165] Even in the post-colonial context, in which the attitudes of newly independent governments towards non-state justice practices and institutions have varied, the legacy of the rule of law has endured in a culture of legalities centred on the state.

The point of this quick historical excursus is to underscore the fact that the exclusive association of law with the state is one that is not very old, and as such rooted neither in the concept of law nor in the idea of the state. As discussed in the introduction to this book, legal pluralism's frontal attack of the positivist precept of centralism stands as a denial that the state's capture of law was ever successful. Law, it is argued, has never been a state monopoly: there are many non-state centres and processes that create, interpret, and apply law.[166] It is good to recall that the state is a relatively new concept on the global stage, having

[162] See generally John Hamilton Baker, *An Introduction to English Legal History* (Butterworths LexisNexis 2002). The question of the rise of the rule of law in British constitutionalism, arguably under the decisive influence of Dicey, is a different issue. See: JWF Allison, 'Turning the Rule of Law into an English Constitutional Idea' in Christopher May and Adam Winchester (eds), *Handbook on the Rule of Law* (Edward Elgar 2018); Mark D Walters, 'Dicey on Writing the Law of the Constitution' (2012) 32 Oxford Journal of Legal Studies 21.

[163] Terence Ranger, 'The Invention of Tradition in Colonial Africa', Perspectives on Africa: A Reader in Culture, History, and Representation (1997); Sally Engle Merry, 'Law and Colonialism', 25 Law & Society Review 889–922 (1991).

[164] Martin Chanock, *Law, Custom, and Social Order: The Colonial Experience in Malawi and Zambia* (Cambridge University Press 1985) 4; Martin Chanock, 'The Law Market: The Legal Encounter in British East and Central Africa' in Wolfgang Mommsen and Jaap De Moor (eds), *European Expansion and Law: The Encounter of European and Indigenous Law in 19th- and 20th-Century Africa and Asia* (Bloomsbury Publishing 1992) 279–280.

[165] Merry (n 163) 917–918; Chanock, 'The Law Market' (n 164) 306.

[166] See René Provost, 'Interpretation in International Law as a Transcultural Project' in Andrea Bianchi, Daniel Peat, and Matthew Windsor (eds), *Interpretation in International Law* (Oxford University Press 2015).

become universalised only about one century ago; prior to that point, much of the world lay outside the "concert of civilised nations" and, as such, sidestepped any idea of the capture of law by the state. The state may be the most comprehensive legally based organisation of our time, but there are others as well.[167] It is said that in some parts of Africa, upwards of 90 percent of disputes, including land disputes, are resolved by way of non-state mechanisms.[168] Informal dispute settlement is, in places like Sierra Leone and Liberia, the normal way of dealing with disputes; indeed, despite the fact that state courts are available, to bring a formal legal suit there is considered an anti-social act that can reverberate across a community.[169] An example set in a location closer to the historical roots of the principle of the rule of law is the Valencia Water Tribunal (*Tribunal de les aigües de la Vega de València*), which describes itself as the oldest judicial institution in Europe, having been established in 1238 or even earlier.[170] Its creation of course predates both Spain and Westphalian statehood, and it continues to operate apart from Spanish administration of justice. The concerns embodied in the concept of the rule of law understood in its fuller sense speak to the manner in which law operates in all these legal centres and processes, including those not connected to the state.

Scholarship on the rule of law significantly has ventured beyond the state with respect to one category of legal actors: international organisations. From about the year 2000, more serious consideration was given to claims that the nature of some powers wielded by international organisations justified extending to them the principles of the rule of law. Anti-terrorism measures adopted by the United Nations after the attacks of 11 September 2001 directly affected important rights and interests of individuals. For instance, the Sanctions Committee, authorised by the UN Security Council, listed individuals on no-fly lists or to be targeted for financial restrictions. The justification, execution, and reviewability of these decisions have been challenged as falling short of what would be demanded of a state taking similar measures.[171] Peacekeeping and other international missions

167 Joseph Raz, 'Why the State?' (Social Science Research Network 2013) SSRN Scholarly Paper ID 2339522 2, online: <https://papers.ssrn.com/abstract=2339522> accessed 10 February 2017.

168 Brian Tamanaha, 'A Bifurcated Theory of Law in Hybrid Societies: The Rule of Law and Non-State Justice' in Matthias Kötter and others (eds), *Non-State Justice Institutions and the Law. Decision-Making at the Interface of Tradition, Religion and the State* (Palgrave Macmillan 2015) 4.

169 Mohamed Sesay, 'Hijacking the Rule of Law in Postconflict Environments' (2019) 4 European Journal of International Security 41, 56.

170 See http://www.tribunaldelasaguas.org/es/; Alejandro Valiño and Arcos Valiño, 'Sull'origine del Tribunal de las aguas de Vega de Valencia', online: <http://roderic.uv.es/handle/10550/55882> accessed 10 July 2017.

171 Sherif Elgebeily, *The Rule of Law in the United Nations Security Council Decision-Making Process: Turning the Focus Inwards* (Taylor & Francis 2017); Matthew Happold, 'United Nations Sanctions and the Rule of Law', *The Rule of Law and Its Application to the United Nations* (Nomos 2016); Clemens A Feinäugle, *Hoheitsgewalt Im Völkerrecht: Das 1267-Sanktionsregime Der UN Und Seine Rechtliche Fassung* (Springer-Verlag 2011).

are another instance of international organisations exercising state-like authority over population and territory, sometimes as direct proto-governmental administrator, other times as an external actor whose presence on the territory of a state cannot be derived from the sovereign authority of that state. When such a situation occurs, the fact that a power usually associated with the government is in fact held by an international organisation does not seem a compelling basis to deny the protection and requirements associated with the rule of law in relation to the exercise of such power. The lack of any accountability mechanism to sanction the spread of cholera in Haiti due to the failure of the United Nations to take necessary and available precautions has been cited a one especially glaring example of the need for rule of law principles to apply to international organisations.[172] The internal processes of international organisations provide a final context in which powers are used in a manner that intersects with the values embodied in the rule of law. Organisations like the United Nations are employers that escape the applicability of national labour standards that normally prevent abuses. The United Nations does have internal norms and procedures, but these were repeatedly challenged as falling short of recognised international standards on transparency, independence, and reviewability. Changes were brought that addressed some of these shortcoming, with explicit references to the rule of law.[173] Evan Criddle and Evan Fox-Decent, as part of their exploration of the justification of state sovereignty, suggest that if an international organisation exercises public authority—powers that are other-regarding, purposive, and institutional in nature—then it stands in a fiduciary position vis-à-vis humanity and as such ought to be governed by standards that frame state powers.[174] While Criddle and Fox-Decent turn to human rights norms as a result, their argument can also be taken to point in the direction of the rule of law.

Consideration of the applicability of the rule of law to international organisations is interesting not only in that it dislodged the concept from its original state-centred ambit but also because it triggered a reflection on the substance of the rule of law at the international level.[175] I mentioned at the start of this section that the lack of agreement on the content of the rule of law paradoxically stands as one of its defining features. Within that observable diversity

[172] See: Gian Luca Burci, 'Enforcement versus Immunities in the United Nations: A Rule of Law Perspective', *The Rule of Law and Its Application to the United Nations* (Nomos 2016); Ernst U Tschoepke, 'The UN Administration of Territories: The Mission in Kosovo and the Rule of Law', *The Rule of Law and Its Application to the United Nations* (Nomos 2016).

[173] Clemens A Feinäugle, 'The UN Declaration on the Rule of Law and the Application of the Rule of Law to the UN: A Reconstruction From an International Public Authority Perspective' (2016) 7 Goettingen Journal of International Law 157, 175–178.

[174] Evan J Criddle and Evan Fox-Decent, *Fiduciaries of Humanity: How International Law Constitutes Authority* (Oxford University Press 2016) 283–290.

[175] Machiko Kanetake and André Nollkaemper (eds), *The Rule of Law at the National and International Levels: Contestations and Deference* (2016).

of views, however, when the international rule of law is discussed, it seems that there is a general consensus that the rule of law applicable to states and the rule of law applicable to international organisations cannot be identical. Because of fundamental differences in the foundation, structure, and functions of states and international organisations, there is no question of taking the components of the national rule of law (howsoever defined) and transfer them lock, stock, and barrel to an international rule of law.[176] José Alvarez notes in this respect that courts may well be called to play different roles at the domestic and international levels. In public international law, there are many situations in which there is no possibly of judicial review of the legality of an act, both for jurisdictional reasons (courts have limited rather than general jurisdiction, of an optional rather than compulsory nature) and for functional reasons (the UN Security Council plays a role in responding to threat to international peace that doesn't square easily with judicial review).[177]

A different context in which the concept of the rule of law has been expanded to cover actors beyond the state is international development assistance by international organisations or by state development agencies. Laura Grenfell has tracked the evolution of rule of law policies of organisations like the World Bank and state agencies like DFID (UK) and USAID (US) to show how they went from a position of indifference towards non-state justice mechanisms in the 1990s to an acknowledgment that, at least for some countries, it was absolutely necessary to consider non-state justice to meaningfully strengthen the rule of law.[178] Afghanistan provides an interesting example that straddles development and armed conflict. The main state actor, the United States, initially focussed nearly entirely its development effort to strengthen the rule of law on the official justice system, with very limited concrete impact.[179] From 2010, USAID took more fully into account the fact that 80 to 90 percent of legal disputes in Afghanistan were resolved through non-state justice mechanism, and divided nearly equally its rule of law development assistance between the official and the informal justice sectors.[180] Geoffrey Swenson attributes the failure of this engagement with the non-state justice sector to a misguided sense that there was a justice vacuum that needed to be filled and to the subservience of these efforts to security interests and counter-insurgency strategies.[181] A more thoughtful model

176 McCorquodale (n 145) 289–290; Elgebeily (n 171) 36–46.

177 José Alvarez, 'International Organizations and the Rule of Law' (2016) 14 New Zealand Journal of Public and International Law 25–30.

178 Grenfell (n 156) 24–32.

179 Whit Mason (ed), *The Rule of Law in Afghanistan: Missing in Inaction* (Cambridge University Press 2011).

180 Geoffrey Swenson, 'Why U.S. Efforts to Promote the Rule of Law in Afghanistan Failed' (2017) 42 International Security 114, 125–127.

181 ibid 150–151.

to constructively engage with informal justice actors was advocated by the UN Development Programme (UNDP), calling for the fuller integration of Afghan state and non-state justice into a hybrid model.[182] This speaks to a broader and deeper engagement of UNDP with informal justice systems, including the exploration of avenues to reconcile these with international human rights standards.[183] Tellingly, the hybrid model devised by UNDP in Kabul, although presented as reflecting deeply held Afghan cultural values, triggered an "angry and threatening response from Afghan judicial and state justice institutions" as well as opposition from human rights organisations.[184]

As a guiding principle, the substance of the rule of law must reflect the specific and evolving context of the exercise of public authority to which it is applied, with the shift from state to non-state actors as a fundamental change in context that calls for significant adjustments to facets of the rule of law that some would consider central.[185] In this light, enriched by a legal pluralist understanding of law, the rule of law emerges as a living organism rather than a fixed list of attributes or an idealised image of justice.[186] It follows that the rule of law as related to public authority exercised by rebels would be substantially distinct from that applied to the state or international organisations.

B. Rule of Law in Armed Conflict

War disrupts many of the values and practices that are normally considered fundamental, and as such is a type of contextual transformation that can be expected to translate into a significantly distinct rule of law. The disruptive impact of armed conflict on the rule of law is reflected in both legal regimes that regulate war, international human rights and humanitarian law, in a fashion that speaks directly to an imagined rebel rule of law.

i. Human Rights: Derogation and Margin of Appreciation

International human rights law does not stop producing legal effects during periods of armed conflicts, although the outbreak of war does have a normative impact on the protection of human rights. The precise nature of the relationship

[182] UNDP, Afghanistan Human Development Report: Bridging Modernity and Tradition—Rule of Law and the Search for Justice (2007) 126–132.

[183] UNDP, Informal Justice Systems—Charting a Course for Human Rights-Based Engagement (2013) 88–96.

[184] Ali Wardak, 'State and Non-State Justice Systems in Afghanistan: The Need for Synergy' (2011) 32 University of Pennsylvania Journal of International Law 1305, 1322.

[185] Tobias Berger and Milli Lake, 'Human Rights, the Rule of Law, and Democracy' in Anke Draude, Tanja Börzel, and Thomas Risse (eds), *The Oxford Handbook of Governance and Limited Statehood* (Oxford University Press 2018) 424.

[186] Zumbansen (n 144) 63.

between human rights and international humanitarian law has been the subject of enormous academic and judicial attention over the last several decades. Positions range from the International Court of Justice's approach whereby human rights law is *lex generalis* to international humanitarian law's *lex specialis*, to the European Court of Human Rights jurisprudence in which humanitarian law could inspire the interpretation of human rights but not displace them.[187] There is no longer any debate, if there ever was a serious one, on the fact that human rights remain legally applicable during an armed conflict. The impact of armed conflict on human rights standards can be assessed with greater clarity with respect to the possibility of derogation and the doctrine of the margin of appreciation.

The clear intent of states to manage the impact of war on human rights law can be seen in the inclusion, in the International Covenant on Civil and Political Rights (Art. 4), the European Convention on Human Rights (Art. 15), and the American Convention on Human Rights (Art. 27), of a derogation clause that authorises states to suspend rights and freedoms in "situations of emergency that threaten the life of the nation".[188] While both the European and American regional instruments mention "war" specifically, whereas the Covenant does not, it is a given that armed conflicts are the prototypical emergency that can threaten the life of the nation. The treaty provisions that explicitly provide for the possibility of derogation during a state of emergency include a list of rights that are deemed "non-derogable". Tellingly, the lists of non-derogable rights in the Covenant, the European Convention, and the American Convention do not include due process guarantees that frame the administration of justice and, arguably, constitute an important element of the rule of law.[189] As such, the state of emergency is a direct challenge to the foundational role of the rule of law.[190] Even if the threat to the survival of the political community is averred, however, international human rights law does not allow the jettisoning of the rule of law.

[187] See generally René Provost, *International Human Rights and Humanitarian Law* (Cambridge University Press 2002); Jens David Ohlin (ed), *Theoretical Boundaries of Armed Conflict and Human Rights* (Cambridge University Press 2016).

[188] The African Charter of Human and Peoples' Rights does not mention the possibility of derogation in situations of emergency, and the African Commission has largely resisted claims by states to suspend or limit rights because of an emergency: Fatsah Ouguergouz, *The African Charter on Human and Peoples' Rights: A Comprehensive Agenda for Human Dignity and Sustainable Democracy in Africa* (Martinus Nijhoff Publishers 2003) 423–471; Rachel Murray, *The African Charter on Human and Peoples' Rights: A Commentary* (Oxford University Press 2019) 207.

[189] The Human Rights Committee has offered in its General Comment 29 that due process guarantees that are necessary to ensure protection of non-derogable rights are themselves non-derogable, by necessary implication. See Alex Conte and Richard Burchill, *Defining Civil and Political Rights: The Jurisprudence of the United Nations Human Rights Committee* (Routledge 2016) 40–41. For a fuller consideration of due process guarantees before insurgent courts, see Chapter 3, Section III.

[190] Criddle and Fox-Decent (n 174) 126; Evan J Criddle (ed), *Human Rights in Emergencies* (Cambridge University Press 2016).

The possibility of derogation is constrained: even for rights that are derogable, limitations must be temporary, officially proclaimed, and strictly limited to the exigencies of the situation.[191] The ensuing requirements of necessity and proportionality reinforce the conclusion offered in the previous section regarding the ever-changing requirements of the rule of law, always reflecting the specifics of the circumstances of their application. In war, as the prototypical state of emergency recognised in international human rights treaties, the rule of law must be adapted to reflect the often extraordinary circumstances in which the administration of justice takes place. Human rights treaty provisions on derogation indeed point the way to how to carry out this necessary adjustment, in specifying that any measure taken to limit rights and freedoms during a state of emergency must comply with the state's "other obligations under international law". In this respect, international human rights law is structurally connected to international humanitarian law, as well as to other fields of international law.

The possibility for states to derogate from a number of fundamental human rights, including minimally some rights that will often be taken to form part of the substance of the rule of law, supports the claim that this concept will be transformed significantly by its application to situations of armed conflict. This brief foray into international human rights law has, to this point, focussed on the *state*'s right to suspend fundamental rights and freedoms during an emergency. In the context of the exploration of the relevance of the concept of the rule of law to the rebel administration of justice, this begs the question of whether only a state may derogate during a state of emergency, or whether a non-state armed group may do so as well. This is of course a provocative suggestion, one that does not seem to have been considered in legal doctrine so far. An initial answer might be that the specific provisions of the treaties cited in the previous paragraph refer only to a state declaring a situation of emergency, and therefore that no other entity is competent to do the same. It is well and true that, for example, Article 4 of the Covenant on Civil and Political Rights only envisages that states can derogate, but it is equally true that Article 2 of the same treaty spells out substantive human rights obligations of states, and of no one else. There is thus an issue of "having your cake and eating it too" with the overly facile response resting on the wording of the derogation provisions in the treaties.

Beyond the range of technical explanations that have been offered to justify the applicability of human rights standards to armed opposition groups,[192] the conundrum remains that if rebels exercise public authority in a manner that warrants the application of human rights, the same can be invoked to articulate

[191] See generally Jaime Oraá, *Human Rights in States of Emergency in International Law* (Clarendon Press 1992).

[192] Daragh Murray, *Human Rights Obligations of Non-State Armed Groups* (Hart Publishing 2016) 82–117. This is discussed more fully in Chapter 3, Section III.

a justification for a right to derogate that will mirror that proclaimed in favour of states. For instance, Criddle and Fox-Decent offer a fiduciary foundation for both the imposition of human rights obligations on governments and for the possibility of suspension during a state of emergency. As mentioned earlier, the final chapter of their book interrogates the applicability of a fiduciary construction of sovereignty to international organisations, leading them to conclude that inasmuch as they exercise public authority, organisations ought to be bound by human rights norms. They do not take the extra step of asking what are the implications of this conclusion in situations of emergency, but the justification offered earlier in the book for derogation seems equally transposable to international organisations.[193] Indeed, the need to preserve a minimal degree of social stability as a prerequisite to the enjoyment of human rights is equally applicable to peacekeeping operations. Thus a peacekeeping force maintaining order in a situation of extreme instability or intervening in a conflict zone may not be legally required to ensure human rights as if there were no emergency; to conclude otherwise would both seem unrealistic and to impose on an international organisation a higher obligation than on states.[194]

In a parallel fashion, the public authority approach can be applied to governance by non-state armed groups to justify both the applicability of human rights—or the rule of law—and the possibility of derogation. Indeed, the designation of the entity whose life is protected by derogation in the Civil and Political Covenant and European Convention, the "nation", is not necessarily coextensive with the state. In this respect, the American Convention is explicitly more restrictive, justifying derogation on the need to "protect the independence and security of a State Party". In the two other documents, the "life of the nation" is a looser concept that does not easily justify a narrow focus on the state as its exclusive protector. If the fundamental concern is the protection of minimal social stability as a prerequisite to the enjoyment of human rights, then it seem equally relevant to situations of governance by armed groups. Derogation by insurgents would remain subject to the conditions and limitations applicable in any state of emergency.

Similar questions arise with respect to the margin of appreciation, a human rights doctrine that has had a significant impact on the application of human rights in general, and derogations during a state of emergency in particular. Initially developed by the European Court of Human Rights, the doctrine of the margin of appreciation provides that a state shall be granted a significant degree of deference in the interpretation and application of human rights. In other

[193] Criddle and Fox-Decent (n 174) 123–161, 283–352.

[194] Scott Sheeran, 'Human Rights and Derogation in Peacekeeping' in Evan J Criddle (ed), *Human Rights in Emergencies* (Cambridge University Press 2016) 229.

words, when a human rights body examines whether a measure taken by a government is consistent with its obligations, the assessment ought not to be in the nature of a de novo evaluation but closer to vetting the reasonableness of the position taken by the state. This form of judicial restraint has been justified on the basis of the greater proximity of the national government to the situation at hand (as compared to a supra-national court like the European Court of Human Rights), the greater political legitimacy of governments, as well as the open-textured nature of human rights norms that can accommodate a diversity of legitimate interpretations.[195] The same provocative question arises here again: if an armed opposition group administers justice and, as such, is said to be bound by international human rights law and subject to the rule of law, should the group be granted any margin of appreciation in the application of human rights?

Unlike derogations in a state of emergency, the doctrine of margin of appreciation does not rest on any textual foundation in the treaties.[196] As such, the easy rebuttal identified for derogation, on the basis of the explicit reference to the state in treaty provisions allowing derogations, does not obtain for the margin of appreciation. One might imagine an objection based on the foundation of the public authority wielded by non-state armed groups as opposed to governments. Two reasons can be mentioned to question the persuasiveness of this objection. First, it suggests that governments are granted a margin of appreciation because they have legitimacy, normally linked to their democratic representativeness. This would imply that governments that are in fact not democratic, or more broadly not representative, should be given a smaller margin, or none at all. Andrew Legg, in his comprehensive study of the doctrine, makes a valiant effort to defend such a reading of the jurisprudence of the European Court of Human Rights. He notes that in some of the cases in which the Court relies on the doctrine, like *Dudgeon v. UK*, there are mentions of the government acting carefully and in good faith.[197] Critically, however, he cannot unearth any passage in which the European Court would have noted the unrepresentative nature of a national government as justification for a narrower margin.[198] It would in

[195] Andrew Legg, *The Margin of Appreciation in International Human Rights Law: Deference and Proportionality* (Oxford University Press, Oxford 2012); Yuval Shany, 'Toward a General Margin of Appreciation Doctrine in International Law?' (2005) 16 European Journal of International Law 907; Marisa Iglesias Vila, 'Subsidiarity, Margin of Appreciation and International Adjudication within a Cooperative Conception of Human Rights' (2017) 15 International Journal of Constitutional Law 393.

[196] The doctrine of the margin of appreciation was codified in Protocol 15 to the European Convention of Human Rights in 2013, a development that did not substantively transform the doctrine.

[197] Legg (n 195) 75–79; see also Josephine Asche, *Die Margin of Appreciation Entwurf einer Dogmatik monokausaler richterlicher Zurückhaltung für den europäischen Menschenrechtsschutz* (Springer-Verlag 2018) 179–214.

[198] At most, as noted by Shany, we can note that the European Court *de facto* tends to make wider use of the margin of appreciation with respect to the complex balancing of rights, which tend to arise more often in established democracies of Western Europe than in the newer and more fragile

any case be extremely difficult for a court to classify governments along a spectrum of democracy for that purpose.[199] The second objection to a foundational critique of recognising a margin of appreciation to an armed opposition group speaks to the necessarily unrepresentative nature of such groups. As discussed in the introduction to this book, and as the conflict in Colombia illustrates, no system of governance can be grounded in violence alone. It would be extremely difficult for a rebel group to survive, much less exercise real governance of any kind, without some degree of support from the population. In Colombia, the FARC's behaviour at times attracted support and at other times provoked resistance from the population, and the group was not necessarily less representative than the government at all times and in every respects. With respect to the administration of justice, as shown, there is no evidence to point out that rebel justice was thought inherently inferior to official justice, and indeed in some ways it was felt to be closer to the ideals of the rule of law. Likewise, it is hazardous to claim that the government of Syria is necessarily more representative than some of the armed opposition groups in that conflict.[200] Just like there are decent states and wicked states, there are decent rebels and wicked rebels. It is not obvious that such distinctions provide a solid conceptual basis to dismiss the possible extension of a margin of appreciation to rebel groups.

ii. Humanitarian Law: Occupation as Hostile Relations

Moving from human rights to international humanitarian law, the occurrence of an armed conflict has an impact on the concept of the rule of law in that its connection to state sovereignty is formally disrupted. This is most transparent in the regulation of occupation, when a power other than the territorial state comes to exercise authority over a conquered territory.

The law of occupation, as noted by Eyal Benvenisti, is the mirror image of the concept of state sovereignty, and as such comes to indirectly define sovereignty in international law.[201] Occupation does not signal a transfer of sovereignty, a reflection of the now entrenched norm that sovereign title to territory cannot be

democracies to the East: Yuval Shany, 'All Roads Lead to Strasbourg?: Application of the Margin of Appreciation Doctrine by the European Court of Human Rights and the UN Human Rights Committee' (2018) 9 Journal of International Dispute Settlement 180, 185.

[199] Dominic McGoldrick, 'A Defence of the Margin of Appreciation and an Argument for Its Application by the Human Rights Committee' (2016) 65 International & Comparative Law Quarterly 21, 57.

[200] See the discussion of Syrian Kurdish governance in Chapter 4. More generally, see Nina Caspersen, 'Degrees of Legitimacy: Ensuring Internal and External Support in the Absence of Recognition' (2015) 66 Geoforum 184.

[201] Eyal Benvenisti, *The International Law of Occupation* (2d edn, Oxford University Press 2012) 1–2; see also Aeyal Gross, *The Writing on the Wall: Rethinking the International Law of Occupation* (Cambridge University Press 2017) 17–51.

validly acquired through the use of force. At the same time, it is acknowledged that an occupier can validly exercise some public authority over the territory and population under its control. One aspect of public authority explicitly recognised to an occupying force is the maintenance of public order and civil life (Art. 43, 1907 Hague Regulation), overlapping to a significant extent with the idea of the rule of law. For a very long time, the idea of a trustee has been used to describe the nature of the powers recognised to the occupier.[202] This is of course a particular type of trust, in that it fails to incorporate any sense of intentional delegation from the territorial government in favour of the occupier, much less any sense of confidence from the former in the latter. Instead, the fiduciary dimension of occupation reflects the mere fact of occupation and the corresponding inability of the territorial state to exercise its normal authority in that territory. This is clearly conveyed in Article 42 of the 1907 Hague Regulations, the first treaty codification of the law of occupation, which refers in the French authentic version to a territory "*placé de fait sous l'autorité de l'armée ennemie*" to the extent that this authority "*est établie et en mesure de s'exercer*".[203] The legal regulation of occupation is thus a regime under *jus in bello* that stands wholly insulated from the legality or legitimacy of the presence of the occupier in the given territory, an aspect that would reflect *jus ad bellum*.[204] In this respect, for example, Iraq as an occupier further to its manifestly illegal invasion of Kuwait in 1990 was in principle in the same legal situation as was the United Kingdom after it took control of part of Iraq in 2003. Two ideas interesting for our discussion of rebel governance emerge from this analysis. First, international law explicitly reflects the suggestion that the power to govern, bringing with it the principle of the rule of law, can be dissociated from sovereignty, at least in situations of armed conflict. Second, the recognition of public authority exercised by the occupying force is not tied to the legitimacy of its presence or power.

This sketch of the construction of governance and the rule of law in wartime can be sharpened with three observations. To begin with, the nature and extent of the powers of the occupier have been the subject of intense debate regarding the extent to which an invading state is required to leave in place and enforce the laws of the occupied government. An older construction of the framing idea of the occupier as trustee identified the territorial government as the beneficiary of that trust. In this perspective, the occupier is a place-holder for the territorial government, and as such granted the most limited power to alter existing

202 Adam Roberts, 'What Is a Military Occupation?' (1985) 55 British Yearbook of International Law 249, 259.

203 There is no official English version of this treaty, but this provision can be translated as "Territory is considered occupied when it is actually placed under the authority of the hostile army".

204 Henri Meyrowitz, *Le Principe de l'égalité des belligérants devant le droit de la guerre* (Pedone 1970).

laws and public institutions. This is reflected in Article 64 of the Fourth Geneva Convention, which imposes limits on the occupier's discretion to change the laws of the occupied territory. Over the course of the last century, a competing vision of occupation has come to emerge, whereby the primary beneficiary of the fiduciary powers held by the occupier is the population of the occupied territory. Under the very significant influence of international human rights law, this "transformative occupation" allows or even requires the occupier to bring the legal order of the occupied territory in line with the requirements of the rule of law.[205] Regardless whether the law of occupation has fully evolved to embrace a wholly transformative approach, this is a movement towards a tighter embrace of the rule of law in situations of armed conflict, with a corresponding lesser priority given to concerns of state sovereignty.

A second, related observation touches on the steady widening of the extraterritorial application of human rights. This is, again, a much-contested development, centred in the jurisprudence of the European Court of Human Rights. In a series of cases over the last decade, the European Court has reversed an earlier approach that eschewed, to a large extent, the applicability of state obligations under the European Convention on Human Rights to acts that take place beyond national borders. The military occupation of Iraq and Afghanistan by a number of states party to the European Convention provided an opportunity for the Court to revisit this position, later also applied within the *espace juridique européen,* leading it to conclude in *Georgia v Russia (II)* that any situation meeting the requirements of belligerent occupation under humanitarian law will correspond to human rights jurisdiction.[206] The extension of this approach to contexts beyond the European Convention of Human Rights to other treaties and to customary law, as well as the particulars of when and to what extent these obligations are applicable, remain contentious. That said, it is an evolution that both converges with a "transformative" vision of occupation and insists on the need for enjoyment of rights and freedoms regardless of who has sovereign authority in a given time and place, to place much greater emphasis instead on the identity of the actor with factual capacity to fulfil human rights

[205] Criddle and Fox-Decent (n 174) 192–193; Nehal Bhuta, 'The Antinomies of Transformative Occupation' (2005) 16 European Journal of International Law 721; Adam Roberts, 'Transformative Military Occupation: Applying the Laws of War and Human Rights', Michael Schmitt and Jelena Pejic (eds), *International Law and Armed Conflict: Exploring the Faultlines* (Brill 2007); David Kretzmer, *The Occupation of Justice: The Supreme Court of Israel and the Occupied Territories* (State University of New York Press 2002) 61–72.

[206] ECtHR, *Georgia v Russia (II)*, Appl. No 38263/8, Judgment (Grand Chamber), 21 January 2021, para 196; Marko Milanovic, *Extraterritorial Application of Human Rights Treaties: Law, Principles, and Policy* (Oxford University Press 2011); Gerd Oberleitner, *Human Rights in Armed Conflict* (Cambridge University Press 2015) 220–231.

obligations.[207] It converges as well with a reading of international human rights law that concludes, as noted earlier, that when non-state actors are acting in a position of public authority they should be bound to comply with human rights obligations.[208]

The third and final observation on the construction of the rule of law in times of war centres on the scope of the concept of occupation. Although the very first codification of the law of occupation came about in the Lieber Code and concerned the civil war in the United States, the various humanitarian law treaties that regulate occupation only apply it explicitly to situations of international armed conflict in which a state occupies the territory of another state.[209] In the *RUF Case* before the Special Court for Sierra Leone, the defence advanced the claim that the non-state armed group was an occupying force and as such could require civilians to carry out work and confiscate property. The Court rejected this claim by applying a classical understanding of the concept of occupation, inapplicable to a situation of non-international armed conflict like the war in Sierra Leone.[210] The concept of occupation, however, has evolved over the years and now seems less fully bound to this traditional picture of belligerent occupation. The clearest divergence is found in Article 1(4) of the 1977 Additional Protocol I, which provides that rules applicable to international armed conflicts shall apply to situations of "alien occupation", an expression broader than belligerent occupation that was widely taken as a coded reference to the Israeli-Palestinian situation.[211] More generally, the same provision of Protocol I declares that wars of national liberation in which a people is fighting in furtherance of its right to self-determination are to be deemed international armed conflict. The implication is that the national liberation movement is to be treated in every respect as if it were a state, which would suggest that this party to the conflict can also become an occupying force under international humanitarian law.[212] There is a conceptual hurdle in applying this suggestion, in that the national liberation movement does not have a national territory beyond which it becomes an occupier. This is illustrated by the sole declaration to date that has triggered the application of Article

[207] Marko Milanović and Tatjana Papić, 'The Applicability of the ECHR in Contested Territories' (2018) 67 International & Comparative Law Quarterly 779, 794–799; Yuval Shany, 'The Extraterritorial Application of International Human Rights Law' (2020) 409 Recueil des cours 21.

[208] Andrew Clapham, *Human Rights and Non-State Actors* (Edward Elgar 2013); Murray (n 192).

[209] Benvenisti (n 201) 35–36, 45; Roberts (n 202); Robert Kolb and Sylvain Vité, *Le droit de l'occupation militaire: perspectives historiques et enjeux juridiques actuels* (Bruylant 2009); Rotem Giladi, 'A Different Sense of Humanity: Occupation in Francis Lieber's Code' (2012) 94 International Review of the Red Cross 81.

[210] Special Court for Sierra Leone, *Prosecutor v Sesay, Kallon & Gbao ("RUF Trial")*, Trial Chamber, Judgment, 2 March 2009, SCSL-04-15-T, paras 982–988.

[211] This was meant to overcome applicability issues. See Kretzmer (n 205) 32–40; Benvenisti (n 201) 3.

[212] Yoram Dinstein, *The International Law of Belligerent Occupation* (2d edn, Cambridge University Press 2019) 38.

1(4) of Protocol I, issued in 2015 by the Polisario Front in Western Sahara vis-à-vis Morocco.[213] While there is a physical boundary of sort (a sand berm in the desert) that marks the spheres of power of Morocco and the Polisario, it is hardly a marker of divided sovereignty.

The solution, in accordance with the normative framework of international humanitarian law, is to examine the nature of the relationship between the population and the military force: if it is broadly marked by enmity, if the allegiances of the occupier and the occupied population link to opposing sides of the conflict, then the former should be subject to occupation law. This is indeed consistent with the approach developed by the International Criminal Tribunal for the former Yugoslavia in cases in which the accused objected that they could not be convicted of grave breaches of the 1949 Geneva Conventions because the victims were not "protected persons", defined as nationals of an enemy state. The Tribunal in *Celebici* and *Tadic* concluded that the substance of differing allegiances rather than formal links of nationality ought to guide the application of the Geneva Conventions.[214] The 2015 US Law of War Manual, while offering a general principle of inapplicability of the law of occupation to civil wars, does make an exception for "recognised" belligerents.[215] There have been many suggestions that this reasoning should in fact obtain in all non-international armed conflicts, so that a non-state armed group that find itself exercising authority over a population with which it does not share allegiances should be bound by the law of occupation.[216] One documented example is the relation between the Rwandan Patriotic Front—then an armed insurgent group—and peasants in Rwanda in the early 1990s, described as having shifted from liberation to occupation.[217] A wider concept of occupation seems congruent with the expansion of human rights obligations to non-state actors and to the concept of national liberation

213 Marco Sassòli, 'The Concept and the Beginning of Occupation' in Andrew Clapham, Paola Gaeta, and Marco Sassoli (eds), *The 1949 Geneva Conventions: A Commentary* (Oxford University Press 2015) 19–20.

214 Provost (n 187) 39–40. See *The Prosecutor v Delalic*, Trial Judgment, 16 November 1998, Case No IT-96-21-T (Trial Chamber, ICTY), paras 265–266; *The Prosecutor v Tadic*, Appeals Judgment, 15 July 1999, Case No IT-94-1-A (Appeals Chamber, ICTY), paras 165–168.

215 United States Department of Defense, Law of War Manual, rev'd Dec. 2016, s. 11.1.3.3. See Yael Ronen, 'The Department of Defense Manual: Occupation Chapter' in Michael Newton (ed), *The United States Department of Defense Law of War Manual: Commentary and Critique* (Cambridge University Press 2018) 23–26. On the recognition of belligerency and insurgency, see Robert McLaughlin, *Recognition of Belligerency and the Law of Armed Conflict* (Oxford University Press 2020).

216 Benvenisti (n 201) 59–61; Sivakumaran, *The Law of Non-International Armed Conflict* (n 2) 530. The argument can also be deployed in relation to the state, to argue that the more protective regime of belligerent occupation should obtain when the state is in a hostile relation with its own population on its own territory. The US Supreme Court deployed a variant of this approach in relation to the former Confederate states after the Civil War: see Chapter 4, Section IV.

217 Mahmood Mamdani, *When Victims Become Killers: Colonialism, Nativism, and the Genocide in Rwanda* (Princeton University Press 2001) 186–189.

armed conflict, as discussed earlier. Sandesh Sivakumaran suggests that perhaps not every aspect of the law of occupation can be transposed to non-international armed conflicts, but that a piecemeal approach could identify which aspects can justifiably be found applicable by insurgents in a civil war. One key example he gives is the maintenance of law and order which, if not taken over by the rebels, would simply fail to be enforced at all.[218]

These elements combine to suggest that the rule of law in situations of armed conflict takes on a distinct colour. Substantively, as suggested by the possibility of derogation, its content is likely to have to be adapted to exigencies of war in order to provide realistic guidance that reconciles elements of the rule of law with military necessity. Subjectively, international legal standards attest to the lack of a necessary connection between the rule of law and state sovereignty, allowing for the administration of justice by states other than the sovereign territorial state and opening a door to the maintenance of law and order by non-state actors. In this context, the concept of the rebel rule of law stands as a point of convergence of various norms and trends rather than a fanciful suggestion devoid of any foundation in law or in fact.

C. Elements of a Rebel Rule of Law

The idea of the rule of law detached from the state, applied to a non-state armed group, and adjusted to the realities of armed conflict, hints at a concept of the rebel rule of law. This in turn begs the question of the content of such a concept. It is indeed at this second stage that the realistic and useful character of a proposed rebel rule of law can meaningfully be assessed. In so doing, however, I run up against the broader and largely intractable debate surrounding the content of the rule of law generally, whether it should be "thin" or "thick", and which specific elements can justifiably be included. The main thrust of the analysis in this chapter has been to demonstrate that the concept of the rebel rule of law is viable. Part of the argument is indeed founded on the notion that the rule of law is a variable concept that must be adjusted to different actors and different contexts. Logically, it would seem inconsistent to attempt to map out an objective understanding of the substantive requirements of the rule of law as applied to the rebel administration of justice. In general, the rule of law can be said to be thinner in situations of armed conflict, and distinct in relation to non-state actors. As a result, the elements of a rebel rule of law offered here correspond to a thin version of the concept, leaving space for more demanding components to be argued for when the circumstances allow for them. Finally, the elements of a rebel rule of

[218] Sivakumaran, *The Law of Non-International Armed Conflict* (n 2) 530.

law are not necessarily all derived from the rule of law as applicable to states, so that the former would be a pared-down version of the latter. As we will see, the administration of justice by non-state armed groups brings challenges that in part are unique to them, corresponding to elements of a rebel rule of law that are without equivalent for states. Using the institutions and practices of the FARC in Colombia as a case study, I suggest four elements to a rebel rule of law whereby the administration of justice must be part of a broader system of governance, must be carried in a regular fashion, must include some minimum elements of procedural fairness, and must rest on a narrative of social justice.

i. Broader System of Governance

The rule of law is a concept that situates the administration of justice within a broader framework of legitimacy and accountability in the exercise of public authority. It seems difficult to imagine a system of justice that could correspond to the aspirations of the rule of law if it operates in isolation from other components of public governance, as the law is only one facet of a coherent scheme of justice.[219] This aspect of the rule of law can be taken for granted when the concept is imagined in relation to states, because state governance comprises a wide array of governance practices and institutions. When the administration of justice is envisaged in settings beyond the state, for instance in suggestions that a world court of human rights be established, then the need for the interconnectedness of justice with other facets of governance does become more readily identifiable.[220]

The embeddedness of the rebel administration of justice in a broader system of governance does not necessarily correspond to a "state-within-a-state" established by armed opposition groups. The FARC in Colombia is a good illustration of the complex nature of rebel governance, described earlier as corresponding to a dual strategy of instrumentalisation and marginalisation of official authority.[221]

219 TRS Allan, 'The Rule of Law' in David Dyzenhaus and Malcolm Thorburn (eds), *Philosophical Foundations of Constitutional Law* (Oxford University Press 2016) 207; Robert O Keohane, Andrew Moravcsik, and Anne-Marie Slaughter, 'Legalized Dispute Resolution: Interstate and Transnational' (2000) 54 International Organization 457, 466–468; John Tasioulas, 'The Rule of Law' in John Tasioulas (ed), *The Cambridge Companion to the Philosophy of Law* (Cambridge University Press 2020) 119.

220 See: Philip Alston, 'Against a World Court for Human Rights' (2014) 28 Ethics & International Affairs 197, 206 ("Courts do not function in a vacuum. To be seen as legitimate and to aspire to effectiveness they must be an integral part of a broader and deeper system of values, expectations, mobilizations, and institutions. They do not float above the societies that they seek to shape"); Johanna Speyer, 'Das Gegenteil von Gut Ist Gut Gemeint. Wie Ein Weltmenschenrechtsgerichtshof Die Menschenrechte Schwächt' (2018) 25 Zeitschrift für Internationale Beziehungen 6, 16 (suggesting that states are unlikely to provide that broader shared governance to underpin a world human rights court); Benedetta Berti, 'Rebel Justice? Rule of Law and Law Enforcement by Non-State Armed Groups' in Linda Hamid and Jan Wouters (eds), *Rule of Law and Areas of Limited Statehood* (Edward Elgar Publishing 2021) 135.

221 I rely in this section upon the findings described in Section II.A and II.B.iii, supra, without repeating all the sources cited therein.

Where the government was absent or weaker, the FARC would assume powers more broadly, consistently, and institutionally, but always incorporating community actors. Where the government had a stronger foothold, the FARC would undermine and influence state authorities to orient them in a manner consonant with the rebels' priorities. In all cases, a web of relations was established between the FARC and the population, covering many facets of life. This web of social relations is what constituted, for a segment of the population, the FARC as a legitimate actor to whom individuals could turn to resolve disputes and sanction anti-social behaviour. Indeed, as expressed by some insurgent leaders, the FARC was drawn into the administration of justice in a rather organic fashion, by its mere presence and power combined with its self-image as the embodiment of peasant needs, contributing to the legitimacy and stature of the group within the population. Conversely, their administration of justice could be a burden, and failure to discharge it in a manner that was felt to be adequate by the community could have undermined their authority and, as a result, their strategic effectiveness. This is related to a certain presence of armed groups in a given territory which allows them to exert some authority continuously, to accumulate the social capital required to administer justice.

> *In the case, for example, of a rapist where everyone loathes him, where the population almost wants to lynch him, almost wants to kill him with their own hands, the guerrillas are often forced by the circumstances, to take a radical measure, which is to execute him. Because if the guerrillas don't do it, in some way, they begin to lose legitimacy in the eyes of the population. There are even meetings that take place, for example, in a village, in a community, and at one point someone takes the floor and says: "no, compañero, what's happening is that you are getting very soft. What's happening, compañero, is that lately you are allowing many things to happen and this is getting out of hand". And that's what I think is the most important thing about the relationship between the guerrillas and these people. More than the political affinity of the local population with the guerrilla group, it is the affinity of the population with the activity of the guerrilla, insofar as the group guarantees security for the area.*
>
> *Interview, FARC Commander Edoardo (July 2016)*

This is not to say that the rebels must necessarily "control the territory", meaning that they can exclude government presence. It was already noted in the introduction to this book that the concept of territory cannot be reduced to bare space, land, or terrain, but that it is socially constructed by a combination of power and geography.[222] Territorial control by a non-state armed group is a condition for the application of Protocol II, and sometimes international human rights

[222] Stuart Elden, *The Birth of Territory* (University of Chicago Press 2013) 322–323; Paul Alliès, *L'invention du territoire* (Presses universitaires de Grenoble 1980) 147.

obligations, but not for common Article 3 or customary norms.[223] Even under Protocol II, the territorial control demanded is not absolute, but rather only "such control . . . as to enable" rebels to carry out sustained and concerted military operations and implement the protocol.[224] Territorial permanence rather than control emerges from case studies as the factual condition necessary for a rebel governance to coalesce.[225] The requirement is not that the armed group must be always present but rather that it never be too far, that it can reach a particular population if it so chooses. In Colombia, as in many other civil wars, the government was most often present in some way, not rarely concomitantly with the rebels. Even if there was state military presence, the FARC could withdraw but still be virtually present: if one needed to find the FARC, for instance to bring a dispute, there were often known ways to reach them. In other conflicts, parts of national territory are controlled by the state during the day and by rebels at nighttime.[226] It is clear that the intensity of control over the territory has an impact on the rebel administration of justice: when the state is effectively excluded, as it was in Colombia in the demilitarized zone, or in Sri Lanka in the north-east, then rebels may establish more formal institutions that more closely resemble official courts.[227] In Afghanistan, the Taliban has the military capacity to capture cities, but often decides not to because these are costly operations and the group cannot hold cities when confronted with the superior firepower of the government and its foreign allies; more fundamentally, the Taliban does not need to wrestle control of territory away from the government in order to exert its authority over it:

> The critical point, and one which is often missed in analyses of Taliban control, is that *governance does not come after the capture of territory, but precedes it.* Coercion, coupled with the more popular aspects of Taliban governance such

223 ICRC, Commentary to the 1949 Second Geneva Convention (2016) para 430; Jean-Marie Henckaerts and Cornelius Wiesener, 'Human Rights Obligations of Non-State Armed Groups: An Assessment Based on Recent Practice' in Ezequiel Heffes, Marcos D Kotlik, and Manuel J Ventura (eds), *International Humanitarian Law and Non-State Actors: Debates, Law and Practice* (TMC Asser Press 2020) 213. The ICTY Trial Chamber noted that territorial control was an indicative factor of the degree of organisation of a group, but not an essential factor: *Prosecutor v Haradinaj*, ICTY, Case No IT-04-80-T, Trial Judgment, 3 April 2008, para 60 (ICTY Trial Chamber).

224 ICRC, *Commentary on the Additional Protocols of 8 June 1977 to the Geneva Conventions of 12 August 1949* (International Committee of the Red Cross 1987) para 4466 ("The word 'such' provides the key to the interpretation").

225 Francis O'Connor, 'The Spatial Dimension of Insurgent-Civilian Relations: Routinised Insurgent Space' (Peace Research Institute Frankfurt 2019) 6.

226 Murray (n 192) 144–145.

227 There are even striking examples of rebel groups like the FARC and LTTE, whose courts had a "jurisdiction" that extended even beyond the territory they controlled, with civilians in government-controlled areas crossing into rebel territory to file complaints in insurgent courts: Miranda (n 123); Mampilly (n 1) 119; Aponte González (n 44) 185–187. On the territorial jurisdiction of rebel courts, see Chapter 3, Section II.B.

> as justice, softens the ground. Taliban governance does not supplant the Afghan government but co-opts and augments it, resulting in a hybrid service delivery arrangement.[228]

Hybrid governance, which can be observed in many non-international armed conflicts, can correspond to the rebel administration of justice, in addition to other governance functions in areas like taxation, education, or health. Too often, control of territory is imagined in monopolistic terms, such that the established state monopoly on violence is displaced by an equally monopolistic rebel use of violence. Likewise, inspired by traditional visions of the rule of law, the administration of justice is imagined as a state monopoly that can only be replaced by an armed group monopoly.[229] The study of armed groups in armed conflicts does not support either view: violence is shared, control often overlapping, and the administration of justice susceptible to division, sometimes in complementary terms, between the state and armed insurgents.

Situating the rebel administration of justice within a broader governance of non-state armed groups also speaks to a minimal degree of organisation and structure within the group, echoing another condition for the applicability of international humanitarian law to non-international armed conflicts. A rebel group with weak internal discipline will likely behave in a disordered manner and focus on short-term objectives, all indicators of limited potential for rebel governance.[230] Not all non-state armed groups engage in this type of governance. One extreme example of a group not engaged in governance is the Lord's Resistance Army in Uganda, which appears to live off the population through predatory terror and kidnapping rather than the sort of interactive engagement that underpins governance.[231] More generally, this is one of the elements that mark the rebel administration of justice as different from acts of violence carried out by criminal gangs. At an administrative level, the broader organisational integration of insurgent courts will increase the effectiveness of its decisions, as courts delegate enforcement functions to other governance entities.[232]

[228] Ashley Jackson, 'Life Under the Taliban Shadow Government' (Overseas Development Institute 2018) 25 (emphasis added). The Taliban administration of justice is studied more in details in Chapter 2, Section III.B.

[229] Adam Baczko and Gilles Dorronsoro, 'Pour une approche sociologique des guerres civiles' (2017) 67 Revue française de science politique 309.

[230] Arjona, *Rebelocracy* (n 86) 10.

[231] See Tim Allen and Koen Vlassenroot (eds), *The Lord's Resistance Army: Myth and Reality* (Zed Books 2010); Frank Van Acker, 'Uganda and the Lord's Resistance Army: The New Order No One Ordered' (2004) 103 African Affairs 335.

[232] Bernhard Zangl and Michael Zürn, 'Make Law, Not War: Internationale Und Transnationale Verrechtlichung Als Baustein Für Global Governance' in Berthold Meyer (ed), *Konfliktregelung und Friedensstrategien—Eine Einführung* (Springer 2011) 534.

ii. Stability and Predictability

A second element of the rebel rule of law is a degree of stability and predictability in the application of law.[233] There are both normative and institutional dimensions to this element.

Normatively, the administration of justice can be said to correspond to the rule of law if it sanctions the application of binding rules that are known or knowable to those to whom they are applied.[234] In this respect, the rule of law encompasses the principle of legality or *nullum crimen sine lege*.[235] This can mean either that the armed opposition group is sanctioning customary norms that exist within a given community, or that the group has issued its own rules. Although war is a practice of social disruption, it does not usually entirely displace social structures that preceded it, especially in civil wars. This can be the case as regards norms administered by rebels, corresponding to values shared between the rebels and the general population. In the case of the FARC, they claimed that many of the norms they incorporated into their administration of justice overlapped with peasant values, a reflection of the origins of the movement.[236] At other times or in respect of specific questions, the rebels can issue directives imposing rules of behaviour that must be complied with by the population. Whether these be about crimes, commerce, taxation, and so forth, they could be printed and nailed to trees or simply proclaimed orally during community meetings. Often produced by people without any legal training, they tend to be expressed in simple terms that are well understood by everyone. Non-state armed groups in some other armed conflicts produced considerably more elaborate standards, including the LTTE in Sri Lanka, which promulgated its own civil code and criminal code.[237] In her extensive field work throughout Colombia, Arjona found that 90 percent of the time civilians had a clear expectation of what the rebel rules were and how the group would behave.[238]

The requirement of stability and predictability also has institutional implications. While the ideal of a permanent, fixed, public rebel judicial system is likely unattainable in a great number of armed conflicts, the concept of the rule of law speaks to the need to inscribe the exercise of public authority in legal practices. As such, authority that is exercised without any predictable patterns

233 Raz, *The Authority of Law* (n 151) 214–215.

234 Aguilera Peña, 'Las Guerrillas Marxistas y La Pena de Muerte a Combatientes' (n 56) 222. The principle *nulle poena sine lege* is rendered in the *Codigo penal guerrillero* of 28 May 1961, Article 2 ("Ningún comandante podrá imponer sanción alguna que no esté de acuerdo con el código y conforme a las normas en él contenidas").

235 The principle of legality is also a specific procedural guarantee contributing to the fairness of a trial. This dimension is examined in Chapter 3, Section III.C.vi.

236 Molano (n 53) 334.

237 E Pararajasingham, 'Tamil Eelam Legal System' (2003), online: <http://tamilnation.co/tamileelam/defacto/031030judicial.htm> accessed 21 February 2017.

238 Arjona, 'Wartime Institutions: A Research Agenda' (n 33) 1371.

of who and how decisions are made cannot be said to comport with the rule of law. For instance, the Colombian ELN in its early days was led by commanders who would order executions without any process for matters that reflected their own impulses.[239] The practice of the FARC evolved to be very different from this picture: even without standing institutions, there were known ways of getting the rebel group to become seized of a matter, either because of open meetings on market days or by passing word to a *mosca* (fly), a person "in the know" who could alert the FARC. This is far from filing a motion to initiate an action, but it does convey a sense that justice—at least of a sort—was at hand when it was needed, something like a right of action.[240] This can be contrasted to the courts run by ISIS in Iraq and Syria, in theory accessible to anyone but in fact conditioned on obtaining permission from both the local ISIS chief and from the court itself.[241] In this sense, the rule of law supports individual agency by allowing people to plan their lives.

iii. Minimal Fairness

The institutional and normative dimensions of the stability and predictability of justice lead to the third element of a rebel rule of law: a minimum degree of fairness in the way in which decisions are made. What due process requirements are, in the context of the rebel administration of justice, is a complex question that cannot be fully explored yet. A full answer will require a thorough exploration of the applicability of international human rights obligations to non-state armed groups as well as an articulation of due process rules in the very particular context of the administration of justice on the battlefield.[242] Inevitably, this would enlarge the concept of the rule of law to the thicker end of the spectrum describe earlier, at which human rights and the rule of law become fused. In keeping with the announced ambition to articulate here a thin version of the rebel rule of law, four implications of the requirement of fairness can be suggested, all reflecting the idea that the exercise of authority must be constrained by rules.

A first implication is that rules bind not only those subject to authority but also those who wield it.[243] It reflects a necessary reciprocity between the governed and the governing whereby there is a general expectation on the part of the population that the armed opposition group will abide by its own standards.[244] The fact that, for the FARC as well as for some other armed groups, the administration of

239 Molano (n 53) 332.
240 Zangl and Zürn (n 232) 530–531.
241 Adam Bazcko and others, 'The Rationality of an Eschatological Movement: The Islamist State in Iraq and Syria' (Yale Program on Governance and Local development 2016) 15.
242 These questions are analysed in Chapter 3.
243 Alvarez (n 177) 24.
244 Lon Fuller, 'Human Interaction and the Law' (1969) 14 American Journal of Jurisprudence 1, 24; Arjona, 'Wartime Institutions: A Research Agenda' (n 33) 1374.

justice grew organically from internal discipline to a more public form of justice is one way in which the rules applicable to the population and those applicable to the group are connected. The possibility of complaining to rebel leadership of the behaviour of a member or even of the group as a whole, as did occur at least in some occasions against the FARC in Colombia, is another indication of this element of reciprocity. It reflects, more broadly, the fact that the civilian population retains agency, that it is in a position to embrace or resist rebel justice, even when subjected to the power of an armed group so extreme as ISIS.[245]

A second implication is that the established practices or institutions to administer justice be marked by some degree of impartiality and independence.[246] Impartiality does not mean neutrality, as the rebel administration of justice can surely reflect the broad governance objectives of the armed group just as official justice does that of the state. On the other hand, it means that rules must be applied in a spirit of objectivity as opposed to simply giving effect to preferences of the decider. This reflects the doctrine of the separation of power, said to be implicit in the concept of the rule of law.[247] Separation of power need not be institutional, but minimally must inform a distinct stance of the person when acting as impartial decider as opposed to rebel commander. It is not rare, in non-international armed conflicts, for tribal connections of a party to a dispute to have a decisive influence on the outcome. This was the situation in the Kurdish Region of Iraq, for example, where at least for a time "access to rule of law [was] dependent on ethnic and religious affiliation, tribe, connections, family and relatives, and it [was] very difficult, if not impossible, for an individual to stand up for his rights by himself".[248] Independence signals that the decision-maker has a degree of autonomy in applying the relevant standards to the case at hand. If, on the other hand, the decider is merely a conduit to convey the fiat of the leadership of the armed opposition group, then clearly we cannot speak of any degree of independence. The International Criminal Court (ICC) in the *Bemba* trial found that the "courts-martial" established by the accused within his armed group, the *Mouvement de libération du Congo*, were simply there to overlay a veneer of legitimacy on Bemba's decisions.[249] The study of FARC governance in

[245] See the discussion of ISIS governance in Chapter 2.

[246] Raz, *The Authority of Law* (n 151) 216–217; Zangl and Zürn (n 232) 531–532; Keohane, Moravcsik, and Slaughter (n 219) 459–461.

[247] Allan (n 219) 211.

[248] Danish Refugee Council, *KRI Access, Possibility of Protection, Security and Humanitarian Situation Report* (2017) 45

[249] Witness T-159 testified that "[i]t was well-known that judges were there simply to implement or execute orders, but that these orders had to be dressed in a military or judicial-looking system so that they do not appear to be arbitrary, whether it be within the context of military justice or not, but the truth of the matter is that these were simply orders that the judges were bound to implement and to execute": ICC, *Prosecutor v Jean-Pierre Bemba Gombo*, Trial Judgment, 21 March 2016, ICC-01/05-01/08, at 299–300 note 1861. This specific aspect is not discussed in the Appeals Judgment in the same case: 8 June 2018, ICC-01/05-01/08 A.

Colombia does bring up complaints that sometimes the resolution of a dispute seemed to owe to a personal connection of one of the parties to the FARC (such as having a relative who was a FARC fighter).

A third, related implication is the need to listen to all sides of a dispute before reaching a decision. Again, many informants on the FARC administration of justice confirm that the principle of *audi alteram partem* was part of the regular decision-making process of the group. FARC commanders remarked on the importance of fact-finding more broadly, including the possibility of calling other witnesses and going to inspect the evidence if it could not be brought to the hearing. Conversely, justice practices by ISIS in the territory under its control was said to be chaotic, rushed, one-sided, and so prone to error that the civilian population at times openly resisted it.[250]

Finally, as a fourth implication, fairness speaks to the need for a resolution of the legal issue that is clear and final, to ensure what is sometimes referred to as "legal security". The FARC often issued written decisions to ensure that there would be no further disputes, and at times these were even entered into official ledgers of community dispute settlement mechanisms. In some cases, the FARC allowed for the possibility of an appeal of a decision, including in cases where the death penalty was imposed for a serious crime. Otherwise, there is a sense that it was unwise to ignore a decision by the FARC, for sanction could be quick and harsh.

iv. Narrative of Social Justice

The fourth and final element of the rebel rule of law is discursive: the armed opposition group must relate its administration of justice to objectives that are consonant with social justice. This is related to Joseph Raz's claim that every legal system must claim to have legitimate authority in order to be considered to be a legal system, on the tautological and yet revealing basis that "[t]he claims the law makes for itself are evident from the language that it adopts".[251] In addition to this revelatory dimension, Robert Cover suggested that to refer to something as "law" is to coat it with "a veneer which changes the very nature of that which it covers up".[252] An invocation of the ideology of the rule of law, in order to be persuasive, will demand an exercise of authority that is not evidently partial and unjust.[253] What matters here is the claim itself, not whether it is well-founded or accurate.

[250] See the discussion of ISIS governance in Chapter 2, Section II.

[251] Joseph Raz, *Ethics in the Public Domain Essays in the Morality of Law and Politics* (Clarendon 1995) 215.

[252] Robert M Cover, 'The Folktales of Justice: Tales of Jurisdiction' (1984) 14 Capital University Law Review 179, 181.

[253] EP Thompson, *Whigs and Hunters: The Origin of the Black Act* (Pantheon Books 1975) 263; Mariana Valverde, 'Deepening the Conversation Between Socio-Legal Theory and Legal Scholarship about Jurisdiction', in Stephen Allen and others (eds), *The Oxford Handbook of Jurisdiction in*

Not all armed non-state actors claim the mantle of justice when exercising public authority. Some may have an approach that is more overtly predatory, as in the example of the Lord's Resistance Army mentioned earlier, and others may feel distrustful of the local population that they wish to keep at bay rather than engage by way of justice mechanisms, as the Rwandan Patriotic Front reportedly did during its initial take-over of Rwanda.[254] Alternatively, an armed opposition group that anticipates that it will overturn the government rapidly may not see the need to establish justice practices nor foster in the civilian population the impression that it is already the "real" government of the country. If there is an awareness that military victory is a long way off, sustaining a long time horizon for the rebels, or if the aim is to establish a new state, the non-state armed group will be more likely to embrace the language of social justice to underpin its governance.[255] In two decisions, the Special Court for Sierra Leone found that accountability mechanisms established by non-state armed groups aimed primarily at maintaining internal discipline, and had very little or nothing to do with a wish to sanction international criminal law or to act on the basis of moral, ethical, or religious opposition to behaviour that amounts to violations of the laws of war.[256] UN Secretary-General Kofi Annan suggested that the rule of law should apply to any institution that seeks to promote it, and perhaps we should add, only to them.[257] If, as advanced by Rod Macdonald, "as a technique of social ordering, law is the endeavour of symbolizing human conduct as governed by rules", then it is fundamental that the rebel group itself partake in this symbolising effort.[258] Each armed insurgency produces its own justificatory narrative which is, more often than not, couched in terms that evoke social justice—this is certainly the case for the FARC in Colombia, as can be gleaned from a perusal of internal FARC Regulations described earlier.[259] What social

International Law (Oxford University Press 2019) 179 ("once arguments are produced using certain narrative conventions, then, a particular type of law, a particular jurisdiction with its distinct 'how' of governance, follows").

[254] Mamdani (n 217) 186–189.

[255] See Mampilly (n 1) 215.

[256] SCSL, *RUF Trial* (n 210) para 712: "[T]he RUF disciplinary system functioned essentially to allow the leadership to maintain control over all the RUF fighters and impose and maintain order in RUF-held territory. It failed to systematically deter or regularly and effectively punish crimes against civilians or persons *hors de combat*. The disciplinary process was fundamentally a means of keeping control over their own fighters and was not a system to punish for the commission of crimes". See also SCSL, *Prosecutor v Alex Tamba Brima et al.*, Trial Chamber, Judgment, 20 June 2007, SCSL-04-16-T, para 1739 (http://www.legal-tools.org/doc/87ef08/).

[257] UN Secretary-General (n 147). See also Dieter Fleck, 'Comment—Perspectives on Courts Established by Armed Opposition Groups' in Heike Krieger (ed), *Inducing Compliance with International Humanitarian Law* (Cambridge University Press 2015) 184–185 (suggesting to investigate the political goals pursued by rebel courts).

[258] Roderick A Macdonald, 'Call-Centre Government: For the Rule of Law, Press #' (2005) 55 University of Toronto Law Journal 449, 459.

[259] See the discussion in Section II.B.ii, supra.

justice is, and what the practices in which it is embedded are, will be a reflection of the particular social order that was already present in the community. As noted by James Worrall, any armed group seeking to impose its governance on a population "enters upon a complex socio-political field and must compete with the power and authority of existing actors, norms, traditions, and structures".[260] A successful rebel court system will be one that speaks of justice in the vernacular, whether that reflects accepted religious belief, a discourse of political emancipation, nationalist identity, the effectiveness of witchcraft, or any other system of beliefs that will seem intuitively right to a critical mass of people. This element of the rule of law amounts to an invitation to non-state armed groups to explicitly inscribe their exercise of public authority into such particularised social justice narratives, something that will often dovetail with the very raison d'être of their armed struggle.[261]

A non-state armed group engaged in the administration of justice by way of practices and institutions that incorporate the four elements just sketched out can be said to embody the rule of law. As with all statements of the rule of law, this is an idealised projection. Just as the administration of justice in every state is marred by at least some encroachments of the tenets of the rule of law, it is likely that rebel justice will in some respects fall short of meeting these elements in full. As such, the rule of law remains a set of objectives that must inspire the administration of justice rather than a benchmark that must be met in order for the label "justice" to be used in a legitimate and meaningful way.

III. Rebel Justice and Sovereignty

Whether the rebel administration of justice can be accommodated within a broad conception of the rule of law is only one among several possible approaches to interrogating the fundamental nature of rebel justice. An alternative approach starts from the doctrine of state sovereignty, to enquire whether the suggestion that non-state armed groups may properly be said to administer justice contradicts in a fundamental manner the sovereignty of the state over its population and territory. Given that the rule of law is a concept at the heart of state sovereignty, it is clear that there is some significant overlap between a contestation of rebel justice anchored in the doctrine of the rule of law and one rooted in state sovereignty.[262] In one reading, sovereignty stands for boundless

[260] James Worrall, '(Re-)Emergent Orders: Understanding the Negotiation(s) of Rebel Governance' (2017) 28 Small Wars & Insurgencies 709, 716.

[261] O'Connor (n 225) 16; Michael Gross, *The Ethics of Insurgency* (Cambridge University Press 2015) 73.

[262] See the discussion in Section III.A, infra.

freedom of action for the state and, as such, seems irreconcilable with state authority bounded by the rule of law; in another reading, the rule of law is the very principle that allows for the mediation of social relations that coalesce into a sovereign entity with authority over a population and territory.[263] The *Rechtsstaat* or *État de droit* affirms the sovereignty of the state in acknowledging that the state all at once is constituted by law and makes law possible.[264]

Sovereignty, as can be seen, encompasses more than the rule of law; it is a complex, multifaceted concept that inter alia includes a justification for the authority of the state. Martti Koskenniemi has suggested that "[t]here simply is no fixed meaning, no natural extent to sovereignty at all".[265] In public international law, as expressed in the statement by Max Huber in the *Island of Palmas* award, sovereignty classically has been taken to refer to the idea of independence and the exclusive competence of a state in relation to territory.[266] In other words, sovereignty defines the relation among states and the right of one state to prevent others from exercising authority over its territory. That initial conception of sovereignty has evolved to go beyond the necessary validation of whatever power exists over a people and territory, to encompass the idea of self-determination and human rights.[267] Today, it is understood that sovereignty addresses not only the relations among states (external sovereignty) but also those between a government and people under its control (internal sovereignty). It is in that latter sense that the administration of justice by armed opposition groups may be taken as potentially contradicting the sovereignty of the state.

The concept of sovereignty as recognised in public international law reflects the evolution of governance in Europe over several centuries. It bears emphasising that while statehood as the necessary embodiment of sovereignty was successfully exported to the rest of the world by the "Concert of civilized nations" in the nineteenth and twentieth centuries, its transplant to other geopolitical contexts provoked significant distortions in this concept. The sovereign state in Europe and the sovereign state in a place like Colombia are not only quite different realities but also different constructs. There is, always, a gap between the

263 See David Dyzenhaus' brilliant analysis of the different approaches by Carl Schmitt, Hans Kelsen, and Hermann Heller in his Introduction to Hermann Heller, *Sovereignty: A Contribution to the Theory of Public and International Law* (Oxford University Press 2019).

264 Dyzenhaus, ibid 54.

265 Martti Koskenniemi, *From Apology to Utopia: The Structure of International Legal Argument* (Cambridge University Press 2006) 242.

266 *Case Concerning the Sovereignty the Island of Palmas (Netherlands v USA)*, Award, 4 April 1928, RIAA, vol II, 829, at 838. For a presentation and critique of this classical vision of sovereignty, see Don Herzog, *Sovereignty, RIP* (Yale University Press 2020) xi (sovereignty as "a locus of authority that is unlimited, undivided, and unaccountable to a higher authority").

267 W Michael Reisman, 'Sovereignty and Human Rights in Contemporary International Law' (1990) 84 American Journal of International Law 866, 872; Thomas Risse and Eric Stollenwerk, 'Legitimacy in Areas of Limited Statehood' (2018) 21 Annual Review of Political Science 403.

theoretical construction of sovereignty and its reality on the ground. Whereas the state, like god, is presumed to exercise sovereign authority everywhere across national territory, no state, however powerful, can actually do so at all times and in all places, a phenomenon recognised in a segment of legal doctrine as "areas of limited statehood".[268] The sovereignty of the state in Colombia, as in many other non-Western countries, never followed an evolution similar to the European state that led to presume at least a capacity to exercise authority across the national territory. The concentration of sovereign authority in the state never occurred, leaving other, local sources of power in place still today: Colombia has too much geography for too little sovereignty.[269] The emergence of rebel governance in this type of environment poses a challenge to the idea of sovereignty that is distinct from what it would be in Canada or France. A different understanding of sovereignty will in turn inform the mapping of the doctrine of the rule of law in this context.

The administration of justice by armed rebels, and in particular the administration of criminal justice, is not the only possible challenge to the state's authority in this domain. Once we decide to step away from the notion that states necessarily have a monopoly over the exercise of criminal jurisdiction, the question is whether there is any limit to the exercise of criminal jurisdiction? Why does a particular entity have authority?[270] Can any body or entity exercise criminal jurisdiction? Are there any relevant principles that delimit the binary position between "only States" and "anyone"? Why not the Disney Corporation,[271] a Kansas City dog catcher, the World Chess Federation, the Rolling Stones,[272] any other domestic non-state entity, including the Mafia?[273]

There are three different situations in which this question has already been considered significantly: revisiting the basis of state criminal jurisdiction (compared with the exercise of "criminal justice" by vigilantes);[274] the jurisdiction of

[268] Heike Krieger, 'International Legal Order' in Anke Draude, Tanja Börzel and Thomas Risse (eds), *The Oxford Handbook of Governance and Limited Statehood* (Oxford University Press 2018); Villegas and others (n 113) 15–20.

[269] ibid 27 ("Colombia tiene más geografia que Estado"); see also Sarah Schmid, *Öffentliche Gütererbringung Jenseits Des Staates in Afghanistan Und Kolumbien* (Springer 2019) 267–298; Fernán Gonzales and Silvia Otero Bahamon, 'La presencia diferenciada del Estado: un desafío a los conceptos de gobernabilidad y gobernanza' (Centro de Investigación y Educación Popular 2006), online: <http://www.institut-gouvernance.org/es/analyse/fiche-analyse-237.html> accessed 14 September 2020.

[270] Zachary Hoskins, 'Punishment' (2016) 0 Analysis 1, 10.

[271] Leslie Green, 'The Duty to Govern' (2007) 13 Legal Theory 165, 182.

[272] David Luban, 'Fairness to Rightness: Jurisdiction, Legality, and the Legitimacy of International Criminal Law' in Samantha Besson and John Tasioulas (eds), *The Philosophy of International Law* (Oxford University Press 2010) 579.

[273] Andrew Altman and Christopher Heath Wellman, 'A Defense of International Criminal Law' (2004) 115 Ethics 35, 63.

[274] Christopher Heath Wellman, 'Piercing Sovereignty: A Rationale for International Jurisdiction Over Crimes That Do Not Cross International Borders' in Robin Antony Duff and Stuart Green (eds), *Philosophical Foundations of Criminal Law* (Oxford University Press 2011); Malcolm Thorburn,

other states (in particular universal jurisdiction);[275] and the jurisdiction of international bodies (including the ICC).[276] At each level, what we see is a theory of authority based on duty or responsibility emerging from a situation of moral urgency or necessity, coupled with a principle to try to distribute fulfilment of that duty between multiple capable entities (like complementarity and double jeopardy). The requirement for a situation of necessity or moral urgency renders this account of authority one of "(morally) legitimate authority" rather than merely *de facto* authority. *De facto* authority only requires an "ability to get others to act in ways that they desire even when the subject does not want to do what the agent wants him to do".[277] According to Hobbes, "any entity capable of performing the function of *de facto* authority is necessarily justified and deserves the obedience of the *de facto* subjects", whereas others have argued something more is required.[278] I consider more fully in turn the basis of state jurisdiction and the exercise of jurisdiction by other states or international organisations.

A. Basis of State Jurisdiction

Turning to the basis of state jurisdiction, it is an observable practice for states to resist both internal and external competitors who seek to take the criminal law into their own hands.[279] Although largely assumed in international law as a basis of statehood, the question of why the state should enjoy a monopoly on the permissible use of punishment remains "a central and enduring question of political philosophy".[280] Rebel justice questions the validity of this assumption, suggesting

'Criminal Law as Public Law' in *Philosophical Foundations of Criminal Law*; Malcolm Thorburn, 'Justifications, Powers and Authority' (2008) 117 Yale Law Journal 1070.

275 Luban (n 272); Antony Duff, 'Authority and Responsibility in International Criminal Law' in Samantha Besson and John Tasioulas (eds), *The Philosophy of International Law* (Oxford University Press 2010); Michael Guidice and Matthew Schaeffer, 'Universal Jurisdiction and the Duty to Govern' in François Tanguay-Renard and James Stribopoulos (eds), *Rethinking Criminal Law Theory: New Canadian Perspectives in the Philosophy of Domestic, Transnational, and International Criminal Law* (Hart Publishing 2012).

276 Larry May, *Crimes Against Humanity: A Normative Account* (Cambridge University Press 2005); Altman and Wellman (n 273); Wellman (n 274); Kristen Hessler, 'State Sovereignty as an Obstacle to International Criminal Law' in Larry May and Zachary Hoskins (eds), *International Criminal Law and Philosophy* (Cambridge University Press 2010); Diane Bernard, 'Ne Bis in Idem—Protector of Defendants' Rights or Jurisdictional Pointsman?' (2011) 9 Journal of International Criminal Justice 863.

277 Tom Christiano, 'Authority' in Edward N Zalter (ed), *Stanford Encyclopedia of Philosophy* (Stanford University 2013) 4. The relevance of the concept of jurisdiction to the rebel administration of justice is more fully discussed in Chapter 3, Section II.

278 See discussion in ibid.

279 Wellman (n 274) 465.

280 ibid 465, citing Nozick's *Anarchy, State, and Utopia* (Basic Books 1974). Sabine Gless describes the suggestion of punishment without sovereign as "almost mysterious": Sabine Gless, 'Strafe ohne

that "anyone who seeks to defend State punishment owes us a story of how the State comes to acquire an exclusive, executive right which initially resides either exclusively with the victim or generally with each of us".[281] Early justice systems left dealing with crime to the victims or their family, who took on the role of prosecutor and had to retaliate or seek retribution.[282] This became less and less tenable with the development of larger, more settled societies, as "blood feuds" tended to be destabilising.[283] Slowly, with the evolution of the state apparatus and the wish to solidify the political power of the government, the management of the aftermath of crime was taken over by the state. A traditional justification for this evolution, invoking Locke, suggested that the transfer comes from a voluntary transaction, in the form of a social contract.[284] The image of course stands as a metaphor rather than a description of constitution-building, although it is remarkable that the constitution of the autonomous region of Rojava in Northern Syria, proclaimed by the PYD Kurdish rebels group, is called the "Charter of Social Contract".[285] The dominant contemporary approach provides instead a justification for state exclusive jurisdiction based on two propositions: first, the state is the best able to achieve the aims of punishment; and second, the consequences of vigilantism are so serious for everyone—a Hobbesian state of nature—that *only* the state should be able to exercise criminal jurisdiction even if there are other individuals (the victim or others) who could do it.[286] Although it is an alternative account to state sovereignty, it still justifies the exclusivity of state criminal justice. It not only posits the superior capacity of states in most cases, but also maintains the value of a monopoly. It is precisely the value of this monopoly—the binary position between state monopoly and Hobbesian state of nature—that is challenged by insurgent courts. Many places in which non-state armed groups exercise some degree of governance could be described, as was the territory under PKK control, as "a place without government, yet without disorder".[287] The survey of the administration of justice by the FARC in Colombia certainly questions the necessary validity of these two assumptions.

Souverän?' (2007) 125 Schweizerische Zeitschrift für Strafrecht 24 ("Wenig behandelt, fast rätselhaft erscheint dagegen die Frage nach der *Strafe ohne Souverän*").

281 ibid 467.

282 Tyrone Kirchengast, *Victims and the Criminal Trial Process* (Springer 2016) 12; John H Langbein, 'The Criminal Trial before the Lawyers' (1978) 45 The University of Chicago Law Review 263.

283 Jo-Anne M Wemmers, *Victimology: A Canadian Perspective* (University of Toronto Press 2017) 6.

284 Wellman (n 274) 467.

285 Loqman Radpey, 'The Kurdish Self-Rule Constitution in Syria' (2015) 14 Chinese Journal of International Law 835, 837.

286 See: May (n 276); Altman and Wellman (n 273); Wellman (n 274); Hoskins (n 270).

287 N Abdulla, 'A Kurdish Village Governed by None' *New York Times* (24 August 2010).

An alternative approach that engages with the same ideas of capacity and consequence conceives of jurisdiction as a duty rather than an exclusive right, thus decoupling it from the idea of state sovereignty. Like an individual's duty to rescue a person in peril when the rescue poses no significant risk, the duty to govern reflects a morally urgent task and the capacity to act effectively. Les Green, relying on foundational work by John Finnis, has articulated an argument based in necessity such that "authority should be exercised *when* there is a certain kind of problem to be solved, and that it should be exercised *by* someone who has the effective capacity to solve it".[288] Green gives an example of this duty in situations of belligerent occupation:

> The occupant's duty to govern derives from its duty to preserve the rule of law (if any remnants remain) or to establish it—even if it destroyed it in the first place. . . . If B, the belligerent occupant, cannot actually keep order (for example, because B's forces and agents are incompetent or corrupt or because B's rule provokes massive resistance), then B should withdraw from the territory and let someone else try to rule.[289]

I noted in the earlier discussion of the rule of law that international humanitarian law expressly provides for the authority of the occupying state to administer justice. We see in this approach grounded in a task-efficiency justification that the shift from authority to duty suggests a consequence for the inability to act—the duty to let someone else have a go at it—that was not apparent in the initial reading. Turning back to the rebel administration of justice, it seems undeniable that there is a moral necessity to administer justice in a situation of armed conflict in which the state may not be in a position to effectively do so. Whether a given armed opposition group has the effective capacity to fulfil this duty in a given time and place will not be easy to ascertain. This is indeed a challenge that applies to all possible agents to whom the duty to govern could be imposed, including states.[290] One way of understanding states' perceived exclusive right to govern and exercise jurisdiction is that states are presumed to be capable, unless proved otherwise. On the opposite, no presumption applies to other entities, including non-state armed groups, and capacity must be evaluated on a case-by-case basis. For armed rebels, the capacity to effectively administer justice will be linked to and reflective of their broader approach to governance, presented earlier as the first component of a rebel rule of law.

288 Green (n 271) 169; John Finnis, *Natural Law and Natural Rights* (1979) 246.
289 Green (n 271) 174.
290 Guidice and Schaeffer (n 275) 246. As noted by Green, it is possible that an agent will acquire the necessary capacity in performing the task: Green (n 271) 175.

In this understanding of jurisdiction, as Green notes, "actual social power gives rise to normative power or authority".[291] In public international law, this has at times been presented as a broad principle of *effectivité*, the idea that law and power are mutually reinforcing in that law must be supported by power and power must be reflected in law.[292] The principle of *effectivité* has been the subject of significant scrutiny in international legal writing in French, and to a lesser degree in German and Spanish, but more peripherally in English.[293] This principle seeks to capture and incorporate in law a reality as it is perceived on the ground rather than articulating norms exclusively rooted in concerns of legality and legitimacy. The dissociation of *jus ad bellum* and *jus in bello* is one example of reliance on the idea of *effectivité*, eschewing a more coherent approach whereby an illegal act should not produce legally recognised effects. Legal stability and legal security are values that are also incorporated into public international law, whereby facts and norms are constantly and necessarily in dialogue.[294] The progressive strengthening of international legal normativity has resulted in a thicker regulation that leaves fewer grey zones to manage by way of the consideration of *effectivité*.[295] That said, the administration of justice by non-state armed groups is one such grey zone in which the principle of *effectivité* can be invoked to provide some conceptual scaffolding.

In a series of decisions applying a 1947 treaty of peace imposed upon Italy by the victorious Allies after the Second World War, Franco-Italian and Italian-US Conciliation Commissions were called to make a determination whether the treaty reference to "the laws in force in Italy during the war" included laws adopted by the so-called Salò Republic between 1943 and 1945.[296]

[291] Green (n 271) 169.

[292] Florian Couveinhes-Matsumoto, *L'effectivité en droit international* (Bruylant 2014) para 101.

[293] ibid 38; Charles De Visscher, *Les Effectivités du droit international public* (Editions A Pedone 1967); Jean Touscoz, *Le Principe d'effectivité dans l'ordre international* (R Pichon et R Durand-Auzias 1964); WH Balekjian, *Die Effektivität und die Stellung nichtanerkannter Staaten im Völkerrecht* (Springer 1970) 11–18; Adolfo Miaja de la Muela, 'Nuevas realidades y teorías sobre la efectividad en derecho internacional' (1976) 3 Anuario de derecho internacional 3; Herbert Krüger, 'Das Prinzip Der Effektivität, Oder: Über Die Besondere Wirklichkeitsnähe Des Völkerrechts' *Festschrift für Jean Spiropoulos* (1957); Meinhard Hilf and Saskia Hörmann, 'Effektivität—ein Rechtsprinzip?' in Christian Tomuschat and others (eds), *Völkerrecht als Wertordnung: Festschrift für Christian Tomuschat* (2006); Gleider Hernández, 'Effectiveness' in Jean D'Aspremont (ed), *Concepts for International Law: Contributions to Disciplinary Thought* (Edward Elgar Publishing Limited 2019); Enrico Milano, *Unlawful Territorial Situations in International Law: Reconciling Effectiveness, Legality and Legitimacy* (Brill 2005) 21–54. Some authors in English refer to it as a principle of "effectiveness", although it is more commonly designated as "effectivity" or "*effectivité*": Jean d'Aspremont, '"Effectivity" in International Law: Self-Empowerment Against Epistemological Claustrophobia' (2014) 108 AJIL Unbound 103; Salvatore Zappalà, 'Can Legality Trump Effectiveness in Today's International Law?' in Antonio Cassese (ed), *Realizing Utopia* (Oxford University Press 2012).

[294] Balekjian (n 293) 11–18; Hernández (n 293) 237–239.

[295] Zappalà (n 293) 105.

[296] For discussion, see: Balekjian (n 293) 116–117; Couveinhes-Matsumoto (n 292) paras 264–265; Katharine Fortin, *The Accountability of Armed Groups under Human Rights Law* (Oxford University Press 2017) 264–266.

The Salò Republic was a government headed by Mussolini over the northern part of the country that emerged after the official government of Italy decided to switch over to the Allied side. Although the Salò Republic emerged thanks to the military support of Germany, the commissions concluded that it remained distinct from its German patron.[297] The Italian government in the *Fubini Claim* argued that Salò government acts and decisions couldn't be considered as "laws in force in Italy during the war" because "the concept of 'Law' requires a power of legality which that Government lacked entirely".[298] In that case, the Italian-US Conciliation Commission identified the principle of *effectivité* as central to the determination of the status of an insurrectional government, adopting the statement by Paul Guggenheim that "[t]he seizure of power by belligerents and insurgents in part of the territory of the State conflicts with State positive law, entails the creation of a new provisional legal order".[299] The commission noted:

> It has occurred several times in history that a rival Government was established in an occupied State, either with the recognition of the occupied authorities, or against them and the national Government that has accepted defeat; in that case there exist three simultaneous powers in one and the same State: the power of the legal Government, the power of the rival Government, which is a *de facto* Government, and the limited power of the military occupant which is not to be identified with that of the *de facto* Government.[300]

In that perspective, what matters in the determination of whether an entity is wielding law, is that "the rules it decreed were obligatory for all those who were in actual fact subjected to that legal order and liable to penalties".[301] This is a question that is wholly distinct from the question of the legality of rebel norms pursuant to the domestic law of the territorial state.[302] The line of decisions by the Franco-Italian and Italian-US Conciliation Commissions thus considered that

[297] *Différend Dame Mossé*, Decisions No 144, 17 January 1953, 13 R.I.A.A. 486, 492–493 (Franco-Italian Conciliation Commission), a holding adopted in subsequent decisions of the Italian-US Conciliation Commission.

[298] *Fubini Case*, Decision No 201, 12 December 1959, 14 R.I.A.A. 420, 428 (Italian-US Conciliation Commission). The dissenting Italian member in another case echoed this argument, "to my mind, the concept of 'law' has an exact meaning, implying the 'juridicity' thereof, a quality which the Government of Salò lacked completely": *Treves Case*, Decision No 144, 24 September 1956, 14 R.I.A.A. 262, 271 (Italian-US Conciliation Commission).

[299] *Fubini Case*, ibid at 430, translating Paul Guggenheim, *Traité de droit international public, avec mention de la pratique internationale et suisse*, vol 1 (Georg 1953) 203.

[300] *Fubini Case*, ibid at 429.

[301] ibid at 430.

[302] *Treves Case*, at 267.

the acts and measures of the insurgent order in Salò was part of "the law in force" in Italy during the war.

The principle of sovereignty when informed by the concept of *effectivité* accommodates the possibility that the power to rule may not be bundled together in the hands of a single actor, but instead may be shared among several actors that do not necessarily coordinate their actions. This is in fact entirely consistent with the international legal approach taken to constitutional arrangements in which several levels of government may autonomously exercise authority in a given territory.[303] It avoids radical and to some degree arbitrary choices among several entities that may have effective powers on the territory of a single state. For instance, during the Spanish Civil War, it would have been impossible to make a coherent determination of who "the government of Spain" was and who "the rebels" were, at any given time, if that was meant to provide a realistic reflection of who had effective power to declare and enforce legal rules.[304] Instead, the House of Lords in *The Arantzazu Mendi* merely gave effect to the *de facto* authority of the nationalist forces, while refraining from pronouncing on the identity of the *de jure* government.[305] In the context of the conflict in Colombia, while it could always be said who the government was, it would be a legal fiction to deny that the FARC governed in a meaningful and legally cognisable way in some parts of the country for portions of that war.

As noted by W.H. Balekjian, "If one oversteps the ineluctable necessity of coordination, the unbridled application of the principle of *effectivité* amounts to the negation of international law as a legal order".[306] There is no doubt that the principle of *effectivité* embodies a tension between law and power, between fact and norm, and that if it is pushed to its extreme, it leads to a denial that international law is law at all.[307]

[303] It is interesting to note that US constitutional law accommodates a notion of dual sovereignty in relation to American Indian tribes: US Supreme Court, *Santa Clara Pueblo v Martinez*, 436 U.S. 49, 71–72 (1978) ("As separate sovereigns pre-existing the Constitution, tribes have historically been regarded as unconstrained by those constitutional provisions framed specifically as limitations on federal or state authority").

[304] Note that this is a question distinct from the practice of legal recognition of states or, going back to a previous epoch, recognition of governments. Such a recognition, of a largely political nature, corresponds to a statement that one state or government is willing to engage with another as a peer. See Stefan Talmon, *Recognition of Governments in International Law: With Particular Reference to Governments in Exile* (Clarendon Press 1998) 21–43.

[305] House of Lords (UK), *The Arantzazu Mendi*, [1939] 1 All E.R. 719, 722 (Lord Atkin).

[306] Balekjian (n 293) 15 ("Wenn man die Grenzeder unumgänglichen Koordinationsnotwendigkeit überschreitet, bedeutet die schrankenlose Anwendung des Effektivitätsgrundsatzes die Leugnung des Völkerrecht").

[307] Couveinhes-Matsumoto (n 292) paras 101–102.

B. Exercise of Jurisdiction by Others than the Territorial State

Another context in which the foundation of the state's monopoly on the administration of justice on its territory has been interrogated is the exercise of jurisdiction either by an international criminal tribunal or by a state prosecuting a non-national on the basis of universal jurisdiction. What justifies the jurisdictional claim of the ICC over Omar al-Bashir, for example? There is not, in that case, an easy argument that can be made on the basis of delegation of authority by the state by way of its ratification of the Rome Statute, given that Sudan has not ratified that treaty and the case was referred to the Court by the UN Security Council. Likewise, what was the basis of Senegal's jurisdiction to try Issène Habré in 2016 for crimes against humanity against his own people in Chad? The legal basis involved an agreement between Senegal and the African Union leading to the establishment of an internationalised chamber within the courts of Senegal, acting "on behalf of Africa".[308] The 1949 Geneva Conventions provide for a universally ratified treaty basis for universal jurisdiction over "grave breaches" of international humanitarian law committed during an international armed conflict; the legal foundation for universal jurisdiction over war crimes committed in non-international armed conflicts, genocide, and crimes against humanity, remains without a treaty basis, although states increasingly claim the right to initiate such prosecutions.[309]

The ethos of international criminal law, inspired by the Nuremberg Principles, is that it stands as a universal pledge to proscribe and sanction the violations of values held to be fundamental to the international community as a whole. The challenge is that the "international community" is not a political community, lacking the political institutions that would constitute it as such and which could react in a legitimate and effective way to international crimes. At most, it can be claimed that the international community is a moral community, begging the question of who can act on its behalf.[310] "Are all persons and institutions, simply by being members or groups of members of the moral community, justified in claiming and exercising universal jurisdiction"?[311] Some, like Anthony

[308] See Sofie AE Høgestøl, 'The Habré Judgment at the Extraordinary African Chambers: A Singular Victory in the Fight Against Impunity' (2016) 34 Nordic Journal of Human Rights 147, 150–151.

[309] Jo Stigen, *The Relationship between the International Criminal Court and National Jurisdictions: The Principle of Complementarity* (M Nijhoff 2008) 192. More generally, a state may by treaty allow another state to exercise criminal jurisdiction on its territory. For example, Cuba by treaty gave the United States "complete jurisdiction and control" over part of its territory, providing a basis for US criminal trials in Guantanamo Bay, while reserving "ultimate sovereignty" to Cuba: Kal Raustiala, 'The Geography of Justice' (2004) 73 Fordham Law Review 2501.

[310] Duff (n 275) 600; Kai Ambos, 'Punishment Without a Sovereign? The Ius Puniendi Issue of International Criminal Law: A First Contribution Towards a Consistent Theory of International Criminal Law' (2013) 33 Oxford Journal of Legal Studies 293, 313–314.

[311] Guidice and Schaeffer (n 275) 239.

Duff, argue that there should be universal jurisdiction only in situations in which the state with primary jurisdiction fails to sanction international crimes; if that occurs, then a complementary jurisdiction may be activated so that the wrongdoer is prosecuted by an international tribunal or other state on behalf of the unrepresented political community in the territorial state.[312] For David Luban, the only possible legitimation of the jurisdiction of international tribunals lies in the quality of their administration of justice: "Tribunals bootstrap themselves into legitimacy by the quality of justice they deliver; their rightness depends on their fairness".[313] According to this approach, tribunals generate their own authority by delivering "champagne quality due process and fair, humane punishments".[314] There is an echo of this construction of legitimacy in the way in which the ICC Elements of Crimes define what amounts to a "regularly constituted court": the Elements subsume the constitutive aspects of the tribunal into the due process requirements, such that a court will be found to be regularly constituted if it affords due process.[315] Michael Guidice and Matthew Schaeffer for their part surmise that international criminal law is a polycentric regime in which a plurality of agents is likely to have a role in the application of law. They turn to the idea of jurisdiction as a duty, evoked earlier, as the approach best suited to meet the need for coordination:

> The most that can be done now is to identify who has a duty to do what to help bring about the goals of international criminal law . . . More of course remains to be said about how the duty to govern international criminal law ought to be divided . . . and distributed among state and international legal institutions (including but not limited to the ICC) to reach the goals of international criminal law. . . . [G]iven the moral urgency of international criminal law and the need to develop effective institutions and effective coordination among institutions, the terms in which we ought to assess the moral legitimacy of claims to universal jurisdiction are better cast as institutional duties, and not institutional rights.[316]

This approach is similar to an earlier argument formulated by Kristen Hessler and Onora O'Neill.[317] Hessler and O'Neill advocate trying to identity "all of the potential 'agents of justice' that might be able to work to protect human rights when they are at great risk, such as in corrupt or weak States",[318] rather than

[312] Duff (n 275) 598.
[313] Luban (n 272) 579.
[314] Luban (n 272).
[315] ICC, Elements of Crimes, 9 September 2002, ICC-ASP/1/3 (part II-B), p 34 (http://www.legal-tools.org/doc/3c0e2d/). Somer (n 2) 674. The requirement for a court to be "regularly constituted" under international humanitarian law is analysed in greater details in Chapter 2, Section IV.C.ii.a.
[316] Guidice and Schaeffer (n 275) 248.
[317] Onora O'Neill, 'Agents of Justice' (2001) 32 Metaphilosophy 180.
[318] Hessler (n 276) 49.

focussing on circumstances in which state sovereignty can be pierced. "Agents of justice" can be identified based on their "effective capabilities to achieve justice in the relevant geographical, political and economic circumstances".[319] O'Neill argues that the "value of focussing on capabilities is that this foregrounds an explicit concern with the action and with the results that agents or agencies can achieve in actual circumstances, and so provides a seriously realistic starting point for normative reasoning".[320]

It may be that states will be in a "better epistemological position to investigate and prosecute or have better incentives to balance peace and combat impunity".[321] Consequently, primary but nonexclusive jurisdiction may rest with states, but "for reasons other than an alleged sovereign right to exclude actors, such as how best to achieve the goals of deterrence, anti-impunity or retribution, and reconciliation".[322] This also opens up the possibility that others may also be capable of combating impunity.

This approach is not inconsistent with current international law in two respects. First, prosecution of international crimes is not only regarded as a matter of right but also the subject of obligations. For instance, the Rome Statute recalls that "it is the duty of every State to exercise its criminal jurisdiction over those responsible for international crimes"[323] (although the basis and scope of that criminal jurisdiction is open to argument). Second, the role of reaching the aims of international criminal justice is not vested in one entity. According to Gerhard Kemp:

> [T]he judgment by the ICJ in *Belgium v Senegal* is a good illustration of how the international criminal justice project is best regarded as a comprehensive, multi-layered and complex system that relies on different modalities to reach the same aim: an end to impunity for the worst atrocities. The role of states that are willing to act as forum states for the investigation and possible prosecution of crimes under international law is crucial. Whether it is Belgium, or eventually Senegal, it does not really matter—at least not in terms of the central goals of the international criminal justice project.[324]

However, it is evident that there continues to be a strong assumption that states are the actors on which to the duty to act is imposed, and which cooperate in the

[319] ibid 49.
[320] O'Neill (n 317) 189; see also Hessler (n 276) 49.
[321] Hessler (n 276) 56–57.
[322] ibid 55.
[323] Rome Statute, Preamble para 6.
[324] Gerhard Kemp, 'Taking Stock of International Criminal Justice in Africa—Three Inventories Considered' in Beitel Van Der Merwe (ed), *International Criminal Justice in Africa: Challenges and Opportunities* (Konrad Adenauer Stiftung 2014) 29.

multilayered system. Whether international law extends this duty to prosecute international crimes to non-state entities such as insurgent courts is less clear.

As regards the administration of justice generally, and not only the sanction of international crimes, there are elements in the law of state responsibility that signal that there is no clear incompatibility between public international law and the rebel administration of justice. Article 10 of the UN Articles on the Responsibility of States for Internationally Wrongful Acts provides for the attribution to the state of the acts of an insurrectional movement that becomes the new government, inasmuch as there is "real and substantial continuity" between the insurgents and the government.[325] While the rule is framed as an answer to the question of whether the state should be held responsible for the acts of an insurrectional movement, and not to the broader question of the legality per se of such acts under international law, it does represent an acknowledgment that there are circumstances under which an armed opposition group acts with what comes to be recognised as legally recognised authority. That said, the focus of Article 10 is internationally wrongful acts, whereas the rebel administration of justice includes acts that could be lawful if performed by a legitimate public authority. Clearly, the provision would apply to any violation of rules of human rights or humanitarian law found applicable to insurgent courts, but, like for detention by armed groups, it intersects awkwardly with practices that are consistent with such rules but for the fact that their authors are not an established government. As a result, Article 10 is not obviously illuminating on the possible legitimacy of the administration of justice by armed opposition groups.

Another article provides for the attribution to the state of acts of persons or groups "in fact exercising elements of the governmental authority in the absence or default of the official authorities and in circumstances such as to the call for the exercise of those elements of authority" (Art. 9). The Commentary explains that "Article 9 deals with the exceptional case of conduct in the exercise of elements of the governmental authority . . . without any actual authority to do so".[326] The truly exceptional nature of the circumstances reflected in the provision have been emphasised, corresponding to situations like "revolution, armed conflict or foreign occupation" which result in the total or partial collapse of state authorities.[327] There are three elements that must be established in order for this article to apply, namely: the conduct must effectively relate to an "exercise of elements

[325] James Crawford (ed), *The International Law Commission's Articles on State Responsibility: Introduction, Text and Commentaries* (Cambridge University Press 2002) 118 para 7; see also James Crawford, *State Responsibility: The General Part* (Cambridge University Press 2013) 176; for critique, see Jean D'Aspremont, 'Rebellion and State Responsibility: Wrongdoing by Democratically Elected Insurgents' (2009) 58 International and Comparative Law Quarterly 427.

[326] Crawford, *The International Law Commission's Articles on State Responsibility: Introduction, Text and Commentaries* (n 325) 114 para 1.

[327] ibid.

of governmental authority"; the conduct must have been carried out "in the absence or default of the official authorities"; and the circumstances must have been such "as to call for the exercise of those elements of authority".[328] Article 9 does not define what constitute "elements of governmental authority", but it incorporates the same notion as in Article 5, that is, "if a private person can usually perform the function without the government's authorization or delegation of powers, it is not to be considered 'governmental' ".[329] The archetypal example often given for an exercise of governmental authority is in the exercise of law and order and border/immigration functions by the Komitehs (Revolutionary Guards) in *Yeager v. Iran*.[330] The scenario most commonly associated with the rule proclaimed in Article 9 is that of a *levée en masse*, in which a population spontaneously rises to stop an advancing enemy in the absence of regular troops.[331] Some authors have suggested that this could also cover situations in which rebels assume control over parts of national territory, inasmuch as their goal is one of governance and not merely private gain.[332] If that is so, then there is little doubt that the administration of justice by armed groups would correspond to the exercise of an element of governmental authority covered by Article 9.

This brief foray into the ideas of sovereignty, jurisdiction, and authority in public international law, as illuminated by some insights from philosophy and political theory, suggests that the rebel administration of justice is not inherently incompatible with these notions. This challenges a certain sense that only states, like gods, can both embody the experience of the sacred and demand sacrifice, devotion, and obedience.[333] In this respect, the narrative of insurgency is a project that stands in competition to that of sovereignty.

****

The survey of the administration of justice by the FARC in Colombia suggests that this form of rebel governance is not necessarily incompatible in all its

[328] James Crawford, *The International Law Commission's Articles on State Responsibility: Introduction, Text, and Commentaries* (Cambridge University Press 2002) 114 para 3.

[329] Crawford, *State Responsibility: The General Part* (n 325) 169.

[330] Iran-United States Claims Tribunal, *Yeager v Islamic Republic of Iran*, Award No 324- 10199-1, 2 November 1987, Iran-United States Claims Tribunal Reports, vol 17 (1987-IV), p 103, para 42.

[331] Helmut Philipp Aust, 'Complicity in Violations of International Humanitarian Law' in Heike Krieger (ed), *Inducing Compliance with International Humanitarian Law: Lessons from the African Great Lakes Region* (Cambridge University Press 2015) 464.

[332] Gérard Cahin, 'The Responsibility of Other Entities: Armed Bands and Criminal Groups' in James Crawford, Alain Pellet, and Simon Olleson (eds), *The Law of International Responsibility* (Oxford University Press 2010) 335–336; Tatyana Eatwell, 'Rebel Governors in Areas of Limited Statehood: State Responsibility and Agents of Necessity' in Linda Hamid and Jan Wouters (eds), *Rule of Law and Areas of Limited Statehood* (Elgar 2021); Katharine Fortin, 'The Relevance of Article 9 of the Articles on State Responsibility for the Internationally Wrongful Acts of Armed Groups' in James Summers and Alex Gough (eds), *Non-State Actors and International Obligations* (Brill 2018).

[333] Paul Kahn, *Political Theology* (Columbia University Press 2011).

aspects with the concept of the rule of law. The latter is sufficiently diverse, fluid, and flexible to allow for a meaningful application of its fundamental elements to the rebel administration of justice, to nudge it in the direction of practices that are evolving towards the progressive realisation of the aspirations of the rule of law. This does not necessarily imply the legitimisation of the cause embraced by an armed opposition group such as the FARC, nor of its practices. In this sense, the rebel rule of law operates a function similar to the rule of law more generally when it is applied to the administration of justice by a state: it does not bring with it the condoning of the state or of its actions, quite the opposite since the rule of law is usually brandished to castigate a government for its failures in this regard. One difference is that states have a full international legal personality and are presumed competent to fulfil their legal obligations, although lack of resources and other externalities may excuse incomplete performance. Armed groups, on the other hand, have a legal personality that is only partial, and the idea of the rebel rule of law can be a tool to determine what their obligations should be, in addition to whether they have been met.

Governments fighting against armed opposition groups are eager to delegitimize every facet of the insurgency, and thus to dissociate every form of rebel *de facto* governance from any notion of justice or law. While there may be sound political and even legal reasons for these governments to do so, in following their lead we deprive ourselves of both a yardstick by which to measure and criticise the practices of non-state armed groups and a tool with which to engage in a dialogue with these groups to encourage them to alter their behaviour. The work of organisations like the International Committee of the Red Cross (ICRC) and Geneva Call have established with unimpeachable clarity that humanitarian engagement with armed rebels is feasible and potentially transformative, and the study of the FARC suggests that this can be so for the administration of justice as well.

In a very different context, discussing ways to limit the powers of the President of the United States, Curtis Bradley and Trevor Morrison suggested that the mere fact of having lawyers make arguments grounded in legality could produce an internalisation of its concepts and ultimately exert some pull to comply.[334] Even if the invocation of a legal precept is merely a conceit, it carries what John Elster described as "the civilizing force of hypocrisy", initiating a dialogue on a basis that will always owe something to earlier statements, however disingenuous.[335] The rebel rule of law likewise could play this civilising influence, however slowly and unevenly bringing the administration of justice by armed opposition groups closer to the ideals of the rule of law.

[334] Curtis A Bradley and Trevor W Morrison, 'Presidential Power, Historical Practice, and Legal Constraint' [2013] Columbia Law Review 1097, 1142–1143; Alvarez (n 177) 33.

[335] Jon Elster, 'Strategic Uses of Argument' in Kenneth Joseph Arrow, *Barriers to Conflict Resolution* (WW Norton & Company 1995) 250.

2

Legality of Rebel Courts—Islamic State and Taliban Justice

Ce n'est pas à vous que j'apprendrai que toute justice, dans son principe comme dans son exécution, n'appartient qu'à l'État.

— Charles de Gaulle, Lettre à Jean-Paul Sartre, 19 avril 1967[1]

I. Introduction

The concept of the rule of law, as we have seen, is a notion marked by its elusiveness, the boundaries of which are fated to remain disputed. The rise of the Westphalian state has been in part marked by a narrative of the capture of the idea of the rule of law by the claims of sovereignty, leading to assumptions of a state monopoly on the administration of justice that all too often have remained untested. In the previous chapter, the acknowledgment that non-state armed groups like the FARC have in conflict zones adopted practices and established institutions that fulfil at least parts of what we think of as the administration of justice provided an opportunity to challenge the state's stranglehold on the rule of law. The conclusion that a rebel rule of law is not an oxymoron opens a conceptual door to thinking differently about the administration of justice by armed insurgents, but it does not provide any clear answers as to what binding force should be given to judgments of rebel courts. The response to this distinct question necessarily must reflect existing legal norms applicable to a given actor in a specific context. For non-state armed groups in conflict zones, this means turning to rules of public international law to assess whether they determine with any clarity the legality of insurgent courts. Two subfields of international law appear as especially relevant to an investigation of the legality of courts under public international law: international humanitarian law, as a body of

[1] <http://www.lemonde.fr/archives/article/1967/04/25/toute-justice-dans-son-principe-comme-dans-son-execution-n-appartient-qu-a-l-etat-ecrit-le-general-de-gaulle-a-m-jean-paul-sartre-et-la-reponse-du-president-de-la-republique_3111895_1819218.html?xtmc=sartre_de_gaulle_justice_etat&xtcr=41>.

Rebel Courts. René Provost, Oxford University Press. © Oxford University Press 2021.
DOI: 10.1093/oso/9780190912222.003.0003

rule designed to regulate the behaviour of belligerents in armed conflicts, and international human rights law, as a body of rules especially concerned with the conditions of validity of the administration of justice.

An initial reaction to the question of the legality of insurgent courts under public international law has been that, as a legal regime established by states all sharing a fundamental interest in the maintenance of their sovereignty, it would seem unlikely that international law would countenance any legal validity to the rebel administration of justice. Thus, the statement thirty years ago by Denise Plattner that "[i]t is difficult to conceive of IHL giving insurgents the authority to prosecute and try the authors of violations" stands confirmed by Clapham's assessment in 2019 that "[n]o state really accepts that armed groups are entitled to detain or try anyone".[2] A different line of general denial of the legality of insurgent courts has centred on the unlikelihood that such courts could meet even the most minimal requirements of due process demanded under international law.[3] These general statements of denial of the legality of insurgent justice have often been made without the benefit of a thorough analysis of the legal norms at play, and on the whole are sufficiently dated to raise the possibility that international law has evolved to allow for the possibility, in some circumstances, of the legal recognition of insurgent justice.[4] This is the conclusion, for instance, reached by the Stockholm District Court in the trial of Omar Sakhanh in February 2017, in relation to a rebel court established by the Free Syrian Army in that country.[5] The remainder of this chapter offers an analysis that concludes that international humanitarian law and international human rights do open a door to the lawful administration of justice by non-state armed groups in some but not all situations of armed conflicts. The analysis is complemented by two case studies that might be taken as among the most controversial, if not provocative, instances in which

[2] Denise Plattner, 'The Penal Repression of Violations of International Humanitarian Law Applicable in Non-International Armed Conflicts' (1990) 30 International Review of the Red Cross Archive 409, 415; Andrew Clapham, 'The Limits of Human Rights in Times of Armed Conflict and Other Situations of Armed Violence' in Bardo Fassbender and Knut Traisbach (eds), *The Limits of Human Rights* (Oxford University Press 2019) 315; Liesbeth Zegveld, *Accountability of Armed Opposition Groups in International Law* (Cambridge University Press 2002) 68.

[3] James Bond, 'Application of the Law of War to Internal Conflict' (1973) 3 Georgia Journal of International and Comparative Law 345, 373.

[4] See, inter alia: Jonathan Somer, 'Jungle Justice: Passing Sentence on the Equality of Belligerents in Non-International Armed Conflict' (2007) 89 International Review of the Red Cross 655; Sandesh Sivakumaran, 'Courts of Armed Opposition Groups—Fair Trials or Summary Justice?' (2009) 7 Journal of International Criminal Justice 489; Mark Klamberg, 'The Legality of Rebel Courts during Non-International Armed Conflicts' (2018) 16 Journal of International Criminal Justice 235.

[5] *Prosecutor v Omar Haisam Sakhanh*, Stockholms tingsrätt (Stockholm District Court), B 3787-16, Judgment of 16 February 2017 (hereinafter 'Sakhanh, Stockholm District Court'), online: http://www.ejiltalk.org/wp-content/uploads/2017/03/Stockholms-TR-B-3787-16-Dom-2017-02-16.pdf accessed 18 July 2018, with a partial translation in (2018) 16 *Journal of International Criminal Justice* 403–424; confirmed by Prosecutor v Omar Haisam Sakhanh, Svea hovrätt (Svea Court of Appeal), B 2259-17, Judgment of 31 May 2017 (hereinafter 'Sakhanh, Svea Appeal Court'); leave to appeal was denied by the Supreme Court of Sweden, B 3157-17, 20 July 2017.

armed groups have claimed the mantle of the administration of justice, the so-called Islamic State, or ISIS, in Syria and Iraq, and the Taliban in Afghanistan. As the case studies reveal, even these armed groups that resort to extreme violence against the civilian population rely upon a combination of brutality and bureaucracy that is not entirely inconsistent with the idea of the administration of justice.

II. Islamic State Justice: A Penchant for Paperwork

The Islamic State,[6] also known as the Islamic State of Iraq and the Levant (ISIL), the Islamic State of Iraq and Syria (ISIS), or by its Arabic acronym *Da'esh*, is a Salafi-jihadist militant group whose primary aim is to establish and expand a caliphate based on its fundamentalist interpretation of Sunni Islam.[7] At the height of its power in 2014–2015, the group controlled a vast swath of territory in Syria and Iraq as large as the United Kingdom, exerting control over a population estimated at between six and twelve million people, relying on a sectarian army numbering 30,000 combatants combining local armed insurgencies in Iraq and Syria as well as foreign recruits.[8] By August 2016, the group and its network of military affiliates were believed to be operational in some eighteen countries worldwide, including "official" branches in Algeria, Nigeria, and Afghanistan, and "aspiring" branches in the Philippines, Indonesia, and Bangladesh.[9]

The Islamic State's origins can be traced to the early 2000s, when the group took part in the Iraqi insurgency against American occupation, first under the name of *Jama'at al-Tawhid wal-Jihad* (Organization of Monotheism and Jihad),

[6] I will use the term "Islamic State" and ISIS rather than alternate acronyms (Da'esh, ISIL, ISI) to reflect the group's self-appellation as "al-Dawla al-Islamiyya" ("Islamic State" in Arabic). See Cole Bunzel, 'The Ideology of the Islamic State,' The Brookings Project on US Relations with the Islamic World, No 19, March 2015. See also Mara Revkin, 'The Legal Foundations of the Islamic State' (Brookings Institution 2016).

[7] The Islamic State, Mapping Military Organization, Stanford University, online: http://web.stanford.edu/group/mappingmilitants/cgi-bin/groups/view/1.

[8] Early 2015 is generally accepted as the peak of the Islamic State's control over territory in Iraq and Syria. See, e.g., Pamela Engel, 'ISIS' Caliphate Is Shrinking, and the Terror Group Is about to Lose One of Its Biggest Cities' *Business Insider*, online: <http://www.businessinsider.com/how-much-territory-has-isis-lost-2016-10>. As military pressure against the group intensified in Iraq and Syria, al-Baghdadi sent off scores of his lieutenants to the Libyan city of Surt "as a rearguard base to fall back to if the organization is forced out of Syria": Fawaz A Gerges, *ISIS: A History* (Princeton University Press 2016) 5. See also Micah Zenko, 'How Many Bombs Did the United States Drop in 2015?' (7 January 2016), online: <https://www.cfr.org/blog/how-many-bombs-did-united-states-drop-2015>.

[9] 'Islamic State and the Crisis in Iraq and Syria in Maps' *BBC News* (20 July 2017), online: <http://www.bbc.com/news/world-middle-east-27838034>; 'New Counterterrorism "Heat Map" Shows ISIS Branches Spreading Worldwide' *NBC News* (August 3 2016), online: <http://www.nbcnews.com/storyline/isis-terror/new-counterterrorism-heat-map-shows-isis-branches-spreading-worldwide-n621866>; 'ISIS Now Has a Network of Military Affiliates in 11 Countries Around the World' *New York* (23 November 2014), online: <http://nymag.com/daily/intelligencer/2014/11/isis-now-has-military-allies-in-11-countries.html>.

and then, after pledging allegiance to al-Qaeda, as al-Qaeda in Iraq (AQI).[10] The group faced decline until its involvement in the Syrian Civil War in 2011, a conflict it used "as a training ground and tool for expansion".[11] In April 2013, the group changed its name to the Islamic State in Iraq and Syria (ISIS), and made significant territorial gains, capturing the key Iraqi cities of Falluja[12] and Mosul[13] in January and June 2014, respectively. The assets seized in the occupations, coupled with taxation, ransoms, and foreign donations, brought the group's funds to an estimated $2 billion,[14] and by September 2014, the group's oil revenues alone amounted to $1 million to $2 million a day.[15] With ever greater financial and territorial might, the group rebranded itself again in June 2014, this time as the "Islamic State",[16] proclaiming a worldwide caliphate with absolute political authority over all Muslims.[17] The Islamic State combined an embrace of an extreme and rigid interpretation of Islam with state-like bureaucratic forms.[18] Abu Bakr al-Baghdadi, who had assumed leadership of the group since 2010,[19] later was declared caliph, and called upon all Muslims and jihadi groups to swear fealty to him.[20] After he was killed in a US operation in October 2019, he was succeeded as caliph by Abu Ibrahim al-Hashimi al-Qurashi. As of 2021, although a force

[10] See: William McCants, *The ISIS Apocalypse: The History, Strategy, and Doomsday Vision of the Islamic State* (Macmillan 2015); Ahmed Hashim, 'The Islamic State: From Al-Qaeda Affiliate to Caliphate' (2014) Middle East Policy 21:4 74, online: <http://www.mepc.org/islamic-state-al-qaeda-affiliate-caliphate>. See also Donna Starr-Deelen, *Counter-Terrorism from the Obama Administration to President Trump: Caught in the Fait Accompli War* (Springer 2018).

[11] ibid.

[12] Kirk Semple and Eric Schmitt, 'ISIS Keeps Up Pressure Near Baghdad as Iraqi Troops Hesitate' *New York Times* (17 October 2014), online: <https://www.nytimes.com/2014/10/18/world/middleeast/isis-keeps-up-pressure-near-baghdad-as-iraqi-troops-stumble.html>.

[13] Martin Chulov, 'ISIS Insurgents Seize Control of Iraqi City of Mosul' *The Guardian* (10 June 2014), online: <https://www.theguardian.com/world/2014/jun/10/iraq-sunni-insurgents-islamic-militants-seize-control-mosul>.

[14] Ehab Zahriyeh, 'How ISIL Became a Major Force with Only a Few Thousand Fighters' *Al Jazeera* (19 June 2014), online: <http://america.aljazeera.com/articles/2014/6/19/isil-thousands-fighters.html>.

[15] 'How ISIS Works' *New York Times* (16 September 2014), online: <https://www.nytimes.com/interactive/2014/09/16/world/middleeast/how-isis-works.html>.

[16] 'What Is "Islamic State"?' *BBC News* (2 December 2015), online: <http://www.bbc.com/news/world-middle-east-29052144>.

[17] Michael Pizzi, 'In Declaring a Caliphate, Islamic State Draws a Line in the Sand' *Al Jazeera* (30 June 2014), online: <http://america.aljazeera.com/articles/2014/6/30/islamic-state-caliphate.html>; Radwan Mortada, 'What Does ISIS' Declaration of a Caliphate Mean?' *Al-Akhbar* (30 June 2014), online: <http://english.al-akhbar.com/node/20378>.

[18] Adam Bazcko and others, 'The Rationality of an Eschatological Movement: The Islamist State in Iraq and Syria' (Yale Program on Governance and Local Development 2016) 11–14.

[19] Anthony Shadid, 'Iraqi Insurgent Group Names New Leaders' *New York Times* (16 May 2010), online: <https://atwar.blogs.nytimes.com/2010/05/16/iraqi-insurgent-group-names-new-leaders/?_php=true&_type=blogs&_r=0>.

[20] The declaration of the caliphate, and Baghdadi's caliphhood in particular, were controversial and drew criticism from rival jihadi groups. '"They're Delusional": Rivals Ridicule ISIS Declaration of Islamic State' *CBS News* (30 June 2014, online: <http://www.cbsnews.com/news/theyre-delusional-rivals-ridicule-isis-declaration-of-islamic-state/>.

reduced to 3,000 to 4,000 fighters controlling limited territory, the Islamic State is still active in Iraq and Syria.

A. Islamic State Governance: "Fun, Food, and Services"[21]

The Islamic State rejects the concept of national sovereignty corresponding to the Westphalian state, but nevertheless insists on calling itself a "state" with a monopoly on the use of violence and a "complete social structure".[22] In areas under its control, the Islamic State established a "holistic system of governance" comprising courts, prisons, schools, a police apparatus, as well as humanitarian, religious, and infrastructure projects.[23] At a structural level, the Islamic State government consisted of a hierarchical and centralised top-down chain that began with Baghdadi himself, who held "absolute power" and oversaw all religious and political activities in the caliphate.[24] The caliph, his cabinet advisors, and his two major deputies in Iraq and Syria comprised the executive branch of the leadership, known as the *al-imara* (or "leadership").[25] Each deputy also supervised twelve governors (known as *walīs*) presiding over a local structure akin to a province (*wilayats*) in Iraq and Syria, respectively. Under the auspices of the executive, the government was further divided into a series of "councils" in charge of overseeing the group's military operations, drafting laws and policies, oil sales, counter-intelligence and security activities, and finances.[26] Notably amongst them, the Shura Council, which reported directly to the *al-imara*, acted as the Islamic State's "religious monitor" and could ostensibly dismiss the caliph himself if he failed to govern according to the *Sharī'a*.[27]

21 Vanda Felbab-Brown and others, *Militants, Criminals, and Warlords: The Challenge of Local Governance in an Age of Disorder* (Brookings Institution Press 2018) 64 (a 2015 study of ISIS media outreach concluded: "Come to the Islamic State, is the message. There is fun here, and food, and services").

22 Truls Hallberg Tønnessen, 'The Group That Wanted to Be a State: The 'Rebel Governance' of the Islamic State' in Hendrik Kraetzschmar and Paola Rivetti (eds), *Islamists and the Politics of the Arab Uprising* (Edinburgh University Press 2018) 54–61.

23 Charles Caris and Samuel Reynolds, 'ISIS Governance in Syria' (July 2014) Middle East Security Report 22: 4, *Institute for the Study of War*, online: <http://www.understandingwar.org/sites/default/files/ISIS_Governance.pdf>; see also Richard Barrett, *The Islamic State* (The Soufan Group 2014) at 18.

24 'The Structure of the Islamic State (ISIS)' (8 September 2014), online: http://jcpa.org/structure-of-the-islamic-state/; Husham Al-Hashimi, 'ISIS 2020: New Structures and Leaders in Iraq Revealed' Center for Global Policy (2020), online: https://cgpolicy.org/articles/isis-2020-new-structures-and-leaders-in-iraq-revealed/.

25 Hashim, 'The Islamic State: From Al-Qaeda Affiliate to Caliphate' (n 10).

26 Richard Barrett, 'The Islamic State' The Soufan Group (2014) 31, online: <http://soufangroup.com/wp-content/uploads/2014/10/TSG-The-Islamic-State-Nov14.pdf>.

27 Al-Baghdadi, 'This Is the Promise of Allah' (28 June 2014), online: <https://ia902505.us.archive.org/28/items/poa_25984/ EN.pdf>; CNN, Nick Thompson and Atika Shubert, 'The Anatomy of ISIS: How the "Islamic State" Is Run', *CNN*, online: <http://www.cnn.com/2014/09/18/world/meast/isis-syria-iraq-hierarchy/index.html>.

More broadly, the Islamic State's governance can be divided into two general categories oriented towards administrative and service matters, respectively.[28] The "administrative stream" oversaw courts, recruitment, tribal relations, religious outreach, and elementary education. The "Muslim services" stream, as the name suggests, was in charge of the provision of public services. These included electricity, sanitation, water, mail, construction work, and also a range of health and welfare programs, including subsidised bakeries, soup kitchens, and *zakat* (almsgiving) offices.[29] In Raqqa, there were reports that the group even operated a "Consumer Protection Office", an "Office for Orphans", and a public polio-vaccination campaign.[30] Naturally, the level of sophistication of the Islamic State's governance programs was contingent on the group's level of control and dominance in a given area, with the group's urban strongholds enjoying substantial investments in lasting infrastructure such as sewer lines, dams, and thermal plants.[31] Conversely, rural and disputed areas witnessed "less resource-intensive and less controversial" governance programs such as rudimentary court systems and religious outreach departments.[32]

Underpinning the Islamic State's provision of services was a type of "social contract"[33] based on the act of *bay'ah* (swearing fealty to the caliph). This contract (or *aqd*) gave rise to reciprocal rights and duties between the caliph and his subjects, the terms of which were spelled out in a series of local documents issued by the Islamic State.[34] In early 2016, the group published a constitution-like document entitled *wathīqat al-madīnah* ("documents of the city"), common to the entire caliphate, which "defin[ed] the *Sharī'a* principles and Islamic regulations by which the shepherd and the flock are bound".[35] The thirteen-article *wathīqat*

[28] Our knowledge of the Islamic State's governance structure remains incomplete, but this broad categorisation can be made based on an Aleppo provincial report released by the Islamic State on 24 June 2014, no longer available online. See also Caris and Reynolds (n 23) 14.

[29] ibid at 14; Aaron Zelin, 'The Islamic State of Iraq and Syria Has a Consumer Protection Office', *The Atlantic* (June 2014), online: <https://www.theatlantic.com/international/archive/2014/06/the-isis-guide-to-building-an-islamic-state/372769/ >.

[30] ibid.

[31] In areas where it exerted greatest dominance and had consolidated power, the group also implemented more controversial governance such as religious police and stricter punishments. Caris and Reynolds (n 23) 14.

[32] ibid at 4. These are analysed more fully in the following subsection.

[33] Mara Revkin, 'ISIS' Social Contract. What the Islamic State Offers Civilians' [2016] *Foreign Affairs*.

[34] The Islamic State, 'Wathīqat al-Madīnah' (13 September 2014), issued in Raqqa, online: <http://1.bp.blogspot.com/-Tv8Nm1G1VxM/ VBXdeYnHvpI/AAAAAAAAJi0/Tlt0hnxgVXE/s1600/proxy.jpg>; The Islamic State, 'Wathīqat al-Madīnah' (12 June 2014), issued in Mosul, online: <https://s04.justpaste.it/pdf/Nenwa-justpaste-it-260470.pdf >; The Islamic State, 'Wathīqat al-Madīnah' (17 October 2014), issued in Hit, Iraq, online: <https://web.archive.org/web/20160322234824/; https://twitter.com/HamidHadeed/status/523020667566825472>; The Islamic State, 'Wathīqat al-Madīnah' (2 December 2015), issued in Sirte, Libya, online: <https://web.archive.org/web/20160322234933/;https:/twitter.com/kalsghyr/status/672090395560529920 >.

[35] The Islamic State, Maktab al-Himma, 'Wathīqat al-Madīnah' (25 January 2016), online: <https://web.archive.org/web/20160323000003/>. Subjects of the caliphate are often referred to by the group as *an-Nās* ("the people") or, tellingly, *ri'aya* ("the flock"). Andrew March and Mara Revkin, 'Caliphate

al-madīnah provided a list of basic rights for the "flock" including: "(1) the right to justice and due process of law; (2) the right to security of persons and property; and (3) the right to public goods and services provided by the Islamic State. It also defines their duties: (1) a duty to fulfill obligations required by Islam, including abstention from alcohol and drugs, and (2) a duty of allegiance to the Islamic State".[36]

B. Islamic State Justice

The Islamic State operated official courts across Iraq, Syria, and northern Libya, and proto-courts were reportedly established in the Lebanese border town of Arsal and in the group's *Wilayat* Sinai (Sinai province) in northern Egypt.[37] The establishment of a working administration of justice was a priority for the Islamic State, often before fully controlling a territory, as a way to demonstrate that the group could bring order.[38] Courts were part and parcel of the normalisation of the group's authority:

> The establishment of legal and judicial institutions, within the framework of a distinctive legal order, allowed the Islamic State to justify violence, regulate economic transactions, and impose taxes, offering safety and security and other rudimentary elements of a "social contract" in return. Contrary to popular perception, the Islamic State was not just engaging in a kind of demonstrative performance, merely making things up as it went. There was a method to the madness.[39]

Knowledge of the Islamic State judiciary remains incomplete, but civilians accustomed to the group's governance and documentary evidence suggest that it comprised at least three sections: First, a Bureau of Justice and Grievances, inspired by a seventh-century body with a similar name under the Umayyad Caliphate, supervised the operation of other justice bodies and reported to the caliph and

of Law' *Foreign Affairs* (15 April 2015), online: <https://www.foreignaffairs.com/articles/ syria/2015-04-15/caliphate-law>.

36 Revkin (n 6) 15.

37 Samya Kullab, 'ISIS Running Shariah Court in Arsal in Bid to Win Hearts and Minds' (7 February 2015), online: <http://www.dailystar. com.lb/news/lebanon-news/2015/feb-07/286716-isis-running-shariah-court-in-arsal-in-bid-to-win-hearts-and-minds.ashx>; Yahya Aqeel, 'Sinai Province . . . Courts and Qisas and Application of Hudūd in the Absence of Security' *Rassd* (14 March 2016), online: <https://rassd.com/180142.htm. See also Revkin (n 6) 25.

38 Aaron Zelin, 'The Islamic State's Territorial Methodology' Washington Institute for Near East Policy (2016) 3–4.

39 Felbab-Brown and others (n 21) 64.

the Shura Council.[40] The Bureau also received complaints against the Islamic State's own public officials and combatants. Second, Islamic courts, including a high court located in Mosul, which acted as courts of general jurisdiction over civil, criminal, and security cases. Third, the *Diwan al-Hisba*, which exercised jurisdiction over morality offences referred by the *hisba* police.[41] A form of appeals process also seems to have been in place, with difficult and disputed cases being referred to senior judges in Mosul and death sentences imposed by Islamic Courts being approved by the Bureau of Justice and Grievances.[42] With that said, there are reports that the speed with which Islamic State court rulings were implemented effectively removed any possibility to appeal or revoke a sentence.[43] As regards grievances presented to courts by civilians against Islamic State fighters, although officially encouraged by the group, they required prior approval by the neighbourhood or village chief and permission by the court; as a result, it was suggested that "the only ones to go [to these courts] are those arrested by the Islamic State".[44]

These courts were to some extent tolerated, if not accepted, by residents weary of lawlessness in the caliphate, where "[a]ny law and order was seen as an improvement, even [the Islamic State's] brutal interpretation of [*Sharīʿa*]".[45] Islamic State courts also enjoy a comparative advantage whereby their "legal system is generally [considered to be] more efficient and effective than the available alternative".[46] The Iraqi and Syrian governments were near the bottom of the Corruption Perceptions Index in 2020;[47] other competing armed groups such as the Free Syrian Army were often accused of fraud and graft.[48] As one resident of

[40] Syria Justice and Accountability Centre, 'Judge, Jury and Executioner: The ISIS Bureau of Justice and Grievances' (2020) 3–5.

[41] Aymenn al-Tamimi, 'Aspects of Islamic State (IS) Administration in Ninawa Province: Part III' (23 January 2015), online: <http://www.aymennjawad.org/15961/aspects-of-islamic-state-is-administration-in>; Revkin (n 6) 26.

[42] For example, a property case in Raqqa was transferred to the high court in Mosul after local judges were incapable of convincing a Libyan Islamic State fighter to vacate a house he had illegally expropriated from a resident. Confirmation of death sentences is mentioned in a court document in Syria Justice and Accountability Centre (n 40) 10.

[43] Fariq Al-Amal, 'What Do You Know About the Judicial System of ISIS?' [translated from Arabic], *Sasa Post* (2 February 2016), online: <http://www.sasapost.com/isil-judiciary/>.

[44] Bazcko and others (n 18) 15; Revkin (n 6).

[45] Mikael Ekman (ed), 'ILAC Rule of Law Assessment Report: Syria 2017', online: <http://www.ilacnet.org/wp-content/uploads/2017/04/Syria2017.pdf>, at 132.

[46] Revkin (n 6) 11; Daniel Byman, 'Understanding the Islamic State—A Review Essay' (2016) 40 International Security 127, 141. See also Mona Alami, 'ISIS's Governance Crisis: Social Services' Atlantic Council (1 January 2015), online: <http://www. yementimes.com/en/1847/opinion/4762/ISIS%E2%80%99s-governance-crisis-Social-services.htm>.

[47] Syria was ranked 178th and Iraq was ranked 160th out of 180 countries in the Corruption Perceptions Index (CPI) of 2020: Transparency International, online: <https://www.transparency.org>.

[48] 'Syrian Rebel Command Sacked Over Graft Claims' *Al Arabiya* (27 June 2014), online: <http://english.alarabiya.net/en/News/2014/06/27/Syrian-rebel-command-sacked-over-graft-allegations-.html>.

Aleppo asserted, "[b]efore the Islamic State, it was impossible to get through the day without paying five different bribes. The people were tired of corruption, and the Islamic State offered them a solution".[49] Indeed, both critics and supporters of the Islamic State seem to agree that its institutions were more transparent and less prone to bribery and *wasta* (connections) than the alternative.[50] The group apparently routinely punished its own officials and combatants for misconduct. In one case in the central Iraqi city of Tekrit, one military official was sentenced to ninety-nine lashes for sexually assaulting a young girl.[51] Another Islamic State emir was reportedly dismissed after ridiculing a mentally disabled elderly man for his poor knowledge of the *Sharīʿah*.[52]

In keeping with its spurning of judicial independence, the Islamic State strictly monitored its judiciary through "a top-down bureaucratic chain" that began with the *Sharīʿa* Council, a body that answered directly to Caliph al-Baghdadi.[53] Nominations to judicial offices were reportedly decided by al-Baghdadi himself or his delegate.[54] Under the auspices of the caliph, each province's governor (*walī*) supervised a *Sharīʿa* deputy who himself headed a *Sharīʿa* commission (*hayʾat al-Sharīʿa*) in charge of monitoring local courts and judges.[55] Compliance with the group's official position on legal questions was rigidly enforced, and indeed it was reported that judges were removed and convicted upon disagreement with the group.[56]

> *Daesh authorities would tell people to come to the square to see the 'show' when they had people to punish. They claimed that these people had been convicted by a court. I saw them cut the hand of a thief, but I am not sure that he had really stolen anything. Another time, they threw a man off the top of a silo for being a homosexual.*
>
> *Interview, 'Ali', displaced civilian near Mosul (September 2017)*

Executions were routinely used to inculcate the *Sharīʿa*, with verdicts declared in public squares,[57] often over loudspeakers before a crowd of spectators forced

[49] Revkin (n 6) 11.

[50] Caris and Reynolds (n 23) 18; ibid.

[51] Islamic State, Salah ad-Din Province, Special Security Battalion (March 2015), online: <https://twitter.com/A27660278/status/578830149065420800>; see also Revkin (n 6) 31.

[52] Islamic State, Aleppo Province (17 June 2014), online: <justpaste.it/fvw0>.

[53] Revkin (n 6) 26. See also ibid.

[54] Joana Cook, Haid Haid, and Inga Trauthig, 'Jurisprudence Beyond the State: An Analysis of Jihadist "Justice" in Yemen, Syria and Libya' [2020] Studies in Conflict & Terrorism 1, 12.

[55] March and Revkin (n 35).

[56] See 'Daesh Executes the First Sharīʿa Judge Hamam al-Lafi' *Jordan News* (23 January 2015), online: <http://www.jordanews.com/jordan/32153.html>; 'Facing Internal Criticism for Pilot's Death, ISIS Executes 7' *Al-Akhbar* (6 February 2015), online: <http://english.al-akhbar.com/node/23647>.

[57] Aymenn Al-Tamimi, 'Butchers: Syria's ISIS Crucifying Opponents, Justifying Horror with Qur'an Passages' *PJ Media* (27 March 2014), online: <http://www.aymennjawad.org/14852/isis-use-ofhudud-punishments>; Olivia Becker, 'Islamist Rebels Are Allegedly Crucifying People in Syria'

to attend.[58] *Hudūd* punishments were carried out routinely in the open,[59] and civilian bystanders were invited to take part in stoning the convicted.[60] For lesser *Ta'zīr* punishments, offenders were often compelled to walk in public squares bearing a sign depicting their crime.[61] The prevalence of the imposition of the harshest punishments like executions and amputations is a disputed issue. In contrast to some reports, Human Rights Watch quotes from "Jamal", a civilian interviewed in Sirte, Libya, on life under ISIS:

> People accept the judgments without arguing, for fear of punishment. (. . .) The executions, they are not as frequent as some media report. The amputations, there are very few. But the floggings and imprisonments, there are many cases of that. After the revolution, Sirte had many robberies and killings. But now it is the safest place in Libya. Shops stay unlocked when their owners are at prayer yet no one will dare enter.[62]

This divergence could reflect either the level of attention generated by the shocking violence of public executions and amputations, or the fact that governance approaches varied from one ISIS province to another.[63]

Turning to applicable law, Islamic State courts professed to stringently apply the *Sharī'a*, God's immutable divine law as contained in the Qur'an and the sayings of the prophet (*hadith*).[64] They claimed to follow an originalist interpretation of the Sunni Hanbali school, and issued detailed religious justifications on that basis for punishments like the burning of a captured Jordanian pilot and the boiling to death of traitors.[65] Islamic scholars have rejected such interpretations as unsound and unsupported by any Islamic schools, but that is of course not a

VICE News (30 April 2014), online: <https://news.vice.com/article/islamist-rebels-are-allegedly-crucifyingpeople-in-syria/>.

[58] Revkin (n 6) 25; Islamic State, Raqqa Province, 'Announcement of the Ruling for Drinking Wine' (7 February 2015), online: <https://web.archive.org/web/20150207083631im_/http://i.imgur.com/sJFZhy6.jpg>; Bazcko and others (n 18) 16.

[59] Caris and Reynolds (n 23) 19.

[60] Islamic State, Aleppo Province, 'Implementation of the Hadd Punishment of Stoning Until Death on a Married Adulterer in the Abu Qalqal Region' (12 January 2015), online: <https://web.archive.org/web/20160323224247/https://justpaste.it/Rjm2death>. See also Revkin (n 6) 25–26.

[61] Islamic State, Raqqa Province, 'Ta'zīr Punishment by Tash'hīr in Front of the People' (19 April 2015), online: <https://web.archive.org/web/20160323223638/https:/twitter.com/Raqqa_Sl/status/589561235731046400>. See also Revkin (n 6) 25–26.

[62] Human Rights Watch, '"We Feel We Are Cursed"—Life under ISIS in Sirte, Libya' (2016) 20–21.

[63] Zelin (n 38).

[64] *Sharī'ah* is often contrasted to *fiqh*, which refers to the scholarly interpretations of jurists to elaborate on the details of the *Qur'an* and *hadith*. Unlike the *Sharī'ah*, *fiqh*, as a human endeavour, remains open to debate and change. 'Islamic Law' in John L Esposito (ed), *The Oxford Dictionary of Islam*, online: <http://www.oxfordislamicstudies.com/article/opr/t125/e1107>.

[65] Pouria Askary and Katayoun Hosseinnejad, 'Non-State Courts: Illegal or Conditional?: The Case of Da'esh Courts' (2019) 10 Journal of International Humanitarian Legal Studies 240, 248–253.

question upon which public international law has anything to offer;[66] whether considered as religious norms or legal standards, an armed group is free to dictate its own laws, which remain in all cases subject to the limits imposed by international humanitarian and human rights law. The Islamic State categorically spurned the legitimacy of positive law (*qawanīn wad'īyya*),[67] purporting to adjudicate all disputes "only according to the law of God".[68] The group denied any legitimacy to any state, rejected the idea of state sovereignty and the validity of the international legal order.[69] The Islamic State's disdain for man-made laws ostensibly extended to judges and lawyers as well, who were "among the first people targeted by the Islamic State upon capturing a new area because they symbolize[d] an illegitimate legal order".[70] A fatwah was issued by the group declaring that the legal profession was sinful.[71] Several lawyers accordingly were executed on charges of apostasy and, tellingly, the group's court in Aleppo reportedly bore a sign announcing "No dogs or lawyers allowed".[72]

In line with its condemnation of man-made laws, the Islamic State mostly limited itself to codifying only widely accepted Islamic legal rules.[73] Thus the group selectively codified the few crimes for which the Qur'an specifically provides a punishment (known as *hudūd* crimes), although it also dispensed "discretionary punishments" (known as *ta'zir*) for ones that are not.[74] In areas that fell under its

[66] ibid 254.

[67] "The standard jihadist critique of positive law has been explained in great detail by the al-Qaeda–affiliated scholar Muhammad al-Maqdisi, who has argued that man-made laws are analogous to polytheistic idols and therefore violate tawhīd (the Islamic requirement of a monotheistic belief in God)". Revkin (n 6) 12. See also Abu Muhammad al-Maqdisi, *Kashf Shubhāt al-Mujādilīn 'an'Asākir al-Shirk wa-Ansār al-Qawānīn* (1999), online: <https://archive.org/details/S6d2w,28>.

[68] Al-Battār Media Foundation, Raqqa Province, 'Arrest of a Cell of Extremists' (2015), online: <https://web.archive.org/web/20160323201354/https://s04.justpaste.it/pdf/Btaar-tf-gholah-justpaste-it-953848.pdf>, 5. See also Revkin (n 6) 12.

[69] Bazcko and others (n 18) 26–27.

[70] Revkin (n 6) 12.

[71] Sputnik News, '"Sinful Profession": How Daesh Forced Out Thousands of Lawyers From Syria' (5 August 2017), online: <https://sputniknews.com/middleeast/201708051056211802-syrian-lawyers-forced-to-flee/> accessed 23 July 2020.

[72] See, e.g., Islamic State Media Office, 'Photographic Report: Implementation of the Hadd Punishment on Three Spies, One Lawyer, and One Apostate Ismaili' (8 January 2015), cited in Revkin (n 6) 12; Cole Bunzel, 'The Islamic State's Mufti on Trial: The Saga of the "Silsila 'Ilmiyya"' (2018) 11 CTC Sentinel 14. Tellingly again, upon capturing Raqqa and Mosul, the group issued pamphlets announcing "the release of the people from the rotten shackles of positive law". See The Islamic State, 'Wathīqat al-Madīnah' (13 September 2014), online: <https://web.archive.org/web/20160530071604/http://1.bp.blogspot.com/-Tv8Nm1G1VxM/VBXdeYnHvpI/AAAAAAAAJi0/Tlt0hnxgVXE/s1600/proxy.jpg>; The Islamic State, 'Wathīqat al-Madīnah' (13 September 2014), online: <https://web.archive.org/web/20160530071520/https://justpaste.it/Nenwa>.

[73] Revkin (n 6) 12. The group generally asserted that "that there is no need to write down the rules of the *sharī'a* because they have already been expressed in the primary texts of revelation. For this reason, the caliph is understood as a mere custodian of divine law, rather than a lawmaker himself". ibid.

[74] "These lesser punishments may also be implemented in cases where a person has been accused of a *hadd* crime, but the evidence is insufficient for a conviction". Revkin (n 6) 17. For instance, an alleged thief in western Iraq was given a *ta'zīr* punishment of public whipping, as opposed to the *hadd*

control, the Islamic State issued a public proclamation listing crimes and their punishment. *Hudūd* crimes that were punishable by death included "Blasphemy of God", "Blasphemy of the Prophet", "Blasphemy of Islam", adultery (if married, otherwise punished by 100 lashes and exile), sodomy (for both parties), spying, apostasy, murder, armed robbery causing death (execution by crucifixion); theft was punishable by amputation of the hand; armed robbery by amputation of right hand and left leg; and "terrorizing the people" by exile.[75] The resulting body of criminal law was one that harshly regulated civilians' behaviour in furtherance of the Islamic State's military and ideological aims.[76]

Inconsistently perhaps, the group also took cognizance of the modern-day challenges of twenty-first century governance, on which the *Sharīa* remains largely silent. Relying on the doctrine of *siyāsa shar'iyya*[77] (which roughly translates to "religiously legitimate governance"[78]), the Islamic State enacted a plethora of rules untraceable to the Qur'an or *hadith*, regulating a wide swath of issues ranging from the sale of counterfeit brands,[79] traffic safety,[80] and

punishment of cutting hands, because the evidence against him was insufficient. Islamic State, Furat Province, 'Ta'zīr of a Thief Who Did Not Meet the Conditions for Cutting Off the Hand in the City of Anah' (28 February 2016), a document no longer available online.

[75] See, e.g., the written guidelines issued in Aleppo: Islamic State, Aleppo Province, 'Announcement of the Hudūd' (December 2014), online: <https://web.archive.org/web/20160323231702/http://www.vetogate.com/upload/photo/gallery/79/7/560x1000/921.jpg>; Syria Justice and Accountability Centre (n 40) 11.

[76] "[T]hree general types of punishable offences [can be identified] . . . First, the Islamic State punishes behavior that is perceived as threatening the state. This category includes espionage, treason, collaboration with enemies, corruption or embezzlement of public funds, and spreading disorder (*hirābah*). Many of these offences are construed as acts of apostasy and are therefore punishable by death. Second, the Islamic State punishes crimes against religion or public morality. These include adultery, homosexuality, blasphemy, apostasy, pornography, witchcraft, and selling or consuming drugs, alcohol, or cigarettes. Third, the Islamic State punishes crimes or torts against particular individuals or society as a whole. These include theft, burglary, rape, highway robbery, battery, and murder" [Footnotes omitted]: Revkin (n 6) 18.

[77] Revkin (n 6) 13 ("The doctrine, which is often associated with the medieval Islamic scholar Ibn Taymiyyah, implies a dualistic model of law and governance. First, it requires that *sharīa* courts and judges apply Islamic legal rules in situations where the case or controversy in question can be decisively resolved by the text of the Qur'an or other accepted sources. Second, the doctrine acknowledges that these texts do not contain rules for every conceivable matter, and therefore it allows for religiously legitimate authorities appointed by the state—including market inspectors, military commanders, police officers, and the caliph himself—to issue law-like decisions that meet two necessary conditions: (1) those decisions must be issued with the welfare (maslaha) of the Muslim community in mind and (2) they must not be inconsistent with the divine rules of *sharīa*. The resulting human interpretations of *sharīa* are known as fiqh").

[78] ibid.

[79] Al-Tamimi, 'Archive of Islamic State Administrative Documents' Specimen 2C, online: <http://www.aymennjawad.org/>.

[80] The Islamic State issues tickets for violations including driving without a license, speeding, and parking in prohibited areas. See, e.g., @Syriakm, 'Daesh Issues Drivers Licenses for Motorcycles . . . And Fines for Drivers Who Do Not Carry a License' Tweet (18 January 2015), online: <https://web.archive.org/web/20160323192744/https:/twitter.com/Syriakm/status/556777973982822401>. See also photograph of a ticket issued by the Islamic State for a traffic violation in Raqqa in September 2014,

automobile emissions[81] to university admission systems,[82] rent and price controls,[83] eyebrow-plucking and inappropriate haircuts,[84] and job creation.[85] These also included rather peculiar rules that seemingly have nothing to do with a specific ideology, such as those for drivers (they must carry "a comprehensive repair toolkit" at all times),[86] shop owners (they must not block the pavement with goods without a licence),[87] as well as a general prohibition on playing billiards[88] and rooftop pigeon-keeping.[89] The Islamic State claimed to navigate the restrictions of its uncompromising ideology—and govern virtually every aspect of life under its rule—without falling prey to *bid'ah* (a forbidden "innovation").[90] The group asserted that all of these regulations were uniform across the caliphate, but that claim has been disputed by observers who reported that "the severity of the rules and the degree of enforcement may vary considerably between different provinces".[91]

> *I sold cigarettes to make some money, although I knew that it was prohibited by Daesh. At first, I sold only to people I knew, but later to others as well, which is how I got caught. Daesh fighters took me to prison; they kept me and beat me for a long time until I confessed. They took my fingerprints and told me that they would take my house if I continued to sell cigarettes. If they caught me three times, they would kill me.*
>
> *Interview, 'Khalid', displaced civilian near Mosul (September 2017)*

As regards international humanitarian law, although it rejected the legitimacy of international law, the Islamic State did claim to be in compliance with the Islamic laws of armed conflict.[92] It enacted elaborate guidelines and manuals

online: <https://web.archive.org/web/20160323155408/https://twitter.com/nawaf_boshehry/status/507969365325524992>.

[81] The Islamic State imposes fines on vehicles that fail to meet emissions standards. See, e.g., @modwnatalraqqa, 'Daesh Imposes a Monetary Fine on the Owners of Cars Carrying Fuels That Pollute the Public Roads Unintentionally' Tweet (9 June 2014), online: <https://web.archive.org/web/20160323192923/https:/twitter.com/modwnatalraqqa/status/476128189065216000>.

[82] Al-Tamimi, 'Archive of Islamic State Administrative Documents' Specimen 8G, online: <http://www.aymennjawad.org/>.

[83] Al-Tamimi, 'Archive of Islamic State Administrative Documents' Specimen 1J.

[84] Rukmini Callimachi, 'The ISIS Files: When Terrorists Run City Hall' *New York Times* (4 April 2018).

[85] Al-Tamimi, 'Archive of Islamic State Administrative Documents' Specimen J.

[86] Al-Tamimi, 'Archive of Islamic State Administrative Documents' Specimen 3H.

[87] Al-Tamimi, 'Archive of Islamic State Administrative Documents' Specimen 2R.

[88] Al-Tamimi, 'Archive of Islamic State Administrative Documents' Specimen 1Z.

[89] Al-Tamimi, 'Archive of Islamic State Administrative Documents' Specimen 3T.

[90] Revkin (n 6) 13.

[91] ibid 14.

[92] Other jihadist groups such as al-Qaeda and Jabhat al-Nusra contested the Islamic State's adherence to the Islamic laws of armed conflict. Mohamed al-Najjar, 'Al-Maqdisi Confirms the Deviance of the "Islamic State"' *Al Jazeera* (4 June 2014), online: <http://tinyurl.com/zejcbob>; Ahmed Mansour,

on the subject, "either as official fatwas or independent legal opinions authored by Islamic State–affiliated clerics".[93] Visibly concerned with maintaining an appearance of legality, the group also claimed to deploy Islamic legal scholars to the battlefield to advise its commanders on the legality of their military operations.[94] These rules primarily regulated the conduct of its own combatants, specifying the circumstances under which prisoners of war could be tortured,[95] raped,[96] mutilated,[97] enslaved,[98] or killed. Unsurprisingly, the UN Human Rights Council considers the practices of the Islamic State to have been in contravention of international humanitarian law.[99] Notably, the applicable Islamic State rules on the treatment of civilians were contingent on their religious affiliation, whereby Christians and Jews (as tolerated "people of the book") in theory are granted further protection than *asli* ("original") unbelievers such as the Yazidis. The enslavement of Muslim apostates, on the other hand, remained controversial, but the "consensus leans towards forbidding [their enslavement]".[100]

Not surprisingly again, the Islamic State's justice system flagrantly failed to meet international legal standards. In keeping with its condemnation of the "six tenets of disbelief" associated with democracy, the group explicitly rejected "western concepts" of judicial independence, human rights, separation of

'Al-Julani: The Brotherhood of Egypt Has Deviated . . . And the Islamic State Is "Khawarij" ' *Al Jazeera* (30 May 2015), online: <http://tinyurl.com/j3fouf3>.

93 Revkin (n 6) 22.

94 ILAC (n 45) 131.

95 Torture is generally deemed lawful as 'retributive punishment' for enemies who have done the same. Al-Battār Media Foundation, 'Ruling on the Killing of Muslims and Unbelievers in Conditions of Captivity' (December 2014), online: <https://archive.org/details/hokm_qtl,110–112>.

96 Notably, the raping of Muslim prisoners of war is categorically prohibited. ibid.

97 Abu Bakr al-Madri, 'The Legitimacy of Slaughter and Mutilation of the Bodies of Unbelievers' (5 September 2014), online: <http://web.archive.org/web/20160530095020/https://justpaste.it/gz3j>.

98 Kenneth Roth, 'Slavery: The ISIS Rules' Human Rights Watch (5 September 2015), online: <https://www.hrw.org/news/2015/09/05/slavery-isis-rules>. Generally, all *Kuffar* (unbelievers who refuse to convert) can be lawfully enslaved for the ends of forced labour or sexual exploitation. See, e.g., Richard Spencer, 'ISIL Carried Out Massacres and Mass Sexual Enslavement of Yazidis, UN Confirms' *The Telegraph* (14 October 2014), online: <http://www.telegraph.co.uk/news/worldnews/islamic-state/11160906/Isil-carried-out-massacres-and-mass-sexualenslavement-of-Yazidis-UN-confirms.html>.

99 United Nations Human Rights Council, '9th Report of the Independent International Commission of Inquiry on the Syrian Arab Republic' (5 February 2015), online: <http://www.ohchr.org/EN/HRBodies/HRC/RegularSessions/Session28/Documents/A.HRC.28.69_E.doc>; Independent International Commission of Inquiry on the Syrian Arab Republic, 'Detention in the Syrian Arab Republic: A Way Forward' (8 March 2018) 5 ("[ISIL's] unauthorised mock trials further deprived victims of basic due process guarantees in violation of international humanitarian law and fundamental human rights norms").

100 Islamic State, 'Questions and Answers on Taking Captives and Slaves' (October/November 2014), online: <https://web.archive.org/ web/20160530100043/; https://justpaste.it/saby>. See also Revkin (n 6) 23.

powers, and the rule of law.[101] Lofty rhetoric aside, the reality on the ground remained marred by serious shortcomings undermining due process. Judges were routinely punished and even executed for digressing from the group's official position on legal issues.[102] Others were eager to please the group leaders and prove their allegiance by imposing harsher sentences, particularly in cases involving enemies of the Islamic State.[103] The counterweight to the group's reported efficiency in hearing cases and implementing sentences was a very high rate of judicial errors: the speed with which Islamic State court ordered were carried out effectively removed any possibility to appeal or revoke a sentence, and indeed many were executed wrongfully.[104] Executions reportedly were commonplace, and critics doubt whether *Sharīah* courts even listened to evidence.[105] Reports of torture and systemic delays were also widespread, especially for political prisoners.[106] The Qur'an and Sunnah, the key sources of norms for the Islamic States, focus on crimes and punishments and remain largely silent on questions of procedure corresponding to due process guarantees, which were developed later by classical Islamic scholars.[107] While the group purported to guarantee some rights for detainees, "including a pre-trial detention limit of seven days before the accused person is entitled to a court hearing", arbitrary and extrajudicial detentions were reportedly rife.[108]

[101] Islamic State Committee of Research and Fatwas, 'Clarifying Statement on the Ruling on the Educational System of the Nusayri [Alawite] Government [of Syria]' (November 2014), online: <http://drsc-sy.org/wp-content/uploads/2015/06/ALRAQA1.pdf>.

[102] Revkin (n 6) 26. One judge was, for instance, removed and tried for opposing the group's now infamous immolation of a Jordanian pilot. 'Facing Internal Criticism for Pilot's Death, ISIS Executes 7' *Al-Akhbar* (6 February 2015), online: <http://english.al-akhbar.com/node/23647>. Others have been convicted of witchcraft and treason. Muhamed al-Muhaymid, 'The Islamic State Executes a Sheikh in Error' *al-Hal al-Suri* (16 October 2014), online: <https://7al.me/?p=6572>; 'Daesh Executes the First Sharī'a Judge Hamam al-Lafi' *Jordan News* (23 January 2015), online: <http://www.jordanews.com/jordan/32153.html>.

[103] Fariq Al-Amal, 'What Do You Know About the Judicial System of ISIS?' [translated from Arabic], *Sasa Post* (2 February 2016), online: <http://www.sasapost.com/isis-judiciary/>.

[104] ibid. In one case, a 16-year-old was sentenced to death for allegedly raping a woman in the Manbaj district of Aleppo, only to be exonerated—posthumously—after exculpatory evidence revealed that the two had been fighting over money and that the women had made the allegations as a pressure tactic, causing popular uproar in Aleppo. Another case involved the son of a wealthy merchant in Jarabulus executed on charges of cooperating with the Free Syrian Army (FSA). It was later revealed that the young man had solely been approached by the FSA to convert his gas station into a secret hideout, to which he replied that this place was not suitable for discussing such matters, and the discussion ended there. The Islamic State nonetheless maintained its decision on the basis that discussion amounted to "preliminary approval" for the crime. Revkin (n 6) 26.

[105] Sarah Birke, 'How ISIS Rules' *NYR Daily*, New York Review of Books (9 December 2014), online: <http://www.nybooks.com/daily/2014/12/09/how-isis-rules/>.

[106] Abdul Rahman Salamat, 'Stories from Within ISIS's Judiciary' [translated from Arabic], *Raseef* (July 2015), online: <http://raseef22.com/politics/2015/07/11/judicial-power-in-islamic-state/>.

[107] Askary and Hosseinnejad (n 65) 258–259. There are, of course, more liberal interpretations of the protection of due process under *Sharīa*: Mohamed Mattar, 'Human Rights in Islamic Law, Specifically the Guarantee of Procedural Justice' (2014) 16 European Journal of Law Reform 274.

[108] Revkin (n 6) 27, 31.

> *I was arrested by Daesh because I had an uncle with the Peshmerga [Kurdish forces] and they thought I was giving him information. They kept me in jail for three months. For the first two months, they tortured me but didn't ask me anything. In the third month, I was taken to a judge, with my hands tied behind my back and with a blindfold. I couldn't see the judge or anything else. I said that I hadn't done anything, but I was not allowed to call anyone to confirm that I was telling the truth.*
>
> *Interview, 'Adnan', displaced civilian near Tal Afar (September 2017)*

The Islamic State tenaciously maintained that "there is an Islamic legal basis for every act of violence that it perpetrates" and that all of its members were equally bound by the law, but that assertion seems contradicted by reports of extralegal violence in areas under ISIS rule.[109] As military pressure against the group mounted in Iraq and Syria from 2015, and with reports of increased defections and shortfalls in income, the group became short of both funds and combatants.[110] As a result, the Islamic State was forced to incorporate fighters and judges that fell short of the quality and professionalism of earlier recruits, making it more susceptible to misconduct and bribery.[111] There are reports that, from 2015, the Islamic State employed increasingly unqualified judges. While initially the group's judges consisted solely of trained Islamic scholars, the group later simply offered six-month legal training to otherwise unqualified adjudicators. Judges' lack of legal qualification was also aggravated by their unfamiliarity with the local culture, customs, and norms of the regions to which they were assigned, as many ISIS judges were reportedly "strangers".[112] Indeed,

[109] While it is true that the group routinely punished its own members—the group's court in northern Raqqa even reportedly had a designated weekly time for residents to come forward with complaints—refugees who previously lived under the group's rule report that its judges routinely favoured Islamic State members, by quoting Qur'anic verses or hadiths, including "God prefers those who fight in jihad over those who sit". Associated Press, 'Syrians Who Escaped ISIS Rule Talk about Group's Double Standards' *Al Arabiya Network* (18 January 2016), online: <http://english.alarabiya.net/en/features/2016/01/18/Syrians-who-escaped-ISIS-rule-talk-aboutgroup-s-double-standards-.html>; Aymenn Al-Tamimi, 'Announcement from Islamic State of Iraq and ash-Sham's Tel Abyad Islamic Court' *pundicity Blog* (9 March 2014), online: <http://www.aymennjawad.org/2014/02/announcementfrom-islamic-state-of-iraq-and-ash>. See also Revkin (n 6) 36.

[110] See: Kimiko De Freytas-Tamura, 'ISIS Defectors Reveal Disillusionment' *New York Times* (20 September 2015), online: <http://www.nytimes.com/2015/09/21/world/europe/isis-defectors-reveal-disillusionment.html>; Mona Alami, 'ISIS Is Running Short of Recruits' *Newsweek* (4 March 2015), online: <http://www.newsweek.com/isis-running-shortrecruits-311375>; Patrick Wintour, 'Isis Has Been Financially Weakened, Claim UK and US Military Figures' *The Guardian* (28 April 2016), online: <http://www.theguardian.com/world/2016/apr/28/isis-financially-weakened-coalition-airstrikes-us-uk-military>.

[111] Revkin (n 6) 35. For instance, the group's recruiters directly targeted "street toughs and ex-cons" in Europe. Anthony Faiola and Souad Mekhennet, 'The Islamic State Creates a New Type of Jihadist: Part Terrorist, Part Gangster' *The Washington Post* (20 December 2015), online: <https://www.washingtonpost.com/world/europe/the-islamic-state-creates-anew-type-of-jihadist-part-terrorist-part-gangster/2015/12/20/1a3d65da-9bae-11e5-aca6-1ae3be6f06d2_story.html>.

[112] This was apparent in the case of Abd al-Khaliq Sheikh Mohammed, a 45-year-old who was executed in Jab al-Khafi, a village in Jarabulus, on charges of witchcraft and sorcery. The entire village,

the group's administration appeared eroded by systemic corruption, with high-ranking commanders routinely embezzling money,[113] and some courts "cancelling" convicts' death sentence after receiving a sum of money.[114]

> *Daesh came looking for my cousin, who works in the south of Iraq. They searched the house, destroying everything, and discovered that I had watched a forbidden television channel. They arrested me, blindfolded me, and tortured me to confess that I had a cellphone. When I didn't confess, they took me to the main police station for more torture. After seven days, they released me and told me that they would behead me if I mentioned this to anyone. After a while, I managed to flee to another city.*
>
> *Interview, 'Bassim', displaced civilian near Mosul (September 2017)*

The picture that emerges of the Islamic State's administration of justice remains fragmentary and contested. There is no doubt that it proved unfair in very significant ways, denying due process in the structure of courts that failed to be independent and impartial, preventing parties from enjoying basic procedural rights, applying harsh rules, and imposing excessive and cruel punishments. At the same time, documents captured after the defeat of the Islamic State in Iraq suggest that the group's policing and justice practices did deliver justice in some respects.[115] Unlike official state police and courts, ISIS officials proved willing to intervene for trifling matters of daily life that would have been left unaddressed by the state, because the sums involved were only a few dollars, or they were not legal in a classical sense (for instance, a person insulting their neighbour). Indeed, the Islamic State was so successful in dealing with such matters that people brought them complaints from years before the group assumed power.

except the judge, knew that the man was in fact mentally disabled and was being treated at a psychiatric hospital: Abdul Rahman Salamat, 'Stories from Within ISIS's Judiciary' [translated from Arabic], *Raseef* (July 2015), online: <http://raseef22.com/politics/2015/07/11/judicial-power-in-islamic-state/>.

[113] Lianna Brinded, 'One of ISIS' Most Intractable Enemies Is Its Own Love of Paperwork and Bureaucracy' *Business Insider* (21 December 2015), online: <http://www.businessinsider.com/isis-caliphate-taxes-corruption-paperwork-2015-12>; Erika Solomon, 'Isis Proves Vulnerable to Its Own "Ghost Armies"' *Financial Times* (December 2015), online: <https://www.ft.com/content/fb86019e-a240-11e5-bc70-7ff6d4fd203a>; 'Egyptian ISIS Official Steals Zakat Money . . . And Flees with One Million Syrian Pounds' *Al-Mogaz* (2 February 2015), online: <http://almogaz.com/news/politics/2015/02/02/1850327>.

[114] 'Daesh Sentences a Man and a Woman to Death by Stoning for Adultery . . . And Cancels the Sentence in Exchange for a Settlement' *Al-Khabar Press* (4 February 2014), online: <http://tinyurl.com/j7n5ov>. In another case in Raqqa, a man's death sentence on the charge of adultery was "cancelled" after paying a bribe of ten million Syrian pounds.

[115] Rukmini Callimachi, 'The Case of the Purloined Poultry: How ISIS Prosecuted Petty Crime' *New York Times* (1 July 2018). The elements that follow are taken from this article, based on Islamic State files recovered in Iraq.

Records also suggest that civilians were willing to lay complaints against ISIS fighters, for actions ranging from failing to fully pay for a chicken to torturing suspects in a police station. While some of these complaints were successful (the half-paid chicken), it is difficult to draw more general conclusion as to the effectiveness and fairness of ISIS law and order in other cases and, all the more, in other areas under the group's control.[116]

There is a real danger, because of the use by the Islamic State itself of inhumane punishments as propagande tools, to reduce the administration of justice by the group to a caricature.[117] Burning and boiling people to death are indeed more extreme punishments than those imposed by states, and they do form an important part of the picture. While many and probably most among the local population objected to its violence, they often acknowledged that Islamic State justice was broadly consistent and predictable, in many ways less arbitrary than that of the territorial state.[118] Ultimately, all that can be concluded is that the administration of justice by the Islamic State was flawed in significant and systemic, but not necessarily systematic, ways.

III. Taliban Motorcycle Justice

The Taliban, literally meaning "students" in Pashto, are a predominantly Pashtun Sunni Islamic fundamentalist group currently waging an insurgency against the Western-backed government in Afghanistan.[119] Referring to themselves as the Islamic Emirate of Afghanistan, the Taliban ruled over most of the country from 1996 to 2001, when they were toppled by a US-led invasion for providing refuge to al-Qaeda and Osama Bin Laden.[120] At the height of its power, the group controlled over 90 percent of Afghan territory and enjoyed formal diplomatic recognition by Saudi Arabia, Pakistan, and the United Arab Emirates.[121] Since 2001,

[116] See ILAC (n 45) 133.

[117] Byman (n 46) 129.

[118] Felbab-Brown and others (n 21) 67; Cook, Haid, and Trauthig (n 54) 13.

[119] Fundamentally parochial, the Taliban have repeatedly said that their insurgency or "jihad" is limited to their own country. Barnett Rubin, 'ISIL Won't Get Very Far in Afghanistan—For Now' *Al Jazeera* (2 November 2015), online: <http://www.aljazeera.com/indepth/opinion/2015/11/isil-won-afghanistan-151101062739786.html>. The Taliban should not be confused with Tehreek-e-Taliban in Pakistan, an umbrella organisation of various Islamist militant groups in northwestern Pakistan, not directly affiliated with the Afghan Taliban, with both groups differing greatly in their objectives, histories, and interests. See Scott Shane, 'Insurgents Share a Name, but Pursue Different Goals' *New York Times* (22 October 2009), online: <http://www.nytimes.com/2009/10/23/world/asia/23taliban.html?mtrref=en.wikipedia.org>; see also Ayesha Siddiqa, 'Pakistan's Counterterrorism Strategy: Separating Friends from Enemies' (2001) The Washington Quarterly 34:1 149.

[120] Zachary Laub, 'The Taliban in Afghanistan' *Council on Foreign Relations* (July 4 2014), online: <https://www.cfr.org/backgrounder/taliban-afghanistan>.

[121] While the Taliban successfully took control of Kabul in 1996, it took them another two years (1998) to hold power over 90% of the country. 'The Taliban', Mapping Militant Organizations,

the Taliban have regrouped as an insurgency against the American-backed government in Kabul and the NATO-led "International Security Assistance Force" (2001–2014), as well as its successor "Resolute Support Mission". Unlike the Pakistani Tehreek-e-Taliban, the Afghan Taliban have never been classified or listed as a terrorist organisation by the US government, the United Nations, or the European Union.[122] Numbers are debated, but most current estimates put active membership at between 25,000 and 60,000,[123] while core leadership is thought to consist of 200 to 1,000 individuals.[124] In 2021, the Taliban controlled 75 of Afghanistan's 398 districts, mostly in the country's south and east, with another 187 being contested.[125] In an earlier quarterly report to the US Congress, the Special Inspector General for Afghanistan Reconstruction estimated that the Taliban controlled or contested over 40 percent of the country's districts in which 36 percent of the population reside—more than at any point since their overthrow.[126]

The Taliban's origins can be traced back to the early 1990s, when a faction of the mujahedin—Afghan Islamist fighters who had resisted the Soviet occupation of Afghanistan (1979–1989) with the covert support of the US Central Intelligence Agency and its Pakistani counterpart, the Inter-Services Intelligence[127]—regrouped in opposition to the rampant corruption and factional rivalries that were fragmenting the country since the fall of the Najibullah

Stanford University, online: <http://web.stanford.edu/group/mappingmilitants/cgi-bin/groups/view/367#note42>; Council on Foreign Relations, 'The Taliban Info Guide', online: <https://www.cfr.org/interactives/taliban?cid=marketing_use-taliban_infoguide-012115#!/taliban?cid=marketing_use-taliban_infoguide-012115>.

122 The deterring factor has long been a concern that designating the Afghan Taliban as terrorists would hinder US and Afghan government diplomatic contacts with the group and make peace talks difficult. Ioannis Koskinas, 'Call the Taliban What They Are—Terrorists' *Foreign Policy* (19 February 2015), online: <http://foreignpolicy.com/2015/02/19/call-the-taliban-what-they-are-terrorists/>; Masood Farivar, 'Why Isn't Afghan Taliban on US List of Foreign Terror Groups?' *VOA News* (20 February 2017), online: <https://www.voanews.com/a/afghan-taliban-us-list-foreign-terror-groups/3732453.html>.

123 See: Mujib Mashal, 'How the Taliban Outlasted a Superpower: Tenacity and Carnage' *New York Times* (26 May 2020); Ioannis Koskinas, 'Afghanistan on the Brink, Part 1' (18 February 2016), online:<http://foreignpolicy.com/2016/02/18/afghanistan-on-the-brink-part-1/>; Akmal Dawi, 'Despite Massive Taliban Death Toll No Drop in Insurgency' *VOA News* (6 March 2014), online: <https://www.voanews.com/a/despite-massive-taliban-death-toll-no-drop-in-insurgency/1866009.html>; Antonio Giustozzi, 'Afghanistan: Taliban's Organization and Structure' (LandInfo 2017) 12.

124 'The Taliban', Mapping Militant Organizations, Stanford University (n 121).

125 See the updated and interactive map at <https://www.longwarjournal.org/mapping-taliban-control-in-afghanistan>.

126 Operation Freedom's Sentinel Report to the United States Congress October 1, 2017–December 31, 2017, at p 19, online: <https://media.defense.gov/2018/Feb/15/2001878589/-1/-1/1/FY2018_LIG_OCO_OFS_Q1_DEC2017.PDF>.

127 Laub, 'The Taliban in Afghanistan' (n 120).

regime in 1992.[128] The group's emergence and growth derived chiefly from its firm stance against the strife and disorder that had engulfed the country, with the movement representing "law and order" as a pillar of its ideology.[129] It is generally accepted that early Taliban leadership emerged from Afghan refugees studying at madrasas (religious schools) in Pakistan, funded by Pakistani and Arabic philanthropists wishing to shape the interpretation of Islam in the region.[130] In September 1994, Mullah Mohammad Omar, then a student at Sang-i-Hisar Madrasa near Kandahar, gathered a ragtag group of fifty students to form the group that would later be known as the Taliban.[131] Within months, the movement grew to 15,000, as more students from Pakistani madrasas "announced their intent to restore moral order and justice to Afghanistan".[132] With military and financial backing by the Pakistani Inter-Services Intelligence, the Taliban were able to take control of the strategic town of Kandahar in November 1994, and gradually extended their rule to twelve other provinces over the next months.[133] In September 1996, the insurgents successfully seized Kabul from President Burhanuddin Rabbani, transferred the capital to Kandahar, and declared Mullah Omar head of state.[134] Upon taking control of an area, courts were the first institution established by the Taliban, who brought in their own clerics to sit as judges. According to one senior Taliban leader:

> All the judges that were appointed had to have graduated from Islamic institutions, and needed to be verified in the Hanafi Sharī'a school of law and its principles. They also were required to be able to distinguish between weak and strong points of Islamic jurisprudence. All judges were to set an example themselves in spirit and appearance, and should not have been accused of any crimes, and not be addicted to drugs. These were the key criteria every judge needed to pass, but even the Taliban with their highest aspirations contained individuals whose standards fell short of what they should have been.[135]

[128] Antonio Giustozzi and Adam Baczko, 'The Politics of the Taliban's Shadow Judiciary, 2003–2013' (2014) 1 Central Asian Affairs 199, 201.

[129] "Justice and Order" is even inscribed on their flag and emblem. With regard to their law and order narrative, see Anthony Davis, 'How the Taliban Became a Military Force' in William Maley (ed), *Fundamentalism Reborn?: Afghanistan and the Taliban* (NYU Press 1998) 43–71; Ahmed Rashid, *Taliban: Islam, Oil and the New Great Game in Central Asia* (IB Tauris 2002).

[130] Kamal Matinuddin, *The Taliban Phenomenon: Afghanistan 1994–1997* (Oxford University Press 1999) 17–23.

[131] ibid at 24–27.

[132] Robert D Crews and Amin Tarzi (eds), *The Taliban and the Crisis of Afghanistan* (Cambridge, Harvard University Press 2008) at 4.

[133] See Vanda Felbab-Brown, *Shooting Up: Counterinsurgency and the War on Drugs* (Washington DC, Brookings Institution Press 2010).

[134] Laub, 'The Taliban in Afghanistan' (n 120).

[135] Excerpt from an unpublished document written by a former senior leader of the Taliban, quoted in Alex Strick van Linschoten, 'Mullah Wars: The Afghan Taliban between Village and State, 1979–2001' (PhD Thesis, King's College London 2016) 194.

The administration of justice was a key implement in the Taliban's strategy to solidify their rule over Afghanistan.[136] They remained the ruling entity of the country until their overthrow by US-led coalition forces in 2001, whereupon the group's leadership fled to frontier territories of Pakistan, where they would lay dormant for the next years.[137]

In the early post-2001 years, the Taliban were "little more than roving bands of warrior mullahs who were trying to regroup and relaunch an insurgency", lacking the resources and capacity to instigate a governance apparatus.[138] By 2003, in part due to an increase in funds through narcotics trafficking and a thirst for legitimacy, they began investing greater resources in the provision of governmental services. Visibly conscious that they could not outfight the military forces arrayed against them, the insurgents attempted instead to "outgovern" their enemies, capitalising on the shortfalls of the Kabul government. As the Pentagon withdrew the surge in troops authorised under President Barack Obama starting in 2012, "further drew down its military footprint in 2013, and handed lead security authority over to Afghan forces in June of that year", the Taliban insurgency escalated.[139] It seized Kunduz, its first provincial capital since its defeat, in September 2015.[140] The International Crisis Group reported in 2014 that the group was "increasingly confident" as "ongoing withdrawals of international soldiers have generally coincided with a deterioration of Kabul's reach in outlying districts".[141] Experts estimate that the Taliban and Afghan forces are in a military stalemate, which may explain the willingness of the parties to the conflict to explore a negotiated end to the conflict.[142]

136 Adam Baczko, 'La Guerre par le droit : justice, domination et violence en Afghanistan (2001–2018)' (PhD Thesis, EHESS 2018) 79.

137 'The Taliban', Mapping Militant Organizations, Stanford University (n 121).

138 Antonio Giustozzi, 'Hearts, Minds, and the Barrel of a Gun: The Taliban's Shadow Government' (2012) 3 PRISM Security Studies Journal 71; Antonio Giustozzi, *The Taliban at War: 2001–2018* (Oxford University Press 2019).

139 Experts estimate that that the Taliban and Afghan forces have reached a "military stalemate": Matt Seyler, 'If Goal in Afghanistan "Is Stalemate, We Have Achieved It," Former US Envoy Says' (27 August 2017), online: <http://abcnews.go.com/Politics/goal-afghanistan-stalemate-achieved-us-envoy/story?id=49439993>; see also Laub, 'The Taliban in Afghanistan' (n 120). An independent study commissioned by the Pentagon in 2014 predicted that the insurgency "will become a greater threat to Afghanistan's stability in the 2015–2018 timeframe than it is now": CNA Corporation, 'Independent Assessment of the Afghan National Security Forces' (2014) at 2, online: <https://www.cna.org/cna_files/pdf/DRM-2014-U-006816-Final.pdf>.

140 'Who Are the Taliban?' *BBC News* (29 September 2015).

141 International Crisis Group, 'Afghanistan's Insurgency after the Transition' (12 May 2014) Report No 256, online: <https://www.crisisgroup.org/asia/south-asia/afghanistan/afghanistan-s-insurgency-after-transition>.

142 Matt Seyler, 'If Goal in Afghanistan "Is Stalemate, We Have Achieved It," Former US Envoy Says' (27 August 2017), online: <http://abcnews.go.com/Politics/goal-afghanistan-stalemate-achieved-us-envoy/story?id=49439993>; John R Allen, 'The US-Taliban Peace Deal: A Road to Nowhere' *Brookings* (5 March 2020), online: <https://www.brookings.edu/blog/order-from-chaos/2020/03/05/the-us-taliban-peace-deal-a-road-to-nowhere/> accessed 28 July 2020.

A. Taliban Shadow Governance Post-2001

In the territory that it controls, the Taliban insurgency has been operating "a law-based mode of governance, based on procedural decision making and enforcement".[143] The objective remains the same as it was in the 1990s: to seize Kabul and build an Islamic Emirate based on *Sharī'a*.[144] The Taliban parallel administration includes "shadow governors, judges and health and security officers at the district, provincial and national levels".[145] They provide judicial services and tax lucrative economic enterprises—poppy agriculture and international development projects in particular, but also more mundane things like the operation of mobile telephone companies.[146] Compared to the limited resources of the movement, the Taliban proto-state structure "over-emphasize[s] institutions and formalism", and has been described as "hierarchical and centralized".[147] The Taliban seldom will provide, and much less fund, public services: most often, as in the health and education sectors, the group will co-opt local government officials, so that the Afghan government ends up paying the bill for services delivered by personnel vetted, material sanctioned, and conditions approved by the Taliban.[148] Similar to the 1990s, the group has been able to mobilise over the demand for law and order that was left largely unanswered in rural areas by the Western intervention and the new regime in Kabul, allowing the Taliban to implant themselves throughout Afghanistan. All administrative forms are stamped with the seal of the Islamic Emirate of Afghanistan, "a way to reassert [the Taliban's] interpretation of history, that of a government in exile facing a foreign occupation".[149] The use of official logos, letters, and a standardised approach thus conveys a message of institutionalised authority, "whose behavior is predictable, constrained by rules, and not simply one of pure force".[150]

Knowledge of the post-2001 Taliban governance structure remains a work in progress. We do know that, in every district, a Taliban governor is appointed who himself answers to the Taliban governor of the province. The latter is then

143 Adam Baczko, 'Legal Rule and Tribal Politics: The US Army and the Taliban in Afghanistan (2001–13)' (2016) 47 Development and Change 1412, 1423.

144 Gilles Dorronsoro, 'The Taliban's Winning Strategy in Afghanistan' (2009) Carnegie Endowment for International Peace at 9.

145 Baczko (n 143) 1415.

146 Jelena Bjelica and Kate Clark, 'One Land, Two Rules 1: Service Delivery in Insurgent-Affected Areas, an Introduction' Afghanistan Analysts Network (2018) 6.

147 Baczko (n 143) 1415.

148 For a detailed analysis of Taliban control over education and health, see Ashley Jackson, 'Life Under the Taliban Shadow Government' (Overseas Development Institute 2018) 11–18. Indeed, the Taliban will commonly impose a tax or fee, so that the government also ends up financially supporting the very armed insurgency it is fighting. See Michael Semple, 'Afghanistan's Islamic Emirate Returns: Life Under a Resurgent Taliban' World Politics Review (2018).

149 Baczko (n 143) 1426.

150 Giustozzi and Baczko (n 128) 220.

accountable to a committee in charge of eastern Afghanistan, as well as to the executive body of the leadership in Quetta, Pakistan, known as the Quetta Shura.[151] Within Quetta, Hibatullah Akhundzada ostensibly sits at the apex, followed by "a 19-member Military Commanders' council; a 23-member Military Council that includes commanders from the provinces; a 15-member Judicial Council; a Political Council that acts as liaison with [the Afghan Government] etc.; and a 14-member Financial Council".[152] There are also designated sub-councils in charge of recruitment, veterans' affairs, education, and cultural affairs.

B. Taliban Justice

In 2013, *Al Jazeera* reporter Nagieb Khaja was invited to accompany a Taliban commander in Charkh, Logar Province, an area in which the group operated more or less openly.[153] One event filmed by the journalist was a session of a Taliban court, capturing unique footage of Taliban justice in operation. The case could hardly have been more mundane: a man complained that he had sold some birds on credit to another man, who later refused to pay. The scene takes place in a mosque, with the judge and everyone else sitting on carpets and interjecting their claims in a somewhat chaotic fashion. Remarkably, the claimant is an ordinary villager demanding payment from a Taliban fighter. When the judge finally finds against the Taliban fighter, he gets up and walks in a huff across the back of the mosque, obviously displeased, but not challenging the decision. In its simplicity, the clip gives a sense of the fluidity, efficiency, and ordinariness of much Taliban justice across Afghanistan. Not all Taliban justice follows this pattern, but much of it does.[154]

151 It bears noting that the Taliban leadership has been increasingly fragmented from 2007 onwards, and different 'Shuras' have emerged challenging Quetta's authority. As of mid-2017, these consisted of the Miran Shura, the Peshawar Shura, the Mashhad Shura, and the Rasool Shura, all marked by disagreements over negotiations with Kabul and military alliances. The first two, having declared autonomy from Quetta in 2007 and 2009, respectively, rejoined the group shortly thereafter due to financial bankruptcy, but in the interim the other Shuras had emerged. The Rasool Shura's governance structure is described as "pretty weak and limited", and the Mashhad Shura has not been doing any governance at all. Hence, for the purposes of this memorandum, the fragmentation—on which we have very little information—will not be explored further and the Taliban's shadow governance structure will be deemed unified, with the core of the leadership based in Quetta, and sub-Shuras operating from Peshawar and Miran Shah. See Giustozzi, 'Afghanistan: Taliban's Organization and Structure' (n 123).

152 Shivan Mahendrarajah, 'Conceptual Failure, the Taliban's Parallel Hierarchies, and America's Strategic Defeat in Afghanistan' (2014) Small Wars & Insurgencies, 25:1, 91–121 at 107.

153 Fault Lines, 'This Is Taliban Country' *Al Jazeera* (16 April 2014), online: <https://www.aljazeera.com/programmes/faultlines/2014/04/taliban-country-20144108610575181.html>.

154 The only in-depth analysis of Taliban justice that has been carried out so far is the remarkable doctoral thesis by Adam Baczko, defended at the École de hautes études en sciences sociales in Paris in December 2018: Baczko (n 136). The description in the following pages owes much to Baczko's thesis as well as earlier reports he produced in collaboration with Antonio Giustozzi.

The administration of justice by the Taliban is unique among the case studies in this book in that they are an armed opposition group that previously ruled the country as its government.[155] As the Taliban reorganised after their toppling in 2001, the establishment of a shadow judiciary promptly emerged as their uppermost non-military priority, both as "an instrument of population control and as a means to project [the group] as an effective parallel government".[156] Providing justice—and being seen to do so—indeed corresponds to a key centre of gravity for the insurgency, and is "practically the only quasi-state service that they provide".[157] Press reports on this parallel judiciary only began surfacing in 2007.[158] Rebel *Sharīʿa* courts were operating in the southern provinces of Helmand and Kandahar since at least 2008 (possibly as early as 2004–2006[159]), and Taliban courts were documented in the eastern province of Paktika and the western province of Herat.[160] By 2013, the UN Assistance Mission in Afghanistan (UNAMA) documented "parallel judicial structures" by "anti-government elements" in "all regions of Afghanistan except for the central highlands".[161]

The growth of the Taliban shadow judiciary derives chiefly from the fact that there is often no better alternative, tapping into "the same deep desire for security and the rule of law that helped attract the country to their rule in the mid-1990s".[162] Indeed, the insurgents' provision of justice primarily capitalises on the shortcomings of the formal judicial system in Afghanistan, which even according to the US Department of Defense shows very little progress in becoming fair, transparent, or reliable.[163] It is crucial, in order to understand the place of rebel justice in Afghanistan, to appreciate the extent to which justice in that country was never significantly the business of government. Instead,

[155] Felbab-Brown and others (n 21) 33.

[156] Sarah Schmid, *Öffentliche Gütererbringung Jenseits Des Staates in Afghanistan Und Kolumbien* (Springer 2019) 207–214; Giustozzi and Baczko (n 128) 199.

[157] Kate Clark and Stephen Carter, 'No Shortcut to Stability: Justice, Politics and Insurgency in Afghanistan' Chatham House (December 2010) at p 21.

[158] ibid. With that said, some press reports from 2005 also indirectly hinted at a proto-judicial practice: 'Taliban Kidnap, Threaten to Execute 13 Kidnapped Afghan Police and Officials' *Agence France Presse* (18 June 2005); Rachel Morarjee, 'Afghan Forces Hunt for British Man Kidnapped in Western Afghanistan' *Agence France Presse* (3 September 2005).

[159] Theo Farrell and Antonio Giustozzi, 'The Taliban at War: Inside the Helmand Insurgency' (July 2013) International Affairs 89:4 845.

[160] Tom Blackwell, 'Taliban Rule Returning to Kandahar' *National Post* (October 2008); Tahir Khan, 'Shari'a Court Ruling: Taliban Amputate Thieves Limbs in Herat' *Express Tribune* (21 April 2013); David Isby, *Afghanistan: Graveyard of Empires: A New History of the Borderland* (New York: Pegasus Books, 2011).

[161] UNAMA, 'Mid-Year Report 2013: Protection of Civilians in Armed Conflict,' Kabul, United Nations Assistance Mission in Afghanistan, 2013 at 22; UNAMA, 'Annual Report 2012: Protection of Civilians in Armed Conflict,' Kabul, United Nations Assistance Mission in Afghanistan, 2013 at 13, 25.

[162] Kate Clark and Stephen Carter, 'No Shortcut to Stability: Justice, Politics and Insurgency in Afghanistan', Chatham House, December 2010, p 4.

[163] 'Report on Progress Toward Security and Stability in Afghanistan,' U.S. Department of Defense, December 2012.

informal mechanisms such as jirgas and shuras (both referring to gatherings of elders) mixing local traditions and Islamic teachings have constituted the processes that handle up to 80 percent of legal disputes in civil and criminal matters, ranging from land boundaries disputed between neighbours to murder cases.[164] This reality remains largely unacknowledged by the official justice system which maintains a stance of studied indifference to "traditional justice" despite the fact that the two regimes do informally interact in significant ways.[165] This is not to suggest that the official Afghan court system is unimportant. Although it may handle much fewer issues, it does play a significant role for some important matters like murder and in relation to some individual or groups from minority communities.[166] Decades of war have devastated judicial infrastructures and driven out the country's legal minds.[167] There is widespread consensus that the Afghan government's justice sector is marred—indeed characterised—by systemic corruption, a lack of transparency, insufficient security, weak commitment by judges, chronic understaffing, and limited accessibility (particularly in the countryside).[168]

It is difficult not to consider as a catastrophic failure the international effort to strengthen the official rule of law in Afghanistan in the two decades since the Taliban government was toppled. Laws have been adopted in a chaotic fashion, with statutes more or less imposed by foreign countries in a spirit of complete indifference to local legislation, customs, and sensitivities, for years without any meaningful domestic legislative process or coordination among the various actors. The court system, which was ignored altogether for several years and never managed to implant itself beyond urban centres, remains paralysed by nepotism and corruption, and issues decisions that are largely unenforceable.[169] The

164 This reality is presented with great sophistication in Center for Policy and Human Development, 'Afghanistan Human Development Report 2007—Bridging Modernity and Tradition: Rule of Law and the Search for Justice' (UNDP 2007), online: <https://www.af.undp.org/content/afghanistan/en/home/library/human_development/Af-HDR2007.html> accessed 28 July 2020; see also Noah Coburn, 'Informal Justice and the International Community in Afghanistan' (USIP 2013), online: <https://www.usip.org/publications/2013/04/informal-justice-and-international-community-afghanistan> accessed 28 July 2020; Laura Grenfell, *Promoting the Rule of Law in Post-Conflict States* (Cambridge University Press 2013) 81–85.

165 A proposal to formalise the recognition of traditional justice and integrate it within a hybrid justice regime was furiously rejected by the Afghan judiciary and civil society organisations: Ali Wardak, 'State and Non-State Justice Systems in Afghanistan: The Need for Synergy' (2011) 32 University of Pennsylvania Journal of International Law 1305; Center for Policy and Human Development (n 164) 126; Coburn (n 164) 21.

166 Coburn (n 164) 24–25.

167 Soraya Sarhaddi Nelson, 'Taliban Courts Filling Justice Vacuum In Afghanistan' *NPR* (16 December 2008), online: <http://www.npr.org/templates/story/story.php?storyId=98261034>.

168 Jami Forbes, 'The Significance of Taliban Shari'a Courts in Afghanistan' (2013) 6:5 CTC Sentinel at 13; Integrity Watch Afghanistan, 'Shadow Justice: How the Taliban Run Their Judiciary' Integrity Watch Afghanistan (2012) 10, online: <https://iwaweb.org/wp-content/uploads/2014/12/shadow_justice-how_the_taliban_run_their_judiciary.pdf>.

169 For a damning account, see the contributions in Whit Mason (ed), *The Rule of Law in Afghanistan: Missing in Inaction* (Cambridge University Press 2011).

feeble efforts to build up a working state administration of justice was actually undermined by some aspects of the US "hearts-and-minds" campaign, grounded in an essentialist vision of Afghan society in which governmentality runs though tribal authorities.[170] In a pattern eerily reminiscent of European colonialism in Africa, US forces propped up what they imagined were traditional tribal leaders, including tribal courts, undercutting both the formal court system they were otherwise clamouring for and established community structures of authority and governance.[171] In such a context, Taliban judges have generally been successful at positioning themselves as a faster, fairer, and more efficient alternative than either the moribund governmental justice or the opportunistic and often predatory "tribal" courts propped up by international actors. Traditional jirgas and shuras have an effectiveness that depends on the solidity of the local social fabric and the authority of community and religious leaders, both of which were severely weakened by decades of war and directly targeted by the insurgents.[172] Taliban courts often provide roving support to remote rural regions hitherto ignored by Kabul and are not fixed in urban centres like most government facilities.[173] When it comes to enforcement, the group's intimidating reputation also ranks as a comparative advantage, with most Afghans acutely aware that disobeying a Taliban ruling would likely end with a midnight visit by a guerrilla squad.

Accessibility and efficiency aside, the low cost and high expediency of Taliban courts are also cited as noteworthy advantages over their government counterparts. One resident of Kandahar province tellingly explains: "I don't like our current government at all, and I don't really like the Taliban, either. But I can either spend months in the government court and pay bribes, or I can go to the Taliban and have the matter settled in one day".[174] The one-day mention may be taken as an overstatement: more recent and precise surveys estimate the average times to obtain a decision from a Taliban court to be nine days for a simple unpaid debt, six weeks for family issues like divorce or custody, and three months for more complex property and inheritance disputes.[175] On the other hand,

[170] Baczko (n 136) 163; Geoffrey Swenson, 'Why U.S. Efforts to Promote the Rule of Law in Afghanistan Failed' (2017) 42 International Security 114, 151.

[171] Roberto J González, *Militarizing Culture: Essays on the Warfare State* (Routledge 2016) 153–172; the classic reference is Terence Ranger, 'The Invention of Tradition in Colonial Africa' in Eric Hobsbawm and Terence Ranger (eds), *The Invention of Traditions* (Cambridge University Press 1983).

[172] John Braithwaite and Ali Wardak, 'War, Crime, Justice and Social Order in Afghanistan' in K Jaishankar (ed), *Routledge Handbook of South Asian Criminology* (Routledge 2019) 181; Coburn (n 164) 30.

[173] 'Why the Taliban Are So Strong in Afghanistan' *BBC* (2 February 2012).

[174] Tom A Peter, 'Leery of Courts, Afghans Seek Taliban Justice' *USA Today* (7 March 2012); Dan Murphy, 'Dent in Afghan War Strategy: Why Kandahar Locals Turn to Taliban' *Christian Science Monitor* (6 July 2010).

[175] Ashley Jackson and Florian Weigand, 'Rebel Rule of Law: Taliban Courts in the West and North-West of Afghanistan' (Overseas Development Institute 2020) 6, online: <https://www.odi.org/

there is no exaggeration when it comes to corruption of the Afghan judiciary. To point, Afghanistan was near the bottom of the latest Corruption Perceptions Index in 2020,[176] and its government has been described by Sarah Chayes as a "vertically integrated organised criminal syndicate".[177] Despite receiving over a billion dollars in international development aid since 2001, the state judiciary stands largely scorned by everyday Afghans as the most corrupt part of government, with a common refrain—even in Kabul—being that "to settle a dispute over your farm in court, you must first sell your chickens, your cows and your wife".[178] Perhaps most significantly, the Taliban also enjoy the comparative advantage of religious legitimacy.[179] Against the remote rulings of state courts that often appear "alien and contrary to local customs and norms", the Taliban bring a moralistic rhetoric based on *Sharīʿa*.[180] While the secular codes of law used by Kabul are often unknown, misunderstood, or even disdained, the Taliban apply the familiar and widely accepted code of Islamic law—at least their own Pashtun variation of it.[181]

In its embryonic stages, the Taliban shadow judiciary was typically administered by local commanders and itinerant mullahs sympathetic to their cause, "without an organized and centralized effort to recruit and deploy judges".[182] By 2007, the group had taken its first steps towards establishing a centralised control over its courts, founding a *Qaziano Komitah* ("judicial committee") composed of 20 judges based in Quetta.[183] It is now estimated that the Taliban judiciary comprises over 500 judges, in principle with the qualification of *mawlawis* (fully educated Islamic scholars), supported by local elders with a reputation as effective problem-solvers.[184] Judicial candidates are selected from among graduates of

publications/16914-rebel-rule-law-taliban-courts-west-and-north-west-afghanistan> accessed 28 July 2020.

[176] Ranked 165th out of 198 countries: Transparency International (2020), online: <https://www.transparency.org/en/countries/afghanistan>.

[177] Sarah Chayes, *Thieves of State: Why Corruption Threatens Global Security* (WW Norton 2015) 62.

[178] Azam Ahmed, 'Taliban Justice Gains Favor as Official Afghan Courts Fail' *New York Times* (31 January 2015), online: <https://www.nytimes.com/2015/02/01/world/asia/taliban-justice-gains-favor-as-official-afghan-courts-fail.html>; Center for Policy and Human Development (n 164) 72; Braithwaite and Wardak (n 172) 180.

[179] Rachel Martin, 'Afghan Justice System Fails to Win Public Trust' *National Public Radio* (5 April 2006); Nadjma Yassari, Mohammad Hamid Saboory, and Jan Michiel Otto, 'Sharia and National Law in Afghanistan', *Sharia Incorporated—A Comparative Overview of the Legal Systems of Twelve Muslim Countries in Past and Present* (Leiden University Press 2010).

[180] Integrity Watch Afghanistan (n 168) 35.

[181] Niels Terpstra, 'Rebel Governance, Rebel Legitimacy, and External Intervention: Assessing Three Phases of Taliban Rule in Afghanistan' [2020] Small Wars & Insurgencies 1.

[182] Giustozzi and Baczko (n 128) 207.

[183] ibid.

[184] See: Baczko (n 136) 226; Frank Ledwidge, *Rebel Law: Insurgents, Courts and Justice in Modern Conflict* (Hurst & Company 2017) 69.

Hanafi madrasas by way of a written exam, described as a series of about twenty fact-patterns that the candidates must decide in a period of three hours. They are chosen essentially on the basis of knowledge of *Sharīʿa* jurisprudence, although piousness, good character, and previous experience as a fighter in the armed group are said to play a role as well.[185] Once appointed, Taliban judges enjoy a respectable salary, higher than what most instructors are paid at madrasas.[186]

At a structural level, Taliban courts are integrated into a hierarchal but largely decentralised chain that begins with a central judicial committee based in Pakistan, mentioned earlier, which appoints, moves, and removes judges, manages the administrative dimensions of the justice system, and liaises with the provinces regarding general directives. The central judicial committee seldom gets involved in the substantive activities of the courts.[187] Overseeing the daily activities of the courts are provincial judicial councils, operating under the authority of provincial military commissions that have responsibility for both armed operations and governance activities. Unlike the central judicial committee, provincial military commissions and their judicial councils are closely involved in the day-to-day operation of Taliban justice. Judges are convened to a meeting every Friday to discuss the courts' activities, receive approval by the commission for their decisions, and be informed of the Taliban's directives.[188]

In the grand scheme of the insurgents' judiciary, every district under their control has a trial court, whose decisions may be appealed to the provincial court of appeal. In practice, however, not all provinces have an operational court of appeal, with most disputes concluding at the first instance. In the districts with a lighter Taliban footprint, the local commander handles the simpler cases himself and seeks the intervention of a judge for the more serious or contentious cases.[189] There is a supreme court, which in theory acts as the apex instance of appeal for the entire country, ostensibly sitting in Nauzad, in Helmand province, but with an antenna in Peshawar, Pakistan. The supreme court is said to receive twenty to twenty-five appeals a day from the various provinces of Afghanistan. The uppermost institution within the rebel judiciary is the court of cassation, which has the authority to revise decisions of the supreme court. The court of cassation also sits in Helmand province, Sangin district, but like the supreme court reportedly more often operates over the Pakistani border, beyond the reach of coalition forces.[190]

185 Baczko (n 136) 227–230.

186 Integrity Watch Afghanistan (n 168) 19.

187 Giustozzi, 'Hearts, Minds, and the Barrel of a Gun: The Taliban's Shadow Government' (n 138); Ledwidge (n 184) 68.

188 Baczko (n 136) 210–211.

189 Jackson (n 148) 19.

190 Baczko (n 136) 208–209; Integrity Watch Afghanistan (n 168) 22. The appeals procedures seem quite complex, regulated by a document titled the "Judiciary Courts Administrative Manual": "Letter from the High Office of the Court of the Afghanistan Islamic Emirate to Human Rights Watch, 6

It can take a significant amount of time for a case dealing with a serious crime to proceed through the Taliban judicial apparatus. For example, a man was arrested by the Taliban in early 2018, accused of killing a man in order to steal his motorcycle; it took more than a year for his case to be heard by three different Taliban courts, which eventually confirmed the guilty verdict and sentenced the accused to death by hanging in early 2019.[191]

Turning to the judiciary's technical functioning, the procedure before Taliban courts is best described as structured and comprehensive, but also summary.[192] A systematic rotation of judges across districts and provinces generally sees to the consistency and uniformity of applicable procedures nationwide: judges will normally not spend more than six months in a given district before being transferred to a district in a different province.[193] They are often assisted by local mullahs, also paid by the Taliban, who provide local knowledge and ensure a degree of continuity despite the frequent rotation of judges. Cases can be brought to the court by approaching the judge, via a Taliban command or an elder who has the necessary phone number. There are no written proceedings for simple cases until the issuance of the judgment, though judges often take notes during the trial.[194] For more complex civil cases, the claimant must produce a written statement of claim, to which the defendant also replies in writing, sometimes with the assistance elders or mullahs.[195] Notice of a claim is given by the Taliban either by phone or in writing. If the defendant fails to appear, the Taliban will send someone to bring over the individual, even from areas under government control, with any travel cost to be covered by the reluctant party. This even extends to government officials, who are said to have been given safe-conduct assurances by the Taliban so that they can appear in their court.[196]

The procedure in a Taliban court largely resembles a traditional *Sharīʿa* court hearing, where parties are heard in public before a judge, who then makes his own enquiries. The delivery of a ruling can take only a few days, or up to a month if

June 2020", reprinted in Human Rights Watch, "You Have No Right to Complain: Education, Social Restrictions, and Justice in Taliban-Held Afghanistan" (2020) 76–79.

[191] UNAMA, 'Afghanistan Annual Report 2019: Protection of Civilians in Armed Conflict' (2020) 50. A similar timeline emerges from two capital cases documented by UNAMA in 2020, with one man executed one year after his arrest for kidnapping a child, and another man executed two months after his arrest for kidnapping, robbery and murder: UNAMA, "Afghanistan Mid-Year Report 2020: Protection of Civilians in Armed Conflict" (2020) 13.

[192] Interview with 'Obaid', former Afghan judge in Kabul, Fall 2017.

[193] Giustozzi, 'Hearts, Minds, and the Barrel of a Gun: The Taliban's Shadow Government' (n 138) 74; Ledwidge (n 184) 68. One Taliban appeals judge reports having served in fifty-six different districts, while a trial judge said he has been posted in nine different provinces so far: Baczko (n 136) 213.

[194] Integrity Watch Afghanistan (n 168) 19; Ledwidge (n 184) 69.

[195] Jackson and Weigand (n 175) 4.

[196] ibid.

further investigation and testimonies are felt to be necessary. Lawyers and specialists are not needed, or indeed permitted, though local elders are often invited to superintend the proceedings and negotiate settlements. In line with the tenets of *Sharīʿa*, and chiefly due to the scarcity of written documents in rural Afghanistan, witnesses are central to the group's judicial procedures, and "not having a credible witness will generally compromise a party's case and result in its dismissal".[197] Taliban judges formally subpoena people to testify before them, who generally turn up at court out of fear of reprisals.[198] If not, they are fetched in the manner described previously. The court's decision will not be finalised or made public before having been communicated to the provincial military commission for approval. The chief of the Taliban Laghman province military commission explains the role of this process:

> If a verdict seems problematic, we call in the judge and talk it over. On the basis of this further information, after thinking it over, we order the judge to announce the decision or to change it. [. . .] this doesn't mean that, as a commission, we have the right to meddle in the affairs of others. We have our own restrictions, and these are limits that cannot be ignored. It's a well-defined procedure that allows us to keep track of all decisions to make sure that justice is done for all those who seek it before Taliban courts. A case must be cleared by us in order to ensure that a judge does not have any personal interest in a given case, that it was decided purely on the basis of the situation of the parties.[199]

Once a decision has received the necessary approval, it is deemed "Islamic" and can be written down on paper with the letterhead of the Islamic Emirate of Afghanistan, complete with stamp and signature. Copies of the decision are made for the parties and for the archive kept by the provincial military commission.[200] The procedure allows for appealing to the Military Commission or to the court of appeal, where it exists, though in practice appeals appear to be a rare occurrence since most villagers fear impugning local commanders or offending the judges with the gesture.[201]

Full written transcriptions of major criminal cases, like murder, are usually stored with a serial number, but in most other cases the Taliban simply make a

[197] Integrity Watch Afghanistan (n 168) 21.

[198] David Kilcullen, 'Deiokes and the Taliban: Local Governance, Bottom-up State Formation and the Rule of Law in Counter-Insurgency' in Whit Mason (ed), *The Rule of Law in Afghanistan: Missing in Inaction* (Cambridge University Press 2011) 45.

[199] Taliban military commission chief, interviewed by Baczko in 2011: Baczko (n 136) 218 (my translation).

[200] ibid 211, 216, and 264. Only in very minor cases will there be no written decision; the judge relying on the fact that the decision is rendered in public.

[201] Ashley Jackson and Florian Weigand, 'The Taliban's War for Legitimacy in Afghanistan' (2019) 118 Current History 143, 145; Giustozzi, 'Hearts, Minds, and the Barrel of a Gun: The Taliban's Shadow Government' (n 138) 74; Ledwidge (n 184) 68–69.

note of their sentence. In cases involving land ownership, the written judgment issued by the court is expressly classified as a title.[202] The issuance of incontrovertible decisions on land disputes remains a strenuous task, particularly due to the scarcity of written documents in rural Afghanistan, where illiteracy is also rife and decades of civil war and forced displacement have dislocated many communities. But Taliban courts will even attempt to correspond with (or bribe) the incumbent administration to acquire documents on land ownership, though more often than not there will be no reliable official record.[203] It is a standard practice of the Taliban, when taking over a town, to steal whatever official records are available so that they can be used to decide any future dispute.[204] That said, there is disagreement among Taliban judges as to the weight that should be given to official documents, including judicial decisions of the courts of the regime, touching on matters related to property rights or family law.[205] Other practices include a judicial visit to the disputed land, resorting to "Solomonic" tactics where the reaction of the parties to a decision of evenly splitting the land will be taken as proof of ownership, and asking parties to take an oath on the Qur'an so that their response can be scrutinised as further evidence.[206]

Up until early 2010, the Taliban operated fixed courts in well-known locations, where complainants could approach clerks or judges to file a case.[207] Thereafter, military pressure from the International Security Assistance Force (ISAF) and the growing risk of "night raids" rapidly compelled a transition to mobile courts, overall hindering the accessibility of insurgent justice and considerably shortening trials.[208] With the progressive resurgence of the Taliban, more recent information suggests that some districts have fixed Taliban courts again, some with an adjoining jail.[209] In those districts, where and when Taliban courts sit is public information which everyone seems to have.[210] In districts without a fixed court, Taliban commanders or district governors routinely travel to villages to enquire if anyone needs to lodge a complaint and to distribute mobile numbers to contact judges when necessary.[211] The procedure can take up to a few days before a judge

202 Giustozzi, ibid at 21.
203 Coburn (n 164) 31.
204 Jackson (n 148) 20.
205 Baczko (n 136) 259.
206 Integrity Watch Afghanistan (n 168) 21.
207 ibid at 11.
208 Taliban justice initially faced little opposition by the Afghan government and the NATO-led ISAF, who undervalued its influence amongst villagers, despite being well aware of its existence; by 2010, nonetheless, ISAF attacks on Taliban courts and judges themselves had intensified, forcing the group to convert to mobile courts. ibid.
209 Jackson (n 148) 19; Adam Nossiter, "'I Wake Up and Scream': Secret Taliban Prisons Terrorize Thousands", *The New York Times* (27 February 2021).
210 Jackson and Weigand (n 175) 7.
211 Giustozzi, 'Hearts, Minds, and the Barrel of a Gun: The Taliban's Shadow Government' (n 138) 74; Integrity Watch Afghanistan (n 168) 11.

is informed of a given case, but the alternative would often entail either no dispute resolution or travelling long distances to access government courts. Indeed, already in 2010, government judge positions in sixty-nine districts nationwide were vacant, which meant that villagers had to commute to the provincial capital—often through conflict zones—to access state courts.[212] Despite access to justice programmes supported by various foreign states, the fragilisation of the official court system of Afghanistan has accelerated, and in 2019 there was no state court in 146 districts across Afghanistan, representing nearly 40 percent of the country's 378 districts.[213] The jurisdictional reach of Taliban courts is not limited to territory under the group's military control: courts operate in contested districts, and people bring cases to Taliban courts from government-held areas and even cities.[214]

Logistically, the Taliban judiciary remains overall crude and in want of human resources. Depending on the availability of literate people, judicial clerks are at times employed to assist judges in their work.[215] Otherwise, the only aid enjoyed by most judges consists of fighters serving as bodyguards or personal assistants. There are also reports of butchers working alongside judges to carry out amputations, and physicians and nurses assisting during mutilations to limit the bleeding of the culprits.[216] According to Taliban judges themselves, the workload fluctuates from a few cases a day to about twenty.[217] In contrast, their government counterpart in the province of Kapisa handles 1.9 cases a day, while government courts in the province of Bamyan reportedly adjudicate 1.2 cases daily.[218] Integrity Watch Afghanistan estimates that about 80 percent of cases adjudicated by Taliban judges are civil disputes—mainly water, land/property, and family issues—and the other 20 percent concern criminal accusations like rape, theft, and murder.[219]

As to applicable law, Taliban courts apply the Hanafi school interpretation of *Sharīʿa*, applying the Qur'an and *hadith*, rejecting any type of codification or legislation. A Taliban "Instructions to Judges" that has recently come to light directs judges to consider only the Majallat al-Ahkam al-Adliyya, an

[212] International Crisis Groups, 'Reforming Afghanistan's Broken Judiciary', Asia Report N°195, Brussels, 17 November 2010, p 24.

[213] UNAMA, 'Afghanistan's Fight Against Corruption—Groundwork for Peace and Prosperity', May 2019, p 36.

[214] Florian Weigand, 'Afghanistan's Taliban—Legitimate Jihadists or Coercive Extremists?' (2017) 11 Journal of Intervention and Statebuilding 359, 375–376; Coburn (n 164) 31; Jackson and Weigand (n 175) 3–6.

[215] Integrity Watch Afghanistan (n 168) 16.

[216] See Miles Amoore, 'Afghans Flock to Judge Dread and His Butcher Boys' *The Sunday Times* (23 January 2011).

[217] Integrity Watch Afghanistan (n 168) 18.

[218] ibid.

[219] ibid.

influential nineteenth-century Ottoman codification of Hanafi jurisprudence on civil cases.[220] Because they are constantly on the move and must blend in with the general population, judges usually carry only a copy of the Qur'an and a compilation of *hadith*, although Adam Baczko reports that one Taliban judge showed him an app on his laptop with thousands of Islamic legal texts that could be searched by keywords.[221] This compares favourably to Afghan judges, more than half of whom say that they do not have access to law books and codes, and nearly all of whom have no access to written decisions of the Afghan Supreme Court.[222] Even though the Taliban is linked to the Pashtun community, its leader, Mullah Omar, issued an edict directing judges to strictly apply Islamic law and to disregard Pashtun customs (*Pashtunwali*). While judgments accordingly never refer to any other sources, decisions issued by Taliban courts and comments by judges suggest that it is supplemented, if not often supplanted, by consideration of local custom, common sense, and political expediency, especially in family law matters.[223]

Enforcement of rulings is largely left to the villagers themselves, with Taliban commanders intervening solely when locals are unable or unwilling to deliver. The Taliban has no dedicated police force, and the enforcement of court verdicts, when necessary, is done by its commanders and fighters, who also carry out arrests and investigations.[224] In that regard, the group relies heavily on a network of informants and sympathizers who supply relevant information and can prove rather proactive in tracking down culprits across districts and provinces.[225] Anyone failing to comply with a decision of the Taliban courts is likely to be found out quickly, and punished severely. In particular, someone turning to the state court or even tribal mechanisms to circumvent a final decision of Taliban justice will be dealt with in an exemplary manner. As a result, it is unusual for a decision of the Taliban courts to be resisted.[226] That said, the corollary to that dynamic is that the binding effect of decisions of a Taliban court is subject to the ebb and flow of the movement's influence in an area. Residents who have obtained a decision of the rebel court are conscious of the fact that if the

220 Jackson and Weigand (n 175) 5.

221 Baczko (n 136) 241.

222 Center for Policy and Human Development (n 164) 71.

223 Jackson (n 148) 19; Baczko (n 136) 247–249. The *layeha*, mentioned in the following pages, is not considered to be legislation but rather instructions to fighters that explain what is required under Islamic law.

224 Baczko (n 143) 1427; Ledwidge (n 184) 70.

225 Integrity Watch Afghanistan (n 168) 16.

226 Baczko (n 135) 273 (quoting a Taliban judge in the Dalwat Abad district: 'We'll be very quickly informed if a losing party refuses the court's decision. It hasn't happened yet, but if we heard of such a thing, we would inflict a severe punishment because they are challenging a decision of the holy Qur'an, as I decide according to the holy Qur'an'—my translation).

government and its allies are successful at militarily flushing the Taliban from a district, then the *res* might not be *judicata* after all.[227]

Unsurprisingly, inspired by a strict reading of the *Sharīʿa*, Taliban punishments for crimes are by and large viewed as rigid and harsh, especially for *hudūd* crimes mentioned in the Qur'an. Examples include death by stoning and shooting, lashings, and amputations. Public executions once were not uncommon, carried out "in an exemplary manner to convey a message of severity and moral order to the people", but UNAMA reports that in recent years they have become extremely rare.[228] One Taliban judge in the Province of Ghazni estimated in 2010 that his butchers had severed about forty arms and hands over eighteen months.[229] There are also reports of deviations from established *Sharīʿa* punishments, such as the flogging and shooting of an adulterous pregnant women in Baghdis province in 2010 (when the condign *hudūd* punishment would have been death by stoning).[230] Reliance on imprisonment as a sentence also appears to be rare, though suspects are detained in Taliban-run prisons while the group investigates a given case, generally not exceeding a few days or weeks.[231] With that said, the most stringent punishments seem to be exceptional, with the most theatrical often being heralded by the press. Indeed, Taliban judges appear to proactively avoid circumstances where the heaviest punishments are inevitable, often encouraging weddings and inter-party agreements.[232] The number of capital punishments imposed by rebel courts in Afghanistan seems to steadily decline: in 2016, UNAMA documented thirty-four incidents of parallel justice structure punishments by "anti-government elements", resulting in the deaths of thirty-eight civilians.[233] That number had sunk to twenty-three incidents causing thirty-three deaths in 2017, sixteen incidents causing fourteen deaths in 2018, eight incidents causing six deaths in 2019, and six incidents resulting in four deaths in 2020, despite the enlargement of territory under insurgent control or influence.[234]

[227] See the various civilians quoted in ibid 305–306, 316.

[228] Giustozzi and Baczko (n 128) 222; UNAMA, "Afghanistan Mid-Year Report 2020" (n 191) 13 (documenting about one public execution per year). See also Ledwidge (n 184) 70.

[229] Amoore (n 216).

[230] Bill Roggio, 'Taliban Flog, Execute Pregnant Woman in Afghanistan' *The Weekly Standard* (9 August 2010), online: <http://www.weeklystandard.com/taliban-flog-execute-pregnant-woman-in-afghanistan/article/490451>.

[231] ibid; Nossiter (n 209); Reuters, 'More than 30 Rescued in Afghan Raid on Taliban Prison' (19 November 2017), online: <https://ewn.co.za/2017/11/19/more-than-30-rescued-in-afghan-raid-on-taliban-prison> accessed 16 October 2019.

[232] Baczko (n 136) 269–273.

[233] UNAMA, 'Afghanistan Annual Report 2016: Protection of Civilians in Armed Conflict' (2017) 68. In comparison, Amnesty International counted six executions by the Afghan government in 2016: Amnesty International Global Report, Death Sentences and Executions 2016 at 17, online: <https://www.amnestyusa.org/files/4._embargoed_stats_report.pdf>.

[234] UNAMA, 'Afghanistan Annual Report 2017: Protection of Civilians on Armed Conflict' (2018) 36; UNAMA, 'Afghanistan Annual Report 2018: Protection of Civilians in Armed Conflict' (2019)

Ever conscious of their reputation for fairness and impartiality, the Taliban have also developed vigorous oversight mechanisms within their judicial governance. These comprise a robust internal disciplinary apparatus with two channels of reporting—judges themselves and commanders who operate in the countryside.[235] The latter, separate and independent from the judges, are tasked with collecting information about the performance of judges when they visit villages, talking to the population, picking up rumours, and seeking evidence of misbehaviour. Aware of these practices, Taliban judges are conscious of being under sustained scrutiny.[236] Judges are also required to relay a copy of each of their verdicts and rulings to the provincial military commission.[237] As mentioned, the Taliban judiciary is also "institutionalized" through a centrally managed rotation mechanism, and judges are generally not local to the district they serve. This policy also serves disciplinary purposes, appearing "to be a conscious effort to keep individual judges or commanders insulated from involvement in personal and tribal politicking, from building up personal power bases, and from displaying favouritism and abusing their positions of power in their home districts".[238]

The role of "external" oversight within the Taliban rebel judiciary is essentially fulfilled by community elders who report cases of corruption or misbehaviour to the group's leadership. The weight of these reports varies ostensibly from region to region, contingent on the influence of local commanders and elders within the community. In some areas, complaints can be lodged through what resembles a rudimentary "ombudsman" system.[239] In practice, it appears to simply consist of villagers approaching a local Taliban official to ask him to intercede on their behalf and convey their concerns to a higher Taliban authority. The assessment of Integrity Watch Afghanistan is that "[m]ost villagers will however fear taking such an approach and only those best connected to the Taliban really have this option".[240]

As regards the laws of warfare, the Taliban issued in 2006 a comprehensive manual of rules, called the *layeha*, which was updated twice, in May 2009 and May 2010.[241] The *layeha* reads significantly like a code of military justice or

31–32; UNAMA, 'Afghanistan Annual Report 2019' (n 191) 50; UNAMA, 'Afghanistan Annual Report 2020: Protection of Civilians in Armed Conflict' (2021) 59.

235 Giustozzi, 'Hearts, Minds, and the Barrel of a Gun: The Taliban's Shadow Government' (n 138) 75; Ledwidge (n 184) 71.

236 Integrity Watch Afghanistan (n 168) 28; Baczko (n 136) 218–219.

237 Baczko (n 143) 1428.

238 Integrity Watch Afghanistan (n 168) 28.

239 Kilcullen (n 198) 46–47.

240 Integrity Watch Afghanistan (n 168) 31; Human Rights Watch (n 190) 53.

241 Another version surfaced in 2011, but it appears virtually identical. A translation of the 2010 edition can be accessed in many sources online. I refer to the English translation by the Afghan Analysts Network (AAN), online: <https://www.afghanistan-analysts.org/publication/aan-papers/

field service regulations,[242] and is by and large a set of rules and guidelines for the group's behaviour, admonitions to treat the civilian population justly, and a framework for the operation of Taliban hierarchy. It does not make any reference to or mention of international humanitarian law, which may be interpreted as the Taliban rejecting the legitimacy and applicability of international humanitarian law altogether or that they rely exclusively on Islamic laws of war.[243] At any rate, some of its provisions show respect for humanitarian principles by prohibiting torture, mutilation, kidnapping for ransom, and calling for a minimisation of civilian casualties; others contradict both humanitarian law and *Sharīʿa* law.[244] Experts have cautioned against reifying the text, and some observers have argued that its main purpose is propagandistic, but it is generally accepted to be reflective of the group's idealised organisational framework.[245] While the *layeha* is purported to be distributed widely amongst Taliban cadres and commanders, as evidenced from copies found on dead insurgents, the actual weight that it carries remains unclear given the high illiteracy rate among the group.[246] Be that as it may, there is evidence that the Taliban has taken concrete step towards implementing the *layeha* through two distinct "military justice" mechanisms: the "Nizami Massuls"—"sort of centrally appointed military-political commissar tasked to supervise military operations"[247]—and ordinary courts' disciplining deviances.

The *layeha* underpins a distinct, important function of Taliban courts, that of disciplining the group's own fighters. Judges stand apart from the rest of the movement due to their much higher level of education and relative institutional autonomy. They play a central functional role in relaying the authority of the group's central leadership, located in Pakistan, to even the remotest provinces of Afghanistan. The *layeha* not only lays out many internal disciplinary rules for the group, making up nearly half of the code, but it also affirms the courts' role in enforcing them. It is possible for a civilian to lay a complaint against a Taliban fighter or—admittedly more rarely, but not unheard of—a commander, either directly to a higher-up in the district or province, or by using the hotline or email

the-layha-calling-the-taleban-to-account/>. See Alex Strick van Linschoten and Felix Kuehn, *The Taliban Reader: War, Islam and Politics in Their Own Words* (Oxford University Press 2019) 325.

242 Kilcullen (n 198) 46–47.

243 ibid at 85.

244 Muhammad Munir, 'The Layha for the Mujahideen: An Analysis of the Code of Conduct for the Taliban Fighters under Islamic Law' (2011) 93 International Review of the Red Cross 81, 102.

245 Shivan Mahendrarajah, 'Conceptual Failure, the Taliban's Parallel Hierarchies, and America's Strategic Defeat in Afghanistan' (2014) 25 Small Wars & Insurgencies 107; Kate Clark, 'The Layeha: Calling the Taliban to Account' *Kabul/Berlin: Afghan Analysts Network* (June 2011).

246 Antonio Giustozzi, 'The Taliban's "Military Courts"' (2014) 25 Small Wars & Insurgencies 284, 287.

247 ibid at 288.

of the Taliban Commission for Prevention of Civilian casualties and Complaints. For instance, on 31 July 2019 a civilian bus hit an improvised device on a road near Kandahar, killing twenty-four and wounding eighteen. The Taliban issued a statement on September 3rd that "Immediately following the incident, the Commission for Prevention of Civilians Casualties and Complaints dispatched a team to the site to carry out a comprehensive investigation. With the efforts of this commission, the individual responsible for the incident was identified and detained and the case forwarded to Shariah courts yesterday".[248] There are many reports of fighters and commanders being reprimanded or punished for violating the *layeha* or disobeying orders. That said, judges are also dependent on local commanders for their security and for enforcing their decisions. Some commanders have acquired significant financial or political autonomy from the group's leadership, placing them beyond the reach of this internal control mechanism.[249]

It is difficult to assess precisely how popular the Taliban judiciary is, with most polls being unreliable and divergent.[250] Overall, however, Taliban courts seem to enjoy a particular popularity that the group itself does not. Few Afghans look back at the reign of the Islamic Emirate of Afghanistan and its stringent social policies with nostalgia, and most deplore the fact that the insurgents are responsible for most of the country's terror attacks. As one resident of Paktia province notes, "[w]e don't want to be ruled by them. But we support the Taliban's Islamic courts".[251] However, the number of those who admit to reporting crimes or disputes to the Taliban is negligible. A 2010 survey by Integrity Watch Afghanistan found 2 percent of respondents disclosing that they used a Taliban court.[252] In stark contrast, Shah Jahan Nuri, Afghan member of parliament

248 'Statement by Commission for Prevention of Civilian Casualties Regarding Farah Tragedy' (3 September 2019), online: http://alemarahenglish.com/?p=51111 (where the hotline phone numbers and email are also listed); UNAMA, 'Quarterly Report on the Protection of Civilians in Armed Conflict: 1 January to 30 September 2019', 17 October 2019, at 5; UNAMA, "Afghanistan Annual Report 2020" (n 234) 96. On this Taliban Commission, see Ashley Jackson and Rahmatullah Amiri, 'Insurgent Bureaucracy: How the Taliban Makes Policy' (USIP 2019) 31–36.

249 See Giustozzi, 'The Taliban's "Military Courts"' (n 246); Baczko (n 136) 287–288. Baczko relays the rumor that the Taliban leadership sometimes has dealt with rebellious commanders by leaking their location to US forces, which then carry out the clean up job: ibid 293.

250 "Pollsters cannot work in areas controlled by the Taliban, so most polling is done by cell phone. This introduces a bias toward educated, young, and urban respondents. Results by locality are generally not given. There is no reliable census, and the ethnic distribution of the population is not well known. There is little competition or basis for validating the integrity of polling contractors to prevent them simply from making up results. This begs the question as to why people would trust unknown pollsters in the middle of a civil war": Dorronsoro (n 144) 12.

251 Sami Yousafzai, 'Afghans Take Their Legal Woes to the Taliban Justice System' *Newsweek* (15 April 2013), online: <http://www.newsweek.com/afghans-take-their-legal-woes-taliban-justice-system-62977>.

252 The organisation also acknowledged access barriers, particularly not being able to survey Paktika and Nuristan provinces. Integrity Watch Afghanistan, 'Afghan Perceptions and Experiences of Corruption, A National Survey 2010', Kabul at 77; Antonio Giustozzi, 'Justice and State-Building

from Ghazni, estimates that as much as 80 percent of legal disputes in fourteen unsecure districts of his province are adjudicated by the Taliban.[253] Another 2013 report from Tolo News, itself citing an unidentifiable Integrity Watch Afghanistan report, approximates that 50 percent of Afghans have used "traditional courts and courts governed by the Taliban" rather than their governmental counterpart due to corruption.[254] Unsurprisingly, support for the group and their courts is also reported to vary widely across ethnic groups. "It is high in the rural Pashtun areas and among mullahs and fundamentalists. Uzbeks and Turkmen generally despise the Taliban. Support among educated urban Afghans is limited, and is nonexistent among the Shi'a".[255] Finally, there is a sense that embrace of the Taliban administration of justice depends on the type of cases: in private law matters, such as property disputes or civil liability claims, many ordinary Afghans reportedly feel that the decisions are broadly fair and in accordance with Islamic law; in criminal matters, and especially the punishment of spies and informers, there is a much more hesitant embrace of Taliban justice.[256] Overall, as noted by Florian Weigand, people seem to care considerably more about how law is applied (in a fair and predictable manner) than about what law is applied (state law, local traditions, or *Sharīʿa*).[257]

As discussed, the Taliban have proactively organised their judiciary in a non-sectarian manner, characterised by a robust rotation mechanism meant to prevent judges from forming ties with the population, and nominations from outside the region to minimize biases. Although most Taliban are Pashtun, and most Taliban judges too, there is some representation on the bench from other ethnic groups.[258] Accordingly, Taliban judges are generally deemed impartial and not inclined towards any particular ethnic group. The ethnic minorities of Nuristanis and Gujars recurrently win cases against Pashtuns, who make up the bulk of the majority.[259] Shah Jahan Nuri, the previously cited member of Parliament from Ghazni, adds that Hazara people (who are mostly Shi'a) living near but outside Taliban-controlled areas even preferred going to the insurgents'

in Afghanistan: State vs. Society vs Taliban—Reflections on A Survey of the Afghan People, Part 4 of 4' (August 2012), Occasional Paper No 16 at 7.

253 Rahmat Alizada, 'Reign of the Desert Court' *Afghanistan Today* (11 August 2011), online: <http://www.afghanistan-today.org/en/articles/politics/146>.

254 'Corruption in Judicial System Leads People to Traditional Courts: Afghan Integrity Watch' *Tolo News* (19 February 2013), online: <http://www.tolonews.com/afghanistan/corruption-judicial-system-leads-people-traditional-courts-afghan-integrity-watch>; Forbes (n 168) 13.

255 Dorronsoro (n 144) 12.

256 Jackson (n 148) 20; Human Rights Watch (n 190) 59–61.

257 Weigand (n 214) 376.

258 Terpstra (n 181) 19.

259 Baczko (n 143); Baczko (n 136) 325–327.

courts, who they believed would not discriminate against them.[260] Clearly instructed to remain neutral in local tribal and ethnic conflicts, Taliban judges also seem to not take into account social statuses, having ruled against powerful and influential figures in some key land decisions. "[B]y treating individuals equally, Taliban justice tends to reduce a collective conflict to an individual dispute, effectively depoliticizing social relations".[261]

Be that as it may, the Taliban's juridical success also has its limits. The insurgents' courts have attained negligible penetration in urban centres, and are largely viewed as being too intent on resorting to violence, or indeed more stringent interpretations of the *Sharī'a*.[262] The notable exception to their perceived fairness concerns "political" cases involving alleged spies or government officials, where arbitrary executions remain rife, despite *layeha* rules to the contrary and some evolution towards slower, more rigorous trials even for such cases.[263] There is evidence of some corruption and cronyism within the Taliban judiciary, but also that the group's leadership has been proactively making an effort to rein them in through their aforementioned internal and external oversight mechanisms. As discussed, their appellate system appears to be inefficient and frail, with most villagers afraid of offending the judge—and suffering the consequences thereof—with the filing of an appeal.[264] While members of non-Pashtun Sunni minorities sit on and appear before Taliban courts, Shi'a minorities generally steer clear of these courts applying Hanafi jurisprudence, part of Sunni Islam.[265] Another group that fares less well before Taliban courts are women, who will rarely venture to bring a case in their own name, and whose claims are more likely to be considered as non-justiciable "private" matters.[266] On the other hand, the fact that a woman can bring a case to court at all is presented as significant progress, as is the application of *Sharī'a* as opposed to local traditional norms such as *Baad* (the giving of a virgin girl to another party to settle a dispute).[267] Here, as in everything, the assessment of the rebel administration of justice is a comparative exercise, and it is not clear that Taliban justice comes out worse for women than the misogynistic reality of jirgas and shuras or of the official court system of Afghanistan.[268]

260 As Baczko and Giustozzi point out, this pattern might be specific to Ghazni province, where ethnic relations are often perceived as more harmonious than the rest of the country: Giustozzi and Baczko (n 128) 206.

261 ibid.

262 Ledwidge (n 184) 72.

263 Jackson (n 148) 19; Human Rights Watch (n 190) 59–61.

264 Giustozzi, 'Hearts, Minds, and the Barrel of a Gun: The Taliban's Shadow Government' (n 138) 74.

265 Baczko (n 136) 328.

266 ibid 340–341; Human Rights Watch (n 190) 63–65.

267 Wardak (n 165) 420.

268 Center for Policy and Human Development (n 164) 97; Jackson and Weigand (n 175) 6–8.

Aside from the obstacles to lodging appeals and sporadic reports of corruption, the summary nature of their justice is also widely regarded as a liability. As mentioned, the transition from fixed to mobile courts entailed a significant shortening of trials—particularly in bad security areas contested with the government—where due process guarantees are seriously undermined. "Many villagers appreciated the quick justice provided by the Taliban, where trials would very rarely last more than two weeks, but when many trials started getting resolved in one hour or even less the room for incautious sentences grew to the point that many villagers saw this as a major liability".[269] The growing military strength of the Taliban has allowed for the re-establishment of fixed rebel courts in more districts and, as explained earlier, a more deliberate pace to the administration of justice by the Taliban.[270]

In sum, notwithstanding its setbacks, the judicial practices of the Taliban can be described as mature and effective, at least by Afghan standards. Characterised by predictable procedures and systematic enforcement of verdicts, the Taliban judiciary has managed to outweigh social divides and reduce private disputes to legal affairs, while objectivising the scope of the insurgency nationwide. Reaching out to marginal regions historically ignored by the central government, and through their accessibility and proven effectiveness, Taliban courts have generally been successful at expanding the movement's base across ethnic and tribal boundaries. The fact that the insurgents consistently threaten to punish any villager who takes a case to a government court is also a significant factor, although there is still a possibility of forum shopping and relitigation between state and rebel justice. This is not necessarily the justice that most Afghans would wish for, but there is overwhelming consensus that the administration of justice by the Taliban outperforms that of the state.[271]

IV. Legality of Rebel Courts under International Law

The analysis of the administration of justice by the Islamic State and the Taliban reveal a significant engagement with this form of governance even by groups

[269] Jackson (n 148) 11.

[270] Jackson and Weigand (n 175) 7.

[271] Ali Obaid, 'One Land, Two Rules (3): Delivering Public Services in Insurgency-affected Dasht-e Archi District in Kunduz Province' (Afghanistan Analysts Network 2019), online: <https://www.afghanistan-analysts.org/en/reports/economy-development-environment/one-land-two-rules-3-delivering-public-services-in-insurgency-affected-dasht-e-archi-district-in-kunduz-province/> accessed 28 July 2020 ("All the respondents said the Taleban 'out-govern' the Afghan administration particularly in the justice sector in addressing disputes among local people. This is largely because the government justice system is effectively paralysed"); Felbab-Brown and others (n 21) 33; Terpstra (n 181) 16.

that are more closely associated in the public imagination with arbitrary and extreme, if not irrational, use of violence. Indeed, as with many non-state armed groups, the establishment of insurgent courts does not imply that the groups do not at the same time resort to extrajudicial executions and other forms of abuses. The approach adopted in public international law, unlike that reflected in much popular discourse about armed groups, has been to assess the conduct of groups and individuals in a piecemeal fashion, to establish whether a particular act or practice amounts to a violation of a binding norm of international law. In the context of the international legal regulation of armed conflicts, there is no equivalent to the designation of a group as a criminal organisation or *association de malfaiteurs* found in a number of domestic legal systems. The fact that groups like the Islamic State and the Taliban do commit war crimes, crimes against humanity, genocide, and sundry massive and systematic violations of human rights does not in itself lead to any necessary conclusion as to the legal characterisation of their administration of justice under international law. Such behaviour will certainly inform the analysis of the legal character of rebel justice, but once a situation has been found to rise above the threshold of applicability of international humanitarian law, we must turn to the specific standards of that body of rules for norms that can determine the legality of the rebel administration of justice. As we will see, international law does not provide a straightforward, unambiguous answer to the question of whether the rebel administration of justice is legal or illegal. The remainder of this section scrutinises normative fragments in international humanitarian law, international human rights law, and international criminal law that do provide some signposts for the analysis. The conclusion is that international law does open a space for the rebel administration of justice, albeit only in some circumstances and under certain conditions.

A Categories of Conflicts and Equality of Belligerents

Before turning to the rules that relate directly to the legality of insurgent courts, two framing comments are in order regarding the characterisation of situations under international humanitarian law and the principle of equality of belligerents. Each will inform nearly every aspect of the analysis of specific rules of humanitarian law in the pages that follow.

i. Legal Categories of Armed Conflicts

For better or for worse, we have taken to differentiating in international law among several different types of armed conflicts, each regulated by its own specific set of rules. There is nothing natural or ineluctable about the categories of conflicts that have been entrenched in international law. Rather, the typology stands as an extension of the legal construction of war as a form of violence that ought to be differentiated from other forms of violence, despite the fact that the one and the other may not feel particularly distinct to their victims. Central to the differentiation of war from other forms of violence is the uniqueness of the state as the central actor and creator of the international legal system. Despite some narrowing of the gap in the regulation between, on the one hand, international armed conflicts and, other the other, non-international armed conflicts, they remain subject to different legal rules. Within non-international armed conflicts, situations to which only Common Article 3 of the 1949 Geneva Conventions applies remain much more thinly regulated than the conflicts to which Additional Protocol II applies. The need to underscore this somewhat basic notion in the context of a discussion of the rebel administration of justice arises from the singular focus on non-international armed conflicts in the limited existing literature on the subject, combined to some examples of judicial decisions in which these differences have been overlooked.[272]

While many, perhaps even most, of the situations in which non-state armed groups have established their own courts have been non-international armed conflicts, there are some international armed conflicts in which the same has been observed. For instance, during World War II, that emblematic international armed conflict, there were tribunals run by the resistance that judged and indeed executed individuals as France was being liberated. In one case documented in *Life Magazine*, a resistance court in Grenoble in 1944 sentenced six young men to death for having served in the Vichy regime militia, the whole process taking place under the eyes of US troops.[273] This was far from a unique event, as about 10,000 individuals are thought to have been executed in France during the *épuration* ("cleansing"), the period between liberation and the effective assertion of governmental authority by the newly liberated French government.[274] Returning to both the Islamic State and the Taliban, the nature of the conflicts in Syria/Iraq and Afghanistan has shifted over time from international to non-international, meaning that they were governed by the law applicable to international armed conflicts at least some of the time. The same could be said of the operations of Kurdish groups in the initial phase of the conflict in Iraq from 1991, coextensive with the hostilities taking place in the south of Iraq and in Kuwait between coalition forces and Iraqi government troops.[275]

[272] For instance, the decision of the US Supreme Court in *Hamdan v Rumsfeld*, 548 US 557 (2006).
[273] John Osborne, 'Death at Dusk in Grenoble' *Life Magazine* (2 October 1944) 69.
[274] See: Denis Salas, 'La Transition démocratique française après la seconde guerre mondiale' (2019) 29 Histoire de la justice 215, 216; Peter Novick, *The Resistance versus Vichy: The Purge of Collaborators in Liberated France* (Columbia University Press 1968).
[275] For a discussion of Iraqi Kurdish groups, see Chapter 4, Section I.

Rebel courts can also be envisioned in a different sort of international armed conflict, pursuant to Article 1(4) of Additional Protocol I. According to this provision, wars of national liberation fought by a people against a colonial, racist, or alien regime are to be characterised as international armed conflicts and subject to the full application of the 1949 Geneva Conventions and Additional Protocol I. In 2015, the Polisario Front issued the only declaration under Article 96(3) of Protocol I that has been accepted by Switzerland as the depository of the Geneva Conventions, with the consequence that the lingering conflict between the Polisario Front and Morocco over the territory of Western Sahara became deemed an international armed conflict.[276]

The full legal implications of this classification remain contested. Under the terms of Article 1(4), the conflict simply becomes an international armed conflict, and the full array of relevant norms becomes applicable to all belligerents, the state as well as the national liberation movement. This is specified in Article 96(3) of Protocol I, which provides that the declaration of acceptance by the non-state group means that the latter "assumes the same rights and obligations as those which have been assumed by a High Contracting Party to the Conventions and this Protocol". Despite a rather absolute statement that the plain meaning of the treaty should be accepted, that is, that the non-state liberation movement has the same rights and obligations as the state, even the ICRC in its commentary noted that this calls for some modulation.[277] For instance, the Conventions and Protocol often make reference to nationality, which will be awkward to transpose to national liberation wars, in which a notion of allegiance will be better suited.[278] Likewise, the regime of belligerent occupation cannot be transposed to the exercise of authority of a national liberation movement over a territory and population without some alterations to treaty provisions.[279] Coming back to the administration of justice, all of this begs the question of the extent to which a national liberation movement, as a non-state entity, is granted a right to establish its

[276] Andrew Clapham, 'The Concept of International Armed Conflict' in Andrew Clapham, Paola Gaeta, and Marco Sassoli (eds), *The 1949 Geneva Conventions: A Commentary* (Oxford University Press 2015) 19–21. The text of the Polisario Front declaration (in the original French) can be found at <https://www.eda.admin.ch/dam/eda/fr/documents/aussenpolitik/voelkerrecht/geneve/150626-GENEVE_en.pdf>.

[277] ICRC, *Commentary on the Additional Protocols of 8 June 1977 to the Geneva Conventions of 12 August 1949* (ICRC and Martinus Nijhoff 1987) paras 3767–3769, where the ICRC notes that Article 7 (on meetings of High Contracting Parties) and Part VI (final provisions) are inapplicable to national liberation movements.

[278] ibid para 117 (for example, Article 100 of Convention III and Article 118 of Convention IV mention the fact that prisoners of war and civilian detainees do not have the same nationality as the detaining power).

[279] Marco Sassòli, 'The Concept and the Beginning of Occupation' in Andrew Clapham, Paola Gaeta, and Marco Sassoli (eds), *The 1949 Geneva Conventions: A Commentary* (Oxford University Press 2015) paras 55–56 (suggesting that occupation would only relate to territory not associated with the people fighting for national liberation).

own courts under international law. Does the movement have rights and duties equivalent to that of an occupying state to administer justice in occupied territory? This would imply, inter alia, meeting the heavy demands of procedural justice codified in Article 75 of Additional Protocol I. Does the very idea of national liberation war in fact suggest that the national liberation movement acquires full sovereign authority over any territory that it comes to control, bringing with it a degree of autonomy in administering justice that international law otherwise recognises only to states vis-à-vis their own national territory? Does that seem realistic given the fact that, despite the exalted status given under international humanitarian law to national liberation movements, they remain otherwise largely similar to other non-state armed groups? The limited judicial governance of the Polisario Front in Western Sahara and the scant practice of other states in relation to the Saharaoui territory and population give pause for reflection in this respect.[280]

ii. Equality of Belligerents

These observations bring up a second framing comment on the principle of the equality of belligerents, a foundational notion of international humanitarian law that has played a significant role in the doctrinal discussion of the rebel administration of justice.[281] It has been invoked explicitly by some armed groups, such as in the FMLN doctrine in the context of the civil war El Salvador:

> In applying Protocol II to the Salvadoran conflict, the United Nations implicitly recognized that there exist in El Salvador two political-military powers in confrontation which both have the same rights and the same obligations under humanitarian norms of war. As a consequence of this equality of rights the highest level world organization has been overseeing the respect for prisoners of war, the war-wounded, health personnel and the military hospitals of both parties.[282]

The principle of equality of belligerents warrants that states have the same rights and obligations pursuant to *jus in bello* regardless of the lawfulness of the resort to armed hostilities by one or the other state under *jus ad bellum*. The principle

[280] See generally Juan Soroeta Liceras, *International Law and the Western Sahara Conflict* (Wolf Legal Publishers 2014).

[281] Note the reference to equality in the titles of two of the handful of articles published on the legality of rebel courts: Somer, "Jungle Justice: Passing Judgment on the Equality of Belligerents in Non-International Armed Conflict" (n 4); Ezequiel Heffes, 'Generating Respect for International Humanitarian Law: The Establishment of Courts by Organized Non-State Armed Groups in Light of the Principle of Equality of Belligerents' (2016) 18 Yearbook of International Humanitarian Law 181.

[282] FMLN Secretariat for the Promotion and Protection of Human Rights, 'The Legitimacy of Our Methods of Struggle' (FMLN 1988) 4.

is meant to make clear that modern international humanitarian law is fully insulated from older just war theories, according to which by definition only one side in a given conflict could be fighting justly, and only the just side was entitled to the benefit of rules on restraints on war under the law of nations.[283] The principle of equality of belligerents is further meant to reflect the principle of the sovereign equality of states, all endowed with the same international legal personality despite radical differences that may exist among states as regards their military and political power. At the core of the principle of equality of belligerents is the idea of reciprocity, corresponding to the acknowledgment that the fact that the laws of war are equally binding on all states during an armed conflict plays a vital rule in stimulating compliance by belligerents. This remains so despite statements aiming to underplay the significance of reciprocity in international humanitarian law in the name of a desire for the humanisation of the laws of war.[284]

The extent to which the principle of the equality of belligerents also obtains in non-international armed conflicts is a matter of considerably less certainty. There are two differences between international and non-international conflicts that stand as obstacles to the straightforward transposition of the principle of equality of belligerents to the latter type of conflicts. The first is that there is no equivalent for the internal use of force to the *jus ad bellum* applicable to the use of force by states in their international relations. There are some restrictions to the type and degree of force that can be used in a non-international armed conflict, but these reflect a *jus in bello interno* rather than a *jus ad bellum internum* or a *jus contra bellum internum*.[285] As a result, in relation to internal armed conflicts, we do not find a suggestion that one side to the conflict, and only one side, could be fighting justly against an unjust opponent, thus calling into question the equal applicability of international humanitarian law and justifying the need for a principle of equality of belligerents. The second difference between international and non-international armed conflicts that bears on this principle is the underlying doctrine of the sovereign equality of states, which is taken to demand that the same rights and obligations be applicable to all states party to an armed conflict. There is, of course, no suggestion of sovereign equality as between a non-state armed group and a state engaged in a non-international armed conflict. On the contrary, Common Article 3 includes a specific statement that its application to a situation "shall not affect

[283] The classic treatment of this principle remains Henri Meyrowitz, *Le Principe de l'égalité des belligérants devant le droit de la guerre* (Pedone 1970).

[284] I have analysed this at length in René Provost, *International Human Rights and Humanitarian Law* (Cambridge University Press 2002) 121–238.

[285] See: Tom Ruys, 'The Quest for an Internal Jus Ad Bellum: International Law's Missing Link, Mere Distraction or Pandora's Box?' in Claus Kreß and Robert Lawless (eds), *Necessity and Proportionality in International Peace and Security Law* (Oxford University Press 2019); Claus Kreß, 'Towards Further Developing the Law of Non-International Armed Conflict: A Proposal for a Jus in Bello Interno and a New Jus Contra Bellum Internum' (2014) 96 International Review of the Red Cross 30.

the legal status of the Parties to the conflict". This was reassurance demanded by states to ensure that no intimation of a legitimate status for non-state armed groups could be derived from the fact that they have rights and obligations pursuant to the Geneva Conventions. The underlying equality of states that is taken as a foundation for all of international humanitarian law is thus not only not proclaimed for non-international armed conflicts, but the final paragraph of Common Article 3 stands as an intended rebuttal of any suggestion to that effect.[286]

One element that has been invoked to support a principle of equality of belligerents in non-international armed conflicts is the fact that the treaty provisions specifically addressing this category of conflicts do not articulate different rights and obligations for state and non-state actors.[287] Common Article 3, for example, provides that "each Party to the conflict shall be bound to apply" the set of rules that are enumerated in the provision. Likewise, Additional Protocol II provides standards applicable in non-international armed conflicts without distinguishing between the state and non-state parties to the conflict.

The ICRC had proposed an article in the draft of Protocol II that specified that "[t]he rights and duties of the parties to the conflict under the present Protocol are equally valid for all of them", but its inclusion was rejected by states.[288] The ICRC nevertheless maintains in its commentary to the Protocol that its "rules grant the same rights and impose the same duties on both the established government and the insurgent party", an assertion the foundation of which has been rightly questioned in view of its rejection by states in Geneva.[289] For some humanitarian standards, such as the prohibition of directly targeting civilians or the illegality of certain weapons, few objections can be raised to equal applicability. For others, however, it can be unrealistic to expect that non-state armed groups can comply because they lack some of the attributes of states (for instance, for some of the finer institutional implications of command responsibility), or it can be objectionable because it would give armed groups powers that are thought reserved to the state by reason of its sovereignty.[290] The administration of justice is clearly one area in which objections of this nature have been made.[291]

One facet of the regulation of non-international armed conflicts that casts a large shadow over suggestions of equality between state and non-state belligerents

[286] ICRC, *Commentary on the Second Geneva Convention* (Cambridge University Press 2017) paras 888–896.

[287] See, e.g., Anne-Marie La Rosa and Carolin Wuerzner, 'Armed Groups, Sanctions and the Implementation of International Humanitarian Law' (2008) 90 International Review of the Red Cross 327, 328.

[288] ICRC, *Commentary on the Additional Protocols of 8 June 1977 to the Geneva Conventions of 12 August 1949* (n 277) paras 4442–4443.

[289] Somer (n 4) 660–661.

[290] Marco Sassòli, *International Humanitarian Law: Rules, Controversies, and Solutions to Problems Arising in Warfare* (Elgar 2019) 208.

[291] As noted in the quote from Plattner in the Introduction to this chapter: Plattner (n 2).

is the relevance of the concept of combatant and the immunity associated with it in the law of international armed conflicts. To recall, in an international armed conflict, those with the status of combatant enjoy a privilege, meaning that "they have the right to participate directly in hostilities" (Article 43(2), Additional Protocol I) and therefore cannot be prosecuted for merely taking part in hostilities. A belligerent that would impose accountability upon enemy soldiers on that basis under its domestic law would in so doing violate international law.[292] The very notion of combatant is hard to pin down in the law of non-international armed conflict, with Common Article 3 and Additional Protocol II not using the term.[293] It is generally taken as a given that state forces are composed of combatants, and usually accepted as well that insurgent fighters can be civilians directly participating in hostilities or combatants. This does not necessarily imply a combatant privilege leading to immunity as described earlier for international armed conflicts. Even for the armed forces of the state, there floats a haze in international humanitarian law applicable to non-international armed conflicts as to whether they benefit from combatant immunity under international law. The debates, rather, usually centre around the possibility of embracing combatant privilege for non-state fighters, something that is clearly not a part of existing humanitarian law.[294] This leaves the matter to be regulated by the domestic law of the state, which invariably will criminalise the taking up of arms against the government. This results in radical asymmetry as between state and non-state belligerents, as the former will be operating legally pursuant to domestic law, whereas the latter will be committing a crime merely by taking part in hostilities. While this obtains under domestic law, because of its significance in non-international armed conflicts, it nevertheless renders somewhat hollow any claim that the state and non-state armed group can have equal rights and obligations under international humanitarian law.

In part, the challenge posed by the principle of equality of belligerents in international humanitarian law reflects the construction of the concept of equality. Its import, in the doctrine that invokes it in a discussion of the legality of rebel courts, is that non-state armed groups necessarily have the same right to establish courts as do states. Equality as it emerges from the ways in which it is invoked in discussions of the laws of war evokes an idea of equality as necessarily grounded in sameness.[295] Basically, belligerents can be equal if they are the same, which

[292] This privilege of course does not imply immunity for acts that constitute war crimes, crimes against humanity, or genocide.

[293] See generally Gérard Aivo, *Le Statut de combattant dans les conflits armés non internationaux: étude critique de droit international humanitaire* (Bruylant 2013).

[294] Emily Crawford, *The Treatment of Combatants and Insurgents under the Law of Armed Conflict* (Oxford University Press 2010) 513–520; Sandesh Sivakumaran, *The Law of Non-International Armed Conflict* (Oxford University Press 2012) 513–520.

[295] I have explored this issue in René Provost, 'The Move to Substantive Equality in International Humanitarian Law: A Rejoinder to Marco Sassòli and Yuval Shany' (2011) 93 International Review of the Red Cross 437.

of course raises some eyebrows—and questions—when we ask whether a principle of equality obtains as between state forces and insurgent groups during a non-international armed conflict. Indeed, in looking at the Geneva Conventions and Protocols as well as customary law, it does seem that the applicability of the laws of war turns to some degree on the insurgents' ability to remake themselves as a proto-state or government-in-waiting hoping to replace the administration currently controlling the state. We see traces of this in the requirement that an armed group must control part of the national territory and be equipped with structures of command and institutions enabling it to apply humanitarian law (Article 1, Additional Protocol II). The notion of equality that this recalls is the one first advanced by liberal feminist legal scholars in the 1970s, essentially arguing that if women were treated like men, then justice would be achieved. Later, critical feminists savaged this idea, mocking the suggestion that turning women into men was really the solution to the denial of equality for women. Women, they noted, simply *are* different from men, and so the solution must be one of acknowledging these differences and arriving at a regime which reflects a diversity of gender rather than imposing a male model as the necessary reference point and structuring concept.[296] We find something of a similar trend in the discussion of the principle of equality under international humanitarian law: however much we might push to make non-state armed groups more like states, having courts with due process and so on, in the end they are *not* states at all. But equality doesn't necessarily entail turning women into men or insurgent groups into states: we can abandon a claim to sameness without jettisoning the idea of equality. What this brings us to is a conclusion that there can be a principle of substantive equality that infuses humanitarian law even if the obligations of different types of actors are not identical.

Importantly, a shift from formal to substantive equality in humanitarian law applicable to internal conflicts does not necessarily deny the reciprocal nature of such obligations. The much-maligned notion of reciprocity has often been reduced to merely an excuse handed to one side of the conflict to justify its own unwillingness to comply with humanitarian standards. A deeper study of the phenomenon suggests not only that it has not been widely rejected but also that it retains a critical function in the creation and application of humanitarian norms. The danger here is to define reciprocity as merely tit-for-tat, meaning that belligerents' obligations must be the same (formal equality) and that bindingness is conditioned upon compliance by the other side. On the opposite, we do not

[296] For an overview of this evolution, see Margaret Jane Davies, *Asking the Law Question* (4th edn, Thomson Reuters 2017) 240–266. This of course reflects a binary construction of gender that in turn became the target of criticism by Queer theory, but that critique only further amplifies the point being made here: Carl Stychin, *Law's Desire: Sexuality and the Limits of Justice* (Routledge 1995) 140–155.

need to cling to a model of sameness of obligations in order to retain the benefit of reciprocity as a tool to induce compliance.[297] We must all at once reject an impoverished idea of reciprocity and reclaim the notion as capturing a broader normative dynamic whereby the obligations of all participants in a legal regime are interconnected. Public international law, structured around states deemed sovereign equals, may not appear especially receptive to such an arrangement. The idea of common but differentiated responsibilities and obligations is one which has made progress in recent years, especially in the field of international environmental law. Under such a model, insurgents and the state may be held to distinct obligations, but compliance by one side is nevertheless taken as pulling compliance by the other. Ultimately, this opens the door to adopting rules on insurgent warfare which reflect the legitimate interest of non-state armed groups, without having to abandon the normative *acquis* found in Common Article 3, Protocol II, and customary law applicable to governmental armed forces.[298] This will prove significant in discussing the legality of the rebel administration of justice, for it allows for the articulation of rights and obligations of insurgents that are related to but not necessarily identical to those of states.

B. Rebel Courts in Legal Context

The interpretive space created by an understanding of the principle of equality of belligerents reflecting asymmetrical reciprocity calls for an analysis of norms of international humanitarian law governing the administration of justice to map the content of these norms as they relate to non-state armed groups.

Although non-state armed groups may establish courts in the context of an international armed conflict, the treaty provisions that have been taken to bear most directly on the legality of rebel courts are ones directly applicable to non-international armed conflicts. The first is Common Article 3(1)(d), which provides that "the following acts are and shall remain prohibited at any time and in any place whatsoever with respect to the above-mentioned persons: [. . .] (d) the passing of sentences and the carrying out of executions without previous judgment pronounced by a regularly constituted court, affording all the judicial

[297] See Marco Sassòli and Yuval Shany, 'Should the Obligations of States and Armed Groups under International Humanitarian Law Really Be Equal?' (2011) 93 International Review of the Red Cross 425.

[298] For a fuller development, see René Provost, 'Asymmetrical Reciprocity and Compliance with the Laws of War' in Benjamin Perrin (ed), *Modern Warfare: Armed Groups, Private Militaries, Humanitarian Organizations, and the Law* (UBC Press 2012); see also Anna Evangelidi, 'Restraint in Bello—Some Thoughts on Reciprocity and Humanity' in Mats Deland, Mark Klamberg, and Pål Wrange (eds), *International Humanitarian Law and Justice: Historical and Sociological Perspectives* (Routledge 2018).

guarantees which are recognized as indispensable by civilized peoples". The second provision playing a central role in discussions of rebel justice in conflict zones is the chapeau of Article 6(2) of Additional Protocol II, providing that "[n]o sentence shall be passed and no penalty shall be executed on a person found guilty of an offence except pursuant to a conviction pronounced by a court offering the essential guarantees of independence and impartiality".

These two provisions directed at the regulation of internal conflicts can immediately be related to their equivalent applicable to international armed conflicts, Article 75(4) of Additional Protocol I, which holds that "[n]o sentence may be passed and no penalty may be executed on a person found guilty of a penal offence related to the armed conflict except pursuant to a conviction pronounced by an impartial and regularly constituted court respecting the generally recognized principles of regular judicial procedure". There are similarities and differences in the formulations of these treaty articles that will help to delineate the legality of insurgent justice. In addition, other norms of international humanitarian law as well as international human rights law and international criminal law will complement the analysis and confirm that non-state armed groups may legally establish courts in some circumstances under certain conditions.

The remainder of this section contextualises these fragments of legality by situating the rebel administration of justice within a spectrum from permission to obligation (i) and assessing the regulatory reach of the provisions quoted in the previous paragraph (ii).

i. A Spectrum of Obligations

International humanitarian law, as the field of international law devoted to the regulation of armed conflicts, is the primary point of reference in an investigation of the legality of the rebel administration of justice. In significant ways, its interpretation and application are influenced and complemented by other norms of public international law. Taken in a holistic manner, international law can possibly provide a range of possible answers to the question of whether insurgent courts are legal: it could declare that for a non-state armed group to establish courts is a violation of international law; it could contain no clear answer, maintaining an agnostic stance on rebel justice; it could establish a protected right for armed groups to administer justice; and finally, it could impose an obligation on rebels to do so.[299] The analysis that follows indicates that an initial reading of treaty standards signals that rebel courts are not prohibited, that international law grants armed opposition groups a right to establish their own

[299] Sassòli, *International Humanitarian Law: Rules, Controversies, and Solutions to Problems Arising in Warfare* (n 290) 486–495; Anne Quintin, *The Nature of International Humanitarian Law: A Permissive or Restrictive Regime?* (Edward Elgar Publishing 2020) 2–10 (in terms of "strong" and "weak" permission under humanitarian law).

courts, and that rebels may in some cases be under a duty to administer justice (a). The general question of the legality of establishing any type of rebel court is then linked to related duties under international law touching on the duty to prosecute war crimes (b), the duty to ensure respect of humanitarian law (c), the duty to respect and secure human rights (d), and the import of the doctrine of command responsibility in international criminal law (e).

(a) From Prohibition to Obligation

A Prohibition for Rebels to Administer Justice? The starting point of an analysis of the legality of rebel courts under international law is to enquire whether there exists a norm that provides for their outright illegality. A positive answer would make irrelevant all the other questions raised earlier, to leave open to discussion only the elements of this wrongful act and the possibility that it constitutes a war crime. At the outset, it is useful to underscore that, in most domestic legal systems, it is illegal for armed groups to establish courts, most visibly for criminal and other public law matters. Even for private law matters, for which private arbitration is an option in many jurisdictions, the involuntary nature of rebel jurisdiction, the fact that its operation is not subject to any form of control by state courts, and its integration into what could be termed a criminal enterprise, all seem difficult to reconcile with the domestic law of most states. The study of ISIS and Taliban courts highlights the integral role of violence at the hands of armed actors, for all categories of decisions, in a manner that seems obviously not compatible with Iraqi, Syrian, or Afghan law.[300] This leads, for example, UNAMA to state in its 2018 report on the protection of civilians that[301]

> [a]nti-Government Elements continued to adjudicate criminal and civil cases according to parallel justice structures, particularly in areas under their control where civilians had very limited access to legal judicial mechanisms. [. . .] Punishments carried out by Anti-Government Elements are criminal acts pursuant to the laws of Afghanistan and amount to human rights abuses. Moreover, severe punishments such as executions can constitute serious violations of international humanitarian law and amount to war crimes. UNAMA urges Anti-Government Elements to immediately cease running parallel justice structures, which have no basis under Afghan law, and stop imposing punishments on civilians. UNAMA reiterates that the Government bears the ultimate

[300] Judicial, as opposed to political, pronouncements of the illegality of rebel justice under domestic law are rare, because factual circumstances seldom bring the issue to courts. One example is the decision of the Supreme Court of Colombia in the case of FARC Commander Arteta Davila, convicted for acts of "private justice" that amounted to "a grave breach of public order and public security". See Chapter 4, Section IV.

[301] UNAMA, 'Afghanistan Annual Report 2018" (n 234) 31–32.

responsibility to protect fundamental human rights in Afghanistan and must prioritize the suppression of all such illegal procedures.

Even if all aspects of insurgent justice in the Afghan conflict corresponds to a violation of domestic law, however, does it amount to a violation of international law as concluded in this UN report?

As we can see in the last sentence of the passage from the UNAMA report, the principle of international law that is often invoked as implicitly negating the legality of insurgent justice is sovereignty. As a foundation and consequence of statehood, sovereignty implies the right of a state to be independent, that is to exercise to the exclusion of any other state the functions of the state, of which jurisdiction is a central one.[302] The claim that a state monopoly over the administration of justice on national territory can be derived from the principle of sovereignty was examined earlier, leading to the conclusion that such a reading of sovereignty cannot be countenanced under international law.[303] As a result, the principle of sovereignty cannot be understood to imply the illegality of the rebel administration of justice.

Turning more specifically to the law of armed conflicts, there is only one norm of international humanitarian law that could possibly be taken as pronouncing on the illegality of rebel justice: the prohibition in Common Article 3(1)(d), for non-international armed conflicts, and in Article 75(4) of Additional Protocol I, for international armed conflicts, of the passing of sentences by a court that is not "regularly constituted". If the reference to a "regularly constituted" court is understood to imply that it must be established pursuant to the national or state law in force at the time, then the creation and operation of criminal courts by non-state armed groups is indeed prohibited by international humanitarian law in conflicts to which Common Article 3 or Additional Protocol I apply. There is, in a large measure, a consensus that the reference to a "regularly constituted" court in Common Article 3 was indeed originally to be understood in the sense of a court established pursuant the national law of the state, thus implying the illegality of the establishment of rebel courts.[304] This is the position adopted by the ICRC in its study of customary humanitarian law, in which it comments on Rule 100 dealing with fair trial guarantees that "[a] court is regularly constituted if it has been established and organized in accordance with the laws and procedures

302 *Case Concerning the Sovereignty the Island of Palmas (Netherlands v USA)*, Award, 4 April 1928, RIAA, vol II, 829, at 838. The external sovereignty of the state, including its responsibility to maintain law and order on its territory free from intervention by other states, is affirmed in Article 3 of Additional Protocol II: ICRC, *Commentary on the Additional Protocols of 8 June 1977 to the Geneva Conventions of 12 August 1949* (n 277) paras 4497–4501.

303 See the discussion Chapter 1, Section III.

304 ICRC, *Commentary on the Additional Protocols of 8 June 1977 to the Geneva Conventions of 12 August 1949* (n 277) para 4600.

already in force in a country".[305] Rule 100 is presented by the ICRC as applicable in both international and non-international armed conflicts, and no discussion is offered of the possibly distinct implications of this norm in different type of conflict, nor is the statement linked to any evidence of state practice that would support its customary status.[306] How the reference to a "regularly constituted" court should be understood is in fact subject to significant debate in contemporary international law. I will unpack this expression presently in Subsection (iv), to suggest that the very narrow understanding suggested by the ICRC does not appear warranted, and as a result that the requirement of a regularly constituted court does not amount to the declaration of the outright illegality of rebel courts.

A Right for Rebels to Administer Justice? If, as I have just suggested, a proper reading of international humanitarian law does not suggest a norm declaring insurgent justice to be illegal, are there on the contrary elements that proclaim a right for non-state armed groups to establish their own courts? The most significant element in this regard, it has been suggested, is the elimination of an explicit requirement that a court be "regularly constituted" in Article 6(2) of Additional Protocol II. In the newer provision that covers some of the same ground as Common Article 3, albeit for a category of armed conflicts defined more restrictively, the only qualities required for a court to adjudicate criminal offences related to the conflict is that it offer "essential guarantees of independence and impartiality". The Svea Court of Appeal, in the *Sakhanh* trial, accepted the Stockholm District Court's conclusion that the shift in the formulation of the norm from the Geneva Conventions to Additional Protocol II implies that "a non-state actor in some situations must be able to establish their own courts".[307] While it may be overstated to say that this change of language "unequivocally" recognises a right for armed opposition groups to establish courts, it is undeniable that it represents a space in which an argument can be advanced that rebel courts are allowed under international law.[308] As we will see in the following pages, the aggregation of various norms in adjoining fields of international law does support the recognition of a composite norm validating the legality of insurgent courts, at least in some circumstances.

A Duty for Rebels to Administer Justice? Moving further along the spectrum of obligatoriness, does international law impose a duty upon non-state armed groups to administer justice in the territory over which they have control? It may seem odd to raise that question after discussing the existence of a prohibition and a right to create courts, as a finding of a duty to do so may reasonably be taken to

[305] ICRC, Customary International Humanitarian Law Database, Rule 100, online: <https://ihl-databases.icrc.org/customary-ihl/eng/docs/v1_rul_rule100> accessed 17 July 2019.
[306] Somer (n 4) 672.
[307] Sakhanh Appeal Judgment (n 5) 3; Sakhanh Trial Judgment (n 5) para 27.
[308] Heffes (n 281) 189.

infer the existence of a right and the inexistence of a prohibition. The ordering reflects the significant uncertainty that obtains in the interpretation of norms in relation to this question. For example, in 2018 the UN Special Rapporteur on Extrajudicial Execution concluded that rebel courts are legal under international law but clarified that she was "not suggesting that all [non-state armed groups] should be under the obligation to deliver policing functions or justice".[309] Several international legal norms in fact may be taken to suggest the possibility of an affirmative duty for insurgents to establish courts and administer justice, at least in some circumstances: the duty to prosecute war crimes, the duty to ensure respect for international humanitarian law, the duty to ensure human rights, and the doctrine of command responsibility under international criminal law. Each is addressed in turn.

(b) Duty to Prosecute War Crimes

If a duty to prosecute war crimes were found to apply to non-state armed groups, then a duty to create courts and administer criminal justice to that extent at least would necessarily follow. It is not easy to articulate a compelling argument that such a duty currently exists for armed groups under international law. There is a limited duty of states to investigate and prosecute grave breaches of the Geneva Conventions (Arts. 49/50/129/146) and Additional Protocol I (Arts. 85 and 86). According to these provisions, a state party has an obligation to search for authors of grave breaches of the Conventions and to "bring such persons, regardless of their nationality, before its own courts". This obligation is limited in a number of ways salient to the present enquiry. To begin with, it provides for an option to extradite rather than prosecute, a choice that is presented as a discretionary matter for the state, limited only by the requirement that there be some state or international tribunal seeking jurisdiction over an alleged perpetrator of grave breaches.[310] Linking this to insurgent justice, this aligns with the suggestion commonly made that if a non-state armed group detains an individual suspected of having committed a grave breach or other international crime, it should simply hand him over to the national state, a third state, or an international tribunal for prosecution, thus denying the necessity of rebel justice in this regard. The duty to prosecute or extradite imposed by the Geneva Conventions is also limited to a small class of "grave breaches", a list of

[309] Agnès Callamard, Report of the Special Rapporteur on Extrajudicial, Summary or Arbitrary Executions on Armed Non-State Actors: The Protection of the Rights to Life, UN Doc A/HRC/38/44 (2018) 16 para 74.

[310] ICRC, *Commentary on the Second Geneva Convention* (n 286) para 2988. See Luigi Condorelli, 'Il Sistema della repressione dei crimini di guerra nelle Convenzioni di Ginevra del 1949 e nel Primo Protocollo addizionale del 1977' in Pierluigi Lamberti Zanardi and Gabriella Venturini (eds), *Crimini di guerra e competenza delle giurisdizioni nazionali: atti del convegno, Milano, 15–17 maggio 1997* (Giuffrè 1998).

specific crimes that leaves out significant violations of humanitarian law such as sexual crimes. Other violations, under the same provisions, are subject to a duty to "suppress" and not "repress", corresponding to an obligation to adopt measures that need not be criminal prosecutions before a court.[311] Further, the grave breaches regime is applicable only to international armed conflicts, leaving out the non-international armed conflicts in which the rebel administration of justice is a more prevalent phenomenon. Some have argued for the enlargement of the grave breaches regime to all armed conflicts, based on the perceived general rapprochement between the laws applicable to international and internal conflicts, but there is consensus that this cannot be justified at the moment either as interpretation of the Geneva Conventions or as customary international law.[312]

Within these limitations, there is a positive obligation to prosecute or extradite authors of grave breaches. What is its relevance, if any, to non-state armed groups? Seeing as this is relevant only to international armed conflicts, the only possible impact on non-state armed groups would be in national liberation armed conflicts as defined in Article 1(4) of Additional Protocol I. Indeed, whereas Articles 49/50/129/146 of the Geneva Conventions refer only to "High Contracting Parties", meaning only states, Article 86(1) of the Protocol stipulates that "High Contracting Parties and the Parties to the conflict shall repress grave breaches". The change in language was specifically meant to address the possibility that an armed conflict deemed international would take place between a state and a national liberation movement, and that the latter would be under a duty to prosecute or extradite authors of grave breaches.[313] For a national liberation movement like the Polisario Front in Western Sahara, for example, this implies a duty to prosecute or extradite authors of grave breaches in that conflict, which would demand that the Polisario Front have its own court system. This is a narrow but nevertheless remarkable acknowledgment of non-state justice on the part of the 174 states that are parties to Additional Protocol I.

Beyond the limited conventional duty to extradite or prosecute grave breaches, the ICRC suggests that there is a customary obligation for states to prosecute authors of war crimes more broadly defined, applicable in international as well as non-international armed conflicts.[314] While there are episodes in the practice of international bodies and academic opinions that support such a view, the general

[311] ICRC, ibid paras 3004–3008.

[312] ibid paras 3013–3015; ICTY, *Prosecutor v Tadic*, IT-94-1 (1995), Decision on Interlocutory Appeal on Jurisdiction, para 80. This is confirmed by the restriction of the grave breaches regime to international armed conflicts in the Rome Statute, Article 8(2)(a). See Lindsay Moir, 'Grave Breaches and Internal Armed Conflicts' (2009) 7 Journal of International Criminal Justice 763.

[313] Michael Bothe and others, *New Rules for Victims of Armed Conflicts: Commentary on the Two 1977 Protocols Additional to the Geneva Conventions of 1949* (2d edn, Nijhoff 2013) 594.

[314] ICRC (n 305) Rule 158.

sense is that there is little state practice and opinio juris that can be found to provide a foundation for a customary duty of states to prosecute war crimes at large, whether in international or non-international armed conflict.[315] Seeing the uncertainty as it relates to a duty for states, it seems rather fanciful to entertain the claim that such a duty might exist for non-state armed groups under international humanitarian law.[316]

(c) Respect and Ensure Respect of International Humanitarian Law

A different bundle of humanitarian law obligations is derived from the duty to "ensure respect" for international humanitarian law formulated in Common Article 1 of the Geneva Conventions. The provision itself is explicitly directed at "High Contracting Parties" and thus cannot be read to be directly relevant to any obligation of non-state armed groups. This is so even in Article 1(1) of Additional Protocol I, despite the use of the more encompassing "parties to the conflict" in many other provisions of the treaty, thus apparently excluding national liberation movements from its ambit. There is no mention of the duty to ensure respect in Additional Protocol II. Under treaty law, it seems clear that the duty to ensure respect is limited to states. The position of the ICRC, which seems to garner general support in the academic literature, is that the customary equivalent to the duty to ensure respect in Common Article 1 does extend to all parties to an armed conflict, including any non-state armed group.[317] The reasoning is that insurgents are bound to comply with international humanitarian law, which generates obligations of an *erga omnes* character for all actors, bringing armed groups within the normative reach of the duty to ensure respect. Although Common Article 1 is included in the four 1949 Geneva Conventions and Additional Protocol I but not Additional Protocol II, the duty to ensure respect is considered applicable in situations of non-international as well as international armed conflicts.[318] At the

[315] Payam Akhavan, 'Whither National Courts? The Rome Statute's Missing Half: Towards an Express and Enforceable Obligation for the National Repression of International Crimes' (2010) 8 Journal of International Criminal Justice 1245, 1258–1262; M Cherif Bassiouni and Edward M Wise, *Aut Dedere Aut Judicare: The Duty to Extradite or Prosecute in International Law* (M Nijhoff 1995); Christian Maierhöfer, *'Aut dedere—aut iudicare' Herkunft, Rechtsgrundlagen und Inhalt des völkerrechtlichen Gebotes zur Strafverfolgung oder Auslieferung* (Duncker & Humblot 2006); International Law Commission, 'Final Report on the Obligation to Extradite or Prosecute (Aut Dedere Aut Judicare)' (2014) UN Doc A/69/10 160–161.

[316] Jan Willms, 'Courts of Armed Groups—A Tool for Inducing Higher Compliance with International Humanitarian Law?' in Heike Krieger (ed), *Inducing Compliance with International Humanitarian Law* (Cambridge University Press 2015) 158–162; Hannes Jöbstl, 'Bridging the Accountability Gap—Armed Non-State Actors and the Investigation and Prosecution of War Crimes' [2020] Journal of International Criminal Justice 18–19.

[317] ICRC (n 305) Rule 139; ICRC, *Commentary on the Second Geneva Convention* (n 286) paras 153–154; Robin Geiß, 'The Obligations to Respect and Ensure Respect' in Andrew Clapham, Paola Gaeta, and Marco Sassòli (eds), *The 1949 Geneva Conventions: A Commentary* (Oxford University Press 2015) 116.

[318] Andreas Frutig, *Die Pflicht von Drittstaaten zur Durchsetzung des humanitären Völkerrechts nach Art. 1 der Genfer Konventionen von 1949: auf dem schmalen Grat zwischen Recht und Moral*

level of treaty obligations, the duty to ensure respect applies to the 1949 Geneva Conventions as a whole, including Common Article 3. The duty is, in this regard, directly applicable in non-international armed conflicts governed by Common Article 3. Given that such conflicts correspond to a wider category that also includes armed conflicts governed by Additional Protocol II, all situations rising above the level of internal disturbances and tensions call for application of the duty to ensure respect of international humanitarian law by all parties to the conflict. Under customary international humanitarian law, the ICRC concludes that the duty to ensure respect applies to all of humanitarian law, by all parties to the conflict.[319]

Turning to substance, the duty to "respect" humanitarian law implies rules and institutions to regulate the actions of any actor whose conduct is attributable to a belligerent.[320] For states as much as for non-state armed groups, this implies a disciplinary regime to sanction violations, which in turn demands a process that meets the requirements of fundamental justice. The duty for belligerents to "respect" humanitarian law would thus already lead to some form of rebel administration of justice, at least as it relates to the internal discipline of the non-state group. More generally, the duty reflects the requirement that armed groups be organised and under responsible command.[321]

The duty to "ensure respect" for its part is understood to have both internal and external dimensions, with the former garnering a stronger consensus than the latter. As for internal aspects of the duty to ensure respect, most directly relevant to the issue at hand, this includes an obligation on the part of belligerents to take steps to prevent and sanction violations of international humanitarian law by actors whose behaviour cannot be attributed to the belligerent. For both state and non-state belligerents, this is a due diligence obligation reflecting the degree of effective authority they wield over a population and territory.[322] This obligation is linked to the duty to repress grave breaches and suppress other violations of humanitarian law. There are normative and institutional implications to the due diligence requirement to ensure respect, including the adoption of rules proscribing acts contrary to humanitarian standards and the establishment of procedures to sanction any violation. For states, this has been expressed as

(Helbing Lichtenhahn 2009) 311; Birgit Kessler, *Die Durchsetzung der Genfer Abkommen von 1949 in nicht-internationalen bewaffneten Konflikten auf Grundlage ihres gemeinsamen Art. 1* (Duncker und Humblot 2001).

319 ICRC (n 305) Rule 139.

320 ICRC, *Commentary on the Third Geneva Convention* (Cambridge University Press 2020) paras 176–182.

321 ICRC, *Commentary on the Second Geneva Convention* (n 286) para 154. This group duty is linked to the doctrine of superior or command responsibility, relevant to individual criminal responsibility, to which I turn shortly.

322 Geiß (n 317) 118.

a requirement that humanitarian law be incorporated into domestic law and that domestic organs, including courts, act to ensure compliance by way of a *dédoublement fonctionnel*.[323] Once it is agreed that non-state armed groups are subject to the duty to ensure respect, it follows that the groups must likewise adopt rules and operate institutions that will prevent and punish violations of international humanitarian law by any actors, whether or not their actions can be imputed to the armed groups. In so doing, rebels must of course not breach other applicable international legal standards, including other rules of humanitarian law as well as international human rights law. The duty to ensure respect would in all likelihood translate into a duty to operate some form of administration of justice for a non-state armed group that has authority over a population and territory.

The more contentious external dimension of the duty to ensure respect also has some relevance to the rebel administration of justice. The holding that Common Article 1 imposes obligations on states for events taking place in areas that are not under their authority was embraced by the International Court of Justice in its *Advisory Opinion on the Construction of a Wall in the Palestinian Territory*, in which the Court held that all states party to the Geneva Conventions had a duty to ensure respect of the Conventions by Israel in the occupied territories.[324] While some scepticism has been expressed that the implications of this obligation should be so universalised, it seems considerably more difficult to object to its implication for the territorial state, especially if it is a party to the conflict. The territorial state is thus under a due diligence obligation to ensure respect of humanitarian law by the armed opposition groups that are fighting on its territory. While this of course does not mean that any rebel war crime becomes attributable to the state, it implies that the states must refrain from contributing to such violations by its actions or inactions. In the context of the rebel administration of justice, for example, the fact that the Democratic Republic of Congo (DRC) blocked a flight arranged by the United Nations to bring defence attorneys to assist in a trial before a court of the rebel Mouvement de Libération du Congo could amount to a breach of the DRC's obligation to ensure respect.[325] In the maximalist position adopted by the International Court of Justice (ICJ), the

[323] Luigi Condorelli and Laurence Boisson de Chazournes, 'Quelques remarques à propos de l'obligation des États de "respecter et faire respecter" le droit international humanitaire "en toutes circonstances"' in Christophe Swinarski (ed), *Études et essais sur le droit international humanitaire et sur les principes de la Croix-Rouge en l'honneur de Jean Pictet* (Nijhoff 1984) 25.

[324] ICJ, *Advisory Opinion on Legal Consequences of the Construction of a Wall in the Occupied Palestinian Territory*, [2004] ICR Rep. 136, 199–200. This conclusion is challenged in separate opinions by Judges Higgins (at 217) and Kooijmans (at 232–234). For competing views, see: Théo Boutruche and Marco Sassòli, 'Third States' Obligations Vis-à-Vis IHL Violations under International Law' (Norwegian Refugee Council 2016); Michael N Schmitt and Sean Watts, 'Common Article 1 and the Duty to "Ensure Respect"' (2020) 96 International Law Studies 22.

[325] The episode is described in Willms (n 316) 149–150.

prohibition by the United States of training in international humanitarian law for the LTTE and PKK would likewise amount to a violation of its duty to ensure respect.[326]

(d) Respect and Secure Human Rights

In addition to a duty to prosecute and an obligation to ensure respect of international humanitarian law, a distinct yet related source of obligations may be relevant to a duty for insurgents to establish courts: the duty to respect and ensure or secure human rights. The broad question of the applicability of international human rights law to non-state actors is complex and contested. A more fulsome analysis of the issue will be offered in Chapter 3, but suffice it to say for now that there is a solidifying consensus in the practice of international organisations, non-governmental organisations, and states that at least some human rights obligations are imposed on non-state actors under international law.[327] A position that international human rights law is applicable to non-state armed groups in situations of armed conflicts does not necessarily bring with it a conclusion that such groups are bound to behave as if they were states. As discussed in Chapter 1, whereas the principle of state sovereignty under international law provides full legal personality to an entity once it has emerged as a state, the legal personality of rebels is at best partial and variable. The extent to which a non-state armed group is bound to comply with international human rights law will likewise be variable, reflecting the specific circumstances of the situation, such as the capacity of the group and its degree of authority over territory and population. In non-international armed conflicts in particular, the nature and extent of the human rights obligations of insurgents will be interconnected with the human rights obligations of the territorial state. As rebels solidify their hold over parts of national territory, to the extent that they engage in governance in these areas, the intensity of the state's human rights obligations will abate as a reflection of the latter's diminishing ability to govern in such places. In

[326] See the discussion of the US Supreme Court decision in *Holder v Humanitarian Law Project*, in Chapter 4, Section III.B.

[327] In 2021, forty-four UN independent human rights experts affirmed that "**at a minimum**, armed non-State actors exercising either government-like functions or *de facto* control over territory and population must respect and protect the human rights of individuals and groups": 'Joint Statement by independent United Nations human rights experts on human rights responsibilities of armed non-State actors', 25 February 2021. See Cédric Ryngaert and Jean d'Aspremont, Third Report of the ILA's Non-State Actors Committee (2014), online: <http://www.ila-hq.org/en/committees/index.cfm/cid/1023>; Daniele Amoroso, 'Armed Opposition Groups' (and Foreign Fighters') Abidance by International Human Rights Law: The Issue of Compliance in Syria and Iraq' in Andrea de Guttry, Francesca Capone, and Christophe Paulussen (eds), *Foreign Fighters under International Law and Beyond* (Springer 2016); Andrew Clapham, 'Human Rights Obligations for Non-State-Actors: Where Are We Now?' in Fannie Lafontaine and François Larocque (eds), *Doing Peace the Rights Way: Essays in International Law and Relations in Honour of Louise Arbour* (Intersentia 2019); Daragh Murray, *Human Rights Obligations of Non-State Armed Groups* (Hart Publishing 2016) 157–171.

international human rights law, the condition of applicability of obligations for states is expressed in terms of jurisdiction: the state owes a duty to respect and ensure or secure human rights to any individual under its jurisdiction.[328] For human rights law, jurisdiction is primarily—but not exclusively—territorial. The state is presumed to exercise full jurisdiction over national territory, a presumption that can be rebutted in situations of armed conflicts in which an insurgent has wrestled control away from the state over part of this territory. Even in such circumstances, however, the European Court of Human Rights has explained on several occasions that the jurisdiction of the national state does not fall into abeyance with respect to territory no longer under its control; rather, as the Court explained, for example, in *Ilascu v. Moldova and Russia*, the state maintains jurisdiction, but the obligations that are due pursuant to international human rights law are modulated to reflect the limits of the state's *de facto* authority.[329]

The transposition of this approach to non-state armed groups in zones of armed conflicts is very challenging. The central difficulty comes from the fact that an armed group does not have a defined territory to which its very existence is wedded, in the way that the state owes its very existence to having a defined national territory.[330] There is as a result no presumption that an armed group has jurisdiction over any territory whatsoever; instead, jurisdiction will reflect the factual authority exercised by a group over a territory. This understanding of jurisdiction for non-state armed groups echoes the development of the extraterritorial applicability of human rights obligations of states. In recent years, an evolution spearheaded by the European Court of Human Rights has found that a state will have jurisdiction beyond its national territory in circumstances in which it comes to have authority over persons or territory. The key reference remains the decision of the European Court in *Al-Skeini v. UK*, in which the Court found that a state acquires extraterritorial jurisdiction "when, as a consequence of lawful or unlawful military action, [it] exercises effective control of an area outside that national territory".[331] Effective control is a question of fact, and will primarily reflect the military presence of a state in a given area. A second, distinct basis of extraterritorial jurisdiction is grounded in "agent authority and control", applicable in particular to situations in which a person is detained abroad by a state's agents. When a state has jurisdiction on the basis of area control, the entire range of substantive rights must be secured, whereas in the case of agent control

[328] E.g., Art. 2, International Covenant on Civil and Political Rights; Art. 1, American Convention on Human Rights; Art. 1, European Convention of Human Rights.

[329] ECTHR, *Ilascu v Moldova and Russia*, Appl. No 48787/99, [2004] ECHR 318, para 333. The implications for the territorial state of a modulated duty to ensure human rights in territory under rebel control are more fully explored in Chapter 4, Section IV.

[330] Montevideo Convention on the Rights and Duties of States, No 3802, (1933) 165 League of Nations Treaty Series 19, Art. 1.

[331] ECTHR, *Al-Skeini v UK*, Appl. No 55721/07, 7 July 2011, para 138.

like detention, only those rights relevant to the given situation will need to be secured by the state.[332]

When considering the operationalisation of human rights obligations of non-state armed groups, the approach devised by the European Court of Human Rights provides signposts that can usefully guide the analysis of where and when an armed group is bound to respect and ensure human rights to the civilian population. This seems broadly consistent with the practice of states vis-à-vis *de facto* authorities, governments that have not been recognised by other states but that nevertheless wield effective control over part or all of the territory of a state. This approach has allowed states to all at once demand compliance with human rights from the likes of the authorities of the Turkish Republic of Northern Cyprus or of Somaliland while at the same time refraining from giving any formal recognition to these entities.[333] On that basis, a non-state armed group would have jurisdiction when it exercises effective control over an area or if it detains an individual and consequently would be bound to respect international human rights law. It bears repeating that jurisdiction does not imply exclusivity; as the European Court of Human Rights noted in *Ilascu*, several agents with human rights obligations can have overlapping and complementary jurisdictions over a given population and territory.[334] This is consonant with data from field surveys of governance by armed groups which found that, even in very difficult situations like that related to the Islamic State in Syria and Iraq or the Taliban in Afghanistan, the state rarely disappears altogether from areas under partial or total rebel control.

Once it is accepted that non-state armed groups in situations of armed conflicts can come to exercise jurisdiction over parts of the civilian population, they will be subject to a range of obligations pursuant to international human rights law. The breadth and depth of obligations imposed by international human rights law will reflect the intensity and scope of territorial authority armed groups wield over a civilian population. Various nomenclatures have been developed in global and regional human rights regimes to articulate the various strands of obligations flowing from human rights norms. While these nomenclatures vary more in terms of accent than substance, perhaps the most sophisticated version is the one devised by the African Commission on Human and Peoples' Rights in *SERAC v. Nigeria*.[335] In that case, the African Commission offered that human

332 ibid paras 137–138. There are similar, albeit less fully articulated, developments in other human rights regimes: Yuval Shany, 'The Extraterritorial Application of International Human Rights Law' (2020) 409 Recueil des cours 21, 77–101.

333 This is very well analysed by Murray (n 327) 120–137.

334 *Ilascu v Moldova and Russia* (n 329).

335 *The Social and Economic Rights Action Center and the Center for Economic, and Social Rights v Nigeria*, Communication 155/96 (2001). Other nomenclatures include: Special Representative of the Secretary-General on the Issue of Human Rights and Transnational Corporations, 'Guiding Principles on Business and Human Rights: Implementing the United Nations 'Protect, Respect

rights standards of all types, civil and political as well as economic, social, and cultural, generate four levels of obligations for states, corresponding to duties to respect, protect, promote, and fulfil human rights.[336] Very briefly, the duty to "respect" refers to the fact that the state itself must not be the immediate source of the denial of enjoyment of fundamental rights and freedoms. The duty to "protect" speaks to the need to shield individuals and groups from violations of human rights by other actors, including the adoption of legislation and the availability of effective remedies. The duty to "promote" demands that the state take measures to ensure a social and cultural environment that nurtures fulfilment of human rights, including public education and awareness campaigns. Finally, the duty to "fulfil" requires that the state take positive steps to realise human rights, which may imply that the state itself provide the means to allow individuals and groups to enjoy their human rights. Arguably, there are elements of the administration of justice that intersect with all four levels of obligations, but the duties to respect and protect may be said to be most central to the issue of whether, in some circumstances, non-state armed groups in conflict zones have a duty to establish rebel courts.

In many ways, in relation to the administration of justice by non-state armed groups in conflict zones, the duties to "respect" and "protect" human rights recall the duties to "respect" and "ensure respect" of international humanitarian law, with the difference that human rights law has a wider field of application than humanitarian law. As to the duty of armed groups to "respect" human rights, requiring that the groups themselves not be the source of violations of fundamental rights and freedoms, it implies internal policies and practices designed to ensure rights-compatible behaviour by the groups and their members. Adopting an internal code of conduct like the Taliban *layeha* or the FARC Disciplinary Regulation would thus be a practice going towards fulfilment of the duty to respect, although it is perhaps conceivable that compliance could be achieved by a very disciplined armed group without such a formalised, written code of conduct.[337] In addition to standards of behaviour, the duty to respect human rights calls for mechanisms that will impose sanctions for any member of the armed group that denies the rights of others, whether civilians or co-belligerents. Here again, the formal and detailed

and Remedy' Framework' for consideration by the Human Rights Council. UN Doc A/HRC/13/31, 21 March 2011; UN Committee on Economic, Social and Cultural Rights, 'General Comment 14', UN Doc E/C.12/2000/4 (2000); Inter-American Court of Human Rights, *Velásquez Rodríguez v Honduras*, Merits, Judgment, (ser. C) No 4 (1988) paras 164–177. The labels and divisions do vary, but not clearly the cumulative duties imposed upon states by international human rights standards.

[336] Ibid paras 43–47.

[337] For a discussion of the Taliban *layeha*, see Section III.B, supra; for the FARC Disciplinary Regulation, see Chapter 1, Section II.B.ii.

internal disciplinary process of the FARC stands as a good example of measures that are an element of the duty to respect human rights.[338] These norms, practices, and institutions echo the features that are required of an armed opposition group in order to justify the application of international humanitarian law to a non-international armed conflict.[339] It goes without saying that the proclamation of policies and practices does not in itself correspond to respecting human rights: such norms must substantively conform to human rights and be actually put into practice by the groups. Seeing as some violations of human rights proscribed by rebel codes of conduct correspond to serious crimes that may attract severe sanctions, possibly even capital punishment, it leads to conclude that non-state armed groups must have institutions that can internally administer justice fairly. In a limited but significant way, then, the duty of armed groups to "respect" human rights implies a certain duty to establish insurgent justice mechanisms.

The duty to "protect" human rights to some extent mirrors the duty to "ensure respect" of international humanitarian law and corresponds to a broader set of obligations than the duty to "respect" human rights. While the latter addresses limitations to the full enjoyment of fundamental rights and freedoms that originate in the behaviour of the armed group itself, the duty to protect human rights imposes an obligation for the group to take action to ensure that the behaviour of third parties does not produce the same effect. Actions required of armed groups under this heading span the full spectrum of possible measures, including legislative, institutional, judicial, and administrative steps.[340] These measures must relate to every possible stage of human rights violations, from prevention to punishment and remedy. The Inter-American Court of Human Rights articulated the implications of this dimension of the duty to protect human rights in its landmark *Velásquez Rodríguez* judgment, finding a duty for states "to organize the governmental apparatus and, in general, all the structures through which public power is exercised, so they are capable of ensuring the free and full enjoyment of human rights".[341] For the Court, it goes without saying that the governance apparatus and structure must include a functioning judicial system, as it makes clear in the paragraph that follows in the judgment: "The obligation to ensure the free and full exercise of human rights is not fulfilled by the existence of a legal system designed to make it possible to comply with this obligation—it also requires the government to

[338] See Chapter 1, Section II.B.ii.

[339] Tilman Rodenhäuser, *Organizing Rebellion: Non-State Armed Groups under International Humanitarian Law, Human Rights Law, and International Criminal Law* (Oxford University Press 2018) 40–42, 52–54.

[340] Committee on Economic, Social and Cultural Rights (n 335) para 33; Murray (n 327) 186.

[341] *Velásquez Rodríguez* (n 335) para 166.

conduct itself so as to effectively ensure the free and full exercise of human rights".[342] This also reflects the distinct human right to an effective remedy, entrenched in all major human rights treaties and in customary international law.[343] For states, then, the duty to protect ineluctably leads to the requirement of a functioning and effective judicial system. Is it so for non-state armed groups as well? The starting point is different, as the sovereignty underpinning the construction of state obligations under international human rights law leads to presume that it is the sole source of public authority on national territory. For armed opposition groups, on the opposite, there is a presumption that the sovereign state remains present, albeit its ability to exercise authority in all parts of national territory may be subject to factual limitations. For both state and non-state actors, limited available resources and external constraints can offer justification for partial and progressive implementation of human rights: *à l'impossible nul n'est tenu*, such that if an insurgent group simply does not have the institutional capacity to administer justice in territory under its control, it does not have a legal obligation to so.[344] The rebels that lack capacity but have jurisdiction nevertheless remain under a duty to protect human rights. In such a situation, they must deliver on that obligation indirectly, by allowing the state to run courts that offer the effective remedies that are required to permit full enjoyment of rights and freedoms. When, however, non-state armed groups in control of parts of national territory come to develop a broader system of governance, then the administration of justice must be part of that governance. The Islamic State, for example, established a broad governance regime touching on many aspects of life under its effective control in Syria and Iraq, from traffic safety to consumer protection. If, as I have suggested earlier, there is a solidifying consensus that non-state armed groups are bound by international human rights law, then the associated obligation to "protect" human rights would mean that ISIS had a duty to establish its own courts and administer justice in the territory under its control.

(e) *Command Responsibility*

A final potential source of obligations requiring that non-state armed groups establish courts reflects the doctrine of command responsibility in international criminal law. This doctrine relates to individual duties and possible international

[342] Ibid para 167. See also Human Rights Committee, General Comment No 31 'Nature of the General Obligation on State Parties to the Covenant', UN Doc CCPR/C/21/Rev.1/Add.13 (2004).

[343] Dinah Shelton, *Remedies in International Human Rights Law* (3d edn, Oxford University Press 2015) 58–80.

[344] This is expressed most explicitly with regard to economic, social, and cultural rights, but the principle obtains for civil and political rights as well: Committee on Economic, Social and Cultural Rights, "General Comment No 3: The Nature of State Parties Obligations (article 2 para 1)", UN Doc E/1991/23 (1990); Murray (n 327) 191–192; Rodenhäuser (n 339) 189–193.

criminal responsibility of commanders, but it may nevertheless indirectly speak to the right or duty of non-state armed groups to administer justice.[345] Under international humanitarian law, Additional Protocol I specifies that military commanders have a duty to prevent and suppress breaches of the Geneva Conventions and Protocol (Art. 87), as distinct from the belligerent's own duty to do the same (Art. 86). This corresponds to the doctrine of command responsibility under international criminal law, imposing individual criminal liability for a commander who fails to prevent, repress, or refer a violation of international humanitarian law.[346] It was codified in Article 28 of the Rome Statute, but had been applied previously by the ICTY, the ICTR, and in other international and domestic war crimes trials, and is listed by the ICRC as a customary humanitarian norm.[347] This doctrine is applicable equally to commanders or superiors of state and non-state forces, exercising effective military or civilian authority *de jure* or *de facto*, in international as well as non-international armed conflicts.[348]

The link between command responsibility and the rebel administration of justice were a central element of the *Bemba* trial before the ICC, in which the accused invoked, inter alia, that he had repressed war crimes committed by his subordinates by having them prosecuted before a court of his own armed opposition group. In an *amicus curiae* brief submitted to the ICC, Amnesty International took the positions that the accused, Jean-Pierre Bemba, could not rely on judicial mechanisms internal to his Mouvement de Libération du Congo to sanction violations of international law carried out by troops under his command; instead, he should have referred the matter to the state on whose territory the events took place, to a third state willing to act on the basis of universal jurisdiction, or to an international tribunal.[349] The ICC Pre-Trial Chamber, ruling in a preliminary manner on the confirmation of charges, broadly disagreed with the approach advocated by Amnesty International, a position confirmed in the 2016 trial judgment in the case: the ICC discounted a request made at the time by Bemba to the UN Secretary-General to open an international investigation into crimes committed in the region, finding it too little too late. On the other hand, it

345 See: Somer (n 4) 685; Willms (n 316) 160.

346 Guénaël Mettraux, *The Law of Command Responsibility* (Oxford University Press 2009).

347 ICRC (n 305) Rule 153; Mettraux (n 346) 3–35.

348 William Schabas, *The International Criminal Court: A Commentary on the Rome Statute* (2d edn, Oxford University Press 2016) 607–618; Cyril Laucci, 'Article 28. Responsabilité des chefs militaires et autres supérieurs hiérarchiques' in Julian Fernandez and Xavier Pacreau (eds), *Statut de Rome de la Cour pénale internationale: commentaire article par article*, vol 1 (2d edn, Éditions Pedone 2019) 1105–1108; Sandesh Sivakumaran, 'Command Responsibility in Irregular Groups' (2012) 10 Journal of International Criminal Justice 1129.

349 ICC, *Prosecutor v Jean-Pierre Bemba Gombo*, Amnesty International, Amicus Curiae Observations on Superior Responsibility submitted pursuant to Rule 103 of the Rules of Procedure and Evidence, 20 April 2009, ICC-01/05-01/08-406, paras 22–23, online: <http://www.legal-tools.org/doc/9efb78/>.

gave particular weight to "the availability of a functional military judicial system within the MLC through which [the accused] could have punished the crimes committed".[350]

Does the accepted duty of commanders of non-state armed groups to prevent or punish war crimes necessarily imply a need to create courts internal to the group, similar to what existed in the non-state armed group in the *Bemba* case? While there is a clear requirement that the punishment imposed by a commander be proportional to the crime, such that a very serious war crime would call for criminal responsibility rather than mere disciplinary measures, that does not ineluctably lead to the necessity of courts within a rebel group.[351] The individual commander may not have the authority to initiate a prosecution before a court of the group, or the factual circumstances may make a prosecution impossible or inopportune, or the group may simply not have any such courts. It goes without saying that the sanctions imposed by a commander must themselves not amount to violations of international law, including all the requirements for the regular constitution and fair operation of rebel courts.[352] These elements underscore the fact that the focus on individual criminal responsibility requires that the accused not be made to bear the consequences of any failure on the part of the group. Accordingly, courts have interpreted flexibly the commander's duty to repress or punish to include the possibility of referring the crimes of subordinates to competent authorities that are not those of the armed group but rather those of the national state, of third states, or of an international tribunal.[353] While it is not possible to interpret the doctrine of command responsibility as imposing a duty for non-state armed groups to create courts, even for the narrow purpose of sanctioning international crimes committed by members of the groups, the jurisprudence analysing that doctrine does imply that a rebel court is a licit tool to fulfil the commander's duty to repress or punish crimes of subordinates.

The conclusion to draw from the survey of norms related to the rebel administration of justice in international humanitarian law, international human rights law, and international criminal law is that there is very little to support a position that views rebel courts as a violation of international law. At the very least, the

[350] ICC, *Prosecutor v Jean-Pierre Bemba Gombo*, Decision Pursuant to Article 61(7)(a) and (b) of the Rome Statute in the Charges of the Prosecutor against Jean-Pierre Bemba Gombo, 15 June 2009, ICC-01/05-01/08, paras 497, 501; ICC, *Prosecutor v Jean-Pierre Bemba Gombo*, Trial Judgment, 21 March 2016, ICC-01/05-01/08, paras 206–209, 402, 597, 727–733. This specific aspect is discussed in the Appeals Judgment in term of Bemba's material ability, thus implicitly confirming his legal ability: ICC, *Prosecutor v Jean-Pierre Bemba Gombo*, Appeals Judgment, 8 June 2018, ICC-01/05-01/08 A, paras 167–169.

[351] Mettraux (n 346) 262.

[352] Alessandra Spadaro, 'Punish and Be Punished? The Paradox of Command Responsibility in Armed Groups' (2020) 18 Journal of International Criminal Justice 1, 18–27.

[353] This flexibility explains, in part, the overturning of Bemba's conviction by the ICC Appeals Chamber: ICC, Bemba Appeals Judgment (n 350) paras 167–173. See Jöbstl (n 316) 20–21.

composite normative scheme that emerges validates a right for non-state armed groups in situations of international and non-international armed conflicts to establish their own courts. Indeed, the duty to ensure compliance with international humanitarian law and the duty to secure human rights suggest that, in certain circumstances at least, armed group may have a duty to administer justice. This provides a critical context for the analysis of the provisions of the Geneva Conventions and Protocols that speak more directly to the rebel administration of justice.

ii. A Focus on Crimes and a Nexus with the Conflict

In the limited body of literature discussing the legality of courts of non-state armed groups under public international law, two rules of international humanitarian law have played a central role in the analysis: the prohibition in Common Article 3 of the 1949 Geneva Conventions of judgments passed by a court that was not "regularly constituted, affording all the judicial guarantees which are recognised as indispensable by civilized peoples" and its equivalent in Article 6(2) of Additional Protocol II referring to a "court offering the essential guarantees of independence and impartiality".[354] Given the focus on rebel courts in situations of armed conflicts, in this literature as well as in the present analysis, the turn to these provisions is entirely understandable and indeed justified. That said, these rules are limited in ways that are sometimes noted in that literature, but without fully exploring the implications of such limitations.[355] Before turning, in the following subsection, to the requirements of regular constitution and independence and impartiality, it is important to explore the implications of the apparent focus on criminal law in Common Article 3 and Article 6 of Protocol II and the necessity of a nexus to the conflict. In the following pages, I argue that these treaty provisions and international humanitarian law generally should be taken to govern not only the criminal sanction of war-related acts by rebels (e.g. punishing informants) but also the repression of ordinary crimes (e.g. the theft of a cow) and even the administration of justice beyond the criminal law (e.g. family issues or unpaid debt).

Turning first to Common Article 3, the rule proclaimed covers only a limited form of criminal jurisdiction. The provision prohibits "the passing of sentences and the carrying out of executions" against "persons taking no active part in the hostilities", unless it is done by a court that is regularly constituted. The drafting

[354] See: Somer (n 4); Sivakumaran, 'Courts of Armed Opposition Groups—Fair Trials or Summary Justice?' (n 4); Parth Geiji, 'Can Insurgent Courts Be Legitimate under International Law?' (2013) 91 Texas Law Review 1525; Willms (n 316); Heffes (n 281). The criminalisation of violations of these provisions in the Rome Statute is usually invoked as a supplementary rule.

[355] Two recent notable contributions are: Murray (n 327); Katharine Fortin, *The Accountability of Armed Groups Under Human Rights Law* (Oxford University Press 2017).

history of the 1949 Geneva Conventions suggests that the concern behind the initial inclusion of this provision was the prevention of summary justice, including summary executions, in conflict zones.[356] There was, during and in the immediate aftermath of World War II, no shortage of deficient and expedited forms of justice to sanction crimes committed during the war, with executions not rarely the penalty meted out as a result. In reaction to the abuses committed in the name of the administration of justice, the draft of the Geneva Conventions included elaborate guarantees applicable to criminal prosecutions of prisoners of war (Arts. 102–108, Third Geneva Convention) and civilians under occupation (Arts. 64–78, Fourth Geneva Convention), the two categories of individuals felt to be most at risk in that regard. It must be borne in mind that, in the ICRC's initial draft of the 1949 Geneva Conventions, it was proposed that the rules devised for international armed conflicts also be applied to situations of non-international armed conflict, whether completely, in their principles, or by analogy.[357] This proposal proved unacceptable to states at the diplomatic conference during which the Geneva Conventions were negotiated, and in the end Common Article 3 was adopted with the view to provide a skeleton (a "convention in miniature") of the most essential humanitarian protections in times of internal conflict.[358] This explains the narrow scope of the rule entrenched in Common Article 3, focussing only on criminal prosecution, with a special concern touching the imposition of capital punishment. As noted by the ICRC:

> Sentences and executions without previous trial are too open to error. "Summary justice" may be effective on account of the fear it arouses—though that has yet to be proved—but it adds too many further innocent victims to all the other innocent victims of the conflict. All civilized nations surround the administration of justice with safeguards aimed at eliminating the possibility of judicial errors. The Convention has rightly proclaimed that it is essential to do this even in time of war. We must be very clear about one point: it is only "summary" justice which it is intended to prohibit. No sort of immunity is given to anyone under this provision. There is nothing in it to prevent a person presumed to be guilty from being arrested and so placed in a position where he can do no further harm; and it leaves intact the right of the State to prosecute, sentence and punish according to the law.[359]

[356] Sivakumaran, 'Courts of Armed Opposition Groups—Fair Trials or Summary Justice?' (n 4) 496.

[357] ICRC, *Commentary on the Second Geneva Convention* (n 286) paras 388–391.

[358] ICRC, *Commentary on the Fourth Geneva Convention* (ICRC 1958) 34.

[359] ibid 39.

There is no denying that the prosecution of crimes is an essential facet of rebel governance in many armed conflicts. As the case studies of the Islamic State and the Taliban illustrate well, it has important implications both for public security within the community and, of course, for any person brought to court to face charges. On the other hand, as again the case studies make abundantly clear, this leaves out the rebel administration of justice in all other areas, from family law to private law issues, aspects of the ordinary life of the population the importance of which cannot be overstated.[360] A priori, the reference to "regularly constituted" in Common Article 3 does not apply to these non-penal facets of insurgent justice.

The second treaty provision that can be taken to speak directly to the rebel administration of justice, Article 6 of Additional Protocol II, is, if anything, even narrower than Common Article 3. Article 6(2) of the Protocol in part reprises the same expressions to refer to matters falling within the ambit of criminal law, to provide that "no sentence shall be passed and no penalty shall be executed on a person found guilty of an offence". There is no doubt that the references to "sentence", "penalty", and "guilty of an offence" limit the scope of the rule to criminal prosecutions.[361] Attention also needs to be paid to Article 6(1), where it is specified that "This Article applies to the prosecution and punishment of criminal offences related to the armed conflict". In addition to reiterating the exclusively criminal law focus, paragraph 1 explicitly restricts its reach to those offences that are "related to the conflict". This requires a definition of the relationship to the conflict that is sufficient to bring a matter under the purview of Article 6. It also begs the question of whether such a relationship is an implied condition of application of Common Article 3.

At a general level, the requirement that a crime be related to the conflict in order for its prosecution and punishment to be governed by Common Article 3 and Article 6 of Protocol II reflects the broader applicability of international humanitarian law to any situation, whether an international or a non-international armed conflict. While much of the attention is naturally focussed on defining thresholds of applicability of the various humanitarian law regimes to a situation, it is important to keep in mind that humanitarian law aims to regulate the conduct of hostilities and, as much as possible, the protection of victims of war from the consequences of armed hostilities, but not necessarily to govern every aspect of life in situations to which it is applicable. In other words, international humanitarian law does not entirely displace other relevant and applicable legal regimes, be they the domestic law of the state or other fields of international law such as

[360] See Katharine Fortin, 'The Application of Human Rights Law to Everyday Civilian Life Under Rebel Control' (2016) 63 Netherlands International Law Review 161, 163–164.

[361] The language is even more clearly criminal in the French version, which refers to '*condamnation*', '*peine*', and '*coupable d'une infraction*'.

international human rights law. This is reflected in a number of other provisions in treaty law, including Articles 2 and 5 of Additional Protocol II and Article 75(1) of Additional Protocol I.[362] Early on in its work, in the *Tadic* Interlocutory Decision, the ICTY Appeal Chamber warned against an overly restrictive understanding of the applicability of Common Article 3, whether in geographical or temporal terms or in requiring a link to armed engagements on the battlefield rather than to the armed conflict more broadly.[363] In the discussions of Article 75(1) of Protocol I, which were derived from the text of what became Article 6 of Protocol II, the United States and Australia proposed an amendment that would have limited the reach of the provision to "activity in relation to the armed conflict", a proposal which was ultimately rejected.[364] While there is a danger in giving an overly narrow interpretation to what can be considered "related to the conflict", lest in so doing we curtail the protection offered by humanitarian law, there is a clear consensus that it cannot become all-encompassing. Thus, Article 75(1) of Protocol I is deemed applicable to any person "[i]n so far as they are affected by" an international armed conflict, which could be understood as near-universal applicability; the ICRC Commentary notes:

> When there is armed conflict, all those who find themselves in the territory of the countries at war or in occupied territory, are affected in some way or another. This is very probably not what was intended, particularly because of the words "in so far"; it cannot therefore be denied that there are persons who are not affected in the sense of this article. In general those who contravene the normal laws of the State (ordinary criminals) and who are punished on these grounds, are not "affected" within the meaning of this article. On the other hand, if security measures are taken against certain individuals because of their attitude, whether true or alleged, with regard to the conflict, Article 75 certainly applies to them.[365]

As a reflection of the general limitation of the applicability of international humanitarian law, the "normal administration of justice" would not be subject to its rules.[366] The prosecution by the state of an individual who has committed auto theft to support a drug habit or triggered a brawl in a bar as a result

[362] See also the ICC Elements of Crimes for Article 8(2)(c) of the Rome Statute which provide that "the conduct took place in the context of and was associated with an armed conflict": Knut Dörmann, *Elements of War Crimes under the Rome Statute of the International Criminal Court: Sources and Commentary* (Cambridge University Press 2003) 383.

[363] ICTY, *Prosecutor v Tadic*, Decision on the Defence Motion for interlocutory Appeal on Jurisdiction, IT-94-AR72, 2 October 1995, para 69.

[364] Bothe and others (n 313) 516.

[365] ICRC, *Commentary on the Additional Protocols of 8 June 1977 to the Geneva Conventions of 12 August 1949* (n 277) para 3011.

[366] Bothe and others (n 313) 517.

of drunkenness would not be governed by Common Article 3 or Article 6 of Additional Protocol II, even if the incident occurred in a conflict zone, even if participants professed allegiance to different factions of that conflict.[367] Does that also hold true of the "normal administration of justice" by non-state armed groups? Or should we consider that *anything* done by armed groups in zones of conflict is *necessarily* related to the conflict, *ex officio*? At one level, we can note that the non-legal literature on insurgent governance suggests that all exercises of public authority by an armed group are part of its insurgency strategy, even if there is often not a unique, hostility-driven rationale for something like the rebel administration of justice.[368] It is not easy to show how punishment of the sale of counterfeit branded clothing or of rooftop pigeon-keeping by the Islamic State contributes to advancing its insurgency.[369] What clearly must be resisted, however, is an answer that reflects a vision of insurgents as outlaws, such that everything they do is by definition marked by illegality. As explored in Chapter 1, this may be so under the domestic law of the state, but there is no norm of international law that supports such an all-encompassing illegality. What is needed is a principled approach grounded in norms of international humanitarian law that effectively maps the boundary between the ordinary, everyday life that goes on even in conflict zones and the policies, practices, and acts that are sufficiently related to the conflict to justify the application of humanitarian law.

This very question has been explored in the field of international criminal law, by defence counsels who have sought to exploit the vagueness of the reach of international humanitarian law to challenge its applicability to certain facts and, as a result, deny that an impugned act could constitute a war crime. This has given rise to a requirement, in international criminal law, that there be a nexus between a crime and an ongoing armed conflict. The nexus requirement was progressively developed in the caselaw of the ICTY and ICTR, and these courts' articulation on the subject remains authoritative today.[370] The starting point is that not all crimes committed in a time and place in which an armed conflict is occurring will be considered war crimes, and conversely, that war crimes may be perpetrated in locations and at times removed from armed hostilities by individuals who are not combatants.[371] The ICTY Appeals Chamber offered a cogent statement of principle in its *Kunarac* judgment:[372]

[367] Provost, *International Human Rights and Humanitarian Law* (n 284) 99.

[368] Zachariah Cherian Mampilly, *Rebel Rulers Insurgent Governance and Civilian Life during War* (Cornell University Press 2011) 3–6, 234; Fortin (n 355) 42–47.

[369] See Section II.B, supra.

[370] See Guénaël Mettraux, 'Nexus With Armed Conflict' in Antonio Cassese (ed), *The Oxford Companion to International Criminal Justice* (Oxford University Press 2009).

[371] See: Antonio Cassese, 'The Nexus Requirement for War Crimes' (2012) 10 Journal of International Criminal Justice 1395; Harmen van der Wilt, 'War Crimes and the Requirement of a Nexus with an Armed Conflict' (2012) 10 Journal of International Criminal Justice 1113.

[372] ICTY, *Prosecutor v Kunarac*, Appeals Judgment, IT-96-23, 12 June 2002, para 58.

> What ultimately distinguishes a war crime from a purely domestic offence is that a war crime is shaped by or dependent upon the environment—the armed conflict—in which it is committed. It need not have been planned or supported by some form of policy. The armed conflict need not have been causal to the commission of the crime, but the existence of an armed conflict must, at a minimum, have played a substantial part in the perpetrator's ability to commit it, his decision to commit it, the manner in which it was committed or the purpose for which it was committed. Hence, if it can be established, as in the present case, that the perpetrator acted in furtherance of or under the guise of the armed conflict, it would be sufficient to conclude that his acts were closely related to the armed conflict.

The concept is framed quite broadly, the nexus possibly attaching to the agent's ability, intent, manner, or purpose in relation to an act. One might argue that there is a tension between the requirement that the action be "closely related" to the conflict and the finding that this can correspond to acts merely done "in furtherance of" or "under the guise of" (the authentic French version of the judgment may be ever looser, "*dans l'optique de servir*" and especially "*sous le couvert*") the conflict. The ICTY in *Kunarac* went on to identify some elements that may be relevant to the determination of the nexus, including whether the perpetrator is a combatant, the victim a non-combatant, if they are linked to opposing sides of the conflict, if the actions serve military aims, and if this was done as part of the perpetrator's official duties.[373] In the jurisprudence of the ICTY and ICTR, the nexus requirement was interpreted in a flexible manner, demanding more than simply taking advantage of the occurrence of a conflict but not going so far as requiring that an act be part of combat or an official policy or practice of a belligerent.[374]

How does the administration of justice by non-state armed groups fit into this understanding of the scope of international humanitarian law? To begin with, what is put into question is the extent of the applicability of humanitarian law to criminal prosecutions before rebel courts. For crimes that are directly connected to the conflict, such as the punishment of providing information to the enemy carried out by the Islamic State and the Taliban, there seems to be no room to argue that this is not directly connected to the conflict in a manner that meets the nexus requirement. Is there a nexus, however, for rebel prosecutions of cattle thieves or abusive husbands? Even more broadly, beyond criminal law, is the administration of justice in relation to the travails of ordinary life, divorces and

373 ibid para 59.
374 van der Wilt (n 371) 1119.

alimony, contractual disputes, conflicts over lands, and so forth, carried out by armed groups "in furtherance of" or "under the guise of" the conflict? Doubtless, if there were no conflict, there would be less chances of a breakdown of state authority and thus fewer opportunities for rebel justice, but the jurisprudence suggests that this is not a sufficient connection to the conflict.[375] It is significant, for this analysis, that the agents carrying out rebel justice are either combatants or closely linked to the insurgents. In addition, the fact that the rebel administration of justice reflects a policy or at least accepted practice of armed groups, fulfilled by individuals as part of their official duties within the group, further strengthens its nexus to the conflict. Most often, the accused appearing in a rebel court is not a member of the group, and his or her allegiance to the group certainly cannot be presumed. The trial by an armed group of one of its own members is, as we have seen even for groups like the Islamic State and the Taliban, not unheard of.[376]

It was traditionally understood that international humanitarian law did not regulate the relations within a given belligerent side but only those that crossed lines of allegiance.[377] This view has been challenged in recent doctrinal analysis, including the influential ICRC commentary of Common Article 3 in which the organisation affirms that if members of an armed force are tried by their own party to the conflict, that procedure should be governed by humanitarian law.[378] The issue came to a head before the ICC in the *Ntaganda* trial, in which the accused was charged with sexual violations of child soldiers who belonged to his own group. The Appeals Chamber embraced what it acknowledged was an enlargement of the scope of protection to hold that "international humanitarian law does not contain a general rule that categorically excludes members of an armed group from protection against crimes committed by members of the same armed group".[379] Even in

[375] Manuel J Ventura, 'Automatic International Criminal Liability for Unlawful Confinement (Imprisonment) as a War Crime? A Potential Consequence of Denying Non-State Armed Groups the Power to Detain in Non-International Armed Conflicts' in Ezequiel Heffes, Marcos Kotlik, and Manuel J Ventura (eds), *International Humanitarian Law and Non-State Actors: Debates, Law and Practice* (Springer 2019) 161–162.

[376] See Sections II.B and III.B, *infra*.

[377] SCSL, *Prosecutor v Sesay, Kallon and Gbao ('RUF Trial')*, Trial Judgment, SCSL-04-15-T, 2 March 2009, para 1453 ("The law of international armed conflict was never intended to criminalise acts of violence committed by one member of an armed group against another, such conduct remaining first and foremost the province of the criminal law of the State of the armed group concerned and human rights law. In our view, a different approach would constitute an inappropriate reconceptualisation of a fundamental principle of international humanitarian law. We are not prepared to embark on such an exercise").

[378] ICRC, *Commentary on the Second Geneva Convention* (n 286) paras 569–571; Sivakumaran, *The Law of Non-International Armed Conflict* (n 294) 249.

[379] ICC, *Prosecutor v Ntaganda*, Appeal Judgment on Challenge to Jurisdiction, ICC-01/04-02/06 OA5, 15 June 2017, para 63. This was presaged by the judgment of the ICTY Appeals Chamber in *Prosecutor v Kvočka*, Judgment, Case No IT-98-30/1-A, 28 February 2005, paras 560–561, finding that Common Article 3 applies to an individual detained and mistreated by his own armed group.

such cases, for the Appeals Chamber, the nexus requirement can be applied in a manner that will "sufficiently and appropriately delineate war crimes from ordinary crimes".[380] When the case was returned to the Trial Chamber for judgment, the court found that the rape and sexual slavery of young boys and girls directly participating in hostilities in the same armed group as the accused were acts "associated with" an armed conflict and thus met the nexus requirement.[381] This is an important development for the rebel administration of justice, because it suggests that the application of humanitarian law no longer turns on an overarching relation of hostility among parties to an interaction or practice. This opens a door to applying humanitarian law to the court-martial by an armed group of one of its own members and, more generally, to the administration of justice vis-à-vis a civilian population that is not hostile to the rebels.[382]

As a reflection of the concept of sovereignty, statehood in public international law corresponds to multifaceted and complex governance in which war is but one episode. When a state becomes embroiled in an armed conflict, some but not all public governance becomes related to the conflict. Non-state armed groups, on the other hand, have a legal existence that is wholly wedded to their ability to carry out sustained and concerted military operations reaching a minimal threshold of armed violence. The fact that they reflect broader or longstanding religious, political, ideological, or any other non-state authority is legally immaterial to their legal recognition as armed groups under international humanitarian law.[383] As a result of the inherent link between the legal recognition of an armed group and armed hostilities, it is possible to conclude that the exercise of public authority through the administration of justice by an armed group in a conflict zone will always be related to the conflict. This is the conclusion reached by the ICRC in a recent report:

> [T]he way in which non-State armed groups exercise control over, and interact with, persons living in territory under their de facto control is inherently linked to the conflict in question. The armed conflict plays a substantial part in the group's ability to control the lives of those living under its control and the manner in which such control is exercised. As a result, IHL applies and

[380] ibid para 68.

[381] ICC, *Prosecutor v Ntaganda*, Trial Judgment, ICC-01/04-02/06, 8 July 2019, para 986.

[382] Cóman Kenny and Yvonne McDermott, 'The Expanding Protection of Members of a Party's Own Armed Forces under International Criminal Law' (2019) 68 International & Comparative Law Quarterly 943.

[383] The one exception corresponds to a national liberation movement under Art. 1(4) of Additional Protocol I, whose legal status does turn on a link to a people under colonial domination, alien occupation, or a racist regime.

therefore protects persons living in territory under the de facto control of non-State armed groups.[384]

This does not imply that wartime state authority is likewise always related to the conflict because, to return to a point made earlier in relation to equality of belligerents, states and armed groups *are* different, in fact as in law.[385]

One context in which state authority is detached from sovereignty, belligerent occupation, can provide helpful guidance as to the proper characterisation of the administration of justice in a conflict zone. Under Article 43 of the 1907 Hague Regulations, the occupying force has the duty to "take all steps in his power to restore and ensure, as far as possible, public order and safety, while respecting, unless absolutely prevented, the laws in force in the country". This corresponds to a wide duty to take actions, including the administration of justice, in order to ensure the continued application of law in all areas. It has long been noted that the English translation of the authentic French text of the Hague Regulations suffers here from a serious error, suggesting a much narrower substantive scope to the obligation: in French, the duty relates to "*l'ordre et la vie publics*", literally "public order and life". The idea of "public life" is obviously much broader than "public safety", encompassing "social functions and ordinary transactions that make up everyday life".[386] "Public order", for its part, reflects not only the military security interests of the occupying force and the application of the laws of war but security and general safety of society at large. It speaks not only to the application of ordinary criminal law but more generally of all laws and regulations required to maintain order within society. The ongoing nature of the duty is underscored by the dual obligations to restore and maintain, with the latter signalling that steps must be taken by occupying authorities to ensure that there is no progressive deterioration of life under occupation. All of these obligations are not obligations of result but rather of conduct, meaning that the occupier is required to take reasonable steps to meet these requirements.[387] Bringing this back

[384] ICRC, Report on International Humanitarian Law and the Challenges of Contemporary Armed Conflicts (2019) 53, online: <https://www.icrc.org/en/document/icrc-report-ihl-and-challenges-contemporary-armed-conflicts>.

[385] See this Section IV.A.ii, supra. Thus the critique of the ICC *Al Madhi* decision by Bill Schabas that sometimes "rebels" are democratically elected and adopt measure that could otherwise have been described as war crimes fails to convince, because the agent making such decisions would not be recognised as an armed group under international humanitarian law. Without an armed group, there is obviously no question of a nexus. William Schabas, 'Al Mahdi Has Been Convicted of a Crime He Did Not Commit' (2017) 49 Case Western Reserve Journal of International Law 75, 97.

[386] Eyal Benvenisti, *The International Law of Occupation* (2d edn, Oxford University Press 2012) 78, quoting from the *travaux préparatoires* of the Hague Regulation ("des fonctions sociales, des transactions ordinaires, qui constituent la vie de tous les jours"); Yoram Dinstein, *The International Law of Belligerent Occupation* (2d edn, Cambridge University Press 2019) 99, 101.

[387] Marco Sassòli, 'Legislation and Maintenance of Public Order and Civil Life by Occupying Powers' (2005) 16 European Journal of International Law 661, 664–665.

to the administration of justice, there is no doubt that the occupier is required to establish or maintain a system of courts to enforce applicable laws. This stands confirmed by Article 54 of the Fourth Geneva Convention, which prevents the occupier from altering the status of judges, as well as Articles 64 and 66 of the same convention on the continued operation of local tribunals and possible constitution of military courts by the occupying force. All of this can be understood as a form of incorporation by reference of domestic law by the law of belligerent occupation, leading to conclude that all relations between occupier and the civilian population are governed by humanitarian law.[388] If goes without saying that this is so without any regard for the lawfulness of the occupation itself, in accordance with the principle of strict division between *jus ad bellum* and *jus in bello*.

Despite the fact that belligerent occupation norms are directly applicable only to international armed conflicts, they do provide helpful guidance for the legal characterisation of the relationship between a non-state armed group and the civilian population during a non-international armed conflict. A central obstacle is the fact that there is no broad concept of occupation in internal conflicts nor an equivalent to Article 43 of the Hague Regulations imposing a duty upon armed opposition groups to restore and ensure public order and life. While there isn't an express conventional framework, we have seen earlier that the duty to ensure respect of international humanitarian law and the duty to secure human rights can be taken as an authorisation, if not a requirement, for non-state armed groups to administer justice in territory under their control. If the rebel administration of justice corresponds to a right or duty under international law as a reflection of the authority exercised by armed groups during armed conflicts, then the argument that was made vis-à-vis belligerent occupation can be advanced here: if the public governance practices of rebel groups are in furtherance of their duty to ensure respect for international humanitarian law or, even more broadly, to secure human rights, then they are by definition closely related to the armed conflict. This echoes the most recent formulation of the nexus requirement by the ICC, in the *Ntaganda* judgment, in which the Trial Chamber finds that the act "must have been closely linked to the hostilities or *be related to the control carried out over a certain part of the territory by the relevant party to the conflict*".[389] In *Al-Hassan*, the ICC Pre-Trial Chamber applies this to rebel police and judicial

[388] Éric David, *Principes de droit des conflits armés* (6e éd., Bruylant 2019) 248 ("on peut considérer que toutes les relations entre organes de l'occupant et population de l'occupé relèvent du droit des conflits armé"); David Kretzmer and Yaël Ronen, *The Occupation of Justice: The Supreme Court of Israel and the Occupied Territories* (2d ed., Oxford University Press 2021) 49–50 ("Given the Court's view that the military commander derives authority and powers from the rules of public international law dealing with belligerent occupation, it would seem that each and every act of the military should be examined to see whether it complies with these rules").

[389] Ntanganda Trial Judgment (n 381) para 732 (emphasis added).

governance, finding a sufficient nexus in the fact that the conflict provides the foundation of authority of the armed group over Timbuktu, whether exercised by military or civilian arms of the group.[390] As a result, the administration of justice by non-state armed groups in situations of armed conflicts would be governed by international humanitarian law, whether it relates to criminal or civil matters, whether it involves members of the group, combatants from the government or other non-state groups, or civilians.[391]

The conclusion that the rebel administration of justice at large meets the nexus requirement that triggers the applicability of international humanitarian law does not mean that the specific language of Common Article 3 and Article 6 of Additional Protocol II can be overlooked. It can, however, guide the interpretation to be given to these two provisions. Clearly, the explicit references to criminal law in both articles directs that they cannot be taken to govern the operation of insurgent courts in non-penal matters. In Common Article 3, the references to criminal law are unqualified, meaning that the norms can relate to the prosecution and punishment of any underlying offence. The conclusion just reached that the rebel administration of justice is closely related to the conflict means that there is no reason to limit on a different basis the application of Common Article 3; it will apply to any penal proceedings before insurgent courts. How should we understand the statement in Article 6(1) of Protocol II that it applies "to the prosecution and punishment of criminal offences related to the conflict"? Does "related to the conflict" qualify the criminal offence or the prosecution and punishment? While the expression certainly covers the criminal repression of active participation in hostilities, there is no basis to restrict its ambit so narrowly. Indeed, the expression echoes the nexus requirement applicable to humanitarian law as a whole, and the building blocks of that requirement identified in the jurisprudence of international tribunals discussed earlier can also help to guide the interpretation of Article 6(1). A central concern underpinning this provision is to allow the normal operation of domestic criminal law inasmuch as it is unrelated to the conflict. In particular, it allows for the eventuality of an armed conflict geographically limited to a portion of national territory, leaving largely undisturbed the application of criminal law in the rest of the country.[392] If, however, the individual's ability, intent, manner, or purpose in relation to a crime is

390 ICC, *Prosecutor v Al-Hassan*, Décision de la Chambre préliminaire relative à la confirmation des charges, ICC-01/12-01/18, 13 November 2019, paras 222–225 (available only in French).

391 The ICRC reaches the same conclusion in a recent policy report: ICRC, International Humanitarian Law and the Challenges of Contemporary Armed Conflicts (n 384) 53. Note that this does not deny the important insight that, for the civilian population, life goes on in many respects unaffected by the conflict. Just as citizens do not deal with the state on a daily basis, civilians do not deal with armed groups constantly, in every respect. See Fortin (n 355) 55–56.

392 ICRC, *Commentary on the Additional Protocols of 8 June 1977 to the Geneva Conventions of 12 August 1949* (n 277) para 4490; Fortin (n 355) 49.

related to the conflict, then that would meet the condition imposed by Article 6(1).[393] A relation to the conflict can also be grounded in the prosecuting authority, if the prosecution and punishment are meted out for reasons connected to the conflict. Thus, if a state uses ordinary criminal law, for instance criminal libel or vagrancy, as a tool to persecute individuals for reasons related to the conflict, such as perceived allegiance to the enemy, then that is not a case of the ordinary operation of criminal law unrelated to the conflict. On the contrary, this should be viewed as "the prosecution and punishment of criminal offences related to the conflict". This is consistent with the stated aim to provide protection to persons "deprived of their liberty for reasons related to the armed conflict" included in Articles 2(2), 5(1), and 6(5) of Protocol II. Reasons related to the conflict can be taken in an objective sense, as elements of the crime with a nexus to the conflict, or in a subjective sense, as motives of the authorities for depriving individuals of their liberty.

These standards can play out differently for state and non-state belligerents, reflecting their distinct nature and position. As noted by Katharine Fortin, the reference in Articles 5 and 6 of Protocol II to "prosecutions and punishment of criminal offences related to the conflict" implies that *some* prosecutions will *not* be so related.[394] This will indeed be the case for states, whose existence and operation are not wholly rooted in armed conflict, and who may continue to govern in parts of national territory not affected by war. The implications are different for non-state armed groups, following the conclusion reached in the previous paragraph, in that any penal prosecution by an armed group systematically would be related to the conflict and subject to the requirements laid out in Article 6. Thus, in *Al-Hassan*, the ICC Pre-Trial Chamber rejected a defence argument that the prosecution of adultery or the sale of alcohol by a court of Ansar Dine and al-Qaeda in the Islamic Maghreb in Timbuktu was unrelated to the conflict; the Chamber noted that the required nexus ties the prosecution—rather than the underlying crime itself—to the armed conflict, and that in this case all governance measures applied by the armed group in Timbuktu were in the context of and associated with the conflict.[395] The conclusion that the same rule of Protocol II has different implications for state and non-state actors does not run afoul of any principle of equality of belligerents.[396] As explored earlier, a more flexible

[393] See Bothe and others (n 313) 647.

[394] Fortin (n 360) 178.

[395] ICC Al-Hassan (n 390) paras 415, 486. This is thus not necessarily a claim that *everything* done by an armed group in territory under its control has a nexus to the conflict, but rather more narrowly that the administration of justice by rebels in such circumstances does have such a nexus, regardless of the nature of the underlying crime or civil dispute. The two questions seem conflated in Schabas (n 385) 93–98.

[396] As argued, inter alia, by ibid 98; Elvina Pothelet, 'Life in Rebel Territory: Is Everything War?' *Armed Groups and International Law* (20 May 2020), online: <https://armedgroups-internationallaw.org/2020/05/20/life-in-rebel-territory-is-everything-war/> accessed 25 May 2020.

vision of substantive rather than formal equality allows for reciprocity to operate despite the normative asymmetry between the parties to the conflict.[397] It also brings closer the obligations of occupying state and armed group controlling territory, a different form of equality that does not rest on reciprocity.[398] Finally, this interpretation produces greater coherence between Common Article 3 and Article 6 of Additional Protocol II, in that the explicit reference to prosecution and punishment related to the conflict in the latter matches the implicit nexus requirement applicable to the former.

The conclusion that the administration of justice by non-state armed groups in all areas of criminal law is governed by Common Article 3 and Article 6 of Additional Protocol II is important, and yet it leaves out a vast swath of insurgent justice concerned with non-penal matters. As we saw in the surveys of the administration of justice by the Islamic State and the Taliban, as indeed is true for many other armed groups, the impact of insurgent courts may be felt in an even more pervasive manner in relation to matters of private law, family law, labour law, and so forth. Two points may be raised in this respect. First, pursuant to the interpretation proffered earlier, the very nature of a non-state armed group operating courts in the context of an armed conflict implies that its relationship to the civilian population is related in this respect to the conflict. As a consequence, the rebel administration of justice in non-penal matters is likewise related to the conflict and, as a result, governed by international humanitarian law. Even if Common Article 3 and Article 6 of Additional Protocol II do not apply directly, other norms of humanitarian law can have an impact on insurgent justice beyond criminal law. The second point is that international human rights law, which remains applicable even in situations of armed conflict of one type or another, can provide enormous insight into the boundaries of the lawful administration of justice by any actor. Indeed, whereas it can be said that the construction of the experience of war by humanitarian law is flattened by conflict-driven imperatives, human rights law offers a broader perspective that can encompass a fuller range of human experiences.[399] At the same time, humanitarian norms more effectively incorporate the dynamics of hostile relations that are consonant with warfare and that will affect relations among and between civilians and combatants. The human rights standards on the administration of justice can play an important role in the regulation of insurgent justice, but there is a danger in construing their import as displacing or replacing international humanitarian

[397] See Section IV.A.ii, supra.

[398] Provost, 'Asymmetrical Reciprocity and Compliance with the Laws of War' (n 298).

[399] Fortin (n 355) 58–59; Marco Sassòli, 'L'administration d'un Territoire Par Un Groupe Armé Peut-Elle Être Régie Par Le Droit?' in Michel Hottelier, Maya Hertig Randall, and Alexandre Flückiger (eds), *Etudes en l'honneur du Professeur Thierry Tanquerel. Entre droit constitutionnel et droit administratif: questions autour du droit de l'action publique* (Schulthess 2019) 270 (arguing that the applicability of human rights justifies a narrow nexus under humanitarian law).

law. The more promising approach is to attempt to enrich each by reference to the other, to braid together a regime that can meaningfully and effectively move wartime justice closer to the ideals of both human rights and humanitarian law.[400]

C. The Constitution of Rebel Courts

Having clarified the legal context in which the administration of justice by non-state armed groups in conflict zones can be situated, the analysis now moves to a closer study of standards that impose specific requirements in the establishment of insurgent court. Accordingly, this section identifies the attributes that are associated with the concept of a "court" under humanitarian law (i), explores the ways in which a court may be considered to have been "regularly constituted" (ii), and addresses the institutional implications of a demand that courts be independent and impartial (iii).

i. What Constitutes a "Court"?

As can be gleaned from the case studies in each chapter of this book, "justice" at the hands of armed groups can take many forms. In one of the earliest discussions of the rebel administration of justice, James Bond argued that the reference to a "regularly constituted court" in Common Article 3 should not be taken too literally: "Guerrillas, after all, are not apt to carry black robes and white wigs in their back pack. Any proceeding they convoke will necessarily be ad hoc".[401] It turns out that reality paints a more complex picture. In Sri Lanka, LTTE courts sat in formal courthouses, often the former state courthouses, complete with a large sign on the building, a coat of arms in the courtroom, lawyers required to wear robes, and all the accoutrements of a British-inspired judicial system (except for the wigs). Kurdish courts of the YPG in Rojava, Syria, and of the KRG in Iraq, as well as Islamic State courts, likewise often had a fixed and well-identified location, albeit perhaps with less attention to formal markers of courthouse decorum. Taliban justice more often roams the countryside, the court being largely subsumed into the person of the judge periodically riding in to preside at proceedings in villages and towns. Finally, apart from one limited period and area in which something closer to a judicial bureaucracy was established, FARC justice tended to be more informal and reactive, fusing to varied degrees with communal justice practices. In the limited scholarly discussion of the rebel administration of justice, much of the attention has been focussed on how to interpret the expressions "a regularly constituted court" and "a court offering the

[400] Provost, *International Human Rights and Humanitarian Law* (n 284) 343–350.
[401] Bond (n 3) 372.

essential guarantees of independence and impartiality", respectively, in Common Article 3 and Article 6(2) of Additional Protocol II. The central analytical query in that doctrine is what makes a court "regularly constituted", or the identification of "the essential guarantees of independence and impartiality". But the norms also raise another question: What constitutes a "court" for the purposes of the administration of justice in times of armed conflicts? Can we affirm, with equal assurance and no need for a qualifier, that the court-administered justice offered by the LTTE and the popular assemblies convened by the FARC all correspond to the concept of a "court" as included in humanitarian law? One might be tempted to offer that if a body has been regularly constituted, or if it is found to offer the essential guarantees of independence and impartiality, then it can be considered to constitute a court for the purposes of international humanitarian law. This is perhaps what led Justice Alito in his dissent in *Hamdan v. Rumsfeld* to claim that, under Common Article 3, "[t]he first requirement [of a 'court'] is largely self-explanatory".[402] Two elements give pause before agreeing to this proposition: first, as we will see presently, there is a degree of imprecision as to the precise substance of the concept of regular constitution and essential guarantees of independence and impartiality, so that they may not be the desired source of clarity for the associated notion of a court. Second, it would be to overlook the reality that a court is a concept not devoid of all legal substance, some of which goes beyond the notions of regular constitution and independence and impartiality. As a result, it is necessary to unpack the concept of a "court" and see how it relates to the rebel administration of justice in all its varied forms.

(a) *The Idea of a Court*

At the outset, it is helpful to be reminded that the introduction of a requirement that a judgment and punishment be issued by a (regularly constituted) court in Common Article 3 aimed at the proscription of summary executions. In this respect, as it emerges very clearly from the ICRC commentary of the Geneva Conventions, the requirement of a court decision was linked to the prohibition of the taking of hostages, often leading to executions in reprisals.[403] During World War II, there were many cases of execution of hostages by Germany, while the British and US war manuals both authorised the same practice, so this was far from an academic concern.[404] A distinct but related question touched on

402 *Hamdan v Rumsfeld* (n 272) 726.

403 ICRC, *Commentary on the Fourth Geneva Convention* (n 358) 39.

404 Reprisal executions were authorised by Art. 358(d) of the 1940 US Manual on Rules of Land Warfare FM 27-10 ("The offending forces or populations generally may lawfully be subjected to appropriate reprisals. Hostages taken and held for the declared purpose of insuring against unlawful acts by the enemy forces or people may be punished or put to death if the unlawful acts are nevertheless committed"). For references to post-war decisions on the legality of reprisal executions by courts of various states, see Provost, *International Human Rights and Humanitarian Law* (n 284) 197, 235.

the legality of executing partisans having committed hostile acts against occupying troops. German forces resorted to summary execution of partisans in a quasi-systematic fashion, which gave rise to war crimes prosecutions before Allied tribunals after the war. The relevant decisions of US Military Tribunals in Nuremberg can generously be characterised as uneven. In the *Hostages Case*, the US Tribunal concluded that partisans, like spies, could be shot upon capture, with no mention of a trial, while civilian hostages could not be executed without a fair trial, unless necessity demanded so.[405] In the *High Command Case*, the US Tribunal did find that captured *francs-tireurs*, or partisans, could be punished by death only if proven guilty of hostile acts, but what process was required is unclear:

> It has been urged in this trial that there is no rule of international law that guerrillas be brought to trial before a court and that this order authorizing their disposition on the arbitrary decision of an officer is therefore not illegal. There may be some doubt that trial before a court is in fact required under international law.[406]

The Tribunal found that leaving the matter to the discretion of a junior officer did not meet what was required under the laws of war, which can be taken to imply that a quasi-judicial hearing before a superior officer would be lawful.[407] At a different level, it is known that Winston Churchill initially favoured the summary execution of the Nazi leadership at the close of the Second World War, and only relented in favour of an international tribunal after Franklin D. Roosevelt and Joseph Stalin insisted otherwise.[408] As this context makes clear, the inclusion of a reference to a "court" in Common Article 3 was not a statement of an obvious and universally embraced standard, but rather a determined push to impose a particular type of institution in decisions touching on the administration of criminal justice in the context of armed conflicts.

405 US Nuremberg Military Tribunals, *US v List* (the 'Hostages' Case), *in Trials of War Criminals Before the Nuernberg Military Tribunals under Control Council Law No 10*, Vol 11 (USGPO 1950) 757, 1244–1245, 1250–1253.

406 US Nuremberg Military Tribunals, *US v von Leeb* (the 'High Command' Case), *in Trials of War Criminals Before the Nuernberg Military Tribunals under Control Council Law No 10*, Vol 11 (USGPO 1950) 1, 523.

407 Kevin Jon Heller, *The Nuremberg Military Tribunals and the Origins of International Criminal Law* (Oxford University Press 2011) 210–211 ("Unfortunately, the tribunals were maddeningly vague concerning what the 'accepted trial requirements' actually were"); August von Knieriem, *The Nuremberg Trials* (H Regnery Company 1959) 379–398 (a partial but nevertheless detailed and interesting critique of the tribunals caselaw on hostages).

408 Ian Cobain, 'Britain Favoured Execution over Nuremberg Trials for Nazi Leaders' *The Guardian* (26 October 2012).

A court is thus a thing of substance in the optics of Common Article 3, and presumably in that of other provisions of the Geneva Conventions and Protocols as well as under customary humanitarian law. The question then becomes: What are the attributes that differentiate a court from other institutions and practices? A lawyer might be forgiven the reflex of immediately invoking images of large buildings, possibly fronted by many columns, in which individuals perform highly choreographed functions, perhaps wearing a fixed attire like robes and even wigs. What this speaks to is the intimate connection between the identification of the attributes of a court and the construction of the concept of law. As I explored in Chapter 1, a narrow positivistic understanding of law (not entirely uncommon in the humanitarian law field) supports a necessary and monopolistic association of law and the state that, in turn, locates the administration of justice in the operation of state courts.[409] This point will become central in the discussion of what constitutes a "regularly constituted" court, but it also has a bearing on the very construction of the idea of a "court". As pointed out in the discussion of the rule of law, the complete takeover of the idea of law by the state may have been achieved in a narrative sense in the Western construction of the state, but it appears neither justified nor verified by a deeper analysis of the ways in which legal norms operate in society, even in Western societies. A fuller account of the nature and function of legal norms by way of a pluralistic understanding of law provides a foundation for an analysis of the ways in which a range of actors invoke varied legal regimes to ensure legal security in a given community.[410] Without the conceptual tools provided by legal pluralism, as noted by Brian Tamanaha, legal analysis struggles to account for the fact that in many places much of what we designate as law is administered by institutions and practices independent from the state, whether because state institutions like courts are dysfunctional (a common occurrence in conflict zones) or for cultural and historical reasons.[411] Afghanistan, as we saw, is one example where the state never occupied more than a limited space in the resolution of disputes, be they civil or penal. The recognition of the protean nature of law and legal institutions does not necessarily imply the demise of the notion of formal law, as indicated by the constitutional recognition of legal orders of different natures in the laws of countries like Colombia or South Africa.[412]

[409] Chapter 1, Section III.A.

[410] I explore this in René Provost, 'Interpretation in International Law as a Transcultural Project' in Andrea Bianchi, Daniel Peat, and Matthew Windsor (eds), *Interpretation in International Law* (Oxford University Press 2015).

[411] Brian Tamanaha, 'A Bifurcated Theory of Law in Hybrid Societies: The Rule of Law and Non-State Justice' in Matthias Kötter and others (eds), *Non-State Justice Institutions and the Law. Decision-Making at the Interface of Tradition, Religion and the State* (Palgrave Macmillan 2015).

[412] See: Daniel Bonilla Maldonado, *La Constitución multicultural* (Siglo del Hombre Editores 2006); Christa Rautenbach, 'South Africa: Legal Recognition of Traditional Courts—Legal Pluralism

Rather than importing a model derived from state-centrism, the concept of a court in relation to the administration of justice in zones of armed conflict must be constructed on a functional basis. It is suggested that the concept of a court reflects a combination of attributes linked to the actors, the basis of decisions, and the process. Each is discussed in turn in the next subsections.

(b) Oracles of the Law

The judge is, in some but not all legal traditions, a towering figure that defines in many ways the idea of a court. In the celebrated words of Blackstone, judges "are the depositaries of the laws; the living oracles, who must decide in all cases of doubt, and who are bound by oath to decide according to the law of the land".[413] Even Western legal traditions embrace to greatly varying degrees the notion of the judge as the oracle of the law, to say nothing of other legal traditions tied to distinct religious, political, or cultural environments.[414] Given the global reach of international humanitarian law, with the Geneva Conventions having been universally ratified, it would be unjustified to adhere to an overly rigid construction of the concept of a court reflecting a narrow legal heritage. Thus the critique levelled by ONUSAL and America's Watch that FMLN courts in El Salvador were unlawful because presided over by individuals who had not been trained in the law must be resisted.[415] Some non-state armed groups may perhaps count lawyers among their members, but by and large that is an unusual profile for a rebel fighter, to say the least.[416] Even more unusual is the example offered by the LTTE in Sri Lanka, which established its own Tamil Eelam Law College and required judges and lawyers to be graduates of this college or of one of Sri Lanka's law faculties.[417] Some armed groups inspired by religious ideologies like the

in Action' in Matthias Kötter and others (eds), *Non-State Justice Institutions and the Law. Decision-Making at the Interface of Tradition, Religion and the State* (Palgrave Macmillan 2015).

[413] William Blackstone, *Commentaries on the Laws of England, Volume 1: A Facsimile of the First Edition of 1765–1769* (University of Chicago Press 1979) 59.

[414] See generally John Philip Dawson, *The Oracles of the Law* (Greenwood Press 1978).

[415] ONUSAL, 'Third Report of the United Nations Observer Mission in El Salvador', UN Doc A/46/876-S/23580 (1992) para 112; Americas Watch, 'Violation of Fair Trial Guarantees by the FMLN's Ad Hoc Courts' (1990) 18 ("A judge whose task is to apply the law should know and be able to understand it. Yet, there apparently is no express requirement that ANY member of these ad hoc courts have any legal training or competency. That the fate of persons charged with capital offences should be decided by persons apparently unskilled in the law is appallingly indecent and utterly deprives the accused of a basic guarantee necessary for his or her defense"); Zegveld (n 2) 72; Tathiana Flores Acuña, *The United Nations Mission in El Salvador: A Humanitarian Law Perspective* (Kluwer Law International 1995) 60.

[416] Thus the FMLN objected that "the type of tribunal and law required by Protocol II have to be adapted to the conditions and capacity of the contending party; the particular mechanisms necessary for defense must be adjusted to the real possibilities of the zone where the trial is held. One cannot insist, for example, that the defense counsel be a licensed attorney when in the region no one exists with this specialization": FMLN Secretariat for the Promotion and Protection of Human Rights (n 282) 20.

[417] See Chapter 3, Section II.

Islamic State and the Taliban will usually favour individuals who have received religious rather than legal training, in part a reflection of the norms being applied by the courts.[418] Not rarely, judicial functions will simply be among the duties assigned to military commanders regardless of their lack of legal training or education in general, as was the case for the FMLN and the FARC, for example.

Reliance on individuals lacking any legal training to act as decision-makers in the administration of justice is not, as such, an especially novel or reactionary proposition. It is good to be reminded that even in the legal tradition most closely attached to a vision of the judge as oracle of the law, the common law, the jury of "twelve men good and true" was and still is entrusted with the central decision of the guilt or innocence of the accused, despite their lack of any legal training. They performed this function, at least in the initial phases of the common law that would now be labelled transitional justice, under the watchful eyes of clerics sitting as judges, following the precise written instructions of the political leader (the royal writs).[419] Remaining in the same legal tradition, we could also mention that the highest court of appeal in the United Kingdom, the House of Lords, saw until the nineteenth century cases decided by peers that did not necessarily have the benefit of any legal training.[420] For Blackstone, this was offset by the peers' "delicacy of sentiment, so peculiar to noble birth".[421] In South Carolina (United States), nearly three-quarters of magistrates lacking any legal training preside over a wide range of civil disputes and lesser criminal offences, including trials by jury. The justification for this state of affairs is simply that there aren't enough trained lawyers to fill these judicial posts.[422] In Afghanistan, only 11 percent of state judges have a law degree, with another 44 percent trained only in *Sharīʿa* meaning that nearly half of judges lack any legal education at all.[423] The fact that rebel justice will in some conflict zones be done by way of popular assemblies

[418] Regine Schwab, 'Insurgent Courts in Civil Wars: The Three Pathways of (Trans) Formation in Today's Syria (2012–2017)' (2018) 29 Small Wars & Insurgencies 801, 808. The Mouvement national de liberation de l'Azawad in Mali adopts a similar practice by coopting local cadis to act as judges: Pascal Bongard, 'Words to Deeds: A Research Study of Armed Non-State Actors' Practice and Interpretation of International Humanitarian and Human Rights Norms—the National Movement for the Liberation of Azawad' (Geneva Call 2021) 40, online: <https://words2deeds.org/wp-content/uploads/2021/03/Case-Study-The-National-Movemen.pdf>.

[419] H Patrick Glenn, *Legal Traditions of the World: Sustainable Diversity in Law* (5th edn, Oxford University Press 2014) 239 ("The judges had to be who they were, since there wasn't anybody else, and the procedure was just right, for post-conquest circumstances").

[420] John Philip Dawson, *A History of Lay Judges* (Harvard University Press 1960) 177(the last recorded judicial vote by a lay peer was in 1883).

[421] Blackstone (n 413) 12.

[422] Joseph Cranney, 'These SC Judges Can Have Less Training than Barbers but Still Decide Thousands of Cases Each Year' *Post and Courier* (27 November 2019), online: <https://www.postandcourier.com/news/these-sc-judges-can-have-less-training-than-barbers-but/article_deeac12e-eb6f-11e9-927b-5735a3edbaf1.html> accessed 2 December 2019.

[423] Center for Policy and Human Development (n 164) 70–71. Even more starkly, one ICC judge, Fumiko Saiga, did not have any formal legal education.

convened by an armed group thus does not seem so irreconcilable with the concept of a court as evidenced in the practice of states.

The question of the legal requirement that a particular kind of individual, possibly trained in the law, preside over the administration of justice has sometimes been considered in the context of the recognition of decisions of foreign jurisdictions. In some cases in which double jeopardy was invoked, or in applying the principle of complementarity under the Rome Statute, the question of whether alternative justice mechanisms could be considered as functional equivalent of courts has been analysed. In the discussions of how the ICC should interpret Article 17 of the Rome Statute in relation to alternative justice mechanisms, institutions like the *gacaca* in Rwanda, *mato oput* in Uganda, or *Pashtunwali* in Afghanistan have attracted some criticism for failing to ensure due process in various ways, but not necessarily for falling short of what is functionally required to act as a court.[424] This is so despite the fact that *gacaca* judges did not have legal training, indeed many were illiterate, and yet could impose life sentences.[425] In a different context, the Divisional Court of England and Wales considered a request for extradition presented by the government of Rwanda against individuals who had been previously tried by *gacacà* courts in that country. In its 2017 judgment, the Divisional Court found that there may be due process concerns regarding the *gacaca* proceedings but that this "does not amount to a lack of jurisdictional competence".[426] In other words, an alternative justice mechanism like the *gacaca* could be considered equivalent to a court for the purposes of *ne bis in idem*.

It is with this in mind that must be considered the statement by the Stockholm District Court in the *Sakhanh* case that one requirement for the legality of a rebel court is that "the court is staffed by personnel which before the outbreak of the conflict were appointed in a regular manner as judges or officials of the judicial system".[427] In that case, Sakhanh was accused of carrying out the capital punishment imposed by rebel judges who had been judges in the Syrian state judiciary. There is no basis in international law for this requirement. It appears to

[424] Alexander KA Greenawalt, 'Complementarity in Crisis: Uganda, Alternative Justice, and the International Criminal Court' (2009) 50 Virginia Journal of International Law 107; Linda M Keller, 'Achieving Peace with Justice: The International Criminal Court and Ugandan Alternative Justice Mechanisms' (2007) 23 Connecticut Journal of International Law 209; Mark A Drumbl, *Atrocity, Punishment, and International Law* (Cambridge University Press 2007) 87–94. The relation of rebel justice to complementarity under the Rome Statute is further considered in Chapter 4, Section II.C.

[425] Pietro Sullo, *Beyond Genocide: Transitional Justice and Gacaca Courts in Rwanda* (Springer 2018) 173. On the prevalence of adjudicators without legal training in customary courts, see UNDP, 'Informal Justice Systems—Charting a Course for Human Rights-Based Engagement' (UNDP-UN Women-UNICEF 2013) 61–62.

[426] *Rwanda v Ntezíryayo*, [2017] EWHC 1912, para 478.

[427] Sakhanh Trial Judgment (n 5) para 38. The Svea Court of Appeal in the case does not appear to refer to or endorse this particular requirement, deciding the matter on other points.

have been taken from the expert statement by Mark Klamberg, but in fact he addressed a different model situation, in which the state's courts continue to operate even in areas under rebel control.[428] Such situations, if they are not usual, are by no means unknown in non-international armed conflicts. The FARC, for instance, often permitted state courts to keep operating in zones under its control, preferring to impose restrictions on what cases they could deal with.[429] If insurgents refrain from stopping the operation of state courts, then the latter obviously retain their status as "courts", subject to further conditions that they afford due process and adjudicate in an independent and impartial manner. The establishment by non-state armed groups of their own, autonomous courts is an entirely different model situation, and even a creative interpretation of applicable public international law standards does not lead to require that defectors from the state judiciary be found to sit as rebel judges. It would imply that judicial legitimacy is somehow *ad hominem*, and that judges can "go rogue" and bring with them the mantle of justice despite severing their link to the state. What's more, it is in the nature of the judicial function that governments tend to appoint as judges individuals who profess loyalty to the sovereign authority of the state, and the happenstance in the *Sakhanh* case that the sentence was imposed by judges who had defected is, in fact, an extremely rare example.[430] In the majority of armed conflicts, imposing this requirement would amount to preventing the establishment of any insurgent court. In Syria, for example, discrimination against Kurds means that there were nearly no Kurdish judges sitting in the courts of the regime.[431]

Even states give themselves much flexibility in the staffing of courts in conflict zones.[432] At most, it might be suggested that the fact that rebel courts are presided over by former state judges may be a factor in determining the independence

428 Mark Klamberg, 'Possibility of a Non-State Actor to Establish Courts, Issue Sentence and Avoid Criminal Responsibility for Acts That Otherwise Would Constitute War Crimes' (2016) SSRN Scholarly Paper 20, online: <https://papers.ssrn.com/abstract=2914188> accessed 10 August 2019. See also Somer (n 4) 677 (quoting an ICRC delegate during the negotiations of Protocol II to the same effect).

429 See Chapter 1, Section I.B.iii.

430 The Syrian conflict is one in which it is reported that a number of judges defected to the insurgency and presided over rebel courts: United Nations Independent International Commission of Inquiry on the Syrian Arab Republic, 'Memorandum: Response to the Swedish Prosecution Authority', Nationella Operativa Avdelningen, Sakkunnigutlåtande COI-rapport, diarienr: 5000-K132600-16 (12 October 2016) para 6. One can think of the US Civil War as another situation in which many federal judges appointed by the US Government switched allegiance and continued sitting as Confederate judges: William Robinson, *Justice in Grey; A History of the Judicial System of the Confederate States of America* (Harvard University Press 1941). That situation is considered in some details in Chapter 4, Section IV.

431 Ekman (n 45) 127.

432 Benjamin Disraeli reportedly went so far as to claim that "in the state of martial law there can be no irregularity in the composition of the court, as the best court that can be got must be assembled", *cited in* William Winthrop, *Military Law and Precedents* (2d edn, US Government Printing Office 1920) 835.

and impartiality of the court in some cases.[433] Even here, there is more than a little irony in deriving this from the *Sakhanh* case, given how notoriously lacking in independence and impartiality have been the courts of Bashar Al-Assad's regime. Indeed, accepting appointment as a judge in such a brutally repressive regime suggests a willingness to compromise that is precisely the opposite of the qualities one associates with the judicial functions.[434] One might be forgiven for viewing more positively the FMLN code that reportedly provided "concrete rules for selecting an independent and impartial tribunal from among the population. It establishes that the defense counsel should be selected by virtue of his conduct and the solidity of his ethical principles. Obviously it does not exclude a specialist in law from being chosen where one is found".[435] Integrity, independence, impartiality, and compassion are qualities that have been identified as central to the judicial function, and one might expect to find them in a range of individuals not limited to those previously appointed to the bench by the state, or even trained in the law.[436]

(c) The Concept of Law

In addition to the identity of the decision-makers, another attribute distinguishing a "court" from other institutions is the basis of decision. In the analysis of how the concept of the rule of law relates to the rebel administration of justice, I suggested that one element of a rebel rule of law is a degree of stability and predictability of decisions.[437] The normative implication of this speaks to the fact that the court decides on the basis of norms that were known or knowable to the individuals to whom they are applied. This is expressed in penal matters by the maxim *nullum crimen sine lege*, but it obtains in non-criminal matters as well. A court properly so conceived must arrive at its decisions by applying "law", as opposed to pure morality, the decider's whim, or simply arbitrariness.[438] The key question, then, becomes how the concept of law should be defined in this context. Leaving aside philosophical investigations of the ontological nature of law that have fascinated and frustrated thinkers through the ages, the question

[433] Klamberg (n 4) 23–24.

[434] The dilemmas faced by Syrian judges were explained by former Syrian judge Khaled Shehab Eddin as an expert witness in the *Sakhanh* trial: Nationella Operativa Avdelningen, Förhör med Shehab Eddin, Khaled, diarienr: 5000-K132600-16 (23 March 2016) 28–29, 33; Raymond Wacks, 'Judges and Injustice' (1984) 101 South African Law Journal 266, 267–268 (the first question to ask about judging in an unjust system is "what is the judge doing in such a system?"); David Dyzenhaus, *Hard Cases in Wicked Legal Systems: Pathologies of Legality* (2d edn, Oxford University Press 2010).

[435] FMLN Secretariat for the Promotion and Protection of Human Rights (n 282) 20.

[436] Robert J Sharpe, *Good Judgment: Making Judicial Decisions* (University of Toronto Press 2018) 249–269.

[437] See Chapter 1, Section II.C.ii.

[438] Duncan Kennedy, *A Critique of Adjudication (Fin de Siècle)* (Harvard University Press 1997) 3 (Judges "are supposed to 'submit' to something 'bigger' and 'higher' than 'themselves'").

can be framed in more pedestrian terms as the range of norms that a rebel court could invoke, under international law, as the basis of its decision. The *Sakhanh* case here again provides an interesting jumping-off point. In its judgment, the Stockholm District Court found that non-state armed groups could legally establish a court if "the court applies the law that existed before the outbreak of the conflict, or at least not laws that differ considerably in stricter direction from the legislation that existed before the outbreak of the conflict".[439] This reflects the fact that, in the Court's view, "it is only states, in accordance with their respective constitutional rules, that may impose criminal law".[440] At trial, Sakhanh had testified that the men he was accused of executing had been convicted of the murder and rape of civilians under the relevant Syrian law, which provides for the death penalty for these crimes. Does international law require that a rebel court apply the law of territorial state as a condition of its legality?

Article 6(2)(c) of Additional Protocol II affords some elements of an answer in providing that "no one shall be held guilty of any criminal offence on account of any act or omission which did not constitute a criminal offence, under the law, at the time when it was committed". This provision is of course limited to the administration of justice in criminal matters, leaving out an enormous part of the rebel administration of justice in non-penal matters, but it nevertheless offers a statement of principle that can be enlightening. The initial ICRC draft of Article 6(2)(c) was inspired by Articles 99 of the Third Geneva Convention and 67 of the Fourth Geneva Convention, and Article 15(1) of the International Covenant on Civil and Political Rights.[441] The ICRC draft did not mention "law" but simply referred to an act which was an offence. The German Democratic Republic proposed, at the onset of negotiations in 1974, the addition of a reference to "national or international law" to fully align the text with Article 15(1) of the Covenant and to cover the possibility of prosecution of international crimes that were not offences under domestic law.[442] Despite some opposition, the German amendment was adopted, but it triggered lingering discussions regarding what would be covered by the expression "national and international law".[443] Nigeria had proposed the addition of a reference in the chapeau of Article 6(2) to a court "whose jurisdiction is based on a recognizable body of law" because, it explained, "[i]t was only logical that if rebels could organize themselves

[439] Sakhanh Trial Judgment (n 5) paras 31, 38.

[440] ibid para 30. The Court derives this from the expert testimony of Professor Mark Klamberg: Klamberg (n 428) 10.

[441] ICRC, *Commentary on the Additional Protocols of 8 June 1977 to the Geneva Conventions of 12 August 1949* (n 277) para 4604.

[442] The *travaux préparatoires* of Protocol II are conveniently collated in Howard S Levie, *The Law of Non International Armed Conflict: Protocol II to the 1949 Geneva Conventions* (Martinus Nijhoff Publishers 1987) 246, 250 (Meeting of Committee I, 20 March 1975, CDDH/I/SR.33, para 38).

[443] ibid 278 (Meeting of Committee I, 4 June 1976, CDDH/I/SR.63, paras 60 [Spain] & 62 [GDR]).

sufficiently to observe the Protocols, and thereby enjoy their protection, they could also organize a recognizable body of law".[444] Argentina objected that the newly added reference to "national law" was confusing because "[i]t was indeed unlikely that a Government which was a party to a non-international armed conflict would recognize the idea of rebel law as 'national law'".[445] A proposition was made to amend the text to remove "national and international" to leave the reference to "law" unqualified, presumably to include rebel law. The *travaux préparatoires* are somewhat difficult to follow, but it seems that this proposed deletion was put to a vote and rejected.[446] Despite this rejection, however, some confusion in the conference secretariat seems to have resulted in the English draft subsequently omitting the words "national and international" before "law", while the French version maintained a reference to "*le droit national ou international*".[447] No one seems to have noticed the discrepancy, and both English and French versions were adopted by consensus by the Conference Plenary without any discussion of this issue.[448] This speluncean detour into the *travaux* of Additional Protocol II was necessary because we find ourselves in the unusual position of having two equally authentic versions of Protocol II that diverge in a critical manner.[449]

There is no doubt that the reference to the sanction of a criminal offence "under the law" in the English version lends itself to a wider definition of what might be encompassed by the term "law" than the mention in French of "national and

[444] ibid 258 (Meeting of Committee I, 20 March 1975, CDDH/I/SR.34, para 20).

[445] ibid 282 (Meeting of Committee I, 7 June 1976, CDDH/I/SR.64, para 54).

[446] ibid 290 (proposed amendment rejected by a vote of 35 to 3, with 4 abstentions: Report of Committee I, Third Session, CDDH/I/Rev.1, Official Records vol 10 at 131).

[447] The English version adopted by Committee I and the one sent by the Drafting Committee to the Conference Plenary Meeting both include the mention of "national and international law". The qualifiers are missing from a Pakistani proposed amendment introduced at the Plenary and focusing on the death penalty, which might have been the source of the confusion: ibid 293 (CHHD/427, 31 May 1977, Official Records vol 4 at 36).

[448] ibid 294–303.

[449] While only the French and English versions of the 1949 Geneva Conventions are authentic (Art. 55/54/133/150), the Arabic, Chinese, English, French, Russian, and Spanish versions of the Additional Protocols are equally authentic (Art. 102, Protocol I; Art. 28, Protocol II). See Bothe and others (n 313) 647 ("Without questioning in any way the legal principle that the texts in all six languages are equally authentic one cannot avoid giving some account of the linguistic reality. During the Conference in the Plenary, in the Committees and also in the Working Groups the most used language was English. Informal discussions between delegates who spoke another language in the official meetings were also mostly conducted in English. The same was true of drafts which very often were written during such informal meetings. In view of the composition of the staff of the Conference, French texts were frequently available earlier than English texts. Nevertheless amendments to these French texts were often written also in English, but soon translated into French. Spanish and Russian versions usually were distributed with some delay. As to the relationship between the two main languages of the Conference, one cannot say that a hierarchy can be established. The precedence of a version in English can only be accepted in those cases in which such version has been called authentic and the Drafting Committee was asked to bring the French text into line with an original English text").

international law". While, as one might expect, some states have objected to the suggestion of rebel law in this context, others have considered that the provision does justify giving recognition to what is occurring in practice. Thus the United Kingdom, in its Manual on the Law of Armed Conflict, noted the difference between the French and English versions of Additional Protocol II and concluded that "law" was wide enough to include not only national and international law but that "[i]t could also be wide enough to cover 'laws' passed by an insurgent authority".[450] This has been linked to some extent to a discussion of the legality of detention by armed groups during non-international armed conflicts, which is taken to imply that the groups have some internal law validating and regulating such detention.[451] The United Nations has maintained a degree of fuzziness on the question of whether non-state armed groups may enact their own laws: the UN Mission in El Salvador (ONUSAL) during the civil war in that country criticised aspects of laws promulgated by the FMLN, in a manner that suggested that the armed group could indeed enact such norms;[452] on the other hand, the UN Assistance Mission in Afghanistan (UNAMA) in its annual reports refers to Taliban justice as an illegal usurpation of justice under Afghan law and calls for the group to put an end to it.[453] The ICRC in its commentaries on Additional Protocol II and Common Article 3 is unambiguous in accepting the law-making capacity of non-state armed groups, finding that both state and insurgent law could be characterised as "national law" coexisting in the territory of the state.[454] The alternative position embraced by the Stockholm District Court in *Sakhanh*, which would require a rebel court to apply state law, seems inconsistent with the thrust of the analysis of international humanitarian law up to this point, and would force the application of standards that were designed for state courts

450 UK Ministry of Defence, *The Manual of the Law of Armed Conflict* (Oxford University Press, Oxford 2005) para 15.42 note 94. See also Sivakumaran, 'Courts of Armed Opposition Groups—Fair Trials or Summary Justice?' (n 4) 507.

451 Andrew Clapham, 'Detention by Armed Groups Under International Law' (2017) 93 International Law Studies 1, 28; Frédéric Mégret, 'Detention by Non-State Armed Groups in NIACs: IHL, International Human Rights Law and the Question of the Right Authority' in Ezequiel Heffes, Marcos D Kotlik, and Manuel J Ventura (eds), *International Humanitarian Law and Non-State Actors: Debates, Law and Practice* (TMC Asser Press 2020). The 2016 US Law of War Manual acknowledges that detention by an armed group would likely constitute criminal kidnapping under domestic law but that "detention during non-international armed conflict by non-State armed groups is not prohibited by international law", without specifying the inference that this would reflect rebel law: United States Department of Defense, *Law of War Manual* (2016) 1064 para 17.17.2.

452 ONUSAL (n 415) 28–29; Zegveld (n 2) 70–71. Significantly, both sides of the war in El Salvador acknowledged the applicability of Additional Protocol II to the conflict: FMLN Secretariat for the Promotion and Protection of Human Rights (n 282) 3–4.

453 See the passage quoted earlier from UNAMA (n 301).

454 ICRC, *Commentary on the Additional Protocols of 8 June 1977 to the Geneva Conventions of 12 August 1949* (n 277) paras 4605–4606; ICRC, *Commentary on the Second Geneva Convention* (n 286) para 714.

with different levels of resources, operating in a very different context, with possibly vastly distinct social, political, cultural, or religious aims.[455] This is of central significance for the rebel administration of justice in non-criminal matters, to which neither Common Article 3 nor Article 6 of Protocol II apply. The fact that, while not all armed groups enact their own laws, many do so, especially in situations in which they come to assume a governance role in zones under their control or influence, means that international law must address and regulate this phenomenon rather than pretend it just doesn't exist.

A court is an institution that functions on the basis of law, which includes, as we have seen, the possibility of insurgent law. It is important to underscore the fact that such rebel law is subject to the requirements and limitations emanating from both international humanitarian law and international human rights law. Thus an insurgent law like that of the Islamic State that discriminates on the basis of religion, for instance, might be law, but it is nevertheless in violation of international law. Conversely, it would seem perverse to insist that rebel courts apply the wicked laws of an unjust regimes, as surely would be the case for Syria, or even state laws that are less progressive than that of the armed opposition group, such as the LTTE rules against discrimination on the basis of caste or in favour of gender equality. Just like sovereignty can be understood as responsibility, the recognition of law-making autonomy for non-state armed groups in armed conflicts is one that comes with a bevy of obligations. As such, to open to the possibility of rebel law is to broaden the regulatory palette with which international law aims to orient the behaviour of armed groups in a manner more consistent with the protection of the victims of war. A distinct point rarely made in this respect touches on the other type of law explicitly mentioned in the French version of Article 6(2)(c) of Protocol II: international law. There are examples of rebel courts given the jurisdiction to sanction war crimes and other serious violations of international law.[456] It seems impossible to fault an insurgent court for applying rules that sanction violations of values central to the international community as a whole.

(d) Of Courts and Cathedrals

Does the idea of a court imply the necessity of a courthouse? Religious allegories are not infrequent in legal analysis, and the cathedral has from time to time been used as a metaphor for the idea of law and the role of courts.[457] In some

[455] We could also note that the Court does not close the door entirely to rebel laws, but only to that which "differ considerably in stricter direction" from state law (Sakhanh Trial Judgment (n 5) paras 31, 38). It is not easy to fathom what "differing in stricter direction" might mean apart from imposing harsher penalties for exactly the same crime. In reality, as we can see with Islamic State and Taliban laws, rebel law often goes its own way, making comparisons with state law very difficult.

[456] See, e.g., FMLN Secretariat for the Promotion and Protection of Human Rights (n 282) 17.

[457] Linda Mulcahy, *Legal Architecture: Justice, Due Process and the Place of Law* (Routledge 2010) 19. On the proximity in the representations of law and religion more broadly, see Douglas Hay,

suggestions that the rule of law must be built brick by brick like a cathedral, there is a sense of the monumental dimension of the administration of justice. This is indeed translated into a practice, in many places, of courthouses with impressive architecture that structures the performance of legal rituals central to the social life of the law.[458] As architect Paul Katsieris has suggested, "[a] society looks to a law court, as well as other public buildings, to personify the community's state of being with respect to matters of justice".[459] A palace of justice is designed to glorify the operation of law just as a cathedral is meant to celebrate the glory of god. In this vision, "courts are centrally located, locally anchored, spatially discrete and architecturally symbolic", communicating a theory of authority and shaping the justice that is delivered.[460]

In the discussion of the rebel administration of justice, there are fleeting hints of some discomfort with the absence of a special place associated with, if not designed for, the administration of justice, a sense that justice is not something that can be dispensed anywhere in any fashion. Thus Jonathan Somer and to a degree Sandesh Sivakumaran evoke with some trepidation the "intriguing possibility of portable courts".[461] This shines a light on a dimension of the discussion of rebel justice that is never acknowledged, that these "kangaroo courts" can never fulfil the function performed by "real courts" because they are simply too informal, in all senses of that word. Of course, as previously mentioned, there *are* rebel courts that conform to such expectations of form attaching to the operation of justice. Most spectacularly (pun intended), the LTTE courts were as formalistic as any state courts, down to the coat of arms on the wall and the gowns required of lawyers. But the LTTE stands as an exception in that regard, a reflection of the stability and longevity of the group's governance over the north-east of Sri Lanka. More frequently, insurgent justice is dispensed in places not consecrated for the administration of justice, whether in schools, mosques, or other public buildings, or even just outside in the open.

'Property, Authority and the Criminal Law' in Douglas Hay (ed), *Albion's Fatal Tree: Crime and Society in Eighteenth-Century England* (Verso 1975) 29–30.

458 Richard Mohr, 'In Between: Power and Procedure Where the Court Meets the Public Sphere' in Marit Paasche and Judy Radul (eds), *A Thousand Eyes: Media Technology, Law, and Aesthetics* (Henie Onstad Art Centre 2011).

459 Paul Katsieris, 'The Design of the Commonwealth Law Courts Building, Melbourne' (1999) 1 Journal of Social Change and Critical Inquiry, online: <http://pandora.nla.gov.au/nph-wb/20000123130000/http://www.uow.edu.au/arts/joscci/kastieris.html> accessed 9 September 2019.

460 Mulcahy (n 457) 12; Mariana Valverde, 'Deepening the Conversation Between Socio-Legal Theory and Legal Scholarship about Jurisdiction', in Stephen Allen and others (eds), *The Oxford Handbook of Jurisdiction in International Law* (Oxford University Press 2019) 175, referring to Bruno Latour, *The Making of Law: An Ethnography of the Conseil D'Etat* (Polity 2010).

461 Somer (n 4) 688; Sivakumaran, 'Courts of Armed Opposition Groups—Fair Trials or Summary Justice?' (n 4) 506–507.

As suggested in Mariana Valverde's notion of chronotopes of law, there are both place and time dimensions to the idea of justice.[462] The unstated and largely unacknowledged requirement that a court must have a designated and visible seat must be resisted. There is in fact nothing intriguing about the possibility of portable courts, as that is precisely the way to describe state courts for long periods of their existence. Whether the itinerant eyre courts going from town to town in England or the aptly named Circuit Courts of Appeals in the United States, it is not difficult to find examples of formal state courts that did not have a fixed location. More generally, the association of courts with courthouses is a relatively recent and culturally contingent phenomenon. In many places in the past and in some still today, law is administered outdoors, on moot hills, under oak trees, or in the market place, for reasons of visibility or convenience.[463] The image of the Taliban judge riding into town on his motorcycle is but a variation of the English assize court judge arriving by train to be ceremonially welcomed by the county sheriff in the 1960s.[464] In the Democratic Republic of Congo, government mobile courts have played a central role in the prosecution of war crimes and crimes against humanity committed in the context of the conflict in that country, by being able to be deployed rapidly and in remote locations.[465] In Burma/Myanmar, the Karen National Liberation Army combines fixed courts of different levels with "mobile judges" who can be called to provide village-level justice.[466] As noted by Alessandra Spadaro, there is no reason to presume that mobile courts are less apt to deliver due process; on the opposite, they might be better suited to the constantly shifting reality of insurgency.[467]

To be intriguing, we might push the idea further and envisage the possibility of MSF-inspired *juges sans frontière*, independent and impartial trained jurists who would participate in insurgent justice remotely, sitting in proceedings by way of a live video link.[468] This would in fact align with the current trend towards the increasing digitalisation of courts, which occupy a virtual as well as a situated space.[469] It would likewise mirror a growing practice of hybridisation of courts dealing with war crimes, in which the bench is composed of a mix of national

[462] Mariana Valverde, *Chronotopes of Law: Jurisdiction, Scale and Governance* (Routledge 2015) 18.
[463] Mulcahy (n 457) 6–7.
[464] Sir Basil Nield, *Farewell to the Assizes: The Sixty-One Towns* (Garnstone Press 1972) 6.
[465] Christian M De Vos, *Complementarity, Catalysts, Compliance: The International Criminal Court in Uganda, Kenya, and the Democratic Republic of Congo* (Cambridge University Press 2020) 239–245.
[466] Brian McCartan and Kim Jolliffe, 'Ethnic Armed Actors and Justice Provision in Myanmar' (Asia Foundation 2016) 25.
[467] Spadaro (n 352) 26.
[468] There are organisations called *Avocats sans frontière* and Lawyers Without Borders, but I am not aware that they provide this type of remote legal assistance to rebel courts in conflict zones.
[469] On the "dematerialisation of the courthouse", see Mulcahy (n 457) 162–183.

and foreign judges.[470] Armed opposition groups like the Islamic State have proven savvy users of social media, and it is not as fanciful as might be thought to suggest that they could be connected for this purpose to people well outside the conflict zone. Whether armed groups would be willing to do so is, of course, an entirely different question.

In conclusion, the suggestion that non-state armed groups can or must establish courts in some circumstances under international humanitarian law reflects an expectation that these are particular types of institutions that are defined by specific features. Who can act as a decision-maker, what norms will guide the process, and what institutional design corresponds to a court are elements that have a defined and yet flexible substance. A balance is both desirable and possible between that which makes courts instruments of justice and the ideals that are simply unattainable for non-state armed groups operating in conflict zones.

ii. "Regularly Constituted" Courts

A second, distinct, requirement stemming from Common Article 3 is that the court passing the possibly capital sentence be "regularly constituted". The one element of consensus about this requirement is that the notion of a "regularly constituted" court is left largely undefined in the Geneva Conventions and in international humanitarian law generally. I first explore the most plausible interpretation of that expression before considering its relation to the human rights standard that a tribunal be "established by law".

(a) Regularly Constituted Courts in Humanitarian Law

In a report on the state of Ireland in the 1880s, the Earl of Carnarvon bemoaned that "the greatest mischief lay in the informal courts" established by the Irish National League to handle land disputes in its effort to undermine British rule and resist the injustice of English courts: "And when I say 'informal' courts, perhaps I should say 'formal', for they were formal in every respect except that they were secret.... They were regularly constituted, went into evidence on each side in a regular manner, and under a system of carefully drawn rules, proceeded by written records, and were in complete communication with the Central Body in Dublin".[471] This example, taken from a very different setting, makes the point that we can think of a court as regularly constituted despite the fact that

[470] Harry Hobbs, 'Towards a Principled Justification for the Mixed Composition of Hybrid International Criminal Tribunals' (2017) 30 Leiden Journal of International Law 177; Frédéric Mégret, 'In Defense of Hybridity: Towards a Representational Theory of International Criminal Justice' (2005) 38 Cornell International Law Journal 725.

[471] Sir Arthur Hardinge, *The Life of Henry Howard Molyneux Herbert, Fourth Earl of Carnarvon, 1831–1890*, vol 3 (Humphrey 1925) 252; cited in Donald Jordan, 'The Irish National League and the "Unwritten Law": Rural Protest and Nation-Building in Ireland 1882–1890' (1998) 158 Past & Present 146, 161.

it operates in violation of the national law of a state. In the context of the interpretation of the expression "regularly constituted" in Common Article 3 of the Geneva Conventions, the first question would be to assess whether this is a concept defined in international humanitarian law. The only other use of the expression "regularly constituted court" can be found in Article 75(4) of Additional Protocol I, which refers to an "impartial and regularly constituted Court", but without providing any further specificity to the expression. Article 66 of the Fourth Geneva Convention for its part uses the expression "properly constituted court" to describe non-military courts in occupied territory, although the equally authentic French version uses "*régulièrement constitués*" in both Common Article 3 and Article 66. The ICRC commentary explains that a properly or regularly constituted court "definitely excludes all special tribunals" in favour of ordinary military tribunals established "in accordance with the recognized principles governing the administration of justice".[472] This actually does little to dim the uncertainty surrounding the notion of a regularly constituted court, as it is not specified whether these "recognized principles" are those derived from public international law or from the domestic legal order of the occupying state.

The United States, because of both its history and its constitutional framework, has had a very significant although not unique engagement with this issue. Since the mid-nineteenth-century occupation of Mexico by US troops, it has been the accepted practice that a commander may establish military commissions that have a broad jurisdiction over ordinary criminal offences normally dealt with by civilian courts as well as over violations of the laws and customs of war, inasmuch as they are all geographically and temporally connected to the theatre of war or zone of occupation.[473] There are two aspects of this practice that have some significance for the construction of the concept of a regularly constituted court under international humanitarian law: the fact that military commissions are an emanation of the executive rather than the legislative branch, and the invocation of the laws of war as the foundation of the authority to establish such courts. Unlike courts-martial with jurisdiction over members of the US military, there was for more than a century and a half of their existence no statutory basis for the establishment of military commissions. The executive power to create these court was felt to fall under the power to conduct hostilities in times of war, not a matter for the legislature.[474] A similar pattern was followed in the United Kingdom, where courts operating in Germany after World War II to try enemy soldiers for war crimes were established not by a statute of Parliament but by

[472] ICRC, *Commentary on the Fourth Geneva Convention* (n 358) 340.
[473] Winthrop (n 432) 834–835; Detlev F Vagts, 'Military Commissions: A Concise History' (2007) 101 American Journal of International Law 35.
[474] Winthrop (n 432) 831, 835.

royal warrant pursuant to the royal prerogative, in other words a purely executive decision.[475] In the United States, this power is seen to emanate not only from constitutional law but also from what is referred to as the "common law of war".[476] The legality of military commissions under domestic and international law was challenged in a series of cases before the US Supreme Court, most significantly the *Quirin*, *Yamashita*, and *Hamdan* cases, leading to judgments that illuminate the concept of a regularly constituted court.[477]

In *Quirin*, dealing with a group of German saboteurs arrested on US soil during World War II, President Roosevelt had issued a proclamation establishing a military commission to try the men and to block access to regular courts. The US Supreme Court, in denying *habeas corpus*, rejected an argument that the court ought to have been established by statute, seeming to find that the constitution incorporated into US law not only the substantive war crimes under international law but also the wherewithal to sanction them.[478] In *Yamashita*, related to the prosecution of the commander of Japanese forces in the Philippines, the Supreme Court rejected a claim that *Quirin* implied that the military commission created for Yamashita was subject to the Articles of War, a statute offering various guarantees he was denied. Instead, the majority held that the commission "was not convened by virtue of the Articles of War, but pursuant to the common law of war".[479] Unusually for such a case at the time, this triggered a vigorous dissent from Justice Rutledge, protesting that "the tribunal, specially constituted for the particular trial" was not in accord with basic concepts of American law.[480]

After a half-century of abeyance, military commissions were revived to deal with the presumed authors of the 9/11 attacks, leading to a challenge by one Guantanamo Bay detainee, Salim Hamdan. In its 2006 decision, the US Supreme Court found that, in some respects, matters broadly stood as they did for *Yamashita*, with commissions still expressly regulated neither by the US Constitution nor by statute.[481] One important change since the previous decisions in 1946, however, was the adoption of the 1949 Geneva Conventions and, with it, the explicit requirement of a "regularly constituted court". Justice Stevens for the Court recalled the excoriation of specially constituted tribunals

475 United Nations War Crimes Commission, *Law Reports of Trials of War Criminals*, vol XV (HMSO 1949) 28–29 (also on the legal basis of Australian and Canadian war crimes courts); APV Rogers, 'War Crimes Trials under the Royal Warrant: British Practice 1945–1949' (1990) 39 International & Comparative Law Quarterly 780, 788–89 (offering a detailed analysis of the British decision to proceed without a statute).

476 See, e.g., Lawrence Lauer, 'The International War Criminal Trials and the Common Law of War' (1945) 1 St. John's Law Review 18.

477 *Ex Parte Quirin*, 317 US 1 (1942); *In Re Yamashita*, 327 US 1 (1946); *Hamdan* (n 272).

478 *Quirin*, ibid, 28–29.

479 *Yamashita* (n 402) 20.

480 ibid 44–45. See also *Duncan v Kahanamoku*, 327 U.S. 304 (1946).

481 *Hamdan* (n 272) 590.

in the *Yamashita* dissent and linked it to the ICRC commentary of Common Article 3 whereby the notion of a regularly constituted court "definitely excludes all special tribunals", to conclude that a tribunal not established by law could not be regularly constituted.[482] This idea is framed more broadly by Justice Kennedy in his concurring opinion:

> Whatever the substance and content of the term "regularly constituted" as interpreted in this and any later cases, there seems little doubt that it relies upon the importance of standards deliberated upon and chosen in advance of crisis, under a system where the single power of the Executive is checked by other constitutional mechanisms. All of which returns us to the point of beginning—that domestic statutes control this case.[483]

In dissent, Justice Alito basically agrees with this approach, arguing that the domestic law of the state in question is the only possible body of law that could regulate the regular constitution of court, but interpreting US law as offering that support.[484] On the opposite, Justice Thomas, arguing that "the common law of war is flexible, responsive to the exigencies of the present conflict, and deferential to the judgment of military commanders", held that the mere longevity of this practice, more than 150 years, shows that military commissions are regularly constituted.[485] In reaction to the striking down of military commissions by the Supreme Court, Congress enacted the *Military Commissions Act* of 2006 to provide the statutory foundation that a majority of the Court considered necessary for a court to be regularly constituted.[486] Strikingly, the Act sought to preempt any further discussion of the issue under consideration by explicitly stating that the military commissions thus validated were "regularly constituted court" under Common Article 3.[487] The *Military Commissions Act* of 2009 stepped back from this jurisdictional overreach by eliminating this language, leaving it to

[482] ibid 632.
[483] ibid 637.
[484] ibid 727 ("In order to determine whether a court has been properly appointed, set up, or established, it is necessary to refer to a body of law that governs such matters. I interpret Common Article 3 as looking to the domestic law of the appointing country because I am not aware of any international law standard regarding the way in which such a court must be appointed, set up, or established, and because different countries with different government structures handle this matter differently. Accordingly, "a regularly constituted court" is a court that has been appointed, set up, or established in accordance with the domestic law of the appointing country").
[485] ibid 691, 720–721.
[486] Military Commissions Act of 2006, 10 U.S.C. §§948a–950w.
[487] ibid §948b(f) ("**Status of Commissions Under Common Article 3.** A military commission established under this chapter is a regularly constituted court, affording all the necessary 'judicial guarantees which are recognized as indispensable by civilized peoples' for purposes of common Article 3 of the Geneva Conventions"). See Carlos Manuel Vázquez, 'The Military Commissions Act, the Geneva Conventions, and the Courts: A Critical Guide' (2007) 101 American Journal of International Law 73.

courts to determine whether the revamped military commissions correspond to regularly constituted courts pursuant to international humanitarian law.[488]

The conclusion that most members of the US Supreme Court arrived at, that a regularly constituted court must be established pursuant to the domestic law of the relevant state, mirrors the ICRC statement of the corresponding customary international law norm.[489] Some have taken this to imply that non-state armed groups cannot regularly constitute a court pursuant to Common Article 3, as it would be extremely unlikely that national law would authorise a rebel court.[490] The evolution of the jurisprudence of the US Supreme Court examined earlier can be taken to challenge a rigid equation between the regular constitution of courts and statutory authorisation under the domestic law of a state. To do so would, for instance, present a challenge to the legality of international courts like the ICTY or ICTR that were not established pursuant to the domestic legal order of any given state.[491] The central concern animating the requirement that criminal law be administered by a regularly constituted court is not the defence of state sovereignty but rather the humanitarian protection of those tried in conflict zones. Returning to the statement by Justice Rutledge in *Yamashita* against ad hoc courts created specifically to try one person, and to Justice Kennedy's reflection in *Hamdan* that a requirement of regular constitution speaks to the need for advanced and deliberate consideration of the means to administer justice in a manner that prevents abuses, we can agree that states normally carry out such deliberation by way of legislation, although in unusual circumstances perhaps they could do so otherwise. Non-state armed groups, for their part, are less systematically reliant on legislation, although some may indeed have fixed rules that capture such deliberate consideration. If a court was established pursuant to rebel law, then it could meet the requirement of a regularly constituted court.[492] Otherwise, rather than a focus on formal outcomes of deliberative processes, the analysis should investigate whether the court was established with a broad mandate to administer justice by way of a norm of general application, as opposed to being a tool devised to arrive at a specific result in a given case. Thus, states and non-state armed groups can be taken to both be able to regularly constitute

488 David Weissbrodt, 'International Fair Trial Guarantees' in Andrew Clapham and Paola Gaeta (eds), *The Oxford Handbook of International Law in Armed Conflict* (Oxford University Press 2014) 436.

489 ICRC (n 305) Rule 100 ("A court is regularly constituted if it has been established and organized in accordance with the laws and procedures already in force in a country").

490 La Rosa and Wuerzner (n 287) 340; Somer (n 4) 671–672; Sivakumaran, 'Courts of Armed Opposition Groups—Fair Trials or Summary Justice?' (n 4) 498; ICRC, *Commentary on the Additional Protocols of 8 June 1977 to the Geneva Conventions of 12 August 1949* (n 277) para 4600.

491 Dieter Fleck, 'Comment—Perspectives on Courts Established by Armed Opposition Groups' in Heike Krieger (ed), *Inducing Compliance with International Humanitarian Law* (Cambridge University Press 2015) 181 note 1.

492 ICRC, *Commentary on the Second Geneva Convention* (n 286) para 714.

courts, even if through somewhat different means. As such, this exemplifies the type of substantive rather than formal equality of belligerents discussed earlier.[493]

(b) Courts Established by Law in Human Rights Law

The question of whether a court is regularly constituted pursuant to Common Article 3 is related to the human rights standard that a court be "established by law". International human rights law remains applicable during armed conflicts, even if the obligations it imposes must be adapted to the specificity of these unusual circumstances. Both treaty and customary human rights norms related to due process require that a judicial decision be taken by a court established by law. Thus Article 14(1) of the International Covenant on Civil and Political Rights provides in part that "In the determination of any criminal charge against him, or of his rights and obligations in a suit at law, everyone shall be entitled to a fair and public hearing by a competent, independent and impartial tribunal established by law". One crucial difference between the humanitarian law norm of a regularly constituted court and the human rights standard of a court established by law is that whereas the former, as noted earlier, is applicable only with respect to criminal matters, the former cover both civil and penal matters. The ambiguous reference in Article 14(1) of the Covenant to "a suit at law" is clarified by the French version which employs the expression "*des contestations sur ses droits et obligations de caractère civil*".[494] The human rights requirement of a court established by law thus equally applies to the rebel administration of justice in non-criminal matters, which is a very significant dimension of insurgent governance in many armed conflicts, as we saw in the case studies of the Islamic State and the Taliban.

Turning to the substance of the human rights norm that a civil or criminal court must be "established by law", it has been interpreted to normally require that states provide for the constitution of their courts by way of statutes adopted by the relevant legislative body, as opposed to a fiat of the executive branch.[495] One limited exception accepted by the Human Rights Committee under the Covenant on Civil and Political Rights relates to religious or customary courts, although their jurisdiction is to be limited and under supervision

[493] See Section IV.A.ii, supra.

[494] Human Rights Committee, General Comment 32 (Article 14), UN Doc CCPR/C/GC/32 (2007) paras 16–17. See Sarah Joseph and Melissa Castan, *The International Covenant on Civil and Political Rights: Cases, Materials, and Commentary* (Oxford University Press, Oxford 2013) 434; William Schabas, *U.N. International Covenant on Civil and Political Rights: Nowak's CCPR Commentary* (3rd edn, NP Engel Publisher 2019) 361–363. The American Convention on Human Rights specifies in its equivalent provision that it applies to "the determination of his rights and obligations of a civil, labor, fiscal, or any other nature".

[495] Human Rights Committee, ibid, para 3; IACtHR, *Caso Barreto Leiva v Venezuela*, Judgment, 17 November 2009, para 76; ECtHR, *Coëme and Others v Belgium*, Appl. Nos 32492/96, 32547/96, 32548/96, 33209/96, and 33210/96, Judgment, 22 June 2000, para 98.

of state courts.[496] In an *amicus curiae* brief submitted to the ICC in the *Bemba* trial, Amnesty International argued that a "competent authority" in Article 28 of the Rome Statute must be interpreted to conform to the human rights requirement of a court established by law and that a court of a non-state armed group would not normally meet this condition.[497] The ICC Trial Chamber in its decision did not directly address the impact of this human rights norm, but it did hold against the accused that "he was the competent authority to investigate and prosecute the crimes", and that his failure to empower members of his group to do so attracted responsibility pursuant to Article 28 of the Rome Statute.[498] On appeal, the Appeals Chamber found that the Trial Chamber had erred in appreciating factual limits to a remote commander's material ability to establish a court-martial to sanction violations by his troops, thus implicitly proclaiming the legal right, indeed duty, to do so.[499] In a different context, the ICTY Appeals Chamber in the *Tadic* case considered a defence argument that the Tribunal itself was not "established by law" because its creation resulted from a resolution of the UN Security Council rather than from a statutory instrument enacted by a legislative body. The ICTY found that a court could be "established by law" by a range of decision-making bodies that was not limited to legislative assemblies, inasmuch as it was set up in a manner consistent with the rule of law requirements respecting fair trial guarantees.[500] The ICTY decision does stand as a rebuttal of the principle that a court established by law can only be established by way of national legislation, in the domestic legal order of a state; rather, the international context of the creation of the ICTY means that this norm corresponds to a different establishment process. If the international community is not structured around a tryptic of executive, legislative, and judicial branches that mirrors the constitutional orders of states, then necessarily a "court established by law" must correspond to a different process.

This finding can be transposed to the establishment of courts by non-state armed groups, in the sense that these groups typically do not have a constitutional structure that replicates that of states. It follows that, for armed groups, the process to constitute a "court established by law" will not necessarily entail the

496 Human Rights Committee, ibid, para 32. For example, the *Dina* customary court system in Madagascar, which imposed capital punishment further to summary trials failing to meet fair trial guarantees, was not seen as established by law: Human Rights Committee, Concluding Observations on Madagascar (2007) UN Doc CCPR/C/MDG/CO/3 para 16.

497 Amnesty International (n 349) 15–16. The one exception conceded there are the courts of the Confederate States during the US Civil War.

498 *Bemba Trial Judgment* (n 350) para 733.

499 *Bemba Appeals Judgment* (n 350) paras 167–169. The deduction is warranted on the basis of the deference due on appeal to the Trial Chamber as trier of facts, whereas no such deference obtains in relation to questions of law: ICC, *Prosecutor v Lubanga*, Appeals judgment, 1 December 2014, No ICC-01/04-01/06 A 5 paras 16–28.

500 *Tadic Interlocutory Appeal Judgment* (n 312) paras 41–47.

enactment of a statute. The European Court of Human Rights considered a situation that bears many similarities to the rebel administration of justice in *Ilascu v. Moldova and Russia*, in which the applicant challenged the legality of their detention and treatment pursuant to decisions of the courts of the "Moldavian Republic of Transdniestria", an autonomous entity not recognised under international law. With respect to the legality of such courts under the European Convention on Human Rights, the Court noted:

> In certain circumstances, a court belonging to the judicial system of an entity not recognised under international law may be regarded as a tribunal "established by law" provided that it forms part of a judicial system operating on a "constitutional and legal basis" reflecting a judicial tradition compatible with the Convention, in order to enable individuals to enjoy the Convention guarantees.[501]

The European Court found that legal requirements for what constitutes a court must take into account the existence of an armed conflict, such that what may be needed for a court to be established by law by an armed opposition group in a conflict zone would not necessarily correspond to the full array of requirements normally demanded of states in peacetime.[502] All of these elements seem to align with those associated with the concept of a "regularly constituted court" pursuant to Common Article 3 and international humanitarian law more generally, centrally the need for deliberate consideration by an established authority to constitute a court of general jurisdiction that will apply "law" broadly defined.

iii. Judicial Guarantees of Independence and Impartiality

The requirement that a court be regularly constituted is not the only one set by Common Article 3 as a condition of the lawfulness of the imposition of a sentence and the carrying out of execution in an armed conflict. In addition, the provision requires that the court afford "all the judicial guarantees which are recognized as indispensable by civilized peoples". This element is also found in Article 6(2) of Additional Protocol II, which demands "a court offering the essential guarantees of independence and impartiality". This requirement raises two distinct questions, which will be discussed in turn: first, what is the relationship between the condition that a court be "regularly constituted" and its

[501] *Ilascu* (n 329) para 460; ECtHR, *Güzelyurtlu v Cyprus and Turkey*, Grand Chamber, Judgment, Appl. No 36965/07, 29 January 2019, paras 248–249. See Willms (n 316) 156. On the issue of the exhaustion of local remedies, the European Court has seemed to show itself open to the possibility that an applicant may be required to seek remedies before the courts of a non-state entity before turning to the Strasbourg court: Chapter 4, Section II.D.

[502] ECtHR, *Hassan v UK*, Grand Chamber, Judgment, Application No 29750/09, 16 September 2014, paras 104–106.

ability to afford judicial guarantees? And second, how are the concepts of judicial independence and impartiality to be understood under international law when applied to the courts of non-state armed groups?

(a) Fairness as Rightness

In the formulation codified in Common Article 3, to repeat the full statement of the rule, a lawful conviction and sentence must be issued by "a regularly constituted court, affording all the judicial guarantees which are recognized as indispensable by civilized peoples". The formulation adopted in 1977 in Article 6(2) of Protocol II differs in significant ways from Common Article 3, referring to "a court offering the essential guarantees of independence and impartiality", but omitting any mention of the regular constitution of the tribunal. A third variant is used in Article 75(4) of Additional Protocol I, applicable to an international armed conflict, requiring that a conviction be "pronounced by an impartial and regularly constituted court respecting the generally recognized principles of regular judicial procedure". The least that can be said is that the use of different formulations in these three treaty provisions casts a degree of uncertainty as to the institutional features required of a court under humanitarian law.

One approach to resolve this uncertainty, adopted by the ICRC in its commentaries to Protocol II and Common Article 3, holds that the requirement that the court be regularly constituted simply has been abandoned in Protocol II. For the ICRC, the need for regular constitution "is replaced by" the need for independence and impartiality.[503] The rationale for this interpretation rests on the assumption that a court can only be "regularly constituted" if it is established pursuant to the laws of the state, which is surely unlikely. As a result, if insurgents are ever to be able to administer justice in territory under their control, then the regularly constituted requirement must be jettisoned in favour of independence and impartiality. This seems an awkward approach in at least two ways: first, it goes beyond a teleological interpretation of the Conventions and Protocol II, to instead posit a conclusion (armed groups must be able to establish courts) that is neither stated in nor derivable from the instruments in order to justify a particular reading of Common Article 3 and Article 6(2) of Protocol II. The second problem is that Additional Protocol II was not adopted to amend or change the Geneva Conventions, but rather to supplement them. There is nothing in the text or in the *travaux préparatoires* of Protocol II that suggests an intent to delete the regularly constituted requirement found in Common Article 3. It is important to remember that the scope of application of the Protocol is narrower than that of

503 ICRC, *Commentary on the Additional Protocols of 8 June 1977 to the Geneva Conventions of 12 August 1949* (n 277) para 4600; ICRC, *Commentary on the Third Geneva Convention* (n 320) para 729; Payam Akhavan, 'Judicial Guarantees' in Andrew Clapham, Paola Gaeta, and Marco Sassòli (eds), *The 1949 Geneva Conventions: A Commentary* (Oxford University Press 2015) 1223.

Common Article 3, such that any armed conflict governed by the newer Protocol will *also* be governed by Common Article 3. There would be a certain paradox, if not contradiction, in loosening the institutional requirement for the regular constitution of courts in an armed conflict that is defined more narrowly in part on the basis of a demand that armed groups be more structured and responsible.[504] In its study of customary humanitarian law, the ICRC in Rule 100 maintains both requirements of a regular constitution and independence and impartiality for international as well as non-international armed conflicts, a position that appears to mirror more accurately the interplay of Common Article 3 and Article 6(2) of Protocol II.[505]

A slightly different approach is taken in the Elements of Crimes adopted pursuant to the Rome Statute of the ICC. The Statute itself, in Article 8(2)(c)(iv), provides for jurisdiction over serious violations of Common Article 3, formulating the requirement for a "regularly constituted court" with the same wording as the Geneva Conventions. One can note that the drafters of the Rome Statute did not slavishly transpose the wording of the Geneva Conventions in this provision, as they eliminated in the latter part of that sentence the reference to "civilized peoples" that is found in the older treaty. Pursuant to Article 9 of the Rome Statute, the Assembly of States Parties may adopt Elements of Crimes to "assist the Court in the interpretation and application of articles 6, 7 and 8". The Elements of Crimes must be consistent with the Rome Statute (Art. 9(3)) and, as such, are not binding on the Court. It is fair to say, however, that they are considered highly persuasive.[506] The Elements of Crimes related to Article 8(2)(c)(iv) subsume the requirement that the court be "regularly constituted" into the requirement touching on due process:

> War Crime of Sentencing or Execution Without Due Process [. . .]
>
> 4. There was no previous judgement pronounced by a court, or the court that rendered judgement was not "regularly constituted", that is, it did not afford the essential guarantees of independence and impartiality, or the court that rendered judgement did not afford all other judicial guarantees generally recognized as indispensable under international law.[507]

The argument here is no longer that the rule has changed so that the requirement for a court to be "regularly constituted" has been replaced by one that it be independent and impartial, as suggested by the ICRC in its commentary, but rather

504 Art. 1(1), Additional Protocol II.
505 ICRC (n 305) Rule 100 Commentary.
506 Dörmann (n 362) 8.
507 ibid 408.

that the requirement of regular constitution be interpreted as met if a court is independent and impartial.

The challenge in Rome was that the crimes in non-international armed conflicts were primarily defined in relation to the more universally agreed-upon Common Article 3, but that Additional Protocol II had come to supplement international humanitarian law in significant ways that should be reflected in international criminal law. An initial Belgian proposal for this Element of Crime had clearly differentiated three situations that would correspond to a violation of Article 8(2)(c)(iv): there was no previous judgment; the court was not regularly constituted; the court did not afford essential guarantees of independence and impartiality.[508] Somehow, during the negotiation process, this accurate rendering of the rule was mushed into the paragraph reproduced earlier, which introduces significant confusion in the elements of this particular crime. Under the Elements of Crimes, there is no longer any independent substance associated with the requirement of regular constitution, which is wholly subsumed into that of independence and impartiality. As noted by Somer, there is here clearly a tension between the binding wording of the Rome Statute and the interpretation suggested by Elements of Crimes.[509] More than an inconsistency, it seems difficult not to conclude that the position adopted in the Elements of Crimes is incoherent, something that did not seem to trouble the ICC Pre-Trial Chamber in *Al-Hassan* when it endorsed this approach.[510]

The basic and obvious point is that the substance of the requirement of regular constitution of a court is quite different from that of independence and impartiality: one relates to the process whereby a decision to create a court is taken, and the other to the institutional features of this court. It is not hard to find examples of courts established in the most regular way that fail to afford basic guarantees of independence and impartiality, as in the previous example of the official courts of Syria under Bashar Al-Assad. Conversely, it is not unimaginable that a court might well be independent and impartial and yet fail to have been regularly constituted. Vigilante justice could perhaps be done with independence and impartiality, but it would not be the product of a regularly constituted body. The point is, as explored in the previous subsection, that the regular constitution of courts and their independence and impartiality are mutually reinforcing features that contribute to the fair administration of justice. This also ties back to the relevance of the human rights norm that tribunals be not only independent and impartial but also "established by law". No one seems to have suggested that, under

[508] 'Proposal by Belgium concerning article 8, paragraph 2 (c) (iv) of the Statute of the International Criminal Court', UN Doc PCNICC/1999/WGEC/DP.13 (28 July 1999), online: <https://www.legal-tools.org/doc/e51c85/pdf/>.

[509] Somer (n 4) 675.

[510] ICC, *Al-Hassan* (n 390) para 376.

human rights law, if a court is shown to be independent and impartial, then *ipso facto* it becomes established by law.

As noted by Miriam Gur-Arye and Alon Harel, criminal law is an "agent-dependent enterprise", in that it matters not only how well justice is done but also who is doing it.[511] What the requirement of regular constitution in Common Article 3 and Article 8(2)(c)(iv) of the Rome Statute conveys is a sense that rightness is not wholly reducible to fairness.[512] This echoes the need for justice to be administered by institutions and practices established through deliberate consideration by an established authority, forming part of the broader governance by non-state armed groups. As a result, the creation of a court able to afford guarantees of independence and impartiality is a requirement distinct from its regular constitution.

(b) Institutional Requirements of Independence and Impartiality

Turning to substance, what are the institutional features of a rebel court that will be demanded to show that it can afford judicial guarantees of independence and impartiality? The wording used to describe the required guarantees varies from one provision to the next. It can be noted that the reference to "judicial guarantees which are recognized as indispensable by civilized nations" in Common Article 3 sought to capture an international minimum standard that would avoid the variations found among national legal systems at the time. In 1949, there was no binding international human rights instrument that could provide a common statement of judicial guarantees, and "civilized nations" was the accepted shorthand to ensure that basic norms such as the presumption of innocence would obtain everywhere.[513] The fact that Article 8(2)(c)(iv) of the Rome Statute eliminates the last three words ("by civilized nations") and the Elements of Crimes' outright replacement of these words by a reference to international law do not correspond to a change in the law, but are merely a reflection of the evolution of international legal context in which Common Article 3 must be interpreted. As was made explicit during the drafting of Article 6(2)

[511] Miriam Gur-Arye and Alon Harel, 'Taking Internationalism Seriously: Why International Criminal Law Matters' in Jens David Ohlin and Frédéric Mégret (eds), *Oxford Handbook of International Criminal Law* (Oxford University Press 2018).

[512] See the discussion, Chapter 1, Section III.B, including the argument by David Luban that courts can give themselves legitimacy by the fairness of the justice they provide: David Luban, 'Fairness to Rightness: Jurisdiction, Legality, and the Legitimacy of International Criminal Law' in Samantha Besson and John Tasioulas (eds), *The Philosophy of International Law* (Oxford University Press 2010) 579.

[513] See *Diplomatic Conference for the Establishment of International Conventions for the Protection of Victims of War*, Vol II-B (Geneva, 1949) 83; ICRC, *Commentary on the Second Geneva Convention* (n 286) para 705; on civilisation as a common standard in international law, see Martti Koskenniemi, *The Gentle Civilizer of Nations: The Rise and Fall of International Law, 1870–1960* (Cambridge University Press 2002) 132–136.

of Additional Protocol II, all these varied statements can be taken today as reflecting the essential guarantees of independence and impartiality as entrenched in international human rights law, most particularly in Article 14 of the ICCPR, as adjusted to reflect the particular context of an armed conflict.[514]

The twin requirements of independence and impartiality are interdependent and overlap to some extent. Thus, the fact that the corresponding provision in Additional Protocol I, Article 75(4), omits the mention of independence to refer only to "an impartial and regularly constituted court", is not taken to signal a different standard. That said, particular attributes have been associated with guarantees of judicial independence, on the one hand, and of judicial impartiality, on the other.

Independence speaks to the autonomy of a court in its consideration of cases. In particular, in international human rights law, various bodies have underscored the need for an arm's-length relationship between courts and the executive and legislative branches of government. This translates into rules dealing with the appointment, tenure, and removal of judges such that the position is not so fragile as to make its holders susceptible to pressures from the coequal branches of government.[515] If a judicial body is structured in a manner that allows the leadership of non-state armed groups to simply direct what decisions are issued, then there is no sense of independence, and indeed the body in question can hardly merit the label of a court.[516] For instance, witnesses in the *Bemba* trial before the ICC testified that the courts-martial created within the *Mouvement de liberation du Congo* were largely a charade meant to hide the fact that judges were merely executing orders issued by their superiors.[517] As suggested in Chapter 1, this negates one of the building blocks of the rebel rule of law. Of course, this vision of independence reflects the administration of justice by states through a formal court system operating in peacetime. Non-state armed groups, even when they are institutionally sophisticated and exercise broad governance authority, rarely will be constituted in separate and coequal branches of government. As we can see in the operation of the courts of the Islamic State and the Taliban, for example, the rebel administration of justice remains marked by the context of armed hostilities in

[514] Bothe and others (n 313) 748.

[515] Human Rights Committee, General Comment 32 (n 494) 5–6. See also UN Basic Principles on the Independence of the Judiciary, adopted by the Seventh United Nations Congress on the Prevention of Crime and the Treatment of Offenders held at Milan from 26 August to 6 September 1985 and endorsed by General Assembly resolutions 40/32 of 29 November 1985 and 40/146 of 13 December 1985; Amal Clooney and Philippa Webb, *The Right to a Fair Trial in International Law* (Oxford University Press 2021) 82–105.

[516] ibid at 6 ("A situation where the functions and competencies of the judiciary and the executive are not clearly distinguishable or where the latter is able to control or direct the former is incompatible with the notion of an independent tribunal").

[517] ICC, *Prosecutor v Jean-Pierre Bemba Gombo*, Trial Judgment, 21 March 2016, ICC-01/05-01/08, at 299–300 note 1861.

its design, objectives, and operation. Even in groups like the LTTE that have distinct military and political wings, the division does not carry with it any notion of a judicial branch that stands apart from the rest of the movement.[518]

Is it possible, in that context, to have a rebel court that would be considered independent? Transposing the substance of judicial independence to armed groups, we can already note that rebel courts need not be entirely disconnected from such groups in order to be independent, no more than state courts need to be disconnected from the government apparatus. Insurgent courts may be an arm of the rebellion just as state courts may be an arm of the sovereign authority of the state. In both cases, there is no legitimate expectation that the court will be neutral vis-à-vis the policies of the government or armed group.[519] Courts are, after all, a tool of governance. It takes political and social capital to make people obey summons and respect decisions of a court, and that political and social capital will surely be found at least in part in the more general authority of the armed group as a whole rather than only in the rebel courts themselves.[520] The model offered by the House of Justice in Houran, a court jointly established by nearly 100 armed groups in Southern Syria which was said to demand that judges have no affiliation with any armed group, thus would be rather unique, possibly as a reflection that it handled not only individual cases but also disputes among the different armed groups.[521] More commonly, rebel judges will be linked to the armed group but exercise their judicial authority with a degree of autonomy from its hierarchy.

One type of state courts that could reasonably be thought to provide a better comparator to insurgent courts are military courts, because they are attached to the armed forces and they are designed to operate, at least some of the times, in situations of armed hostilities. The question of the independence of courts-martial has attracted significant attention and criticism, especially in their consistency with human rights requirements that courts be independent and impartial. Considerable work has been done in this respect by the United Nations, first under the aegis of the Sub-Commission on the Promotion and Protection of Human Rights and its Special Rapporteurs Louis Joinet Emmanuel Decaux,

[518] See Chapter 3, Section I.C.v.

[519] Sassòli, 'L'administration d'un territoire par un groupe armé peut-elle être régie par le droit?' (n 399) 271.

[520] Coburn (n 164) 26.

[521] Geneva Call, 'Administration of Justice by Armed Non-State Actors (Report from the 2017 Garance Talks)' (Geneva, 2018) 10 (statement by Esmat Alabasi). External observers noted that armed groups divided the number of judges each could appoint to the Houran House of Justice, casting some doubt as to their independence: Marika Sosnowski, 'The Syrian Southern Front: Why It Offers Better Justice and Hope than Northern Front' *Syria Comment* (9 July 2015), online: <https://www.joshualandis.com/blog/the-syrian-southern-front-why-it-offers-better-justice-and-hope-than-northern-front-by-marika-sosnowski/> accessed 15 August 2018. The Houran House of Justice is discussed in Chapter 4, Section V.

and later by successive Special Rapporteurs on the Independence of Judges and Lawyers appointed by the Human Rights Council.[522] In the context of the administration of justice by state armed forces, independence has been understood to relate to the status of judges and autonomy of the military judiciary. As regards status, in some countries, military justice is administered by civilian judges (e.g. Belgium, France), while in others the court is composed of service members but they are accorded protections similar to civilian judges (e.g. Russia, Turkey, Spain); in the majority of countries, however, judges do not have special status and remain subject to the chain of command and military discipline (e.g. Argentina, Brazil, Cameroun, United States, Israel).[523] In many cases, national law envisages the possibility that operational officers and enlisted men, rather than officers with legal training attached to the armed forces legal services or judge advocate general, can serve as decision-makers on judicial panels or juries.[524] As regards the autonomy of military justice, external interference can take place at the level of the laying of charges, confirmation of the judgment, and possibility of appeal. Here again, state practice remains widely variable, from outright interference (e.g. China, Cameroon) to a process of confirmation of decisions by political authorities (e.g. Egypt, Ireland, Chile).[525]

No particular distrust of the independence of military courts can be discerned in international humanitarian law. Article 84 of the Third Geneva Convention provides in a very strict manner that "a prisoner of war shall be tried only by a military court", unless the detaining state's own troops may be tried by a civilian court. The ICRC Commentary makes clear that the latter is the exception rather than the rule and that the fact that the court will be trying an enemy is not incompatible with it independence.[526] The same provision specifies that in all cases the court must "offer the essential guarantees of independence and impartiality as generally recognised". A similarly positive disposition towards military courts is evident in Article 66 of the Fourth Geneva Convention, under which civilians in occupied territory may be tried by the "properly constituted, non-political military courts" of the occupying power for offences against its security. The rationale for favouring military courts in situations of occupation is the fact that an

522 See especially: Report submitted by Mr. Emmanuel Decaux to the Sub-Commission on the Promotion and Protection of Human Rights on the administration of justice through military tribunals, UN Doc E/CN.4/Sub.2/2004/7; Report of the Special Rapporteur Gabriela Knaul on the independence of judges and lawyers, UN Doc A/68/285 (2013).

523 Knaul Report, ibid paras 26–28; Geneviève Giudicelli-Delage, 'Les garanties procédurales et le droit au recours-rapport de synthèse' in Elisabeth Lambert-Abdelgawad (ed), *Juridictions militaires et tribunaux d'exception en mutation: perspectives comparées et internationales* (Archives contemporaines 2008) 466; Georg Nolte and Heike Krieger, 'Comparison of European Military Law Systems' in Georg Nolte (ed), *European Military Law Systems* (Walter de Gruyter 2003) 156–171.

524 See, e.g., Art. 25, United States Uniform Code of Military Justice, 10 U.S.C. §825.

525 Giudicelli-Delage (n 523) 466–467.

526 ICRC, *Commentary on the Third Geneva Convention* (n 320) paras 3600–3604, 3614.

occupying force will necessarily bring along its own courts, in order to deal with the inevitable offences and crimes committed by its own forces; as such, these courts will be available in situ, an option preferable to moving civilians charged with an offence to the national territory of the occupant or, one presumes, to the creation of civilian courts of the occupying forces.[527] The role of military courts was left untouched in Additional Protocol I, despite a provision that significantly augmented the due process guarantees owed to anyone prosecuted for an offence related to the conflict, a notion broad enough to include both prisoners of war and civilians in occupied territory (Art. 75(4), Additional Protocol I). All these provisions apply only to situations of international armed conflicts, with no explicit reference to military courts in Common Article 3 or Additional Protocol II.

The picture of the independence of military tribunals that emerges from the jurisprudence of international human rights bodies is radically different. The caselaw of the European Court of Human Rights, the Inter-American Court and Commission of Human Rights, and the African Commission of Human and Peoples' Rights is replete with findings that military courts fail to meet the requirement of independence under international human rights law. Key flashpoints have focussed on the lack of insulation of military investigators, prosecutors, and judges from the chain of command within the army, on whether violations of human rights should properly fall within the jurisdiction of military courts, on a practice of transferring the prosecution of civilians to military tribunals in situations of emergency or under anti-terrorism measures, and on the observance of due process guarantees in military justice.[528] It is interesting to note, in that respect, that a number of states have entered reservations aiming to exclude their military justice system from the full application of human rights conventions.[529] Despite repeatedly concluding to the inadequacy

[527] ICRC, *Commentary on the Fourth Geneva Convention* (n 358) 340.

[528] See Knaul Report (n 522) 8–19 for a survey of various decisions touching on all these points. See also Christina M Cerna, 'The Inter-American System and Military Justice' in Alison Duxbury and Matthew Groves (eds), *Military Justice in the Modern Age* (Cambridge University Press 2016); Frederico Andreu-Guzman, 'Les tribunaux militaires et juridictions d'exception dans le système onusien des droits de l'homme' in Élisabeth Lambert Adbelgawad (ed), *Juridictions militaires et tribunaux d'exception en mutation: perspectives comparées et internationales* (Archives contemporaines 2008); Julie Daniel, 'Les tribunaux militaires et juridictions d'exception à l'épreuve de la jurisprudence de la Cour européenne des droits de l'homme' in Élisabeth Lambert Adbelgawad (ed), *Juridictions militaires et tribunaux d'exception en mutation: perspectives comparées et internationales* (Archives contemporaines 2008); Élisabeth Lambert Adbelgawad, 'Les tribunaux militaires et juridictions pénales spéciales sous le contrôle de la Commission africaine des droits de l'homme et des peuples' in Élisabeth Lambert Adbelgawad (ed), *Juridictions militaires et tribunaux d'exception en mutation: perspectives comparées et internationales* (Archives contemporaines 2008); Jeanine Bucherer, *Die Vereinbarkeit von Militärgerichten Mit Dem Recht Auf Ein Faires Verfahren Gemäß Art. 6 Abs. 1 EMRK, Art. 8 Abs. 1 AMRK Und Art. 14 Abs. 1 Des UN-Paktes Über Bürgerliche Und Politische Rechte* (Springer 2010) 37–101.

[529] Peter John Rowe, 'How Well Do International Human Rights Bodies Understand Military Courts?' in Alison Duxbury and Matthew Groves (eds), *Military Justice in the Modern Age*

of military courts under human rights law, regional human rights courts have not gone so far as to conclude that military courts are inherently unable to meet the requirements of independence and impartiality.[530]

As always, the delineation of the institutional requirements for state courts under international law must be adapted to the reality and limitations of the administration of justice by non-state armed groups. The fact that armed groups are never as large and complex a governance apparatus as a state has been underscored already. Where the state operates on the basis of many internal divisions, among branches of government and within each branch among various services, insurgents tend to have organisational structures that are both more fluid and more integrated. Thus, as noted by Daragh Murray in his lucid exploration of the human rights obligations of non-state armed groups, the entire discussion of military justice in human rights law is coloured by the assumption that there is an available civilian justice system operating in parallel.[531] Nowhere is this more evident than in the Inter-American doctrine of the "right to the natural judge" (*derecho al juez natural*), meaning that the state must offer a particular justification to remove a case from the civilian court in favour of a military one.[532] More broadly, this view reflects a conviction that, in a democratic state, the constitutional role of the armed forces must be limited to national security.[533] Save for a few armed opposition groups, the rebel administration of justice will rarely involve distinct institutions devoted to civilian and military justice, a reflection of the fact that the insurgents are, more than anything else, a military organisation. Even for non-state armed groups that do have judicial mechanisms for offences by members of the group that are distinct from the civilian administration of justice, such as the FARC in Colombia or the YPG in Syria, the "civilian" arm of rebel justice remains more fully integrated into the structures of the armed group than the equivalent state-run civilian courts. It follows that the strand of decisions by human rights bodies resisting the jurisdiction of military

(Cambridge University Press 2016) 26 (reserving states include France, Azerbaijan, Czech Republic, Slovakia, Spain, Armenia, Moldova, Portugal, and Russia).

530 See, e.g., African Commission of Human and Peoples' Rights, *Civil Liberties Association v Nigeria*, Comm. No 218/98 (2001) para 44 ("a military tribunal per se is not offensive to the rights in the Charter nor does it imply an unfair or unjust process", although in that case, the Commission does conclude that the court fails to meet the requirement of the African Charter); Rowe, ibid 33–35.

531 Murray (n 327) 210–214.

532 Christian Steiner and Marie-Christine Fuchs (eds), *Comentario Convención americana sobre derechos humanos* (2d edn, Konrad Adenauer Stiftung 2019) 274; Bucherer (n 528) 115–133.

533 ECtHR, *Mustafa v Bulgaria*, Judgment, Appl. No 1230/17, 28 November 2019, para 35 ("[La Cour] rappelle que la place particulière qu'occupe l'armée dans l'organisation constitutionnelle des États démocratiques doit être limitée au domaine de la sécurité nationale, le pouvoir judiciaire relevant pour sa part, en principe, du domaine de la société civile"). See Fionnuala Ni Aolain, 'Principle 29. Restrictions on the Jurisdiction of Military Courts' in Frank Haldemann and Thomas Unger (eds), *The United Nations Principles to Combat Impunity: A Commentary* (Oxford University Press 2018).

courts over certain types of offences or certain categories of individuals cannot easily be transposed to insurgent courts.

The human rights jurisprudence insisting that military judges and prosecutors must be detached to some extent from the regular chain of command when carrying out judicial functions seems important to consider for insurgent courts.[534] Here again, the findings related to state courts-martial must be adapted, such that a demand for a military bench and bar wholly autonomous from the rest of the armed forces is surely unrealistic for non-state armed groups. To that can be added that the administration of military justice in many states still relies on decision-makers in the regular chain of command, with a power to review or confirm by superior officers.[535] If, however, a rebel court is merely an emanation of the rebel leadership such that a decision in a given proceeding is predetermined by someone other than the judge, whether directly or indirectly, then such a court does not meet the requirement of independence under international law. Thus, reports that Islamic State judges have been punished or even executed for issuing decisions that did not conform to what the group's leadership thought ought to be decided corresponds to a lack of judicial independence, a regime in which fear of displeasing leaders rather than objective assessment of a case drives decision-making.[536] The Taliban model of administration of justice is less obviously contrary to the demands of independence. Judges are appointed by a distinct section of the central authority and operate in a manner connected to the civil administration branch rather than to military operations. On the other hand, as described earlier in this chapter, both branches are joined in the Taliban provincial military committee, which approves every decision of the courts before they are finalised. It is interesting to consider the justification of this function by the head of the Taliban military commission for the province of Laghman:

> As the head of the military commission, I am in charge of the whole province. Upon the advice of the [provincial] judicial council, I appoint all judges in the province. But as I told you, it doesn't mean that I control judges' minds. As in any organisation, there must be someone in charge, to give directions, and in this case it's me. That's all. There is no question of control that would bring me a personal benefit or anything like that.[537]

[534] See: ECtHR, *Findlay v United Kingdom*, Appl. No 22107/93, 25 Sept. 2001, paras 74–80; Supreme Court of Canada, *R v Généreux*, [1992] 1 S.C.R. 259, 263.

[535] See generally: Alison Duxbury and Matthew Groves (eds), *Military Justice in the Modern Age* (Cambridge University Press 2016); Élisabeth Lambert-Abdelgawad (ed), *Juridictions militaires et tribunaux d'exception en mutation: perspectives comparées et internationales* (Archives contemporaines 2008).

[536] See Chapter 2, Section II.B.

[537] Baczko (n 136) 211 (my translation). The extent to which this corresponds to Taliban practice is challenged by Human Rights Watch (n 190) 62.

Taliban military commanders and fighters, for their part, are strictly prohibited by Rule 64 of the *layeha* from becoming involved in any way in a case before the courts.[538] Thus, as regards independence, Taliban justice is a model that is not so far from the structure of courts-martial used in many countries. As we have seen, the conformity with international human rights law of some aspects of such courts-martial has been contested, but the model has not been rejected outright. In *Al-Hassan*, the ICC Pre-trial Chamber noted with apparent concern that Ansar Dine/al-Qaeda in the Islamic Maghreb judges were armed and subject to the superior authority of the group's commander.[539] These are elements underscoring the incorporation of judges into the armed group, something that is unsurprising in this exceptional context and which does not per se signal lack of sufficient independence. The participation of the president of the Timbuktu Islamic Court in a "crisis committee" that took strategic military decisions is more troubling, and could indicate that there was not a distance between the taking of military decisions and the administration of justice that is required for a court to be independent.[540]

The requirement that a court be impartial raises fewer legal complexities, even though it may set a condition of legality that will not rarely be tested in the practice of insurgent courts. As with the requirement of independence, the fact that some of the applicable provisions of international humanitarian law such as Common Article 3 predate the appearance of international human rights law should not be taken to suggest that impartiality has different meanings in humanitarian law and human rights. The link to human rights was made explicit in the negotiations of Article 6 of Additional Protocol II.[541] As a result, despite the fact that Common Article 3 and Article 6 of Protocol II only apply to a narrow class of criminal trials before insurgent courts, the requirement of impartiality can be understood in a consistent manner across the board for the rebel administration of justice in general. Impartiality speaks to the need for the decision-maker to avoid favouring one side over the other for reasons unrelated to the substance or procedure of the case. It bears repeating here the comment made earlier in relation to independence, to wit, the requirement of impartiality (or independence) does not imply neutrality vis-à-vis the objectives or policies of the non-state armed group to which a court belongs. As an emanation of armed

[538] The rule reads: "64. Mujahidin commanders and individuals are not allowed to intervene in public disputes. They are not allowed to recommend anyone to a judge, or go to court with them. They cannot take sides in any disputes". On the *layeha*, see Section III.B, *infra*.

[539] ICC Al-Hassan (n 390) paras 426–427. The Chamber incorporates these elements to its discussion of the impartiality of the rebel court, but it seems more properly understood as relevant to independence.

[540] ibid paras 424. The decision is both preliminary and heavily reacted, making it difficult to form a clear picture of the precise significance of this role.

[541] Bothe and others (n 313) 745.

groups, insurgent courts are a tool of rebel governance that is no more designed to challenge that governance than state courts are to challenge state sovereignty. Within the framework of that governance, however, international law requires that justice be administered in an impartial manner, for non-state courts as much as for state ones.

The canon of interpretation of the requirement of judicial impartiality, embraced by bodies and tribunals in international human rights as well as humanitarian law, distinguishes between the subjective and objective components of impartiality.[542] The subjective element speaks to the state of mind of the decision-maker. Judges must not harbour bias, prejudice of preconceptions with respect to a case before them, such as to favour the interests of one party over the other. Neither can they have any sort of personal interest, much less involvement, in the case at bar. Subjective bias must be shown to exist in fact, as reflected in the behaviour of the judge during the proceedings, the language used and arguments relied upon in the decision, or any other concrete sign of a lack of partiality before, during, or after the proceedings.[543] The justice system must include a process whereby claims of partiality can be lodged so as to impugn a decision issued in such circumstances.[544] The objective element of impartiality refers not to the state of mind of the decision-maker but to the appearance, for a reasonable observer, that the court is or could be biased. This will typically relate to the identity, status, or function of the decision-maker, and can overlap to a degree with the requirement of independence. The concern at play in relation to objective impartiality is to maintain the confidence of the parties and of the public at large in the fairness of the administration of justice. Thus, there are many decisions of human rights courts that have found that the partial or complete military composition of a court can, in some circumstances, create an appearance of partiality in addition to a lack of independence.[545] In a different setting, the fact that more than a quarter of *gacaca* judges were removed for having themselves taken part in the genocide can legitimately render suspect the entire community court structure.[546] For insurgent courts, the operation in Iraqi Kurdistan of two sets

[542] See: Human Rights Committee, General Comment No 32 (n 494) para 21; Knaul Report (n 522) para 44; ECtHR, *Findlay v UK* (n 534) para73; ICTR, *Prosecutor v Nahimana*, Appeal Judgment, ICTR-99-52-A, 28 November 2007, paras 47–50; Steiner and Fuchs (n 532) 279; Clooney and Webb (n 515) 109–110; Louise Doswald-Beck, 'Judicial Guarantees under Common Article 3' in Andrew Clapham, Paola Gaeta, and Marco Sassòli (eds), *The 1949 Geneva Conventions: A Commentary* (Oxford University Press 2015) 472–473; ICRC, *Commentary on the Second Geneva Convention* (n 286) para 703.

[543] See IACtHR, *Duque v Colombia*, Sentencia (Exceptiones preliminaries, fondos, reparaciones y costas), 26 February 2016, paras 159–166; ECtHR, *Kyprianou v Cyprus*, Appl. No 73797/01, 15 December 2005, paras 119, 129–133.

[544] Steiner and Fuchs (n 532) 280.

[545] ECtHR, *Ergin v Turkey*, Appl. No 47533/99, 4 May 2006, para 45; Knaul Report (n 522) para 45.

[546] Sullo (n 425) 176, 184.

of parallel court structures, each associated with a political party that to some extent reflected a particular tribal identity, strongly suggested an appearance of partiality of the courts vis-à-vis members of the opposing party or tribe.[547] On the other hand, the Taliban's reported practice of continuously rotating judges and preventing them from sitting in an area to which they had connections, in addition to a process of judicial oversight and the availability of avenues for civilians to lay a complain about a Taliban judge, are elements that conform to the requirement of impartiality.[548]

V. Conclusion

Whether international law recognises that non-state armed groups can lawfully establish their own regime of administration of justice in zones of armed conflict is a question the answer to which is complex and polycentric. As the previous pages have illustrated, it involves a combination of elements drawn from international humanitarian law, international human rights law, international criminal law, and parts of general public international law. One aspect on which no uncertainty remains is that the legality of justice practices of armed groups cannot be assessed purely on the basis of a few words in Common Article 3 and Article 6 of Additional Protocol II, provisions that regulate only a fraction of what falls within the ambit of the rebel administration of justice.

To begin with, the analysis shows that an oversimplified reading of the requirement that courts must be regularly constituted must be resisted. Indeed, there is little basis to conclude that insurgent courts cannot be regularly constituted. Regular constitution can be achieved by non-state armed groups by means other than legislation, inasmuch as it corresponds to a deliberate decision by an effective authority to establish a general process to apply identified "law" broadly defined. Justice, whether in the hands of states or armed groups, can neither be improvised nor ad hoc; it must form an integral and fixed part of a broader regime of governance. In the practice of armed groups, it can correspond to rebel legislation to create formal courts as well as to a set rebel policy to convene popular assemblies under defined conditions. Whatever the type of justice institutions and practices, and whatever form the deliberate decision of the rebel group may take, it must in all cases correspond to the requirement of regular constitution. This is so even in non-international armed conflicts that are regulated by Additional Protocol II and not merely by Common Article 3. To underscore the point, despite the fact that Article 6 of Protocol II does not

547 See Chapter 4, Section I.C.
548 See Chapter 2, Section III.B.

mention that courts must be regularly constituted, this requirement flowing from Common Article 3 does not disappear if and when the conflict reaches the threshold of Protocol II. Common Article 3 *also* governs this narrower class of non-international armed conflicts, and the very notion of a court speaks to some form of regular constitution.

All courts must offer guarantees of independence and impartiality, whether in a non-international armed conflict of one type or another, or in an international armed conflict. The requirement of independence and impartiality, touching on the decision-making process, is distinct from the requirement of regularly constitution, reflecting the establishment of the court. There is thus no basis, either statutory or conceptual, in the fusion of these elements suggested in the ICC Elements of Crimes. The effective gutting of the requirement regarding regular constitution in the Elements of Crimes amounts to a serious dilution of judicial fairness that must be resisted. Finally, the requirements of regular constitution and independence and impartiality are not different according to the type of armed conflict to which these treaty rules apply. Variations in the legal standards depends on agent, not type of conflict. For non-state armed groups, the demands of legality for insurgent courts are the same in a Common Article 3 conflict as they are in a Protocol II conflict. Conversely, the interpretation of the Geneva Conventions and Protocols do not suggest that the rebel administration of justice can only be legal in situations to which Additional Protocol II is applicable. While conditions of applicability of the Protocol such as an internal disciplinary system and territorial control are often coextensive with the type of rebel governance and institutionalisation that can sustain insurgent justice, they are not systematically present. There are examples of non-international armed conflicts, such as much of the conflict in Colombia, in which the armed group does not control territory but nevertheless exerts effective authority.

How exactly a court can be regularly constituted by a non-state armed group does not necessarily mirror what states must do to regularly constitute a court. Likewise, the implications of the duty to provide judicial guarantees of independence and impartiality will likely be different for states and for armed groups. Both concepts historically have evolved in relation to the institutional and normative practices of states, and as such are reflections of the exercise of authority by the state. When we acknowledge that non-state actors—whether international organisations or non-state armed groups—in some circumstances may come to wield public authority, the regime regulating the exercise of that authority must be adapted to reflect the reality and capacities of these non-state actors. This is so for many human rights norms, as we will see presently in the next chapter, including the requirements that courts be regularly constituted and offer judicial guarantees of independence and impartiality. As I have aimed to sketch in this chapter, the key is to balance the meaningful and effective protection of the interests protected by these legal standards with the constraints imposed on non-state armed groups by the conflict.

More broadly, the attempt to translate for non-state armed groups the requirements under international law for the rebel administration of justice seeks to provide better and clearer guidance to armed groups (and states) and to capture a practice that is happening in conflict zones but that has largely escaped the scrutiny it deserves under international humanitarian law and human rights. Ultimately, the aim is to incentivise non-state governance practices that bring rebel justice closer to the ideals enshrined in human rights law but that prove elusive during armed conflicts. As with all of international humanitarian law, this is the art of the possible, mixing elements that are more humanitarian to others than owe to military necessity or the stark realities of warfare. The critique of humanitarian law that it serves to legitimise (some) violence remains apt in the context of the rebel administration of justice, in that it may legitimise (some) forms of justice that remain far from what we would wish for. The alternative is to reject altogether the possibility of the rebel administration of justice or, more likely, impose conditions that will be all but impossible to meet for the vast majority of armed groups in the vast majority of conflicts. The value of a compromise approach is that it provides a foundation to differentiate insurgent justice that is justice only in name, as was broadly the case for ISIS courts that were neither regular nor independent and impartial, from that which is imperfect but not flawed in every respect, as is the case for courts run by the Taliban. The conclusion that an armed group has regularly constituted courts offering guarantees of independence and impartiality does not mean that a decision issued by such a court is fair and, accordingly, lawful. Justice administered by regularly constituted courts, state and non-state alike, may yet flounder at the implementation stage on the shoals of due process requirements. Indeed, the possibility of regularly constituted insurgent courts must imperatively and systematically be tempered by the requirements of procedural fairness, to which the analysis now turns.

3

Rebel Jurisdiction, Due Process, and Tamil Tiger Justice

La justice militaire est à la justice ce que la musique militaire est à la musique.

— Georges Clémenceau

The conclusion that international law allows non-state armed groups to legally constitute their own court system raises as many questions as it answers. The decision for rebels to become engaged in the administration of justice will normally correspond to a position, most likely an order, adopted or issued by those wielding the levers of power within the armed group. There is comparative simplicity to this decision when contrasted with the messy reality of actually administering justice, combining the need to determine the what, who, where, and how of operating a justice system with the complexity, variety, and contradictions of human existence and social relations traversed by the chaotic and polarising reality of war. At that level, the questions become more particularised, and the promise of a legal analysis aiming at systematic pronouncements of principles more fraught. At the same time, the idea of law as a set of norms shared among different agents and even separate communities demands that all practice, however diverse, be integrated into a broader conversation. Law does not ensure coherence, much less produce sameness, but it does provide the vocabulary for a conversation aimed at managing our differences. In that spirit, the analysis now turns to some of the consequential what, who, where, and how questions alluded to just above. The first three—What? Who? Where?—form a set that can be grouped under the idea of jurisdiction, mapping the reach of the rebel administration of justice as envisaged or permitted under public international law, discussed in Part II. The last—How?—addresses the particular constraints that have emerged in international humanitarian and human rights law on the procedural guarantees that must attach to the exercise of jurisdiction by any court, discussed in Part III. The elaborate and longstanding administration of justice by the Liberation Tigers of Tamil Eelam in the north-east of Sri Lanka, described in Part I, will be used as a key reference point to illustrate the analysis of the answers to these various questions.

Rebel Courts. René Provost, Oxford University Press. © Oxford University Press 2021.
DOI: 10.1093/oso/9780190912222.003.0004

I. Purr Curiam: Tiger Justice in Sri Lanka

A. Origins and Evolution of the LTTE

The Liberation Tigers of Tamil Eelam (LTTE), also known as the "Tamil Tigers", and the government of Sri Lanka were engaged in a conflict described as "one of the world's most intractable civil wars" from 1983 until the military defeat of the LTTE in May 2009.[1] The war was brutal and is estimated to have caused a total 80,000 to 100,000 casualties.[2] Although active hostilities commenced in 1983 (six years after the establishment of the LTTE), the root causes of the conflict run far back to the colonial era.[3] Indeed, the years leading up to the conflict are not only important to appraise the causes of the conflict but also central to understand the origins and evolution of the LTTE itself, which seemed to emerge in response to tensions between the Sinhalese majority and the Tamil minority.

From the late 1920s onwards, political ruptures between the Sinhalese majority and Tamil minority started emerging. Upon gaining independence from British rule in 1948, the conflicting ideologies of the Sinhalese and Tamil politicians and the development of party politics led to the propagation of Tamil separatist sentiments as well as Sinhala nationalist thinking.[4] In the wake of early ethnic discourse, the Tamil parliamentarian S.J.V. Chelvanayakam and his party, the Ilankai Thamil Arasu Kachchi, became ardent advocates of an autonomous state and self-determination for Tamils and were harsh critics of Sinhalese peasant settlements in the Eastern provinces of Sri Lanka, arguing that the "Sinhalese were colonising the rich agricultural districts in Tamil provinces".[5]

The early 1950s saw a rise in Sinhala nationalism, which facilitated and then was furthered by the election of Prime Minister Solomon Bandaranaike in 1956. The introduction of the Official Language Act (also referred to as the Sinhala Only Act) declared Sinhala as the official language of Sri Lanka and created

[1] Asoka Bandarage, *The Separatist Conflict in Sri Lanka: Terrorism, Ethnicity, Political Economy* (Routledge 2009) 1.

[2] 'Up to 100,000 Killed in Sri Lanka's Civil War: UN' *ABC Australia* (20 May 2009), online: <http://www.abc.net.au>; 'Sri Lanka Starts Count of Civil War Dead' *Al Jazeera America* (28 November 2013), online: <America.aljazeera.com>.

[3] Sri Lanka, known as Ceylon until 1972, became a colony of the British entirely from 1815 until it gained independence in 1948. For a compelling political history of Sri Lanka, see Nira Wickramasinghe, *Sri Lanka in the Modern Age: A History* (Oxford University Press 2015).

[4] Rudhramoorthy Cheran (ed), *Pathways of Dissent: Tamil Nationalism in Sri Lanka* (SAGE Publications India 2009) xxii. The Sri Lankan population of over 21 million is composed of 74.9% Sinhalese densely spread in the south, west, and central parts, 11.1% Sri Lankan Tamils predominant in the northern and eastern parts, 9.3% Muslims, and 4.1% Indian or Estate Tamils: Sri Lanka, Department of Census & Statistics, 'Census of Population and Housing of Sri Lanka, 2012—Table A3: Population by district, ethnic group and sex' (Study) (Colombo: Department of Census & Statistics).

[5] A Jeyaratnam Wilson, *S.J.V. Chelvanayakam and the Crisis of Sri Lankan Tamil Nationalism, 1947–1977: A Political Biography* (Hurst 1994) 149; Bandarage (n 1) 40.

many barriers for Tamils in gaining future employment, engaging in administration, and joining other professions in the country.[6] More broadly, it made "language . . . the focal point of a new ethnic consciousness of two rival nationalisms".[7] The Official Language Act marked the ascension of political discourse to a community-level ethnic problem. Sinhalese mob assault on a sit-down protest against the Act in Colombo, ethnic violence in other parts of the country, and violence against Tamil peasant settlements in Gal Oya, Ampara were critical to the growing nationalist discourse.[8]

Fearing continued ethnic violence, Prime Minister Bandaranaike entered into a pact with Chelvanayakam, offering to establish a Tamil speaking regional council and recognise Tamil as a national minority language. However, Bandaranaike abrogated the pact in 1958, as a result of giving in to increasing pressure from Sinhala nationalists. This abrogation led to a massive civil disobedience movement spearheaded by the Tamil opposition party, degenerating into ethnic riots resulting in 500 to 600 deaths.[9] Soon after, Prime Minister Bandaranaike was assassinated, with his widow replacing him. Continued political chaos and governmental changes in Sri Lanka did not help curb the growing discontent among ethnic minorities. To add to the problems, the introduction of a language-based standardisation policy in the early 1970s to control state university entrance was interpreted by many Tamils as an assault against their community, adding to a push by the government to reduce the presence of Tamils in the public service and the military.[10] Concurrently, Sri Lanka was faced with severe economic crises, with lack of employment leading to youth unrest.

Two aspects of Sri Lanka's 1972 constitution (which established Sri Lanka as a republic) precipitated Tamil political separatism. First, it gave Buddhism primacy as the state's religion, which fuelled stronger demands for a separate state for the mostly Hindu Tamils. Second, it created Sri Lanka as a unitary state, which prompted the existing Tamil political parties to come together to form the Tamil United Front in May 1972 (which then became the TULF in 1975). This is thought to have signalled that "[w]hat was originally conceived [of] as political opposition to certain government policies had . . . blossomed into a demand for a sovereign, separate, socialist state of Tamil Eelam".[11]

In 1976, the Tamil United Liberation Front Party held a convention and adopted the *Vadukkoddai* Resolution, reaffirming its call for the establishment

6 Sri Lanka, *Official Language Act* No 33 of 1956.

7 KM De Silva, *Managing Ethnic Tensions in Multi-Ethnic Societies: Sri Lanka, 1880–1985* (University Press of America 1986) 172–173.

8 See Bandarage (n 1); Wickramasinghe (n 3) 280–285.

9 Bandarage (n 1) 50.

10 Eva Gerharz, *The Politics of Reconstruction and Development in Sri Lanka: Transnational Commitments to Social Change* (Routledge 2014) 21.

11 Cheran (n 4) xxviii.

of a separate Tamil state. Meanwhile, many Tamil youth, educated and unemployed, grew increasingly frustrated by the perceived ineffectiveness of political action.[12] Given the fruitless efforts of Tamil political leaders, the youth "felt that peaceful political agitation by the old men had got nothing for the Tamils, and it was the boys' turn to secure rights for the Tamils".[13] The Tamil Students League, which had organised protests against the government's university entrance policies, became the Tamil Youth League and later the Tamil New Tiger under the direction of Velupillai Prabhakaran.[14] The LTTE was formed on 5 March 1976 when the Tamil New Tigers joined forces with another Tamil armed group led by S. Subramaniam.[15] The membership of the new LTTE also overlapped with that of the Tamil Youth Front, the military wing of the Tamil United Liberation Front.[16]

For a period of several years, more than a dozen Tamil militant groups operated in parallel, including the Tamil Eelam Liberation Organisation. Many incidents, including the 1981 burning of the Jaffna library and its unique holdings of Ceylon Tamil culture, marked a steady escalation of tensions. By 1983, the LTTE emerged as the biggest and dominant Tamil militant group.[17] In July 1983, LTTE militants killed thirteen Sri Lankan soldiers in Jaffna, marking the transformation of the conflict from an internal disturbance to an armed conflict, referred to by the LTTE as the 'First Eelam War'. Critically, the killings triggered a series of violent mob attacks carried out by Sinhalese against Tamils throughout Sri Lanka (referred to as 'Black July'), which resulted in the death of hundreds of Tamils, forced evictions from home, offices, and factories, and victimisation of many Tamil civilians living all over the country.[18] The violence also aggravated matters at the political level, prompting the government to ban the Tamil United Liberation Front political party. This created a vacuum of Tamil representation, into which stepped the LTTE to become the main voice for the Tamil community and the dominant force in the insurgency.[19] After a brief attempt at forming a coalition of Tamil groups, the LTTE forced all other groups to submit, executing members of the Tamil Eelam Liberation Organisation and others who resisted.

[12] ibid xxxi.

[13] Shaheen Akhter, 'Ethnic Conflict in Sri Lanka: Domestic, Regional and International Linkages (1983–1993)' (PhD Dissertation, Quaid-i-Azam University Department of International Relations, 2007) 107, *cited in* Syed Rifaat Hussain, 'Liberation Tigers of Tamil Eelam (LTTE)' (2012) 4 Criterion Quarterly n 40.

[14] Joanne Richards, 'An Institutional History of the Liberation Tigers of Tamil Eelam (LTTE)' (Graduate Institute of International and Development Studies—CCDP 2014).

[15] DR Kaarthikeyan, 'The Tamil Tigers of Sri Lanka' in Albrecht Schnabel and Rohan Gunaratna (eds), *Wars from Within: Understanding and Managing Insurgent Movements* (2d edn, Imperial College Press 2015) 276. Richards (n 14) 12.

[16] Richards (n 14) 12.

[17] Bandarage (n 1) 77–109.

[18] Wickramasinghe (n 3) 299–301.

[19] Gerharz (n 10) 24–26; Bandarage (n 1) 110–111.

In only a few years, the LTTE led by Prabhakaran went from being a small band of Tamil youth engaged in sporadic acts of guerrilla warfare to a large organised armed group with military cadres, an administrative hierarchy, a governance structure, and regulatory codes.[20]

Many attempts were made to achieve a political solution via peaceful negotiations between the government and the LTTE. The first attempt were negotiations held in Bhutan upon the intervention of India and a three-month ceasefire starting on 18 June 1985. The LTTE demands were outlined in the 'Thimpu Principles', which the government refused given their denial of Sri Lankan sovereignty over parts of its territory and population.[21] India played a significant role in this phase of the conflict, with the government of Indira Gandhi initially providing some financial and logistical support for the Tamil rebellion. This support came to an end with the election of Rajiv Gandhi as Prime Minister of India in 1987. That year, India and Sri Lanka signed a peace accord that provided for the immediate deployment of an Indian Peacekeeping Force in the north-east of Sri Lanka to disarm the LTTE and end armed hostilities, in return for significant political compromises in favour of Tamils.[22] Political disagreement about the peace accord emerged nearly immediately, and the LTTE never did significantly disarm. Tensions between the LTTE and the Indian Peacekeeping Force deteriorated into open conflict (known as the 'Second Eelam War') within a few months, leading to a military stalemate. Resentment against the peacekeepers grew among both Tamils, because of the behaviour of Indian troops, and Sinhalese, because of fear of infeudation towards India, paradoxically leading the government to provide military support to the LTTE in its fight against the Indian forces.[23] The situation was only resolved by the withdrawal of the Indian Peacekeeping Force in 1990. The Indian withdrawal allowed the LTTE to take control of Jaffna and much of the north of the country, in which it started to provide some public services, not rarely in tandem with the government. Violence and conflict did

[20] See: Richards (n 14) 15; Wickramasinghe (n 3) 302–303; Suthaharan Nadarajah and Dhananjayan Sriskandarajah, 'Liberation Struggle or Terrorism? The Politics of Naming the LTTE' (2005) 26 Third World Quarterly 87; Kristian Stokke, 'Building the Tamil Eelam State: Emerging State Institutions and Forms of Governance in LTTE-Controlled Areas in Sri Lanka' (2006) 27 Third World Quarterly 1021; Zachariah Cherian Mampilly, *Rebel Rulers Insurgent Governance and Civilian Life during War* (Cornell University Press 2011) 93–108.

[21] Tamil Delegation to Thimpu Talks, 'The Thimpu Declaration' Statement (1985), online: <http://tamilnation.co/conflictresolution/tamileelam/85thimpu/thimpu10.htm>. The principles were: recognition of the Tamils of Ceylon as a nation; recognition of the existence of an identified homeland for the Tamils in Ceylon; recognition of the right of self-determination of the Tamil nation; and recognition of the right to citizenship and the fundamental rights of all Tamils in Ceylon.

[22] See Shantha K Hennayake, 'The Peace Accord and the Tamils in Sri Lanka' (1989) 29 Asian Survey 401.

[23] Wickramasinghe (n 3) 303–306; Mampilly (n 20) 105; Richards (n 14) 40; Bandarage (n 1) 133–155.

endure, however, including the mass eviction of 75,000 to 100,000 Muslims from Jaffna and the assassination of Rajiv Gandhi by the LTTE in May 1991.[24]

By the early 1990s, the LTTE had gained extensive control in northern Sri Lanka and created a military stalemate with the government.[25] The period of what is known as the 'Third Eelam War' (1995–2001) led to severe economic losses and increasing unemployment, poverty, and drain of human resources.[26] A change in government in Colombo, supported by favourable international conditions and the intervention of Norway, opened the door to the Ceasefire Agreement of 2002. Between 2002 and 2006, the ceasefire resulted in a fragile but effective status quo that afforded the rebels unimpeded control of a sizeable portion of Sri Lanka's territory. In March 2004, the commander for the LTTE forces in Eastern Sri Lanka (Karuna) broke away from the LTTE, claiming that the interests of Eastern Tamils were ignored.[27] To add to the LTTE's strategic woes, the tsunami of 26 December 2004 resulted in massive losses to the naval and manpower of the LTTE. More generally, the northern and eastern areas of Sri Lanka suffered a humanitarian catastrophe, prompting the LTTE and the government to enter into a difficult aid-sharing agreement.[28] With the 2005 election of Mahinda Rajapaksa as President, the government announced its official suspension of the ceasefire agreement, leading to the bloodiest phase of the conflict between the government and the LTTE between 2006 and 2009 (the 'Fourth Eelam War'). Ultimately, the LTTE was completely defeated, albeit not without tens of thousands more civilian casualties and credible claims of war crimes committed by both sides of the conflict. The Sri Lankan Army reported the death of LTTE leader Velupillai Prabhakaran on 18 May 2009, marking the end of the thirty-year-long war.

B. LTTE Governance

The LTTE was headed by a central governing committee overseeing a military wing, a political wing, an international secretariat, and a peace secretariat.[29] The central governing committee was headed by founder and leader, Prabhakaran, who generally wielded absolute authority over every facet of the LTTE.

24 See generally Bandarage (n 1).
25 Stokke (n 20) 1022.
26 Bandarage (n 1) 168–169.
27 Abhayraj Naik, 'Sarendib's Sorrow: Sri Lanka's Continuing Conflict' (2008) 4 Socio-Legal Review 66, 80.
28 Jude Lal Fernando, 'Lost Lives and a Missed Political Opportunity: The Politics of Conflict and Peace in Post-Tsunami Sri Lanka' (2015) 3 Asian Journal of Peacebuilding 137.
29 Kaarthikeyan (n 15) 282–283, 303.

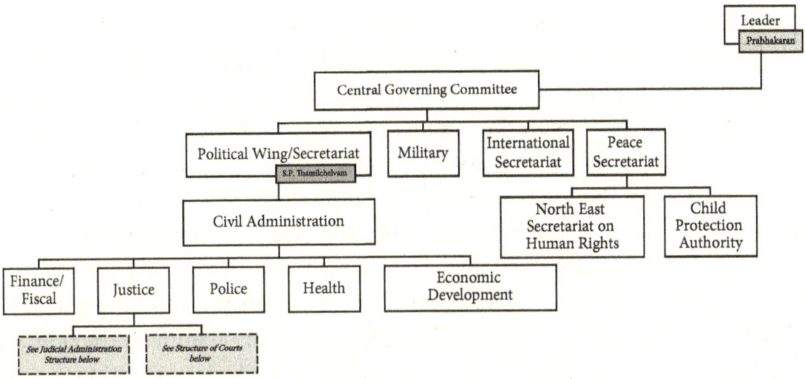

Figure 3.1 LTTE Governance Structure

The military wing of the LTTE was a comprehensive assortment of cadres divided into ground, naval, and airborne forces. It also included the Black Tigers (suicide commandos), Tiger Cubs, the Liberation Tigers Women's Front, and its own military intelligence unit, the Tiger Organization Security Intelligence Service.[30] LTTE cadres were bound by a code of ethics preventing smoking, consuming alcohol, and romantic involvement. The rigid training and the deep sense of loyalty was a distinct feature of the Tamil Tigers, embodied in the infamous cyanide capsule worn around each cadre's neck to enable them to commit suicide rather than suffer capture and risk divulging information.[31] In addition to trained fighters, the LTTE also relied on a 'civil militia' that was often deployed to collect weapons left behind and evacuate injured cadres.[32]

The political wing of the LTTE was initially a political office, functioning independently from the military wing, comprised of the several members of the civil military administration, and tasked with the primary duty of assisting the military wing. During the early stage of war (1983–1987), the territory under the LTTE's control was minimal, and the civil administrative functions within the Jaffna peninsula were primarily carried out by government appointees.[33] By the year 1987, the LTTE had gained sufficient control in the north and announced the establishment of the 'Tamil Eelam Secretariat' and the taking over of civil

[30] Richards (n 14) 13–30. See also DBS Jeyraj, 'Issues: Pottu vs. Karuna: Clash of the "Ammans"' *The Sunday Leader (Sri Lanka)* (14 March 2004), online: <http://www.thesundayleader.lk>.

[31] Visakesa Chandrasekaram, *The Use of Confessionary Evidence Under the Counter-Terrorism Laws of Sri Lanka: An Interdisciplinary Study* (Amsterdam University Press 2018). See also TS Subramaniam, 'Wearing Death Around Their Necks' *The Hindu* (19 May 2009), online: <http://www.thehindu.com>.

[32] See 'Situation Report-II—Expanding Tiger Civil Service' *Sunday Times (Sri Lanka)* (9 June 2002).

[33] Mampilly (n 20) 109–111; Bandarage (n 1) 129.

administrative functions in the area. When the Indian Peacekeeping Force withdrew from Sri Lanka in the late 1980s, the LTTE was "in the process of replacing the government's administration with its own courts, transport, food distribution, and media . . ."[34] With the gradual breakdown of government services in LTTE-controlled areas, the remaining idle government officials continued to be paid a salary from the government for the limited purpose of maintaining the "last slender link of bureaucracy" and "[to not] sever the authority" over areas under the LTTE control.[35] Despite government efforts, the LTTE reinforced its presence by restructuring its political wing within the two administrative districts of Jaffna and Vanni.[36] S.P. Thamilchelvam was appointed the political wing leader to oversee the operations of the LTTE civil administration, a position he held until his death in 2007.[37]

Responsibility for health, education, and economic development was shared between the government of Sri Lanka and the LTTE.[38] Despite the LTTE's desire for a separate Tamil Eelam State, the emergence of LTTE governance in zones under its control or influence was not coupled with the systematic removal of official governance. Thus, the LTTE did not replace government offices like the land registry and the births and deaths registry, which continued to operate without interference.[39] Likewise, health and education continued to be delivered by the government throughout the war in LTTE-controlled areas. A similar openness to some degree of co-existence was also shown by the government. The decisions of the chief governmental official of the area, the government agent, were taken 'in consultation' with the LTTE.[40] Consequently, a kind of multilayered governance took shape, with multiple actors sharing public authority.[41] For instance, though funds were allocated for maintenance of roads and infrastructure by the government, the work was carried out under the supervision of the LTTE. That said, it was a fragile co-existence, and the exercise of power by the LTTE was often met by counter-insurgency measures by the government. For example, in response to the LTTE decision to issue its own vehicle licence plates and impose

[34] Bandarage (n 1) 129.

[35] SC Sardeshpande, *Assignment Jaffna* (Lancer Publishers 1992) 19.

[36] Mampilly (n 20); Stokke (n 20). Neeran, 'The Civil Administration in Tamil Eelam' *Ilankai Tamil Sangam* (website) (10 May 1996), online: <http://www.sangam.org/ANALYSIS_ARCHIVES/civil.htm>.

[37] See generally Iqbal Athas, 'Situation Report: SLAF Regains Its Image with Powerful Strike' *Sunday Times (Sri Lanka)* (4 November 2007); Lasantha Wickrematunge, 'Sri Lanka Kills Rebel Leader' *Time* (2 November 2007), online: <http://content.time.com/time/world/article/0,8599,1679817,00.html>.

[38] Richards (n 14) 46.

[39] Interview with 'Abhay' (government agent under the LTTE) (October 2017); Interview with 'Niranjan' (lawyer who practiced in LTTE courts) (October 2017).

[40] Interview with 'Abhay' (government agent under the LTTE) (October 2017); Neeran (n 36).

[41] Nelson Kasfir, Georg Frerks, and Niels Terpstra, 'Introduction: Armed Groups and Multi-Layered Governance' (2017) 19 Civil Wars 257.

rationing measures, the government placed an embargo on all fuel supplies.[42] As a result of the embargo on essential goods, scarcity of fuel, and the closure of the A9 road (which connects Jaffna to the Central Province), the LTTE was able to exert control over the civilian population by monitoring the distribution of fuel, operating public transport services via road and sea routes where fares were prescribed and collected by the LTTE, controlling the black market of essential goods resulting in exorbitant prices, and manning entry and exit points to the LTTE-controlled areas.[43] In the years that followed, the LTTE developed significant governance capacity in the fields of economic development, education, taxation, and banking. In many ways, the LTTE looked and behaved more like a state than a non-state armed group, including in the administration of justice.

Although an early kind of policing was established in the mid-1980s as soon as the LTTE started to control territory, a more formal police force was inaugurated in 1990 when the LTTE took control of the Jaffna Peninsula.[44] A decade later, there were fourteen LTTE police stations, and a further two were opened in Trincomalee and Batticaloa in conjunction with court expansion in 2002.[45] According to an interview with the 'Inspector General of Police of Tamil Eelam', the police service included divisions on crime prevention, traffic, personnel, transport, communication, forensics, and investigation.[46] He clarified that the primary function of the LTTE police was to maintain law and order, but that it also took part in the 'freedom struggle'. After visiting the area at the time, Zachariah Mampilly also reported that the LTTE police force was widely respected for its incorruptibility and its contribution to local stability.[47]

C. LTTE Justice

Gaining a coherent and comprehensive understanding of the LTTE justice system is difficult for three reasons. First, LTTE courthouses, administrative structures, and archives were destroyed with great zeal and efficacy by

42 Bandarage (n 1) 129; Daya Somasundaram, 'Parallel Governments: Living Between Terror and Counter Terror in Northern Lanka (1982–2009)' (2010) 45 Journal of Asian and African Studies 568; Neeran (n 36).

43 Interview with 'Abhay' (government agent under the LTTE) (October 2017).

44 Niels Terpstra and Georg Frerks, 'Governance Practices and Symbolism: De Facto Sovereignty and Public Authority in "Tigerland"' (2018) 52 Modern Asian Studies 1001, 1014–1020; Mampilly (n 20) 116; Iqbal Athas, 'Inside Vanni: Tiger Police Force—Problem for Peace (Situation Report)' *Sunday Times (Sri Lanka)* (9 June 2002), online: <http://www.sundaytimes.lk/020609/index.html>.

45 Athas (n 44).

46 ibid.

47 Mampilly (n 20) 116. This is complemented by a discussion of the possibility of civilian resistance to LTTE rule in the north-east: Nimmi Gowrinathan and Zachariah Mampilly, 'Resistance and Repression under the Rule of Rebels: Women, Clergy, and Civilian Agency in LTTE Governed Sri Lanka' (2019) 52 Comparative Politics 1.

the advancing Sri Lankan army in the last phase of the civil war in 2008–2009, leaving only very limited fragments in private collections. Second, individuals who played a role in the administration of justice by the LTTE were killed, disappeared, interned, or exiled following the bloody end of the conflict. Those interned, if they have been freed, remain under close surveillance by the state intelligence service even more than a decade later and are still extremely reluctant to discuss anything related to the LTTE. Those who left Sri Lanka to resettle in other countries (Canada, the United Kingdom, and India have the largest Sri Lankan Tamil diaspora communities) will likely not have divulged their link to an entity internationally designated as a terrorist organisation because it would have disqualified their claim to asylum. Even today, many in the diaspora fear that the more militant LTTE supporters among them would look askew at anyone talking about the LTTE courts. Finally, in more explicit and strident terms than other governments confronted with rebel justice, the government of Sri Lanka has categorically dismissed the notion of an LTTE court system as wholly extralegal.[48] According to then Chief Justice Sarath N. de Silva, the LTTE had no mandate to exercise judicial functions, as opposed to consent-based conciliation or mediation for dispute resolution. In this view, under the Sri Lankan Constitution, judicial power is an exercise of sovereignty vested in the people which only the government of Sri Lanka has the mandate to perform.[49] Accordingly, the LTTE courts are often referred to locally as "kangaroo courts", a travesty of the judicial function embodying lawlessness rather than justice.[50]

These difficulties explain the gap between the scale and duration of the justice practice of the LTTE and the precision of its description offered here. Evidence is drawn from a number of studies on the LTTE relying on research carried out during the ceasefire period between 2002 and 2008, none of which are dedicated to the administration of justice, as well as fieldwork carried out in Sri Lanka, in addition to surviving documents produced by the LTTE itself.

[48] Chris Kamalendran, 'The Inside Story of LTTE Courts' Sunday Times (Sri Lanka) (8 December 2002), online: <http://www.sundaytimes.lk/021208/news/courts.html; "Independence of Judiciary Maintained—Rauff Hakeem" Global Tamil News—உலக தமிழ்ச் செய்திகள் (5 June 2011), online: <http://dev.globaltamilnews.net/GTMNEditorial/tabid/71/articleType/ArticleView/articleId/62155/language/en-US/Independence-of-judiciary-maintained--Rauff-Hakeem.aspx>.

[49] Kamalendran (n 48). Laila Nasry, 'LTTE Has No Judicial Authority—CJ' *Sunday Times (Sri Lanka)* (14 November 2004), online: <http://sundaytimes.lk/021208/news/courts.html> ("These courts are not consistent with our constitution and they cannot exist under our hierarchy. Our courts are fully functional in those areas and we do not recognise any other courts. The people too should not go there [. . .] We must maintain our courts because that is what holds for governance. Legal systems, courts, police are all incidence of governance. If there is an erosion then there is no state. This is the danger of it"—CJ Sarath N. de Silva).

[50] Col R Hariharan, 'Downside of Rajiv Assassination' *The Island* (24 August 2016), online: <http://www.island.lk>.

i. Evolution and Structure

The LTTE court system emerged progressively over a period of two decades, starting with vigilance committees and mediation boards before law courts were created. Indeed, given the significant differences between the iterations of adjudicative bodies, perhaps it is contentious to characterise, in hindsight, the earlier forms as predecessor courts. On the other hand, as the deficiencies of the earlier bodies are stated (for example, by the head of the LTTE's judicial division) as being one of the motivations for the court system that emerged, it seems reasonable to consider them together.[51]

(a) Evolution

Vigilance committees reportedly were created by the LTTE's political division following the LTTE's 1986 ban on competing Tamil armed groups. The committees operated in the Jaffna Peninsula and were responsible for monitoring anti-LTTE activities. This period is understood as characterised by rule by terror rather than rule by law. According to the ex-chief of the crime division of the Kilinochchi LTTE police station: "Before the LTTE courts were established, if complaints were made to LTTE leaders against rapists and murderers, the accused were arrested and killed in public by shooting in the head".[52] For their part, the conciliation/mediation boards (*inakkai sabha*) were established in 1984 to resolve disputes among individuals in the regions controlled by the LTTE. The boards were presided over by retired civil servants, schoolteachers, and other local intellectuals.[53] As the LTTE expanded in capacity as an organisation and increased its territorial control, the conciliation boards were not sufficient to meet the demand for justice.[54] According to the LTTE, "the Courts evolved from these Boards which were lacking in legal acumen suitable for dealing with complex issues".[55]

Around 1990, a separate judicial division of the LTTE was established.[56] In April 1990, a member of the Sri Lankan Parliament was reported as explaining

[51] 'Tamil Eelam Judiciary Said a Basis for Rebuilding Northeast' *TamilNet* (30 October 2003), online: <http://www.tamilnet.com/art.html?catid=79&artid=10277>.

[52] Srinath Prasanna Jayasuriya, 'ත්‍රස්තවාදය අවසන් කර අදට වසර 4යි: එදා කිලිනොච්චි කොටි පොලීසියේ "අපරාධ" ස්ථානාධිපති කතා කරයි' [It's 4 Years Since the Defeat of Terrorism: The Ex-crime Division Chief of the Kilinochchi Police Speaks] *Lankadeepa (Sri Lanka)* (12 May 2012), online: <http://www.lankadeepa.lk>; Interview with 'Abilashini' (who was involved in establishing the LTTE courts in the 1990s) (December 2018).

[53] Interview with 'Niranjan' (lawyer who practiced in LTTE courts) (October 2017); Amantha Perera, 'Justice According to the Tiger' *The Sunday Leader* (3 October 2004), online: <http://www.thesundayleader.lk>; Mampilly (n 20) 109; Stokke (n 20).

[54] 'Tamil Eelam Judiciary Said a Basis for Rebuilding Northeast' (n 51).

[55] LTTE, 'The Judicial System of Tamil Eelam: Its Structure, Functions and Duties of Officials in Charge' (~1999) 16 (undated LTTE document, on file with author).

[56] Interview with 'Abilashini' (who was involved in establishing the LTTE courts in the 1990s) (December 2018).

that the LTTE had launched simultaneous campaigns to take over the law and order functions in the northern and eastern provinces by, on the one hand, ordering the closure of 'regular' courts and, on the other hand, establishing civil courts in rural areas of the two provinces.[57] One such court was already reported as having commenced hearing civil cases at the Eppadikottan colony in the Ampaara District.[58] Soon after, in 1993, the LTTE court system was established in Kilinochchi, as control over Jaffna territory was continuously being exchanged between the Sri Lankan Army and the LTTE.[59] According to one informant, the LTTE courts were often set up in the same buildings as had been occupied by the Sri Lankan courts and "had the accoutrements of formal courts".[60] The slow expansion of the LTTE court structure was not always aligned with LTTE control of territory. An early report indicates that an LTTE court existed in Kokkadicholai village, near Batticaloa, as early as 1998, at a moment when the group did not have military control of the area.[61]

The development of formal LTTE courts during the 1990s seemed to come as a reaction to both internal and external factors: on the one hand, the creation of the LTTE judicial system was motivated by "the perceived failure of the Sri Lankan Constitution to provide protection for minority rights".[62] On the other hand, as mentioned, the development of formal courts seemed also to have responded to inadequacies in earlier LTTE attempts at providing justice mechanisms. Mediation boards were dismantled and replaced by "a fully-fledged legal system"[63] due to complaints directed at the "disorganised approach to administering justice" and a recognition that the administration of justice was an important part of the LTTE's relationship with the civilian population it sought to control.[64] Mampilly also mentions an early system of land courts, established primarily for revenue generation purposes, whose function was taken over by regular courts when they were established.[65]

With the 2002 ceasefire agreement, new courts became necessary due to the rise of litigation with several Tamils returning to their homeland, resulting in the opening of new courts and expanding the LTTE judicial system.[66] LTTE justice

[57] Senadhira Sugeeswara, 'LTTE Control Is Increasing' *India Abroad* (13 April 1990) 21.

[58] ibid.

[59] Perera (n 53); Tyron Devotta, 'The Rule of Law in Tiger Territory' *Sunday Times (Sri Lanka)* (27 February 2005), online: <http://www.sundaytimes.lk/050227/news/20.html>.

[60] Interview with 'Prabashini' (former lawyer at the Chavakachcheri Court House) (October 2017).

[61] PS Suryanarayana, 'An Eelam Outpost' (1998) 15 *Frontline*, online: <https://frontline.thehindu.com/static/html/fl1501/15010540.htm>.

[62] Richards (n 14) 44; Stokke (n 20) 1029.

[63] Chris Kamalendran, 'Inside Story of Eelam Courts' *Sunday Times (Sri Lanka)* (14 November 2004).

[64] Mampilly (n 20) 117.

[65] ibid.

[66] Perera (n 53); E Pararajasingham, 'Tamil Eelam Legal System' (2003), online: <http://tamilnation.co/tamileelam/defacto/031030judicial.htm> accessed 21 February 2017. Chris Kamalendran, 'LTTE

expanded into the eastern province in November and December 2002, with the opening of rebel courts in the Batticaloa and Trincomalee districts.[67] This expansion was contemporaneous with the Oslo peace talks, in the course of which the LTTE agreed not to operate law-and-order mechanisms in areas outside its control. It seems that although the question of law and order was discussed in the peace talks, the discussions were limited to LTTE police rather than LTTE courts.[68] According to the LTTE, by 2005, over 32,000 cases had been tried by the district courts and 1,500 by the Court of Appeals.[69] The LTTE courts operated until nearly the end of the war in May 2009, after which the Sri Lankan judicial system was re-established in the entire national territory for the first time since 1987.[70]

Despite the development of a formalised court system, there is some indication of a number of parallel practices. First, there are indications that a military court system existed, where disciplinary and penal complaints against cadres were tried by officials appointed by the LTTE.[71] Likewise, it is reported that civil disputes between two LTTE cadres would be resolved in a military court rather than in the District Court.[72] As these military proceedings were not carried out in public, little information could be found about them beyond general statements that they were expedited and harsh.[73] Second, although it is only supported by

Opens First "Court" in East' *Sunday Times (Sri Lanka)* (24 November 2002), online: <http://www.sundaytimes.lk/021124/front/ltte.html>.

[67] 'LTTE "Law Courts" in the East from Friday' *Sunday Times (Sri Lanka)* (10 November 2002), online: <http://www.sundaytimes.lk/021110/> ("From next Friday [15 November 2002], LTTE 'Courts of Law' will commence functioning in the East. The Sunday Times learns that confirmation of this move has even reached the head office of the Sri Lanka Monitoring Mission in Colombo. Initially, these 'courts' will be in the areas where 'Police Stations' have already been set up"); Kamalendran (n 66). 'LTTE Opens First Thamileelam Court in Trincomalee District' *TamilNet* (2 December 2002), online: <https://www.tamilnet.com/art.html?catid=13&artid=7925>.

[68] Kamalendran (n 66) ("The Sunday Times learns that the issue of LTTE 'courts' will not be taken up at the upcoming peace talks in Oslo, but the issue of LTTE 'police stations' will be taken up as Prime Minister Ranil Wickremesinghe has assured SLMC leader Rauff Hakeem that it would be taken up").

[69] US State Department, 'These Tigers Don't Purr: Analysis of the Tamil Tiger Police and Judiciary', Diplomatic Cable No 05COLOMBO1396_a, 10 August 2005, para 8, online: <https://wikileaks.org/plusd/cables/05COLOMBO1396_a.html>; 'LTTE Opens First Thamileelam Court in Trincomalee District' (n 67).

[70] 'Judicial System to Be Revived in Kilinochchi, Mullaitivu' *The Sunday Observer (Colombo)* (21 February 2010).

[71] LTTE Judge Thambirasa Varathiswaran, in Kamalendran (n 63); Tharanga Ratnaweera and Lasitha Duminda, 'කොටි උසාවියේ නඩු ඇසූ කයිලාසා කතා කරයි' *Divaina* (21 October 2012), online: <http://www.divaina.com>. [Divaina, 'Kailasa']; 'தமிழீழ நீதிமன்றம்—ஓர் அறிமுகம் [Tamileelam Law Courts—An Introduction]' விடுதலை புலிகள் [Liberation Tigers] (June 1993), online: <https://eelamview.files.wordpress.com/2008/09/33.jpg> [Liberation Tigers, 'Tamileelam Courts'].

[72] Perera (n 53).

[73] Jayasuriya (n 52); Divaina, 'Kailasa' (n 71); US State Department, 'These Tigers Don't Purr' (n 69) para 10.

anecdotal comments, it seems that the vigilance committees may have been restructured but not entirely abolished: that is, there are some suggestions emerging from the interviews that certain unspecified crimes against the LTTE or the Tamil nation were dealt with directly by LTTE cadres rather than brought to the courts.[74] Third, in 2004, the LTTE established the North East Secretariat on Human Rights (NESOHR), a body attached to the Peace Secretariat rather than the justice system.[75] NESOHR had three main functions: to receive, investigate, and resolve human rights complaints, including those of migrants and prison inmates; to run educational programmes on the protection of human rights for schools, the police, the military, and the judiciary; and to advise authorities on human rights issues, including assessing legislation and practices.[76] Interestingly, NESOHR received complaints against both the Sri Lankan state and the LTTE, on issues that included forced disappearances, extrajudicial killings, and the recruitment of child soldiers.[77] Finally, although the LTTE court system played a prominent role in dispensing justice during the conflict in Sri Lanka, informal dispute resolution methods remained very much in place within the northern and eastern provinces.[78] The LTTE, being a powerful political actor, continued to be involved in informal dispute resolution mechanisms throughout its zone of control.[79] LTTE cadres participated in informal dispute resolution amongst the *grama sevakas* (officials appointed by government for civil administration at a village level), priests, and police officers.[80] During the period of the ceasefire, in areas under government military control, the LTTE operated political offices where civilians could present complaints about private or public matters; the LTTE was heavily involved in managing disputes relating to domestic violence, substance abuse, property, and family issues.[81]

[74] Interview with 'Abilashini' (who was involved in establishing the LTTE courts in the 1990s) (December 2018). Such crimes would likely correspond first and foremost to charges of spying on behalf of the government.

[75] For a description of the work of NESOHR by its secretary, see Naguleswaran Malathy, *A Fleeting Moment in My Country: The Last Years of the LTTE de-Facto State* (Clear Day Books 2012).

[76] See <https://web.archive.org/web/20070115174131/http://nesohr.org/background-goals/>.

[77] NESOHR, 2005 Annual Report (July 2005) 7, online: <https://web.archive.org/web/20060616194446/http://nesohr.org/annual-reports/>.

[78] See generally Craig Walters, 'Community Mediation and Social Harmony in Sri Lanka' (2013) The Asia Foundation, Paper No. 4, online: <http://www.lse.ac.uk/internationalDevelopment/research/JSRP/downloads/JSRP4-Theories-in-Practice-Sri-Lanka.pdf>.

[79] 'Informal Dispute Resolution in the North East and Puttalam' (2007) Centre for Policy Alternatives, online: <http://www.cpalanka.org/wp-content/uploads/2007/8/Informal_Dispute_Resolution.pdf>.

[80] ibid.

[81] Eva Gerharz, 'Between Order and Chaos' in Siri Hettige and Eva Gerharz (eds), *Governance, Conflict and Development in South Asia: Perspectives from India, Nepal and Sri Lanka* (SAGE Publications India 2015) 195–200. See also US State Department, 'Tigers Gradually Expand Network of Control in the East, as Security Forces Watch and Muslims Fret', Diplomatic Cable No 02COLOMBO2133_a, 14 November 2002, online: <https://wikileaks.org/plusd/cables/02COLOMBO2133_a.html>.

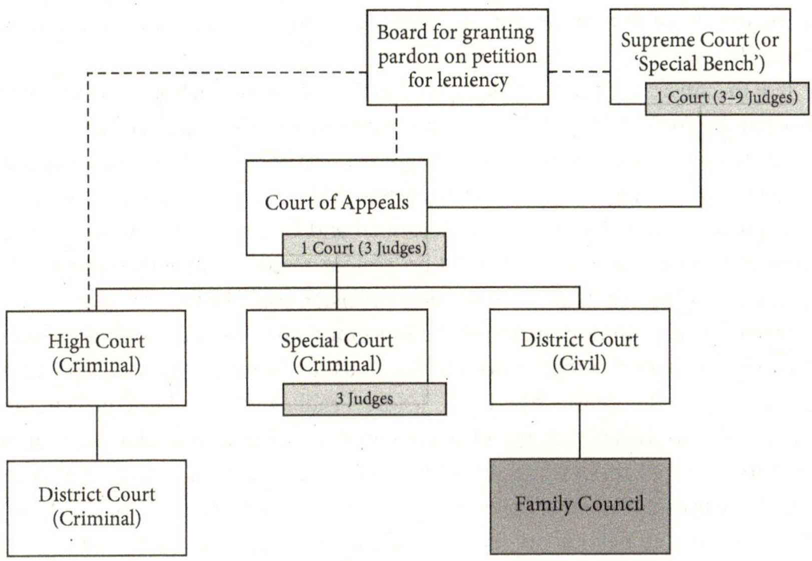

Figure 3.2 LTTE Judicial Structure

(b) Structure

According to an undated LTTE publication titled 'The Judicial System of Tamil Eelam: Its Structure, Functions and Duties of Officials in Charge', the judicial system was constituted as shown in Figure 2.

The expansion of the court system meant that it eventually consisted of seventeen courts, including six District Courts, two High Courts with civil and criminal divisions, a Special Court, a Court of Appeals, and a Supreme Court (sometimes referred to as 'Special Bench'). Magistrate courts do not appear in all descriptions of the structure.[82] The resulting structure is 'nearly identical' to the Sri Lankan court system, save for the existence of a lower tier of magistrate courts in the government system.[83] As will become clear in the description of the functions of each court and of judicial officers, this hierarchical structure facilitated both judicial and administrative oversight. That is to say, the higher courts (especially the Supreme Court) were not only the final appellate court, but

[82] According to TamilNet, a seventh district court was established as of 2006, but there is some doubt as to its existence: 'Tamileelam Legislature Enacts Child Protection Act' *TamilNet* (25 October 2006), online: <http://www.tamilnet.com/art.html?catid=13&artid=20025>. Tamil Centre for Human Rights, 'Study Mission to Vavuniya, Vanni, Mullaitivu and Jaffna by Representatives of TCHR in April–May 2003' (2003), online: <http://www.tchr.net/report_studymission_2003.htm>. One example of mention of magistrates courts is in Iqbal Athas, 'Inside Vanni: Expanding Tiger Civil Service (Situation Report)' *Sunday Times (Sri Lanka)* (9 June 2002), online: <http://www.sundaytimes.lk/020609/index.html>.

[83] US State Department, 'These Tigers Don't Purr' (n 69) para 8.

its officers were responsible for overseeing the judges in the lower courts more generally.

For the most part, it seems that the civil and criminal jurisdictions were kept separate by the creation of civil and criminal courts, at least for trial level. The Court of Appeals and the Supreme Court heard appeals from both civil and criminal courts. One informant suggested that perhaps even within a court hearing both kinds of matters, different judges would hear criminal and civil cases.[84] However, another informant indicated that there might be 'various reasons' why judges might hear both criminal and civil cases, but no more precision could be found.[85]

Appellate jurisdictions included the Supreme Court and the Court of Appeals. The Supreme Court initially was referred to as the 'Special Bench', composed of three judges, all appointed by LTTE leader Prabhakaran. Its basic jurisdiction was similar to the apex courts of many countries, sitting in final appeal for all matters.[86] It appears that the size of the Supreme Court was enlarged at some point to a normal bench of five judges, growing to a maximum of nine judges.[87] More unusually, beyond its familiar role as a court of ultimate appeal, the Supreme Court also appointed and transferred judges "in consultation with the officials in charge" and "offer[ed] advice in judicial and legal matters" (although to whom is not altogether clear).[88] The appointment and transfer role was carried out by the Chief Justice and a fellow Supreme Court Judge, who also acted as Official in Charge of Judges, and his/her deputy (the Chief Justice being responsible for Judges of the High Courts, Special Court and District Courts, and the Deputy being responsible for the Judges of the Court of Appeals). Supreme Court judges also oversaw disciplinary complaints against lower-court judges and attorneys. The Court of Appeal was constituted by a bench of three judges and "functions as the court which has jurisdiction in respect of appeal cases tried by the High Courts, District Courts and the Special Court".[89] The LTTE leader, Prabhakaran, directly appointed judges to the Court of Appeals. Although an appeal could be filed easily upon payment of a small fee (equivalent to about $10), less than 3 percent of trial-level decisions were appealed.[90]

There were three kinds of trial-level courts, namely: a Special Court, High Courts, and District Courts. The Special Court sat in a bench of three judges, selected by the Chief Justice of the Supreme Court, to try criminal cases that arose

[84] Interview with 'Abilashini' (who was involved in establishing the LTTE courts in the 1990s) (December 2018).

[85] Interview with 'Tharmi' (LTTE lawyer then judge) (December 2018).

[86] LTTE, 'The Judicial System of Tamil Eelam: Its Structure, Functions and Duties of Officials in Charge' (n 55) 4; Pararajasingham (n 66) 2.

[87] Interview with 'Partheepan' (former LTTE judge) (October 2017).

[88] LTTE, 'The Judicial System of Tamil Eelam: Its Structure, Functions and Duties of Officials in Charge' 4.

[89] ibid 4.

[90] Perera (n 53).

out of "incidents that happened in special circumstances".[91] Little is known as to what such special circumstances might correspond to, but it can be speculated that it covered issues related to the security of the LTTE. The High Court, sitting in Kilinochchi and Mullaithivu, had "the jurisdiction to try certain criminal cases according to the terms of the Court of Appeals Act", apparently corresponding to the most serious crimes passable of capital punishment, such as treason, murder, rape, and arson.[92] Criminal and Civil District Courts were the courts of primary jurisdiction in their respective fields, including on matters that fell within the competence of magistrate courts in the Sri Lankan court system.[93] The judges of the High Courts and District Courts were appointed by the Chief Justice of the Supreme Court in consultation with the head of the judicial division, Pararajasingham, who occupied the position equivalent to Minister of Justice in the LTTE administration.[94] By 2009, there were a total of six District Courts sitting in Kilinochchi, Mallavi, Jeyapuram, Puthukkudiyiruppu, Trincomalee, and Batticaloa.[95] The Kilinochchi District Court sat as a civil court on Mondays and Tuesdays, whereas the last two days of the week were reserved for criminal cases.[96] Although in the initial phase prior to 1996 the District Court benches consisted of three judges, from at least 1999, only a single judge presided.[97] Family disputes brought to the District Courts, Civil Division were first steered towards the Family Council, a subsidiary judicial body tasked with attempting to mediate a resolution.[98] In penal matters, in the early phase of the LTTE court system, a person sentenced to pay a fine over Rs100,000 (about $1,000) or to serve a prison term of more than five years could write a letter of apology to LTTE supreme leader Prabhakaran asking for a lesser sentence; and on Maaveerar Naal (a day of commemoration of the LTTE militants who died in battle), the LTTE leader would grant full pardon to selected prisoners.[99] In a later phase, a 'Board of review of petitions for leniency' was established to hear petitions for pardon or reduction of sentence, with the ultimate decision on all sentences resting with Prabhakaran.[100]

Turning to the make-up of the LTTE judiciary, it appears that most judges were connected to the movement either as former fighting cadres or as persons

91 LTTE (n 88) 14.

92 LTTE, 'The Judicial System of Tamil Eelam: Its Structure, Functions and Duties of Officials in Charge' (n 55) 6; US State Department, 'These Tigers Don't Purr' (n 69) para 8; Pararajasingham (n 66) 2.

93 LTTE, ibid; Interview with 'Partheepan' (former LTTE judge) (October 2017).

94 US State Department, 'These Tigers Don't Purr' (n 69) para 8.

95 Pararajasingham (n 66).

96 Perera (n 53).

97 Interview with 'Vithushini' (former court clerk) (October 2017).

98 Kamalendran (n 48); LTTE, 'The Judicial System of Tamil Eelam: Its Structure, Functions and Duties of Officials in Charge' (n 55) 9.

99 Liberation Tigers, 'Tamileelam Courts' (n 71). No corroboration of this practice could be found.

100 LTTE, ibid 7–8.

who were politically connected to the group.[101] The LTTE presentation pamphlet on the court system offers, somewhat ambiguously, that "[j]udges are selected among the members who have dedicated their services and live [*sic*] to the interest of the general public, and appointed on the basis of merit".[102] One implication is that no non-Tamil or Muslim could be appointed to the bench, resulting in a judiciary that failed to reflect significant segments of the civilian population under the authority of the LTTE.[103] All those appointed to sit as judges had received a formal legal education. Prior to the establishment of the law college, the University of Jaffna offered classes to teach law to cadres so that they could become judges and lawyers.[104] After the LTTE established its own law college in 1992, it moved to select graduating students to follow a special course taught by senior lawyers for those destined to be appointed to the bench, possibly followed by a stint as judicial assistant.[105] This represents a departure from the British-inspired model of appointing senior lawyers to the bench, and indeed no established attorney nor anyone who had held a judicial appointment to the courts of Sri Lanka was named to sit as a judge on an LTTE court.[106] Some lawyers objected that LTTE judges were too young and inexperienced and could be manipulated by senior barristers, but it is difficult to determine whether this is really a critique of an approach to the judicial function that resembles that in Continental Europe. Consistent with other facets of the LTTE's progressive approach to gender equality, there were approximately the same number of women and men appointed to the bench.[107] Sitting judges were required to undertake continuing legal education courses, generally taught by senior lawyers who had trained at the University of Colombo and were practicing in parts of the country controlled by the Sri Lankan government. The continuing education courses tended to focus on precedential cases from Sri Lanka, India, and other foreign jurisdictions.[108]

[101] Interview with 'Vijitha' (lawyer who appeared in LTTE courts) (October 2017); Interview with 'Abilashini' (who was involved in establishing the LTTE courts in the 1990s) (December 2018).

[102] LTTE, 'The Judicial System of Tamil Eelam: Its Structure, Functions and Duties of Officials in Charge' (n 55) 19.

[103] US State Department, 'These Tigers Don't Purr' (n 69) para 12. The LTTE was of course quick to respond that this was the equivalent to the Sri Lankan constitution, which was "the indubitable expression of Sinhala Buddhism supremacy in this island, drawn up by the Sinhalese for the Sinhalese": Pararajasingham (n 66) 1.

[104] Interview with 'Parameswaran' (former lecturer, University of Jaffna) (October 2017).

[105] LTTE, 'The Judicial System of Tamil Eelam: Its Structure, Functions and Duties of Officials in Charge' (n 55) 18; Interview with 'Partheepan' (former LTTE judge) (October 2017); Interview with 'Vijitha' (lawyer who practiced before LTTE courts) (October 2017).

[106] Interview with 'Abilashini' (who was involved in establishing the LTTE courts in the 1990s) (December 2018).

[107] Interview with 'Vithushini' (former court clerk) (October 2017); Interview with 'Manodi' (Colombo human rights researcher) (October 2017).

[108] Interview with 'Partheepan' (former LTTE judge) (October 2017).

ii. Judicial Process

The unique nature of the trial process was a significant theme emerging from the interviews. Specifically, it seems that the LTTE court process was 'inquisitorial' (as opposed to the adversarial process of the Sri Lankan courts).

Although no complete account of the LTTE inquisitorial process exists, several key features emerged from the interviews. First, the parties and witnesses were examined by the judge(s) as part of the initial assessment of a dispute or prosecution. Apparently on a model reminiscent of the *juge d'instruction* in continental Europe, it seems that enquiries and interrogations were carried out in chambers "to uncover the truth", in particular to determine if a party or witness "failed to speak the truth".[109] Second, perhaps as a result of the inquisitorial process, the presence of lawyers may not have been strictly necessary. Whether a lawyer was present seemed to depend on whether they were requested to be there by their client.[110] Third, there were further mechanisms for verifying the truth of testimony and documentary evidence. Specifically, again reminiscent of the practice of *juge d'instruction*, it was reported that judges sometimes sent officials to undertake investigations to verify a witness's or party's account.[111] Fourth, according to an LTTE pamphlet on its court system, there was a 'Committee of Experts of Handwriting and Fingerprints', whose duty it was to "find the truth of documents in respect of the signature of them . . . in relation to documents received by Courts in civil and criminal cases".[112] The committee was made up of "the official in charge of legislation, a member of the police, and a handwriting expert".[113]

Rules of judicial procedure and evidence were set out in the Code of Civil Procedure, the Code of Criminal Procedure, and the Evidence Act, all enacted by the LTTE.[114] No copy of the Code of Civil Procedure could be found, but the Code of Criminal Procedure and the Evidence Act are very detailed statutes containing, respectively, 363 and 162 articles. While they were said by the LTTE to be inspired by English common law, they also sought to reflect Tamil culture, including precolonial customary norms such as the *Thesawalamai* in Jaffna and the *Mukkuwa* in Batticaloa.[115] In some ways there are clear divergences from English common law, for example, there is no principle against the admission of hearsay evidence, something that rankled some Sri Lankan–trained

109 Interview with 'Partheepan' (former LTTE judge) (October 2017); Interview with 'Vithushini' (former court clerk) (26 October 2017).
110 Interview with 'Partheepan' (former LTTE judge) (October 2017).
111 Interview with 'Prabashini' (former lawyer at the Chavakachcheri courthouse) (October 2017).
112 LTTE, 'The Judicial System of Tamil Eelam: Its Structure, Functions and Duties of Officials in Charge' (n 55) 8.
113 ibid.
114 LTTE, Code of Civil Procedure, mentioned in ibid 17; LTTE, Code of Criminal Procedure (2004), on file with the author; LTTE, Evidence Act (1995), on file with the author.
115 LTTE, 'The Judicial System of Tamil Eelam: Its Structure, Functions and Duties of Officials in Charge' (n 55) 17; Pararajasingham (n 66) 3–4.

lawyers.[116] In penal matters, procedural guarantees entrenched in human rights law were protected (e.g. presumption of innocence, protection against double jeopardy, inadmissibility of evidence obtained under duress or by torture).[117] With the exception of the investigatory phase that took place in chambers, informants generally reported that cases were heard in open court, the exception being crimes of a sexual nature which were heard *in camera*.[118] It seems that court proceedings were conducted mostly, but not exclusively, in Tamil.[119] Lawyers from the south (that is, outside LTTE-controlled areas) could and did appear before LTTE courts, usually intervening in English.[120] No informant had any experience of proceedings being conducted in Sinhala, probably a reflection that all judges were Tamil and unlikely to fluently understand Sinhala.[121]

Decisions of LTTE courts were issued in writing and a copy kept in the archives at the various courthouses, all of which were destroyed in the last phase of the conflict. Once a judgment was issued, its enforcement was the responsibility of the police in criminal cases and of an entity designated as the 'Fiscal' in civil cases.[122] Anyone displeased with a decision of the District Court, High Court or Special Court could appeal to the Court of Appeals by way of a procedure that was simple and inexpensive.[123] As mentioned earlier, it seems that few litigants or convicted persons availed themselves of this rights.[124] Judgments of the Court of Appeals could in turn be appealed to the Supreme Court.

116 Interview with 'Lojini' (lawyer who appeared before LTTE courts) (October 2017). It can be noted that many legal systems allow some forms of hearsay evidence: Kai Ambos, *Treatise on International Criminal Law*, vol III: International Criminal Procedure (Oxford University Press 2016) 474–477; Christoph Safferling, *International Criminal Procedure* (Oxford University Press 2012) 495–499.

117 Interview with 'Sharmi' (Senior State Counsel); Interview with 'Kajenthini' (former LTTE lawyer); Interview with 'Abilashini' (who was involved in establishing the LTTE courts in the 1990s) (December 2018); Interview with 'Tharmi' (former LTTE lawyer then judge) (December 2018).

118 Interview with 'Partheepan' (former LTTE judge) (26 October 2017); Interview with 'Sharmi' (Senior State Counsel); Interview with 'Kajenthini' (LTTE lawyer); Interview with 'Abilashini' (who was involved in establishing the LTTE courts in the 1990s) (December 2018).

119 Interview with 'Sharmi' (Senior State Counsel); Interview with 'Kajenthini' (LTTE lawyer); Interview with 'Abilashini' (who was involved in establishing the LTTE courts in the 1990s) (December 2018)) (who was under the impression that all proceedings were in Tamil).

120 Interview with 'Kajenthini' (LTTE lawyer).

121 Interview with 'Sharmi' (Senior State Counsel); Interview with 'Kajenthini' (LTTE lawyer); Interview with 'Abilashini' (who was involved in establishing the LTTE courts in the 1990s) (December 2018).

122 LTTE, 'The Judicial System of Tamil Eelam: Its Structure, Functions and Duties of Officials in Charge' (n 55) 9.

123 ibid 4; Interview with 'Abilashini' (who was involved in establishing the LTTE courts in the 1990s) (December 2018).

124 Perera (n 53).

iii. Legal Practice

The practice of law in LTTE jurisdictions was highly controlled by the group, from the qualifications needed to become an attorney to the conditions under which lawyers worked.

The LTTE is perhaps unique among rebel groups in having established its own college of law to train its members to become attorneys and judges. The first LTTE legal education initiative was in early 1990, when classes were introduced at the University of Jaffna to teach law to cadres to enable them to become judges and lawyers.[125] Very quickly, when the LTTE established its authority over parts of the Vanni in 1992, Prabhakaran decided that the creation of a college of law for the movement was a priority.[126] It seems that the law college was initially started at Kilinochchi before moving to Mullaithivu.[127]

Although it was predominantly cadres or former cadres who initially trained in the LTTE college of law, this was not a formal precondition for admission, and civilians soon came to be admitted as well.[128] Newly admitted students were divided into two streams: 'Internal students' included those who had been LTTE fighters and students recently graduated from high school, while 'external students' included university graduates and individuals with at least seven years' experience working for the government or non-governmental organisations.[129] The course of study was five continuous terms over three years for internal students, while external students had to sit three term exams over that same period, completed for all by a one-year articling position.[130] In 2004, the head of the LTTE judicial division is quoted as saying that there currently were twenty-five students registered in the college of law, and that a total of 150 had passed as lawyers, presumably since the college's inception.[131]

The structure of the curriculum seems to have been based in part on the curriculum of the Sri Lankan Law College, with changes made to incorporate Tamil language and culture as well as historical and customary laws.[132] It seems that

125 Interview with 'Parameswaran' (former lecturer, University of Jaffna) (October 2017).

126 LTTE, 'The Judicial System of Tamil Eelam: Its Structure, Functions and Duties of Officials in Charge' (n 55) 21; Pararajasingham (n 66).

127 Interview with 'Vijitha' (lawyer who appeared in LTTE courts) (October 2017); Interview with 'Tharmi' (former LTTE lawyer then judge); Interview with 'Suboshini' (lecturer, University of Colombo); Interview with 'Sharmi' (Senior State Counsel); Interview with 'Kajenthini' (former LTTE lawyer) (December 2018); Interview with 'Abilashini' (who was involved in establishing the LTTE courts in the 1990s) (December 2018); Perera (n 53).

128 Interview with 'Abilashini' (who was involved in establishing the LTTE courts in the 1990s) (December 2018); Interview with 'Suboshini' (lecturer, University of Colombo).

129 LTTE, 'The Judicial System of Tamil Eelam: Its Structure, Functions and Duties of Officials in Charge' (n 55) 22.

130 ibid 8, 21; Interview with 'Tharmi' (former LTTE lawyer then judge); Interview with 'Abilashini' (who was involved in establishing the LTTE courts in the 1990s) (December 2018).

131 Perera (n 53).

132 Interview with 'Divya' (lecturer, University of Colombo); Interview with 'Suboshini' (lecturer, University of Colombo); Interview with 'Abilashini' (who was involved in establishing the LTTE courts in the 1990s) (December 2018).

despite the importance of the Tamil language, many of the courses were taught in English.[133] The course curriculum appears to have followed a pattern that will be familiar to anyone with legal training:[134]

First Year	Second Year	Third Year
Criminal Law	Civil Procedure Code	Evidence Act
History of Law and Legal System	Criminal Procedure Code	Law of Trust Property
Roman Dutch Law	Commercial Law, Accountancy, and Management	Administrative Law
English Law	Law of Property Act	Trade Practices Act
Constitutional Law	Law of Thesawalamai	International Law
Human Rights and Rules	Family Law	Law of Notarial Instruments
Jurisprudence	Police Act	Sales Tax Act
Law of Torts	Personal Act	Forensic Medicine and Criminology
Tamil Language and Literature	Land Act	English Language
English Language	English Language	

As is suggested by the course listing, and confirmed by an informant, the curriculum of the college of law extended beyond LTTE law. Thus, questions from Sri Lankan, Indian, Malaysian, and British law were studied in classes; indeed, constitutional law was taught even though 'Tamil Eelam' itself did not have a constitution.[135]

It seems that legal education through the law college, although not wholly free, was inexpensive: one informant estimates having paid Rs10,000 (about $100) over the three years.[136] There reportedly were scholarships or bonded-placement options available. For example, one informant understood that it was open to students, in exchange for free education, to agree to work for the LTTE legal unit following graduation, which would mean that they would be paid a lower salary or be required to take on pro bono cases.[137]

The practice of law before LTTE courts was not restricted to graduates of the group's own college of law. Established lawyers in areas that came under LTTE authority, who had trained in one of the recognised faculties of law and the law college in Sri Lanka, could continue to practice law. Likewise, lawyers from outside LTTE-controlled areas admitted to practice in the Sri Lankan courts were able to appear before LTTE courts. In both cases, these lawyers were required

[133] Interview with 'Suboshini' (lecturer, University of Colombo) (October 2017).

[134] LTTE, 'The Judicial System of Tamil Eelam: Its Structure, Functions and Duties of Officials in Charge' (n 55) 23–24.

[135] ibid 21; Interview with 'Tharmi' (LTTE lawyer then judge) (December 2018).

[136] Interview with 'Tharmi' (former LTTE lawyer then judge) (December 2018); Interview with 'Kajenthini' (former LTTE lawyer) (December 2018).

[137] Interview with 'Kajenthini' (former LTTE lawyer) (December 2018).

to first take an oath similar to the one taken by graduates of the LTTE college of law upon being called to the bar.[138] No informant offered the precise wording of the oath, although one indicated that it included a promise not to knowingly defend the guilty.[139] It goes without saying that not many lawyers from the rest of Sri Lanka would be willing to travel to the LTTE area and submit to this requirement.

The fees charged by lawyers practicing in LTTE courts were tightly regulated by the group, as a reaction against the high cost of lawyers in the rest of the country that was seen to contribute to the unfairness of the justice system.[140] Thus, not only did the LTTE impose a fee structure, greatly limiting how much attorneys could charge for their services, but also all fees were paid through the court registry to ensure strict abidance with this regulation.[141] For instance, a lawyer could not demand more than Rs500 ($5) for appearing before the Court of Appeal, and most procedures did not cost more than Rs150 ($1.50).[142] If even these modest fees proved too much for indigent parties to a case, legal aid would be provided free of charge by the LTTE legal division.[143] The lawyers responsible for providing legal aid seemed to be those that received free or subsidised education at the LTTE college of law.[144]

iv. Applicable Law

Formally, the operation of LTTE courts was based on the 'laws of the LTTE'. In practice, this seems to have meant that the courts applied a combination of pre-existing national law and a number of statutes adopted by the LTTE on the basis of British, Sri Lankan, Indian, and Malaysian laws.[145]

The LTTE had a 'legislative branch' or secretariat that was responsible for drafting new laws, operating in a manner that was independent of the judiciary

138 Interview with 'Tharmi' (former LTTE lawyer then judge) (December 2018); Interview with 'Sharmi' (Senior State Counsel) (December 2018). Interview with 'Lojini' (lawyer who appeared before LTTE courts) (October 2017); Interview with 'Parameswaran' (former lecturer, University of Jaffna) (October 2017).

139 Interview with 'Lojini' (lawyer who appeared before LTTE courts) (October 2017); Interview with 'Tharmi' (LTTE lawyer then judge) (December 2018). According to this informant, lawyers could defend their clients to the full extent of the law and would not be found to have defended a guilty client if the client was subsequently convicted.

140 LTTE, 'The Judicial System of Tamil Eelam: Its Structure, Functions and Duties of Officials in Charge' (n 55) 19.

141 See Perera (n 53).

142 Interview with 'Lojini' (lawyer who appeared before LTTE courts) (October 2017); US State Department, 'These Tigers Don't Purr' (n 69) para 8.

143 Interview with 'Suboshini' (lecturer, University of Colombo); Interview with 'Kajenthini' (former LTTE lawyer); Interview with 'Abilashini' (who was involved in establishing the LTTE courts in the 1990s) (December 2018).

144 Interview with 'Suboshini' (lecturer, University of Colombo); Interview with 'Kajenthini' (former LTTE lawyer); Interview with 'Abilashini' (who was involved in establishing the LTTE courts in the 1990s) (December 2018).

145 Kamalendran (n 48); Perera (n 53).

but wholly subservient to the overall LTTE leader, Prabhakaran.[146] The initiative for a law to be drafted was said to come "at the request of respective fields", which could be taken to refer to the various branches of the LTTE administration. After being prepared by the legislative branch, all draft laws were reviewed by a 'Committee for the review of legislation' composed of officials in charge of political affairs, intelligence, finance, police, justice, women, orphans, and refugees. The LTTE was not a democratic institution, and these members were not elected but rather chosen by Prabhakaran because they were "outstanding members of society who have set their mark in [various] fields including law". After passing the review stage, each draft law was sent to Prabhakaran for his final approval before being "published as the law of the land".[147] According to informants, there were programmes for lawyers to facilitate people's awareness of the laws generally, and the media was used to distribute the Penal Code of Tamil Eelam.[148]

According to a LTTE pamphlet, at least nineteen pieces of legislation were enacted by the group.[149] An incomplete list includes: Tamil Eelam Legal Code (1993); Penal Code of Tamil Eelam (1994); Law of Evidence (1995); Code of Civil Procedure (date unknown); Law for Appointing a Lawyer to the Appeal Court of Tamil Eelam (2001); Code of Criminal Procedure (2004); Act for the Protection of Tamil Eelam Children (No. 4 of 2006); Tamil Eelam Land Act (2006).[150]

The Penal Code of Tamil Eelam, for example, was drafted based on a combination of existing Sri Lankan criminal law and *Thesawalamai* customary law, amended to reflect LTTE ideology and "meet the needs of the people".[151] Thus, the LTTE created new offences for conduct it deemed anti-social behaviour, such as adultery.[152] The *Thesawalamai* itself, which was a body of customary norms that was applicable by Sri Lankan courts to the Tamil inhabitants in the province of Jaffna and to all land situated within Jaffna, was "recast . . . with amendments relevant to the caste system and the liberty of Tamil women".[153] Specifically, the Tamil Eelam Civil Code sought to modify the *Thesawalamai* law to, for instance,

[146] LTTE, 'The Judicial System of Tamil Eelam: Its Structure, Functions and Duties of Officials in Charge' (n 55) 7, 18.

[147] ibid 7, 18, 20.

[148] Interview with 'Tharmi' (former LTTE lawyer then judge) (December 2018); Interview with 'Abilashini' (who was involved in establishing the LTTE courts in the 1990s) (December 2018); Interview with 'Parameswaran' (former lecturer, University of Jaffna) (13 October 2017).

[149] LTTE, 'The Judicial System of Tamil Eelam: Its Structure, Functions and Duties of Officials in Charge' (n 55) 18.

[150] Copies on file with author, except for the Code of Civil Procedure and Land Act. The latter is mentioned in VS Sambandan, 'The "Tamil Eelam Lands Act" Once Again Highlights a Key Issue of the Conflict—Control of Land' *Frontline* (7 April 2006), online: <http://www.frontline.in/static/html/fl2306/stories/20060407001605300.htm>.

[151] Interview with 'Parameswaran' (former lecturer, University of Jaffna) (13 October 2017).

[152] S. 206, Penal Code of Tamil Eelam; Interview with 'Lojini' (lawyer who appeared before LTTE courts) (October 2017).

[153] LTTE, 'The Judicial System of Tamil Eelam: Its Structure, Functions and Duties of Officials in Charge' (n 55) 18.

allow married women to sell property without the husband's consent.[154] Further, according to one informant, the practice of dowry was also banned.[155] The approach of the LTTE to abolish such traditional practices was applauded by some, including many women, but was not met with favour by all segments of the civilian population.[156] There is no denying that laws adopted by the LTTE were more progressive on question of gender equality. In that respect, the post-conflict resumption of the application of Sri Lankan law in the north-east signalled a regression for the status of women, and a decade later activists are still pushing for amendments to at least bring back the protection of women to what it was under the LTTE.[157]

The 'Act for the Protection of Tamil Eelam Children', enacted in 2006, offers an interesting example of more targeted legislation by an armed opposition group. The Act offers a broad statement of children's rights:

> 05. The Rights of children include right to live or exist, to get a name, to have links with the parents, to enter one's own country, to express ones [*sic*] ideas, to obtain information, to exchange them, to think, to preserve one's religious faith, to meet others, to form a union, to get together, to preserve one's privacy, to engage in rest, recreation, sports and cultural activities, to learn, to get protection from sexual and other forms of exploitation, and also to participate in social activities.[158]

The Child Protection Act also contains provisions prohibiting the enlistment of children under the age of seventeen in the armed forces of the LTTE(s. 39), prohibiting the deployment of soldiers under the age of eighteen (s. 40), regulating the employment of children (s. 54), providing parental responsibilities, and imposing penalties for child offenders (ss. 49–53). It generally provides that all official decisions related to children shall be taken in their best interest (s. 73).[159] The LTTE had a reputation for being among the most ruthless armed groups using child soldiers, and accordingly was criticised for blatant child rights abuses. The adoption of the Child Protection Act can be seen as a response to international pressure. At the same time, the LTTE announced its commitment to discontinue the recruitment of child soldiers and adopted an action

154 'Tamil Eelam Judiciary Said a Basis for Rebuilding Northeast' (n 51).

155 Interview with 'Ajanthan' (political economist) in Colombo (20 October 2017).

156 Danesh Jayatilaka and Kopalapillai Amirthalingam, *The Impact of Displacement in Dowries in Sri Lanka* (Washington DC: Brookings-LSE, 2015); Malathy (n 75) 105–115.

157 Although, for obvious reasons, these claims are never presented to the current government in such a fashion: Interview with 'Sachiv' (lawyer who trained LTTE judges and lawyers) (October 2017).

158 S. 5, Act for the Protection of Tamil Eelam Children, in an English version that seems to have been prepared by the LTTE, online: <http://theirwords.org/?country=LKA>.

159 ibid.

plan to release enlisted children.[160] Although the Act was promulgated, there is conflicting evidence as to whether the law was ever fully implemented and enforced.[161]

Another intriguing LTTE instrument is the NESOHR Charter, promulgated in 2005.[162] It contains a very long and detailed list of fundamental rights and freedoms, covering civil and political rights as well as economic, social, and cultural rights, with specific rights for women, children, prisoners, aliens, workers, disabled people, elders, and internally displaced people. It draws much of its language directly from international human rights and humanitarian law instruments, for example borrowing the text of Article 2(1) of the International Covenant on Economic, Social and Cultural Rights to formulate the obligations of "the State" (presumably a reference to the putative state of Tamil Eelam). Indeed, the Charter lists the first objectives of NESOHR as the promotion and recognition of human rights as guaranteed in the Universal Declaration of Human Rights and all the main UN human rights treaties. The breadth of fundamental rights and freedoms covered by the NESOHR Charter compares very favourably with nearly any constitutional bill of rights. One informant was under the impression that the LTTE had "adopted every single thing from international [law]" because they "did not have any issues with international [standards]".[163] Two informants indicated that the LTTE (through a statement by Mr. Balasingam) attempted to accept being bound by international humanitarian law, but that it was not effective due to the LTTE's non-state status.[164] That said, the normative status of the NESOHR Charter within the LTTE legal order is not altogether clear. It does not appear to be a statute adopted through the legislative process described earlier, much less a constitutional document. Instead, it appears to have been drafted by the NESOHR itself, which suggests that it represents a political statement of the standards that would guide the NESOHR in its activities.[165] It is telling that none of the judges, lawyers, or litigants in the LTTE judicial system mentioned the existence of this document during the fieldwork. Accordingly, it is not considered to be a legal source for the purposes of the following analysis.

160 Jo Becker, 'Child Recruitment in Burma, Sri Lanka and Nepal' in Simon Reich and Scott Gates (eds), *Child Soldiers in the Age of Fractured States* (University of Pittsburgh Press 2010).

161 Compare: *Report of the Secretary-General on children and armed conflict in Sri Lanka UNSC*, UN Doc S/2007/758 (2007); LTTE Child Protection Authority, Report on Children and Armed Conflict in the Northeastern Part of the Island of Sri Lanka (August 2006), on file with the author; Malathy (n 75) 90.

162 The English version of the NESOHR Charter is available at <https://tamilnation.org/tamileelam/nesohr/051001Charter-English.pdf>.

163 Interview with 'Suboshini' (lecturer, University of Colombo) (October 2017).

164 Interview with 'Divya' (lecturer, University of Colombo) (October 2017); Interview with 'Sharmi' (Senior State Counsel) (December 2018).

165 HR Group Meets to Finalize Charter, 1 August 2004, online: <https://www.tamilnet.com/art.html?catid=13&artid=12576>. The presentation format of this document does not follow the set format adopted for all other available LTTE laws.

v. Overall Assessment of LTTE Justice

The general impression derived from assessments of the LTTE administration of justice by independent observers is that it gained significant social acceptance during its years of operation, but also that there were limits to what could be expected from it.

It is clear, both from the history and the governance structure set out in the preceding that the LTTE courts were embedded in the non-state armed group and as such were an important institution for the furthering of the objective of establishing a Tamil Eelam State. Despite this, or perhaps precisely because of this, a recurrent theme that emerged from the interviews with informants was the importance of the independence of the court system from the other branches or wings of the LTTE. One informant who had been a LTTE judge repeatedly emphasised the independence of the courts from the LTTE police, as demonstrated by the fact that that complaints or accusations filed by the police were not merely accepted but were checked carefully and clarified before any summons was issued and, further, judges would 'scold' the police in court for mistaken or false accusations.[166]

The ability to use a rebel court to control the power of the armed group itself always stands as the acid test of the court's autonomy and resilience. The responses from informants were varied as to the extent to which LTTE cadres were subject to proceedings before its courts and what process applied. On the one hand, some responses suggested that cadres were *not* subject to cases or complaints in the regular courts. For example, one informant gave the impression that the regular courts did not get any cases involving cadres.[167] Another informant was under the impression (although not based on personal experience) that LTTE cadre cases were handled by either Thamilselvan (the head of the political wing) or Prabhakaran (the overall leader of the LTTE), depending on the seriousness of the case.[168] This is confirmed in an interview with the LTTE Inspector General of Police, who explained:[169]

> Our leader (Mr Prabhakaran) is committed to the "rule of law". If there is misconduct on the part of one of our cadres, the section head is required to withdraw their cyanide capsule/identification tag and hand over the person to us. We will fully investigate the matter and send in a report. It is only if they are cleared that they will be re-enlisted.

All of this could be understood as reflecting the existence of a parallel military justice system that handled disciplinary and criminal sanctions against LTTE

[166] Interview with 'Tharmi' (LTTE lawyer then judge) (December 2018).
[167] Interview with 'Lojini' (lawyer who appeared before LTTE courts) (October 2017).
[168] Interview with 'Sharmi' (Senior State Counsel) (December 2018).
[169] Athas (n 44).

cadres.[170] However, a number of responses signalled that in other ways cadres were subject to the jurisdiction of regular LTTE courts. Informants reported that not only was it possible to bring cases against cadres in the regular courts but that "there was no special fear in bringing a case against a cadre" and that the law applied equally against cadres (e.g. speeding fines were issued against cadres).[171] Over the period of their operation, the LTTE courts and the judiciary reportedly remained independent and free from duress.[172] When making decisions, it is thought that the courts generally followed due process and judgments were pronounced after an objective examination of facts. Above all, informants' overwhelming impression was that the courts were impartial, that a party's links to the LTTE did not affect the outcome of cases, and that all parties were treated equally before the court. All informants asked about discrimination responded that "everyone is equal before the court".[173] In terms of whether there was any apparent discrimination against Muslims or Sinhalese peoples, informants were under the impression that no Muslims or Sinhalese people had come before the LTTE courts.[174] We can only speculate that, in all likelihood, this indicates a complete lack of trust on their part in the fairness of LTTE courts towards non-Tamils.

Suggestions of the independence of LTTE courts should not be overstated. At one level, it seems that there was a close connection between the courts and LTTE leadership at least in terms of oversight. For example, one informant noted that care was taken by judges (particularly in the writing of judgments) because they were sometimes required to give justifications for their judgments to leader Prabhakaran.[175] On the other hand, the general impression was that there was little political interference. One informant suggested that political interference would only occur in response to undue delays.[176] More broadly, another surmised that this was because the LTTE leadership was "not interested" in the court cases, which perhaps reflected the rarity of politically significant cases.[177]

[170] Interview with 'Tharmi' (LTTE lawyer then judge) (December 2018).

[171] Interview with 'Abilashini' (who was involved in establishing the LTTE courts in the 1990s) (December 2018); Interview with 'Parameswaran' (former lecturer, University of Jaffna) (October 2017).

[172] KW Gunawardena, 'භීෂණ සමයේ දණ්ඩ නීතිය (Penal Law during Times of Terror)' *Divaina (Sri Lanka)* (16 January 2012), online: <http://www.divaina.com> [Divaina, 'Penal Law']; Divaina, 'Kailasa' (n 71); Kamalendran (n 48).

[173] Interview with 'Tharmi' (LTTE lawyer then judge); Interview with 'Suboshini' (lecturer, University of Colombo); Interview with 'Kajenthini' (LTTE lawyer) (December 2018).

[174] Interview with 'Tharmi' (LTTE lawyer then judge); Interview with 'Divya' (lecturer, University of Colombo); Interview with 'Suboshini' (lecturer, University of Colombo); Interview with 'Sharmi' (Senior State Counsel); Interview with 'Kajenthini' (LTTE lawyer); Interview with 'Abilashini' (who was involved in establishing the LTTE courts in the 1990s) (December 2018).

[175] Interview with 'Tharmi' (LTTE lawyer then judge) (December 2018).

[176] Interview with 'Vithushini' (former court clerk) (October 2017).

[177] Interview with 'Lojini' (lawyer who appeared before LTTE courts) (October 2017).

In many ways, for the civilian population, Sri Lankan courts provided a comparator by reference to which the LTTE courts could be described. As with many rebel court systems, there was a broad sense that LTTE courts were more efficient, less expensive, and less vulnerable to corruption than their Sri Lankan counterparts.[178] For example, land disputes were the most frequent type of civil cases brought before LTTE courts: according to a 2005 assessment by the US embassy in Colombo, "simple property disputes in government courts could take from one to ten years to settles, whereas LTTE courts consistently settled disagreements in one court date and often mediate disputes rather than proffering court rulings".[179] The fact that some Tamils from government-controlled areas travelled to LTTE territory to petition the rebel court is sometimes mentioned as indicative of the positive impression it created among the civilian population.[180] The feelings towards LTTE administration of criminal law, however, are more ambivalent. The group imposed harsher punishments than the state for some crimes (such as rape) and criminalised behaviour that was not subject to prosecution under Sri Lankan law (such as caste discrimination).[181] There is some degree of confusion in analyses of the LTTE between sentences imposed by the group's courts and its continuous reliance on extrajudicial violence and executions.[182] Thus, while the Penal Code of Tamil Eelam—like that of Sri Lanka—allowed for capital punishment for a limited number of crimes, the death penalty was very seldom applied.[183] One former LTTE judge told me that in his eight years as a judge he had never issued a death sentence.[184] Of course, the suggestion that rebel courts can act in accordance with the rule of law cannot be taken to import that the corresponding armed group as a whole becomes infused with the principles of the rule of law. This certainly did not seem to be the case for the LTTE.

When the civil war ended in 2009, a great curtain fell across the north-east of Sri Lanka to cover much of what had occurred during the conflict. The governance activities of the LTTE were thus largely effaced, including the years of operation of the various courts of the armed group. All judicial archives were systematically destroyed, meaning that no official records exist for tens of thousands of court decisions related to every facet of social life, from land ownership to divorce. The official governmental line is that "there is no there there": it is simply a legal black

178 Interview with 'Tharmi' (former LTTE lawyer then judge) (December 2018).

179 US State Department, 'These Tigers Don't Purr' (n 69) para 9; Perera (n 53).

180 Divaina, 'Penal Law' (n 172).

181 LTTE, 'The Judicial System of Tamil Eelam: Its Structure, Functions and Duties of Officials in Charge' (n 55) 20; Francesca Bremner, 'Recasting Caste: War, Displacement and Transformations' (2013) 2 International Journal of Ethnic & Social Studies 31, 47.

182 Jayasuriya (n 52).

183 US State Department, 'These Tigers Don't Purr' (n 69) para 10, mentions that only four people had been sentenced to be executed by LTTE courts by 2005.

184 Interview with 'Partheepan' (former LTTE judge) (October 2017).

hole that remains unacknowledged in the law of Sri Lanka.[185] While this may be manageable in Colombo, where lawyers gave me incredulous looks when I asked about the possibility of invoking an LTTE court judgment before Sri Lankan courts, things are different in what used to be rebel-held areas. Thus, the Chavakachcheri District Court, near Jaffna, accepted judgments and orders from LTTE courts as evidence favouring the plaintiff in a 2017 case. The judgment also seems to acknowledge that the defendant accepted that the LTTE courts had concluded the case on behalf of the plaintiff.[186] The decision is said not to be unique, suggesting that LTTE law may live still despite the demise of the non-state armed group.

II. The Jurisdiction of Rebel Courts

In Chapter 29 of the 1225 version of the *Magna Carta*, protection is granted to any free man against punishment "except by the lawful judgment of his peers and by the law of the land".[187] There are two distinct guarantees in this important provision, the first reflecting the fairness of the proceedings and the second the legitimacy of rules under which punishment is ordered.[188] These two guarantees are echoed in critiques regularly directed at the rebel administration of justice by both the international community and territorial states: the former typically focusses the lack of due process in rebel court trials, whereas the latter more often reject the legitimacy of such courts, regardless of the fairness of the proceedings. Indeed, states engaged in armed hostilities against armed groups often insist that the groups lack legitimate authority to administer justice in any way whatsoever, even to sanction crime or misconduct by the insurgents' own fighters.[189]

Whether non-state armed groups have any authority under public international law to administer justice turns, generally, on the application of the concept of jurisdiction in relation to rebel justice (A) and, more specifically, on the concept of jurisdiction over subject-matter (B), personal jurisdiction (C), and territorial jurisdiction (D).

185 Interview with 'Abilashini' (who was involved in establishing the LTTE courts in the 1990s) (December 2018).

186 Chavakachcheri District Court (Sri Lanka), Case L/7159/2003, 18 September 2017, at 14, on file with the author.

187 Magna Carta 1225, British National Archives, online: <https://www.nationalarchives.gov.uk/education/resources/magna-carta/magna-carta-1225-westminster/>.

188 See Nathan S Chapman, 'Due Process of War' (2018) 94 Notre Dame Law Review 639, 654–656.

189 See: Sandesh Sivakumaran, *The Law of Non-International Armed Conflict* (Oxford University Press 2012) 557–558; Jan Willms, 'Courts of Armed Groups—A Tool for Inducing Higher Compliance with International Humanitarian Law?' in Heike Krieger (ed), *Inducing Compliance with International Humanitarian Law* (Cambridge University Press 2015) 149–150; Louise Doswald-Beck, 'Judicial Guarantees under Common Article 3' in Andrew Clapham, Paola Gaeta, and Marco Sassòli (eds), *The 1949 Geneva Conventions: A Commentary* (Oxford University Press 2015) 491.

A. The Idea of Rebel Jurisdiction

Generally, the idea of jurisdiction speaks to the legitimacy of an authority both to say what the law is in a given time and place for some people (normative jurisdiction), and to take steps to ensure compliance with this law (enforcement jurisdiction). The suggestion of rebel jurisdiction was previously evoked as part of the discussion of the compatibility of the rebel administration of justice with the idea of the rule of law.[190] In that discussion, it was noted that the notion of sovereignty cannot be taken to necessarily imply a state monopoly over the administration of justice. There are circumstances, sometimes formally recognised in international law, in which entities other than the sovereign state have the authority to exercise jurisdiction. These entities can be other states, for instance during belligerent occupation, or international organisations, acting as peacekeepers or administering international criminal law, or even non-state actors in situations in which the state is unable to perform its governance functions or when an insurrectional movement succeeds in toppling the government to take its place. The conclusion reached earlier was that the idea of the rule of law and existing principles of various branches of public international law leave open the possibility that non-state armed groups may have jurisdiction over a population and territory. Rebel jurisdiction must be given a sharper definition so that it can operate its function in coordinating jurisdictions of other agents, primarily the territorial and other states.[191]

Rebel jurisdiction, in its normative dimension, speaks to the possibility of rebel law. This opens the possibility of rebel groups satisfying the requirements, under international humanitarian law and human rights law, concerning the legal proscription of criminal offences and the constitution of tribunals.[192] As noted in Chapter 2, the interpretation of Article 6(2)(c) of Additional Protocol II is complicated by the fact that the English and French official versions differ markedly. The French incorporates a qualifying reference to 'national or international law' whereas the English refers simply to 'law' unqualified. On its face, the English version appears broad enough to include the law of non-state armed groups. This view is supported by the *travaux préparatoires*, as well as subsequent interpretations adopted by the ICRC and the United Kingdom. A similar conclusion was reached in the analysis of the human rights requirement that civil and criminal judicial decisions be taken by a "tribunal established by law".[193] Decisions of the

[190] See the discussion in Chapter 1, Section III.

[191] On the contested and polysemic meaning of jurisdiction in international law, see: Marko Milanovic, *Extraterritorial Application of Human Rights Treaties: Law, Principles, and Policy* (Oxford University Press 2011) 19–53; Mariana Valverde, 'Deepening the Conversation Between Socio-Legal Theory and Legal Scholarship about Jurisdiction', in Stephen Allen and others (eds), *The Oxford Handbook of Jurisdiction in International Law* (Oxford University Press 2019).

[192] See the discussion in Chapter 2, Section IV.C.i.

[193] See the discussion in Chapter 2, Section IV.C.ii.b.

ICC, the ICTY, and the European Court of Human Rights all conclude that this requirement does not necessarily point to state law as the sole form of 'law' that can provide a basis for the establishment of a court. Accordingly, international law (for the ICTY) and the law of non-state armed groups (for the ICC and the European Court) could equally be considered as 'law' for this purpose.

Beyond the interpretation of the word 'law' in various treaties, the imposition of a growing range of obligations on armed groups under international humanitarian law, international human rights law, and international criminal law often corresponds to practices that imply some form of rebel law-making. It also echoes the legal agency of national liberation movements formally recognised under Article 96(3) of Protocol I, whereby *pacta sunt servanda* is a principle applicable to these non-state actors.[194]

The notion that rebel authority may be recognised under international law in certain circumstances, and the conclusion that armed groups can make laws, coalesce in the concept of rebel jurisdiction.[195] The reality that must be managed by invoking the concept of jurisdiction isn't that conflict zones under the authority of armed groups are lawless, but on the contrary that there may be an overabundance of laws in such zones. The recognition of the law-making power of non-state armed groups does not imply that they have an unfettered discretion to create law to bind everyone, at all times, in all places, and in all respects. No more so than states. The concept of jurisdiction is the legal device used to map the limits of the normative power of states and armed groups.

The principle of *effectivité* in international law signals that the factual ability to wield power over population and territory is linked to its legal recognition, albeit not in a reductive formula that simply coats any effective exercise of raw power with a legitimating veneer of legality.[196] If, as suggested by Robert Cover, law is contested because it is a veneer that transforms the very nature of the social patterns it covers, then the nature of these social patterns will necessarily impose constraints as to what may be designated as law.[197] For any agent, state as well as non-state, power and jurisdiction are not coextensive, but states do benefit from a presumption of jurisdiction reflective of their sovereignty over territory. As a result, some—but not all—forms of extraterritorial exercise of authority by a state will be captured in jurisdictional terms and, conversely, a state will retain some—but not all—jurisdiction over its national territory even in situations in

194 Robert McCorquodale, 'Defining the International Rule of Law: Defying Gravity?' (2016) 65 International and Comparative Law Quarterly 277, 297.

195 On the relation between the concepts of power, authority and jurisdiction, see Lea Raible, *Human Rights Unbound: A Theory of Extraterritoriality* (Oxford University Press 2020).

196 Hans Kelsen, *General Theory of Law and State* (Transaction Publishers 1949) 219.

197 Robert M Cover, 'The Folktales of Justice: Tales of Jurisdiction' (1984) 14 Capital University Law Review 179, 181; EP Thompson, *Whigs and Hunters: The Origin of the Black Act* (Pantheon Books 1975) 260–264.

which it loses the ability to effectively wield its authority on parts or all of its territory. To address concerns of legal certainty in international relations, international law strikes a balance between power and law through the concept of jurisdiction, informed by the principle of *effectivité*.[198] If the idea of law speaks to the nature of social practices, the notion of jurisdiction speaks to the identification of who can act in the name of the community in relation to place, time, action, and actor. When confronted with multiple, overlapping claims of authority, as will typically be the case in situations of armed conflicts involving non-state armed groups, jurisdiction is the device aiming at the principled coordination of the exercise of power through law.[199]

In public international law, jurisdiction has been developed in relation to the state, as a corollary to the notion of sovereignty. It is often said that state jurisdiction is primarily territorial, reflecting the rootedness of sovereignty as an attribute of statehood.[200] The link of state jurisdiction to territory, however, has never been viewed as a significant limiting factor. As famously declared by the Permanent Court of International Justice in *The Lotus Case*, "[f]ar from laying down a general prohibition to the effect that States may not extend the application of their laws and the jurisdiction of their courts to persons, property and acts outside their territory, it leaves them in this respect a wide measure of discretion which is only limited in certain cases by prohibitive rules".[201] For nearly a century, the validity of this permissive approach to jurisdiction has been debated by international lawyers, and to some extent limited by more recent decisions of the International Court of Justice. However, state practice continues to affirm a general openness to states extending the applicability of their national laws beyond the confines of their sovereign territory.[202] Having said that, state practice also seems to support a requirement for some form of genuine, or real and substantial, link to the state to underpin the application of criminal or civil laws beyond national territory. Such a link can be established by the nationality of a person involved in the act or practice engaging the application of the law, whether as

198 See Florian Couveinhes-Matsumoto, *L'effectivité en droit international* (Bruylant 2014) paras 100–101, for a more sophisticated articulation of these ideas.

199 See: Malcolm Thorburn, 'Criminal Law as Public Law' in Antony Duff and Stuart Green (eds), *Philosophical Foundations of Criminal Law* (Oxford University Press 2011) 33; Michael Giudice and Matthew Schaeffer, 'Universal Jurisdiction and the Duty to Govern' in François Tanguay-Renaud and James Stribopoulos (eds), *Rethinking Criminal Law Theory: New Canadian Perspectives in the Philosophy of Domestic, Transnational, and International Criminal Law* (Bloomsbury Publishing 2012) 239; Antony Duff, 'Authority and Responsibility in International Criminal Law' in Samantha Besson and John Tasioulas (eds), *The Philosophy of International Law* (Oxford University Press 2010) 595.

200 James Crawford, *Brownlie's Principles of Public International Law* (9th edn, Oxford University Press 2019) 440.

201 PCIJ, *The Case of the SS "Lotus"*, (1927) PCIJ Ser. A No 10, 19.

202 Crawford (n 200) 441–442; Robert Jennings and Arthur Watts, *Oppenheim's International Law*, vol 1: Peace (Oxford University Press 2008) 478–479.

author or victim of a crime or delict, or party to a contract. A less precisely defined link consistently invoked by states as a basis for extraterritorial jurisdiction is the protective or security principle, whereby an act carried out abroad by non-nationals may be subject to a state's law if it is seen as affecting a fundamental interest of the state. The printing of counterfeit money and the planning of a coup d'État are the classic examples of this widely accepted protective principle, which includes military and political security.[203] An even more general principle, the effects doctrine, is invoked in light of the holding of the PCIJ in the *Lotus Case* that the fact that the effects of the criminal negligence by the officer of the watch on the French ship were felt on the Turkish ship was sufficient to ground Turkey's criminal jurisdiction over the French officer. The breadth of the effects doctrine can be grasped from Judge Learned Hand's statement that, already by 1945, "it is settled law . . . that any state may impose liabilities, even upon persons not within its allegiance, for conduct outside its borders that has consequences within its borders which the state reprehends".[204] This has been relied upon, in particular but not exclusively, by the United States to extend its antitrust legislation to foreign corporations operating abroad.[205] Finally, this is completed by universal jurisdiction, giving all states authority to prosecute a limited number of international crimes, pursuant to treaties like the Geneva Conventions or under customary law.

This rapid overview of state jurisdiction under public international law brings up two points that will be germane to a discussion of rebel jurisdiction. First, effective authority does not necessarily limit jurisdiction in every way. At a normative level, international law allows states to regulate behaviour in places that are not under their control, and in some cases by agents that have no link of allegiance to the state claiming jurisdiction. Some form of link to the state claiming jurisdiction has been posited, but its precise nature remains disputed. Second, there are no jurisdictional monopolies in international law. In other words, it is a given that multiple states may legitimately claim jurisdiction to regulate the same act by the same agent. This includes, in an undisputed way, criminal law, such that it is accepted that an individual may be convicted of the same crime in relation to the same act by different jurisdictions.[206] It also covers regulation in civil matters, allowing for example the double taxation of corporate income by multiple states.[207] Far from an aberration, "the coexistence of overlapping

[203] Crawford (n 200) 446; Jennings and Watts (n 202) 470; Cedric Ryngaert, *Jurisdiction in International Law* (2d edn, Oxford University Press 2015) 114–119.
[204] *US v Aluminium Co. of America*, 148 F.2d 416 (Second Circuit Court of Appeals, 1945) 443.
[205] Crawford (n 200) 447–448.
[206] Double jeopardy, or *ne bis in idem*, proscribes only multiple prosecutions by the same jurisdiction. As such, its application to ICC prosecutions is an exception created by that treaty. See the discussion in Chapter 3, Section III.C.i.d, *infra*, and in Chapter 4, Section II.B.ii.
[207] Crawford (n 200) 441.

jurisdictions is acceptable and convenient".[208] This of course results in potential conflicts of laws, but public international law is mostly silent, or at least recondite, as to the way such conflicts ought to be resolved. Arguments have been advanced to identify an overlapping jurisdictional principle or an ordered hierarchy among different bases of jurisdiction, but general international law remains unsettled on this question.[209] How these two points about state jurisdiction carry over to illuminate rebel jurisdiction will be discussed in the following subsections, in which the jurisdiction of non-state armed groups *ratione loci*, *ratione materiae*, and *ratione personae* are examined.

B. Territorial Jurisdiction of Armed Groups

As mentioned, while state jurisdiction is said to be primarily territorial, there are widespread and accepted grounds evidencing a genuine connection to the state that can justify the extraterritorial application of a state's laws. The transposition of these principles to the jurisdiction of non-state armed groups in zones of armed conflict raises a number of challenges. If jurisdiction is primarily territorial, what is the territory in question for armed groups engaged in hostilities? Is the possibility of extraterritorial jurisdiction accepted for state equally applicable to non-state armed groups? Each question is briefly addressed in turn.

For states, the anchoring of jurisdiction in territory is all at once a reflection of sovereignty, affirming the legitimacy of the state's authority within its national borders, and a coordinating principle, aiming to limit overlapping jurisdictional claims by different states over a single place. When evoked in relation to rebel jurisdiction, this emerges as problematic in at least three distinct ways. First, there is no equivalent for armed groups to a 'defined territory' that underpins the very existence of an independent state, as proclaimed in the 1933 Montevideo Convention.[210] Second, jurisdiction is a legitimating device, affirming the legitimacy of the exercise of power by a state in a given place, while states in drafting the Geneva Conventions and Protocols were intent on refraining from any express or implied recognition of legitimacy to non-state armed groups.[211] Third, while there might not be a preordained priority for territorial jurisdiction when several jurisdictional claims compete, it is generally understood that the fact that jurisdiction is 'primarily' territorial gives it a comparative advantage; applied to

[208] Jennings and Watts (n 202) 457.

[209] Ryngaert (n 203) 145–187. The matter largely has been left to be regulated by conflict of laws or private international law under the domestic law of the given state: ibid 20–22.

[210] Convention on the Rights and Duties of States, (1933) 115 LNTS 19, Art. 1(b).

[211] This is captured in the last paragraph of Common Article 3 ("The application of the preceding provisions shall not affect the legal status of the Parties to the conflict") and in Art. 3(1), Additional Protocol II.

rebel jurisdiction, this would suggest some form of superiority for insurgent justice over state law in territory under the authority of armed groups.

The territorial jurisdiction of rebel justice more heavily relies on the insurgents' ability to effectively project their authority than is the case for state jurisdiction. If jurisdiction remains primarily territorial, for armed groups that will mean that they can claim jurisdiction over the territory and population over which they exercise a degree of control. The fact that the geographical boundaries of such a territory can fluctuate isn't, as such, an obstacle to finding that there is a territorial basis for rebel jurisdiction. Put in a different way, it fuses rebel groups' normative jurisdiction (or jurisdiction to legislate) and enforcement jurisdiction (or jurisdiction to adjudicate and enforce). This study has raised, at several points, the issue of the extent of territorial control or authority required to underpin the rebel administration of justice.[212] The position defended has been that rebel justice is not preconditioned on the insurgents' ability to exclude government forces from an area, because governance is not necessarily coextensive with military dominance. There are indeed conflicts, such as the war in Sri Lanka, in which insurgents have been able to exclude any military presence by the government in a swath of national territory, but that is a comparatively unusual situation. In many more conflicts, the state can concentrate overwhelming military force in a zone to preclude any military presence by armed groups, but it cannot do so in all parts of national territory affected by the conflict. In wars such as Colombia or Afghanistan, the effective authority of armed groups has extended to areas that significantly exceed any zones from which it can prevent any state military presence. More than comparing the military might of the government and an armed group in a given area, it is probably more significant to compare the relative effectivity of state and rebel governance.

The fluid nature of 'rebel territory' as compared to the fixed boundaries of state territory is also a reflection of human mobility in conflict zones. There is a recurring pattern observed in many conflicts, confirmed in the studies of Colombia, Afghanistan, and Sri Lanka, of individuals crossing over to an area of rebel authority in order to lay a complaint or present a claim before rebel courts. Conversely, a Kurdish judge related that men wishing to circumvent restrictions on polygamous marriage in the Kurdish Region of Iraq slip into territory under the control of the central Iraqi government to celebrate the polygamous marriage before returning to the KRI, where it will be recognised.[213] This forum shopping may be for ideological reasons (support for the rebel cause), because it relates to a matter that is not or differently handled by state law (for instance, the enforcement of contracts related to illegal activities, such as drug transactions), as

[212] See, e.g., Chapter 1, Section II.C.i.

[213] Interview with Judge 'Siryan' (September 2017).

a means to relitigate a dispute that was not resolved by the state court to one party's satisfaction, or because of the comparative efficiency and affordability of the rebel administration of justice. The phenomenon remains limited, but it does attest to the interconnectedness of the territorial jurisdiction of the state and that of armed groups. Of course, such patterns of forum shopping can also be observed in relation to the territorial jurisdiction of different states. Conflicts between state jurisdictions are negotiated through mutual recognition, comity, and doctrines such as *forum non conveniens* (for civil matters) and *male captus bene detentus* (for criminal matters, more controversially), reflecting common practice more than set rules of customary international law.[214] Save for the more unilateral doctrine of *male captus, bene detentus*, it seems unlikely that these other cooperative approaches can play a significant role in mediating competing territorial jurisdictional claims of states and armed groups.

While rebel jurisdiction mostly remains limited to the territory under its authority, there are examples of extraterritorial extensions, for both normative and enforcement jurisdiction. As regards the former, the LTTE offers a fascinating example of rebel extraterritorial legislation that mimics the practice of states. In 2006, the LTTE adopted the Act No 4 for the Protection of Tamil Eelam Children, a wide-ranging statute that prohibits, inter alia, the sexual exploitation of children (Art. 36).[215] The preliminary provisions of the Act include Article 13, on territorial reach: "Any offence against which action could be taken under this Act committed outside Tamil Eelam could also be taken when the offender is present within the boarders [*sic*] of Tamil Eelam taking into consideration the Tamil Eelam Criminal Procedure Act 14 of 2004".[216] This extraterritorial application of the LTTE Children Act mirrors a trend among countries that do not typically extend their criminal law outside national territory, such as Canada, to criminalise the sexual exploitation of children abroad as part of sex tourism.[217] While many countries require a link of nationality,

214 Ryngaert (n 203) 20–22. *Male captus, bene detentus* is a doctrine whereby a tribunal will have jurisdiction over individuals if they are present in court, regardless of any due process flaws in the process of bringing them to court. See Paul Michell, 'English-Speaking Justice: Evolving Responses to Transnational Forcible Abduction After Alvarez-Machain' (1996) 29 Cornell International Law Journal 383; Julien Cazala, 'L'adage "male captus bene detentus" face au droit international' [2007] Journal du droit international 837.

215 Discussed earlier (n 158). For background on the LTTE and child protection, see LTTE Child Protection Authority (n 161); Malathy (n 75) ch 9 (Malathy was the Director of the LTTE Child Protection Authority, and the author of this report).

216 This is taken from an English translation that seems to have been prepared by the LTTE itself, online: <http://theirwords.org/?country=LKA>.

217 Naomi L Svensson, 'Extraterritorial Accountability: An Assessment of the Effectiveness of Child Sex Tourism Laws' (2006) 28 Loyola of Los Angeles International and Comparative Law Review 641; Danielle Ireland-Piper, *Accountability in Extraterritoriality: A Comparative and International Law Perspective* (Edward Elgar Publishing 2017) 15–16; Benjamin Perrin, 'Taking a Vacation from the Law? Extraterritorial Criminal Jurisdiction and Section 7(4.1) of the Criminal Code' (2009) 13 Canadian Criminal Law Review 175.

which is awkward—but not impossible—to translate for a group like the LTTE, others have taken the broader approach encouraged by many to seize jurisdiction vis-à-vis residents, bringing us closer to a temporary territorial link found in the LTTE Children Act.[218] Of course, this specific example is a case of double criminality, as the criminalisation of sexual exploitation of children not only aligns with Sri Lankan law but also with international law.[219] A much tighter link to the territorial jurisdiction of an armed group would be required for conduct like caste discrimination, criminalised under insurgent law but not in the law of the state.

As regards enforcement jurisdiction, the judicial cooperation mechanisms normally available among states to ensure that decisions of courts are not thwarted by a party skipping to another jurisdiction, whether through INTERPOL notices or extradition requests in criminal matters, or petitions for recognition of foreign judgments in civil matters, will normally not be available for the rebel administration of justice.[220] However, that does not necessarily mean that insurgent justice has no enforcement reach beyond the geographical boundaries of its effective authority. In the Sri Lankan context, Mampilly comments that "the Tigers had an impressive ability to influence daily life even in towns outside their nominal control".[221] One extraterritorial enforcement strategy in Sri Lanka is described as such:

> The judges in the LTTE-run courts have devised extrajudicial methods to ensure that their sentences on those who fall outside their court's jurisdiction are implemented. Such persons who are unwilling to accept the verdicts find that their relatives or friends in Kokkadicholai are taken hostage until such time as they comply with the sentence.[222]

This approach echoes the practice of prison gangs that rely on the collectivisation of responsibility to extend the reach of their power to tax or collect unpaid debts even beyond the walls of the prison and into broader society.[223] This is not to suggest that such approaches are lawful—taking hostages for any reason is a clear

[218] Svensson (n 217) 655.

[219] See: Art. 360B, Penal Code of Sri Lanka, online: <https://www.lawnet.gov.lk/penal-code-consolidated-2/>; Art. 4, Optional Protocol to the Convention on the Rights of the Child on the sale of children, child prostitution and child pornography, UN Doc A/RES/54/263 (2000), requiring states to criminalise the sexual exploitation of children whether it occurs nationally or transnationally.

[220] For a discussion of the recognition of rebel court laws and judicial decisions by other states, see Chapter 4, Section III.

[221] Mampilly (n 20) 119.

[222] Suryanarayana (n 61).

[223] René Provost, 'Putting the "Con" Back in the Constitution: The Social Order of the Underworld—How Prison Gangs Govern the American Penal System, by David Skarbek, New York, Oxford University Press, 2014' (2017) 49 Journal of Legal Pluralism and Unofficial Law 87.

violation of both international humanitarian and human rights law—but rather to warn against concluding too easily that the power of armed groups is caged in by the (limited) territory they control.

C. Subject-Matter Jurisdiction of Armed Groups

What, if anything, can a non-state armed group regulate through law? Does it have any law-making agency, or is it required to simply rely upon the law that was in place when it came to wield authority over a territory and a civilian population? For armed groups, the imposition of legal standards is much more than the policing of certain activities in a manner that allows for effective control, although it is certainly that too. Cover captures this sentiment with pithy eloquence: "[t]he legitimating objective of jurisdiction . . . is prophetic not bureaucratic".[224] The adoption of legal standards of any kind are thus, for rebels, not so much the imposition of a rulebook as the conveying of the values and aspirations that justify the resort to armed violence and sketch the promise of an alternative society inspired by these values and aspirations.[225] As always, law is a central tool of governance, and the jurisdictional claims of an armed group cannot be dissociated from its insurgency. For that reason, rebel jurisdiction is systematically resisted and rejected by the territorial state, which would be expected to ascribe no legal validity or effect to rebel laws.[226] The question is whether this outright rejection is reflected in international law. The argument advanced here is that there is no norm of international law that denies all law-making authority to non-state armed groups, although it does signal some limits related to subject-matter.

International law doesn't speak explicitly to the law-making practice of non-state armed groups. This is so despite the fact that such practice is common and varied, touching on the entire gamut of subject-matters from the ecological management of forest to the right to education of children.[227] The one part of international law that addresses overlapping jurisdictions and conflicting interests in conflict zones is the law of belligerent occupation. The international law of occupation was previously evoked as part of the discussion of the rule of law, to signal

[224] Cover (n 197) 189.

[225] Ashley Jackson, 'Life Under the Taliban Shadow Government' (Overseas Development Institute 2018) 8.

[226] The recognition of the rebel administration of justice and rebel laws under national law is discussed in Chapter 4, Section IV.

[227] On environmental protection by armed groups, see Jonathan Somer, 'Environmental Protection and Non-State Armed Groups: Setting a Place at the Table for the Elephant in the Room' *Toxic Remnants of War Project Blog* (4 Dec. 2015), online: <http://www.toxicremnantsofwar.info/environmental-protection-and-non-state-armed-groups-setting-a-place-at-the-table-for-the-elephant-in-the-room/>. An example of rebel norms related to children's rights is the LTTE Child Protection Act mentioned above.

that state sovereignty does not negate the possibility that an actor other than the territorial state may administer justice. Indeed, the 1907 Hague Regulations and the 1949 Fourth Geneva Convention recognise that the occupying power may (indeed must) lawfully administer justice during its occupation, even though its very presence may be without any legitimacy under *jus ad bellum*.[228] As concisely put by Eyal Benvenisti:

> The law that regulates the administration of occupied territories must confront the inherent conflict of interests that exists between occupant and occupied. The occupation administration must attend to at least three sets of interests: its own security interests, the interest of the ousted government, and those of the local population, which may be different from the interest of their legitimate government.[229]

There is no suggestion that the international law of belligerent occupation can directly apply to rebel control over territory in the context of a non-international armed conflict. Rather, the passage from Benvenisti highlights the striking similarities between the tensions that must be managed in situations of belligerent occupation and those in areas under insurgent authority. In both types of situations, a new actor wrestles effective authority away from the established government and must govern, in a manner that will ineluctably reflect, to varying degrees, the interests of the *de facto* ruler, civilian population, and the government. The starting point, in Article 43 of the 1907 Hague Regulations, is that the occupier has a duty to "re-establish and maintain, as far as possible, public order and public life, while respecting, unless absolutely prevented, the laws in force in the country".[230] While the language might suggest a hands-off approach towards existing law, the provision on the contrary has been interpreted and applied in a manner that condones legislation by the occupier on almost anything that is reasonably justified.[231] The Hague Regulations are complemented by several

[228] See the discussion in Chapter 1, Section II.B.ii.

[229] Eyal Benvenisti, *The International Law of Occupation* (2d edn, Oxford University Press 2012) 69.

[230] The authentic French speaks of the duty: "de rétablir et d'assurer, autant qu'il est possible, l'ordre et la vie publics en respectant, sauf empêchement absolu, les lois en vigueur dans le pays." On the misleading nature of the English translation most commonly used, 'public order or safety', see the discussion in Chapter 2, Section IV.B.ii.

[231] Yoram Dinstein, *The International Law of Belligerent Occupation* (2d edn, Cambridge University Press 2019) 120; Benvenisti (n 229) 77–93; David Kretzmer and Yaël Ronen, *The Occupation of Justice: The Supreme Court of Israel and the Occupied Territories* (2d edn, Oxford University Press 2021) 140–143; Yutaka Arai-Takahashi, *The Law of Occupation: Continuity and Change of International Humanitarian Law, and Its Interaction With International Human Rights Law* (Brill 2009) 91–113; Marco Sassòli, 'Legislation and Maintenance of Public Order and Civil Life by Occupying Powers' (2005) 16 European Journal of International Law 661, 673–682.

provisions in Geneva Convention IV, particularly Article 64. Although Article 64 provides, in its first paragraph, that the "penal laws of the occupied territory shall remain in force" except "where they constitute a threat to its security", its seconds paragraph states that the occupier "may, however, subject the population of the occupied territory to provisions which are essential to enable the Occupying Power to fulfil its obligations under the present Convention, to maintain the orderly government of the territory". Once again, the initial language might be read as supporting a limited right to suspend penal law, but the subsequent paragraph's much wider formulation, without any reference to penal law, is generally taken to have widened the occupier's power to legislate broadly in civil as well as criminal matters.[232] This recognition of increasing legislative authority for the occupier mirrors the evolving construction of the role of the state in the last century, shifting from a laissez-faire approach in favour of greater state intervention in social and economic life. The emergence of a thickening web of obligations under international human rights law, and especially the growing acceptance that occupied territory falls under the human rights jurisdiction of occupying states, likewise results in a vision of occupation as transformative, calling for more rather than fewer changes to applicable law.[233]

Even if the international law of belligerent occupation is not directly applicable to rebel authority over territory and population in situations of non-international armed conflict, it is notable and relevant that international humanitarian law has evolved towards the greater protection of the interests of the civilian population, to the general detriment of the protection of the interests of the absentee or ineffective national government. This is especially so if, as explored in the previous chapter, both international humanitarian law and international human rights law reasonably can be understood to impose a responsibility upon non-state armed groups to respect and ensure respect of, or secure, individual interests and rights under both international human rights and humanitarian law. Such a responsibility calls for the application of laws to re-establish and maintain public order and public life in territory under the authority of armed groups, covering criminal as well as civil matters.[234]

[232] Dinstein (n 231) 126–127; Benvenisti (n 229) 95–101; Arai-Takahashi (n 231) 115–136; Sassòli (n 231) 670.

[233] ECtHR, Georgia v Russia (II), Judgment (Grand Chamber), Appl. No 38263/08, 21 January 2021, para 196 (where there is belligerent occupation under humanitarian law there is jurisdiction under human rights). The key precedent here is the US-led Coalition Provisional Authority in Iraq, which, as belligerent occupier, adopted a 'torrent' of new laws: Dinstein (n 231) 127. See also Sassòli (n 231) 667–668; Robert Kolb and Sylvain Vité, *Le droit de l'occupation militaire: perspectives historiques et enjeux juridiques actuels* (Bruylant 2009) 283–295.

[234] See Daragh Murray, *Human Rights Obligations of Non-State Armed Groups* (Hart Publishing 2016) 231–236.

i. Criminal Law Jurisdiction

Security is a public need that is often imperilled in situations of armed conflict of any type, corresponding to a threat to the fundamental interests of the civilian population. Expressed in human rights terms, insecurity is a central and all-encompassing menace to a wide range of individual and collective rights. From the perspective of civilians, the maintenance of public order is a central public good. There are examples in conflicts as different as Colombia and Afghanistan of civilians demanding of the FARC or the Taliban that they sanction petty or serious crimes in the community in a context in which the state is unwilling or unable to act. Conversely, if an armed group wields a degree of authority over a territory and population, insecurity will be a factor limiting its ability to effectively project its power. While there are some groups that operate on a frankly predatory model, such as the Lord's Resistance Army in Uganda, it is much more usual for groups to engage in governance practices that will garner support from the civilian population, including providing basic security through the administration of criminal justice.[235] This raises a general question as to the body of law that a rebel group may use as the statement of applicable penal law writ large (a), as well as the lawfulness of conflict-specific crimes created by many armed groups (b).

(a) Applicable Law

With regard to the identification of the basic body of criminal law which a non-state armed group may apply, two basic issues can be identified. First, can an armed group depart from the state-sanctioned criminal law that was in force prior to gaining authority in a given territory, whether by invoking a different existing body of law or by legislating its own criminal law? Second, do non-state armed groups have autonomous jurisdiction to enforce international criminal law in the territory under their authority?

Turning first to general criminal law, there are cases in which armed groups establish their own courts to administer criminal justice but retain as applicable law the criminal laws of the state against which they are fighting. For example, in the Syrian armed conflict, several rebel groups linked to the Free Syrian Army operated courts that applied the Syrian Penal Code. In the Kurdish region of Syria, the PYD also applies the state penal code, but an effort has been undertaken to reform parts of it. A similar approach is followed in the Kurdish Region of Iraq, where courts apply the Iraqi Penal Code save for some limited changes introduced by the KRG. Likewise, in the initial phase of the conflict in Sri Lanka,

[235] See Ana Arjona, *Rebelocracy: Social Order in the Colombian Civil War* (Cambridge University Press 2016) 56; Jeremy M Weinstein, *Inside Rebellion: The Politics of Insurgent Violence* (Cambridge University Press 2006) 163–197.

the LTTE simply continued to apply the established national penal code in its own courts. Although in Colombia, criminal justice was administered by the FARC is a considerably less formalised manner, mostly through popular assemblies convened under the authority of the local commander, it is reported that the substantive law applied was "95% the official law of the state", with divergence touching more significantly question of procedure and sentencing.[236] The PKK offers a variation of this approach, declaring in its constitutional KCK Charter that there are three bodies of law applicable to territory under its authority: the law of the European Union, unitary state law, and democratic confederal law. The latter refers to the PKK's own rules, but 'unitary state law' is taken to be Turkish, Syrian, or Iraqi law according to the location of the crime in question.[237] Swedish courts in the *Sakhanh* case held that the application of state law was a necessary condition of legality for the rebel administration of justice, but, as previously discussed in Chapter 2, there is no basis in international law for such a narrow interpretation of the principle of legality.[238]

Unsurprisingly, many armed opposition groups engaged in an armed struggle with the state will not feel that their courts should serve as extensions of the state's legal agenda, and accordingly have adopted criminal law that diverges from state law. Several Islamist non-state armed groups established courts that relied upon *Sharīʿa* as applicable law. Of course, as *Sharīʿa* does not refer to an institutionalised source of law about which there is agreement, these courts differed as to their conception of *Sharīʿa* to be applied: ISIS and Taliban courts applied their own, often radical, interpretation of the *Sharīʿa*, whereas other courts have applied the Unified Arab Code, a comparatively more moderate codification of *Sharīʿa* endorsed by the League of Arab States.[239] Other armed groups proceeded to adopt more comprehensive criminal laws that reflected the group's ideology and general approach to the repression of crime. One relatively elaborate example is the Public Legal Code 2060 (2003/2004) adopted by the Communist Party of Nepal—Maoist (CPN-M) and applied by the movement's

236 Mario Aguilera Peña, *Contrapoder y Justicia Guerrillera: Fragmentación Política y Orden Insurgente En Colombia (1952–2003)* (IEPRI 2014) 107.

237 See the description of the PKK legal system in Chapter 4, Section I.A.

238 See the discussion in Chapter 2, Section IV.C.i.c.

239 Thomas Pierret, 'L'Instance Islamique du Sham—Une « voie moyenne » salafiste contre la radicalisation jihadiste' (2018) 181 Archives de sciences sociales des religions 219, 232–234; Mikael Ekman, 'ILAC Rule of Law Assessment Report: Syria 2017' (International Legal Assistance Consortium 2017) 78–79, online: <http://www.ilacnet.org/wp-content/uploads/2017/04/Syria2017.pdf>. The more fundamentalist Nusra Front objected to the use of the Unified Arab Code as not wholly consistent with *Sharīʿa*, and therefore refused to participate in the court that used that source: Neil MacFarquhar, 'A Battle for Syria, One Court at a Time' *The New York Times* (13 March 2013) . On the Unified Arab Code, see Maxwell Martin, '"The Unified Arab Code—A Study and Assessment" by the Islamic Sham Organization' *Wilayat Nowhere* (5 December 2014), online: <https://wilayatnowhere.wordpress.com/2014/12/05/document-summary-the-unified-arab-code-a-study-and-assessment-by-the-islamic-sham-organization/> accessed 31 January 2020.

courts during its armed insurgency.[240] This is a twenty-page document divided into eleven distinct chapters, each containing up to ten sections, some of which are subdivided into multiple paragraphs. There is a three-paragraph preamble, and the whole has a structure and formulation that is broadly similar to statutes enacted by states. Section 3 ('Some facts about Offences') contains a basic statement framing the criminological approach of the group, and is quoted here in full to provide a flavour of the Code:

1. Crime is the by-product of a society. The desire for a crimeless society without establishing a classless, stateless and lawless communist society, is a mere illusion. Hence, crime will be committed in a society like ours in spite of every effort to minimize them. Therefore, it shall be our objective to control, minimize and punish them according to the gravity of the crime by changing the behavior and vision about crime and criminals, instead of aspiring for a crimeless society.
2. Criminal punishment must be productive, creative, dedicated to the nation and rehabilitative.
3. The commission of crime is natural and, therefore, we should bear in mind that not the criminal but the crime should be eliminated. Criminals should not be destroyed but rehabilitated.
4. The source of crime is the society itself. Attention shall be paid to ensure that it is not the crime but the source of crime which is investigated and that not the crime but the source of crime is eliminated.
5. Crime is a matter of level of class awareness and also a kind of human nature. Therefore, the commission of crime should not be taken as unusual but as natural, a punishment theory should not be retributive i.e. "tit for tat" but we shall be flexible to allow a pardon i.e. it is human nature that instigates the commission of crime- the nature which instigates to commit a crime is the subject of the extreme hatred and the struggle be carried out against it is without compromise.
6. The root cause of crime is personal interest. Therefore, efforts shall be made to emancipate from personal interest, and emphasis be made to build relations based on the community and good will.
7. Crimes are also committed because of social norms and tradition which mystifies [sic] the subject matter; therefore, it is necessary to present the subject matter naturally and objectively.
8. The other causes of the crime are suppression, hatred, hopelessness, prejudice and ill treatment; they shall be eliminated gradually from the society.

[240] On file with the author. This is an unofficial translation that seems to have been prepared by the CPN-M.

9. Law is not the ultimate instrument to prevent crime and there is no such possibility. It is merely an instrument to control crime and to reform the criminal. It is nothing more than this.

The Code then proceeds to list a number of standard offences against the (CPN-M) 'government', against persons, and against property. There is no capital punishment, and the harshest sentence is ten years' imprisonment with hard labour, applicable to first-degree murder (s. 6(4)). The Code also includes a limited set of basic procedural rules applicable to criminal trials (s. 20).

The LTTE sets the high-water mark for wide-ranging law-making by a non-state armed group. In the criminal sphere, the LTTE adopted a full-length Penal Code of Tamil Eelam in 1994.[241] The Code is derived from the Sri Lanka Penal Code and also incorporates elements from British and Indian law, as well as aspects of the *Thesawalamai*, the customary law of Tamils in the Jaffna Peninsula.[242] The LTTE Penal Code is divided into 26 chapters containing 439 sections, with the official printed version extending over 214 pages. It includes as the most severe crimes murder, sexual violence, treason, cast-related crimes, and drug trafficking. Penalties include capital punishment, imprisonment with or without harsh labour, and fines.[243] As compared to Sri Lankan law, some penalties under the LTTE Penal Code are more severe, for instance for sexual assault, while others are more lenient, including those for minor crimes. In 2004, the LTTE adopted an equally comprehensive Code of Criminal Procedure, divided into 19 chapters containing 363 articles. The whole, with an annex that includes 17 different model procedural forms, extends to 136 pages.[244]

These different examples illustrate the varied scope of jurisdiction *ratione materia* exercised by non-state armed groups in conflict zones. The language of the CPN-M Penal Code suggests the possibility of a rebel penal code that is driven by an ideology that may not align with that of the Nepalese state but is still well within the range of approaches that are adopted by different governments in their equivalent legislation. Indeed, the CPN-M Code may be considered more progressive and liberal than many state criminal codes. Likewise, the LTTE Penal

[241] On file with the author. The Code is in Tamil, and there is no known English translation.

[242] Pararajasingham (n 66) 5; on the Thesawalamai, see Kumaravadivel Guruparan, 'Customary Law of Stateless Nations: Some Observations on the Question of Who Can Reform the Thesawalamai, the Customary Laws of the Tamils in Sri Lanka' (2016) 7 Jindal Global Law Review 49.

[243] Mampilly (n 20) 117. In a 2003 interview, the Head of the Tamil Eelam Judicial Division indicated that "[w]e are in the process of reviewing provisions in the Penal Code that permit capital punishment in the light of the increasing trend against it", although it is not know whether any changes were ever made before the conflict ended in 2008: Pararajasingham (n 66) 5. Art. 52 of the Penal Code of Sri Lanka includes the possibility of capital punishment, although by the early 2000s it had not been applied for many years.

[244] On file with the author. The Code is in Tamil, and there is no known English translation.

Code signals distinct choices in policy and ideology, for instance the treatment of caste discrimination as a major crime, but there seems to be little in international law that could be used to impugn such an approach. The social and cultural proximity of an armed group to the civilian population, when contrasted with the government sitting in a distant capital, will sometimes result in rebel law addressing issues that were not visible, or perhaps not significant, to the official regime. For instance, the FARC *Manual de convivencia ciudadana* provided in Article 6 that "[p]eople who deceive the community with tales of witchcraft, sorcery, and all kinds of magic and divination will be treated as antisocial" and punished with a fine.[245]

At the same time, rebel jurisdiction *ratione materia* remains subject to the constraints of international humanitarian law and especially international human rights law. Thus, the more disproportionate or discriminatory use of criminal law by armed groups like the Islamic State would run afoul of such binding international legal standards. For example, the Islamic State's proscription of apostasy (arguably directly forbidden by the Qur'an) as a *hudūd* crime, runs directly contrary to the customary protection of freedom of religion and conscience under international humanitarian law as well as international human rights law.[246] Conversely, it is important to underscore that a non-state armed group implementing state law that runs contrary to international human rights or humanitarian law would not be shielded from responsibility for such violations. Indeed, the direct subjection of armed groups to international law implies that it has an autonomous responsibility to refuse to implement state norms contrary to international law, and possibly to replace them with its own norms that do align with the requirements of public international law. The limits thus imposed by international human rights and humanitarian law mark the outer boundaries of what may be regulated by criminal law, whether the state's or the insurgents', leaving a vast area in which an armed group can adopt and implement its own penal standards to the extent that it wields effective authority over a territory and population.

(b) Treason and Participation in the Conflict

Two specific types of offences often sanctioned by insurgent legal orders have been seen as particularly problematic: the punishment of 'treason', covering a

[245] Lorena Carrillo, '"¡Juntos, pero no revueltos!" (o de cómo se ha concertado la regulación social en medio de la guerra) El Caso de la región de El Pato, San Vicente del Caguán, Colombia. 1956–2016' (Master's Thesis, Colegio de Michoacan 2016) 158.

[246] Art. 2(1), Additional Protocol II. On ISIS practice in this respect, see Mara Revkin, 'The Legal Foundations of the Islamic State' (Brookings Institution 2016) 17. On ISIS justice more generally, see Chapter 2, Section II.B.

range of acts against the security of the non-state armed group, and of taking part in hostilities against the group, corresponding to the possibility that an armed group would punish government soldiers merely for participating in the state repression of armed insurgency. Neither type of rebel norm corresponds to an obvious violation of international human rights or humanitarian law, raising questions about their legality under international law more generally.

Non-state armed groups systematically punish 'treason', corresponding to some form of collaboration with the enemy, whether the government or any other hostile entity. As the 1994 Penal Code of Tamil Eelam illustrates, treason against the group is always included as one of the gravest crimes, if not the most injurious one. It will normally be punished with the most severe sanction, whether long terms of imprisonment with harsh labour (as in the CPN-M Code) or capital punishment (as in the LTTE Code).[247] Collusion with the enemy presents an existential threat in any armed conflicts such that its repression is seen as an absolutely imperative. In his original and compelling study of treason in war, Shane Darcy notes that "[f]or parties to an armed conflict, collaborators may present as significant a threat to their ability to wage conflict as the combatants of the opposing side".[248] This explains the contempt, if not moral outrage, directed at those who collude with the enemy in wartime.

Perhaps because this is behaviour considered to be beyond the pale, the punishment of treason by armed insurgents has often been a point of tension for the rebel administration of justice. The Taliban, for instance, include in the *laheya*, their code of conduct, a long section on the treatment of spies that regulates the punishment of "the one who strives to disseminate evil" (Art. 17). The *laheya* spells out the type of proof that is required for a conviction and limits the power to order the execution of spies to the imam, the judge, or the provincial governor.[249] Despite these clear rules and a judiciary that is well-structured and normally disciplined, the summary execution of alleged spies by Taliban commanders in contradiction with these rules remain common in Afghanistan.[250] Overall, most cases of capital punishment ordered by the Taliban are said to be connected to espionage.[251] The FARC offer an even more extreme example. Their administration of justice in criminal matters never was institutionalised to a high degree, consisting of a very basic process leading

247 See Mario Aguilera Peña, 'Las Guerrillas marxistas y la pena de muerte a combatientes. un examen de los delitos capitales y del "juicio revolucionario"' (2014) 41 Anuario colombiano de historia social y de la cultura 201, 216.

248 Shane Darcy, *To Serve the Enemy: Informers, Collaborators, and the Laws of Armed Conflict* (Oxford University Press 2019) 131.

249 Kate Clark, 'The Layeha: Calling the Taliban to Account' (Afghan Analysts Network 2011).

250 Human Rights Watch, "You Have No Right to Complain: Education, Social Restrictions, and Justice in Taliban-Held Afghanistan" (2020) 59–61; Adam Baczko, 'La Guerre par le droit : justice, domination et violence en Afghanistan (2001–2018)' (PhD Thesis, EHESS 2018) 294–300; Jackson (n 225) 19.

251 Baczko (n 250) 269.

to a decision by the regional commander for lesser crimes, or convening popular assemblies for more serious crimes like murder or sexual assault. People suspected of acting as spies for the state or for paramilitary groups, known as *sapos*, most often benefitted neither from the highly structured and ritualised courts-martial process applicable to FARC fighters suspected of a crime, nor from the community-based process applicable to regular crimes by civilians. Instead, informants suggest that anyone suspected of collaborating with the enemy was liable to be executed on the order of the local FARC commander, with no due process to speak of.[252] The question of applicable due process is distinct, and will be analysed in the next section, leaving the need to determine whether international law imposes limits on the ability of armed groups to criminalise espionage or collaboration with the enemy.

In general, the punishment of spies or collaborators in times of armed conflicts has been pursued with particular harshness by both state and non-state belligerents. Darcy's comprehensive study of the question suggests that nearly all sides in every conflict have sought to punish espionage, often in a deliberately public manner in order to deter as much as possible anyone from engaging in this practice.[253] The consistent state practice regarding the criminality of collaboration with the enemy in war is reflected in the uniquely ambiguous status of spies in international humanitarian law. The ambiguity comes from the fact that information-gathering is a necessary and important aspect of any military campaign, such that all belligerents engage in espionage in one form or another. At the same time, as mentioned, being the target of spying by the enemy belligerent is a considerable security threat, and therefore is resisted with all available means. As noted by Hersh Lauterpacht, this duality is reflected in international law: "Although a belligerent acts lawfully in employing spies and traitors, the other belligerent, who punishes them, likewise acts lawfully".[254] Under humanitarian law applicable to international armed conflicts, privileged combatants and civilians that engage in espionage in enemy or occupied territory are explicitly denied the protection otherwise given to them as prisoners of war or protected persons.[255] Despite some occasional claims to the contrary, the withholding of special protection under international humanitarian law for those who engage in espionage does not imply that espionage is, in itself, a war crime.[256] On the other

[252] Interview with FARC commander German (January 2018). See also Aguilera Peña (n 247) 222–223, 436.

[253] Darcy (n 248) 131.

[254] Hersch Lauterpacht, *Oppenheim's International Law*, vol 2 (7th edn, Longmans 1952) 422.

[255] Art. 5, Fourth Geneva Convention; Art. 46, Additional Protocol I. See also Jean-Marie Henckaerts and Louise Doswald-Beck (eds), *Customary International Humanitarian Law*, vol 1: Rules (Cambridge University Press 2005), Rule 107.

[256] Lauterpacht (n 254) 426, 575. The European Court of Human Rights in *Kononov v Latvia* mistakenly mentions, in passing, that 'war treason' by civilians in occupied territory is a war crime: ECHR, *Kononov v Latvia*, Judgment (Grand Chamber), Appl. No 36376/04, 17 May 2010, para 204; Darcy (n 248) 151.

hand, seeing the near-universal practice sanctioning it, there is no basis to doubt the jurisdiction of states to make espionage a crime under their domestic law.[257]

In the context of belligerent occupation, international humanitarian law explicitly envisages that the occupier may make changes to local law to ensure its security (Art. 64, Fourth Geneva Convention). Here again, it is established and accepted practice for the occupier to declare that espionage and any form of collaboration with the enemy is an offence subject to prosecution and punishment.[258] This is indirectly confirmed by Article 30 of the 1907 Hague Regulations, which specifies that a spy cannot be punished without a previous trial, a now-customary requirement that replicates international human rights law in this respect.[259] Specifically in the context of occupation, Article 68 of the Fourth Geneva Convention allows the application of the death penalty to persons guilty of espionage "provided that such offences were punishable by death under the law of the occupied territory in force before the occupation began". This unusual pairing of the legislative power of the occupier and the local law in force at the start of occupation was hotly debated at the 1949 diplomatic conference and several states, including the United States, entered reservations to reserve the right to apply the death penalty in occupied territory regardless of local law.[260] Given that, even today, it appears that half of all states retain the possibility of capital punishment for wartime espionage, the limitation imposed by Article 68 is far from a clear prohibition of the death penalty for this crime during belligerent occupation.[261] As commented by Darcy, "[t]hat the execution of spies is lawfully permitted in certain circumstances may contribute to a general perception of broader permissibility, particularly on the part of non-state armed groups".[262]

The power to sanction espionage reflects an agent's status as a belligerent in an armed conflict rather than statehood, as exemplified by the fact that states are practically unanimous in not only sanctioning espionage or collaboration with the enemy in wartime but also in accepting that an occupier may do so even in the absence of sovereign authority to underpin such repression. If it is accepted that non-state armed groups have jurisdiction to adopt any laws at all, it would seem to follow

257 Darcy (n 248) 133–134.

258 Dinstein (n 231) 123; Benvenisti (n 229) 95–101; ICRC, *Commentary on the Fourth Geneva Convention* (ICRC 1958) 337.

259 See ECHR, *Kononov v Latvia* (n 256) para 204.

260 ICRC, *Commentary on the Fourth Geneva Convention* (n 258) 345. Several of the reserving states, including Australia, Canada, Netherlands, New Zealand, and the United Kingdom, later withdrew this reservation. See Claude Pilloud, 'Reservations to the Geneva Conventions of 1949—Part II' (1976) 16 International Review of the Red Cross 163, 184–185 (noting that "[i]n effect, the fears of the States which made this reservation are illusory. There is no country, it appears, which in war-time does not have laws punishing with death the crimes listed in Article 68").

261 Darcy (n 248) 157.

262 ibid 156.

that, as a matter of course, it would include prohibiting acts endangering the group's security. Without some basis in international law to counter the recognition of the jurisdiction of armed groups in this respect, it seems difficult to deny that they can indeed prohibit collaboration and espionage in territory under their effective authority. It goes without saying that this is purely under international law, and that one would expect that this criminal repression of espionage by an insurgent would constitute a violation of the domestic law of the state. There is no contradiction in recognising under international law that an armed group may adopt such rules and that the territorial state may punish it under national law. This approach is analogous to the use of armed force by non-state actors in a non-international armed conflict, which may lawfully be punished by the local state as a crime under municipal law, despite not violating international law.[263]

For the civilian population, this can result in a conflict between the law of the non-state armed group and the law of the state. Daragh Murray notes that "the law of the state would prohibit collaboration with the armed group, while the law of the armed group would prohibit collaboration with the state, resulting in a patently unworkable situation".[264] The first thing to note is that, while there is a tension between these two laws, it does not place civilians in a dilemma, as these are all 'negative' obligations of abstention, such that a civilian that does not become involved in collaboration will run afoul of neither rebel nor state law. Secondly, the tension thus created between the laws of the state and non-state armed group parallels exactly the tension between the law of the occupying state and that of the territorial state, accepted under international humanitarian law. This is a state of affairs that is taken as reflecting the fact that effective authority over occupied territory is exercised by an agent other than the sovereign state, similar to that which obtains in a non-international armed conflict in which an armed group wields effective authority over part of national territory. Thirdly, as examined earlier, overlapping and possibly contradictory jurisdictions are an ineluctable fact of the life of international relations, captured by private international law or conflict of laws, such that an overlap and tension between the law of the territorial state and rebel law would not appear per se especially remarkable.[265]

The second crime established by rebel law that has been seen as problematic is the criminalisation of directly taking part in hostilities. In other words, can non-state armed groups make it a crime for individuals to be involved in armed hostilities against them, either as part of the armed forces of the state or as a member of another armed group? This would possibly lead an armed opposition group

[263] Liesbeth Zegveld, *Accountability of Armed Opposition Groups in International Law* (Cambridge University Press 2002) 36–37.

[264] Murray (n 234) 226; see also Darcy (n 248) 166.

[265] See the discussion supra (n 208) and accompanying text.

to prosecute soldiers captured on the battlefield for conduct that was fully consistent with international humanitarian law, a possibility that is taken as especially injurious by governments involved in non-international armed conflicts. The question of the rebel criminalisation of mere participation in hostilities by government or enemy soldiers was first raised by Jonathan Somer in his landmark study of insurgent justice.[266] The one example he gives refers to the prosecution and execution of 'informers' by the CPN-M in Nepal, although Article 4(4) of the CPN-M Code (on "offences against Peoples' Government") is not wholly clear as to whether it sanctions mere participation in hostilities by government soldiers or a more specific offence.[267] The Taliban *layeha* is more explicit in this regard with an entire section on the treatment of enemy prisoners (Arts. 9–16).[268] Different rules apply depending on whether the individual is "a soldier, policeman, or other official of the enslaved government", a "contractor", or "an infidel fighter", but in all cases execution is one of the contemplated courses of action. There are references in the *layeha* to "the judgment for execution" (Art. 10) in cases where individuals "are proven guilty of any of the aforementioned activities by the provincial judge" (Art. 11), as well as the exceptional right for mujahedin to summarily execute an enemy prisoner captured on the battlefield if he cannot be transferred to a safe place without endangering the life of the mujahidin (Art. 13). Taken together, these provisions suggest that the sanction of mere participation in hostilities is one available course of action for the Taliban.[269] In practice, although some government soldiers captured by the Taliban are interned or even executed, the dominant trend seems to be that they are released upon a promise not to rejoin the Afghan army.[270] In contrast, the Islamic State has carried out many mass and individual executions of captured government soldiers, sometimes killing several hundred at a time.[271] In the case of the Islamic State, there seems to be no pretence that this was preceded by any type of judgment. Many, if not most, non-state armed groups do not claim to criminalise mere participation in hostilities by government soldiers.

[266] Jonathan Somer, 'Jungle Justice: Passing Sentence on the Equality of Belligerents in Non-International Armed Conflict' (2007) 89 International Review of the Red Cross 655, 686.

[267] ibid 686 footnote 140. Art. 4(4) of the CPN-M Code punishes "whoever commits or attempts to conspire or join the enemy", although capital punishment was not used by this group.

[268] See Clark (n 249) 4–5.

[269] It bears noting that the summary execution envisaged by Art. 13 of the *layeha*, even if restricted to exceptional circumstances, nevertheless remains a clear war crime.

[270] See for a recent example, Najim Rahim and Rod Nordland, 'Taliban Capture about 150 Afghan Soldiers after Chase into Turkmenistan' *The New York Times* (18 March 2019) A4.

[271] Heather Saul, 'Iraqi Soldier Survives ISIS Mass Execution by Lying on Floor—And Pretending to Be Dead' *The Independent* (3 September 2014). In the early days of the Syrian conflict, it was reported that the Free Syrian Army regularly executed government soldiers for mere participation in hostilities: United Nations Independent International Commission of Inquiry on the Syrian Arab Republic, 'Memorandum: Response to the Swedish Prosecution Authority', Nationella Operativa Avdelningen, Sakkunnigutlåtande COI-rapport, diarienr: 5000-K132600-16 (12 October 2016) para 8.

There is no doubt that municipal law does not contemplate that non-state armed groups may criminalise conduct in furtherance of a defence of the nation by state armed forces. Any such criminalisation would be treated as a domestic crime committed by armed insurgents. What is less clear is whether international law authorises or prohibits the exercise of rebel jurisdiction *ratione materiae* in this fashion. It may be surprising, but international humanitarian law does not include any provision that explicitly provides authorisation to a state to criminalise the taking up of arms against its legitimate government. Common Article 3, for instance, remains mute on the subject, leaving unspecified the offences for which a "judgment pronounced by a regularly constituted court" must be obtained. Article 6(5) of Additional Protocol II provides that "[a]t the end of hostilities, the authorities in power shall endeavour to grant the broadest possible amnesty to persons who have participated in the armed conflict". This provision has generated a debate as to whether the amnesty so envisaged could cover war crimes.[272] On its face, the wording of the provision refers to amnesty for participation in the conflict, implying a legal capacity to impose criminal responsibility for this behaviour. No doubt, governments in Geneva in 1949 as much as in 1977 took it as a given that states could criminalise the taking up of arms against the established government, and indeed such laws are to be found in most if not all states.[273] Note, however, the noncommittal formulation used in Article 6(5) of Protocol II to designate who can grant amnesty: 'the authorities in power'. There is, after all, a possibility that an armed opposition group will defeat the established government, and in such a situation the humanitarian invitation to grant as wide an amnesty as possibly for mere participation in hostilities would certainly obtain in favour of members of the armed forces of the former regime.

One might be tempted to invoke the principle of the equality of belligerents to suggest that if one side in a non-international armed conflict can criminalise participation in hostilities, then so should the other.[274] A rigid application of the principle of equality to explain the scope of obligations of state and non-state belligerents in the context of non-international armed conflicts was previously rejected in Chapter 2.[275] The positions of the sovereign government and that of armed insurgent with respect to jurisdiction over direct participation in hostilities is different, reflecting distinct starting points. The government is presumed to have jurisdiction over the entire national territory, thereby giving it authority

[272] See Sivakumaran, *The Law of Non-International Armed Conflict* (n 189) 505–509.
[273] A few state laws or constitutions provide a right to rebel in exceptional circumstances: Tony Honoré, 'The Right to Rebel' (1988) 8 Oxford Journal of Legal Studies 34, 42–43; Annyssa Bellal, 'What Are "Armed Non-State Actors"? A Legal and Semantic Approach' in Ezequiel Heffes, Marcos D Kotlik and Manuel J Ventura (eds), *International Humanitarian Law and Non-State Actors: Debates, Law and Practice* (TMC Asser Press 2020) 33–34.
[274] There is a nod in that direction in Somer (n 266) 686.
[275] See the discussion in Chapter 2, Section IV.A.ii.

to impose demands on anyone within its borders. The prohibition of rebellion in national law creates a normative blanket that covers at least the whole of the territory of the state. When individuals take up arms against the state, they do so while subject to the state's jurisdiction. Rebel jurisdiction over direct participation, on the other hand, is limited by the territorial reach of the armed group's effective authority; by definition, a soldier engaged in hostilities against insurgents will not be doing from a position of subservience to the authority of the armed group. For that reason, it is suggested that the criminalisation of direct participation in hostilities by non-state armed groups falls beyond their jurisdiction *ratione materiae*.

(c) Crimes against International Law

A final question related to penal subject-matter jurisdiction for non-state armed groups is their legal capacity to prosecute individual authors of crimes against international law such as war crimes, crimes against humanity, and genocide. Three somewhat distinct scenarios can be envisaged. First, cases in which the individual who has committed an international crime is a member of the very armed group that could or would prosecute him. For example, in 1991, during the conflict in El Salvador, a patrol belonging to the FMLN managed to shoot down a low-flying US Air Force helicopter in a remote part of the country. The pilot was killed in the crash, but two US soldiers survived and were captured. The rebel patrol commander ordered both men to be shot. This was contrary to the FMLN code of conduct, and the group prosecuted its own fighters for what it labelled 'war crimes'.[276] The second scenario covers situations in which a non-state armed group detains members of another non-state armed group who have committed international crimes. A current example is the Kurdish Regional Government, which holds a number of Islamic State fighters who have been linked to acts of genocide against members of the Yazidi community. High-ranking members of the KRG have expressed a keen interest in setting up a penal accountability mechanism so that these international crimes do not go unpunished, and accordingly have sought support from third states and international organisations.[277] The third scenario concerns crimes against international law committed by members of the state armed forces who at a later point come to

[276] Commission on the Truth for El Salvador, 'From Madness to Hope: The 12-Year War in El Salvador', UN Doc S/25500 (1993) 168–169; Deborah Tyroler, 'El Salvador: Killings of U.S. Military Advisers by Rebels Acknowledged' (1991), online: <https://digitalrepository.unm.edu/noticen/4951>, quoting a FMLN communique saying the two rebels "are accused of committing a war crime, of violating the FMLN's principles and codes of war conduct, and of violating the Geneva protocol of the FMLN, and of violating the Geneva protocol".

[277] Interviews with Fallah Mustafa Bakir (Foreign Minister of KRG) and Safeen Dizayee (KRG Spokesman), Erbil, September 2017. Opposition from the central Iraqi government has meant that the KRG's request for support has fallen on deaf ears so far.

be detained by an armed opposition group. This corresponds to the underlying facts of the prosecution of Omar Sakhanh before Swedish courts: he was prosecuted for taking part in the execution of seven government soldiers who had been convicted of murder and rape of civilians by a tribunal of the Free Syrian Army.[278] In that case, the rebel court apparently based its jurisdiction on the Syrian Penal Code, but one can imagine a similar situation in which murder and sexual assault are prosecuted as war crimes. These three scenarios raise a number of different questions. One relates to the jurisdiction *ratione personae* of insurgent courts in relation to members of other non-state armed groups and, in particular, of soldiers of the armed forces of the state. Another question reflects the physical location of the crime against international law and whether rebel jurisdiction *ratione loci* for such crimes extends beyond the geographical reach of the non-state group's effective authority. Although both aspects are intertwined to some extent with the jurisdiction *ratione materiae* of insurgent courts, I leave them aside for now to consider only the issue of subject-matter jurisdiction of these courts over crimes against international law.

The question concerning the jurisdiction *ratione materiae* of rebel courts relates only to the execution dimension of this jurisdiction, as opposed to its normative aspect. War crimes, crimes against humanity, and genocide are all recognised as crimes under customary international law, such that they will necessarily be applicable to any action, anywhere, by anyone. The question is whether rebel courts are excluded from the list of possible mechanisms that can impose individual criminal responsibility for such crimes. Views of that nature certainly have been expressed in the past. In the context of the civil war in El Salvador, for instance, it is reported that the ICRC rebuffed the FMLN's attempt to devise practices that could meet due process requirements: "the ICRC stated that in the presence of serious violations of humanitarian law, the rebels should have recourse to the national system of the administration of justice".[279] The denial that international law grants non-state armed groups jurisdiction to prosecute war crimes was said to have found "wide recognition in international

[278] *Prosecutor v Omar Haisam Sakhanh*, Stockholms tingsrätt (Stockholm District Court), B 3787-16, Judgment of 16 February 2017 (hereinafter 'Sakhanh, Stockholm District Court'), online: <http://www.ejiltalk.org/wp-content/uploads/2017/03/Stockholms-TR-B-3787-16-Dom-2017-02-16.pdf> accessed 18 July 2018, with a partial translation in (2018) 16 *Journal of International Criminal Justice* 403–424; confirmed by Prosecutor v Omar Haisam Sakhanh, Svea hovrätt (Svea Court of Appeal), B 2259-17, Judgment of 31 May 2017 (hereinafter 'Sakhanh, Svea Appeal Court'); leave to appeal was denied by the Supreme Court of Sweden, B 3157-17, 20 July 2017.

[279] Tathiana Flores Acuña, *The United Nations Mission in El Salvador: A Humanitarian Law Perspective* (Kluwer Law International 1995) 61 n 247. This is broadly similar to the position embraced by Amnesty International in its *amicus curiae* brief in the *Bemba* trial before the ICC: ICC, *Prosecutor v Jean-Pierre Bemba Gombo*, Amnesty International, Amicus Curiae Observations on Superior Responsibility submitted pursuant to Rule 103 of the Rules of Procedure and Evidence, 20 April 2009, ICC-01/05-01/08-406, paras 22–23, online: <http://www.legal-tools.org/doc/9efb78/>.

practice".[280] It is suggested that such views reflect a broader refusal to recognise any form of rebel administration of justice and that the evolution of international practice analysed in Chapter 2 leads to the conclusion that there is no sound reason today to exclude crimes against international law from the subject-matter jurisdiction of rebel courts. Such a conclusion is founded on the very nature of crimes against international law: these crimes are recognised as offensive to humanity as a whole and are purely grounded in public international law. As such, they are the basis of universal state jurisdiction, such that the prosecution of war crimes, crimes against humanity, or genocide is rooted in international law as opposed to the prosecution of ordinary crimes by the state, based in its own sovereignty. As put by Anthony Colangelo, for crimes against international law, "[t]he primary lawgiver . . . is the international legal system, and individual states exercising universal jurisdiction merely act as decentralized enforcement vehicles for that lawgiver".[281] In this view, jurisdiction over crimes against international law is not for the state to share or not. This explains why the UN Security Council can defer a case to the ICC or that any state may prosecute a war crime under universal jurisdiction, neither of which involves consent or delegation by the territorial state. This sends us back to the question of who is, in Onora O'Neill's evocative formulation, an 'agent of justice' that can act on behalf of humanity.[282] The possible options are certainly not limited to states and will in any case depend on the agent's actual ability to administer justice. Whether or not this corresponds to a duty to govern, the answer should be grounded in task-efficacy as a central—but not exclusive—criterion.[283]

Rebel jurisdiction over crimes against international law is implicitly regulated by international law in relation to war crimes committed by an armed group's own members. As a reflection of the doctrine of command responsibility under international criminal law and of the duty to respect under Common Article 1 of the Geneva Conventions, the group has an affirmative obligation to take steps to sanction war crimes committed by its own members. In many circumstances, the only realistic option to effectively and lawfully do so is to establish an insurgent court with jurisdiction over crimes against international law.[284] The lawfulness of a

[280] Zegveld (n 263) 67–68; Denise Plattner, 'The Penal Repression of Violations of International Humanitarian Law Applicable in Non-International Armed Conflicts' (1990) 30 International Review of the Red Cross Archive 409, 415.

[281] Anthony J Colangelo, 'Double Jeopardy and Multiple Sovereigns: A Jurisdictional Theory' (2008) 86 Washington University Law Review 769, 796–797.

[282] Onora O'Neill, 'Agents of Justice' (2001) 32 Metaphilosophy 180, 189; Giudice and Schaeffer (n 199) 239. This is linked to the discussion of rebel justice and sovereignty in Chapter 1, Section III.B.

[283] Giudice and Schaeffer (n 199) 245; Leslie Green, 'The Duty to Govern' (2007) 13 Legal Theory 165, 173.

[284] ICC, *Prosecutor v Jean-Pierre Bemba Gombo*, Decision Pursuant to Article 61(7)(a) and (b) of the Rome Statute in the Charges of the Prosecutor against Jean-Pierre Bemba Gombo, 15 June 2009, ICC-01/05-01/08, paras 497, 501; ICC, *Prosecutor v Jean-Pierre Bemba Gombo*, Trial Judgment, 21 March 2016, ICC-01/05-01/08, paras 206–209, 402, 597, 727–733; ICC, *Prosecutor v Jean-Pierre*

jurisdictional claim by insurgent courts over war crimes stands further buttressed by the duty to ensure respect under customary humanitarian law, covering crimes by individuals not falling under the responsibility of the group.[285] The grounding of jurisdiction over crimes against international law directly in public international law, as opposed to necessarily via the national law of a state, is confirmed by the formulation of the principle of *nullum crimen sine lege* in Article 6(2)(c) of Additional Protocol II. As noted previously, while the English version of the Protocol ambiguously refers to "a criminal offence, under the law", the French version leaves no doubt that the crimes may be established by international law: "*un acte délictueux d'après le droit national ou international*".[286] At the level of jurisdiction *ratione materiae*, there seems to be no valid reason to exclude crimes against international law from the jurisdiction of courts of non-state armed groups. Whether this is limited as to place or person will be considered presently.

The claims of many armed groups in non-international armed conflicts to administer criminal justice have been vigorously resisted by territorial states in the name of sovereignty. While each state remains undoubtedly largely free to criminalise the rebel administration of penal justice under its domestic law, public international law imposes no outright barrier to this form of rebel governance. Rebel criminal jurisdiction can lawfully cover a range of ordinary crimes (whether or not criminalised by the law of the state), crimes against the security of armed groups, and crimes against international law. For the reasons articulated earlier, insurgents may not pretend to criminally sanction mere participation in hostilities by other belligerents, including the state armed forces, corresponding to a form of legal asymmetry in that respect. Beyond this specific limit, in substance and in process, the whole rebel administration of criminal justice remains subject to the requirements of international human rights law. As such, the creation of any crime violating established fundamental rights and freedoms, whether by discrimination or otherwise, would amount to the illegal exercise of subject-matter jurisdiction by a non-state armed group.

ii. Civil Law Jurisdiction

What little attention has been paid to the rebel administration of justice has focussed, nearly exclusively, on matters of criminal law, no doubt because this is

Bemba Gombo, Appeals Judgment, 8 June 2018, ICC-01/05-01/08 A, paras 167–169. This was considered in Chapter 2 as part of the discussion of a wider duty for armed opposition groups to administer justice: Chapter 2, Section IV.B.i.

[285] Henckaerts and Doswald-Beck (n 255) Rule 139; Zegveld (n 263) 67–68; Murray (n 234) 222–223.

[286] Michael Bothe and others, *New Rules for Victims of Armed Conflicts: Commentary on the Two 1977 Protocols Additional to the Geneva Conventions of 1949* (2d edn, Nijhoff 2013) 746–747. This provision is analysed more fully in Chapter 2, Section IV.C.ii in relation to the question of whether 'law' in this context can cover the law of non-state armed groups.

perceived to be the most blatant and frontal assault on the sovereignty of the state. What might be termed, in contrast, civil law jurisdiction, encompassing here all non-criminal private and public law issues from family law to contracts, administrative law to property, has nearly entirely escaped analysis. This is so despite the fact that, in war as much as in peace, very few people get caught in the application of criminal law, while everyone relies nearly continuously on civil law norms. Admittedly, criminal law has a normative effect that extends much beyond its formal application in specific circumstances, conditioning behaviour in a much broader and more sustained manner than the dockets of rebel courts might suggest. In addition, civil and criminal jurisdictions eventually join up at the enforcement stage, if only as a threat in the case of noncompliance with decisions related to civil matters. Still, it is suggested, the administration of justice by non-state armed groups in non-criminal law matters is a phenomenon of considerable significance that ought to be examined much more closely, including by legal scholars. I offer some preliminary thoughts on its context, form, and substance as an invitation to study this practice more systematically than I can do here.

The regulation of insurgent jurisdiction in civil matters under public international law is limited. None of the relevant treaties, whether related to international humanitarian law or international human rights law, explicitly speaks to the possibility that armed opposition groups might claim jurisdiction over such issues. This question is related to the legality for such groups to establish their own courts, examined in Chapter 2. Much of the relevant standards examined there, from the duty to prosecute to the doctrine of command responsibility, relates to the administration of justice in criminal rather than civil matters. The general duty to 'respect and ensure respect' of international humanitarian law, arguably applicable to non-state armed groups under customary international law, might be said to imply a degree of insurgent jurisdiction in civil matters.[287] Nearly all of the obligations imposed on armed groups under Common Article 3 and Additional Protocol II relate to the security of person or property in a manner that evokes the conduct of hostilities and, to a more limited extent, criminal jurisdiction. One can point to Article 4(3)(a) of Protocol II, which requires that children be provided with an education, as imposing a duty that implies a regulatory framework of some kind, even if simply permissive. This duty applies to *de jure* and *de facto* authorities over a territory and seems to provide a foundation for the adoption of rebel norms dealing with the education of children inasmuch as it corresponds to the effective authority of insurgents.[288] This would

[287] Henckaerts and Doswald-Beck (n 255) Rule 139 (on the customary status of the duty to ensure respect).

[288] ICRC, *Commentary on the Additional Protocols of 8 June 1977 to the Geneva Conventions of 12 August 1949* (International Committee of the Red Cross 1987) 1377–1378.

provide a basis, for example, for the LTTE Act for the Protection of Tamil Eelam Children, providing a right to education for grades 1–11 (Art. 25), with specific provisions for homeschooling (Art. 26), special needs and low-income children (Arts. 27–28), measures to discourage dropping out (Art. 30), and limiting house chores during study hours (Art. 31). Aside from this quite narrow jurisdictional head, one may wonder whether an armed group that wields effective authority over a territory and population can lawfully dispense entirely with any engagement with non-criminal matters.

Does the broad duty to ensure respect in international humanitarian law envisage a working civil law justice system in war zones as a minimal humanitarian need? The life-goes-on dimension of life in war-affected communities, reflecting daily travails like the neighbour's cow trampling a field or a drunken brawl causing an injury, corresponds to an unabating need for dispute resolution mechanisms. If none is available, people will take matters into their own hands, leading us back to the field of criminal law. This explains why, in many non-international armed conflicts, the civilian population will at times be the party demanding that the local armed group become involved in the administration of justice in civil matters.[289] As mentioned earlier, the fundamental need for a working civil law justice system is captured in the occupier's duties to ensure public order and public life (*'l'ordre et la vie publics'*) in the context of belligerent occupation (Art. 43, Hague Regulations), and "to maintain the orderly government of the territory" (Art. 64, Fourth Geneva Convention).[290] The duration of belligerent occupation has been identified as a key factor in this respect: "The longer the occupation lasts, the more compelling the need to weigh the merits of a whole gamut of novel legislative measures designed to ensure that societal needs in the occupied territory do not remain too long in a legal limbo".[291] The same would obtain in situations in which official justice in civil matters becomes ineffective because of insurgent authority over a territory: the longer state courts are not functional, the greater the social need for a replacement insurgent justice system. Here, again, no claim is made that these norms devised for international armed conflicts are applicable to internal conflicts, but they do convey recognition, at international law, of the undeniable importance of an active civil jurisdiction in conflict zones.

[289] This is the pattern that led the FARC to become involved in settling private disputes. See Chapter 1, Section I.B.iii.

[290] On the limited duty to maintain local laws in force at the start of occupation, see the discussion supra (n 231) and accompanying text.

[291] Dinstein (n 231) 128; Adam Roberts, 'Prolonged Military Occupation: The Israeli-Occupied Territories Since 1967' (1990) 84 American Journal of International Law 44, 52; Vaios Koutroulis, 'The Application of International Humanitarian Law and International Human Rights Law in Situation of Prolonged Occupation: Only a Matter of Time?' (2012) 94 International Review of the Red Cross 165.

The legality of rebel jurisdiction in civil matters stands further reinforced by the applicability of international human rights standards. If human rights obligations are considered applicable to non-state armed groups in situations in which they wield effective authority over a territory, a premise discussed in more details in the next section, then they are required to protect individuals and communities against violations stemming from private actors. As articulated by the Inter-American Court of Human Rights in its landmark judgment in *Velásquez Rodríguez*, this includes the operation of a legal system capable of ensuring the free and full exercise of human rights.[292] It was noted in Chapter 2 that this obligation for armed groups is modulated by their capacities, so that if a group is unable to administer justice, then it has an obligation to allow state justice to continue operating.[293] Because state courts are unlikely to apply rebel laws, the insurgents' normative jurisdiction depends on its involvement in the administration of justice: rebel law can be judicially applied only through rebel courts. If an armed group can and does administer justice in civil matters, however, then its normative jurisdiction at least in part derives from international human rights law, which both authorises and limits the civil jurisdiction of that armed group. To return to the example of the LTTE Child Protection Act, for example, its provision dealing with the special educational needs of disabled children would reflect and be grounded in the human rights of these children as guaranteed in the UN Convention on Persons with Disabilities (Art. 24) and in customary international law. Considering the breadth of fundamental rights protected in international human rights law, this corresponds to a very wide rebel jurisdiction in civil matters.

The practice of non-state armed groups in armed conflicts with respect to civil jurisdiction varies enormously. Some groups simply go along with the civil law of the state, unless there is a specific norm that is seen as incompatible with insurgent ideology or governance. Reportedly, for example, the YPG in Rojava essentially has continued to apply official Syrian law.[294] Sometimes, insurgents will adopt their own standards in relation to some matters and leave others to the laws and courts of the state. The FARC in Colombia, for instance, were not keen to become involved in family law matters and so steered civilians towards state institutions whenever they were available.[295] Other armed opposition groups seem much more absolute in rejecting state jurisdiction in civil matters. Taliban judges do not apply the laws of the state of Afghanistan in any area, objecting to the very concept of state legislation.[296]

292 Inter-American Court of Human Rights, *Velásquez Rodríguez v Honduras*, Merits, Judgment, (ser. C) No 4 (1988) paras 164–177.
293 See Chapter 2, Section IV.B.ii.
294 See Chapter 4, Section I.B.
295 Carrillo (n 245) 166–167.
296 Baczko (n 250) 241.

There is little doubt that many states would resist a finding that international law affords non-state armed groups any jurisdiction over civil matters, at least in relation to an armed conflict on their own territory. However, if the choice is between state-sanctioned chaos due to non-functioning official courts and rebel-administered justice reflecting the effective authority of armed groups, there is little in international humanitarian and human rights law that justifies privileging the former to the detriment of the latter.

Rebel law-making takes many varied forms. Some armed groups like the Taliban and Islamic State deny, for ideological reasons, that they make law at all, claiming instead to be applying a purer, unadulterated form of *Sharīʿa*. In some other cases, even without any ideological objection to law-making, there is little form to speak of, such as the FARC's significant reliance on local customs or common sense as understood by the civilian population and applied in popular assemblies or by commanders sitting as single decision-makers in makeshift courts. More formal, albeit variable in its content between regions, was the *Manual de convivencia* eventually adopted by the FARC in Colombia. As explained in Chapter 1, this was a document that was initially developed in collaboration between the armed group and local assemblies in the Caqueta province and later transplanted to other areas under FARC control.[297] A few versions of the *Manual de convivencia* have survived, revealing that they tend to be quite short, no more than about seventy provisions, drafted in plain, descriptive and accessible language.[298] Other groups with more stable, exclusive and long-lasting authority carried out more ambitious law-making exercises. The KRG in Iraq is one example, although its near-governmental status may perhaps be taken to be too close to that of an independent state to be indicative of the practice of non-state armed groups in general. The LTTE may be a better example. It adopted some statutes that are similar in form to those of officially recognised governments, for example, the 1995 Law of Evidence that contains 162 articles running over 115 printed pages.[299] Even more ambitious are the LTTE Penal Code and Code of Criminal Procedure, described in a previous subsection, each including hundreds of articles.[300] There are mentions of LTTE Civil Code and Code of Civil Procedure in some of the documentation produced by the group during the war, but no existing copy of these codes could be found during the fieldwork for this project.

[297] Carrillo (n 245) 154–172.

[298] See Ariel Fernando Ávila Martínez and Juan Diego Castro León, 'Los Retos En Convivencia, Administración de Justicia y Seguridad Rural En El Posconflicto' [2015] Cuadernos de análisis Friedrich Ebert Stiftung 1, 43–44, for a copy of the Manual de Convivencia for FARC Frente 32; Carrillo (n 245) 193–197, 203–211 for copies of the FARC manuals for El Pato and La Macarena.

[299] On file with the author.

[300] See supra (n 241) and accompanying text.

Still in the context of Sri Lanka, the LTTE changes to the *Thesawalamai* are an interesting example of some of the challenges related to forms of rebel legislation in non-international armed conflicts. The *Thesawalamai* is a compilation of the customs of the Tamils of the Jaffna Peninsula that predates the emergence of Sri Lanka as an independent state or as a unitary political territory. In 1707, during the Dutch colonial period in what was then the island of Ceylon, a Dutch official named Claas Isaaks wrote down Tamil customs applicable in the north-east, with very little input from local communities. Nearly a century later, in 1799, the *Thesawalamai* was given official recognition as applicable local law by the new colonial ruler, the United Kingdom. An English version of the Dutch compilation was prepared, from which was derived a translation into Tamil.[301] The *Thesawalamai* has not meaningfully been changed by the Sri Lankan Parliament since the country became independent in 1948 and has been continuously applied by the government courts.[302] It contains a range of applicable norms on property, inheritance, adoption, gifts, mortgage, sales, loans, as well as obviously outdated sections on slavery and the sale of children.[303] The *Thesawalamai* is a striking example of the 'invention of tradition' so brilliantly described by Terry Ranger in the context of African colonialism, whereby European administrators driven by a sense of respect for their own tradition set out to write down what they felt were local mores, resulting in a body of reified rules crystallising the converging interests of colonial rulers and local elites more than the complex and flexible body of norms that was applied in precolonial times.[304] The *Thesawalamai* does not fit easily in the all-encompassing claims to legislative sovereignty expressed by states. Indeed, Kumaravadivel Guruparan persuasively argues that "in the eyes of the Tamil people, if the Sri Lankan Parliament is to enact a reform process to the *Thesawalamai*, it will be inherently illegitimate", because there is little meaningful representation of the Tamil minority in that legislative body.[305] There are echoes here of the relationship between Indigenous peoples and their legal traditions, a form of law that can both be truly 'legal' and at the same time partly escape the law-making authority of the state.[306] In that

301 The evolution of the Thesawalamai is described in Henry Wijayakone Tambiah, *The Laws and Customs of the Tamils of Jaffna* (Women's Education Research Centre 2009).

302 Guruparan (n 242) 52.

303 HF Mutukisna, *The Tésawalamai; Or the Laws and Customs of the Malabars of Jaffna: Promulgated by the Dutch Government of Ceylon in the Year 1707, and Referred to in the Government Regulation No. 18 of December 9, 1806* (GJA Skeen, Government Printer 1891).

304 Terence Ranger, 'The Invention of Tradition in Colonial Africa' in Eric Hobsbawm and Terence Ranger (eds), *The Invention of Traditions* (Cambridge University Press 1983) 212, 261–262.

305 Guruparan (n 242) 55.

306 A claim by a state to freely alter the legal tradition of an Indigenous people would seem contrary to the right of peoples to self-determination as recognised in international law: Jessie Hohmann and Marc Weller, *The UN Declaration on the Rights of Indigenous Peoples: A Commentary* (Oxford University Press 2018) 143–146.

context, the LTTE modernisation of the *Thesawalamai* to eliminate references to slavery, remove caste discrimination, and ensure gender equality might seem comparatively more legitimate inasmuch as it was an entity more closely related to the Tamil community than the government of Sri Lanka.

The range of subjects covered by insurgent jurisdiction in civil matters is very wide. Rebels norms are known to have related to, inter alia:[307] public governance (the form of local authority, its powers, electoral process, deliberation procedures, finances, minimal gender representation), transport (speed limits, public transports, regulation of the taxi industry), land use planning (regulation of agriculture, deforestation, erection of new buildings, location of houses of worship and religious services), health (public sanitation, rules on proximity of polluting activities to sources of potable water, provision of medical services), education (appointment of teachers, maintenance of schools, operating hours, curriculum, gender-specific standards), environmental protection (norms specifically referring to global warming and climate change, sustainable farming, protection of endangered species of flora and fauna, prohibition of logging precious wood, use of genetically modified seeds), hunting and fishing (what species, with what tools or weapons, at what time, and in what places), labour relations (minimum wage, fair conditions of work including hours and safety), consumer protection (fair pricing, sale of counterfeit goods), commercial licensing, sports, culture, family (marriage, polygamy, divorce, alimony, adoption, inheritance), and lifestyle (personal appearance including length of hair, beard; prohibition of earrings for men, (short) skirts for women, long pants for men, selling or drinking alcohol, smoking cigarettes, consumption of drugs, listening to music, sexual relations including infidelity, same-sex relations). In some ways, insurgent jurisdiction extends beyond matters covered by state law, including the regulation of activities illegal under state law such as prostitution or drug trafficking, which have been regulated like any other activity in some insurgent jurisdictions (e.g. by the FARC and the Taliban).[308] The prohibition of witchcraft in the FARC *Manual de Convivencia* offers a different model, covering a concern that simply did not merit regulation in the eyes of the official legislator.[309] Unlike state jurisdiction, rebel jurisdiction does not tend to be comprehensive, covering all issues; it tends, rather, to mirror the common concerns of the local population and the priorities of the non-state armed group. That said, it is in fact difficult to think of something that has not been seized upon by rebel jurisdiction in one armed conflict or another. There does not seem to be any norm of public international

[307] These are taken from the different case studies in each of the four chapters of this book.

[308] Nicolás Espinosa Menéndez, 'La Justicia guerrillera en Colombia. Elementos de análisis para los retos de la transición política en una zona de control insurgente (el caso del Piedemonte amazónico)' [2016] Estudios latinoamericanos 87, 95.

[309] Carrillo (n 245) 193 (Art. 6, Normas de convivencia comunitaria, region de El Pato).

law that removes non-penal subject-matters as per se beyond the jurisdiction of non-state armed groups. On the other hand, international human rights law will impose on armed groups, as it does for states, very significant limitations as to the content of rebel norms on any given subject.

In conclusion, the jurisdiction *ratione materiae* of non-state armed groups in criminal and civil matters knows few identifiable limitations under public international law. There does not seem to be any norm of international law that requires insurgents to retain the laws of the state if they come to assume effective authority over a territory and population. On the other hand, unlike for belligerent occupiers in situations of international armed conflicts, there is no explicit norm of international law that affirms the law-making power of armed groups in areas under their authority. That said, the need expressed in Article 43 of the 1907 Hague Regulations to establish and maintain public order and public life in occupied territory seems equally relevant to rebel areas in non-international armed conflict. The fundamental need for public governance equally obtains in internal conflicts and stands buttressed by the duty to ensure respect of international humanitarian law and to secure human rights. With the limited exception related to the criminalisation of direct participation in hostilities by government soldiers, the limits imposed under international law on rebel jurisdiction relate not to subject-matter itself but to the substance of norms and the manner in which they are administered by insurgents.

D. Personal Jurisdiction of Armed Groups

Non-state armed groups have, in various armed conflicts, exercised jurisdiction over different categories of persons, whether in relation to penal or civil matters. Are there, under public international law, limits to the personal jurisdiction of armed groups that would place some persons beyond the reach of the rebel administration of justice? Distinct arguments, of variable depth and persuasiveness, relate to four categories of persons: a group's own fighters, civilian persons (whether physical or corporate), members of other armed groups, and members of the official armed forces of a state (whether the territorial state or other states).

The jurisdiction of non-state armed groups over their own members would seem to pose the least difficulty, and yet even that has given rise to opposition.[310] During the civil war in Nepal, for example, the United Nations Office of the High Commissioner for Human Rights in that country urged the CPN-M rebel group to "set up an internal mechanism at the national level to oversee

[310] Doswald-Beck (n 189) 491.

internal investigations into allegations of abuses by CPN-M cadres".[311] Noting that this armed group had, at least on one occasion, taken the exceptional step of handing over to the state three of its own members accused of killing a civilian, the United Nations insisted that processes internal to the group "cannot substitute for criminal investigations by police, independent investigations and prosecutions carried out in a state court".[312] It should be noted that handing over individuals to state courts is not always an option, not only for obvious political reasons (this would be seen as a betrayal by other members of the group) but also for legal reasons if, as is not rarely the case in war-afflicted countries, the state's own administration of justice is marred by violations of human rights. Under the principle articulated by the European Court of Human Rights in *Soering*, sometimes borrowing the refugee law label of *non-refoulement*, the surrender of an individual to an actor likely to deny fundamental rights of that individual would be a violation of human rights law.[313] The jurisdiction *ratione personae* of non-state armed groups over their own members reflects the requirement that armed groups be under responsible command.[314] As noted by the ICRC in its commentary to Additional Protocol II, the idea of responsible command implies "imposing a discipline in the name of a de facto authority", which in turn speaks to jurisdiction over members of the non-state group.[315] The duty to 'respect' international humanitarian law under Common Article 1 and customary law, applicable to all categories of armed conflicts and belligerents, likewise points to a requirement of responsible command and internal discipline.[316] This is reinforced by the doctrine of command responsibility in international criminal law, whereby a superior or commander in an armed opposition group will be held criminally accountable for failing to sanction war crimes committed by subordinates. As discussed in Chapter 2, this doctrine has been codified in Article 28 of the Rome Statute and was applied by the ICC to the leader of a non-state armed group in the *Bemba* trial, in which the availability of a rebel court was a key element.[317] The ineluctable conclusion is that insurgent jurisdiction *ratione personae* extends, without any possible doubt, to an armed group's own members.

[311] UN Office of the High Commissioner for Human Rights in Nepal, 'Human Rights Abuses by the CPN-M—Summary of Concerns' (September 2006) 8.

[312] ibid at 3–4, 8.

[313] ECHR, *Soering v United Kingdom*, Appl. No 14038/88, 7 July 1989.

[314] Art. 1(1), 1907 Hague Regulations; Art. 4(A)(2)(a), Third Geneva Convention; Art. 1, Additional Protocol II. These cover non-state armed groups in both international and non-international armed conflicts.

[315] ICRC, *Commentary on the 1977 Additional Protocols* (n 288) 1352.

[316] ICRC, *Commentary on the Second Geneva Convention* (Cambridge University Press 2017) para 154.

[317] See Chapter 2, Section IV.B.i.

Rebel jurisdiction over civilians represents the assertion of juridical authority that has been the most widespread in zones of armed conflicts and consequently the most systematically resisted by states. From the point of view of many non-state armed groups, claims of jurisdiction over the civilian population are a central tool of governance that can both ensure security for the group and amount to the provision of a public good that can elicit local support for the insurgency.[318] The production of a mix of obedience and support are thus the objectives pursued by the application of rebel justice to civilians. Strangely perhaps, this central feature of non-international armed conflict is something of a legal black hole in international humanitarian law, which does not explicitly address the modalities of the exercise of non-violent power by armed groups over the civilian population. The concern of states that explains this silence is, of course, that any degree of regulation inevitably brings with it a degree of legitimation.

Despite the absence of any provision that explicitly speaks to rebel jurisdiction over civilians, several norms implicitly confirm that the extension of jurisdiction *ratione personae* to the civilian population is lawful under international law. A first norm is the duty to prosecute or extradite authors of war crimes, claimed by the ICRC to be a customary standard applicable in international as well as non-international armed conflicts.[319] As war crimes may be committed by civilians, extending the duty to prosecute to armed groups would implicitly also confer jurisdiction *ratione personae* over civilians.[320] As noted in Chapter 2, however, there is some doubt as to whether sufficient state practice and *opinio juris* underpin a claim that this has indeed matured into a customary obligation for states, undermining any possible extension to non-state armed groups.[321] There is surer footing for the claim that the duty to 'ensure respect' for international humanitarian law is applicable to armed groups under customary law.[322] This duty corresponds to an obligation to prevent and punish violations of humanitarian law in situations under the effective authority of an armed group.[323] Such violations, as noted, could have been carried out by combatants or civilians. There is thus not just a right but a duty, under customary international law, for

[318] Arjona, *Rebelocracy* (n 235) 45–47.

[319] Henckaerts and Doswald-Beck (n 255) Rule 158.

[320] René Provost, *International Human Rights and Humanitarian Law* (Cambridge University Press 2002) 79–89.

[321] Chapter 2, Section IV.B.i.

[322] Henckaerts and Doswald-Beck (n 255) Rule 139; ICRC, *Commentary on the Second Geneva Convention* (n 316) paras 153–154; Robin Geiß, 'The Obligations to Respect and Ensure Respect' in Andrew Clapham, Paola Gaeta, and Marco Sassòli (eds), *The 1949 Geneva Conventions: A Commentary* (Oxford University Press 2015) 116.

[323] Luigi Condorelli and Laurence Boisson de Chazournes, 'Quelques Remarques à Propos de l'obligation Des États de "respecter et Faire Respecter" Le Droit International Humanitaire "En Toutes Circonstances"' in Christophe Swinarski (ed), *Études et essais sur le droit international humanitaire et sur les principes de la Croix-Rouge en l'honneur de Jean Pictet* (Nijhoff 1984) 25.

insurgents to claim jurisdiction over civilians, at least in relation to violations of humanitarian law. This is echoed and amplified by the wider duty to 'ensure' or 'secure' human rights, understood to be applicable to non-state armed groups wielding authority over a civilian population. Once human rights law is understood to impose obligations directly upon armed groups, a point more fully explored in the next section, there is a duty to protect fundamental rights and freedoms against violations at the hands of anyone, including members of the civilian population. The duty is captured in the corresponding individual right to a remedy under treaty and customary law.[324] For example, in many parts of Colombia in which the FARC was a dominant presence, organised criminal bands engaged in drug trafficking were an important source of violations of fundamental rights attaching to the person and property of the civilian population.[325] Fulfilment of the duty to protect human rights can be done by allowing the state's judicial system to operate in territory under rebel authority, or by establishing insurgent courts with jurisdiction over civilians. Given that there will be situations, such as in Colombia or Sri Lanka, where the state is unable to administer justice, the duty to protect human rights implies a rebel jurisdiction *ratione personae* over the civilian population.

The applicability of human rights obligations to non-state armed groups reflects a jurisdiction over civilians that covers a much wider spectrum of interests than those protected under international humanitarian law. It also brings up the question of rebel jurisdiction over corporations, both to regulate and to constitute them. There is an emerging consensus that corporate actors are sometimes involved directly or indirectly in the commission of human rights violations, not rarely in situations of armed conflict. For instance, there have been credible reports that transnational corporations were involved in massive and systematic violations of human rights in the non-international armed conflicts in Sudan and Colombia.[326] Corporate actors may also fall under the jurisdiction of armed groups in relation to environmental regulation or consumer protection, two fields in which rebels in various conflicts have adopted binding standards. The Kurdish Regional Government has established a Kurdistan Board of Investment to encourage foreign ventures in the region, regulated by Investment Law No.

[324] See Dinah Shelton, *Remedies in International Human Rights Law* (3d edn, Oxford University Press 2015) 58–80.

[325] Arjona, *Rebelocracy* (n 235) 93.

[326] See: Carlos Lopez and Sonia Ost, 'UNCHR in South Sudan Points to Oil Companies' Complicity in Gross Human Rights Abuses' *Opinio Juris* (15 March 2019), online: <https://opiniojuris.org/2019/03/15/united-nations-commission-on-human-rights-in-south-sudan-points-to-oil-companies-complicity-in-gross-human-rights-abuses/> accessed 17 February 2020; Adriaan Alsema, 'Chiquita Guilty of Crimes against Humanity in Colombia?' *Colombia News | Colombia Reports* (3 February 2017), online: <https://colombiareports.com/chiquita-guilty-crimes-humanity-colombia/> accessed 17 February 2020.

4 of 2006.[327] This also converges with longstanding discussions of the possibility of criminal accountability for corporations involved in the commission of crimes against international law, now recognised in Article 46C of the Statute of the African Court of Justice and Human Rights, as amended by the Malabo Protocol.[328] There may be limits related to territorial jurisdiction that curtail rebel jurisdiction, but otherwise once the idea of rebel jurisdiction is accepted, there seems to be no reason to exclude corporations—whether local or foreign—from the reach of insurgent justice.

The possibility that non-state armed groups may not only regulate corporations but also constitute them may seem (yet again) outlandish. Within the parameters that have delimited the present study, namely, the administration of justice by non-state armed groups in situations of armed conflicts, there is no known example of a group adopting their own legal norms to provide for the registration of local or foreign corporations. In Iraqi Kurdistan, the national Companies Law 21 (1997) of Iraq is relied upon locally to register new corporations in the KRI, which are thereafter subject to taxation by the KRG.[329] In north-east Sri Lanka, the LTTE-controlled Bank of Tamileelam operated eleven branches between 1994 and 2009, receiving deposits and clearing cheques with other state-approved banks, without a licence from the Sri Lankan Central Bank. The bank was reportedly not owned directly by the LTTE, and its specific corporate structure is not known.[330] In a slightly different setting, some unrecognised governments not in situations of armed conflict have adopted company laws that allow for new companies to be registered. For example Somaliland, an autonomous territory not recognised internationally, enacted a company law inspired by US model law in 2018.[331] It is interesting to note that the United Kingdom and Australia both have statutes that provide for the recognition of corporations established under the laws of a non-recognised foreign entity, framed broadly enough to encompass a company law that would be adopted by a non-state armed group wielding authority over a territory.[332]

327 Available at <http://kurdistaninvestment.org/docs/Investment%20Law.pdf>.

328 See: Carsten Stahn, 'Liberals vs Romantics: Challenges of an Emerging Corporate International Criminal Law' (2018) 50 Case Western Reserve Journal of International Law 91; Joanna Kyriakakis, 'Corporations before International Criminal Courts: Implications for the International Criminal Justice Project' (2017) 30 Leiden Journal of International Law 221.

329 General Directorate for Company Registration, KRG Ministry of Trade and Industry, 'Services and Information', online: <https://www.crkrg.org/en/services-information/>.

330 Geert De Clercq, 'Tamileelam Bank' *Reuters* (16 March 2004) <https://www.sangam.org/articles/view/?id=260> accessed 17 February 2020 (there is a mention of 'the LTTE's many companies', but no detail is given); 'LTTE Operated 11 Bank Branches in North before Its Defeat' *Deccan Herald* (15 February 2010); Mampilly (n 20) 110.

331 Somaliland Company Law No 80/2018, online: <http://www.somalilandlaw.com/somaliland_company_law.html>.

332 UK Foreign Corporations Act, 1991 c44 s 1; Australia Foreign Corporations (Application of Laws) Act, Act No 183 of 1989 (s 9(1) refers to "entities created, organised or operating under the law

Claims of jurisdiction *ratione personae* by a non-state armed group over the member of a different armed group raise different issues. It is not rare, in situations of both international and non-international armed conflicts, that there are multiple armed groups directly participating in the conflict either as distinct belligerent parties or in association with a state belligerent. Can an armed group prosecute members of another group who have been captured? As a matter of practice, it is notable that the YPG in Rojava (in Syria) and the KRG in Iraq both detain significant numbers of Islamic State fighters captured on the battlefield, some of whom have already been prosecuted and convicted by the courts of these two Kurdish entities. In Colombia, there were at some point five distinct non-state armed groups and fourteen paramilitary groups, some loosely associated under the umbrella of the *Autodefensas unidas de Colombia*, variously fighting each other and the state armed forces in changing patterns.[333] For the FARC, being a member of a paramilitary group was usually sufficient ground for summary execution, without the need for a very elaborate procedure.[334] As a matter of law, the limits of insurgent jurisdiction *ratione materiae*, discussed in the previous pages, suggest that a non-state armed group could not criminalise mere participation in hostilities by enemy fighters because, by definition, they would not be doing so from a position of subservience to the authority of the armed group.[335] However, it was argued that no such limit obtains in relation to crimes against international law committed by members of other non-state armed groups.[336] This would suggest that while insurgent jurisdiction is limited in relation to subject-matter and place, there is no obstacle to an armed group claiming personal jurisdiction over members of other groups. This conclusion is buttressed by the highly unusual position adopted by France that French nationals who had gone to Syria to join the Islamic State and were later captured by Kurdish forces should be prosecuted by Kurdish courts in Rojava for the crimes against international law that they committed.[337] The United Kingdom, albeit in a more ambiguous fashion, seems to subscribe to the French position.[338]

applied by the people in a foreign state or place"). See Thomas D Grant, *The Recognition of States: Law and Practice in Debate and Evolution* (Greenwood Publishing Group 1999) 67–70.

333 Arjona, *Rebelocracy* (n 235) 94–95.

334 Interview with FARC Commander Edoardo (July 2016).

335 See supra (n 275) and accompanying text.

336 See supra (n 286) and accompanying text.

337 See: Le Point Magazine, 'Le gouvernement souhaite que les djihadistes françaises soient jugées en Syrie' *Le Point* (4 January 2018), online: <http://www.lepoint.fr/monde/le-gouvernement-souhaite-que-les-djihadistes-francaises-soient-jugees-en-syrie-04-01-2018-2183934_24.php> accessed 18 July 2018.

338 The UK Foreign Office has said that British ISIS fighters should be prosecuted "in the most appropriate jurisdiction, which will often be in the region where their offences have been committed": Dan Sabbagh, 'Syrian Kurds to Put ISIS Fighters from Dozens of Countries on Trial' *The Guardian* (6 February 2020), online: <https://www.theguardian.com/world/2020/feb/06/

Confronted with the refusal of the states of nationality of foreign fighters to repatriate them, the Kurdish authority in Rojava stated that it was engaged in bilateral talks with these governments to obtain support for prosecution before its non-state courts.[339] This example is remarkable in that claims of personal jurisdiction over members of another armed group are not only not resisted but in fact solicited by other states, despite a link of nationality between the detained individuals and these foreign states.

The jurisdiction *ratione personae* of non-state armed groups over their enemy seems lawful in the case of non-state fighters, but does that extend to members of state armed forces (including troops of the territorial state)? This question was addressed in *Sakhanh*, insofar as Sakhanh raised, as a defence, that the killing of the members of the Syrian armed forces was legitimate as it had been preceded by a judgment of a court of the rebel Free Syrian Army. It could also relate to troops of a foreign state, either in the context of a transnational non-international armed conflict between a state and an armed opposition group located abroad (for instance the 2006 conflict between Hezbollah and Israel), or in a purely internal armed conflict in which the local state has invited foreign troops to support its war effort (for instance the ongoing conflict in Afghanistan). It was suggested earlier, in the discussion of rebel jurisdiction *ratione materiae*, that the state and armed opposition group are not in equal positions under international law, owing to the fact that the state is presumed to have jurisdiction over the whole of its national territory, while insurgents can come to acquire jurisdiction over territory in which it wields effective authority. This explains why a state may lawfully criminalise direct participation in hostilities by rebels but that the reverse does not hold. With respect to other matters, such as crimes against international law or violations of rebel law committed while in captivity, there is no obstacle at the level of subject-matter jurisdiction. The understandable opposition, if not outrage, of governments at the suggestion that rebel courts may have jurisdiction over their soldiers seems to reflect a conviction that armed groups and the state are

syrian-kurds-to-put-isis-fighters-from-dozens-of-countries-on-trial> accessed 19 February 2020. The refusal or hesitation by some other governments to repatriate their own nationals in similar circumstances suggest that they share the stance adopted by France, a position criticised by the United States: 'A Washington, Américains et Européens étalent leurs divisions sur le sort des djihadistes détenus en Syrie' *Le Monde.fr* (14 November 2019), online: <https://www.lemonde.fr/international/article/2019/11/14/washington-critique-l-attitude-de-pays-europeens-sur-le-sort-de-leurs-djihadistes-detenus-en-syrie_6019200_3210.html> accessed 18 February 2020. The broader legal significance of this recognition of insurgent justice by third states is discussed in Chapter 4, Section III.

[339] Hind Hassan, 'Thousands of Foreign ISIS Fighters in Syria Will Go on Trial Starting in March' *Vice* (19 February 2020), online: <https://www.vice.com/en_us/article/pkezqy/thousands-of-foreign-isis-fighters-in-syria-will-go-on-trial-starting-in-march> accessed 19 February 2020.

in fundamentally different positions, under the law. While that is often the case under domestic law, there is nothing in international humanitarian law that replicates this radical legal asymmetry. Need it be reminded, there is no accepted concept of privileged belligerency in the law of non-international armed conflict, no equivalent to Article 43(2) of Additional Protocol I that proclaims a protected right to directly participate in hostilities in an international conflict, even for members of the state's armed forces.[340] When Swedish courts examined the legality of the conviction by a Free Syrian Army court of several soldiers for murder and rape, they did not seem especially troubled by the assertion of rebel jurisdiction *ratione personae* over government combatants.[341] In that case, in a pattern that is quite common, there was no obvious alternative forum to ensure accountability for the crimes allegedly committed by these soldiers. Altogether, these elements suggest that there is no norm of international law that places state combatants beyond the jurisdiction *ratione personae* of insurgent justice.

There seems to be no basis, in international humanitarian law or in other fields of international law, to exclude any specific category of individuals from the jurisdiction *ratione personae* of insurgent justice. Rebel courts may thus claim jurisdiction, in penal or civil matters, over a group's own members, civilian individuals or corporations, fighters from other groups, or members of the armed forces of the territorial or third states. As we saw previously, there are limits to rebel jurisdiction in relation to subject-matter, and the whole is constrained by the limited reach of jurisdiction *ratione loci* discussed above.

In conclusion, the very idea of insurgent jurisdiction may seem provocative, if not simply an oxymoron. Once the reality of the rebel administration of justice in conflict zones is acknowledged, and once it is accepted that its blanket illegality under municipal law is not reflected in international law, then the concept of jurisdiction becomes a necessary legal device to map out the nature and extent of insurgent justice. Jurisdiction is a contested and imprecise notion in public international law when applied to state powers, and so it should come as no surprise that the guidance it offers for the authority of non-state armed groups is incomplete. Nevertheless, as seen in the preceding pages, claims and objections related to the extension of rebel justice to certain subject-matters, persons, and places can be critically examined through the lens of jurisdiction in a manner that clarifies the analysis of their legality under international law.

[340] Gérard Aivo, *Le statut de combattant dans les conflits armés non internationaux: étude critique de droit international humanitaire* (Bruylant 2013). The broader implications of this are discussed in Chapter 2, Section IV.A.ii.

[341] *Sakhanh* (n 278).

III. Due Process in Rebel Courts

The recurring, central critique of the rebel administration of justice is that it fails to afford the minimal procedural fairness without which law and courts are merely a façade hiding the arbitrary use of power. Some have argued that non-state armed groups in conflict zones are structurally unable to deliver the procedural guarantees that are the defining feature of genuine administration of justice, and therefore that rebel courts can never be lawful or legitimate.[342] We have seen in Chapter 2 that the argument for the outright illegality of insurgent justice under international humanitarian and human rights law is not persuasive, and indeed international law seems to leave open the possibility that armed groups may regularly constitute courts. That conclusion in turn demands an articulation of the procedural guarantees that will then be required under international law as the minimal qualities that define the fair administration of justice.

The content of due process standards applicable to rebel courts operating in situations of armed conflicts combines elements of international humanitarian law and international human rights law, which have developed over time. Common Article 3 was the earliest to define the procedural guarantees demanded of regularly constituted courts, albeit vaguely as those "recognized as indispensable by civilized peoples". The substance of due process was sharpened considerably with the adoption of the two Additional Protocols in 1977, each offering a catalogue of procedural guarantees applicable in international (Art. 75(4), Protocol I) and non-international (Art. 6, Protocol II) armed conflicts. The intervening emergence of human rights obligations into positive international law explains the move to greater specificity, and indeed the two protocols directly borrowed from Articles 14–15 of the International Covenant on Civil and Political Rights (ICCPR).[343] The iteration of due process in human rights law is thus relevant to the rebel administration of justice in two different ways: first, as a relevant guide to the interpretation of the Geneva Conventions and Protocols, and second, as obligations directly applicable to non-state armed groups under public international law. Unless some element of humanitarian law dictates otherwise, the interpretation of procedural guarantees applicable to insurgent justice will be presumed to be similar under both bodies of norms.

Because international human rights law occupies a central place in defining procedural guarantees, it is important to establish, more clearly than has been done so far, the basis upon which human rights law is applicable to non-state armed groups (A). The analysis then turns to consider the ways in which due

[342] Zegveld (n 263) 72–73; Cedric Ryngaert and Jean d'Aspremont, 'Third Report on the Responsibility of Non-State Actors' (International Law Association 2014) 7.

[343] ICRC, *Commentary on the 1977 Additional Protocols* (n 288) 1398.

process guarantees must be adapted to the specific context of the administration of justice in conflict zones, for both state and non-state justice (B). The specific elements of a fair trial applicable to rebel justice are thereafter mapped out (C).

A. Sources of Applicable Procedural Obligations for Non-State Armed Groups

Which due process guarantees are legally required before an insurgent court depends on the sources of such obligations. The starting point of any conversation on obligations arising out of international law for non-state armed groups must necessarily be international humanitarian law. How exactly humanitarian law can directly bind armed groups is sketched as a preamble to an explanation of why the applicability of human rights standards is an important issue, leading to discuss the relationship of human rights to non-state armed groups.

As mentioned, public international law includes different catalogues of due process guarantees that vary significantly. For international armed conflicts, Article 75(4) of Additional Protocol I includes an extensive list of procedural guarantees benefitting anyone affected by the conflict. This supplements the provisions, often articulated in more details, benefitting prisoners of war (Arts. 82–106, Third Geneva Convention) and those applicable in situations of belligerent occupation (Arts. 65–77, Fourth Geneva Convention). The scope of due process guarantees in Article 6 of Additional Protocol II, applicable to non-international armed conflicts in which armed groups control at least part of national territory, is less extensive than those included in Article 75(4) of Protocol I. Finally, the sliding scale under international humanitarian law concludes with Common Article 3, applicable to the most limited situations of armed conflict, in which there is no list but rather a general reference to procedural guarantees recognised under international law. We might stop and ponder for a moment how these treaty norms, agreed upon by most states, relate to non-state armed groups. Such groups can be active in both international and non-international armed conflicts, and in all cases will be parties to armed conflicts without having ratified any of the relevant treaties.

How do we explain the binding character of humanitarian law treaties for non-state armed groups?[344] The closest one gets to formal ratification of a treaty in this context is the declaration by a national liberation movement that it undertakes to apply the Geneva Conventions and Protocol I, thus creating legally binding

[344] For a detailed discussion, see Katharine Fortin, *The Accountability of Armed Groups Under Human Rights Law* (Oxford University Press 2017) 178–203.

obligations under these instruments (Art. 96(3)(c), Protocol I). This is the rarest of occurrences, with a single valid declaration having been made (by the Polisario Front) since the Protocol's adoption in 1977.[345] Some unilateral declarations have been issued by armed groups declaring their intention to abide by the Geneva Conventions, in a manner that is not entertained by these conventions and therefore remains extra-conventional.[346] Otherwise, the bindingness of humanitarian law conventions for non-state armed groups is typically explained as deriving from a state's ability to create rights and obligations in international law for individuals and groups under its jurisdiction, often referred to as the 'legislative jurisdiction' theory.[347] There is little doubt that states intended armed groups to be bound by Common Article 3 and Additional Protocol II, as evident from the references to 'parties to the conflict' as opposed to the 'High Contracting Parties'.[348] On the other hand, invoking the state's authority to create obligations for its nationals may not be the approach most likely to generate compliance by an armed group at war with that state. Alternatively, the approach skips over the question of bindingness for the group and focusses instead on obligations of individuals.[349] This approach is buttressed by the solidification of international criminal law into positive international law, including the listing of the deprivation of the "rights of fair and regular trial" as a grave breach of Protocol I (Art. 85(4)(e), Protocol I; Art. 8(2)(a)(vi), Rome Statute) and the criminalisation in the Rome Statute of violation of a right to be tried by a regularly constituted court under Common Article 3 (Art. 8(2)(c)(iv), Rome Statute). The individualising approach is more persuasive when applied to crimes that correspond to individual action, but less so vis-à-vis a practice like the administration of justice that is collective and institutional in its approach. The aim of the requirement of the regular constitution of courts and respect for procedural guarantees is to orient the behaviour of belligerents, whether state or non-state, much more than individual combatants.

345 See Andrew Clapham, 'The Concept of International Armed Conflict' in Andrew Clapham, Paola Gaeta, and Marco Sassoli (eds), *The 1949 Geneva Conventions: A Commentary* (Oxford University Press 2015) 19–21.

346 Sandesh Sivakumaran, 'Binding Armed Opposition Groups' (2006) 55 International & Comparative Law Quarterly 369, 387–388. Unilateral declarations by armed groups remain the exception rather than the rule, and as such cannot be taken as a satisfactory explanation of the source of obligations under humanitarian law. Otherwise, as provided by paragraph 3 of Common Article 3, parties to a non-international armed conflict may enter into a special agreement to make the Geneva Conventions more broadly applicable to the conflict: ICRC, *Commentary on the Second Geneva Convention* (n 316) paras 868–887. Of course, this take the binding nature of Common Article 3 as a starting point rather than provide an explanation for it.

347 Jann K Kleffner, 'The Applicability of International Humanitarian Law to Organized Armed Groups' (2011) 93 International Review of the Red Cross 443; Sivakumaran, 'Binding Armed Opposition Groups' (n 346) 381.

348 ICRC, *Commentary on the Fourth Geneva Convention* (n 258) 37.

349 Kleffner (n 347) 449–451.

A final variation relies on the idea of *effectivité* to derive the bindingness of conventional obligations from the *de facto* control exercised by armed groups over a certain territory and population. The idea here is that ratification of the treaties binds the state, regardless of the identity of the governing authority. When armed groups come to wield state-like authority, they then take over *de facto* as a governing entity of the state under international law.[350] As mentioned briefly in Chapter 1, this is reflected in the International Law Commission Articles on State Responsibility covering the exercise of governmental authority in the absence of the state (Art. 9) and situations in which an insurrectional movement becomes the government of the state (Art. 10).[351] While the administration of justice certainly constitutes an element of governmental authority, both provisions are retrospective in nature and ultimately geared towards imposing responsibility on the state rather than explaining the existence of international obligations for armed groups. Ultimately, the binding nature of conventional obligations for non-state armed groups under the Geneva Conventions and Protocols remains caught in a paradox: while there is a universal consensus that armed groups are indeed bound by these treaties, public international law fails to provide a fully satisfactory explanation for this binding character.[352] In many ways, the sword that cuts through the Gordian knot of the basis of treaty obligations for armed groups under the Geneva Conventions has been the invocation of customary law. Because custom is not grounded in the express consent of the state, we escape the state-centric logic of treaty obligations in favour of a disembodied international community that can more easily encompass non-state actors like armed groups.[353]

The theoretical hurdles to explaining the binding nature of humanitarian treaties for armed groups are compounded when one turns to human rights treaties. Whereas it was agreed upon, from the moment when non-international armed conflicts were first regulated with the adoption of Common Article 3 in 1949, that states intended to create treaty obligations for armed insurgents, no such intent was present at the adoption of the main human rights conventions. On the contrary, rooted in the atrocities committed during World War II, human rights law was presented as erecting a bulwark against abuses of fundamental

350 Roger Pinto, 'Les règles du droit international concernant la guerre civile' (1965) 114 Recueil des Cours 453, 528.

351 See Chapter 1, Section III.B. See Fortin (n 344) 249–254; Kleffner (n 347) 451–454.

352 ICRC, *Commentary on the Second Geneva Convention* (n 316) paras 527–530.

353 As noted by Kleffner, even this explanation is not beyond challenge if only state practice is taken as grounding custom, as did the ICRC in the preparation of its landmark study on customary humanitarian law: Kleffner (n 347) 454–455; Fortin (n 344) 324–330; Anthea Roberts and Sandesh Sivakumaran, 'Lawmaking by Nonstate Actors: Engaging Armed Groups in the Creation of International Humanitarian Law' (2012) 37 Yale Journal of International Law 107; Robert McCorquodale, 'An Inclusive International Legal System' (2004) 17 Leiden Journal of International Law 477.

rights and freedoms by governments.[354] Even more than for humanitarian law, the suggestion that non-state actors like armed groups could be tasked with the duty to protect human rights was opposed as the usurpation of the legitimate, sovereign authority of the state. Before turning to consider the possible sources of human rights obligations for non-state armed groups in conflict zones, one may ask whether a turn to human rights law is indeed necessary in the context of the rebel administration of justice, or whether on the opposite international humanitarian law offers a sufficient foundation for legal analysis. After all, as noted previously, the Geneva Conventions and Protocols do provide for due process guarantees before insurgent courts in both international and non-international armed conflicts.

Nevertheless, three distinct reasons justify the legal significance of directly applicable human rights obligations. First, while procedural guarantees included in Additional Protocols I and II were inspired by human rights treaties and are therefore often very similar, human rights law has developed to a considerably greater extent than humanitarian law. This is so both because human rights law is continuously applicable, as opposed to the applicability of humanitarian law limited to situations of armed conflicts, and because of the significantly greater institutionalisation of human rights enforcement, with courts and other bodies producing a stream of opinions expanding and refining the substance of all protected human rights. Consequently, as a matter of volume, there is simply more human rights law than humanitarian law, at least when it comes to due process guarantees. Human rights can of course be invoked as an aid to interpreting humanitarian law, but there are limits to importing though interpretation obligations that are not binding on a legal actor.

Second, humanitarian law was designed to regulate relations across the battlefield, marked by hostility. It was not intended to apply to a belligerent's treatment of its own combatant or—at least in international armed conflicts—to its own civilian population. Some obligations are framed in more all-encompassing terms for non-international armed conflicts, being applicable "at any time and in any place whatsoever" (Common Article 3; Art. 4, Protocol II), and the ICC has found that war crimes can be committed within an armed group, at least in regard to the sexual abuse of child soldiers.[355] Still, humanitarian law in general requires

[354] See: Samuel Moyn, *The Last Utopia: Human Rights in History* (Harvard University Press 2010) 44–83; Thomas Buergenthal, 'The Normative and Institutional Evolution of International Human Rights' (1997) 19 Human Rights Quarterly 703.

[355] ICC, *Prosecutor v Ntaganda*, Appeal Judgment on Challenge to Jurisdiction, ICC-01/04-02/06 OA5, 15 June 2017, para 63–65. This approach was extended in a decision of the Constitutional Court of Colombia to a female FARC fighter who was subjected by the group to a forced abortion by involuntary caesarean: Corte constitucional, Sentencia SU599/19, 11 December 2019, at 58–63, online: <https://www.corteconstitucional.gov.co/Relatoria/2019/SU599-19.htm> accessed 26 February 2020.

a nexus to the conflict, and procedural guarantees in Article 6 of Protocol II are declared applicable to prosecutions 'related to the armed conflict'; as such, humanitarian law is not meant to entirely displace the application of ordinary law. Thus, a standard reading of humanitarian law would not deem it applicable to the prosecution of a fighter before a court-martial of his own group.[356] Likewise, the prosecution before LTTE courts of a civilian who committed sexual exploitation of a child may be taken to lack the nexus to the conflict that underpins the applicability of humanitarian law. I argued in Chapter 2 that the nexus requirement for the rebel administration of justice should be interpreted very broadly, but a conclusion that human rights law is directly applicable avoids that debate entirely with respect to due process guarantees.[357]

Third, procedural guarantees set out in the Geneva Conventions and Protocols are expressly declared to be applicable to criminal prosecutions. One of the recurring themes of this book has been the significance of the rebel administration of justice in non-penal matters, from family law to labour law, disputes in contracts, delicts, property, and so on. These are matters of great importance such that civil trials may result in great injustice if carried out without due process. Unlike humanitarian law conventions, human rights treaties declare due process guarantees to be applicable to both penal and civil matters.[358] Beyond these three main points, further reasons may be invoked as justifying the relevance of directly applying human rights obligations on armed groups, such as the greater availability of supervisory mechanisms under international human rights law, but the point has been made that there is indeed legal significance to the applicability of human rights law to armed groups.

Whether international human rights law binds non-state armed groups directly remains a highly contested issue, although there seems to be a progression towards greater acceptance that it does impose obligations on these groups in some situations.[359] The central concern fuelling resistance to the *de jure*

[356] SCSL, *Prosecutor v Sesay, Kallon and Gbao ('RUF Trial')*, Trial Judgment, SCSL-04-15-T, 2 March 2009, para 1453. That standard view has been challenged by the ICRC in its recent commentary: ICRC, *Commentary on the Third Geneva Convention* (Cambridge University Press 2020) paras 581–583.

[357] See the discussion in Chapter 2, Section IV.B.ii.

[358] Sarah Joseph and Melissa Castan, *The International Covenant on Civil and Political Rights: Cases, Materials, and Commentary* (Oxford University Press, Oxford 2013) 434.

[359] See: Lindsay Moir, *The Law of Internal Armed Conflict* (Cambridge University Press 2002) 194 ("By contrast, human rights obligations are binding on governments only, and the law has not yet reached the stage whereby, during internal armed conflict, insurgents are bound to observe the human rights of government forces, let alone those of opposing insurgents"); Zegveld (n 263) 53 ("The main feature of human rights is that these are rights that people hold against the state only"); Tilman Rodenhäuser, *Organizing Rebellion: Non-State Armed Groups under International Humanitarian Law, Human Rights Law, and International Criminal Law* (Oxford University Press 2018) 118; Zakaria Daboné, *Le droit international public relatif aux groupes armés non étatiques* (Schulthess 2012) 322–332.

application of human rights law to armed groups is that, to an extent even greater than humanitarian law, it will legitimate their authority.[360] Others have argued that a turn to human rights is unnecessary and unjustified given that humanitarian law is the *lex specialis* in situations of armed conflicts, although we have just seen that in the case of due process guarantees there are gaps that would not be covered by humanitarian law.[361] Organisations like the ICRC still maintain a cautious stance when considering the possible applicability of human rights to non-state armed groups.[362]

It is difficult to argue that human rights treaties directly impose duties on non-state armed groups.[363] Many have pointed out that the language of human rights conventions is expressly directed at the imposition of obligations on *states* vis-à-vis persons under their jurisdiction, in contrast to the much more open formulation in the Geneva Conventions and Protocols.[364] The language of human rights treaties thus appears inimical to arguments invoked previously in relation to humanitarian law conventions, according to which states have a 'legislative jurisdiction' that enables them to create rights and obligations for non-state actors directly under public international law. Indeed, Katharine Fortin's close analysis of the *travaux préparatoires* of several major human rights treaties concludes that there is no evidence of any intent to create obligations for non-state armed groups under these treaties.[365] Arguments have been advanced on the basis of armed groups exercising *de facto* powers of the state, to suggest that the state's treaty obligations should transfer over to *de facto* authorities.[366] In some situations, someone exercising *de facto* authority might be deemed to do so on behalf of the state, in which case an argument could be made that treaty obligations are carried over to the non-state actor. However, in situations of armed conflicts in which non-state armed groups are at war with the state, in a manner somewhat

360 Andrew Clapham, *Human Rights Obligations of Non-State Actors* (Oxford University Press 2006) 53–54; Murray (n 234) 10; Andrew Clapham, 'Focusing on Armed Non-State Actors' in Andrew Clapham and Paola Gaeta (eds), *The Oxford Handbook of International Law in Armed Conflict* (Oxford University Press 2014) 786–787.

361 See Derek Jinks, 'International Human Rights Law in Time of Armed Conflict' in Andrew Clapham and Paola Gaeta (eds), *The Oxford Handbook of International Law in Armed Conflict* (Oxford University Press 2014) 662–663; Christian Tomuschat, 'The Applicability of Human Rights Law to Insurgent Movements', *Krisensicherung und Humanitärer Schutz* (Berliner Wissenschafts-Verlag 2004) 575 ('IHL takes precedence whenever there is a conflict between the two sets of norms').

362 See, e.g., ICRC, 'International humanitarian law and the challenges of contemporary armed conflicts: Recommitting to protection in armed conflict on the 70th anniversary of the Geneva Conventions' (ICRC 2019) 43–44.

363 See Rodenhäuser (n 359) 170–176.

364 ibid 115; Zegveld (n 263) 38–39.

365 Fortin (n 344) 238–239. Some treaties have language that is more amenable to a conclusion that they aim to create obligations for non-state actors, such as the Optional Protocol to the Convention on the Rights of the Child on the Involvement of Children in Armed Conflict, but they do not relate to due process guarantees: ibid 226–238.

366 Murray (n 234) 134–137.

similar to situations of belligerent occupation, it is more difficult to persuasively argue that this reasoning should obtain to justify the bindingness of treaty obligations initially consented to by the territorial state.[367]

The position of armed groups in relation to customary human rights law is quite different. For custom, there is of course no singular formulation of norms that can come to necessarily limit their reach to state actors. Neither is customary law broadly grounded in a theory of express consent by a given state to the binding effect of human rights, reflecting instead a more diffuse embrace by the international community, based on a general practice primarily of states but also, to some extent, of other actors.[368] Non-state armed groups have a measure of international legal personality, as evidenced by the fact that they undeniably have obligations pursuant to international humanitarian law, and it is possible that they could be the bearer of obligations under international human rights law. Not every legal person is bound by every customary norm, however, as some are obviously addressed only to some actors, very often states. The question then remains whether armed groups are bound by customary human rights, more precisely those providing for due process guarantees. There is growing consensus in the practice of international organisations and academic writing that the principle of *effectivité* mandates that when non-state armed groups acquire sufficient authority over a territory and population, then they should be bound to exercise it in conformity with customary human rights.[369] The reasoning is well-illustrated by the following passage from Special Rapporteur Ben Emmerson's report on abuses carried by the Islamic State:

> Some still argue that human rights, as a body of law, can only bind States, and cannot or should not apply to non-State armed groups. However, as the Special Rapporteur has previously highlighted in other contexts, a central tenet of international human rights law is that it must keep pace with a changing world. Human rights apply at all times, inherently belong to individuals and are key to individual dignity. Increasingly, non-State armed groups control parts of territories in which populations live. This is the case with ISIL, which now controls large swathes of territory in which millions of individuals live; it has declared itself a "State", and runs both a civil and a military administration, including the establishment of a "court" system. The threshold for ISIL to be bound by human rights obligations has clearly been met. [. . .]

367 Noam Lubell, 'Human Rights Obligations in Military Occupation' (2012) 94 International Review of the Red Cross 317, 336.

368 See International Law Commission, 'Draft Conclusions on Identification of Customary International Law with Commentaires', UN Doc A/73/10 (2018) 130–132.

369 Fortin (n 344) 242–245; Murray (n 234) 120–137; Rodenhäuser (n 359) 158–159; WH Balekjian, *Die Effektivität und die Stellung nichtanerkannter Staaten im Völkerrecht* (Springer 1970) 205.

> In addition, where ISIL engages in violations that are unrelated to the conflict and not direct consequences of it, the governing legal framework should be international human rights law. In practice, this means that ISIL is legally bound to respect freedom of expression, freedom of assembly and freedom of movement. These rights should be protected without discrimination on any of the grounds prohibited by international law. The right to a fair trial should also be guaranteed.[370]

Tilman Rodenhäuser's survey of the practice of independent experts, of the UN Human Rights Council, and of the UN Security Council attests to the fact that, more and more, states are joining in affirming that armed groups do have human rights obligations under customary international law.[371] The conditions under which this occurs and the breadth of the obligations thus imposed are subject to debate, but it is suggested that when armed groups are in a position to effectively administer justice through the operation of regularly constituted courts, then it is beyond challenge that customary human rights law requires compliance with recognised due process guarantees. The rebel administration of justice is thus regulated by a combination of procedural requirements derived from both international humanitarian law and international human rights law.

B. Justice under Stress: Due Process in Conflict Zones

Before we can map out a detailed list of the procedural guarantees required by an insurgent court operating in conflict zones, there are a number of structural questions that need to be addressed. A first question reflects the significance of the particular context in which insurgent courts operate: while human rights norms are primarily designed to regulate the administration of justice in ordinary circumstances, international humanitarian law is tailored to address the specific context of armed conflicts. To what extent do due process requirements in war differ from those applicable in peace, for states as well as non-state armed groups? A second question touches on the identity of the agent administering justice and its impact on applicable due process norms: Are rebel courts and state courts bound by international law to offer the same procedural guarantees, or does law vary according to the legal actor administering justice? The exploration of these two themes will pave the way to the articulation of a number of

370 Ben Emmerson, 'Report of the Special Rapporteur on the promotion and protection of human rights and fundamental freedoms while countering terrorism', UN Doc A/HRC/29/51 (2015) 10.

371 Rodenhäuser (n 359) 159–169.

organising principles that can structure the mapping of due process guarantees before insurgent courts.

i. Due Process in War and Peace

The administration of justice is a process embedded in a web of more general social practices. Despite the fact that the interests embodied in due process guarantees may be constant, it would be illusory to conclude that their protection can remain unaffected by fundamental changes in the broader social context. Situations of armed conflict correspond to the radical alteration of fundamental features of social order, as reflected in the very existence of a legal regime—international humanitarian law—dedicated to the regulation of social relations in such a context. It follows naturally that due process guarantees in times of war will be, to some extent, distinct from those applicable in peace time. The linking of human rights and humanitarian law with respect to due process guarantees brings up once again the significance of derogation in situations of emergency, including armed conflicts, under international human rights law. The possibility of different due process standards in war and peace applies equally to state and non-state justice. This suggests that the most adequate comparator for an analysis of insurgent justice before rebel courts is the due process guarantees applicable to state military courts in wartimes.

The existence of a derogation regime in situations of emergency under the main universal and two regional human rights conventions was noted in Chapter 1 as part of the argument that the rule of law is a concept the content of which can vary in situations of armed conflicts.[372] Turning now specifically to the due process guarantees entrenched in these treaties, there is a degree of ambiguity as to the recognised impact of the occurrence of a situation like an armed conflict. The ICCPR as well as the American and European Conventions on Human Rights all include a list of rights from which no derogation may be justified on the basis of an emergency. The list of non-derogable provisions varies significantly from one treaty to the next, with the European Convention (Art. 15(2)) having the shortest list and the American Convention (Art. 27(2)) the longest. All three lists include the principle of legality or *nullum crimen sine lege*, but none includes the provision on due process guarantees in the list of non-derogable rights. The possible inclusion of due process guarantees as non-derogable rights was discussed and rejected in the negotiations leading to the adoption of each of these three instruments.[373] The *travaux préparatoires* indicate that most states were sceptical that at least some fair trial guarantees, such as the right to a public trial, could be

[372] See Chapter 1, Section II.B.i. As was underlined in that earlier discussion, the African Charter of Human and Peoples' Rights does not include a derogation clause.

[373] Stephanos Stavros, 'The Right to a Fair Trial in Emergency Situations' (1992) 41 International & Comparative Law Quarterly 343, 347–348.

fully respected in wartime.[374] The decision to omit due process provisions from the list of non-derogable standards is significant, signalling the inevitability that the occurrence of an emergency like war will have an impact on the substance of due process that can be protected under international law.

Importantly, the derogability of due process provisions does not suggest that the interests protected by fair trial guarantees become irrelevant in times of war. As noted by the Inter-American Court of Human Rights:

> This does not mean, however, that the suspension of guarantees implies a temporary suspension of the rule of law, nor does it authorize those in power to act in disregard of the principle of legality by which they are bound at all times. When guarantees are suspended, some legal restraints applicable to the acts of public authorities may differ from those in effect under normal conditions. These restraints may not be considered to be non-existent, however, nor can the government be deemed thereby to have acquired absolute powers that go beyond the circumstances justifying the grant of such exceptional legal measures.[375]

The wartime loosening of due process requirements under human rights law is limited by three factors. First, all derogation provisions mention that states must otherwise respect "other obligations under international law". 'Other obligations' include, in situations of armed conflicts, international humanitarian law. It is clear that there can be no derogation of due process guarantees protected by Common Article 3 or Article 6 of Additional Protocol II in non-international armed conflicts, and under Article 75(4) of Additional Protocol I in international armed conflicts.[376] It goes without saying that the onslaught of war cannot justify suspending respect of treaty obligations only applicable in precisely this circumstance. In addition, the reference to 'other obligations' means that there is a ratcheting up of non-derogable human rights obligations for states that are parties to several human rights treaties, such that a non-derogable standard under any treaty becomes so for every treaty.[377] On the other hand, the fact that fair trial guarantees are also recognised under customary international law has not been considered to limit derogation.[378]

[374] ibid; Jaime Oraá, *Human Rights in States of Emergency in International Law* (Clarendon Press 1992) 91.

[375] IACtHR, *Advisory Opinion on Habeas Corpus in Emergency Situations*, OC-8/87, 30 January 1987, para 24; IACtHR, *Advisory Opinion on Judicial Guarantees in States of Emergency*, OC-9/87, 6 October 1987, paras 25–30.

[376] Stavros (n 373) 348–351.

[377] See, e.g., ECtHR, *Brannigan and McBride v United Kingdom*, Appl. No 14553/89, 25 May 1993, paras 66–73 (on the linking of Art. 15 of the European Convention and Art. 4 of the Covenant).

[378] If a due process guarantee came to be considered as a *jus cogens* norm, then it would become non-derogable: Human Rights Committee, General Comment 29 (States of Emergency), UN Doc CCPR/C/21/Rev.1/Add.11 (2001) para 11. That said, the right to a fair trial is generally not seen as

Second, deviation from ordinary due process guarantees in situations of war is limited by the requirement that measures be "strictly required by the exigencies of the situation". There is thus no justified wholesale suspension of fair trial guarantees, but rather a possible limitation to the extent justified by the specifics of the situation in relation to a given right. While there may be some degree of discretion granted to the derogating authority, or a 'margin of appreciation' in the European context, it is nevertheless curtailed by a principle of proportionality.[379] It can be expected that, due to their nature, some rights will be less affected by the exigencies of the situation (e.g. the presumption of innocence) than others (e.g. the right to a public trial). Much will depend on the specific context, including the intensity of armed hostilities and the capacity of the non-state armed group.[380]

Finally, a third factor limiting derogation from due process guarantees in wartime is their link to non-derogable rights. The limitation is explicit only in Article 27(2) of the American Convention on Human Rights (ACHR), which adds to the list of enumerated non-derogable provisions "the judicial guarantees essential for the protection of such rights". Thus, for example, the protection of the non-derogable rights to life or humane treatment would be negated by a sentence to death or cruel or unusual treatment further to a trial not meeting due process requirements. What judicial guarantees are 'essential' for such purpose is once again objectively indeterminate; the specific elements of due process that are required to effectively ensure the protection of non-derogable rights will depend on the nature of the right in question and the specifics of the context.[381] There is no equivalent statement in the derogation provisions of the ICCPR or the European Convention. The Human Rights Committee, in its General Comment 29, has advanced that the same principle implicitly obtains under the Covenant.[382] In what has been described as the most contentious aspect of this General Comment, the Committee holds that without judicial guarantees, non-derogable rights cannot be meaningfully protected.[383] Considered in a holistic

a peremptory norm: Stefan Trechsel, 'The Character of the Right to a Fair Trial' in John D Jackson and Sarah J Summers (eds), *Obstacles to Fairness in Criminal Proceedings: Individual Rights and Institutional Forms* (Hart 2018) 20–22.

[379] See, e.g., IACtHR, *Galindo Cardenas v Peru*, Judgment, 2 October 2015, paras 198–199; Christian Steiner and Marie-Christine Fuchs (eds), *Comentario Convención Americana Sobre Derechos Humanos* (2d edn, Konrad Adenauer Stiftung 2019) 843–844.

[380] See: Delphine Hayim, 'Le Concept d'indérogeabilité en droit international: une analyse fonctionnelle' (Institut de hautes études internationales et du développement 2012) 279; Amal Clooney and Philippa Webb, *The Right to a Fair Trial in International Law* (Oxford University Press 2021) 46–49.

[381] Steiner and Fuchs (n 379) 847.

[382] Human Rights Committee, General Comment 29 (n 378) paras 15–16. See Clooney and Webb (n 380) 137–138.

[383] Joseph and Castan (n 358) 917.

fashion, the derogation regime for due process guarantees under human rights treaties suggests a clear acceptance that the occurrence of an armed conflict may lower the legal requirements of a fair trial.[384] At the same time, a degree of fairness must be protected at all times, through standards that will vary according to the given right at stake and the context of its application.

Returning to international humanitarian law, the segmentation of armed conflicts into distinct legal categories implies that contextual differences matter. One of the ways in which such a difference matters in humanitarian treaties is in terms of the different catalogues of due process guarantees that attach to different armed conflicts. Common Article 3, with its very general reference to "judicial guarantees which are recognised as indispensable by civilized peoples", does not provide much specificity in this regard. Conversely, the fact that Article 6 of Protocol II and Article 75(4) of Protocol I provide different lists of procedural guarantees that must be respected during, respectively, non-international and international armed conflicts, does appear significant in at least two ways. The first is that, seeing as Common Article 3 and Protocol II relate to internal conflicts, even if the scope of application of the former is somewhat wider, the meaning to be given to 'indispensable guarantees' under Common Article 3 should be derived from Article 6 of Protocol II.[385] It does not seem justified to flesh out the substance of procedural guarantees under Common Article 3 primarily by referring to Article 75(4) of Protocol I, as did the US Supreme Court in *Hamdan*.[386] The fact that due process guarantees are recognised under customary human rights law does not per se erase or deem irrelevant the differences between international and non-international armed conflicts, and thus cannot justify such equivalence either.[387] Second, because the fair trial provisions in both protocols were drafted in tandem, any discrepancy between them should be regarded as meaningful. Unusually, Article 75(4) of Protocol I was drafted on the basis of Article 6(2) of Protocol II, with Article 14 of the ICCPR as the central source.[388] The general approach was that "the same text would be used unless there was a reason for changing it inherent in the differences between

384 As mentioned, the African Charter of Human and Peoples' Rights does not include any kind of derogation provision. The African Commission on Human and Peoples' Rights has taken the view that this means that no derogation of due process guarantees is permitted under the Charter, even in situations of emergency and armed conflict: African Commission on Human and Peoples' Rights, Principles and Guidelines on the Right to a Fair Trial and Legal Assistance in Africa, DOC/OS(XXX)247 (2003) 23.

385 ICRC, *Commentary on the Second Geneva Convention* (n 316) para 706; ICRC, *Commentary on the 1977 Additional Protocols* (n 288) 1396.

386 United States Supreme Court, *Hamdan v Rumsfeld*, 548 U.S. 557, 633 (2006). This link is criticised by Justice Kennedy in his concurring opinion, at 654.

387 Contrary to a passing remark in Jelena Pejic, 'Conflict Classification and the Law Applicable to Detention and the Use of Force' in Elisabeth Wilmhurst (ed), *International Law and the Classification of Conflicts* (Oxford University Press 2012) 86.

388 ICRC, *Commentary on the 1977 Additional Protocols* (n 288) 1397.

international and non-international armed conflicts".[389] Some, but not all, elements found in Articles 14 and 15 of the Covenant that had been omitted from Article 6 of Protocol II were inserted into Article 75(4) of Protocol I. Altogether, not only the wording but also the silences of Article 6 of Protocol II provide important guidance as to the proper understanding of the relationship between human rights and humanitarian law due process standards applicable to the rebel administration of justice in situations of non-international armed conflicts.

One significant laboratory of state practice of administering justice in conflict zones relates to the operation of military commissions or courts-martial.[390] Like insurgent courts, these are justice institutions and practices that are embedded into a military governance structure, designed to deliver justice in very challenging circumstances. Military justice speaks to a certain equilibrium that states have sought to maintain between military effectiveness and the requirements of fundamental justice.[391] For that reason, military courts must not only afford fairness but also be "prompt, portable and flexible".[392] In part, rebel justice represents an attempt to administer justice in similar circumstances, and the functional attributes desired for military justice will be equally needed for the operation of insurgent courts. There are, however, certain fundamental differences between military and rebel courts, beyond the obvious point that the former are operated by states and the latter not. A key difference is that military justice operates in the shadow of the regular administration of justice. The fairness of a military battlefield trial will always be compared to the fairness of a civilian trial in the courts of the very same state that are normally available. This explains, in large part, the fraught relationship between human rights monitoring bodies and military justice, which is very often found to be falling short of fair trial requirements.[393] The mistrust of military courts and the preference for civilian justice is nowhere clearer than in the consensus among human rights bodies that military courts should in principle have limited jurisdiction over civilians.[394] In conflict zones

[389] 'Report of Committee III, Fourth Session', CDDH/407/Rev.1, reprinted in Howard S Levie, *Protection of War Victims: Protocol 1 to the 1949 Geneva Conventions*, vol 4 (Oceana 1981) 71–72.

[390] The parallel was previously made with respect to the requirement of judicial independence and impartiality in Chapter 2, Section IV.C.iii.

[391] Michael R Gibson, 'International Human Rights Law and the Administration of Justice through Military Tribunals: Preserving Utility While Precluding Impunity' (2008) 4 Journal of International Law and International Relations 1, 13.

[392] Michael R Gibson, 'Military Justice in Operational Settings, Peacekeeping Missions and Situations of Transitional Justice' in Alison Duxbury and Matthew Groves (eds), *Military Justice in the Modern Age* (Cambridge University Press 2016) 385–386.

[393] Peter John Rowe, 'How Well Do International Human Rights Bodies Understand Military Courts?' in Alison Duxbury and Matthew Groves (eds), *Military Justice in the Modern Age* (Cambridge University Press 2016) 26.

[394] ibid 30–32; Steiner and Fuchs (n 379) 271–275; Christina M Cerna, 'The Inter-American System and Military Justice' in Alison Duxbury and Matthew Groves (eds), *Military Justice in the Modern Age* (Cambridge University Press 2016).

in which armed groups operate a justice system, there is no alternative civilian or rearguard justice to which rebel courts could be meaningfully compared.[395] One aspect of humanitarian law related to military courts that does seem interesting and relevant for the rebel administration of justice is a certain level playing field between due process guarantees afforded to a state's own soldiers and those that must be granted to prisoners of war. Thus, for example, Article 106 of the Third Geneva Convention provides that a prisoner of war shall have the right to appeal a decision "in the same manner as the members of the armed forces of the Detaining Power".[396] A similar pattern can be observed in some situations of belligerent occupation, for instance in the Palestinian occupied territories where—in theory—similar rules of procedure and evidence apply to the prosecution of Palestinians before military courts as apply to Israeli soldiers before courts-martial.[397] At a minimum, an argument can be made that if circumstances in a conflict zone allow certain procedural guarantees to be respected vis-à-vis an armed group's own fighters, this corresponds to a benchmark that should obtain for other trials.

ii. Due Process before Non-State Courts

The combination of the rule of law and state sovereignty has given rise to a principle of separation of powers and the emergence of structuring principles for the administration of justice, including the necessity of courts marked by independence and impartiality. As we saw in Chapter 1, the concept of the rule of law is open-textured and can be developed to encompass, in its 'thick' version, basic constitutive elements of due process.[398] Indeed, the catalogue of due process guarantees that we find entrenched in human rights instruments is a description of how courts function, or at least should ideally do so. Due process and the judicial function as embodied in state administration of justice are thus mutually constitutive and, as a result, somewhat circular: courts are entities that embody due process and due process is the manner in which courts operate. But the administration of justice is not limited to the operation of state courts, no

395 With respect to the courts of the state against which an armed group is fighting, there is no foundation in international law to a comparative exercise to determine which of the state and rebel justice systems is fairer, so that the less fair one would be required to defer to the fairer one. As discussed in Chapter 2, international humanitarian law does not recognise fairness as the only legitimising foundation of jurisdiction in conflict zones.

396 See also Arts. 102, 103 and 108 of the Third Geneva Convention so similar links.

397 Kathleen Cavanaugh, 'The Israeli Military Court System in the West Bank and Gaza' (2007) 12 Journal of Conflict & Security Law 197, 209. The opposite pattern can be observed in post-genocide Rwanda, where those accused of genocidal crimes against Tutsis were tried before *gacaca* courts that fell significantly short of recognised due process requirements, while those accused of so-called 'revenge crimes' against Hutus were prosecuted before military courts that afforded fuller due process guarantees: Pietro Sullo, *Beyond Genocide: Transitional Justice and Gacaca Courts in Rwanda* (Springer 2018) 169.

398 See the discussion in Chapter 1, Section II.A.

more than law is the exclusive prerogative of the state. As noted in the earlier discussion of the rule of law, the capture of the idea of law and the administration of justice by the state is both recent and incomplete. Legal pluralism has highlighted how there are countless sites in society in which legal norms are produced and applied by a range of actors, most of whom have no link to the state.[399] Concerns of procedural and substantive fairness that animate the rule of law and are represented, in part, in due process guarantees will also be found in these sites removed from the operation of state courts. What fairness in general, and procedural fairness in particular, demand will necessarily depend on the specific decision-making process. Fairness in the distribution of assignments in the workplace or in the granting of kosher or halal certificates to butcher shops can be achieved without turning these decision-making processes into judicial ones.[400] Rod Macdonald offered a compelling rejection of the idea that procedural fairness could be reduced to a set of fixed and universal propositions derived from judicial adjudication, arguing instead that:

> [T]he specific requirements of procedural fairness must be tied to particular decisional processes, and may be derived from the inherent principle of each . . . [P]rocedural fairness requires more than positivistic adherence to a finite set of pre-existing rules; procedural fairness also requires the acquisition and application of tacit knowledge relating to the uses, limits and purposes of each social ordering process.[401]

Of course, the focus of this book is neither managerial work assignment nor religious certification but rather the administration of justice by non-state armed groups in civil and penal matters. Armed groups sometimes do so through courts, or at least judicial practices, which correspond to a particular type of decisional process. Macdonald's insight does not become irrelevant, however, in rejecting a one-size-fits-all approach to procedural fairness. It begs the question of whether any 'court' is the same type of social ordering process, of whether differences among courts may translate into a measure of difference as regards procedural fairness.

That due process requirements may vary depending on context is recognised in international human rights law, and has been more significantly discussed in

[399] See, e.g., Martha-Marie Kleinhans and Roderick A Macdonald, 'What Is a Critical Legal Pluralism?' (1997) 12 Canadian Journal of Law and Society 25; John Tasioulas, 'The Rule of Law' in John Tasioulas (ed), *The Cambridge Companion to the Philosophy of Law* (Cambridge University Press 2020) 122–123.

[400] On employment fairness, see Robert Leckey, 'Employing Fairness' (2003) 18 Canadian Journal of Law & Society 45.

[401] Roderick A Macdonald, 'A Theory of Procedural Fairness' (1981) 1 Windsor Yearbook of Access to Justice 3, 33.

two different settings: in the context of the application of the principle of complementarity in international criminal law and in relation to certain extradition cases. In relation to the implementation of individual responsibility under international criminal law, the ICTY, ICTR, and ICC have considered the relation between due process guarantees offered by an international tribunal and those afforded by national law. In referral cases before the ICTY and ICTR, the tribunals have enquired whether the accused could expect to receive a fair trial before national courts, generally finding that the same guarantees should be offered at both levels in order to justify referrals.[402] Before the ICC, where the logic is reversed under Article 17 of the Rome Statute, the question was raised whether the failure to afford the accused due process guarantees in a national prosecution should be considered as constituting a situation in which the state is unwilling or unable to prosecute. Academic opinions have been deeply divided on this question, but the ICC Appeals Chamber in *Al-Senussi* noted that "the Court was not established to be an international court of human rights, sitting in judgment over domestic legal systems to ensure that they are compliant with international standards on human rights".[403] Accordingly, the Appeals Chamber concluded that a case would not be admissible before the ICC "merely because domestic proceedings do not fully respect the due process rights of a suspect", but only in extreme cases in which "violations of the rights of the suspect are so egregious that the proceedings can no longer be regarded as being capable of providing any genuine form of justice".[404] The discussion of due process is coloured by the jurisdictional purpose of the analysis, but it nevertheless signals a degree of flexibility in the construction of the procedural requirements of a fair trial under international law depending on whether it takes place before a national or international court.

A similar pattern may be observed in relation to attempts to block extradition to jurisdictions alleged to suffer from weaker or absent procedural guarantees. The European Court of Human Rights has considered many petitions of that nature since its landmark decision in *Soering v. UK*, and has striven to devise a measured position vis-à-vis what due process shortcomings should prevent

[402] ICTY, *Prosecutor v Stankovic*, Decision on referral of case under Rule 11bis, Case No IT-96-23/2-PT, 17 May 2005, para 55. See Yvonne McDermott, *Fairness in International Criminal Trials* (Oxford University Press 2016) 151–155.

[403] ICC, Prosecutor v Gaddafi and Al-Senussi, 'Judgment on the appeal of Mr Abdullah Al-Senussi against the decision of Pre-Trial Chamber I of 11 October 2013 entitled "Decision on the admissibility of the case against Abdullah Al-Senussi"', Case No ICC-01/11-01/11 OA 6, 24 July 2014 (Appeals Chamber) para 219.

[404] ibid paras 219, 230. See William A Schabas and Mohamed El Zeidy, 'Article 17: Issues of Admissibility' in Otto Triffterer and Kai Ambos (eds), *Rome Statute of the International Criminal Court: A Commentary* (3d edn, CH Beck 2016) 818–819; Frédéric Mégret and Marika Giles Samson, 'Holding the Line on Complementarity in Libya: The Case for Tolerating Flawed Domestic Trials' (2013) 11 Journal of International Criminal Justice 571; McDermott (n 402) 155–165.

extradition.[405] Thus in *Ahorugeze v. Sweden*, the applicant fought a request that he be extradited to Rwanda to stand trial on charges of genocide arguing, inter alia, that procedural fairness rights protected under Article 6 of the European Convention on Human Rights (ECHR) would not be respected before Rwandan courts.[406] Although the European Court is the very kind of human rights court that the ICC denied being, the former has devised a test that is very close the stance adopted by the latter in *Al-Senussi*. Under the European Convention, extradition may not be granted only if there is a risk of a "flagrant denial of justice" in the requesting country:

> A flagrant denial of justice goes beyond mere irregularities or lack of safeguards in the trial procedures such as might result in a breach of Article 6 if occurring within the Contracting State itself. What is required is a breach of the principles of fair trial guaranteed by Article 6 which is so fundamental as to amount to a nullification, or destruction of the very essence, of the right guaranteed by that Article.[407]

Although this is once again in the context of jurisdictional analysis, reflecting the extraterritorial application of the ECHR, the test adopted by the Strasbourg court does not signal a rigid uniformity of due process guarantees across different courts. The 2017 UK appeal decision in *Rwanda v. Nteziryayo* provides a rare example of a case where the high threshold set by that test was met.[408] That decision reviewed in extraordinary details the domestic prosecution of different categories of crimes before Rwandan courts, to conclude that there was a real risk that there would be a flagrant denial of justice if the extradition requests were granted. The representation of the Rwandan justice system in extradition proceedings in the United Kingdom suggested that there was a real risk of a wholly inefficient—indeed, at times just plain inactive—defence, as well as a pattern of direct political manipulation of judges by the executive branch in cases deemed 'important'.[409]

The occasions in which different jurisdictions interact so that due process guarantees become a point of comparison do not signal a rigid uniformity of procedural fairness under international law. A concern that was expressed by Louise Arbour during the negotiations of the Rome Statute was that, without some flexibility reflecting different capacities of states, there would be a radical asymmetry

[405] ECtHR, *Soering v UK*, (1989) 11 EHRR 439 para 113.
[406] ECtHR, *Ahorugeze v Sweden*, Appl. No 37075/09, Judgment, 27 October 2011. See also ECtHR, *Othman (Abu Qatada) v UK*, Appl. No 8139/09, Judgment, 17 January 2012, paras 260–261.
[407] *Ahorugeze*, ibid para 115.
[408] *Rwanda v Nteziryayo*, [2017] EWHC 1912 (Queen's Bench Admin.).
[409] ibid paras 370–379.

in the application of complementarity such that the ICC would more easily conclude that less developed countries were unable to prosecute "essentially for reasons of poverty".[410] A different point is made by Mirjan Damšaka to support the need for standards of procedural fairness to vary as between national and international prosecutions in light of the particular nature, function and position of international criminal tribunals:

> If international criminal justice ought to follow the traditional domestic cynosure, this does not require, however, that fairness demands be identical in both contexts. To be sure, 'fair trial' rights of international human right documents apply to both national and international justice. But they are couched in broad terms, leaving ample room for differences in regard to procedural arrangements supposed to flow from these rights, and, by the same token, also ample room for their adjustment to special circumstances and peculiar difficulties in which criminal courts go about their business. Imagine only the variety of demands that could plausibly be said to follow from the presumption of innocence.[411]

This is a refutation of the absolutist position defended by Americas Watch many years ago when it rejected the FMLN's claim that due process guarantees must be "adapted to the conditions and capacity of the contending party"; for Americas Watch, this amounted to making compliance with fair trial guarantees depend on the 'convenience' of the parties to the conflict.[412] No system that claims to administer justice can lawfully do away with due process guarantees, but the specific procedural requirements of a fair trial under international law must be adapted to reflect the fact that non-state armed groups are not states.[413]

What emerges from this consideration of the application of fair trial guarantees by non-state actors in situations of armed conflict is that public international law imposes flexible requirements that must be adapted to the specifics of each distinct decisional process. Even for the same actor, the specific implications of due process guarantees may vary according to context, as illustrated by the

[410] Quoted in Schabas and El Zeidy (n 404) 828.

[411] Mirjan Damaška, 'Reflections on Fairness in International Criminal Justice' (2012) 10 Journal of International Criminal Justice 611, 615.

[412] Americas Watch, 'Violation of Fair Trial Guarantees by the FMLN's Ad Hoc Courts' (1990) 13; FMLN Secretariat for the Promotion and Protection of Human Rights, 'The Legitimacy of Our Methods of Struggle' (FMLN 1988) 20.

[413] This model of reconciliation of fair trial guarantees and legal pluralism can also be found in Colombian constitutional law, in which Indigenous jurisdictions are constitutionally recognised. The Constitutional Court has held that due process guarantees protected under the Constitution cannot be applied to Indigenous jurisdictions as they are to regular state court, but must be adapted to reflect Indigenous 'cosmovision' and practices: Corte constitucional, Sentencia T-349/96 (1996) s 2.4.2.3; Corte constitucional, Sentencia T-196/15 (2015) s II.3; Jorge Roa Roa, 'Pluralismo jurídico y mecanismos de coordinación entre los sistemas de justicia indígena y el sistema nacional de justicia en Colombia' [2014] Revista Derecho del Estado 101.

accepted dissimilarities between regular and military justice, or between civil and criminal trials, albeit all administered by states.[414] This suggests that a mapping of procedural fairness requirements for the rebel administration of justice will result in legal standards that may be different than those imposed on states and still subject to possible variation from one armed group to another.

C. Fair Trial Guarantees before Rebel Courts

What constitutes a fair trial under international law has been one of the most contested human rights issues of the last half century. In the European human rights regime, for example, more than half of all cases from 1959 to 2019 dealt with Article 6 on the right to a fair trial, more than those dealing with all other rights combined.[415] The very nature of the right in question has been contested, whether it corresponds to a global, unitary right to a fair trial, or whether each of the specific procedural guarantees mentioned in treaty provisions are stand-alone individual rights. What could be termed the *soupe versus potage* due process conundrum has been discussed most directly in relation to Article 6 of the European Convention of Human Rights.[416] The jurisprudence of the European Court is far from clear or consistent, but its general thrust is that there is a single composite right to a fair trial, with specific due process guarantees standing as markers of what constitutes a fair trial.[417] As a result, as noted by the Grand Chamber in *Beuze*:

> 120. The fairness of a criminal trial must be guaranteed in all circumstances. However, what constitutes a fair trial cannot be the subject of a single unvarying rule but must depend on the circumstances of the particular case (. . .). The Court's primary concern, in examining a complaint under Article 6 § 1, is to evaluate the overall fairness of the criminal proceedings[...]
>
> 121. As the Court has found on numerous occasions, compliance with the requirements of a fair trial must be examined in each case having regard to the development of the proceedings as a whole and not on the basis of an isolated

[414] On the greater procedural demands of due process in criminal cases, see ECtHR, *Moreira Ferreira v Portugal*, Appl. No 19867/12, 11 July 2017, paras 66–67.

[415] ECHR, 'Violations by Articles and by States 1959–2019' (2019), online: <https://www.echr.coe.int/Documents/Stats_violation_1959_2019_ENG.pdf> (11,543 cases dealing with Art. 6 out of a total of 22,535 cases). The same is said to be true of cases before the Inter-American Court of Human Rights: Steiner and Fuchs (n 379) 263.

[416] The difference is explained by François Laplantine and Alexis Nouss, who point out that "[la soupe] est respectueuse de ses composantes qu'elle laisse intactes dans un bouillon sobre et tolérant. Le potage, lui, broie, mélange, passe, bref il fusionne, visant à l'homogène" : François Laplantine and Alexis Nouss, *Métissages: De Arcimboldo à Zombi* (Pauvert 2001) 533. Sadly, the English language makes thin gruel of such culinary and conceptual distinctions, and translates both terms as 'soup'.

[417] Trechsel (n 378) 26; Ryan Goss, 'The Undermining of Article 6 ECHR' [2019] European Yearbook on Human Rights 295, 297–304.

consideration of one particular aspect or one particular incident, although it cannot be ruled out that a specific factor may be so decisive as to enable the fairness of the trial to be assessed at an earlier stage in the proceedings. In evaluating the overall fairness of the proceedings, the Court will take into account, if appropriate, the minimum rights listed in Article 6 § 3, which exemplify the requirements of a fair trial in respect of typical procedural situations which arise in criminal cases. They can be viewed, therefore, as specific aspects of the concept of a fair trial in criminal proceedings in Article 6 § 1[.]

122. Those minimum rights guaranteed by Article 6 § 3 are, nevertheless, not ends in themselves: their intrinsic aim is always to contribute to ensuring the fairness of the criminal proceedings as a whole.[418]

Under such a holistic approach, it is possible that the shortcomings of some procedural aspects of a trial might be offset by other due process guarantees to result in a trial that is sufficiently fair to meet the requirements of human rights law.[419] A global understanding of the right to a fair trial is further buttressed by the fact that the relevant provisions in the ICCPR (Art. 14(1)) as well as the European (Art. 6(1)) and American (Art. 8(1)) Conventions cover both civil and criminal proceedings, but list most specific guarantees only in relation to criminal trials. It is clear that some of the listed guarantees are nevertheless also elements of a fair trial in civil proceedings, for example, the right to legal aid for custody disputes or the right to examine witnesses in delictual or torts litigation.[420]

The sobering judgment passed by Stefan Trechsel with respect to the protection offered by Article 6 of the European Convention seems apt for the different iterations of that norm across human rights and humanitarian law treaties: "the right to a fair trial is a fuzzy panacea, a cluster of rights, not exclusively reserved for the accused, a vague ideal, more a shell than a guarantee of substance".[421] The very general formulation used in Common Article 3 and the non-exclusive list offered in Article 6(2) of Protocol II, confirmed by the general statement offered in Rule 100 of the ICRC customary law study, suggest that the same judgment applies to the right to a fair trial under humanitarian law.[422] This is endorsed

418 ECtHR, *Beuze v Belgium*, Appl. No 71409/10, Grand Chamber Judgment, 9 November 2018, paras 120–121.

419 For a critical view, see Ryan Goss, *Criminal Fair Trial Rights: Article 6 of the European Convention on Human Rights* (Bloomsbury Publishing 2014) 139–159. The Human Rights Committee has adopted a similar approach under the ICCPR: William Schabas, *U.N. International Covenant on Civil and Political Rights: Nowak's CCPR Commentary* (3d edn, NP Engel Publisher 2019) 371–372.

420 Trechsel (n 378) 22–23.

421 ibid 35.

422 In the chapeau of Art. 6(2), the list of essential guarantees is preceded by "in particular". Likewise, in the chapeau of Art. 75(4), the list is given as "generally recognized principles of regular judicial procedure, which include the following". For the ICRC customary law study, see Henckaerts and Doswald-Beck (n 255) Rule 100.

with respect to Common Article 3 by the commentary to the ICC Elements of Crimes, suggesting that the ICC should consider whether "the cumulative effect of factors with respect to guarantees deprived the person or persons of a fair trial".[423] With this caveat in mind, the analysis now moves to consider specific fair trial guarantees applicable to insurgent courts in conflict zones. For the reasons explained in the previous subsection, Article 6 of Additional Protocol II is taken as the central point of reference, interpreted in light of textual differences and contextual applications of Common Article 3, Article 75(4) of Additional Protocol I, and corresponding provisions of human rights treaties.

i. Judicial Independence and Impartiality

Independence and impartiality are among the institutional features that differentiate courts from other decision-making processes. In that respect, this twin concept was previously discussed as a constitutive element of a 'regularly constituted court' under international humanitarian law.[424] The particular place and function of this requirement are not easy to delineate because of the shifting formulations used in the relevant treaty provisions. In Common Article 3, the regular constitution of courts is one element, and the provision of indispensable (but unspecified) judicial guarantees, another. In Article 6(2) of Additional Protocol II, the reference to regular constitution is omitted in favour of "a court offering the essential guarantees of independence and impartiality" that are defined, "in particular", by six specific guarantees. The drafting is paradoxical in that the six guarantees so articulated do not, in fact, speak to independence or impartiality, but rather cover other elements of a fair trial. Although Article 6 of Protocol II was inspired by Article 14 of the ICCPR, that treaty is much clearer in articulating a right to a fair hearing by an independent and impartial tribunal established by law. Likewise, Article 75(4) of Additional Protocol I much more unambiguously differentiates the discrete elements of this requirement in demanding "a conviction pronounced by an impartial and regularly constituted court respecting the generally recognized principles of regular judicial procedure", principles that are thereafter listed in a non-exhaustive way. For the reasons articulated in Chapter 2, the regular constitution of courts and their independence and impartiality are distinct institutional requirements under both Common Article 3 and Protocol II. At the same time, beyond their institutional dimensions, guarantees of independence and impartiality operate as a fundamental element of due process. In other words, even in situations in which the regularly constituted courts are structured in a manner that allows them to

[423] Knut Dörmann, *Elements of War Crimes under the Rome Statute of the International Criminal Court: Sources and Commentary* (Cambridge University Press 2003) 408–409.
[424] See the discussion in Chapter 2, Section IV.C.iii.

operate in an independent and impartial way, there may be individual cases in which that requirement is not met. It is this more ad hoc side of independence and impartiality that is considered here in the context of the operation of insurgent courts.

Armed conflicts are situations in which the independence and impartiality of courts are subject to particular stress because some of the issues they consider are tied to the security of the state, if not its very survival. For state courts, this is a difficult phase that must be weathered; for insurgent courts, this very context is part of their raison d'être, something that will condition their structure as well as their daily operations. Despite this challenging environment, the guarantees of independence and impartiality are absolutely essential features of a fair trial, without which the practice cannot properly be labelled the administration of justice. For both independence and impartiality, a delicate balance must be attempted between the essential needs of a just process and a realistic understanding of constraints imposed by armed hostilities.

As for independence of the court, it corresponds to objective and subjective characteristics. Leaving aside institutional implications examined in Chapter 2, such as the appointment process, security of tenure, or the degree to which courts are fully integrated into the military apparatus of the armed group, judicial independence has been taken to reflect both autonomy and non-interference. Independence as autonomy translates into a sufficiently wide sphere of activity within which judges may operate with some liberty. As noted in Article 8 of the UN Basic Principles on the Independence of the Judiciary, "members of the judiciary are like other citizens entitled to freedom of expression, belief, association and assembly".[425] There is a large body of jurisprudence, in particular by the Inter-American and European Courts of Human Rights, that delineates the extent to which a state may restrict or sanction public pronouncements by judges, but it is accepted that extrajudicial public statements by a judge regarding a specific case undermine at least the appearance of independence of the judiciary.[426] It may be that in the context of an armed conflict and with respect to courts that are often closer to a model of military tribunals, the freedom of judges to express their opinions publicly on matters of general interest may be reduced. The general sense that one gets from description of the social atmosphere in territory under LTTE control in Sri Lanka, for example, does not suggest a wide embrace

[425] UN Basic Principles on the Independence of the Judiciary, adopted by the Seventh United Nations Congress on the Prevention of Crime and the Treatment of Offenders held at Milan from 26 August to 6 September 1985 and endorsed by General Assembly resolutions 40/32 of 29 November 1985 and 40/146 of 13 December 1985.

[426] See, e.g., Report of the Special Rapporteur Diego García-Sayán on the Independence of Judges and Lawyers, UN Doc A/HRC/41/48 (2019) 9–11; Jorge Antonio Climent Gallart, 'La Jurisprudencia del TEDH sobre aa libertad de expresión de los jueces' (2018) 25 Iuris Tantum Revista boliviana de derecho 524.

of freedom of expression for cadres involved in the administration of justice. On the other hand, the limits preventing judges from speaking publicly about cases in which they are involved seems equally valid in relation to the rebel administration of justice. If the judicial function is to remain such, it must imply a duty of restraint specific to that office.

Independence as non-interference is a guarantee against a more direct threat to the fairness of judicial proceedings. It translates into negative and positive obligations for the authority overseeing the operation of courts. As formulated by the Inter-American Court of Human Rights in *Atala Riffo*:

> [O]ne of the main objectives of the separation of public powers is to guarantee the independence of judges, for the purpose of preventing the judicial system and its members from being subject to wrongful restrictions in the exercise of their role by bodies foreign to the Judicial Power or even by senior judges that carry out review or appeal duties. Moreover, the guarantee of judicial independence includes guarantees against external pressures, and therefore the State must abstain from undue interference with the Judiciary or its members, that is, in relation to a specific judge, and must prevent such intrusions and investigate and sanction those who commit them.[427]

In its negative dimension, independence as non-interference corresponds to a duty for the governing authority to refrain from "any restrictions, improper influences, inducements, pressures, threats or interferences, direct or indirect, from any quarter or for any reason".[428] It is not difficult to find egregious examples of interference by the leadership of some armed groups into how specific cases are decided. A particularly glaring example was the manipulation of the courts-martial of the *Mouvement du libération du Congo*, where judges reported to the movements' leader Jean-Pierre Bemba at the end of each hearing to obtain his instructions.[429] The punishment of Islamic State judges who issued decisions that displeased the leadership is another clear example of a lack of independence. Likewise, the ICC Pre-Trial Chamber in *Al-Hassan* found that some matters felt to be 'important' by the leaders of Ansar Dine/al-Qaeda in the Islamic Maghreb were decided by the group's leader and then dressed up as judgments of the Timbuktu Islamic Court.[430] That said, perhaps surprisingly, the independence of

[427] IACtHR, *Atala Riffo v Chile*, Judgment, 24 February 2012, para 186 (footnotes omitted).

[428] UN Basic Principles on the Independence of the Judiciary (n 425) Art. 2. See also Steiner and Fuchs (n 379) 275–277; Clooney and Webb (n 380) 87–89.

[429] ICC, *Prosecutor v Jean-Pierre Bemba Gombo*, Trial Judgment, 21 March 2016, ICC-01/05-01/08, at 299–300 note 1861.

[430] ICC, *Prosecutor v Al-Hassan*, Décision de la Chambre préliminaire relative à la confirmation des charges, ICC-01/12-01/18, 13 November 2019, para 420 (available only in French). This being a preliminary decision, with a heavily redacted public version, the facts are not very detailed.

insurgent courts is a factor often mentioned favourably by civilians under rebel authority, at least in comparison with the official courts of the state. The LTTE, the FARC, and the Taliban were all described by at least some informants as operating in a manner that was free from direct interference from the leaders of these armed groups. There is also a positive dimension of independence as non-interference, requiring the overseeing authority to prevent and punish any improper influence on the court from third parties, including popular acclaim or criticism of decisions.[431]

While the guarantee of independence speaks to the relation of the court to external actors, that of impartiality speaks to the position of the decision-maker relative to the parties. A lack of independence necessarily impedes impartiality, but the reverse is not always true. Impartiality implies that the decision-maker in a given case will approach the issues and the evidence free from favour, bias, or prejudice. It is agreed in both international humanitarian law and human rights law that there are both objective and subjective facets to the requirement of impartiality.[432] The subjective element speaks to the actual state of mind of the decision-makers, as evidenced in their words or actions or in any connection that they may have to the parties or issues at stake in a case before them.[433] For example, more than a quarter of *gacaca* judges in Rwanda were found to have been involved in genocide-related crimes, basically amounting to perpetrators arranging to judge themselves.[434] Judicial corruption corresponds to a rampant violation of the right to an impartial tribunal in its subjective dimension. As illustrated by the annual survey carried out by Transparency International, there is a certain correlation between situations of armed conflict and the prevalence of corruption.[435] Such correlation certainly exists in many of the countries that are the focus of case studies in this book: not rarely, as noted as part of the description of the administration of justice by various armed groups, insurgent governance succeeds in this way

[431] Judicial Integrity Group, Commentary on the Bangalore Principle of Judicial Conduct (UN Office on Drugs and Crimes, 2007) 43.

[432] See: Human Rights Committee, General Comment 32 (Article 14), UN Doc CCPR/C/GC/32 (2007) para 21; Report of the Special Rapporteur Gabriela Knaul on the independence of judges and lawyers, UN Doc A/68/285 (2013) para 44; ECtHR, *Findlay v United Kingdom*, Appl. No 22107/93, 25 Sept. 2001, para 73; ICTR, *Prosecutor v Nahimana*, Appeal Judgment, ICTR-99-52-A, 28 November 2007, paras 47–50; Steiner and Fuchs (n 379) 279; Doswald-Beck (n 189) 472–473; ICRC, *Commentary on the Second Geneva Convention* (n 316) para 703; Clooney and Webb (n 380) 106–124; Schabas (n 419) 369–370.

[433] See IACtHR, *Duque v Colombia*, Sentencia (Exceptiones preliminaries, fondos, reparaciones y costas), 26 February 2016, paras 162; ECtHR, *Kyprianou v Cyprus*, Appl. No 73797/01, 15 December 2005, paras 119, 129–133.

[434] Sullo (n 397) 176, 184; Jacques Fierens, 'Gacaca Courts: Between Fantasy and Reality' (2005) 3 Journal of International Criminal Justice 896, 910–912.

[435] See Transparency International, Corruption Perception Index 2019 (2020), online: <https://www.transparency.org/cpi2019>.

precisely because the official justice system is dysfunctional. Thus, it is a recurring comment from informants that the courts of the LTTE, the FARC, and the Taliban were free of corruption, in stark contrast to the state-run courts in Sri Lanka, Colombia, and Afghanistan, respectively. This is not to suggest that insurgent courts can never be corrupt or partial. Rather, the point is that impartiality is a fairness requirement that seems achievable for a non-state armed group in a conflict zone.

The objective facet of impartiality speaks to whether the court appears to be biased to a reasonable independent observer. As noted in Chapter 2, there is an institutional dimension that poses significant challenges for the rebel administration of justice: the question is whether a reasonable observer could conclude that a rebel court appears impartial in dealing with a matter relating to either the group or one of its members.[436] I related in that earlier discussion that this approximates in some ways the situation of military tribunals, whose impartiality has been the subject of extensive critical analysis by human rights bodies. The study of insurgent courts in a variety of armed conflicts suggests that it is indeed very difficult for the civilian population to feel confidence in the impartiality of these courts. The expression of open hostility by judges of the rebel-run Timbuktu Islamic Court, for example, fails to convey the expected judicial detachment corresponding to impartiality.[437] The acid test of judicial impartiality for rebel courts are cases involving a claim by a civilian against a member of the group. Informants were divided as to whether LTTE cadres could ever be brought before the group's courts in the normal course of business. Likewise, there were cases where civilians reportedly hesitated before bringing to the FARC an issue involving one of its fighters. In Iraqi Kurdistan, tribal and political connections are said to sometimes matter enormously to the effectiveness of KRI courts. On the other hand, there are consistent reports of villagers complaining to Taliban judges of the behaviour of the group's fighters, including a unique example in which proceedings ultimately unfavourable to a Taliban fighter were filmed by an independent journalist.[438] Objective impartiality of rebel courts seems possible but difficult in cases involving a group's own fighters. It may well be that such cases will often be marred by a lack of impartiality and, as a consequence, result in a violation of applicable international law. That said, cases involving an armed group's own fighters are a small fraction of the roll of rebel courts. The practice of insurgent courts suggests that impartiality in most cases is an attainable due process guarantee.

[436] See Chapter 2, Section IV.C.iii.

[437] ICC, *Al-Hassan* (n 430) para 427; ECtHR, *Kyprianou* (n 433) para 130.

[438] Fault Lines, 'This Is Taliban Country' *Al-Jazeera* (16 April 2014), online: <https://www.aljazeera.com/programmes/faultlines/2014/04/taliban-country-20144108610575181.html>.

ii. Right to Be Informed Promptly of the Charges

The right of anyone brought before a court to be informed promptly of the specific charges against them is explicitly protected by Article 6(2)(a) of Additional Protocol II. This is a basic and universally recognised fair trial guarantee declared applicable to a widely defined range of judicial proceedings by various treaty provisions under international humanitarian and human rights law.[439] Indeed, there is intense cross-referencing among these various sources in the doctrine and jurisprudence in both fields of international law. The right to be promptly informed of the charges is an essential element of the "necessary right and means of defence" that are otherwise the focus of Article 6(2)(a). This right is distinct from the right to be informed of the reasons for an arrest or detention (Art. 75(3), Protocol I) and from the right to be tried within a reasonable time (Art. 14(3)(c), ICCPR), neither of which are mentioned in Additional Protocol II.

The due process requirement to inform an accused without delay of the particulars of the alleged offence must be interpreted in light of its link to the right to mount an effective defence. Unless the accused has been informed of the specific facts (cause of the offence) and the precise legal rule which they are claimed to have violated (nature of the offence), it is impossible to prepare an effective defence or to decide whether to plead guilty.[440] This requirement, particularly the articulation of the relevant legal standard, may be difficult for non-state armed groups to meet, as some groups apply informal, unwritten, or vaguely formulated standards. The FARC, for instance, had basically no legislation and tended to rely on community-based standards. A different model is that of the Taliban or the Islamic State who claimed to apply 'pure' *Sharī'a* standards. The answer is not to require the formalisation or codification of rebel law, but rather to enquire whether a person in a conflict zone under the effective authority of a rebel group could reasonably appraise what conduct was prohibited. For instance, as there is little doubt that civilians are aware that passing information to the government is severely punished by all armed groups, there would not be an issue of a lack of specificity of legal standards. Likewise, many of the common

[439] These provisions include: Art. 75(4) of Protocol I; Arts. 96 & 105(4) Third Geneva Convention; Arts. 71 & 123(2) Fourth Geneva Convention; Art. 14(3)(a), Covenant on Civil and Political Rights; Art. 6(3)(a), ECHR; Art. 8(2)(b), ACHR. The African Charter of Human and Peoples' Rights is the only major instrument that does not mention this procedural right (Art. 7), although the African Commission has held that one must understand the nature of the accusations: African Commission on Human and Peoples' Rights, Communication No 301/05, *Haregewoin Gabre-Selassie and IHRDA (on behalf of former Dergue Officials) v Ethiopia*, 7 November 2011, para 231; African Commission on Human and Peoples' Rights, Principles and Guidelines on the Right to a Fair Trial and Legal Assistance in Africa (n 384) 13.

[440] See ECtHR, *Pélissier and Sassi v France*, Appl. No 25444/94, Judgment, 25 March 1999 (Grand Chamber) para 84; IACtHR, *Tibi v Ecuador*, Judgment, 7 September 2004, para 187; David Harris and others, *Harris, O'Boyle and Warbrick's Law of the European Convention on Human Rights* (4th edn, Oxford University Press 2018) 468; Steiner and Fuchs (n 379) 294; Schabas (n 419) 387–389; Clooney and Webb (n 380) 266–272.

crimes punished by insurgent courts, such as theft or sexual assault, would undoubtedly have been known to be prohibited acts by everyone concerned. On the other hand, an accusation that is overly vague will not permit the adequate preparation of an effective defence. The procedural guarantee here mirrors the broader requirement of the rule of law that laws be knowable by those on whom they will be imposed. As regards the factual elements, all material facts must be disclosed in a "clear, detailed and precise description", again with a view to meaningfully allow their contestation by the accused if need be.[441]

At a formal level, an accused must be told of the specifics of the alleged offence as a matter of course, without having to petition for it. This can be done in writing or orally but, as specified in some of the equivalent human rights treaty provisions, in a language that the accused can understand.[442] Protocol II requires that an accused be informed of the particulars of the offence "without delay", a standard that leaves room for interpretation and adaptation to different circumstances. It is clear that 'without delay' evokes a shorter time span than the 'reasonable time' within which the trial must take place under the relevant human rights instruments. Louise Doswald-Beck relies on decisions of the UN Human Rights Committee and the European Court of Human Rights to conclude that, under international humanitarian law applicable to non-international armed conflicts, this must be done in a matter of days, rather than either hours or weeks.[443] The point of the limited delay is to allow a challenge by the accused to continued detention, if they are detained while awaiting trial. In a general manner, armed hostilities can constitute a context in which the administration of justice may be expected to slow down, but there are clearly limits as to what type of delay can be countenanced under an obligation to inform 'without delay' that is designed to be applied in situations of armed conflict under Article 6 of Protocol II. For armed groups, this might translate into a few more days to convey the required information, but would not extend to weeks or months of pre-trial detention without charge.[444] Under what the Inter-American Court of

[441] IACtHR, *Firmín Ramírez v Guatemala*, Judgment, 20 June 2005, para 67. See McDermott (n 402) 63–66.

[442] Art. 14(3)(a), Covenant on Civil and Political Rights; Art. 6(3)(a), European Convention on Human Rights; UN Human Rights Committee, General Comment 32 (n 432) para 31; ECtHR, *Pélissier and Sassi* (n 440) para 53.

[443] Doswald-Beck (n 189) 476.

[444] Note that this does not entirely correspond to the question of detention by armed groups in non-international armed conflict for security reasons, as opposed to detention in the course of the rebel administration of justice. See: Frédéric Mégret, 'Detention by Non-State Armed Groups in NIACs: IHL, International Human Rights Law and the Question of the Right Authority' in Ezequiel Heffes, Marcos D Kotlik, and Manuel J Ventura (eds), *International Humanitarian Law and Non-State Actors: Debates, Law and Practice* (TMC Asser Press 2020); Jelena Pejic, 'Procedural Principles and Safeguards for Internment/Administrative Detention in Armed Conflict and Other Situations of Violence' (2005) 87 Int'l Rev. Red Cross 375.

Human Rights has labelled the 'principle of correlation', the information communicated to the accused serves to bracket the possible conviction that may result from a trial, unless the defence is provided an adequate opportunity to react to new information or new charges over the course of the proceedings.[445]

As mentioned previously, the right to be informed without delay of the particulars of the offence is a due process guarantee distinct from the right to be tried within a reasonable time. Although that requirement is found in Article 14 of the ICCPR, which served as the inspiration for Article 6(2) of Protocol II, it was excised from the text of the latter. Indeed, when the drafting committee adapted the text of Article 75(4) of Protocol I to international armed conflicts, it added some of the human rights procedural guarantees that had been discarded from Protocol II, but this did not lead to the inclusion of a right to trial within a reasonable time under Protocol I either. As noted by Yukata Arai-Takahashi, this is a due process guarantee that has been more widely accepted as derogable under human rights treaties in situations of emergency such as armed conflicts.[446] Seeing the silences of both protocols, and noting the inconsistent state practice invoked by the ICRC to support its conclusion of the customary status of this requirement, Arai-Takahashi concludes there is some doubt that such a norm does apply to non-international armed conflicts. There is no doubt that this could be a significant concern with respect to non-state armed groups exerting stable exclusive authority over a territory for a long period of time, such as the LTTE in Sri Lanka or the KRG in Iraq, because of the possibility of lengthy pre-trial detention. However, in many, if not most, armed conflicts, armed groups are neither interested nor equipped to detain individuals for long periods of time; indeed, the unfairness of rebel trials more often will reflect the rapidity with which rebel courts move from indictment to conviction, as was the case in the *Sakhanh* trial.[447] Still, despite the absence of a specific provision on the right to a trial within a reasonable time, it is suggested that at some point the mere passage of time will result in unfairness. The criteria devised under human rights standards to assess what amount of time is reasonable could be relevant, including the complexity of the issue, the conduct of the accused and prosecution, and of course the general context.[448] The LTTE itself acknowledged that this was a significant concern, stating that "[w]e have rules of laws which state that cases should not be extended for a period of more than six months and therefore, accordingly, judgment could

445 IACtHR, *Firmín Ramírez* (n 441); ECtHR, *Pélissier and Sassi* (n 440) para 54; Clooney and Webb (n 380) 272–280.

446 Yutaka Arai-Takahashi, 'Law-Making and the Judicial Guarantees in Occupied Territories' in Andrew Clapham, Paola Gaeta, and Marco Sassòli (eds), *The 1949 Geneva Conventions: A Commentary* (Oxford University Press 2015) 469–470.

447 *Sakhanh* (n 278) 39 para 62 (delay of forty-one hours between detention and execution suggests a manifestly unfair trial).

448 McDermott (n 402) 52–63; Schabas (n 419) 392–396.

be obtained by the people as early as possible".[449] This is expressed in terms that cover both penal and civil matters, which is not surprising given that unfairness due to delay could arise in both areas of law under rebel jurisdiction.

iii. Presumption of Innocence

The presumption of innocence is a fundamental due process guarantee that was not explicitly mentioned in the 1949 Geneva Conventions but that is listed in Article 6(2)(d) of Additional Protocol II and Article 75(4)(d) of Additional Protocol I. The language used in the two protocols tracks very closely the statement of the presumption of innocence in the major universal and regional human rights conventions.[450] While not included in the list of non-derogable human rights in any of these treaties, the Human Rights Committee and the Inter-American Commission on Human Rights have held that no emergency can justify suspension of the presumption of innocence.[451] This is a recognised feature of nearly all legal systems, and, unsurprisingly, the ICRC concludes that it is entrenched in customary international law applicable to both international and non-international armed conflicts.[452] This is a broad procedural guarantee that overlaps with other due process norms such as the protection against self-incrimination. With respect to the rebel administration of justice, three aspects of the presumption of innocence call for a brief discussion, related to the burden of proof, the mindset of judges, and prejudicial statements by public officials.

First, the presumption of innocence is reflected in the apportionment of the burden of proof in criminal prosecutions. It is a grave denial of the right to a fair trial to require that the accused establish that they did not commit the crime they are alleged to have committed. Rather, the burden falls upon the prosecution to proffer compelling evidence of the guilt of the accused.[453] This is in turn linked to the standard of proof that the prosecution must meet, meaning that no reasonable trier of fact would be left with a reasonable doubt as to the guilt of the accused. Under the principle of *in dubio pro reo*, any lingering element of doubt must be taken to favour the accused.[454] If, however, the accused invoke specific elements in their defence, for instance by claiming an alibi, then there is no violation of the presumption of innocence in requiring them to adduce evidence of the necessary facts.[455] The presumption of innocence applies, in the

[449] LTTE, The Judicial System of Tamil Eelam (n 55) 19.

[450] Art. 14(2), ICCPR; Art. 6(2), ECHR; Art. 8(2), ACHR; Art. 7(1)(b), African Charter of Human and Peoples' Rights.

[451] Human Rights Committee, General Comment 29 (n 378) para 11; IACnHR, Report on Terrorism and Human Rights, OAS Doc OEA/Ser.L/V/II.116 (2002) para 247.

[452] Henckaerts and Doswald-Beck (n 255) Rule 100.

[453] See, e.g., IACtHR, *Ruano Torres v El Salvador*, Judgment, 5 October 2015, para 127.

[454] ECtHR, *Tsalkitzis v Greece (No 2)*, Judgment, Appl. No 72624/10, 19 October 2017, para 60.

[455] Harris and others (n 440) 462–463; Clooney and Webb (n 380) 206–216; Schabas (n 419) 383–385.

wording of Protocol I and II, to "anyone charged", meaning that it will kick in at the latest from the moment of the laying of charges, and perhaps even earlier, but not in the purely investigative phase that may have preceded it.[456] If a person is detained on remand for an extended period of time, likely years rather than months, then it can amount to a punitive act that runs afoul of the presumption of innocence.[457] The study of the practice of rebel courts suggests that very few have a sophisticated approach to matters of procedure and evidence. Prosecutions are rarely framed by an explicit acknowledgment of the presumption of innocence in favour of the accused, or of the burden or proof of the prosecution, or of a standard of proof beyond reasonable doubt. The description of prosecutions before courts of the Islamic State offers an example of proceedings that fall woefully short of the presumption of innocence, with convictions resting on very little evidence proffered in court. Not all non-state armed groups are like the Islamic State, however, and the practice of many rebel courts in seeking out evidence and aiming for a fair and balanced assessment does not seem radically divergent from the administration of justice before the courts of many states. A proactive engagement with armed groups that operate courts with due process requirements could offer the presumption of innocence as a procedural and evidentiary framework that would not require enormous changes for many rebel justice systems but nevertheless contribute to greater or more consistent procedural fairness.

A second aspect of the presumption of innocence is related to the appropriate mindset of the decision-maker in criminal proceedings, whether they are judges or members of the community sitting as a jury or a popular assembly. To presume someone innocent implies that these decision-makers entertain no preconceived notion as to the guilt of the accused.[458] Thus, statements by judges expressing or implying the guilt of the accused while a trial is still ongoing, whether expressed in court as part of judicial proceedings or in extrajudicial statements to the media or in public, violate the presumption of innocence.[459] Less directly, the fact of placing the accused in a metal cage in the courtroom, or to require them to wear clothing identifying them as inmates, has been taken to suggest that they are guilty before the trial has been completed.[460] Thus, the practice of the FARC

[456] Harris, ibid 461; Clooney and Webb, ibid 202; Schabas, ibid 383.

[457] Rachel Murray, *The African Charter on Human and Peoples' Rights: A Commentary* (Oxford University Press 2019) 226; Louise Doswald-Beck, *Human Rights in Times of Conflict and Terrorism* (Oxford University Press 2011) 347; Steiner and Fuchs (n 379) 292.

[458] IACtHR, *Ruano Torres* (n 453) para 127; ECtHR, *Barberà, Messegué and Jabardo v Spain*, Judgment (Plenary), Appl. No 10590/83, 6 December 1988, para 77.

[459] Harris and others (n 440) 465; ECtHR, 'Guide on Article 6 of the European Convention on Human Rights—Right to a Fair Trial (Criminal Limb)' (Council of Europe 2020) 67–68.

[460] Human Rights Committee, *Karimov v Tajikistan*, UN Doc CCPR/C/89/D/1108 (2007) para 7.4; ECtHR, *Valyuzhennich v Russia*, Judgment, Appl. No 10597/13, 26 March 2019, paras 32–35.

of tying an accused to a tree during a court-martial would suggest guilt and as such breach the presumption of innocence, unless there were specific security concerns that might exceptionally justify such a measure.[461] Otherwise, the requirement of an open mind of the decision-maker in criminal trials before rebel courts does not seem unduly onerous or challenging to implement. There seems to be no reason to warrant that this aspect of the presumption of innocence should not apply in full to the rebel administration of justice.

A third implication of the presumption of innocence concerns prejudicial statements by public officials from the executive or legislative branches of government. The right to be presumed innocent implies that the authorities must not behave in a manner that undermines the regular judicial process that must make a determination of the guilt or innocence of a person accused of having committed a crime. In particular, officials must refrain from any public prejudicial statement, whether oral or written, that suggests that the accused is guilty.[462] Public officials, whether they are elected to a political office or attached to the police force, routinely make announcements to inform the public that someone has been arrested and charged with an offence. There is indeed a legitimate interest in keeping the public informed of ongoing criminal investigations. In order to avoid violating the right to the presumption of innocence of any accused, however, public officials must do so "with all the discretion and reserve necessary".[463] Any public statement by a representative of the state that proclaims or suggests the guilt of an accused prior to the final judgment of a court will breach the presumption of innocence. The European Court of Human Rights has insisted that the choice of words and the context in which they are issued and interpreted matter greatly to the determination of whether they go beyond indicating that a person has been accused to instead signal that they are guilty.[464] Statements found in violation of the presumption of innocence have ranged from officials declaring that "they were sure" that the accused had committed the crime to others that merely implied so.[465] For the European Court, "[i]t suffices, even in the absence of any formal findings, that there is some reasoning to suggest that the official regards the accused as guilty".[466] Statements such as describing the

[461] See Chapter 1, Section I.B.ii.

[462] Doswald-Beck (n 189) 475; Murray (n 457) 225; Harris and others (n 440) 466; Steiner and Fuchs (n 379) 292; Joseph and Castan (n 358) 477; Clooney and Webb (n 380) 217–227.

[463] ECtHR, *Allenet de Ribemont v France*, Judgment, Appl. No 15175/89, 10 February 1995, para 38.

[464] ECtHR, *Ismoilov v Russia*, Appl. No 2947/06, 24 April 2008, para 166; ECtHR, *Y.B. v Turkey*, Appl. No 48173/99 & 48319/99, 28 January 2005.

[465] Human Rights Committee, *Gridin v Russia*, UN Doc CCPR/C/69/D/770/1997 (2000) para 3.5; ECtHR, *Allenet de Ribemont* (n 463) para 41.

[466] ECtHR, *Butkevičius v Lithuania*, Appl. No 48279/99, 62 June 2002, para 49. See also Human Rights Committee, *Karimov & Nusatov v Tadjikistan*, UN Doc CCPR/C/89/D/1108 & 1121/2002 (2007) para 7.4.

accused as 'bad men' can be taken as encouraging the public to believe that the accused are guilty and as interfering with the unbiased assessment of fact by the competent tribunal.[467] There is no need to prove that the court in fact presumed them to be guilty in a later trial.[468] The fact that the accused were later acquitted does not negate the possibility that the presumption of innocence was violated.

Applying this standard to the rebel administration of justice, it is likely that the overwhelming majority of criminal cases decided by insurgent courts will not arouse the interest of the armed group's leadership, and as such appear unlikely to trigger this type of prejudicial statements. This nevertheless leaves a small subset of politically sensitive cases, such as those of informants or enemies of one ilk or another. For such cases, it may prove much more likely that the insurgent leaders will not refrain from speaking to the guilt of the accused, because of the strained context of armed hostilities, because rebel courts are a part of the insurgent movement and because there is less of a culture and structure of division of powers within an armed group as compared to state governments. For such politically sensitive prosecutions, as is the case for terrorist trials before state courts, the presumption of innocence may set demands that prove difficult to meet for non-state armed groups.[469]

iv. Necessary Rights and Means of Defence

Article 6(2)(a) of Additional Protocol II requires that an accused, before and during the trial, be afforded "all necessary rights and means of defence". Although this expression was transposed to Article 75(4)(a) of Additional Protocol I, what exactly is included in the 'necessary rights and means of defence' is not defined in those treaties. The vagueness of this humanitarian law notion stands in contrast with the approach adopted in the major human rights instruments, in which an elaborate list of specific rights and means of defence is given.[470] Even other parts of humanitarian law covering judicial proceedings against prisoners of war (Arts. 96, 99, and 105, Third Geneva Convention) and civilians in occupied territory or interned (Arts. 72 and 123, Fourth Geneva Convention) contain comparatively fuller articulations. There was a proposal at the diplomatic conference in Geneva to spell out some of the finer implications of the 'necessary rights and means of defence' in Article 75(4) of Protocol I, but this was largely resisted by states.[471]

467 ECtHR, *Allenet de Ribemont* (n 463) para 41; Doswald-Beck (n 457) 346.

468 Joseph and Castan (n 358) 478.

469 Doswald-Beck (n 189) 475.

470 This includes Art. 14(3) of the Covenant on Civil and Political Rights, Art. 6(3) of the European Convention on Human Rights, and Art. 8(2) of the ACHR. Only the African Charter of Human and Peoples' Rights opts for a general reference to "the right to defence", specified to include the right to counsel (Art. 7(1)(3)).

471 Arai-Takahashi (n 446) 467–468; Levie (n 389) 31, 36, 41–42, 50, 58 (including a remark by Canada that 'the purpose of the Conference was not to draft a Convention on Human Rights', at 55).

More recently, when states negotiated the Elements of Crimes under the Rome Statute related to the violation of Common Article 3, there was again a proposal to list what rights and means of defence were required in order for a conviction to be consistent with judicial guarantees recognised as indispensable, finding inspiration in corresponding human rights provisions.[472] This was rejected, with one state articulating that "[t]he judicial guarantees must be those recognized by international humanitarian law, which takes into consideration the nature of the war; it would be inappropriate to adopt those of international human rights law, which are intended to apply during peacetime".[473] The proper guide to interpret judicial guarantees under Common Article 3 is Article 6(2) of Protocol II, it was noted, without which the "high thresholds appropriate to normal situations" would apply to emergency situations like armed conflicts.[474] It thus seems difficult (for once) to follow Sandesh Sivakumaran in concluding, on the basis of selective references to these same sources, that "[t]he key point . . . is that states did not contest the proposed list of rights and means of defence on the basis of inapplicability to, or impracticality in, internal armed conflicts".[475] On the contrary, there is a pattern of consistent rejection of a fixed content to the 'necessary rights and means of defence' in international humanitarian law.[476] This rejection does not, of course, empty the concept of any content under humanitarian law, nor does it suggest that the corresponding specific articulations of elements related to the rights of the defence in human rights law are irrelevant to the interpretation of Article 6(2)(a) of Protocol II. Rather, the consistent withholding of a fixed list indicates that there is a fluid content to the necessary rights and means of

[472] Proposal Submitted by Costa Rica, Hungary and Switzerland on Article 8 paragraph 2(c) of the Rome Statute of the International Criminal Court, UN Doc PNCC/1999/WGEC/DP.10 (19 July 1999) 3, online: <https://legal-tools.org/doc/bb9a6e/pdf> ("The right to be afforded before and during the trial all necessary rights and means of defence, which includes the following pre-trial and trial minimum guarantees: The right to be brought promptly before a judge or other officer authorized by law to exercise judicial power; The right to be entitled to take proceedings before a court, in order that that court may decide without delay on the lawfulness of his detention and order his release; The right to have adequate time and facilities for the preparation of his defence and to communicate with counsel of his own choosing; The right to defend himself/herself in person or through legal assistance; The right to be tried without undue delay; The right to present and examine witnesses; The right to an interpreter").

[473] Colombia, Comments on the Proposal Submitted by Costa Rica, Hungary and Switzerland on Article 8 paragraph 2(c) of the Rome Statute of the International Criminal Court, UN Doc PNCC/1999/WGEC/DP.15 (29 July 1999) 5, online: <https://legal-tools.org/doc/9c032f/pdf>.

[474] ibid. The possibility of future progress with respect to due process guarantees is mentioned as a further consideration. It is reported that some states feared that a list would devalue any rights no included, while others felt that a denial of one right of means of defence should not amount to a war crime: Knut Dörmann, 'War Crimes under the Rome Statute of the International Criminal Court, with a Special Focus on the Negotiations on the Elements of Crimes' (2003) 7 Max Planck Yearbook of United Nations Law 341, 399.

[475] Sandesh Sivakumaran, 'Courts of Armed Opposition Groups—Fair Trials or Summary Justice?' (2009) 7 Journal of International Criminal Justice 489, 504–505.

[476] Parth Geiji, 'Can Insurgent Courts Be Legitimate under International Law?' (2013) 91 Texas Law Review 1525, 1548.

defence that corresponds to what is feasible and reasonable to ensure an effective defence in the context of a non-international armed conflict, even as it relates to prosecutions before state courts.

Notwithstanding this fluidity, several elements corresponding to the necessary rights and means of defence are commonly identified, namely: the right to counsel; the right to present a full defence; the right to a public trial; and the prohibition of double jeopardy. Each is analysed in turn to assess its implications for the administration of justice by non-state armed groups in a situation of armed conflict.

(a) Right to Counsel

Perhaps the most striking silence in the statement of due process guarantees in Article 6(2) of Protocol II and Article 75(4) of Protocol I relates to the right of an accused person to benefit from legal counsel. From a human rights perspective, this is considered a fundamental component of the right to present one's case before a court. As expressed by the European Commission of Human Rights, counsel is present "to ensure that both sides of the case are actually heard" and to act as "the watchdog of procedural regularity".[477] There is no doubt that it can be an important aspect of the fairness of judicial proceedings before insurgent courts.

Every general human rights convention includes the right of an accused to, in the formulation used in Article 14(3)(d) of the ICCPR, "defend himself in person or through legal assistance of his own choosing". This is an expression of the broad principle of *audi alteram partem*, corresponding to a right to present argument so that the decision-maker can arrive at an informed and fair decision, and a right to choose to do so either directly or through counsel. Thus, the practice of Islamic State courts in and around Mosul whereby the accused would be brought to court but basically not allowed to present their case fails to meet the most basic requirements of the right to a defence.[478] The right to present one's own case may be limited if the accused is disruptive or uses the court as a platform to engage in political diatribes, possibilities more relevant to the operation of international criminal tribunals than insurgent courts.[479] The Covenant, like the regional conventions, frames this right in a criminal law context, but it has been interpreted to apply to a range of judicial proceedings determining issues of significance to the lives of the parties. For instance, this has been applied to constitutional litigation, immigration matters, employment, family, and so

[477] ECnHR, *Ensslin, Baade & Raspe v Federal Republic of Germany*, Appl. No 7572/76, Decision of 8 July 1978, at 114.
[478] See the descriptions of court hearings provided by informants in Chapter 2, Section II.B.
[479] McDermott (n 402) 73–77.

on.[480] The right to the assistance of a legal counsel covers every phase of proceedings, including pre-trial aspects and appeals, as made clear by the mention in Article 6(2)(a) of Protocol II that the rights of defence apply "before and during his trial".[481] This right has been deemed applicable beyond the regular courts of the state. For instance, the African Commission on Human and Peoples' Rights found in *Achutan v. Malawi* that the right to counsel applied to the Southern Regional Traditional Court, a customary court with a recognised jurisdiction under Malawian law.[482] Likewise, the *gacaca* courts established by the government of Rwanda after the 1994 genocide were criticised for failing to guarantee the right to legal counsel.[483]

For courts established by armed insurgents, there are a number of specific aspects of the right to counsel that may pose great challenges. These include the rights to freely choose a legal counsel, to receive free legal assistance if unable to pay for it, to communicate freely, and to be given adequate time and facilities. The interpretation of these rights is guided by the overarching principle of the equality of arms between the parties, whereby whatever rights and resources are available must be fairly apportioned.[484]

The right to freely choose a legal counsel speaks to the nature and extent of the freedom being so recognised and the qualifications associated with the function of legal counsel. All general human rights conventions join in affirming an accused's right to assistance from a legal counsel "of his own choosing". This freedom of choice is also recognised for civilian detainees in occupied territory (Art. 72, Fourth Geneva Convention) and prisoners of war (Art. 105, Third Geneva Convention) in situations of international armed conflicts. There is no mention of any right to counsel in either Additional Protocol, so this silence of course covers any possible freedom of choice in the matter. All relevant instruments in human rights and humanitarian law impose limits on the free choice of counsel, for example, where the accused refuses to choose one and the seriousness of the case or an inability to defend oneself requires that a counsel be present to defend the interests of the accused.[485] In state practice, the

[480] Human Rights Committee, General Comment 32 (n 432) para 10; African Commission on Human and Peoples' Rights, Principles and Guidelines on the Right to a Fair Trial and Legal Assistance in Africa (n 384) 7 ("An accused person or a party to a civil case has the right to an effective defence or representation"); Steiner and Fuchs (n 379) 302; Joseph and Castan (n 358) paras 14.33–14.36.

[481] Human Rights Committee, General Comment 32 (n 432) para 37; Doswald-Beck (n 457) 358; Harris and others (n 440) 473–475; Clooney and Webb (n 380) 334–341.

[482] African Commission on Human and Peoples' Rights, *Achutan v Malawi*, Comm. No 64/92, 68/92, 78/92, 8th ACHPR AAR Annex VI (1994–1995) para 10.

[483] Sullo (n 397) 177–178.

[484] Human Rights Committee, General Comment 32 (n 432) para 13; Murray (n 457) 231–232; Joseph and Castan (n 358) paras 14.21–14.28.

[485] Human Rights Committee, ibid para 37; Doswald-Beck (n 189) 476.

freedom to choose a legal counsel commonly has been restricted in relation to military tribunals, in a manner that often has been found to violate international human rights law.[486] Thus, imposing a specific counsel upon an accused against their wishes, or even forcing a choice among a very limited number of possible counsels, has been taken to deny the protected freedom of choice in human rights law.

An inability to freely choose counsel is rarely mentioned among the grievances levelled at the rebel administration of justice. One example relates to the FMLN during the conflict in El Salvador, which recommended that when a trial took place in contested territory, the identity of the defence counsel be kept confidential, even from the accused. The rationale offered by the group was that a person designated as legal counsel before a rebel court was likely to face retaliatory action by the government.[487] This was harshly criticised by Americas Watch in a report on FMLN courts, finding that the group's prevalent practice of anonymous defenders made a farce of the right of an accused to legal counsel.[488] While it is undeniable that neither choosing nor even knowing the identity of the defender can significantly interfere with the rights of the defence, the possible mistreatment by the government of those who act as defenders is a legitimate concern for an armed group. It may well be that any mistreatment meted out by a state against a civilian for merely acting as counsel before a rebel court is a violation of international law. Be that as it may, if the threat of mistreatment is real, then resorting to anonymous defenders may not be an unreasonable response, in the circumstances, to reconcile the accused's right to counsel and the defender's right to bodily integrity. The courts operated by the LTTE offer a different example of a rebel court system in which legal counsel played an active role but for which the research did not unearth any complaints about restriction to the free choice of counsel.

Who do human rights instruments envisage can provide 'legal assistance'? In particular, does the right to 'legal counsel' necessarily imply a person with a formal legal education, and even admitted to the Bar with relevant practical experience? The courts of the LTTE, to return to that example, could meet even the most expansive interpretation of this requirement, in part because the group established and operated its own college of law to train lawyers and also permitted members of the Sri Lankan Bar to appear before its courts. While the example is not unique (one could also mention the courts operated by the KRG in Iraq), the reality in many situations of non-international armed conflict is that there are few or no lawyers available. The FARC, for instance, mostly wielded authority in parts of Colombia that were remote, with few people having received a university education of any kind, fewer

486 Doswald-Beck (n 457) 360.
487 FMLN Secretariat for the Promotion and Protection of Human Rights (n 412) 20.
488 Americas Watch (n 412) 21–22.

still in law. How does the human rights requirement of 'legal assistance' translate for trials by popular assemblies or decisions by local FARC commanders? In one of its documents, the FMLN insisted that "the particular mechanism necessary for defence must be adjusted to the real possibilities of the zone where the trial is held. One cannot insist, for example, that the defence counsel be a licensed attorney when in the region no one exists with this specialization".[489] Other groups such as the Islamic State and the Taliban have objected to lawyers for ideological reasons, and thus exclude them from judicial proceedings even if they may be available.[490]

This raises the question of whether others, with different qualifications, can provide a functional alternative to formally qualified lawyers to offer legal assistance. The language used by the ICCPR and the ECHR is not very specific in this regard, referring to "legal assistance", while the African Charter of Human and Peoples' Rights uses the word "counsel", and the ACHR the expression "legal counsel". There is no doubt that, in an ordinary context, this is interpreted as referring to licenced attorneys.[491] It is interesting to note that the word used in the Spanish version of the American Convention was the subject of debate during the negotiation of that treaty. The initial draft spoke of the right to be "*defendido por un abogado*", but that was felt to be too narrow and ignored the reality that, in many Latin American countries, individuals who are not licensed attorneys provide legal assistance. The Spanish text was therefore changed to refer instead to the right to be "*asistido por un defensor*", a broader notion.[492] The African Commission on Human and Peoples' Rights has held that "the right to be defended by counsel" (Art. 7(1)(3), African Charter) must be interpreted in a manner that reflects "the fact that in many States the number of qualified lawyers is low", to accommodate legal assistance by paralegals.[493] Seeing this, there seems to be no valid reason to insist on a rigid requirement that those appearing before an insurgent court benefit from the assistance of licenced attorneys or even those formally trained in the law. Alternatively, a requirement that the counsel

[489] FMLN Secretariat for the Promotion and Protection of Human Rights (n 412) 20.

[490] Baczko (n.250) 263.

[491] See Human Rights Committee, *Vasilskis v Uruguay*, Comm. No 80/1980, UN Doc CCPR/C/18/D/80/1980 (1983), holding that the state could not appoint an army officer with no legal training to defend an accused before military courts, even if lawyers were too intimidated to appear for the defence. See Clooney and Webb (n 380) 333–334.

[492] Secretaria general de la Organización de los Estados americanos, Conferencia especializada interamericana sobre derechos humanos—Actas y documentos (Washington DC, 1969) 201 ("el concepto 'defensor' cubre ampliamente todos los aspectos y que puede ser un abogado o no. Que como en los Estados Unidos el defensor tiene que ser abogado ahí está cubierto el concepto 'abogado', pero que en los países latinoamericanos el defensor puede ser otra persona"), online: <http://www.oas.org/es/cidh/docs/enlaces/Conferencia%20Interamericana.pdf>. See also Steiner and Fuchs (n 379) 297. Negotiations essentially took place in Spanish, and the English version of the American Convention was not altered to reflect the change in Spanish, retaining the expression 'legal counsel'.

[493] African Commission on Human and Peoples' Rights, Principles and Guidelines on the Right to a Fair Trial and Legal Assistance in Africa (n 384) 8.

"be selected by virtue of his conduct and the solidity of his ethical principles", as suggested by the FMLN, seems not entirely inappropriate.[494] Ultimately, counsel must be able to provide meaningful advice, and what that is will mirror the nature of the court itself. A state court applying formal law may well normally call for a licenced attorney with a university legal education, but a popular assembly applying community norms will require someone with local knowledge, while a religious court applying *Sharī'a* will require someone with religious training. The whole is subject to the principle of equality of arms, meaning that whatever type of qualification one side enjoys must be accessible to the other.[495]

There are a number of procedural rights that are ancillary to the right to counsel, including the right of an indigent accused to receive free legal assistance, the right to communicate in confidence, and the right to adequate time and facilities, that are of potential significance for the rebel administration of justice. The suggestion that a non-state armed group could be required to set up some sort of legal aid programme in a conflict zone may well seem unrealistic. As is often the case in relation to the rebel administration of justice, reality has overtaken what may appear unrealistic, and the LTTE offers one concrete example of an armed group that imposed a system whereby all lawyers were paid through the court registry, with clients in civil or penal matters paying only a small court fee (equivalent to $20) that could be waived altogether if that amount proved too much.[496] However, the LTTE is exceptional in the structure and longevity of its insurgent court system; most armed groups embrace justice practices with a lesser degree of formality, often without trained attorneys to act as legal counsel. In such situations, the assistance provided by counsel might not be monetised, or compensation might be due in forms that may not require a legal aid programme. A key notion derived from the intense discussion of the right to free legal assistance under human rights conventions is that this must be provided either when the issue before the court is of great significance or when parties are notably unable to defend themselves, whether in civil or criminal cases.[497] In prosecutions that might result in the death penalty, for example, or in cases in which young children are parties, there must be effective legal assistance provided.[498] Arguably, this should form part of the right to counsel under the necessary right and means

494 FMLN Secretariat for the Promotion and Protection of Human Rights (n 412) 20.

495 Murray (n 234) 217.

496 Kamalendran (n 63) 5; Mampilly (n 20) 118.

497 Murray (n 457) 217; Steiner and Fuchs (n 379) 300–303; Schabas (n 419) 402–404; Clooney and Webb (n 380) 343–350.

498 Joseph and Castan (n 358) para 14.52; Murray (n 457) 217. As noted recently by the Inter-American Court of Human Rights, this is also linked to the qualifications of the defender, such that appointing law students to defend a case that led to the imposition of the death penalty violated the right to the assistance of legal counsel under the ACHR: IACtHR, *Girón v Guatemala*, Judgment, 15 October 2019, para 109.

of defence in Article 6 of Protocol II.[499] If a group does not have the material resources to offer such assistance, it could allow a civil society organisation to provide this kind of essential legal assistance, on a model similar to the practice before Israeli military courts in the occupied Palestinian territories.[500]

The ability of a party to a case to freely and privately communicate orally or in writing with their counsel is a key feature of the right to receive legal assistance, expressed most explicitly in the ACHR (Art. 8(2)(d)) but implied under all human rights instruments.[501] The Third Geneva Convention likewise recognises the right for the counsel of a prisoner of war to "freely visit the accused and interview him in private".[502] While this has been curtailed, *de jure* or *de facto*, before some state military tribunals, there seems to be no reason to suggest that a right to communicate with counsel should not be fully applicable to proceeding before insurgent courts as an integral element of the right to counsel.[503]

Finally, the right to time and facilities adequate to sufficiently prepare a defence is another recognised dimension of the right to counsel under human rights law.[504] Because insurgent justice tends to be much more expedited than state justice, the requirement for sufficient time is a critically important norm. What 'adequate time' corresponds to is a matter that must be assessed in light of the specific circumstances, both of the case and of the context of the proceedings.[505] Clearly, for criminal cases, the gravity of the offence and the severity of the punishment are central aspects. If a trial before a rebel court resulted in the imposition of the death penalty after only a few hours or even a few days following the initial indictment, as occurred in the *Sakhanh* case, then it can hardly be claimed that the defence was afforded 'adequate time'.[506] Interestingly, the Third Geneva Convention sets a minimum preparation time of two weeks before the opening of a trial against a prisoner of war (Art. 105§3), a standard that could be taken as a helpful benchmark.[507] As for 'adequate facilities', insurgent courts

[499] Doswald-Beck (n 189) 477.

[500] Yesh Din, 'Backyard Proceedings: The Implementation of Due Process Rights in the Military Courts in the Occupied Territories' (Tel Aviv, 2007) 104–107.

[501] Human Rights Committee, General Comment 32 (n 432) para 34; Steiner and Fuchs (n 379) 297–298; Murray (n 457) 230; Schabas (n 419) 390–392; Clooney and Webb (n 380) 360–364.

[502] Art. 105§3, Third Geneva Convention. The first element is also recognised in Art. 72 § 1, Fourth Geneva Convention, in relation to occupied territory.

[503] For example of restrictive practices before military courts, see Yesh Din (n 500) 107–113 (on Israeli occupation courts), and Jennifer Elsea, 'The Military Commissions Act of 2009 (MCA 2009): Overview and Legal Issues' (Congressional Research Service 2014) 24 (on US military commissions). See also Doswald-Beck (n 189) 477–478.

[504] Art. 14(3)(b), Covenant on Civil and Political Rights; Art. 6(3)(b), ECHR; Art. 8(2)(c), ACHR.

[505] See Human Rights Committee, General Comment 32 (n 432) paras 32–33; Doswald-Beck (n 457) 357; McDermott (n 402) 92; ECtHR (n 459) 75–76; Schabas (n 419) 389–390; Clooney and Webb (n 380) 279–304.

[506] *Sakhanh* (n 278) 39 para 62 (delay of forty-one hours between detention and execution).

[507] The ICRC notes in its recent commentary that this two-week period is preceded by at least another week to allow the Protecting Power to find an advocate, meaning that the minimal period

often operate under rather spartan conditions, such that facilities are minimal for all parties and for the court itself. Adequate time and facilities are taken to include a right to timely access to any document or other evidence that forms part of the prosecution's case for criminal trials.[508] Access to legal materials, which would normally form part of adequate facilities for regular courts, can again pose enormous challenges in conflict zones where law libraries are few and far between. Still, one can mention the example of the Taliban judge explaining that he has thousands of volumes on *Sharīʿa* on his laptop, searchable by keywords.[509] As always, the guiding principle is equality of arms: if one side has access to such resources, then the same must be granted to the other.

(b) Right to Present a Full Defence

A second fundamental element of the necessary rights and means of defence is the right to present a full defence. It is a protection related to the right to be present at one's own trial, relegating to exceptional circumstances the lawful occurrence of a trial *in absentia* during which a full defence is much less likely to be advanced. The right to be present at trial is explicitly recognised in Articles 6(2)(e) of Protocol II and 75(4)(e) of Protocol I, mirroring a right expressly protected under the ICCPR (Art. 14(3)(d)) and considered as implied under other human rights instruments.[510] Seeing the inherent fragility of the rebel administration of justice, there seems to be no reason to limit the full applicability of this norm to insurgent courts. In any case, the prosecution of individuals *in absentia* by armed groups, if it takes place at all, is not a significant practice.

The right to present a full defence is centrally concerned with the ability of an accused or a party to a civil case to adduce documentary and testimonial evidence supporting their claim and to challenge any such evidence put forward by the prosecution or the adverse party. This right is spelled out in Article 75(4)(g) of Protocol I, which borrows the exact wording from Article 14(3)(e) of the ICCPR and Article 6(3)(d) of the ECHR: "Anyone charged with an offence shall have the right to examine, or have examined, the witnesses against him and to obtain the attendance and examination of witnesses on his behalf under the same

is actually three weeks from notification of the indictment: ICRC, *Commentary on the Third Geneva Convention* (n 356) para 4115.

[508] Murray (n 457) 229.

[509] Baczko (n 250) 241.

[510] See: African Commission on Human and Peoples' Rights, Principles and Guidelines on the Right to a Fair Trial and Legal Assistance in Africa (n 384) 16; ECtHR (n 459) 53–55; Doswald-Beck (n 457) 365–366; Payam Akhavan, 'Judicial Guarantees' in Andrew Clapham, Paola Gaeta, and Marco Sassòli (eds), *The 1949 Geneva Conventions: A Commentary* (Oxford University Press 2015) 1229–1230; Clooney and Webb (n 380) 446–480.

conditions as witnesses against him".[511] Critically, this right is not mentioned in Article 6(2) of Protocol II, but it is so central to the protected 'necessary rights and means of defence' mentioned there that some ability to adduce and challenge evidence must be afforded in order for a trial to meet the minimal standard of fairness.[512] Informants described being brought before Islamic State courts in and around Mosul but not being allowed to call any witness, amounting to the denial of a right to present a defence that ineluctably taints the entire trial as unfair.[513]

The right to present a full defence in general, and the right to call and cross-examine witnesses in particular, have been construed once again in light of the principle of equality of arms. Indeed, as can be gleaned from the last segment of the norm quoted in the preceding paragraph, the equality of procedural rights between prosecution and defence is expressly affirmed. Human rights bodies have given much significance to this facet of the right, and some have even suggested in relation to the ICCPR that "article 14(3)(e) is not concerned with the right to call witnesses per se; it is concerned with equality of rights to call witnesses as between the defence and the prosecution".[514] While it is true that the Human Rights Committee has at times insisted on the equality aspect, the right to present a full defence corresponds to a reasonable right to call and examine witnesses. This is apparent from repeated statements that this right is qualified, not unlimited, or subject to reasonable limits, but otherwise essential to a fair trial.[515] Accepted limits to the right to call witnesses include a general requirement that the proposed testimony be relevant, possible immunities that some individuals might enjoy against enforced testimony, and material limits reflecting the fact that potential witnesses might be missing, abroad, sick, or dead.[516] Under human rights law, courts are required to make reasonable efforts to secure witnesses, including resorting to international cooperation.[517] As illustrated by the practice of international criminal tribunals that have limited powers of subpoena, it is possible to maintain procedural fairness even in an environment in which other actors are not always inclined to be very cooperative.[518] Insurgent courts may well be at a

[511] Art. 8(2)(f) of the ACHR specifically mentions the right to call expert witnesses, something considered implied under the other instruments: Doswald-Beck (n 457) 365. The African Charter of Human and Peoples' Rights does not mention explicitly the right to call witnesses, but the African Commission has found that it is inferred under the right to defence (Art. 7(1)(3)): African Commission on Human and Peoples' Rights, ibid 16.

[512] Doswald-Beck (n 189) 480–481.

[513] See the descriptions of court hearings provided by informants in Chapter 2, Section II.B.

[514] Joseph and Castan (n 358) 500.

[515] See: Human Rights Committee, General Comment 32 (n 432) para 39; ICRC, *Commentary on the 1977 Additional Protocols* (n 288) 884; Dörmann (n 423) 429; Doswald-Beck (n 457) 365; Steiner and Fuchs (n 379) 303; Schabas (n 419) 406–407; Clooney and Webb (n 380) 511–532.

[516] Murray (n 457) 232–233; Doswald-Beck (n 457) 365.

[517] ECtHR, *Lucic v Croatia*, Appl. No 5699/11, Judgment, 27 February 2014, paras 79–80.

[518] McDermott (n 402) 87–89.

disadvantage when compared to state courts in their ability to procure witnesses legitimately sought by one party, because their authority tends to be territorially more limited and legally more uncertain. The experience of the LTTE described in the earlier analysis of territorial jurisdiction has shown that rebel courts sometimes have an ability to project their authority even beyond the areas under the control of the armed group to secure the presence of witnesses.[519]

Turning to the right to cross-examine witnesses called by the other party, and in particular the defence right to cross-examine prosecution witnesses in criminal trials, one issue of concern is anonymous or 'faceless' witnesses. A study of the Israeli military justice system in the occupied Palestinian territories illustrates the pervasive role played by 'secret evidence' for the administration of justice in a hostile context.[520] Like Israel in the occupied territories, many armed groups gather information by way of a network of collaborators whose safety would likely be threatened by the divulgation of their identity. In other situations, a witness fears the consequences of testifying against a powerful actor who might exert revenge, or punishment by the state for taking part in insurgent justice. Knowing the identity of witnesses is a critically important aspect of the right to cross-examine them, as it can inform whether there are any reasons to suspect the witnesses to be unreliable or untrustworthy.[521] Under international human rights law, it is acknowledged that the right to confront adverse witnesses can be limited by withholding their identity, if this is necessary to protect the life, personal integrity, safety, or liberty of the witnesses or their family.[522] A decision to allow anonymous testimony must be exceptional, taken by the court on the basis of its own appraisal of objective factors, including the identity of the witness.[523] If mitigating factors can be used, such as testifying behind a screen or sharing the identity of witnesses with defence counsel but not the defendant, then it must be done. Finally, as put by the Inter-American Court of Human Rights, "[e]ven when counterbalancing procedures have been adopted that appear to be sufficient, a conviction should not be based either solely or to a decisive extent on anonymous statements".[524] All of this amounts to a flexible approach under human rights law, aiming to reconcile the right to present a full defence with other legitimate concerns of the state or of other

[519] See Section II.D, supra.

[520] Lisa Hajjar, *Courting Conflict: The Israeli Military Court System in the West Bank and Gaza* (University of California Press 2005) 110–111.

[521] For a wide-ranging study of the question, see David Lusty, 'Anonymous Accusers: An Historical & Comparative Analysis of Secret Witnesses in Criminal Trials' (2002) 24 Sydney Law Review 361.

[522] See: ECtHR, *Al-Khawaja and Tahery v UK*, Appl. No 26766/05 & 22228/06, Judgment (Grand Chamber), 15 December 2011, paras 120–125; IACtHR, *Leaders of the Mapuche Indigenous People v Chile*, Judgment, 29 May 2014, para 234.

[523] Steiner and Fuchs (n 379) 303–304; ECtHR (n 459) 94–95; Doswald-Beck (n 189) 480–481; Clooney and Webb (n 380) 513–516.

[524] IACtHR, *Mapuche Case* (n 522) para 247.

individuals.[525] In the context of the rebel administration of justice, it suggests that while a party must normally be allowed to cross-examine witnesses knowing their identity, insurgent courts have a degree of discretion to conceal that identity in a particular case if so demanded by the interest of justice.[526]

(c) Right to a Public Trial

The right to a public trial is a fundamental right that, for the rebel administration of justice, stands at a point of tension: on the one hand, public trials are governance performances, a demonstration by armed groups that they hold authority over a territory and population; on the other, armed hostilities like many other emergencies are situations in which the control of the flow of information yields weighty and often immediate significance, leading many armed groups to avoid open and adversarial exercises like public trials. The right to a public trial is not mentioned in Article 6 of Protocol II nor in Article 75 of Protocol I. The omission is significant because the provision that inspired due process guarantees in the two protocols, Article 14(1) of the ICCPR, does explicitly protect the right to a public hearing for both criminal and civil proceedings. It is likewise included in the procedural guarantees protected under the European (Art. 6(1)) and American (Art. 8(3)) Conventions on Human Rights, and considered as implied under Article 7(1) of the African Charter of Human and Peoples' Rights.[527] An openness of proceedings of sorts in the context of international armed conflicts is granted under the Third (Art. 105) and Fourth (Art. 74) Geneva Conventions, which provide that Protecting Powers must be given access to judicial proceedings against a prisoner of war or a detained civilian in occupied territory.[528] The ICRC, in its study of customary law, relies on this, on the human rights provisions mentioned before, and on a smattering of state practice to conclude

[525] In international criminal law, tribunals have had divergent approaches, with a progressive evolution towards requiring the defence to be appraised of the identity of prosecution witnesses by the beginning of the trial: ICTY, *Prosecutor v Tadic*, Decision on Prosecution Motion for Protective Measures for Witnesses, IT-94-I-T, 10 August 1995, paras 53–86; ICC, *Prosecutor v Katanga*, Judgment on the appeal of the Prosecutor against the decision of Pre-Trial Chamber I entitled 'First Decision on the Prosecution Request for Authorisation to Redact Witness Statements', ICC-01/04-01/07 (OA), 13 May 2008, paras 66–72; Tim Welch and others, 'Witness Anonymity at the International Criminal Court: Due Process for Defendants, Witnesses or Both' (2011) 23 Denning Law Journal 29; Michael E Kurth, 'Anonymous Witnesses before the International Criminal Court: Due Process in Dire Straits' in Carsten Stahn and Göran Sluiter (eds), *The Emerging Practice of the International Criminal Court* (Brill Nijhoff 2009).

[526] Murray (n 234) 217.

[527] See: African Commission on Human and Peoples' Rights, Principles and Guidelines on the Right to a Fair Trial and Legal Assistance in Africa (n 384) 2; Murray (n 457) 44–45.

[528] Canada proposed the inclusion, in the draft of what became Article 6 of Protocol II, of a right for the Red Cross to attend the trial of any person accused in a non-international armed conflict. The proposed text was clearly derived from the right of access granted to Protecting Powers in the Third and Fourth Geneva Conventions, but this was not accepted: Howard S Levie, *The Law of Non International Armed Conflict: Protocol II to the 1949 Geneva Conventions* (Martinus Nijhoff Publishers 1987) 265, 267.

that the right to a public trial is a general requirement under customary humanitarian law. Although there is very little in the sources that suggests an obligation in situations of non-international armed conflicts, the ICRC holds that this is applicable in all categories of armed conflicts.[529]

The capital significance of the public trial was highlighted by Jeremy Bentham, in a passage repeated by many courts since: "Publicity is the very soul of justice. It is the keenest spur to exertion and the surest of all guards against improbity".[530] There are two distinct interests at play that underpin the principle of the openness and transparency of the administration of justice, the first reflecting the right to a fair trial of the parties, and the second the need to maintain public confidence in the judicial system.[531] Both sets of interests seem equally relevant to the operation of insurgent courts. The right to a public trial implies that the hearings are held at a time and in a location broadly accessible to anyone who might wish to attend. Such time and location must be advertised, and attendance may not be limited to a particular category of persons, for instance to relatives of an accused. The human rights treaty provisions on the right to a public trial explicitly provides for the exceptional exclusion of the public and the media "for reasons of moral, public order (*ordre public*) or national security in a democratic society", to protect the privacy of parties, victims, or witnesses, or to the extent strictly necessary for the interest of justice.[532] The Geneva Conventions for their part exceptionally allow for trials *in camera* "in the interest of State security".[533] A decision to restrict public access to a trial must be made by the court for reasons that are themselves made public, and the measures must be limited to what is strictly necessary in the circumstances.[534] The limits of this right have often been tested in relation to military courts or tribunals dealing with terrorism offences. For example, a military court sitting on a military base that is itself closed to the public cannot be considered accessible as required under the right to a public trial.[535] It should be borne in mind that the right to a public trial, like other due process guarantees, is not included in the list of non-derogable rights in the relevant

529 Henckaerts and Doswald-Beck (n 255) Rule 100.

530 John Bowring (ed), *The Works of Jeremy Bentham*, vol 4 (W Tait 1843) 316. Along the same line, one can cite the famous holding of Lord Hewart CJ in *R v Sussex Justices, ex parte McCarthy*, [1924] KB 256, 259: "it is not merely of some importance but it is of fundamental importance that justice must not only be done, but should manifestly and undoubtedly be seen to be done".

531 ECtHR, *Martinie v France*, Appl. No 58675/00, Judgment (Grand Chamber), 12 April 2006, para 39. See: Doswald-Beck (n 457) 354; Steiner and Fuchs (n 379) 312; ECtHR (n 459) 52; Schabas (n 419) 375.

532 Art. 14(1), Covenant on Civil and Political Rights; Art. 6(1), ECHR; Art. 8(5), ACHR. See Human Rights Committee, General Comment 32 (n 432) para 29; Clooney and Webb (n 380) 162–180.

533 Art. 105§5, Third Geneva Convention; Art. 74§1, Fourth Geneva Convention. See ICRC, *Commentary on the Third Geneva Convention* (n 356) paras 4136–4137.

534 ECtHR (n 459) 56–58; McDermott (n 402) 78; Joseph and Castan (n 358) para 14.104.

535 IACtHR, *Castillo Petruzzi v Peru*, Judgment, 30 May 1999, para 172; Doswald-Beck (n 189) 481. For an example, see Yesh Din (n 500) 88.

human rights treaties. In fact, when it was proposed to include the right to a public trial in the list of non-derogable rights, the United Kingdom objected that such a right might be impossible to implement in wartime.[536] It is important to acknowledge that the requirement of a public trial articulated by human rights bodies in relation to 'normal' situations may be unattainable and inappropriate for situations of armed conflict, all the more so for non-state armed groups with a more fragile governance foothold.

One aspect of the right to a public trial that has particular relevance to the rebel administration of justice is the concealment of the identity of judges. The FMLN reported that, during the civil war in El Salvador, "[m]ost of the time we are obliged not to reveal the identity of the members of the tribunal".[537] More recently, informants report that it was a common practice for the accused in Islamic State courts in and around Mosul to be hooded during court proceedings so that they would not see who were the judges.[538] Concealing the identity of judges raises concerns regarding the impartiality of the tribunal, as the parties are deprived of an opportunity to assess whether the judge has a bias or an interest in the case, but it is more broadly a device to make invisible a pivotal element of the judicial process.[539] As such, faceless judges have been seen as an assault on the right to a public trial. There is a significant practice of faceless judges ('*jueces sin rostro*') in Latin America, in the context of the repression of terrorism, insurgency, and drug trafficking, justified by governments on the basis of threats and attacks against judges in these cases.[540] The Inter-American Commission and Court of Human Rights as well as the Human Rights Committee have all taken the view that it is extremely difficult to reconcile the use of faceless judges with the requirement of due process.[541] At the same time, the right to physical integrity of judges and the interests of justice call for measures that allow for prosecutions even under very difficult circumstances. In all the cases that were found to amount to a denial of the right to a fair trial, the use of faceless judges was combined with an array of other violations of due process guarantees. The fact that sitting on the bench of a rebel court is a criminal act under municipal law is a relevant factual and legal consideration. If the threat to insurgent judges is averred, such that they are likely to be the object of immediate and severe measures against their persons either by members of the community

536 Stavros (n 373) 347 (referring to UN Doc E/CN.4/SR.126 [17 June 1949] 4–5).

537 FMLN Commander Nidia Díaz, quoted in Americas Watch (n 412) 11.

538 Interview with 'Adnan' (displaced civilian, near Tal Afar) (September 2017).

539 Human Rights Committee, *Polay Campos v Peru*, Comm. No 577/1994, 6 November 1997, para 8.8.

540 See Luz Estella Nagle, 'Colombia's Faceless Justice: A Necessary Evil, Blind Impartiality or Modern Inquisition' (1999) 61 University of Pittsburgh Law Review 881.

541 IACtHR, *J v Peru*, Judgment, 27 November 2013, paras 184–186; IACtHR, *Castillo Petruzzi v Peru*, 30 May 1999, para 172; IACnHR, Report on Terrorism and Human Rights (n 451) para 261; Human Rights Committee, *Polay Campos* (n 539) para 8.8.

or by government forces, then an absolute ban on anonymous judges seems hard to countenance.[542] At the same time, the impact on the right to a fair trial must be acknowledged, such that any other restriction on due process guarantees would be compounded by the use of faceless rebel judges, making it much easier to conclude that the entire trial was unfair.

A related question, likely unique to the rebel administration of justice, is whether insurgent courts may be directly targeted by the enemy and, if so, whether that can justify refusing to hold public trials. The Taliban is one such armed group that has had to change its practice in reaction to increased targeting by coalition forces. In an earlier phase, many areas had Taliban courts in identified buildings where civilians could go to present their case or to listen in to ongoing trials. Once Taliban judges became high-value targets hounded by US intelligence and special forces, and after many were killed, they had to change their judicial practices.[543] One Taliban judge in the Nahrin district of Afghanistan remarked: "We don't have buildings like a supreme court or a high court marked with big signs proclaiming 'Supreme Court' or 'High Court'. We operate from any building. They can't be targeted by NATO because they are in the middle of populated villages. They're hard to spot".[544] As a result, judges mostly became itinerant, leaving their mobile phone numbers with village elders or local commanders, but always staying on the move. Another Taliban judge in the Qarabagh district, after two of his predecessors were killed by air strikes, commented that "if we stay in the same place too long, it's possible someone will tell the foreign troops or the ANA [Afghan National Army] so that they can quickly attack us".[545] Courts sit in mosques or private houses, at times and in places not advertised to the public. One villager recounted how, in Logar in 2013, he had to walk three hours in the mountain to find a Taliban judge in a remote village. Another recounted how, in Ghazni in 2011, the proceedings took place at night in an attempt to escape enemy surveillance.[546] Of course, Taliban judges, although they belong to a different internal branch of the Taliban, travel under the protection of armed fighters and sometimes will themselves carry a gun for protection.[547]

If we make an analogy with the regular forces of the state, under international humanitarian law, all members of the armed forces are considered combatants, whether or not they carry a weapon. According to Article 43(2) of Protocol I, all combatants are entitled to directly participate in hostilities, meaning that they

542 Doswald-Beck (n 457) 356.
543 Baczko (n 250) 308.
544 ibid 254 (my translation).
545 ibid 255 (my translation).
546 ibid 257.
547 Pål Refsdal, *Taliban: Behind the Masks* (Films Media Group Journeyman Pictures 2010) 26m57s.

themselves can be directly targeted.[548] It follows that a military judge, in an international armed conflict, is a legitimate target. Whether a court in session may be targeted will depend on whether all of those present are combatants, or whether the anticipated harm to civilians is proportional. That said, under the same set of rules, civilian judges are not combatants and may not be targeted.

In non-international armed conflicts, individuals may be targeted for such time as they directly participate in hostilities or, in the interpretation proposed by the ICRC, if they have a 'continuous combat function'.[549] Both direct participation in hostilities and continuous combat function are predicated on carrying out acts that directly cause a minimum threshold of military harm to the enemy.[550] The concept of direct participation in hostilities has been the subject of heated debates, but it seems quite clear that administering justice does not fall within the purview of direct participation in hostilities.[551] Regarding membership, as noted by Gloria Gaggioli, just like every agent of the state is not a member of the armed forces, not every member of a group will be a fighter: "Clearly, membership for the purpose of targeting implies that the individual has a function in the armed wing of the nonstate party to a conflict. Belonging to the political or humanitarian wings of a nonstate party, in the same way as belonging to the political apparatus of a state, does not turn an individual into a military objective for the purpose of IHL".[552] The United States has a wider, more all-encompassing approach to targetability than many other states, whereby "individuals who are formally or functionally part of a non-State armed group that is engaged in hostilities may be made the object of attack because they likewise share in their group's hostile intent".[553] Under this approach, participation in hostilities appears to relate to the group rather than

[548] ICRC, *Commentary on the 1977 Additional Protocols* (n 288) 515.

[549] Nils Melzer (ed), 'Interpretive Guidance on the Notion of Direct Participation in Hostilities under International Humanitarian Law', online: <https://www.icrc.org/eng/resources/documents/publication/p0990.htm> accessed 4 August 2015; Nils Melzer, 'The Principle of Distinction Between Civilians and Combatants' in Andrew Clapham and Paola Gaeta (eds), *The Oxford Handbook of International Law in Armed Conflict* (Oxford University Press 2014) 302–306.

[550] Melzer, 'Interpretive Guidance on the Notion of Direct Participation in Hostilities under International Humanitarian Law' (n 549) 47–58.

[551] For a sample of this debate, see: W Hays Parks, 'Part IX of the ICRC Direct Participation in Hostilities Study: No Mandate, No Expertise, and Legally Incorrect' (2009) 42 NYU Journal of International Law and Politics 769; Dapo Akande, 'Clearing the Fog of War? The ICRC's Interpretive Guidance on Direct Participation in Hostilities' (2010) 59 International and Comparative Law Quarterly 180; Ryan Goodman and Derek Jinks, 'The ICRC Interpretive Guidance on the Notion of Direct Participation in Hostilities Under International Humanitarian Law: An Introduction to the Forum' (2009) 42 NYU Journal of International Law and Politics 637; Michael N Schmitt, 'The Interpretive Guidance on the Notion of Direct Participation in Hostilities: A Critical Analysis', *Essays on Law and War at the Fault Lines* (Springer 2012). Note that there is no contradiction between this conclusion and the suggestion, in Chapter 2, Section IV.B.ii, that the rebel administration of justice as a whole has a nexus to the armed conflict. The nexus is a specific requirement of direct participation in hostilities, but one that must be complemented by the threshold of harm and direct causation.

[552] Gloria Gaggioli, 'Targeting Individuals Belonging to an Armed Group' (2018) 51 Vanderbilt Journal of Transnational Law 901, 912.

[553] US Department of Defense, *Law of War Manual* (2016) para 5.7.3.

to the individual, such that "affiliation with these groups, makes a person liable to being made the object of attack regardless of whether he or she is taking a direct part in hostilities".[554] This may explain the US strategy of directly targeting Taliban judges.[555] Even within this wider approach to targetability, however, this has been criticised as overbroad, on the basis that an armed opposition group with a distinct non-combatant governance structure that does not directly contribute to the ability to conduct military operations cannot be targeted.[556] Thus, the fact that some Taliban judges carried weapons does not permit sidestepping the question of participation in hostilities, especially in a country like Afghanistan where carrying a weapon for personal protection is not unusual.[557] An analogy can be made to a peacekeeping operation that becomes a party to an armed conflict: its military members will be considered targetable combatants, but police officers tasked with law enforcement or training will remain civilians even if they carry a weapon.[558] Considering the dubious legality of directly targeting insurgent courts, it seems a legitimate concern that may inform and limit the human right to a public trial.

There is, under human rights law, a requirement that "any judgment rendered in a criminal case or in a suit at law be made public" (Art. 14(1), ICCPR). This is a right that is independent from the right to a public trial, although both speak to the need for transparency of the administration of justice.[559] The right to have any criminal judgment pronounced publicly is omitted from Protocol II, but it is specifically deemed applicable in international armed conflicts by Article 75(4)(i) of Protocol I. It is certain that, albeit not formulated in a manner that suggests a rigid requirement, the public nature of judicial decisions is an element contributing to the general fairness of a trial in situations of non-international armed conflicts. The requirement that judgments be made public does not imply that judgments take a particular form: so long as the public has access to the reasoning and conclusions of the court, the judgment may be in written or oral form. If written decisions are filed in a registry, then it must be reasonably accessible for anyone interested.[560] The right to a public judgment may be limited to protect

554 US Department of the Army and Department of the Navy, *The Commander's Handbook on the Law of Land Warfare FM 6-27/MCTP 11-10C* (2019) para 2.59.

555 See R Patrick Huston, 'A Practical Perspective on Attacking Armed Groups' (2018) 51 Vanderbilt Journal of Transnational Law 919, 924–925.

556 See: Michael N Schmitt, 'Targeting Non-State "Mixed Groups"' *Articles of War Blog* (5 August 2020), online: <https://lieber.westpoint.edu/targeting-non-state-mixed-groups>; Michael N Schmitt, 'International Humanitarian Law and the Targeting of Non-State Intelligence Personnel and Objects' (2020) 30 Duke Journal of Comparative & International Law 309, 340.

557 The situation is different for armed groups like the FARC, in which judicial proceedings were normally presided by local commanders. These are individuals with continuous combat function that may be directly targeted at any time, including when they are acting as judges.

558 Tristan Ferraro, 'The Applicability and Application of International Humanitarian Law to Multinational Forces' (2013) 95 International Review of Red Cross 561, 600–603.

559 ECtHR, *Artemov v Russia*, Appl. No 14945/03, Judgment, 3 April 2014, para 109.

560 See Human Rights Committee, General Comment 32 (n 432) para 29; Yesh Din (n 500) 85–86; ECtHR (n 459) 58; Harris and others (n 440) 431–432; Schabas (n 419) 379–380.

the interests of children or, in the wider formulation used in the ECHR, in the interests of morals, public order, or national security, or in the interests of justice more generally (Art. 6(1), European Convention). Insurgent courts do tend to make their decisions public, whether in writing in triplicates like the Taliban, or by carrying out punishment in public squares like the Islamic State. Indeed, if an armed group invests in the establishment of a court, then it will likely be in its interest to publicise its decisions to maximise its impact on the broader community for reasons of legal certainty (a public decision can deter challenges) and to affirm its effective authority (confirming the jurisdictional dominance of rebel as opposed to state justice).[561]

(d) *Ne Bis In Idem*

The protection against double jeopardy or *ne bis in idem* is "one of the specific safeguards associated with the general guarantee of a fair hearing in criminal proceedings".[562] It is a right explicitly protected in international armed conflicts under Article 75(4)(h) of Protocol I, but which was not included in the text of Article 6 of Protocol II for internal conflicts.[563] The initial draft of Protocol II prepared by the ICRC in 1974 did include this protection, but its inclusion was resisted by most states, some of which mentioned its problematic relation to judgments of insurgent courts.[564] The protection against *ne bis in idem* is a well-established human rights standard, explicitly protected under Article 14(7) of the ICCPR as well as Article 8(4) of the ACHR. It was not included in the initial version of the ECHR at its adoption in 1950, but was added in 1984 by Protocol 7 to the Convention, which is unique in mentioning that the prohibition of double jeopardy is a non-derogable right (Art. 4(3) of Protocol 7). The African Commission on Human and Peoples' Rights considers that it is implied under Article 7 of the African Charter.[565] In its study of customary international humanitarian law, the ICRC claims that the broad right to a fair trial implies a protection against *ne bis in idem* in both international and non-international armed conflicts (Rule 100).[566] While there are compelling elements to support

[561] Murray (n 234) 219.

[562] ECtHR, *Mihalache v Romania*, Appl. No 54012/10, Judgment (Grand Chamber), 8 July 2019, para 48.

[563] Also in the context of international armed conflicts, Art. 86 of the Third Geneva Convention and Art. 117§3 of the Fourth Geneva Convention protect prisoners of war and civilian internees against double jeopardy.

[564] Meeting of Committee I, 20 March 1975, CDDH/I/SR.33, paras 67 (Pakistan: "Was it to be understood that when a rebel had been condemned or acquitted by a rebel court, he could not longer be arrested or punished for a breach of the national law of the country?"), 35 (Brazil: "It was, however, obvious that such a claim would be dismissed as ridiculous"), 57 (USA), 69 (Iraq), and 71 (Italy), reproduced in Levie (n 528) 245–255. See Bothe and others (n 286) 745.

[565] African Commission on Human and Peoples' Rights, Principles and Guidelines on the Right to a Fair Trial and Legal Assistance in Africa (n 384) 17; Murray (n 457) 245.

[566] Henckaerts and Doswald-Beck (n 255) Rule 100.

a claim that this is indeed a customary human rights norm, and significant state practice related to its application in international armed conflicts pursuant to humanitarian law, there is nearly nothing to substantiate its extension to internal wars.[567] Whether as a hard standard imposing legal obligations or as a looser norm contributing to the overall fairness of a trial, the protection against double jeopardy does seem to be an important facet of the necessary right and means of defence under Protocol II.

Turning to substance, the protection afforded by *ne bis idem* is limited and contested.[568] In the formulation used in Article 75(4)(h) of Protocol I, it safeguards against prosecution or punishment "by the same Party for an offence in respect of which a final judgment acquitting or convicting that person has been previously pronounced under the same law and judicial procedure". In relation to the rebel administration of justice, there are two different scenarios in which *ne bis in idem* may raise specific issues: the repeated prosecution by the same armed group of an individual for the same action, and the prosecution before a rebel court of an individual for an offence for which the person was previously convicted or acquitted by the territorial state's courts.

The first scenario, in which the same entity prosecutes twice, falls closer to the core of the protection against double jeopardy because it is intra-jurisdictional.[569] The prohibition under Protocol I and in human rights treaties covers repeated prosecution for the same 'offence', and not the same fact, conduct, or action. It is a well-accepted limit of *ne bis in idem* that it does not prevent the same jurisdiction from prosecuting an individual twice for conduct which is an element of the *actus reus* of two different offences that have distinguishing features.[570] That said, it is now generally agreed that a single jurisdiction may not prosecute the same person for the same crime before different types of courts, for instance a military prosecution on the heel of a civil conviction or acquittal.[571] This would apply to groups like the LTTE that apparently had distinct civilian and military judicial systems.

The second scenario, in which a person is prosecuted before a rebel court for an offence for which a state court had previously issued a final judgment in acquittal or conviction, raises more challenging issues. As we see in the formulation used in Article 75 of Protocol I, *ne bis in idem* covers the same party prosecuting

[567] Elements of state practice are collated at <https://ihl-databases.icrc.org/customary-ihl/eng/docs/v2_rul_rule100_sectionn>. See Willms (n 189) 162.

[568] Colangelo (n 281) 774; Schabas (n 419) 424–427.

[569] Diane Bernard, 'Ne Bis in Idem—Protector of Defendants' Rights or Jurisdictional Pointsman?' (2011) 9 Journal of International Criminal Justice 863, 865.

[570] ECtHR, *Ramda v France*, Appl. No. 78477/11, Judgment, 19 December 2017, paras 85–97 (prosecutions for attempted murder and terrorism, although in part based on the same conduct, do no violate Protocol 7 of the ECHR). For the range of approaches adopted by different bodies, see Clooney and Webb (n 380) 790–798.

[571] Human Rights Committee, General Comment 32 (n 432) para 54.

the same offence under the same law and procedure. In doctrinal discussions of double jeopardy, the norm is often linked to state sovereignty, reflecting the state's right to protect its interests through penal prosecution.[572] Sovereignty is invoked here to explain jurisdiction, but as I argued in Chapter 1, jurisdiction cannot be reduced to an expression of sovereignty, as there are many instances of recognised jurisdictions not linked to sovereign rights.[573] Federal states are an apt illustration that multiple jurisdictions may coexist within a single state, and indeed the United States provides an example of a state in which double jeopardy does not operate as between federal and state prosecutions.[574] A conviction or acquittal relies on a particular law that in turn reflects a particular jurisdiction. The question this begs for insurgent justice is whether rebel jurisdiction can be subsumed into state jurisdiction.[575] My exploration in Chapter 2 of the foundations of insurgent justice in international law, complemented by my discussion of rebel jurisdiction in an earlier section of the current chapter, lead to conclude that the state and the armed group embody different jurisdictions. It follows that *ne bis in idem* does not apply as between state and rebel justice, any more than it does as between different states.[576]

This principle can be sharpened with two additional comments. First, the fact that an armed group may apply in its courts the laws of the state might suggest that the same law, and therefore the same offence, is being sanctioned. I previously rejected the Stockholm District Court's suggestion in *Sakhanh* that, under international humanitarian law, insurgent courts are legally required to apply state law; the principle of legality enshrined in Article 6(2)(c) of Protocol II accommodates the reality that an offence may be created "under the law" through insurgent legislation.[577] If an armed group chooses to apply state law, it does so as an exercise of its own jurisdiction, and not as some constructive delegated authority from the state. Second, there is a category of crimes that is sanctioned by state and non-state armed groups alike as agents of the international community. A state court that prosecutes a person for war crimes, crimes against humanity, genocide, or piracy, especially if it does so under universal jurisdiction, reflects a *dédoublement fonctionnel* whereby it acts as an agent of the international community as a whole. As a result, a rebel court could not prosecute again these

[572] Colangelo (n 281) 836.
[573] See Chapter 1, Section III.
[574] The classic reference is: United States Supreme Court, *Houston v Moore*, 18 US 1 (1820). Note that in the United States, this is explained by a doctrine of 'dual-sovereignty': United States Supreme Court, *Gamble v US*, 139 S. Ct. 1960 (2019).
[575] Anthony J Colangelo, '*Gamble*, Dual Sovereignty, and Due Process' [2019] Cato Supreme Court Review 189, 203.
[576] Willms (n 189) 162; Arai-Takahashi (n 446) 465; Joseph and Castan (n 358) para 14.214; Murray (n 457) 247; Clooney and Webb (n 380) 799–801.
[577] See Chapter 2, Section IV.C.i.

international crimes without violating *ne bis in idem* because it would do so on the basis of the same jurisdiction.[578]

The necessary rights and means of the defence are a composite judicial guarantee that will variously include the right to counsel, the right to present a full defence, the right to a public trial, and the prohibition of double jeopardy. Unlike a peacetime trial before a state court in which will apply the full array of necessary rights and means of the defence as defined under human rights law, a trial before an insurgent court in a conflict zone will require the adaptation of the constituent parts this guarantee to the specific context and institutional capacities of the rebel administration of justice.

v. Individual Criminal Responsibility

The principle of individual responsibility is a basic yet fundamental aspect of the administration of justice in criminal matters, positing a necessary link between moral guilt and punishment. Perhaps surprisingly, it is more systematically and forcefully affirmed in international humanitarian law than in international human rights law. Although not mentioned in Common Article 3, both Article 6(2)(b) of Protocol II and Article 75(4)(b) of Protocol I provide that "no one shall be convicted of an offence except on the basis of individual penal responsibility".[579] The ICRC in its study of customary law found that this was a norm of customary humanitarian law applicable in both international and non-international armed conflicts.[580] The principle of individual criminal responsibility is a specific application, in the context of judicial proceedings, of the more general prohibition against collective punishments proclaimed in Article 4(2)(b) of Protocol II and Article 75(2)(d) of Protocol I.[581] There is no explicit reference to a requirement of individual penal responsibility in either the ICCPR or in the ECHR, but it is included in the ACHR (Art. 5(3)) and the African Charter of Human and Peoples' Rights (Art. 7(2) *in fine*). That said, the Human Rights Committee mentions it as an example of a peremptory norm in its General Comment 29 on states of emergency, and indeed it is a non-derogable right under the American Convention (Art. 27(2)).[582]

[578] See: United State Supreme Court, *US v Furlong*, 18 US 184, 197 (1820); Colangelo (n 575) 195–197. This is reflected in Art. 20(2) and (3) of the Rome Statute.

[579] It was previously applied to the benefit of protected persons under Art. 33§1 of the Third Geneva Convention.

[580] Henckaerts and Doswald-Beck (n 255) Rule 102.

[581] There are prohibitions against collective punishment in Art. 26§6 and 87§3 of the Third Geneva Convention and Art. 33§1 of the Fourth Geneva Convention. The ICRC also considers this to form part of customary humanitarian law: ibid Rule 103. The Rome Statute does not mention collective punishment as an indictable war crime before the ICC, although the statutes of the SCSL and ICTR both did. See generally Shane Darcy, 'The Prohibition of Collective Punishment' in Andrew Clapham, Paola Gaeta, and Marco Sassòli (eds), *The 1949 Geneva Conventions: A Commentary* (Oxford University Press 2015).

[582] Human Rights Committee, General Comment 29 (n 378) para 11.

In the context of armed conflicts, the extrajudicial imposition of collective punishment has been a much more significant challenge than the judicial imposition of a penal sanction on a basis other than individual responsibility. Indeed, up to the end of World War II, belligerents claimed the right to impose collective punishment against the civilian population or prisoners of war in reaction to certain hostile acts, claims that were definitely and unambiguously invalidated by the 1949 Geneva Conventions.[583] In relation to the administration of justice by courts, those of the state or of non-state armed groups, the principle of individual penal responsibility has not given rise to significant contestation. It does not stand in the way of diverse forms of participation justifying the imposition of criminal accountability, as made clear by Article 25 of the Rome Statute, inasmuch as each mode of participation reflects the accused's personal involvement in the crime.[584] The fact that responsibility attaches to the individual author of the crime negates the lawfulness of posthumous convictions.[585] The principle of personal responsibility also prohibits taking measures against family members or friends of a person suspected of a crime, as leverage against that suspect. In *Garcia v. Peru*, the Inter-American Commission of Human Rights noted that putting the wife and children of a person sought by authorities under house arrest amounted to a clear violation of the personal responsibility principle.[586] There is some evidence that LTTE courts had a practice of sanctioning the family or friends of those targeted by judicial proceedings, especially for individuals who were beyond the reach of the group in a zone under government control, in order to 'convince' the latter to subject to insurgent jurisdiction.[587] This practice is a clear violation of the principle of personal responsibility binding insurgent courts under international humanitarian and human rights law.

vi. Principle of Legality

The principle of legality, also expressed as *nullum crimen sine lege, nulla poena sine lege*, reflects the fundamental precept that the limits of permissible

[583] See Military Tribunal of Rome, *In Re Kappler*, (1948) 15 Annual Digest of Public International Law Cases 471, 472 ("if civilian citizens of the occupied State commit criminal acts within the occupied territory which harm the occupying State, and if the search for the culprits proves to be a matter of considerable difficulty, partly owing to the solidarity of the population, it is permissible to impose collective sanctions"). In this case as in general, collective punishments were intertwined in a complex manner with belligerent reprisals, creating significant uncertainty as to the scope of the apparent prohibition of collective penalties under Art. 50 of the 1907 Hague Regulations. See: Provost (n 320) 187–192.

[584] Akhavan (n 510) 1227.

[585] ECtHR, *Magnitskiy v Russia*, Appl. Nos 32631/09 & 53799/12, Judgment, 27 August 2019, para 284. This reasoning led the ICC to terminate cases against Raska Lukwiya and Muammar Qadhafi: Ghislain Mabanga, 'Article 25 Responsabilité pénale individuelle' in Julian Fernandez and Xavier Pacreau (eds), *Statut de Rome de la Cour pénale internationale: commentaire article par article*, vol 1 (2d edn, Éditions Pedone 2019) 1015–1016.

[586] IACnHR, *Garcia v Peru*, Case 11.006, Report No 1/95, OEA/Ser.L/V/II.88 rev.1 Doc. 9 at 71 (1995).

[587] Suryanarayana (n 61).

behaviour must be set by law "so as to safeguard individual liberty from any arbitrary encroachment on the part of the authorities of the State".[588] It is one aspect of the idea of the rule of law which, in relation to the rebel administration of justice, speaks to the need for a minimum degree of stability and predictability of legal norms. As discussed in Chapter 1, this translates into the requirement that norms applied by insurgent courts be sufficiently accessible and comprehensible by the people to whom it will be applied.[589] The rule of law and the principle of legality converge to affirm the need for all citizens to be able to know the limits of their liberty and the consequences of their trespass in order to adjust their behaviour accordingly.[590] The requirement that limits to liberty be set by law in turn begs the question of the nature of such law. In discussing the legality under international law for non-state armed groups to establish their own courts, in Chapter 2, I explored the concept of law that underpins the very notion of a court as well as the requirement, in international humanitarian law, that courts be 'regularly constituted'.[591] In all these contexts, the earlier analysis supported a conclusion that the concept of law at play in these international standards is not restricted to state-issued legislation but can accommodate other types of legal norms, including rules adopted by armed opposition groups, customary norms, and public international law. Likewise, 'law' in relation to the principle *nullum crimen sine lege* should be understood to include norms promulgated by non-state armed groups.

The principle of legality is expressly included in the essential guarantees listed in Article 6(2) of Protocol II, using a formulation that is largely borrowed from Article 15(1) of the ICCPR:

> No one shall be held guilty of any criminal offence on account of any act or omission which did not constitute a criminal offence, under the law, at the time when it was committed; nor shall a heavier penalty be imposed than the one that was applicable at the time when the criminal offence was committed; if, after the commission of the offence, provision is made by law for the imposition of a lighter penalty, the offender shall benefit thereby.[592]

588 Permanent Court of International Justice, *Advisory Opinion on the Consistency of Certain Danzig Legislative Decrees With the Constitution of the Free City*, Series A/B No 65 (1935) 56.

589 See Chapter 1, Section II.C.ii.

590 Claus Kreß, 'Nulla Poena Nullum Crimen Sine Lege', *Max Planck Encyclopedia of Public International Law* (Oxford University Press 2010) 381 para 3.

591 See Chapter 2, Section IV.C.i.(c) and Section IV.C.ii. This is also related to the concept of rebel jurisdiction, discussed in Section II.A, supra.

592 One difference, noted in the earlier discussion in Chapter 2, Section IV.C.i.(c), is that the English version of Article 6(2)(c) omits the qualifier 'national or international' to 'law', whereas it is included in the equally official French version of the same provision (*'d'après le droit national ou international'*) as well as in Article 15(1) of the Covenant and in Article 75(4)(c) of Protocol I.

The principle of legality is so universally followed, both at the national and international levels, that there is no doubt that it should now be read into the broad notion of "judicial guarantees which are recognised as indispensable by civilised peoples" under Common Article 3.[593] The universality of the principle of legality is buttressed by its inclusion in all major human rights treaties, in which it is listed as a non-derogable standard.[594] Claus Kreß suggests that the principle of legality can comprise four aspects: non-retroactivity, certainty, the prohibition against analogy, and the prohibition against unwritten criminal law.[595] In the context of the rebel administration of justice, this can be related to specific concerns that the law be applied by insurgent courts with a degree of stability and that applicable norms be accessible to the civilian population.

One may be forgiven for suspecting that the chaotic nature of war, the fluid extent to which an armed group can exert its authority over a territory and population, and the limited priority granted by insurgent leaders to governance practices as compared to strategic objectives, may result in rebel laws being applied in an erratic, unpredictable manner.[596] To what extent can the rebel administration of justice approximate the requirement, under the principle of legality, that law be fixed, declared, and stable?

A first element to note is the diversity of approaches embraced by non-state armed groups with respect to 'their' applicable law. Not rarely, for practical or ideological reasons, insurgents will rely upon an existing body of law rather than attempt to proclaim their own legal standards. Some groups simply apply state law, as the Free Syrian Army court apparently did in the prosecution that led to the *Sakhanh* decision, in which the court applied the Syrian Penal Code.[597] Some other groups tweak official law to reflect particular priorities or values, but without structurally affecting state law. For instance, the KRG modified Iraqi law to prohibit polygamy, allowed elsewhere in the country, but otherwise largely left the national penal code unchanged. A variation is offered by the unrecognised 'Republic of Nagorno-Karabakh' located on the territory of Azerbaijan, which has adapted Armenian statutes as its own law.[598] International criminal law is another body of state-produced legal standards at times applied by rebel courts,

[593] Kenneth S Gallant, *The Principle of Legality in International and Comparative Criminal Law* (Cambridge University Press 2009) 209–211; Doswald-Beck (n 189) 474. The ICRC considers this principle to be a customary norm applicable in all international and non-international armed conflicts: Henckaerts and Doswald-Beck (n 255) Rule 101.

[594] In addition to Art. 15(1) ICCPR, see: Art. 7(1), ECHR; Art. 9, ACHR; and Art. 7(2), African Charter of Human and Peoples' Rights.

[595] Kreß (n 590) para 1.

[596] Murray (n 234) 209.

[597] *Sakhanh* (n 278).

[598] ECtHR, *Chiragov v Armenia*, Judgment (Grand Chamber), Appl. No 13216/05, 16 June 2015, para 182.

for instance by the FMLN in El Salvador.[599] Both Article 15(2) of the ICCPR and Article 7(2) of the European Convention on Human Rights explicitly provide that the criminal repression of international crimes does not offend the principle of *nullum crimen sine lege*. While these articles were adopted to validate state prosecutions of war crimes and crimes against humanity after World War II, even in situations in which such crimes may have been lawful acts under applicable domestic law, there is no reason to exclude rebel prosecutions from their ambit inasmuch as they match the essence of international crimes.[600] Other groups have turned to religious norms as applicable law, most notably the Islamic State and the Taliban. Relevant *Sharī'a* standards includes *hudūd* crimes, specifically provided for in the Qur'an, and also *ta'zir*, punishment for lesser offences not mentioned explicitly.[601] If this was not the law previously applied by the state, as in Syria, Iraq, and Afghanistan, then it can only be imposed to acts done after a declaration to that effect by the armed group. The same goes for insurgents applying looser customary norms or community standards, as did the FARC and to a certain extent the Taliban, and of course for the outright enactment of entirely new laws, as with the LTTE Penal Code.[602] While the prohibition against retroactive criminal law is quite straightforward, the need for certainty corresponds to a fuzzier concept. A crime must be defined in a way that is express and precise, but human rights bodies have not been extremely strict in this regard.[603] If it can be reasonably foreseeable that an action would be considered as a crime, then there is no violation of the principle of legality.[604] In practice, it is not obvious that this corresponds to a widespread concern for insurgent laws.

A distinct implication of *nullum crimen, nulla poena sine lege* that has particular relevance for the rebel administration of justice is the accessibility of the law to ordinary citizens. Clearly, a crime defined in an express and precise manner by a law that is inaccessible cannot result in a fair trial. Accessibility reflects both publicity and form. As to publicity, armed groups rarely publish an official gazette available in public repositories for anyone to consult, in the manner of state governments, unless they attain the degree of autonomy and stability achieved by

[599] FMLN Secretariat for the Promotion and Protection of Human Rights (n 412) 17–21.

[600] See: ECtHR, *Kononov v Latvia* (Grand Chamber), Appl. No 36376/04, Judgment, 17 May 2010, paras 211–213, 186; Human Rights Committee, *Baumgarten v Germany*, UN Doc CCPR/C/78/D/960/2000 (2003); Doswald-Beck (n 189) 475; Kreß (n 590) paras 25–26; Schabas (n 419) 445–446.

[601] Revkin (n 246) 17; Baczko (n 250) 241.

[602] Alfredo Molano, 'La Justicia guerrillera' in Boaventura de Sousa Santos and Mauricio García (eds), *Caleidoscopio de las justicias en Colombia*, vol. 2 (2001) 334; Baczko (n 250) 247–249; LTTE (n 88).

[603] Akhavan (n 510) 1227; Doswald-Beck (n 189) 474; Steiner and Fuchs (n 379) 331–332; Murray (n 234) 208–209.

[604] ECtHR, *Kokkinakis v Greece*, Appl. No 14307/88, Judgment, 25 May 1993, para 52; Kreß (n 590) para 29 ('In practice, international courts are reluctant to hold that a formulation of a crime falls below that standard').

the KRG in Iraq.[605] As to form, while some domestic law versions of the principle of legality proscribe unwritten penal prohibitions, international law does not require that a crime be proclaimed by way of a written instrument.[606] The criminal repression of violations of the (unwritten) laws and customs of war by international tribunals is a clear rebuttal of any suggestion to the contrary.[607] Whether the rules be oral or written, they need to be stated in a public fashion so that anyone could have access to information sufficient to guide their behaviour. When armed groups apply broadly-based community customs or religious norms, it is difficult to deny that they are accessible. They certainly seem as accessible as the customary international law norms were to an ordinary soldier during World War II, a situation that the European Court of Human Rights found in compliance with the principle of legality.[608] If insurgents keep on applying state law, then obviously it would benefit from any publicity that was attached to the process of official enactment or judicial pronouncement. Finally, in situations in which an armed group legislates its own criminal law, it has a duty to sufficiently publicise it. The LTTE printed and sold copies of its penal code, in a manner that was not so different from the Sri Lankan Penal Code, in addition to organising seminars for lawyers and mentioning new laws in the media.[609] The FARC offers a model of an armed group imposing less wide-ranging and formalised rules, either in the form of a *manual de convivencia ciudadana* or just a short list of offences and punishments. These could be printed and left with a local community leader or committee to be shared with everyone concerned, or the FARC would call a town meeting, close all bars, and force everyone to attend so that the commander could explain what rules would be enforced by the group.[610]

The principle of legality stands tempered by the principle that ignorance of the law is no excuse. The former may require that law be fixed and accessible prior to its application, but the latter reflects the fact that few people in a given society have the ability or inclination to become familiar with the law in all its refinements and complexities.[611] While the rebel administration of justice in different conflict zones often falls short of international legal standards in significant ways, violations of the principle of legality are not high on the list of complaints heard from the civilian population about it. Indeed, in her wide-ranging study of rebel governance during the civil war in Colombia, Ana Arjona found that "in about 90% of all observations, civilians knew what rules they had to follow and stated that they had clear expectations about how combatants would behave".[612]

605 See Kurdistan Parliament, online: <https://www.parliament.krd/english/parliament-activities/legislation/>.

606 Kreß (n 590) para 21.

607 Akhavan (n 510) 1227.

608 ECtHR, *Kononov* (n 600) paras 237–239.

609 See Section I.C.iv, supra.

610 Arjona, *Rebelocracy* (n 235) 177.

611 Gallant (n 593) 20–23.

612 Ana Arjona, 'Wartime Institutions: A Research Agenda' (2014) 58 Journal of Conflict Resolution 1360, 1371.

vii. Self-Incrimination

Both Additional Protocols I (Art. 75(4)(f)) and II (Art. 6(2)(f)) expressly provide that "no one shall be compelled to testify against oneself or to confess guilt", using language that is directly borrowed from Article 14(2)(g) of the ICCPR.[613] The rule against self-incrimination pursues two distinct yet connected aims: the prohibition of torture and other cruel and unusual treatments, and the fairness of judicial proceedings. On the one hand, it is understood that the admission as evidence of a confession obtained by coercion would correspond to a judicial stamp of approval on a conduct that is otherwise rejected as an affront to basic standards of humanity; on the other, it is broadly agreed that an individual subject to torture or mistreatment is likely to say anything to put an end to it, casting an enormous doubt on the reliability of such evidence and, as a result, on the fairness of any conviction resting on it.[614] As such, the rule against self-incrimination can be taken as implied by the combined prohibition of torture and requirement of judicial guarantees recognised as indispensable by civilised peoples under Common Article 3 and, more generally, customary humanitarian law.[615] As noted by the European Court of Human Rights, the presumption of innocence imposes on the prosecution the burden of establishing beyond reasonable doubt the guilt of the accused "without resort to evidence obtained through methods of coercion or oppression in defiance of the will of the accused", justifying the conclusion that the right against self-incrimination be seen as protected under the European Convention despite the absence of an explicit mention of this standard in the text.[616]

Situations of armed conflicts, which in civil wars are often associated with anti-terrorism measures, represent a context in which the protection against torture and other 'enhanced' methods of interrogation is often under significant strain because of the immediate and significant nature of the perceived threat to national security.[617] In human rights law, while due process guarantees are not deemed non-derogable in situations of emergency, the prohibition of torture and other cruel and unusual treatments is non-derogable. The Inter-American Court of Human Rights concluded that the absolute and non-derogable nature of the prohibition against torture

[613] This is matched by Art. 99, Third Geneva Convention, and Art. 8(2)(g) and (3), ACHR. Likewise, Art. 15 of the Convention against Torture mandates the exclusion of any evidence obtained through torture: Convention against Torture and Other Cruel, Inhumane or Degrading treatment or Punishment, opened for signature 10 December 1984, 1465 UNTS 85. The UK Supreme Court held in *R v Reeves Taylor*, [2019] UKSC 51, para 76 that the prohibition of torture in the Convention against Torture includes acts of non-state armed groups exercising control over a civilian population.

[614] Manfred Nowak, Moritz Birk, and Giulinana Monina (eds), *The United Nations Convention against Torture : A Commentary* (2d edn, 2019) 417–419.

[615] ICRC, *Commentary on the Second Geneva Convention* (n 316) para 707; Henckaerts and Doswald-Beck (n 255) Rule 100.

[616] ECtHR, *Pishchalnikov v Russia*, Appl. No 7025/04, Judgment, 24 September 2009, para 71. In a similar fashion, the African Commission on Human and Peoples' Rights considers the right against self-incrimination implied in due process guarantees under Art. 7 of the African Charter of Human and Peoples' Rights: African Commission on Human and Peoples' Rights, Principles and Guidelines on the Right to a Fair Trial and Legal Assistance in Africa (n 384) 16.

[617] Nowak, Birk, and Monina (n 614) 418.

and inhumane treatments necessarily implies that the exclusion of evidence or confessions obtained by coercion is itself non-derogable.[618] There is thus consistency between human rights and international humanitarian law standards in proclaiming the absolute inadmissibility of evidence or confessions obtained by coercion.

The type of coercion that will vitiate self-incrimination is not limited to acts of torture but encompasses both physical and psychological forms of coercion.[619] Individuals undergoing interrogation by officials are presumed to be in a highly vulnerable position, compounded if their detention is related to an armed conflict. Accordingly, if a self-incriminating statement is made by an accused without the presence or assistance or legal counsel, it may be suspected, presumed, or deemed to have been made under coercion.[620] Of course, in relation to the rebel administration of justice, it was noted earlier that legal counsels play a role more variable than in state-run courts, in part as a reflection of the limited availability of trained jurists in many zones under the control of insurgents.[621] The guarantee against self-incrimination reaches back into the pre-trial phase, when suspects are being interrogated by authorities, a phase in which it seems even less likely that legal counsel will be available in a zone under rebel control. Given that legal advice is rarely available, it is suggested that the absence of counsel should not lead to any type of presumption, but rather that the facts of each situation need to be examined to reach a conclusion as to whether any type of coercion was used. This in turn brings up the question of who bears the burden of establishing that a statement or confession was obtained by coercion. The Inter-American Court of Human Rights and the Committee Against Torture have explored this issue fully and concluded that, once a reasonable claim has been made that coercion was used to obtain evidence, then the state has an obligation to investigate the complaint and carries the burden of proving that evidence was given freely by the accused.[622] If self-incriminating testimony or confession is found to have been made under coercion, the dominant trend among human rights bodies is that "the absolute character of the exclusionary rule is reflected on the prohibition of granting probative value not only to the evidence obtained directly under duress, but also to evidence deriving from said act".[623] The 'fruit of the poisonous tree'

[618] IACtHR, *Cabrera García and Montiel Flores v Mexico*, Judgment, 26 November 2010, para 165. See also Human Rights Committee, General Comment 29 (n 378) paras 7, 15.

[619] Human Rights Committee, General Comment 32 (n 432) para 41; Doswald-Beck (n 457) 363; Schabas (n 419) 411; Clooney and Webb (n 380) 619–632. Art. 8(3) of the ACHR refers to "coercion of any kind".

[620] African Commission on Human and Peoples' Rights, Principles and Guidelines on the Right to a Fair Trial and Legal Assistance in Africa (n 384) 16 ("Any confession or admission obtained during incommunicado detention shall be considered to have been obtained by coercion"); Human Rights Committee, General Comment 32, ibid.

[621] See Subsection III.C.iv(a), supra.

[622] IACtHR, *Cabrera García and Montiel Flores* (n 618) para 136; Nowak, Birk and Monina (n 614) 431–432.

[623] IACtHR, ibid para 167; ECtHR, *Jalloh v Germany*, Grand Chamber, Appl. No 54810/00, Judgment, 11 July 2006, para 105; Human Rights Committee, General Comment 32 (n 432) para 6; Committee Against Torture, *GK v Switzerland*, No 219/2002, UN Doc CAT/C/30/D/219/2002, 7 May 2003, paras 3.2, 6.9.

doctrine reflects the absolute incompatibility of the use of physical or psychological coercion against suspects and notions of a fair trial.[624]

There is no doubt that the use of coercion by armed groups in order to obtain self-incriminating confessions or evidence is not a rare occurrence. For example, the study of the administration of justice by the Islamic State reveals a near-systematic recourse to physical mistreatment, often amounting to torture, during investigations leading to prosecutions.[625] The widespread nature of this practice suggests that, even if there was no Islamic State policy to endorse it, there certainly was none to proscribe it. This stands in contrast to the Taliban, whose 2010 *layeha* Code of Conduct for the Mujahedin provides in Article 19:

> Getting confession by force—meaning by beating, threats or abuse—has no credibility and neither can it be used to prove a crime. The interrogator shall be pious and wise in order to avoid forced confessions because, in Shari'a, confessions made by force are unsafe and not credible. Mujahedin must [also] not promise anything to the prisoner in return for a confession that they do not intend to fulfil.[626]

One would be naïve to take from this provision of the *layeha* that the Taliban never use coercion to force confessions. Still, the *layeha* should not be dismissed as pure propaganda: it is a statement of aspiration on the part of the leadership as to how the war should be prosecuted.[627] The LTTE, for its part, was known to rely to a significant extent on intimidation, coercion, and violence against the civilian population, not shying away from brutally executing dissidents and competitors. This was carried out by the military and security wing of the group, while its political wing, which included its justice system, endeavoured to align its practice with human rights standards.[628] In relation to coerced self-incriminating statements, one LTTE Senior District Judge remarked that "[u]nlike in the South we do not accept confession reports".[629] It is true that, in the independent human rights reporting on the LTTE, the use of forced confessions does not figure prominently, while the opposite is true for reports on the government of Sri Lanka. During and after the war, UN bodies and nongovernmental organisations (NGOs) have reported on the repeated torture of those accused of association with the LTTE,

624 Nowak, Birk, and Monina (n 614) 421–423.

625 See Chapter 2, Section II.B.

626 Islamic Emirate of Afghanistan, Code of Conduct for the Mujahedin (2010), English translation by the Afghan Analysts Network (AAN), online: <https://www.afghanistan-analysts.org/publication/aan-papers/the-layha-calling-the-taleban-to-account/>.

627 Clark (n 249) 6. For a recent report on the use of torture by the Taliban to obtain confessions relied upon in subsequent judicial proceedings, see Human Rights Watch (n 250) 58.

628 Report of the Special Rapporteur Philip Alston on Extrajudicial, Summary or Arbitrary Executions—Mission to Sri Lanka, UN Doc E/CN.4/2006/53/Add.5 (2006) paras 22–23.

629 Kamalendran (n 63) 4. Interview with 'Sharmi' (Senior State Counsel) (December 2018); Interview with 'Kajenthini' (former LTTE lawyer) (December 2018); Interview with 'Abilashini' (who was involved in establishing the LTTE courts in the 1990s) (December 2018).

with men and women commonly being subject to rape and other physical abuses until they agreed to sign a blank form or a statement written in a language that they could not understand.[630] Nearly all victims were detained pursuant to the Prevention of Terrorism Act of Sri Lanka, which provides that any confession may be received as evidence unless the accused can prove duress, a burden basically impossible to meet in practice. The UN Committee Against Torture found that nearly 90 percent of convictions under the Prevention of Terrorism Act are based on confessions.[631] This stands as a sober reminder not only of the importance of the protection against self-incrimination but also that state justice cannot always be presumed to be a model which rebel courts should seek to emulate.

viii. Right to Judicial and Other Remedies

Due process guarantees are complex and important, and there is always a risk that the judge presiding over a trial will fail to ensure that the proceedings are fully in compliance. For that reason, the right to have a conviction reviewed by a different court has come to be considered an essential component of due process of law.[632] While this right largely has become recognised in international human rights law, it is harder to gauge its acceptance under international humanitarian law.

Both Additional Protocols I (Art. 75(4)(j)) and II (Art. 6(3)) provide, in identical terms, that "[a] convicted person shall be advised on conviction of his judicial and other remedies and of the time-limits within which they may be exercised". The provision is striking for what it omits, namely, "the right to appeal the judgment to a higher court" (Article 8(2)(h), ACHR).[633] The initial draft of Article 6 of Protocol II prepared by the ICRC had included a right to appeal any sentence, but, according to Michael Bothe, "[t]he idea was, however, abandoned in view of the fact that such a right would oblige the rebels to organise a more complicated judicial system than could reasonably be expected".[634] The ICRC Commentary also explains that, when the Protocols were adopted in 1977, it was felt that domestic law was so variable as regards a right to appeal that it could not be included in a humanitarian law treaty.[635] This was so despite the fact that prisoners of war and civilians in occupied territory convicted of a crime are granted a right to appeal under the Third and Fourth Geneva

[630] See, for instance, the harrowing litany of abuses documented in Human Rights Watch, "We Will Teach You a Lesson"—Sexual Violence against Tamils by Sri Lankan Security Forces (New York, 2013).

[631] Committee Against Torture, Concluding Observations on the Fifth Periodic Report of Sri Lanka, UN Doc CAT/C/LKA/CO/5 (2017) para 31 (noting that this was a recurring concern); Chandrasekaram (n 31).

[632] IACtHR, *Mapuche Case* (n 522) para 169.

[633] Arai-Takahashi (n 231) 544. Art. 14(5) ICCPR speaks of "the right to his conviction and sentence being reviewed by a higher tribunal".

[634] Bothe and others (n 286) 747; the initial draft Protocol II provision is reprinted in Levie (n 528) 245.

[635] ICRC, *Commentary on the 1977 Additional Protocols* (n 288) para 4611; Levie (n 528) 258 (statement by Nigeria: "With regard to the right of appeal . . . the standards laid down were just not workable in most countries").

Conventions.[636] What is expressly guaranteed under the two Additional Protocols is quite limited indeed: a right to be provided with information regarding possible judicial and other remedies that may be invoked to challenge the trial judgment. There is no corresponding obligation on the part of belligerents to create any remedies, so that if there are none, this right comes to nought. Perhaps not surprisingly, the protection offered by this right under Protocols I and II has not generated much meaningful practice, and academic commentary has been mostly devoted to what is not protected in humanitarian law: a right to appeal.

In the more than four decades since the adoption of the Additional Protocols, the right to appeal against a conviction or a sentence has hardened as a norm of international human rights law. The increased recognition of a right to appeal is highlighted by the adoption in 1984 of Protocol 7 to the ECHR, which introduced a right to appeal. This right has generated a significant amount of jurisprudence by various human rights bodies, especially the Inter-American Court of Human Rights and the Human Rights Committee. In the *Mapuche* decision, the Inter-American Court explained that the appeal protected by the right must be ordinary (as opposed to exceptional), accessible (reasonable formalities and costs), effective (allowing rectification of a flawed conviction or unjustified sentence), comprehensive (touching on factual, probative, and legal issues), open to anyone, and itself consistent with due process guarantees.[637] Although Protocol 7 to the European Convention on Human Rights allows for exceptions for "offences of a minor character" (Art. 2(2)), the right to appeal under international human rights law is generally taken to apply to any type of criminal conviction.[638] Thus, the African Commission on Human and Peoples' Rights has interpreted it as covering a judicial decision to commit an individual to a mental institution.[639] In fact, perhaps in view of the uniquely broad formulation of Article 7 of the African Charter of Human and Peoples' Rights, the African Commission has held that there is a protected right to appeal even against a final judgment in civil matters.[640] In contrast, the Human Rights Committee has held that the right to appeal applies only in criminal matters.[641] If the sentence imposed is very grave, and most of all in capital cases, then the right to an appeal must be respected in all its dimensions.[642]

[636] Art. 106, Third Geneva Convention; Art. 73, Fourth Geneva Convention. See Arai-Takahashi (n 231) 532; ICRC, *Commentary on the Third Geneva Convention* (n 356) para 4152; ICRC, *Commentary on the Fourth Geneva Convention* (n 258) 358–359.

[637] IACtHR, *Mapuche Case* (n 522) para 170. See generally Clooney and Webb (n 380) 656–717.

[638] Human Rights Committee, General Comment 32 (n 432) para 45; Doswald-Beck (n 189) 483; Schabas (n 419) 415.

[639] African Commission on Human and Peoples' Rights, *Puhorit and Moore v Gambia*, Comm. No 241/2001 (2003) para 72.

[640] African Commission on Human and Peoples' Rights, *Civil Liberties Association v Nigeria*, Comm. No 101/1993 (1995) para 14. See Murray (n 457) 221.

[641] Human Rights Committee, *I.P. v Finland*, UN Doc. CCPR/C/48/D/450/1991 (1993) para 6.2; Human Rights Committee, General Comment 32 (n 432) para 46.

[642] Human Rights Committee, General Comment 32, ibid para 51; African Commission on Human and Peoples' Rights, Principles and Guidelines on the Right to a Fair Trial and Legal

How does this transpose to the administration of justice by armed groups in situations of armed conflict? The ICRC in its study of customary humanitarian law holds that a right to appeal has become applicable in all categories of armed conflicts, a position Arai-Takahashi initially found 'far-fetched' given the dearth of state practice invoked to support it, but which he now seems to accept.[643] Even if there is a customary human right to appeal, we stumble once more on the non-inclusion of this standard in the list of non-derogable provisions, fragilising its status in situations of emergency like armed conflicts.[644] The most compelling approach would not seem to derive a right to appeal from the protected right to be informed of available judicial and other remedies, but rather to see it as a necessary facet of the more general right to a fair trial, as suggested by the Inter-American Court of Human Rights in *Mapuche*. This is indeed the conclusion reached by the Stockholm District Court in *Sakhanh*, albeit without the benefit of any underlying analysis of the point.[645] Rather than supporting a stand-alone right to appeal, this conclusion suggests that the unavailability of appellate review weakens the overall fairness of any criminal proceedings.

There are examples in the practice of non-state armed groups that come to buttress a sense that due process of law does imply a right to appeal. Most clearly perhaps, the LTTE had an elaborate appellate system, with a court of appeals and a supreme court that would certainly meet the requirement of a right to appeal.[646] Likewise, the judicial system of the KRG in Iraq includes a court of cassation sitting in Erbil, to which lower court decisions may be appealed.[647] Some armed groups establish appellate jurisdictions but the reality of conflict makes them less accessible and effective than one would normally expect under the criteria offered by the Inter-American Court in *Mapuche*. Thus, the PKK reportedly has established a Supreme Court of Justice that can hear appeals from lower court decisions, but it sits in a remote mountainous region that is difficult to access.[648] The Taliban has provincial courts of appeal in most, but not all, provinces of Afghanistan, and its supreme court and court of cassation sitting in Helmand province or in

Assistance in Africa (n 384) 18 (suggesting that an appeal be mandatory for capital cases). See Clooney and Webb (n 380) 672–673.

643 Henckaerts and Doswald-Beck (n 255) Rule 100; Arai-Takahashi (n 231) 544; Arai-Takahashi (n 446) 1445; Akhavan (n 510) 1235. Likewise, Sivakumaran finds unwarranted criticism of rebel courts for failing to allow for an appeal process "given that no such obligation is required of armed groups": Sivakumaran, 'Courts of Armed Opposition Groups—Fair Trials or Summary Justice?' (n 475) 508.

644 The Inter-American Commission of Human Rights has suggested that non-derogable due process guarantees 'may' include a right to appeal: IACnHR, Report on Terrorism and Human Rights (n 451) para 261. Likewise, the African Commission on Human and Peoples's Rights held the right to appeal to be non-derogable: *Amnesty International v. Sudan*, Comm. nos 48/90 (1999) para 37. See Clooney and Webb (n 380) 706–707.

645 *Sakhanh* (n 278) para 34.

646 See Section I.C.ii, *infra*.

647 See Chapter 4, Section I.C.

648 See Chapter 4, Section I.A.

Peshawar, Pakistan, may lie beyond the physical reach of many parties.[649] The FARC provides an example of a much less structured engagement with the administration of justice, especially vis-à-vis the civilian population, in which the possibility of appeal is less assured. On the one hand, the internal Disciplinary Regulations of the FARC granted an explicit right to appeal from a decision of a court-martial against a fighter, first to the Block and then to Headquarters, if a conviction seemed unjust or exaggerated.[650] With respect to the civilian population, lesser offences and non-criminal issues were normally decided by the unit commander upon a basic process, whereas more serious crimes were prosecuted before a popular assembly convened by the FARC. Although FARC civilian justice practices were generally derived from its internal disciplinary rules, there is no evidence of any appellate review process either in civil or penal matters.[651]

* * * * * *

The conclusion that public international law creates an opening for non-state armed groups to regularly constitute their own courts in situations of armed conflict called for the articulation of the manner in which such courts ought to operate. As noted in earlier discussions, courts are particular types of institutions, and one of their defining features is a minimal degree of fairness in arriving at decisions. For state courts, the idea of due process of law has been to a large extent deconstructed into a series of due process guarantees that broadly must be respected in order for a judgment to be regarded as fair. I quoted earlier in this chapter a passage from Rod Macdonald in which he argues that "the specific requirements of procedural fairness must be tied to the particular decisional processes, and may be derived from the inherent principle of each".[652] In the analysis that followed, I endeavoured to map out the elements of procedural fairness that can be derived from a study of the practice of armed groups in administering justice. The resulting map of rebel due process suggests that it is not merely an imitation of state-administered justice, that its non-state and insurgent nature corresponds to procedural standards that can be distinct from those derived from official justice, but also that insurgent justice does not represent a radical schism of the notion of due process of law, that there is significant convergence in what defines a fair trial.

Beyond international law, what must be done in order for a rebel trial to be considered fair, reflecting the inherent principle of insurgent justice, does not correspond to the simple fiat of a rebel ruler, nor even of a fiat combined with

649 See Chapter 2, Section II.B.

650 *Reglemento del Régimen Disciplinario de las FARC*, online: <https://web.archive.org/web/20160403205603/http://farc-ep.co/wp-content/uploads/2013/10/Estatutos.pdf> "CAPITULO III DE LA APELACIÓN. Artículo 9. Todo sancionado, cuando considera injusta la sanción impuesta, tiene derecho a apelar al organismo inmediatamente superior y hasta el Estado Mayor Central [. . .] Artículo 10. Cuando la sanción impuesta sea injusta o exagerada, o por el contrario, tan leve que no corresponda a la gravedad de la falta o delito cometido, podrá ser revocada por el Estado Mayor Central o su Secretario". See Aguilera Peña (n 247) 229–230.

651 See Chapter 1, Section I.B.iii.

652 Macdonald, 'A Theory of Procedural Fairness' (n 401) 33.

contextual elements such as territorial control. The limits, uses, and purposes of insurgent justice must be established by way of a dialogical process between armed group and civilian population. Insurgents who engage in governance practices, perhaps especially those who administer justice in territory under their authority, necessarily become part of the social fabric.[653] One of the revealing insights of the emerging field of rebel governance is the extent to which the civilian population retains agency in its relations with armed groups, sometimes even to the extent that civilian resistance can thwart rebel practices.[654] The administration of justice is one of the processes mediating the governance function of rebels in any community over which they have some authority. If we take at face value the central message of the principle of complementarity proclaimed in the Rome Statute, that there is inherent value in local trials, then that must be adapted to the reality of insurgent justice as well.[655] Sally Engle Merry has persuasively developed the concept of the necessary vernacularisation of international human rights norms, so that legal standards can 'speak' to a wider range of local actors whose behaviour is sought to be nudged. For due process of law in zones of conflict, this takes place through a process of collective bargaining between armed groups and civilians. The interpretation of international humanitarian law and human rights offered here suggests that these legal standards can also be an element of that conversation. Indeed, the rebel administration of justice is a form of dialogue that is not privy to insurgents and civilians; its *rayonnement* extends beyond the conflict zone to engage other national, transnational, and international actors.

[653] The point is made with respect to the Taliban by Jackson (n 225) 26.

[654] Ana Arjona, 'Civilian Resistance to Rebel Governance' in Ana Arjona, Nelson Kasfir, and Zachariah Mampilly (eds), *Rebel Governance in Civil War* (Cambridge University Press 2015) 191; Mampilly (n 20) 66–67; Arjona, *Rebelocracy* (n 235) 41–47.

[655] Mégret and Giles Samson (n 404) 577.

4

The Legal *Rayonnement* of Rebel Justice: Recognition, Complementarity, and Kurdish Courts

> Everybody, of course, by definition, will seek a military solution to the insurgency problem, whereas by its very nature, the insurgency problem is militarily only in a secondary sense, and politically, ideologically, and administratively in a primary sense.
>
> — Bernard Fall, 'The Theory and Practice of Insurgency and Counterinsurgency' (1965) 18 *Naval War College Review* 21, 22

If it is accepted that non-state armed groups can regularly establish courts which exercise their jurisdiction in a manner that conform to due process guarantees under international law, the question arises as to how other actors must recognise such a situation. Recognition speaks to the legal *rayonnement* of the rebel administration of justice, and can be framed in a number of ways. What exactly is being recognised could cover the decision itself, in the criminal context corresponding to double jeopardy and complementarity, and in the civil context to *res judicata* and formal recognition of foreign judgments. Recognition can also be framed in terms of the range of actors it covers, not only an alleged executioner as was the case for Omar Sakhanh but also individuals who acted as judges, lawyers, witnesses, parties, and so on.[1] Finally, the question of recognition raises the issue of who has the right or duty to acknowledge the possible legal effect of the decision of an insurgent court. Could the prosecution of an individual before a rebel court circumvent the jurisdiction of the ICC under the principle of complementarity? Third states, as Sweden discovered with the *Sakhanh* case, may well be confronted with this dilemma. The same goes for the state in whose jurisdiction a rebel court has been operating: Is the state, possibly engaged in armed confrontation against the very armed opposition group running a court, at liberty to entirely deny any legal effect to the decisions of such a court? There are situations

[1] The *Sakhanh* Case is discussed in more details in Section III, infra.

Rebel Courts. René Provost, Oxford University Press. © Oxford University Press 2021.
DOI: 10.1093/oso/9780190912222.003.0005

in which a non-state armed group have exercised control over a significant portion of the nation's territory and population for years and even decades, in which it seems well-nigh impossible to simply erase or ignore myriad judicial decisions taken over the years. Finally, there may even be issues of recognition among armed opposition groups, whereby the activities of the court of one group could be recognised by the court of another. Indeed, still in the *Sakhanh* case, the firing squad which Omar Sakhanh joined reportedly did not belong to the same armed group as the court that had convicted and sentenced these men.

Recognition of the administration of justice by non-state armed groups is a vast legal issue that gives rise to questions under both public international law and the domestic law of any state in which it is invoked. Using the case study of the courts established by Kurdish entities in Iraq, Syria, and Turkey (I), the analysis explores the legal implications of the recognition of insurgent courts internationally by the International Criminal Court and other international tribunals (II), transnationally by third states (III), nationally by the territorial state (IV), and transversally by other armed opposition groups (V).

I. Kurdish Non-State Courts: A Spectrum of Extralegality

There is a multitude of state and non-state groups active in the conflict taking place in and near the territory of Syria, Iraq, and Turkey, and indeed it is quite possible to argue that, from a legal standpoint, several distinct conflicts are ongoing. As mentioned already, some of these groups have established judicial institutions before which individuals have been or could be tried for international or domestic crimes, or used to settle a wide range of non-penal matters. Among the many non-state groups taking part in hostilities in the region, Kurdish entities have been involved in the administration of justice and will be used in this chapter as case studies. Before turning to the specific issue of the possible legal recognition of decisions of insurgent courts, it is useful to briefly sketch what these non-state Kurdish courts look like and on what basis they operate. The PKK in North Kurdistan (in Turkey and Iraq), the YPG in West Kurdistan (in Syria), and the KRG in South Kurdistan (in Iraq) are quite different types of entities, sharing an overlapping ethnic identity but differentiated by language or dialect, ideology, politics, and context. The courts of each Kurdish group will raise distinct legal issue as regards recognition.

I now turn to sketch the PKK, PYD, and KRG and their judicial institutions to attempt to overcome the dominant state narrative of extralegality blanketing everything that non-state armed groups do. While, unsurprisingly, the judicial practice of these three Kurdish groups is far from ideal justice, neither does it emerge as wholly disconnected from a broad notion of the administration of justice.

A. North Kurdistan: The PKK/KCK in Turkey and Iraq

i. PKK Governance

The PKK (Partiya Karkerên Kurdistan-Kurdistan Workers' Party) was formed in 1977 and began its armed struggle in 1984,[2] calling for an independent Kurdish state within Turkey.[3] The overall leader of the PKK is Abdullah Öcalan, currently serving a life sentence in a Turkish prison, while the acting leader of the group is Murat Karayılan.[4] The PKK is also known as the Kurdistan People's Congress (Kongra-Gel) and the Kurdistan Freedom and Democracy Congress (KADEK),[5] and has changed its name several times.[6] The number of armed PKK members varies between 3,000 and 5,000, "mostly split between Turkey and northern Iraq".[7] The group's leadership is based in the northern Iraqi mountain of Qandil.[8] The PKK's most important base, Qandil is spread over a broad expanse of inaccessible mountains 80 kilometres from Turkey, near the Iranian border, while other PKK bases dot the Turkish border. The PKK first arrived there in the early 1980s as a guest of Iraqi Kurds and have exploited the power vacuum that opened up with the 1991 collapse of the Baghdad government.[9] The PKK presents itself as a political party using military means to achieve its goals, but many countries including Turkey, the United States, the United Kingdom, Canada, as well as international organisations like the European Union and NATO have labelled the group a terrorist organisation.[10] The PKK is a highly

[2] Kerim Yıldız and Susan Breau, *The Kurdish Conflict International Humanitarian Law and Post-Conflict Mechanisms* (London: Routledge 2010) at 11 [Yıldız and Breau]; 'Profile: The PKK' *BBC News* (21 March 2013), online: <http://www.bbc.com/news/world-europe-20971100>.

[3] *BBC News*, ibid.

[4] Canada: Immigration and Refugee Board of Canada, *Turkey: The Kurdistan Workers' Party (PKK), including areas of operation and targets, methods of recruitment and activities; state response* (15 June 2012), TUR104075.E, online: http://www.refworld.org/docid/4feadb3e2.html accessed 12 February 2016.

[5] ibid.

[6] The movement has changed names after the frequent closure of its newspapers, TV stations, parties, or associations to avoid members being listed and jailed as terrorists, to rebrand itself after an ideological shift, or to mark the occasional new alliance with left-wing factions. "Despite all the changes of name, which were always proclaimed as new beginnings and promised democratic structures, there were no significant changes in organisation and personnel": International Crisis Group, *Turkey: The PKK and a Kurdish Settlement*, Europe Report N°219 (2012) note 54.

[7] ibid at 12.

[8] ibid at 3 note 20.

[9] ibid at 17.

[10] Yıldız and Breau (n 2) 14. This is a contested label, and some foreign instances have characterised the PKK as a non-state armed group involved in a non-international armed conflict rather than a terrorist organisation. For example, this is the conclusion reached by the Belgian Court of Cassation in January 2020, although the Belgian Foreign Minister maintains his position that the PKK is a

structured fighting force, operating in a number of 'fields' in Turkey comprising three or more Turkish provinces, with a field commander supervising several provincial commanders. Provinces are in turn divided into five or six regions, again each with a regional commander in charge of a number of battalions of between 100 and 170 fighters. Battalions are formed by a number of companies (60–70 fighters) divided into platoons and, ultimately, squads of ten fighters each.[11] Regulations stipulate that there is to be one female and two male companies in each battalion.[12] Squad members elect their own commanders, but command at higher levels is determined by the next echelon up. Discipline within the PKK is presented as strict, and all levels of fighters are required to provide frequent oral reports and, once a year, written reports to the central military command and executive committee of the group.[13] Conversely, any fighter can submit a written report on any issue or member of the PKK, including his superior, and such reports are directly and confidentially communicated to the upper echelons.

The PKK formed the KCK (Koma Ciwakên Kürdistan), "an umbrella organization for all PKK affiliates in Kurdish communities in Turkey, Iran, Iraq, Syria and the diaspora", during its congresses in northern Iraq between 2005 and 2007.[14] The KCK has a detailed forty-six-article Charter according to which KCK governance is separated into executive, legislative, and judicial branches, essentially acting as an alternative to the Turkish state.[15] The constitution-like Charter, which came into force in 2007, grants citizenship on a *jus soli* basis to "anyone who is born in Kurdistan, lives there or is bound to the KCK".[16] This new KCK structure was planned as paving the way for a confederate Kurdish state on the territories of Turkey-Syria-Iraq-Iran.[17] According to the International Crisis

terrorist group: Le Ministre Goffin souligne l'engagement sans équivoque de l'Etat belge contre le terrorisme (29 January 2020), online: <https://diplomatie.belgium.be/fr/newsroom/nouvelles/2020/le_ministre_goffin_souligne_engagement_sans_equivoque_etat_belge_contre_terrorisme>; Thomas Van Poecke, 'The IHL Exclusion Clause, and Why Belgian Courts Refuse to Convict PKK Members for Terrorist Offences' *EJIL: Talk!* (20 March 2019), online: <https://www.ejiltalk.org/the-ihl-exclusion-clause-and-why-belgian-courts-refuse-to-convict-pkk-members-for-terrorist-offences/> accessed 24 June 2020.

[11] An unusually detailed description of the PKK's organisation, policies, and operations is provided in the recently published narrative of 'Deniz Koçer', a former high-level PKK commander: Murat Haner, *The Freedom Fighter: A Terrorist's Own Story* (Routledge 2018) 124–125.

[12] ibid 133.

[13] ibid 130 (noting that female fighters had to produce a third report for the head of the women's executive committee).

[14] See Seevan Saeed, *Kurdish Politics in Turkey: From the PKK to the KCK* (Taylor & Francis 2016).

[15] See the KCK Charter (2007) for details, online: <http://theirwords.org/media/transfer/doc/tr_pkk_hpg_2005_17-e646b19295cb5bf24fc94e66e5de891b.pdf>.

[16] International Crisis Group (n 6) 7.

[17] Turkish National Police, 'Structure of the Terrorist Organization', online: <http://www.egm.gov.tr/EN/Pages/pkk_structure_of_the_terrorist_organization.aspx>.

Group, it is not easy to separate the PKK and KCK, headed by the same top three individuals:

> The KCK, therefore, overlaps broadly with the PKK, with the latter's leaders sometimes using the terms interchangeably. [. . .] Under Öcalan's overarching leadership the KCK is headed by his number two, Murat Karayılan, a Kurd from Turkey. He leads the KCK Executive Committee, in whose name major policy statements are made from his base in the Qandil mountains of northern Iraq. The KCK includes a legislature (the Kongra Gel, People's Congress), headed by Remzi Kartal, another Kurd from Turkey, who is a political refugee in Belgium); an executive, including the 'People's Defence Forces' (Hêzên Parastina Gel, HPG), which is run from the Qandils by Bahoz Erdal (a Syrian Kurd, born as Fahman Hussain); and a judiciary, headed by Sait Avdi, an Iranian Kurd.[18]
>
> The top men in the PKK's current executive committee are also the three top names in the KCK's twelve-person executive committee: Öcalan, Karayılan and PKK cofounder and former insurgent forces chief Cemil Bayık[19]

The legislative branch of the KCK is the Kongra Gele Kurdistan (Kongra Gel, or People's Congress of Kurdistan), consisting of 300 members elected biannually. The Kongra Gel itself is further divided into social, political, ideological, and fiscal parliamentary commissions, in addition to specialised groups for defence and public relations. According to a statement of the chief of the KCK's legislature, the group's institutions operate covertly due to their nature as a revolutionary movement, which prevents them from having public meetings.[20] In addition to the adoption of legislation, the Kongra Gel is empowered to ratify agreements with other states and international organisations, and oversees the group's 'diplomatic representation'. While there is some structural overlap between the PKK and KCK, they appear to operate quite distinctly as the military and civilian arms of the overall push for Kurdish autonomy or independence.

One area in which the PKK has been active internationally is international humanitarian law. The PKK has made a number of unilateral statements that suggest a willingness to engage with international legal standards regulating the conduct of armed hostilities. Thus, in 1995, the PKK issued a formal declaration that it would abide by the 1949 Geneva Conventions and the 1977 Additional Protocol I and that the obligations laid out in these instruments would have "the

[18] International Crisis Group (n 6) 8.
[19] ibid. According to sources from 2015, Cemil Bayık is the KCK executive committee co-president. 'KCK Executive Council Co-President Bayık: Kurds Are Not property of the Turkish State' *ANHA News Agency* (26 February 2016), online: <http://en.hawarnews.com/kck-executive-council-co-president-bayik-kurds-are-not-property-of-the-turkish-state/>.
[20] International Crisis Group (n 6) 8.

force of law within its own armed forces and areas within control".[21] In the same declaration, the PKK indicated that it took measures to disseminate the content of humanitarian law and that "[i]t has adopted a system of discipline to ensure respect for those rules and the punishment of those who break them".[22] The PKK later signed two 'Deeds of Commitment' prepared by Geneva Call, one in 2006 undertaking to refrain from using anti-personnel landmines and the other in 2013 pledging to stop recruiting and using child soldiers.[23] Various entities within the PKK have over the years issued a number of internal codes of conduct that echo the norms of international humanitarian law.[24] One can find, in a number of places in these codes of conduct, references to the 'military courts' of the PKK and the principle that punishment for violations will be determined by a tribunal.[25] The PKK operates courts-martial for a range of issues, including collaborating with the enemy, attempting to leave, having an intimate relationship with another fighter, and so on.[26]

[21] Olivier Bangerter, Internal Control Codes of Conduct within Insurgent Armed Groups, online: <http://www.smallarmssurvey.org/fileadmin/docs/B-Occasional-papers/SAS-OP31-internal-control.pdf>, at 5. It bears noting that Turkey is not a party to Additional Protocol I, but that Syria and Iraq are.

[22] ibid.

[23] Geneva Call, Annual Report 2014—Protecting Civilians in Armed Conflict, 14.

[24] See Murat Haner, Michael L Benson, and Francis T Cullen, 'Code of the Terrorists: The PKK and the Social Construction of Violence' (2019) 27 Critical Criminology 393, 401–412.

[25] For instance, Section 9 of the ARGK ('People's Liberation Army of Kurdistan', a military wing of the PKK) Regulation provides: "**B- Offences that military courts will deal with:** 1- Being an enemy agent within the army.

2- Working to the detriment of the army. 3- Inclining towards treason based on enmity towards the revolution and army. 4- Spreading defeatism and destructiveness within the army. 5- Defeating the tactics of the party (PKK) in war. 6- Sabotaging actions. 7- Incorrectly approaching, insulting or disrespecting the hallowed values of the party (PKK). 8- Incorrectly approaching, insulting or disrespecting the fundamental positions of the party (PKK) and army. 9- Degenerating army life in political terms. 10- Causing great harm to the war in military and political terms or bringing about results that give rise to such harm. 11- Causing needless casualties. 12- Causing the external leakage of the secrets of the party (PKK) and army. 13- Mass desertion from the army and conspiring to desert in mass. 14- Deserting from the army, and preparing to do so. 15- Failure to take responsibility, even though circumstances permit, for the fallen and wounded. 16- Murder with intent or by accident. 17- Treating lightly the values of the party (PKK) and people and disparaging the good name of the people. 18- Harming the people's life and property. 19- Causing destruction among the people to the detriment of the party (PKK) and army. 20- Causing large-scale material loss to the army or causing such offences to occur. 21- Shooting oneself so as to remain outside the war. 22- Insistence in an incorrigible manner on remaining outside the war (throwing oneself on the ground, allowing oneself to be consumed with madness, feigning illness etc.). 23- Entering perverted relationships. 24- Sole or mass desertion from one's formation to another formation. 25- Entering decadent relationships within the army ranks or fostering the same. 26- Engaging in immoral conduct with or molesting others. 27- Departing from the party line and mistreating etc. prisoners and detainees. The above offences are war crimes and common offences and may not be dealt with and concluded by formation, unit or area command at structure meetings. These offences shall, by virtue of decisions of the leadership at the place where they occurred, depending on their circumstances, be referred to the military courts": *ARGK Regulation Prisoner Status and Conduct Towards Prisoners* (Geneva Call—Their Words).

[26] See Aliza Marcus, *Blood and Belief The PKK and the Kurdish Fight for Independence* (New York University Press 2007).

ii. PKK Justice

At an institutional level, the internal judicial system of the PKK in its early years—prior to the KCK system—mainly pivoted around summary trials and capital punishment, essentially of PKK members. From witness statements, it appears that there was very limited due process implemented during the 'trials' and that death sentences were handed down liberally. In particular, a mere accusation of being a spy was sufficient for the group to impose the death penalty, without as much as a pretence of a trial. Beyond that, specific crimes, indiscipline, dissenting, trying to quit the group, and having a sexual or emotional relationship within the group were also punishable by death, and indeed it is reported that there were hundreds of executions.[27] There are also less obviously reliable reports that high-ranking members of the group would order executions as a show of their commitment to the PKK, although such reports are nearly systematically circulated by governments to paint armed groups as wholly indifferent to human life, even that of their own members.[28] During the same period, in regions in which the PKK gained ascendency, people regularly turned to the PKK to settle disputes on issues ranging from unmanageable debt to land title, with the group warning people against using local state courts as it would legitimise Turkey's authority in the region. Official Turkish courts, even if they remained operational, were avoided in favour of the PKK's justice mechanism that was felt to better represent Kurdish values and interests.[29] Rebel courts were often felt to be more effective, as the PKK would not hesitate to use force to implement court decisions if ever someone dared to disobey them.[30]

Substantive changes occurred in the judicial system of the PKK when the KCK Charter was adopted during the group's 11th Congress in 2007.[31] The fundamentals of this new legal system are articulated in Article 27 of the KCK Charter: "The independence of the judiciary forms the basis for democratic popular justice. It represents the people's morality and conscience".[32] On this

27 Peter W Galbraith, *Unintended Consequences: How War in Iraq Strengthened America's Enemies* (New York: Simon and Schuster 2008) 93; Emrullah Uslu, 'Leading PKK Commander Cemil Bayik Crosses into Iran' Publication: Terrorism Focus Volume: 5 Issue: 20, The Jamestown Foundation (20 May 2008), online: <http://www.jamestown.org/single/?no_cache=1&tx_ttnews[tt_news]=4938#.Vs36p9DcBCg>; Gülden Aydın, 'Kandil Dağı'ndan yaşanmış tecavüz hikayeleri' *Hurriyet* (5 February 2006), online: <http://www.hurriyet.com.tr/kandil-dagi-ndan-yasanmis-tecavuz-hikayeleri-3886942>.

28 Compare the report that PKK leader Cemil Bayık ordered the execution of up to 300 PKK members in order "to prove his fidelity to Ocalan" during the 1980s (Uslu, ibid) and the description of the limited use of executions in Haner (n 11) 173–177.

29 Marcus (n 26) 107, 178.

30 ibid.

31 Ozgur Algan, *PKK Teror Orgutunun Kurulusu Faaliyetleri ve Siyasallasma Sureci* (Kara Harp Okulu Savunma Bilimleri Enstitusu, 2012).

32 Unofficial translation by the Geneva Call of the Judiciary part of the KCK Charter, online: <http://www.theirwords.org>.

basis, a three-legged judiciary was established, made up of a "Supreme Court of Justice for defending people's dignity and freedoms, Administrative Courts for securing the order of discipline and duties, and People's Courts for solving public problems".[33] Separately, 'Supreme Military Tribunals' were also formed to try important military cases, with lesser military offences dealt with more informally by 'platform panels' composed of three fighters.[34] The members of the Judiciary Council overseeing the courts are elected within and through the 'Kongra Gel', the highest legislative authority of the KCK. All 'KCK citizens' are given the right to appear in court, or to appoint an attorney to respond to any accusation. One of the distinctive characteristics of the KCK judicial system is that it excludes 'women-related issues' from the jurisdiction of ordinary courts, in favour of a mechanism under the Women's Communal-Confederal Community system (Koma Jînên Bilind-KJB).[35] The KJB judicial organs hear specific matters falling under the KJB Convention, although this document and the details of the KJB judicial organs are not publicly available.

Under the KCK Charter, the highest organ in the KCK Justice System is the Supreme Court of Justice, composed of seven full and two substitute members appointed by the Kongra Gel Chair and approved by the KCK General Assembly. The Supreme Court of Justice acts all at once as the Court of Cassation, the Supreme Board of Judges and Prosecutors, the Constitutional Court, and the Ministry of Justice. Disciplinary matters are heard by the Administrative Courts, while the authority to resolve ordinary private disputes is with the People's Courts. The Supreme Military Court, as the name suggests, oversees matters related to the armed wing of the PKK. There is no separation of powers in the KCK system, and the group's leadership does not believe that society's problems can be solved through laws and court decisions.[36] It is said that the KCK accepts all justice-related submissions through a Yahoo! email address.[37]

Media stories and nongovernmental organisation (NGO) reports signal that the KCK began operating local courts after the 2009 general elections in Turkey.[38] The 7th Democratic People's Congress in Diyarbakır officially established the Regional People's Courts representing the local judicial system, charged with

[33] See *KCK Charter*, online: <http://rojbas1.files.wordpress.com/2011/10/komacivakc3aan-kurdistan.pdf>.

[34] Haner (n 11) 119.

[35] Art. 37 KCK Charter.

[36] KCK Justice Court member Zaman Zervan states that "There is no separation of powers in our system. The fundamental power is people because our system aims at revealing the people's democratic will. We only have the justice court. People debate their own problems in there and look for solutions": 'KCK Adalet Divani: Kurtler mahkemelere gitmesin', online: <http://german.rizgari.com/modules.php?name=News&file=print&sid=31875>

[37] *KCK Adalet*, online: <http://dunyagerceklerim.blogspot.ca/2012/09/kck-adalet.html>

[38] 'PKK/KCK Simdi de 'Adalet Divanı' Kurdu' *Aktifhaber* (18 September 2014), online: <http://www.aktifhaber.com/pkkkck-simdi-de-adalet-divani-kurdu-1047804h.htm> [Aktifhaber].

developing access to justice in all fields. The local court system, to which are appointed thirteen full and four substitute judges, is organised in a number of cities under the authority of the Supreme Court of Justice. An appeal procedure also seems to be in place, as cases that could not be solved by the People's Courts are brought up to a camp in the Kato mountain, near the Syrian border.[39] If the trials heard in the Kato mountain can not be finalised, cases can be brought up before courts within the camps of Qandil, Kaniresh, and Hakurk.[40]

At the outcome of a criminal trial, the tribunal's verdict is issued in writing and also read out in court. The punishment given to a convicted person likewise is communicated in writing. For less important matters, the prosecutors and judges can sometimes be members of municipal councils, executives of a political party, or armed militants assigned from a mountain post.[41] The identity of judges is kept strictly confidential from the public and is only known to parties who appear before the court.

The applicable law in the KCK's courts include statutes, customs, morals, and, in general, traditions. According to the KCK Charter, three types of laws are applied by PKK courts in Kurdistan: European Union law, unitary state law, and democratic confederal law. Accordingly, so long as the unitary states—Iran, Iraq, Turkey, and Syria—recognise the confederal law of the Kurdish people, Kurdish people will recognise their laws.[42] This is of course somewhat of a theoretical proposition, as none of the unitary state recognises KCK law.

An interview conducted by a prominent Kurdish news agency, Ajansa Nûçeyan a Firatê, with a member of the KCK Justice Court, Sores Sankan, exposes the underlying principles of the KCK legal system:

> [Translation] The Courts of Justice work, above all, on the basis of an understanding of justice that is different from that of the state: "I distribute justice". Therefore, there is always ongoing research and debates, which are mostly based on the Leader [Öcalan]'s understanding of societal justice and law. Together with the emergence of the Rojava revolution [in Syria] and furthering the revolutionary process in Northern Kurdistan [in Turkey], our justice is grounded in practice. *As an alternative, our goal is to establish authorities and institutions that will find solutions on-site, wherever problems arises. If a problem arises in a particular place, local people will better understand the nature of that problem, the characters of those involved, who is right and wrong, to ultimately arrive at a*

39 Hasim Soylemez, 'KCK'nin Temyiz Mahkemesi: Kato Dagi' *Aksiyon* (16 February 2016), online: <http://www.aksiyon.com.tr/teror/kck-nin-temyiz-mahkemesi-kato-dagi_528236>.

40 ibid.

41 In Turkish "going to the mountain" is an idiom meaning "going to join the groups hiding there". The expression has been used to describe the PKK members living in mountains in southeastern part of Turkey.

42 KCK Charter (n 15) Preamble para 7§5.

fairer decision. They can reconcile the parties and solve a problem in a permanent way. Otherwise, when you go to courts, as courts' decisions are enforced by force, a problem is not really solved.[43]

Later in the same interview, the judge acknowledges that there are many challenges to the implementation of KCK justice, including accessibility for parties, gathering information, summoning witnesses, and obtaining documents. Reportedly, the most common sanction imposed by KCK courts are fines, although there are also indications that exile, prison terms, and capital punishment may be imposed by these courts.[44] The group reportedly receives a significant share of any fine imposed or award granted by its courts.[45]

Summing up, it appears that the PKK or KCK has a lengthy experience with the administration of justice, and that institutions have been established in a more formal manner. At the same time, the operation of such courts emerges as uneven and still directly tributary to political expediency, with limited guarantees of the independence and impartiality of the courts and fragmentary due process guarantees.

B. West Kurdistan: The PYD/YPG in Syria

i. PYD Governance

Kurdish rule in northern Syria started in earnest in November 2013, when a Syrian Kurdish political party, the Democratic Union Party (Partiya Yekîtiya Demokrat, or PYD) together with allied parties and groups formed a "transitional autonomous government in the three areas that comprise what they call Rojava, or Western Kurdistan".[46] In 2014, the PYD-led political coalition (known as the Rojava Movement for a Democratic Society, or TEV-DEM) officially established a subnational autonomous administration across three mainly Kurdish cantons of Syria, Afrin, Jazira, and Ain al-Arab (Kobani).[47] Their administration

[43] Translated from the original in Turkish: Derya Keje and Kamar Ararat, 'Sankan: Toplum adaleti artik kendi kurumlarinda arayacaktir' *ANFNews* (23 December 2015), online: <http://anfturkce.net/guncel/sankan-toplum-adaleti-artik-kendi-kurumlarinda-arayacaktir>.

[44] There are unconfirmed statement by KCK members to the effect that the death penalty has been abandoned by the group: Selin Ongun, 'Dagdan inmek istemiyoruz diyorlar' *Cumhuriyet* (19 April 2015), online: <http://www.cumhuriyet.com.tr/koseyazisi/257947/_Dagdan_inmek_istemiyoruz_diyorlar_.html>.

[45] İsmail AVCI, 'BDP binasında 'KCK Mahkemesi'nin tutanağı çıktı' *Zaman* (25 November 2011).

[46] Human Rights Watch, *Under Kurdish Rule Abuses in PYD-Run Enclaves of Syria* (2014) at 14; Harriet Allsopp and Wladimir van Wilgenburg, *The Kurds of Northern Syria: Governance, Diversity and Conflicts* (Bloomsbury Publishing 2019) 89.

[47] Amnesty International, *Syria: Arbitrary Detentions and Blatantly Unfair Trials Mar PYD Fight Against Terrorism* (2015); Human Rights Watch, ibid; Robert S Ford and Ali El Yassir, 'The Kurdish PYD & the Challenge of Rebuilding a Syrian State' *Middle East Institute* (25 August 2015).

includes local councils akin to ministries, courts as well as a police force (known as Asayish) responsible for law enforcement and internal security.[48] Each canton maintains its own legislative, executive, and judicial councils, ostensibly selected through a bottom-up democratic process by its citizens. Overseen by a general coordinating council, over twenty-two councils were established at the canton level dealing with issues such as security, justice, and foreign relations.[49] Through these, the Rojava administration has been able to provide services such as "fuel, education, job provision, electricity, water, sanitation, customs, [and] health-care".[50] These services are purportedly managed in a decentralised manner, federating upwards "from communes, to neighbourhood/district councils, to city councils, and then to the cantons."[51]

The PYD's armed wing consists of the People's Protection Unit (YPG) and the Women's Protection Unit (YPJ), responsible for maintaining external security and defending the borders of the Kurdish-held territory.[52] A key US military ally, the YPG remains involved in hostilities with Islamist non-state armed groups. The success of the YPG's fight against the Islamic State, in particular in the successful defence of Kobane in 2015, has been the "foremost driver of legitimacy" for the PYD, internationally and domestically.[53] Following the near-complete withdrawal of US forces from Syria in 2019, Turkey and its allied militias have occupied a 'security zone' in northern Syria that was formerly controlled by Kurdish authorities.

The 'Social Contract' introduced in 2014 acts as a provisional constitution for the Rojava administration, proposing a political system based on participatory democracy, self-governance, minority rights, and secularism.[54] It dedicates many articles to fundamental principles of rights and freedoms that echo the Universal Declaration of Human Rights and other international human rights instruments, while entrenching principles such as the abolition of the death penalty (Art. 26) and the inadmissibility of civilians standing trial before military courts (Art. 70), standards significantly more progressive than that of the Syrian

[48] Human Rights Watch (n 46) 14.

[49] Middle East Institute (n 47); Human Rights Watch (n 46) 14.

[50] Rana Khalaf, 'Governing Rojava—Layers of Legitimacy in Syria' (Chatham House, December 2016) 17, online: <https://www.chathamhouse.org/sites/files/chathamhouse/publications/research/2016-12-08-governing-rojava-khalaf.pdf>.

[51] ibid at 11. See Massoud Sharifi Dryaz, 'Non-State Actors and Governance: Kurdish Autonomy in Syria' in Mehmet Gurses, David Romano and Michael Gunter (eds), *The Kurds in the Middle East: Enduring Problems and New Dynamics* (Lexington Books 2020).

[52] Amnesty International (n 47). The armed wing as a whole is referred to as 'YPG'.

[53] Khalaf (n 50) 12.

[54] In December 2016, the 'Social Contract' was replaced by an updated version, the 'Federal Democratic Rojava Social Contract'. English versions of both the 2014 and 2016 documents are available at <https://rojavainformationcenter.com/background/political-system-documents/>.

state.[55] The PYD further implements a progressive gender-equality standard in its governance, with gender-equal representation in all of its assemblies and the formation of a ministry for 'Women's Liberation'.[56] Remarkably, although constitutional in its function, the Social Contract states no aim to secede from Syria to establish an independent state or join a new transnational Kurdish state; rather, it is presented by the PYD as a model for a federal structure in which Rojava would be a province of a united Syria. More fundamentally, the PYD seeks to implement 'democratic autonomy', a popular self-governance model lately embraced by PKK founder Öcalan on the basis of US libertarian socio-ecologist Murray Bookchin.[57] According to this view, the state, far from an ideal to attain, is the root source of social ills. Instead, the goal is 'democratic confederalism', corresponding to a pluralistic, bottom-up network of local assemblies.[58]

The PYD's relationship with the central government has been described as one of "precarious coexistence", with parallel structures emerging in areas where the PYD and the Syrian regime co-exist.[59] Following the uprisings of 2011, the group marked itself amongst the anti-Assad opposition by its willingness to negotiate, culminating in a non-aggression pact with the regime that has comparatively spared Rojava of Syrian shelling and barrel bombs.[60] The PYD leadership continued to keep discreet lines open with the Assad administration, leading critics to accuse the movement of acting as the regime's proxy.[61] The US troop withdrawal in 2019 and the ensuing Turkish encroachment in what had been Kurdish-held territory forced an even closer relationship between the YPG and the Syrian government. Throughout the war, Syrian state structures continued to function in Rojava, with financial support from Damascus. Many of the Rojava administration's employees were previously employed by the Syrian regime, and

55 Ghadi Sary, 'Kurdish Self-governance in Syria: Survival and Ambition' (Chatham House, September 2016), online: <https://syria.chathamhouse.org/assets/documents/2016-09-15-kurdish-self-governance-syria-sary.pdf>.

56 This gender-equal standard has been largely adhered to, including within the military: T Coughlan, 'Revolutionary Kurdish Feminist Leads Assault on Raqqa' *The Times* (27 May 2016), online: <http://www.thetimes.co.uk/article/revolutionary-kurdish-feminist-leads-assault-on-raqqa-29kdsrgpc>; Pinar Tank, 'Kurdish Women in Rojava: From Resistance to Reconstruction' (2017) 57 Die Welt des Islams 404.

57 Damian Gerber and Shannon Brincat, 'When Öcalan Met Bookchin: The Kurdish Freedom Movement and the Political Theory of Democratic Confederalism' [2018] Geopolitics 1.

58 Office français de protection des réfugiés et apatrides—République française, Relation entre le PYD et le régime syrien depuis le début du conflit (2018), online: <https://ofpra.gouv.fr/sites/default/files/atoms/files/1809_syr_saa_et_ypg_a_kobane_0.pdf>; Joost Jongerden, 'Governing Kurdistan: Self-Administration in the Kurdistan Regional Government in Iraq and the Democratic Federation of Northern Syria' (2019) 18 Ethnopolitics 61, 67.

59 Khalaf (n 50) 9.

60 ibid 5; Burcu Özçelik, 'Explaining the Kurdish Democratic Union Party's Self-Governance Practices in Northern Syria, 2012–18' (2019) 55 Government and Opposition 690, 703.

61 Sary (n 55) 3; Mikael Ekman, 'ILAC Rule of Law Assessment Report: Syria 2017' (International Legal Assistance Consortium 2017) 113, online: <http://www.ilacnet.org/wp-content/uploads/2017/04/Syria2017.pdf>.

continue to receive their government salaries in addition to wages paid by the local administration.[62]

Rojava's relationship with the PKK is murkier.[63] On the one hand, Turkey insists that the PYD and PKK are the same terrorist organisation, and invokes this view as justification for its occupation of part of Syrian territory; the United States, on the other hand, views the PKK as a terrorist organisation and the PYD as one of its close military ally, suggesting that it sees them as quite distinct. The PKK enjoyed a long period of harmonious relations with Syria, until international pressure forced that government to expel the PKK in 1998. It is uncontested that the PYD was established by the PKK in 2003, on the basis of the same platform inspired by Öcalan's ideology. Both PKK and PYD participate in the KCK, as an umbrella organisation grouping Kurdish groups in Turkey, Syria, Iraq, and Iran. That said, the PYD insists that it now operates autonomously and denies any affiliation with the PKK.[64] After the withdrawal of the central government in 2012, pre-existing PKK institutions "seem to have formed the backbone of Rojava's provision of security services", and many of the group's senior members previously fought with the PKK for many years.[65] The PYD's UK representative notes that the Rojava administration resembles the KCK in its approach, but insisted that "the PYD has nothing whatsoever [in common] with KCK ideology . . . none of the Rojava parties or organizations are affiliated with KCK".[66] There is little doubt that the fact of exercising authority over a population and territory for many years has transformed the PYD in ways that now set it apart from the PKK in significant ways.[67]

ii. PYD Justice

Turning to the PYD-run justice system, the Social Contract regulates two types of judicial authority: a Supreme Constitutional Court, empowered to "review legislative acts and executive decisions" and "interpret the articles and underlying principles of the Charter" (Art. 78), and a Judicial Council overseeing the entire judiciary. Articles 63–75 of the Social Contract proclaim the independence of the judiciary as well as a number of principles of fundamental justice such as the presumption of innocence, *nulla poena sine lege*, the protection against illegal searches, and the right to a public trial.[68] Human Rights Watch notes that the

[62] Özçelik (n 60) 703.
[63] Zeynep Kaya and Robert Lowe, *The Curious Question of the PYD-PKK Relationship* (Hurst 2017) 275–287.
[64] Alex MacDonald, 'A Guide to the Kurds in Iraq and Syria' *Middle East Eye* (29 October 2014), online: <http://www.middleeasteye.net/news/kurds-2135687288> [MacDonald]; Suat Oren, 'KCK-ROJAVA/PYD Raporu-1' *Gusam* (1 March 2016), online: <http://gusam.org/2016/03/01/kck-rojavapyd-raporu-1/>; Aldar Khalil, 'Syria's Kurds Are Not the PKK' *Foreign Policy* (15 May 2017).
[65] Khalaf (n 50) 24; Özçelik (n 60) 696.
[66] Khalaf, ibid at 11.
[67] Kaya and Lowe (n 63) 281.
[68] Human Rights Watch (n 46) 68–69.

Charter nevertheless "neglects to stipulate a number of core principles, such as the prohibition on arbitrary detention, the right to prompt judicial review, and the right to a lawyer in criminal proceedings".[69] They also underline that there appears to be no official gazette in which laws can be published.[70] On the other hand, the Social Contract "holds as inviolable the fundamental rights and freedoms set out in international human rights treaties" (Art. 20) and "incorporates the Universal Declaration of Human Rights, the International Covenant on Civil and Political Rights, the International Covenant on Economic, Social and Cultural Rights, as well as other internationally recognized human rights conventions". (Art. 21). Combined with the statement in Article 44 of the Social Contract that the enumeration of rights is not exhaustive, it seems that, at least at the level of norms, the protection given to fundamental rights and freedoms in Rojava compares favourably to that in many states, and in particular Syria.

At an institutional level, different types of civil courts have been established in Rojava: Peace and Consensus Committees, People's Courts, a Constitutional Court, and Justice Councils.[71] Peace and Consensus Committees are local bodies that offer immediate and informal access to justice in civil and criminal matters, at least for less serious ones.[72] The committees are composed of five to nine members chosen among the local community. There is a gender quota for membership in this and all other judicial bodies mandating at least 40 percent female membership. In addition, Peace and Consensus Committees have a women's commission, dealing with matters such as domestic violence, forced marriage, and polygamy.[73] Although Peace and Consensus Committee are linked to the justice system, they are not courts in the traditional sense of the word, blending legal and social norms and mediating rather than imposing a resolution. In one municipality, it was reported that 70 percent of cases brought to the committee were resolved at that level.[74] More serious matters, or things that could not be satisfactorily resolved at the Peace and Consensus Committee level, are dealt

[69] ibid. Art. 73 of the Social Contract actually states that 'No one shall be subjected to arbitrary arrest or detention. No one shall be deprived of his liberty except on such grounds and in accordance with such procedure as are established by law'.

[70] ibid.

[71] Ercan Ayboga, 'The New Justice System in Rojava' *Ecology or Catastrophe* (13 October 2014), online: <http://www.biehlonbookchin.com/justice-system-in-rojava/>.

[72] Asya Abdullah and others, *Revolution in Rojava: Democratic Autonomy and Women's Liberation in Syrian Kurdistan* (Pluto Press 2016) 164–165.

[73] Adam Baczko, Gilles Dorronsoro, and Arthur Quesnay, *Civil War in Syria: Mobilization and Competing Social Orders* (Cambridge University Press 2018) 170; Ekman (n 61) 119. See more broadly Rojava Information Center, 'Der Aufbau Des Demokratischen Systems in Nord- .Und Ostsyrien' (2019) 43–54.

[74] Ramazan Mendanlioglu, 'Großes Potenzial Der Kommunalen Selbstverwaltung Für Die Zukunft' (2019) 201 *Kurdistan Report* 33, 35; Rojava Information Center, 'Hidden Battlefields: Rehabilitating ISIS Affiliates and Building a Democratic Culture in their Former Territory' (2020) 24.

with by the People's Courts, with trial and appeal levels in each region as well as a court of cassation in Qamishli.[75] Each trial court is composed of a panel of five or seven judges appointed by a Justice Commission established in each canton, with judges required to be trained in the law.[76] The four courts of appeal are composed of judges that all must be trained jurists, elected to this position by the members of the trial level People's Court for the canton. Finally, as mentioned earlier, the Supreme Constitutional Court composed of seven judges, all jurists, is tasked with the responsibility to ensure that the executive and lower courts comply with the Social Contract. The ideological slant towards 'democratic autonomy' running though PYD governance in Rojava has translated into a degree of resistance against a model of administration of justice too closely centred on the state. In 2015, in reaction to complaints that the People's Courts were too similar to state courts in their formalism, 'justice platforms' were created as an alternative whereby a popular assembly of up to 300 people could be convened to hear a case and decide upon it by consensus or by vote.[77]

The YPG Rules of Procedure also indicate the existence of military courts within the system, in charge of trying military offences and war crimes. According to Article 18 of the YPG Rules of Procedure, there are two different types of crimes in the military code: "mistakes of war" (war crimes), which are considered serious crimes, and "mistakes breaking the rules" (disciplinary offences). According to the rules, war crimes are to be prosecuted before military courts while disciplinary offences "fall under regular investigation (platforms)." Among others "the use of cruel methods and violence for any reason other than protection" and "acts that aid the enemy" are considered to be war crimes. YPG members charged with these crimes are tried in a military court. Human Rights Watch asserts the existence of detention facilities for prisoners of war controlled by the YPG. YPG spokesman Redur Xelil said that "[t]hose we arrest we treat as prisoners of war, according to the Geneva Conventions. [. . .] In some cases, the YPG had engaged in prisoner swaps with Islamist non-state armed groups".[78]

Special 'Anti-Terrorism' courts also began operating in early 2015, mainly prosecuting Islamic State prisoners detained by the PYD.[79] Headed by a former

[75] 'Peoples' Courts in Autonomous Administrated Regions' *Enab Baladi* (26 January 2016), online: <http://english.enabbaladi.net/archives/2016/01/peoples-courts-in-autonomous-administrated-regions-2/>.

[76] Abdullah and others (n 72) 166; Rojava Information Center, 'The Anti-Terror Trial System in NES' (2021), online: https://rojavainformationcenter.com/2021/03/the-anti-terror-trial-system-in-nes/ ("All the judges and prosecutors working here had been studying law in regime universities but now that a department of law has been opened in the Rojava University, they can also study here").

[77] ibid 170.

[78] Human Rights Watch (n 46) 32.

[79] Kamal Sheikho, 'How Kurds Treat Islamic State Prisoners' *Al Monitor* (16 March 2016), online: <http://www.al-monitor.com/pulse/originals/2016/03/syria-kurdish-areas-anti-terrorism-courts-islamic-state.html>.

Syrian civil court judge, the 'People's Defence Courts' practice are purportedly "inspired by international laws on terrorism", with sentences that range from one year imprisonment for a 'civilian member' and life sentences for leaders or those guilty of murder, with the whole subject to appeal.[80] With the death penalty abolished in Rojava, the courts issued an additional "resolution preventing the use of violence during interrogations as well as physical and psychological abuse in prison. [The Courts] have even given instructions that solitary confinement should not exceed one week".[81] The focus has been on the prosecution of crimes by Syrian fighters that belonged to ISIS and pro-Turkey militias, some 8000 of which had been tried in Rojava by early 2021 leading to 1881 convictions; detained foreign fighters have been a particular concern, and the PYD has shifted from asking their repatriation by their national governments to seeking international support for their prosecution in Rojava.[82]

In parallel to the judicial institutions established by the PYD, official courts of the Syrian government have remained in operation in an uninterrupted fashion in territory under rebel control. Judges, prosecutors, and other court officials have continued to receive their salaries, and no effort seems to have been made by insurgent authorities to present people from bringing civil and criminal cases to these state courts. Judicial decisions applying Syrian law and procedure are being issued, although there is no police force available to enforce such decisions.[83] Notwithstanding the Kurds' perceived links with the Assad regime, PYD-run courts are categorically discredited by the central government. In areas where it coexists with the Syrian state, "the PYD has created parallel structures to that of the regime, urging locals to register with the PYD-run system for their own protection. Yet, the locals are also obligated to use regime courts for official documentation, as the regime does not accredit PYD institutions."[84] State and non-state courts maintain an attitude of mutual non-recognition, which has opened the door to litigants unhappy with the results obtained in one jurisdiction to retry the matter in the other.[85]

There is a significant degree of confusion as to the applicable law before Rojava courts. By default, Syrian law has been applied in criminal and civil matters, but since 2012, there has been an effort by the PYD-led authorities to implement

[80] Rojava Information Center 'The Anti-Terror Trial System in NES' (n 76), noting that about 60 percent of sentences are appealed.

[81] Sheikho (n 79).

[82] Dan Sabbagh, 'Syrian Kurds to Put ISIS Fighters from Dozens of Countries on Trial' *The Guardian* (6 February 2020); Tanya Mehra and Matthew Wentworth, 'New Kid on the Block: Prosecution of ISIS Fighters by the Autonomous Administration of North and East Syria' (International Centre for Counter-Terrorism 2021); 'Report of the Independent International Commission of Inquiry on the Syrian Arab Republic', UN Doc. A/HRC/45/31 (2020) para 77. See Section III.A, infra.

[83] Ekman (n 61) 120–121.

[84] Khalaf (n 50) 19.

[85] Ekman (n 61) 121.

wide-ranging legislative reforms. These changes are reportedly occurring in a "haphazard and non-transparent manner", resulting in considerable uncertainty as to what law is applied in any given case.[86] Here again, the state-sceptic ideology of the PYD has led to the decentralisation of law reform, with the 'justice parliament' of each canton authorised to amend existing laws or adopt new ones.[87] For example, the canton of Jazeera in 2014 adopted a law on the status of women that provided for full gender equality in private and public life, including equal pay, marriage, divorce, and inheritance, in addition to prohibiting forced marriage, honour killings, dowries, and polygamy.[88] Other cantons have related laws that are said to diverge in some ways from this statute.[89] The head of the internal affairs council in Jazeera, Kanan Barakat, also a lawyer, told Human Rights Watch that

> a combination of laws from Syria, Switzerland, the United Kingdom, and Egypt were currently in effect, as well as the Social Contract and what he called 'local customs.' Co-head of the People's Court of Qamishli, Qehreman Issa, gave a similar account. 'We are preparing the laws for Rojava bit by bit,' he said. 'Some laws are from Syria, some from France, the UK.' He explained that, unless there is a change, Syrian law remains in effect but 'at the same time we get inspiration from other laws.' This differed from the view of Asayish general commander Ciwan Ibrahim, who said the Asayish applies Syrian criminal law and the Social Contract.[90]

A representative of the PYD police force noted even more starkly that "[t]he foundation is Syrian criminal law, but we use other sources when it suits us, like Swiss or German law . . . We also use customary law, but this may vary between different places and ethnic communities".[91] Not surprisingly, uncertainty in applicable law creates uncertainty for the subjects of law. One of the prisoners in Qamishli prison told Human Rights Watch, "I don't know what's going on, no one knows the laws", while another one said, "I don't know what law I will be judged under".[92]

[86] Human Rights Watch (n 46) 2; Rojava Information Center 'The Anti-Terror Trial System in NES' (n 76).

[87] Abdullah and others (n 72) 167.

[88] An English translation of the law is available at <https://rojavainformationcenter.com/storage/2019/12/2014-Womens-Law-Basic-Principles-and-General-Principles-for-Women.pdf>.

[89] Rojava Information Center, 'Der Aufbau Des Demokratischen Systems in Nord- Und Ostsyrien' (n 73) 46.

[90] ibid 25.

[91] Carl Drott, 'Syrian Kurdish Areas Under the Rule of Law?' *Carnegie Endowment for International Peace* (7 May 2014).

[92] Human Rights Watch (n 46) 25; Rojava Information Center 'The Anti-Terror Trial System in NES' (n 76).

The Social Contract proclaims that "[t]he independence of the Judiciary is founding principle of the rule of law" (Art. 63), and PYD officials claim that judges enjoy full independence from the leadership of the group. That claim has been disputed by some lawyers who have appeared before the People's courts.[93] They say the courts are primarily PYD-appointed personnel, who serve the interests of the group. "They just sit and discuss the case without going back to the law or investigating or relying on evidence", says one lawyer not affiliated with the PYD.[94] For example, according to Kurdish website Kurdwatch, Husam Hirkuki, the chairman of the court in Afrin, allegedly had close ties to the intelligence service.[95] To make matters worse, there is an admitted shortage of qualified jurists to serve as judges, prosecutors, and defence counsels.

More generally, the PYD-run justice system is reportedly marred by serious shortcomings undermining the right to a fair trial. NGOs such as Amnesty International, Human Rights Watch, and the Carnegie Endowment for International Peace have documented a frail level of rule of law and due process violations in the area of northern Syria under the control of the PYD. The alleged breaches of the rule of law in the region commonly consist of arbitrary arrest and detention practices, investigations and trials on the basis of political opposition, and mistreatment in detention. The PYD security forces deny any arrest on the basis of political motives, claiming instead that detainees are arrested on the basis of criminal acts such as drug trafficking and bomb attacks. That said, individuals associated with Kurdish political parties opposing the PYD, such as the Kurdish Democratic Party of Syria (KDPS), the Yekiti Party, and the Azadi Party, have been repeatedly detained.[96] Human Rights Watch reports that

> [i]n April 2014, a PYD-run court in Afrin convicted 13 people, including five KDPS members, for various bomb attacks in a trial that seemingly failed to meet international standards. The judges apparently convicted the defendants only on the basis of their confessions, and disregarded complaints that investigators had extracted confessions with torture. The police, known as Asayish, regularly failed to present a warrant when making an arrest, according to those arrested or their relatives. Detained individuals either did not know they had the right to a lawyer or they lacked the money to pay for one. This contradicted local officials, who said detainees were promptly granted access to a lawyer. Current and former detainees also complained about the

93 Human Rights Watch (n 46) 14–15; Ekman (n 61) 118.

94 Human Rights Watch ibid.

95 'Afrin: PYD Establishes Courts' *Kurdwatch*, online: <https://kurdwatch.ezks.org/?aid=2553&z=en>.

96 Human Rights Watch (n 46) 1; 'Report of the Independent International Commission of Inquiry on the Syrian Arab Republic' (n 82) para 75.

> length of time in detention before seeing an investigative judge, in two cases more than a month.[97]

This mirrors Amnesty International's findings, on the basis of interviews conducted with detainees during their fact-finding mission to northern Syria. Some detainees were held without any charge or trial up to a year, and their rights "to defend themselves, to see the evidence against them and access to a lawyer and their family" were denied. For example, "[o]ut of five detainees convicted on terrorism grounds interviewed, four said they had been sentenced after grossly unfair trials without any substantiated evidence of their guilt".[98] Others, on the basis of their own recent observation on the ground in Rojava, have directly challenged the findings documented by Human Rights Watch and Amnesty, possibly as a result of improvements put into place since the time of these reports, including better access to legal counsel.[99]

It seems clear that, despite the very open language of the Social Contract, the PYD has authoritarian tendencies and takes a dim view of any attempt to promote political programmes that challenge its 'democratic confederalism' model.[100] On the other hand, some of the criticisms of PYD courts do seem overstated, and the undeniably enormity of the challenge of administering justice in a conflict zone marred by extreme instability cannot be underestimated. While, here again, there are very significant shortcomings to the way in which justice is actually being served, the stated purpose and structure of Rojava courts do seem compatible with the notion of the rule of law as embodied in international humanitarian law and international human rights law.[101]

C. South Kurdistan: The KRG in Iraq

i. KRG Governance

The Kurdistan Region of Iraq (KRI) is a federated area comprising the three Iraqi governorates of Dohuk, Erbil, and Sulaymaniyah in Iraq's north, bordering Syria, Turkey, and Iran.[102] The capital of the region is Erbil.[103] The KRI has its own flag,

[97] Human Rights Watch (n 46) 21.

[98] Amnesty International (n 47).

[99] Abdullah and others (n 72) 172; Mehra and Wentworth (n 82); Rojava Information Center 'The Anti-Terror Trial System in NES' (n 76); Jane Arraf, '"Revenge is for the Weak": Kurdish Courts in Northeastern Syria Take On ISIS Cases', *National Public Radio* (29 May 2019); Liz Sly, 'Captured ISIS Fighters Get Short Sentences and Art Therapy in Syria', *The Washington Post* (14 August 2019).

[100] Özçelik (n 60) 691; Kaya and Lowe (n 63) 279.

[101] Ekman (n 61) 126–127.

[102] Freedom House Report on Iraq—2021, online: <https://freedomhouse.org/country/iraq/freedom-world/2021>.

[103] UK Home Office, Country of Origin Information Report Kurdistan Regional Government Area of Iraq, 21 May 2009 [UK Home Office Report on the KRG].

language, military (*Peshmerga*), and governing structure (the Kurdish Regional Government, or KRG).[104]

The *de facto* autonomy of the KRI started on October 1991 when an uprising against Saddam Hussein resulted in the Iraqi regime's withdrawal of its political, military, and civilian state institutions from the region, where Kurds seized control.[105] After the fall of Saddam Hussein's regime in 2003, the region remained autonomous, without any recognised definition of what its territorial limits were. Indeed, for periods of time, Islamic State control of parts of Iraq meant that the territory of the KRI was not contiguous with territory controlled by the central government.[106] Still today, despite the resumption of Iraqi control over areas that had been held by the Islamic State, there is an effective border called the "green line" between the KRI and the rest of Iraq. Although there is no formal KRG law restricting entrance into the KRI,[107] the entry into the KRI from the rest of Iraq is strictly regulated by KRG authorities, who do not give effect to visas issued by the central Iraqi government.[108] Although airspace is under the control of the central government, entry from other countries or from the air is controlled by the KRG, which issues its own visas not valid for the rest of Iraq. Kurdistan has largely escaped the sectarian violence and terrorist warfare that has afflicted Iraq since the fall of the Baath regime.[109]

Politics in the KRI have been fractious from the moment the region became autonomous, largely driven by tribal and ideological affiliations. In May 1992, the first elections of the Kurdistan National Assembly or Parliament were held in the KRI, resulting in a legislature evenly divided between the Kurdistan Democratic Party (KDP), led by Kurdish President Masoud Barzani, and the Patriotic Union of Kurdistan (PUK), led by former Iraqi President Jalal Talabani. Each party maintained its own government and militia, exercising control over separate segments of the KRI.[110] In early 2006, however, the two parties announced a Unification Agreement to merge their administrations into one.[111] Under the

[104] Freedom House Report 2021 (n 102).

[105] UK Home Office Report on the KRG (n 103); Center for Middle Eastern Strategic Studies, Democracy Process and Problems in Iraqi Kurdistan, Report No:151, April 2013, Ankara-Turkey.

[106] Nancy E Soderberg and David L Phillips, *Task Force Report State-Building in Iraqi Kurdistan*, Institute for the Study of Human Rights, Columbia University, October 2015.

[107] "Citizens (of any ethnicity, including Kurds) crossing into the region from the south were obliged to stop at checkpoints, undergo personal and vehicle inspection, and receive permission to proceed. Officials prevented individuals from entering into the region if deemed a security threat. Entry for male Arabs was reportedly more difficult than for others. The officer in charge at the checkpoint was empowered to decline entry into the region", online: http://www.globalsecurity.org/military/world/iraq/krg.htm>.

[108] Soderberg and Phillips (n 106).

[109] Judicial Reform Index for Iraq: Kurdistan Supplement, Iraq Legal Development Project, October 2006 at 3.

[110] UK Home Office Report on the KRG (n 103). The KDP came to govern the Arbil and Dehuk governorates, while Sulaimaniya was governed by the PUK.

[111] *Kurdistan Regional Government Unification Agreement*, online: <https://www.refworld.org/docid/469cdd7a2.html >.

terms of the Agreement, each party would be assigned a set number of cabinet positions, with posts such as the Speaker of the National Assembly and the Prime Minister rotating periodically between the two. While the PUK-KDP division still lingered in some respects, the unification agreement was partly effective in creating a unified KRG for a period of time.[112] The fracture between the two parties was renewed following the 2017 referendum on independence and the ensuing military debacle in Kirkuk, with the result that the KRI remains a deeply divided society and territory.[113]

The legal status of the KRI under Iraqi law is murky, with successive Iraqi institutions attempting to reclaim the region by way of recognising its autonomy within a federal Iraq. Thus in 2004, the Coalition Provisional Authority issued the Law of Administration for the State of Iraq for the Transitional Period, which "recognized the 'Kurdistan Regional Government'" (Art. 53).[114] A year later a new Federal Constitution of Iraq recognised the KRI and its existing authorities as a "federal region" (Art. 117).[115] The Constitution recognises the right of the KRI to exercise legislative, executive, and judicial powers in all areas save those exclusively devolved to the federal government (Art. 121). It also provides the KRI with a right to a portion of the national revenue from the sale of oil and gas, as the federal government is required to "[distribute] its revenues in a fair manner in proportion to the population distribution in all parts of the country" (Art. 112).[116] Interestingly, the Constitution validates all laws adopted by the KRG and judicial decisions issued by KRG courts since the region gained *de facto* autonomy in 1992, unless they contravene the Constitution (Art. 141).[117]

[112] UK Home Office Report on the KRG (n 103). Notably, a report of the Carnegie Endowment for International Peace on the Unification of Peshmerga published in 2015 confirms that the KDP and PUK maintain separate Peshmerga forces. "Both parties, moreover, exert substantial political influence over additional groups that are under the Ministry of Peshmerga Affairs' nominal authority. On paper, Kurdish President and KDP head Masoud Barzani is the commander in chief of all peshmerga forces, and the PUK's Kosrat Rasul Ali is his deputy. However, Barzani has limited influence over the peshmerga groups in PUK areas, and the same is true for Rasul in relation to the units in KDP regions." Carnegie Middle East Center, Kurdistan's Political Armies: The Challenge of Unifying Peshmerga, 16 December 2015.

[113] Jongerden (n 58) 68.

[114] Human Rights Watch, Caught in the Whirlwind—Torture and Denial of Due Process by the Kurdistan Security Forces, July 2007, Vol 19, No 2 (E), p 14; see also Kurdistan Regional Government (KRG), Global Security, online: <http://www.globalsecurity.org/military/world/iraq/krg.htm>.

[115] Constitution of the Republic of Iraq, Section Five, Powers of the Regions, Chapter One, arts. 116–121, as published in the Iraqi Gazette (al-Waqa'i al-'Iraqiyya), Vol. 4012, December 28, 2005: Judicial Reform Index For Iraq: Kurdistan Supplement (n 109).

[116] In the case of the KRI, this amounts at least to 17%. The same article requires the federal government to "specific[y] an allotment for a specified period for the damaged regions which were unjustly deprived of them by the former regime, and the regions that were damaged afterwards in a way that ensures balanced development in different areas of the country".

[117] John McGarry and Brendan O'Leary, 'Iraq's Constitution of 2005: Liberal Consociation as Political Prescription' (2007) 5 International Journal of Constitutional Law 670.

As things stand today, it is unclear whether the Federal Constitution of Iraq amounts to anything more than empty legal rhetoric, a desperate but largely unsuccessful effort to cling to sovereignty over the KRI.[118] The federal model written into the 2005 Constitution seems to have been largely rejected by later Iraqi governments, which refused to follow through on some of its obligations vis-à-vis the KRI and further resisted any attempt by other parts of Iraq to create their own region.[119] The relationship between the KRG and the central government in Baghdad remains highly antagonistic, afflicted by ongoing feuds over the precise borders of the KRI's territory and its right to control natural resources in disputed areas, most notably the oil-rich region in and around the city of Kirkuk. The two have been locked in a dispute since 2014, when the Kurds began exporting crude oil independently and on their own terms in pursuit of economic independence, leading Baghdad to slash funding for the region in retaliation.[120] With ever greater economic and political independence, the KRG held a non-binding referendum on independence in September 2017 in which more than 90 percent of ballots cast supported the creation of an independent Kurdish state.[121] This triggered an angry reaction from Baghdad that resulted in armed confrontations between Kurdish Peshmerga, Iraqi troops, and Shi'a militias, with the central government recapturing key oilfields and the city of Kirkuk.[122] Still, the two sides have refrained from all-out war, and the KRG remains autonomous. Thus the KRI has been described as "having 'de facto statehood', being an 'unrecognized state' and being a 'quasi-state' ".[123]

ii. KRG Justice

Turning to the administration of justice, the structure of KRI courts follows closely that of the Iraqi federal judiciary.[124] The essence of the KRG's judicial

[118] UK Home Office Report on the KRG (n 103); Judicial Reform Index for Iraq: Kurdistan Supplement (n 109).

[119] Jongerden (n 58) 72 ('the Kurdish autonomous region became an aberration from Baghdad's perspective').

[120] 'Iraqi Kurdistan's Battle with Baghdad over Oil Revenues' *BBC News* (9 April 2015), online: <http://www.bbc.com/news/business-32220764>; 'Baghdad Money Squeeze Tests Limits of Iraqi Kurdistan's Autonomy' *Reuters* (17 March 2014), online: <http://uk.reuters.com/article/kurds-iraq-idUKL6N0MC03S20140317>.

[121] Martin Chulov, 'More than 92% of Voters in Iraqi Kurdistan Back Independence' *The Guardian* (27 September 2017).

[122] Loveday Morris, 'How the Kurdish Independence Referendum Backfired Spectacularly' *The Washington Post* (20 October 2017).

[123] Zeynep N Kaya, 'When sovereignty and self-determination overlap in claims to statehood: The case of Iraqi Kurdistan', in *International Relations and a New Middle East Symposium* (Pomeps 2015) 22 (notes omitted).

[124] One notable exception being the absence of Administrative Courts. Administrative matters can be brought up before ordinary courts in the region. In theory, individuals residing in the KRI have an option of bringing an administrative case before the Administrative Court in Baghdad. However, "in practice it would be unusual for them to do so" because it would be unlikely to result in an effective remedy: Judicial Reform Index for Iraq: Kurdistan Supplement (n 109) 12.

system is set forth in the Judicial Authority Law of December 1992,[125] which established the basis for the judiciary in the region as an autonomous and independent organ of the KRG—replacing the nearly identical Iraqi 1979 Judicial Organization Law (No. 160) as a result.[126] KRG courts were henceforth to sentence in the name of the people of Iraqi Kurdistan, and had authority over all natural and moral persons in the region. Kurdish is given as the language of the courts, but the Arabic language can ostensibly be used when necessary. Independently of any authority derived from the central Iraqi government of the time, two parallel systems of justice were established in the region, controlled respectively by the two main competing Kurdish political parties: the PUK and the KDP each established a Court of Cassation and other courts including a Court of First Instance, a Personal Status Court, and Criminal Courts—all operating in a manner entirely separate from the official Iraqis courts.[127] As mentioned earlier, the competing Kurdish institutions were unified in 2006 further to a power-sharing agreement between the PUK and KDP parties, leading to the integration of the two Kurdish court systems with a single nine-member court of cassation sitting in Erbil.[128] In addition to these 'regular' courts, there are also state security courts (for political offences), military courts (with jurisdiction over the armed forces, known as *Peshmerga*), communal courts (called *komalayeti*), tribal courts (with jurisdiction only over member of a designated tribe), labour court, and juvenile courts. The 'Kurdish Judicial Council', a body formally independent from the executive, is empowered to assign, promote, and transfer new judges and investigate their conduct and efficiency.[129]

Under the Judicial Power Law adopted in 2007 by the Kurdish Parliament, the Court of Cassation is the highest judicial body in the KRI and is separate from its counterpart in Baghdad.[130] The jurisdiction of the Kurdish Court of Cassation and that of the Court of Cassation in Baghdad are respectively limited to the KRI and the rest of Iraq. As a consequence, "neither of the Courts of Cassation has the authority to review or modify a decision of the other Court of Cassation . . . residents of Kurdistan are obliged to bring claims arising in Kurdistan before the Kurdish courts".[131] Under the 2005 Federal Constitution of

125 Law No 14 of 1992, passed by Decree No 44 of December 28, 1992, published in Perleman (Kurdistan Gazette), Vol 7, January 1993.

126 The Judiciary and the law in the Kurdistan Region of Iraq, August 14, 2009, online: <http://gjpi.org/2009/08/14/the-judiciary-and-the-law-in-the-kurdistan-region-of-iraq/>.

127 Dennis Chapman, 'Security Forces of the Kurdistan Regional Government' (US Army War College 2009).

128 ibid; Esraa Mahmood Badr Alsamee, Harlida Abdul Wahab, and Yuhanif Yusof. 'The Application of Federalism in the Kurdistan Region under the Iraqi Constitution 2005' (2020) 7(5) *Journal of Critical Reviews* 172, 174–175.

129 Law No (23) of 2007 Judicial Power Law in Iraqi Kurdistan, Art. 33 [Judicial Power Law].

130 ibid.

131 Judicial Reform Index for Iraq: Kurdistan Supplement (n 109) 5.

Iraq, as part of the general attempt to reclaim authority over the KRI *de jure* if not *de facto*, a Federal Supreme Court is not empowered to review Kurdish law, but may only consider the constitutionality of "national acts or laws" (Art. 93).[132] On the other hand, the court can arbitrate disputes between the central and regional governments. Even this limited jurisdiction remains unrealized as the Supreme Court has never been established, because the Iraqi Constitution requires the adoption of a federal statute with a super-majority that provides Kurds with a *de facto* veto.[133] As a result, the Federal Supreme Court continues to operate pursuant to the previous, transitional constitution, arguably without the powers conferred by the 2005 Constitutional.[134]

Further complicating the divide is the tenuous or virtually non-existent relationship between KRI courts and courts in the rest of Iraq. Despite a joint-committee meant to coordinate the activities of the two, Kurdish and Iraqi federal courts seldom communicate.[135] Judges in the KRG are never invited to attend any judicial conferences or training run for Iraqi judges.[136] "The courts in the rest of Iraq generally do not honor court acts, documents and orders issued by the KRI courts. Allegedly, official documents such as birth or marriage certificates written in Kurdish are not recognized by other courts in Iraq".[137] Instead, official documents in Kurdish must be translated into Arabic and formally recognised by way of a legal procedure in Baghdad, and vice versa in the KRI. There is no institutional link between the courts of the KRG and that of the rest of Iraq, including no right to appeal.[138] When probed about the legal weight of a judgment issued by an Iraqi court, a judge in the KRI described a status that amounts to that of a foreign judgment.[139]

The isolation of Kurdish courts from the rest of Iraq has in turn created a safe haven for many fugitives fleeing federal authorities.[140] KRG officials are reportedly happy to receive politicians wanted by the Iraqi judiciary, actively inviting opponents of the federal government accused of corruption and terrorism to stay in Erbil under the pretext of security and stability available in

132 ibid.

133 See generally David Romano, 'The Iraqi Kurdish View on Federalism: Not Just for the Kurds' in David Romano and Mehmet Gurses (eds), *Conflict, Democratization, and the Kurds in the Middle East* (Palgrave Macmillan 2014) 200.

134 Dawn Walsh, *Territorial Self-Government as a Conflict Management Tool* (Springer 2018) 199; Adnan Amin Qadir, 'The Judicial Review of Law-Making Process in Iraq under the Constitution of Republic of Iraq—2005' (2020) 4 UKH Journal of Social Sciences 37, 44.

135 'Experts: The Abnormal Relationship Between the Kurdistan Region and the Federal Judicial Council has Created a Safe Haven for Fugitives' [in Arabic], *Al Masalah* (12 May 2014), online: <http://almasalah.com/ar/PrintNewspage.aspx?newsid=30038 > [KRI Safe Haven].

136 Interview with Judge 'Siryan', Erbil, September 2017.

137 Chapman (n 127) 214.

138 ibid.

139 Interview with Judge 'Siryan', Erbil, September 2017.

140 KRI Safe Haven (n 135).

the provincial capital, which they in turn use as leverage against Baghdad in negotiations on controversial issues such as oil sales and disputed areas.[141] Most famously, in 2012, the KRG refused to hand over then Iraqi Vice-President Tariq Al-Hashimi, who had been in Erbil when a Baghdad court issued an arrest warrant against him for involvement in terrorist activities.[142] Many observers have concluded that the Maliki government in Baghdad relied on spurious criminal charges to centralise power and get rid of political opponents.[143]

Turning to applicable law, Iraqi laws and regulations were of course applicable in the KRI before the region broke away from Baghdad in 1991. During that period, "[t]he legal system . . . was modelled on the Egyptian system, which in turn was modelled on the French civil law system".[144] Following the 1992 legislative elections in the KRI, the Kurdish parliament, as one of its first acts, issued a decree pertaining to the status of legislation promulgated by the central government in Baghdad. The decree required ministries to "examine the laws, decrees, regulations and directives issued by the central authorities to identify what is not compatible with the welfare of the people of Kurdistan and [to] submit these to the National Assembly for a decision on the legitimacy or otherwise of their enforceability in the Region".[145] The same decree further stated that "[n]o laws, decrees, regulations and directives which were issued or which will be issued by the central government authorities after the withdrawal of the [Baath administration] shall be enforced except after the legitimacy of their enforceability has been confirmed by the Kurdistan National Assembly".[146] In practice, KRG authorities refused to implement Iraqi legislation issued after 1991, choosing instead to promulgate separate laws establishing their new ministries and regulating political, judicial, security, and social matters in the region.[147] With that said, "many of the same Iraqi laws remained applicable in the region".[148] Criminal and civil procedure rules applicable in the region have remained largely unchanged, and KRI courts continue to hear cases pursuant to the Iraqi national Code of

141 ibid.

142 "Although Maliki warned the KRG that the Kurdistan Region would have serious problems if it did not hand Hashemi over, the KRG refused. It explained its position by saying that Hashemi was a guest in the region and Kurdish tradition required that he be treated as such—an interesting logic behind their defiance of the federal judiciary ruling": Alex Danilovich, *Iraqi Federalism and the Kurds: Learning to Live Together* (2014) 80.

143 Romano (n 133) 201.

144 Judicial Reform Index for Iraq: Kurdistan Supplement (n 109) 4.

145 Kurdistan National Assembly, Decree No 11 of 31 August 1991 (Art. 1), published in Perleman (Kurdistan Gazette), Vol 1, September 15, 1991.

146 ibid, art 2.

147 E.g., see the Law on Publications for the Iraqi Kurdistan Region (No 10 of 1993), the Law on Associations for the Iraqi Kurdistan Region (No 18 of 1993), the Law on Parties for the Iraqi Kurdistan Region (No 17 of 1993), and the Weapons Law (No 16 of 1993).

148 Judicial Reform Index for Iraq: Kurdistan Supplement (n 109) 4.

Criminal Procedure (No. 23 of 1971), the Penal Code (No. 111 of 1969), and the Law of Civil Procedure (No. 831 of 1969), as amended.[149]

Under the 2005 Federal Constitution of Iraq, criminal and civil procedure are not areas under exclusive federal jurisdiction (Art. 110). Hence, the KRG has discretion to amend the applicable law, and indeed a number of amendments were made in 2003 and 2006.[150] In family law, Kurdish authorities adopted new statutory conditions on polygamy to make it more restrictive in the KRI than in the rest of country, with a mandatory minimum six months' imprisonment for those who fail to abide by these conditions.[151] The Kurdish Parliament also incorporated significant amendments to the Iraqi Code of Criminal Procedure that guaranteed better protection for detainees at the investigative stage,[152] including the right to be questioned in a language they understand or have an interpreter appointed to them,[153] and the right to engage legal counsel or have legal counsel appointed to them.[154]

One noteworthy and significant area of confusion over the applicable law in the KRI concerns detainees accused of terrorism-related offences, which include captured Islamic State fighters.[155] After being extended three times, the Kurdish counter-terrorism law[156] (No. 3 of 2006) expired in July 2016, thanks to a Parliament suspended amidst political infighting over Massoud Barzani's hanging onto the presidency of the KRG after the expiry of his term.[157] At the time, the Shura (Consultative) Council—a controversial KRG advisory

[149] ibid.

[150] Human Rights Watch, 'Caught in the Whirlwind' (n 114); Global Justice Project: Iraq, Amendments to Criminal Procedure Code No 23 of 1971 in the Kurdistan Region of Iraq, online: <http://gjpi.org/2009/09/21/amendments-to-criminal-procedure-code-no-23-of-1971-in-the-kurdistan-region-of-iraq/>.

[151] Law No 15 of 2008 Amending the Personal Status Law (No 188) of 1959; Report on Joint Finnish-Swiss Fact-Finding Mission to Amman and the Kurdish Regional Government (KRG) Area, 10–22 May 2011

[152] Law No 22 of 2003, Kurdistan Gazette, Vol 45, 10 October 2003 (Suspending Implementation of Articles of the Iraqi Code of Criminal Procedure No 23 of 1971), passed by the Kurdish Parliament on 27 September 2003.

[153] Iraqi Code of Criminal Procedure, Art. 61 (c), amended by CPA/MEM/27 June 2004/03, Section 3 (a).

[154] Iraqi Code of Criminal Procedure, Art. 123, amended by CPA/MEM/27 June 2004/03, Section 3 (b).

[155] Rudaw, '150 boys detained by Kurdish Regional Government on suspicion of joining ISIS' [translated from Kurdish] (30 March 2017), online: <http://www.rudaw.net/sorani/kurdistan/300320173>.

[156] Law No 3 of 2006, Kurdistan Gazette, Vol 61, 16 July 2006. This law is separate and replaced the from anti-terrorism legislation passed by the central government in Baghdad in November 2005: Law on the Combat of Terrorism, No 13 of 2005, Iraqi Gazette, Vol 4009, 9 November 2005).

[157] Vaar Media, 'Kurdistan parliament ratifies amended Iraqi Penal Code' (7 April 2014), online: <http://waarmedia.com/english/kurdistan-parliament-ratifies-amended-iraqi-penal-code/>; Histiyar Qader, 'Getting Away with It? Iraqi Kurdistan's Terrorism Law Expires, Leaving Extremists in Legal Limbo' (13 July 2016), online: <http://www.niqash.org/en/articles/security/5311/>.

committee on legal matters established in 2008[158]—suggested bringing charges pursuant the 'internal security' provisions of Iraq's Penal Code (No. 111 of 1969), until the Kurdish counter-terrorism law was reinstated. Another possibly applicable solution would have been Iraq's heavily criticised[159] counter-terrorism law (No. 13 of 2005), a federal law that could be taken to apply to the whole country. Kurdish prosecutors have nonetheless continued to bring charges under the expired Kurdish counter-terrorism law, seeking higher sentences than the Penal Code's national security provisions would allow.[160] That said, while the federal anti-terrorism stature imposes a mandatory death penalty for all the listed offences, there has been a moratorium on capital punishment in the KRI since 2008.[161] Further adding to the confusion is the lack of clarity as to the applicable jurisdiction; Iraq's Code of Criminal Procedure is generally interpreted as requiring suspects to be tried in the jurisdiction where they are said to have committed the crime.[162] In other terms, most Islamic State suspects should be tried in the Nineveh court system under the control of the federal government. The KRG's official security agency (known as *Asayish*) has nevertheless refused to acknowledge the jurisdictional limit, barring the transfer of cases to federal courts and pressuring Kurdish judges to rule on the cases.[163] The overall result is a confusing legal vacuum governing the detention and prosecution of terrorism suspects, at odds with the KRG's declared desire to hold accountable the authors of crimes against the Yazidis and others.[164]

As regards international humanitarian law and human rights commitments, the KRG still officially maintains its *de jure* status as a region of Iraq, which implies that all treaties ratified by Iraq are applicable within the KRI.[165] In the

158 The rulings of the Council, which holds no legal mandate, have been controversial: in a 2015 decision the same Council had supported Massoud Barzani's hanging onto the presidency. Since the ruling—which was vehemently denounced by most KRI political parties, except Barzani's own—the Council has been viewed more critically, and its rulings have had limited effects.

159 The federal counter-terrorism law had been criticised for providing a minimum sentence of life in prison for any terrorism related offence and for allowing the death penalty for adults. Mushreq Abbas, 'Iraq's Anti-Terrorism Law Criticized' *Al Monitor* (16 April 2013), online: <http://www.al-monitor.com/pulse/originals/2013/04/iraq-terrorism-law-executions-controversy.html>.

160 Human Rights Watch, 'Why Children Are Stuck in Prison in Erbil Without Trial' (27 March 2017), online: <https://www.hrw.org/news/2017/03/27/why-children-are-stuck-prison-erbil-without-trial >.

161 UNAMI and UNHCHR, 'Human Rights in the Administration of Justice in Iraq: Trials Under the Anti-Terrorism Laws and Implications for Justice, Accountability and Social Cohesion in the Aftermath of ISIL' (2020) 4, 12.

162 Rudaw (n 155); Mara Revkin, 'The Limits of Punishment—Transitional Justice and Violent Extremism Iraq case Study' (Institute for Integrated Transitions 2018) 18.

163 Human Rights Watch (n 160).

164 Interview with Fallah Mustafa Bakir, Foreign Minister of the KRI, Erbil, September 2017; Interview with Safeen Dizayee, Spokesperson for the KRG, Erbil, September 2017.

165 See, e.g., Art. 50 ICCPR ("The provisions of the present Covenant shall extend to all parts of federal States without any limitations or exceptions"). Iraq ratified the ICCPR in 1971. The position of the KRG is clearly stated in the website maintained by that entity: <https://web.archive.org/web/20170408034945/http://cabinet.gov.krd/p/p.aspx?l=12&p=180>.

event of secession, the KRG—as a successor government of Iraq—would also arguably remain bound by previous administrations' ratifications of humanitarian treaties.[166] This includes the ICCPR, the International Covenant on Economic, Social and Cultural Rights, the Convention on the Rights of the Child, Convention on the Elimination of All Forms of Discrimination Against Women, as well as the 1949 Geneva Conventions and 1977 Additional Protocol I.[167] In addition, during the time of the *de facto* autonomy of the KRI, the two main Kurdish political parties separately signed Geneva Call deeds of commitment on anti-personnel mines in 2002.[168]

Not surprisingly perhaps, there are reports of serious shortcomings in the administration of justice in the courts of the KRG. Up until the enactment of the Judicial Power Law in 2007, the judiciary enjoyed no *de jure* independence, controlled entirely as it was by the Ministry of Justice and the executive branch.[169] While the Judicial Power Law provided a number of protections including the independence of the Judicial Council (Art. 2) and public trials (Art. 7), the situation on the ground remained far from ideal. Judicial independence continues to be undermined by the political nature of appointments to the bench, by external interferences in trials by the executive branch, political parties, and tribal leaders, and because of corruption.[170] Despite the formal unification of the dual judicial system sponsored by the two main political parties in the KRI, appointments are said to continue to be driven by political affiliation, resulting in lingering public distrust of the court system.[171] Access to justice remains dependent on ethnic and religious affiliations and political and personal connections.[172] *Wasta*, or favouritism, remains a serious concern, as traditional family and religious forces

[166] René Provost, 'Article 73—Cases of State Succession, State Responsibility and Outbreak of Hostilities' in Olivier Corten and Pierre Klein (eds), *Commentary to the Vienna Convention on the Law of Treaties*, vol 2 (Oxford University Press 2011) 1647–1649.

[167] UNAMI, Report on the Protection of Civilians in the Non International Armed Conflict in Iraq: 5 June–5 July 2014.

[168] See: Geneva Call, online: <http://theirwords.org/?country=IRQ>; Middle East Research Institute, Compliance of Armed Forces with International Humanitarian Law, Policy Note, May 2016.

[169] See Judicial Reform Index for Iraq: Kurdistan Supplement (n 109).

[170] Center for Middle Eastern Strategic Studies (n 105); Judicial Reform Index for Iraq: Kurdistan Supplement (n 109); Michael J Kelly, 'The Kurdish Regional Constitutional within the Framework of the Iraqi Federal Constitution: A Struggle for Sovereignty, Oil, Ethnic Identity, and the Prospects for a Reverse Supremacy Clause' (2009) 114 Penn State Law Review 707, 741 ("[c]orruption has long influenced the judiciary in Kurdistan. This is not surprising given the security situation the Kurds had to endure. Nevertheless, a complete lack of judicial independence, party loyalty of the judges, favoritism, and random judgments led to an atmosphere of unpredictability. This atmosphere was exacerbated by a system of courts divided among parties and other entities that neither worked in concert nor toward the ends of justice").

[171] Araz Barwari, 'UN Should Stop Iraqi Kurdistan Ruling Families Abusing the Judiciary System' *Kurd Net Daily News* (6 April 2019), online: <https://ekurd.net/un-should-stop-iraqi-kurdistan-2019-04-06> accessed 2 July 2020.

[172] Danish Refugee Council, KRI Access, Possibility of Protection, Security and Humanitarian Situation Report, 2016.

remain highly influential in Kurdish society, indirectly affecting the decisions of judges.[173] Reports that senior judges have unfairly punished lower-ranking judges for decisions with which they disagreed also indicate that judges are not sufficiently independent from each other.[174] There are also concerns about the qualifications of Kurdish judges, as judicial candidates are precluded from attending the Judicial Institute in Baghdad and do not receive adequate continuing legal education training.[175] There also appears to be a lack of adequate infrastructure for KRG courts, as judicial buildings are in a state of disrepair and lack basic information technology capacities.[176]

A general shortage of personnel and resources means that delays are unpredictable, often extremely lengthy.[177] There are many reports of illegal detention, the use of torture in interrogations, and convictions on the basis of confessions obtained under torture, especially in relation to suspected terrorists[178]—many of whom are children.[179] As mentioned, the lack of clarity as to the applicable law and jurisdiction for terrorism-related offences makes it nearly impossible to prepare a defence,[180] and arguably violates the principle of legality.[181]

Compared to their Iraqi counterparts, Kurdish judges generally enjoy a "relatively secure and stable environment", enabling them to live in their own homes, travel with minimum security precautions, and perform their duties more productively.[182] The KRG also pays a respectable salary to its judges, enabling it to attract well-qualified judicial candidates.[183] The unification of the two competing

173 Judicial Reform Index for Iraq: Kurdistan Supplement (n 109) 23.

174 ibid at 2.

175 ibid at 10.

176 ibid at 17; Interview with Judge 'Siryan', Erbil, September 2017.

177 Report on Joint Finnish-Swiss Fact-Finding Mission to Amman and the Kurdish Regional Government (KRG) Area, 10–22 May 2011; Soderberg and Phillips (n 106).

178 See UK Home Office Report on the KRG (n 103); US State Department Country Report on Iraq (2019), online: https://www.state.gov/reports/2019-country-reports-on-human-rights-practices/iraq/.

179 Human Rights Watch, 'Why Children Are Stuck in Prison in Erbil Without Trial' (27 March 2017), online: <https://www.hrw.org/news/2017/03/27/why-children-are-stuck-prison-erbil-without-trial>.

180 Continued detention by the KRG (rather than the by the Iraqi federal government) also prevents detainees from benefiting from Iraq's (controversial) General Amnesty Law (No 27/2016) enacted in August 2016, which offers amnesty to anyone who can show that they joined ISIS or other extremist groups against their will, and did not commit any serious offense while a member. Being forced to face trial in front of KRG trials may also mean lengthier delays. In addition to the mentioned shortage of resources and personnel, one lawyer representing terror suspects said that he knew of only three KRI judges with expertise in counter-terrorism cases involving child suspects, but that in federal Iraq, where these cases have been frequent since 2003, there is considerably more expertise: Human Rights Watch, 'Why Children Are Stuck in Prison in Erbil Without Trial' (27 March 2017), online: <https://www.hrw.org/news/2017/03/27/why-children-are-stuck-prison-erbil-without-trial>.

181 ibid.

182 Judicial Reform Index for Iraq: Kurdistan Supplement (n 109) 1.

183 ibid.

political parties in 2006 somewhat diminished political factionalism within the region, alleviating but not eliminating pressure on judges to pay heed to the political connections of parties appearing before them. A series of wide-ranging reforms have also been implemented to combat corruption. Amongst them, the 'Kurdistan Integrity Commission', formed in 2011 by an Act of the Kurdish Parliament, has been investigating and prosecuting government officials and judges who abuse their power.[184] One recurring demand of this commission is the establishment of a special anti-corruption court on the model of the Iraqi anti-corruption court, but this has not been done so far.[185]

In conclusion, it is quite difficult to characterise with any degree of clarity the legal nature of the courts of the KRG. At a formal level, there is agreement between the KRG and the federal government of Iraq that the KRI remains a province of Iraq. Even then, the extent to which the KRG can operate autonomously under the terms of the 2005 Federal Constitution of Iraq is considerable, both in deciding its own laws and administering justice in the territory of the KRI. That said, above and beyond the significant autonomy of the KRG within Iraq under federal law, the reality on the ground indicates that the KRG justice system is entirely autonomous for all intents and purposes. In terms of the rule of law, there are severe problems at every level, and it is not unwarranted to describe the situation as one of a flailing self-governing region within a flailing state.

More generally, the structure and operation of courts in Turkey, Syria, and Iraq by the PKK, YPG, and KRG illustrate the complexity of a reality that has often been reduced to a caricature in political discourse and a concept in legal analysis. Not surprisingly, the experience of administering justice by non-state armed groups occupies layers of grey zones that call for a legal analysis rooted in the actual reality of insurgent justice, to the extent that it is possible to appraise it. There is no doubt a need for further ethnographic fieldwork to uncover in greater details the practice of insurgent tribunals like those of these Kurdish entities, but even the limited sketch offered in the preceding pages opens the door to a more balanced and modulated analysis of the interface between the exercise of jurisdiction by rebel courts and the administration of justice by international and national courts.

The finding that Kurdish courts can correspond to the concept of the administration of justice, even if they do so to varying degrees depending on time and place, brings up the question of the extent to which they should be recognised

[184] The basic documents and annual reports of the Kurdistan Integrity Commission are available at <http://despaky.krd/Default.aspx>.

[185] Kurdistan Integrity Commission, '2018 Annual Report' (2019) 14. In February 2021, the KRG Supreme Judicial Council announced its intent to establish such an anti-corruption court: 'Iraqi Kurdistan "to Form" Special Court to Hear Corruption Cases' (22 February 2021), online: https://ekurd.net/iraqi-kurdistan-special-court-2021-02-22.

as such, and if so, by whom. As mentioned in the introduction to this chapter, such recognition can operate internationally, transnationally, nationally, and transversally. The analysis now turns to the international sphere to consider the possible recognition of the rebel administration of justice by the International Criminal Court and other international tribunals.

II. International Recognition: Rebel Courts and International Tribunals

The survey of judicial institutions established by the three Kurdish entities suggests once again that there are enormous challenges to the administration of justice by actors other than states. At the same time, the example of Kurdish administration of justice provides another example of the fact that non-state armed groups can and do claim the language of judicial governance and the rule of law, even if it is as part of a broader endeavour that is not taken as authorised by the domestic law applicable to the territory in question. As mentioned in the opening section of this chapter, a range of actors external to the armed opposition group operating its own courts may be confronted with the need to characterise its legality. These actors include international courts and tribunals such as the ICC and human rights tribunals, but possibly others such as arbitration commissions and the International Court of Justice. The analysis here takes the ICC as a key setting to analyse the implications of the rebel administration of justice under the Rome Statute, given the existence in that instrument of a number of provisions that potentially speak directly to this issue. Human rights tribunals will be briefly considered in the concluding part of this section.

There is at the time of writing no discernable basis for the ICC to exercise jurisdiction over crimes committed in Kurdish areas,[186] but there are other situations over which the Court has jurisdiction and where non-state groups have run their own courts. With the adoption of the Rome Statute in 1998, international criminal law shifted to a model of complementarity whereby the ICC will intervene only if local authorities are unwilling or unable to genuinely investigate and prosecute the authors of crimes falling within the jurisdiction of the Court. But what counts as a national prosecution that could forestall an intervention by the ICC? What if an entity other than a state is willing and able to independently and impartially try the author of an international crime? The proposed creation

[186] An ICC preliminary examination on Iraq was opened in 2014, but it was limited to the actions of UK troops, as Iraq itself is not a party to the Rome Statute. The preliminary investigation was closed in 2020: Office of the Prosecutor, 'Situation in Iraq—Final Report', 9 December 2020.

of a criminal chamber of the African Court of Justice and Human Rights already raises that question, but I want to explore the more radical possibility of a court created in the context of a non-international armed conflict by a sub-state semi-autonomous entity like the KRG or non-state entities like the YPG and PKK. Could the exercise of jurisdiction by a non-state court give rise to 'insurgent complementarity'?

The consideration to be given to the activity of non-state courts by the ICC has already arisen in the preliminary phase of two cases related to the situations in Georgia and in Libya. In the context of a request by the Prosecutor to the Pre-Trial Chamber to authorise an investigation into the situation in Georgia, the fact that the breakaway region of South Ossetia was administering justice in the territory under its control became a contested legal issue. The initial Request by the Prosecutor discussed the existence of national proceedings in Georgia and Russia against authors of crimes that could fall within the jurisdiction of the ICC. In a short addendum to that long discussion, the Prosecutor noted that there was no information that any third state had undertaken proceedings in relation to these crimes, adding that

> it considers South Ossetia to be part of the territory of Georgia and not a State within the meaning of Article 17. Since Article 17 is premised on national investigations or prosecutions 'by a State which has jurisdiction', the Prosecution does not consider that South Ossetian *de facto* authorities would have standing before this Court to lodge an admissibility challenge pursuant to article 19(2)(b).[187]

The Pre-Trial Chamber, in its January 2016 Decision on this request, simply endorsed the Prosecution's statement just quoted to conclude that "any proceedings undertaken by *de facto* authorities of South Ossetia are not capable of meeting the requirements of article 17 of the Statute, due to South Ossetia not being a recognized State".[188] Judge Kovács in a Separate Opinion took issue with the approach adopted by the Prosecutor and the majority of the Pre-Trial Chamber, labelling it an exercise in oversimplification.[189] He noted that there are situations like that of Taiwan where an unrecognised entity does have the capacity to carry domestic prosecutions of crimes within the jurisdiction of the ICC. For Judge Kovács, complementarity cannot turn on the criterion of state

[187] ICC Office of the Prosecutor, 'Request for authorisation of an investigation pursuant to article 15 on the Situation in Georgia', 16 October 2015, ICC-01/15-4-Corr, at 150 para 322.

[188] ICC Pre-Trial Chamber, 'Decisions on the Prosecutor's Request for authorisation of an investigation pursuant to article 15 on the Situation in Georgia', 27 January 2016, ICC-01/15-4, at 18 para 40.

[189] ibid, Separate Opinion of Judge Péter Kovács, 27 January 2016, ICC-01/15-12-Anex-Corr, at 29 para 65.

recognition, but instead calls for a case-by-case approach of the specifics of each situation:

> I cannot exclude, therefore, that is a *de facto* regime passed a proper sentence following the principles of due process of law against an accused person for one or more of the crimes falling within the jurisdiction of the Court, this could furnish a sufficient basis for an admissibility challenge under article 19(2)(a) together with article 17(1)(c) and 20(3) of the Statute.[190]

Ultimately, in the case at hand, there was no evidence that South Ossetian authorities had initiated any investigation or prosecution of the alleged crimes, making the diverging views immaterial in this instance.

The issue of the possible complementarity of courts of armed groups arose more recently in the *Al-Werfalli* case, part of the Libya situation before the ICC further to a referral by the UN Security Council. Mahmoud Al-Werfalli is the commander of a brigade in the self-styled 'Libyan National Army', which, despite its name, is a non-state armed group led by General Haftar engaged in a non-international armed conflict against the government of Libya. He was first accused in 2017 of the war crime of murder for the killing of thirty-three persons, to which additional charges for the murder of another ten persons were added in 2018.[191] In the ICC pre-trial proceedings to confirm the arrest warrant, it emerged that General Haftar had ordered Al-Werfalli's arrest following the initial series of killings so that the armed group's military prosecutor could investigate, but that he was eventually released and allowed to resume his command. Haftar ordered Al-Werfalli arrested again in January 2018 further to the second round of killings covered in the amended arrest warrant, but once more he was released two weeks later.[192] Interestingly, the United States, the United Kingdom, and France issued a joint statement that they welcomed the announcement of the investigation by the group: "We call on the LNA to ensure that the investigation is carried out fully and fairly; and those responsible for the unlawful killings are held to account".[193] The ICC Pre-Trial Chamber, presided by Judge Kovács, determined *proprio motu* that it should consider whether these measures by the 'Libyan National Army' could have a bearing on the admissibility

[190] ibid, at 30 para 66.

[191] ICC Pre-Trial Chamber, *Prosecutor v Al-Werfalli*, 4 July 2018, ICC-01/11-01/17, Second Arrest Warrant.

[192] ibid paras 25–26.

[193] ICC Arrest Warrant for Major Mahmoud al-Werfalli in Libya: Joint Statement by the Governments of France, the United Kingdom, and the United States of America, 18 August 2017, online: <https://www.state.gov/icc-arrest-warrant-for-major-mahmoud-al-werfalli-in-libya-joint-statement-by-the-governments-of-france-the-united-kingdom-and-the-united-states-of-america/>.

of the case before the ICC. More precisely, the question was whether it should be considered that the case against Mr. Al-Werfalli was being investigated in Libya within the meaning of Article 17(1)(a)–(b) of the Rome Statute.[194] Under the well-settled jurisprudence of the ICC, in order for a case to be considered as under investigation, there must be "tangible, concrete and progressive investigative steps" taken by the relevant authority.[195] With respect to Mr. Al-Werfalli, the investigation was too short and was limited to an interview of the suspect, leading the Chamber to conclude that "irrespective of whether the entity exercising authority in the territory controlled by the LNA can be considered a State for the purpose of Article 17 of the Statute, there remains a situation of inactivity".[196] Although the ICC came close to confronting the legal significance of the rebel administration of justice for the operation of complementarity, it ultimately sidestepped the question. These two cases leave little doubt that it is only a matter of time before the ICC is directly confronted with the issue of insurgent complementarity.

In the following section, I focus on the legal impact of insurgent justice on the ICC, by first situating the principle of complementarity in the context of the function of the ICC in the international community (A), then analysing the specific text of the Rome Statute that govern complementarity (B), and finally offering a broader reading of the concept of complementarity that allows for some recognition of insurgent justice by the ICC (C).

A. Insurgent Complementarity: Contextual Approach

The ICC is of particular interest in an exploration of insurgent jurisprudence because it operates in a manner that is tightly connected to the exercise of criminal jurisdiction by states but is also reflective of the supranational nature of the crimes within its jurisdiction. More specifically, the principle of complementarity mandates a broad approach whereby the Court will intervene only in situations in which a state is unwilling or unable to sanction an international crime. As such, the Rome Statute can be taken as furthering a Westphalian construction of the international community composed exclusively of sovereign states, with the ICC exercising powers delegated by states. At the same time, the ICC has jurisdiction over "the most serious crimes of concern to the international community as a whole", specifically the crime of genocide, crimes against humanity, war crimes, and the crime of aggression.[197] These crimes are "pure international

[194] ICC *Al-Werfally* (n 191) para 29.
[195] ibid para 27.
[196] ibid.
[197] Art. 5, Rome Statute.

crimes" because their "criminal character originated in international rather than domestic law, and international rather than domestic legal institutions".[198] By contrast, domestic criminal law (even that applied transnationally) protects domestic societal interests. This is the case notwithstanding that international crimes may be subsequently incorporated into domestic criminal law. This latter kind of domestic criminal law is said to be distinct because it governs "deeds of international rather than merely domestic concern" and they are "laws, moreover, that would not exist without international efforts to establish them".[199] As a result, the ICC can be seen as a embodying a certain tension between a state-centred vision of the rule of law and one that acknowledges the existence of a bundle of interests in the rule of law that are not fully captured by the concept of state sovereignty. The paradoxical nature of ICC jurisdiction designates it as a rich laboratory in which insurgent justice, as another challenge to state monopoly on the rule of law, can be explored.[200]

The interface between the ICC and rebel courts gives rise to many questions. In the remainder of this section, I want to focus on the interpretation of the specific provisions in the Rome Statute that articulate most directly the principles at play in that interface. I will leave aside for the purpose of this discussion other important questions examined earlier that ultimately could have an impact on whether or not the ICC could in a given case 'recognise' a decision by an insurgent tribunal, including whether international humanitarian law recognises a right for non-state armed groups to create their own courts, as well as the substance of due process guarantees that must be accorded by a rebel court to an accused in order for the trial to be considered fair. Instead, I will ask what the proper stance of the ICC should be if we take for granted that non-state armed groups can lawfully establish rebel courts, that all due process requirements were met, and that the accused has committed a crime that falls within the jurisdiction of the ICC. What should the ICC do with respect to the case of an individual captured by armed insurgents and tried by the group for war crimes, crimes against humanity, or genocide, if we assume that the accused was indeed guilty and the trial compliant with all due process requirement?

[198] David Luban, 'Fairness to Rightness: Jurisdiction, Legality, and the Legitimacy of International Criminal Law' in Samantha Besson and John Tasioulas (eds), *The Philosophy of International Law* (Oxford University Press 2010) 572.

[199] ibid. However, even this category of crimes has been criticised by Wellman for "implicitly endorsing the Westphalian outlook" because the invocation of an "international community" it itself reflective of a presumption that "each state enjoys a privileged position of moral dominion over its self-regarding affairs" such that "it is up to each state to decide whether and how to prosecute its own criminals, even those responsible for human rights atrocities": Christopher Heath Wellman, 'Piercing Sovereignty: A Rationale for International Jurisdiction Over Crimes That Do Not Cross International Borders' in RA Duff and Stuart Green (eds), *Philosophical Foundations of Criminal Law* (Oxford University Press 2011) 470.

[200] This is thus to be read in the context of the discussion in Chapter 1, Section III.

As mentioned earlier, the principle of complementarity is a central pillar underpinning the function of the ICC in the international community. Under this principle, the Court acts as a failsafe to ensure accountability for international crimes if and when states in a position to exercise jurisdiction neglect or are incapable of doing so. As highlighted by the negative imperative formulation of Article 17 of the Rome Statute, the general stance is one of deference towards state sovereignty:

Article 17 – Issues of Admissibility

1. Having regard to paragraph 10 of the Preamble and article 1, the Court shall determine that a case is inadmissible where:
   (a) The case is being investigated or prosecuted by a State which has jurisdiction over it, unless the State is unwilling or unable genuinely to carry out the investigation or prosecution;
   (b) The case has been investigated by a State which has jurisdiction over it and the State has decided not to prosecute the person concerned, unless the decision resulted from the unwillingness or inability of the State genuinely to prosecute;
   (c) The person concerned has already been tried for conduct which is the subject of the complaint, and a trial by the Court is not permitted under article 20, paragraph 3;
   (d) The case is not of sufficient gravity to justify further action by the Court.

Paragraph 10 of the Preamble and Article 1 both emphasise that the ICC "shall be complementary to *national criminal jurisdictions*". The language highlighted in Article 17(1) marks the bifurcated approach to the question of admissibility: whereas paragraphs (a) and (b) speak to actions by "a State which has jurisdiction", paragraph (c) more broadly refers to an earlier trial brought to its conclusion, without any explicit reference to a state.[201] Trial Chamber II in *Katanga and Ngudjojo Chui* underscored the distinct interests at stake in this choice of wording:

> This belated inclusion of the *ne bis in idem* principle in article 17(1)(c) as a basis for challenging admissibility is therefore explained essentially by the need to protect the rights of the accused, in contrast to subparagraphs (a), (b), and (d) of the same article, the purpose of which is to safeguard the sovereign rights

[201] The same is rendered by the French version of the Rome Statute, which uses the expression "un État ayant compétence" in paragraphs (a) and (b) and "a déjà été jugée" in paragraph (c).

of States and to ensure that cases brought before the Court are of sufficient gravity.[202]

The diverging purposes of the two legs of the provision suggest that there may be a greater space for some recognition by the ICC of the actions of rebel courts under Article 17(1)(c), to the extent that it can be expressed in terms of protection of the rights of the accused. A priori, it seems much more difficult to imagine doing so under Article 17(1)(a) or (b) if the reference to a "state which has jurisdiction" is indeed taken to signal the pre-eminence of state sovereignty.

That said it is important not to overlook the unusual references, in the chapeau of Article 17(1), to paragraph 10 of the Preamble and Article 1 which proclaim the ICC as complementary to a "national criminal jurisdiction". The notion of a "national criminal jurisdiction" is not defined in the Rome Statute. Many commentaries of Article 17 simply assume that "national criminal jurisdiction" can be equated to "a State with jurisdiction". For example, Jo Stigen takes the view that "according to article 17(1), ICC interference can only be pre-empted by 'a State which has jurisdiction over it' ",[203] and thus concludes that "a case which is not being and has not been investigated or prosecuted by a State with jurisdiction is always admissible".[204] This is consistent with the fact that the ICC has held, in the *Lubanga* case, that "a case would be admissible (...) if those states with jurisdiction over it remain inactive in relation to that case".[205] This understanding is underpinned by a certain view of the ICC's own jurisdiction and its relationship to state jurisdictions. Specifically, it takes as a given that only states have jurisdiction, and so in the face of inactivity of states with jurisdiction, the ICC remains the only other authority able to act. Part of the problem with how to understand the relationship between the ICC and "national jurisdictions" (whether state, internationalised, or non-state) comes from a tension that exists in the Rome Statute in terms of the ICC's own jurisdiction, as mentioned just previously. It can be argued that a reading of ICC jurisdiction that eschews a perspective exclusively rooted in state sovereignty in favour of one balancing state and humanitarian concerns opens the door to a more modulated application of the principle of complementarity in relation to insurgent justice.

[202] ICC Trial Chamber, *Prosecutor v Katanga and Ngudjojo Chui*, 16 June 2009, ICC-01/04-01/07, Reasons for the oral decision of the Motion challenging the admissibility of the Case, para 48. See Diane Bernard, 'Ne Bis in Idem—Protector of Defendants' Rights or Jurisdictional Pointsman?' (2011) 9 Journal of International Criminal Justice 863, 876.

[203] Jo Stigen, *The Relationship between the International Criminal Court and National Jurisdictions: The Principle of Complementarity* (M Nijhoff 2008) 190.

[204] ibid 185. See also Gaiane Nuridzhanian, 'Ne Bis In Idem in Article 20 (3) of the Rome Statute and Non-State Courts' (2019) 18 The Law & Practice of International Courts and Tribunals 219, 224.

[205] ICC Pre-Trial Chamber, *Prosecutor v Lubanga Dyilo*, 24 February 2006, ICC-01/04-01/06, Decision on the Prosecutor's Application for a warrant of arrest, Art. 58, para 29.

B. Insurgent Complementarity: Textual Approach

The Rome Statute may be taken as representing a combination of sovereign and community interests, but the bifurcated approach to admissibility identified in Article 17 remains significant. As such, it is justified to separately examine the implications of the precise wording of paragraphs (a) and (b) of Article 17(1), on the one hand, and paragraph (c), on the other, as was done by the handful of authors who have explored the application of complementarity in relation to courts of non-state armed groups.

i. Article 17(1)(a) and (b)—"A State Which Has Jurisdiction over It"

Turning first to Article 17(1)(a) and (b) of the Rome Statute, which mandate that a case be declared inadmissible by the ICC if it is being investigated or prosecuted or has been investigated "by a State which has jurisdiction over it", it seems that there is not much room to maneuver to argue for the inclusion of rebel court decisions. Jann Kleffner, who has offered the most specific reflection on this issue as part of his sustained work around the principle of complementarity, starts from the simple acknowledgment that no one during the Rome Statute negotiations ever envisaged the possibility that non-state actors could create courts whose decisions might prevent admissibility of a case to the ICC.[206] Kleffner's position is that proceedings by an organised armed group cannot trigger Article 17(1)(a) and (b), irrespective of the basis of such proceedings in international law. This position is based on the text of Articles 17(1)(a) and (b), interpreted in light of its drafting history:

> The term 'State' excludes those investigations, prosecutions and decisions not to prosecute carried out or taken by non-State actors on the sub-statal level, most notably *organized armed groups*, which are parties to non-international conflicts. [Emphasis in original][207]
>
> The provision is quite clear: these investigations and prosecutions or decisions not to prosecute have to be those of 'a State' . . . The simple fact that the proceedings are being carried out by an OAG [organized armed group], rather than a state, removes the case from the ambit of assessment under Art 17(1)(a)

[206] Jann K Kleffner, 'The Law and Policy of Complementarity in Relation to "Criminal Proceedings" Carried Out by Non-State Organized Armed Groups', *The International Criminal Court and Complementarity: From Theory to Practice*, vol II (Cambridge University Press 2012) 708 ('[T]he phenomenon of proceedings carried out by OAGs is conspicuously absent from the wording of the provisions of the Rome Statute relating to complementarity and their drafting history. Nor is there any document of the Court and its organs in the public domain that would suggest that any thought has been given to the possibility of such proceedings and their implications for complementarity').

[207] Jann K Kleffner, *Complementarity in the Rome Statute and National Criminal Jurisdictions* (Oxford University Press 2008) 109.

> and (b) since the two provisions are only triggered if and when proceedings are those conducted by a state.[208]

According to this view, neither the fact that international law (particularly the doctrine of command responsibility) imposes obligations on commanders and superiors of organised armed groups 'to suppress' international crimes, nor that there are instances of organised armed groups establishing suppressive measures via courts, changes the fact that such courts "do not qualify as investigations, prosecutions and decisions not to prosecute by a 'State' ".[209] Leaving aside for now the impact of paragraph (c), Kleffner concludes that "nothing would seem to divest the ICC from the possibility to exercise its jurisdiction in cases where organized armed groups . . . whose proceedings cannot be considered to be conducted 'by a State', carry out proceedings".[210]

More recently, William Schabas and Mohamed El Zeidy have also discussed this issue, in the context of considering situations that may test the limits of what constitutes a 'State' for the purpose of applying Article 17 of the Rome Statute.[211] They note that, of course, 'State' minimally includes a state that can ratify the Rome Statute according to Article 125. In addition, there are references in some articles of the Statute to both state parties and states with jurisdiction over an international crime, for instance Article 18, necessarily implying that there are indeed 'states' that are not party to the Rome Statute. Beyond this rather straightforward interpretation, Schabas and El Zeidy suggest that more difficult questions may arise and that a rigidly narrow construction of the wording of Article 17(1) may undermine the goal of ending impunity for international crimes:

> There may, for example, be entities whose status is contested but which enjoy an undisputed control over territory and have the capacity to exercise jurisdiction. An example is Taiwan, which, although unable to become a State Party in accordance with article 125 of the Statute because of the controversy surrounding its status at the United Nations, might otherwise be granted a limited standing before the Court as a state with jurisdiction within the meaning of article 17.
>
> Less clear-cut examples might concern categories relating to disputed territories, such as Kosovo (which is recognised by many Western Countries but is disputed by Russia), or South Ossetia (which is recognised by Russia,

[208] Kleffner (n 206) 718.

[209] Kleffner (n 207) 110; Nuridzhanian (n 204) 225.

[210] Kleffner (n 207) 110.

[211] William A Schabas and Mohamed M El Zeidy, 'Article 17—Issues of Admissibility' in Kai Ambos and Otto Triffterer (eds), *Commentary on the Rome Statute of the International Criminal Court: Observers' Notes, Article by Article* (3d edn, Nomos Verlagsgesellschaft 2016) 794–795.

> but disputed by the Western Countries). In these situations, the Court might nonetheless be willing to consider arguments as to the entity's standing for the purposes of articles 17 and 19(2), notwithstanding their controversial status under international law.

The case of Taiwan (officially, the 'Republic of China') is interesting because it combines a legal jurisdiction offering all the guarantees of impartiality and independence that are required under international human rights law while not exercising this jurisdiction in a manner that can be construed as delegated or authorised by the purported sovereign, the People's Republic of China. Indeed, it bears noting that the courts of Taiwan fulfil to a significantly greater degree the requirements of impartiality and independence than do the courts of the recognised state, the People's Republic of China.[212] To these examples we can add, in an even more immediate manner, the case of Palestine as an entity with material control over a population and territory as well as a significant degree of international recognition by other states and the United Nations. In February 2021, the Pre-Trial Chamber of the ICC concluded that Palestine had effectively ratified the Rome Statute and become a state party, but that did not determine Palestinian statehood more generally because the ICC "is not constitutionally competent to determine matters of statehood that would bind the international community".[213] This suggests that the notion of a 'state' pursuant to Article 17(1)(a) and (b) may be wider than the corresponding notion under general public international law.[214] One could mention further situations like Western Sahara, Northern Cyprus, and Somaliland as other examples of contested emergence of sovereign states. Of these, it is perhaps the Western Sahara that provides the best example of the challenge of overdetermined categories: that situation is viewed by many as belligerent occupation or a low-level lingering armed conflict, in which the Polisario Front is alternatively considered as an armed opposition group, as the national liberation movement

[212] See World Bank Worldwide Governance Indicators for the rule of law, online: <http://databank.worldbank.org/data/reports.aspx?source=worldwide-governance-indicators>.

[213] Pre-trial Chamber, Situation in the State of Palestine, 5 February 2021, ICC-01/18, Decision on the "Prosecution Request Pursuant to Article 19(3) for a Ruling on the Court's Territorial Jurisdiction in Palestine, para 108.

[214] These questions are vigorously, at times stridently debated in the fifty or so briefs filed before the ICC Pre-Trial Chamber and to which the Prosecutor responded in the document mentioned in the previous note. See: ICC Pre-trial Chamber, Situation in the State of Palestine, 30 April 2020, ICC-01/18, Prosecution Response to the Observations of *Amicus Curiae*, Legal Representatives of Victims, and States. See also: Yaël Ronen, 'ICC Jurisdiction over Acts Committed in the Gaza Strip: Article 12 (3) of the ICC Statute and Non-State Entities' (2010) 8 Journal of International Criminal Justice 3, 17; John Dugard, 'Palestine and the International Criminal Court Institutional Failure or Bias?' (2013) 11 Journal of International Criminal Justice 563; Andreas Zimmermann, 'Palestine and the International Criminal Court Quo Vadis? Reach and Limits of Declarations under Article 12 (3)' (2013) 11 Journal of International Criminal Justice 303.

representing the Sarhrawi people, or as the political party governing the Sahrawi Arab Democratic Republic.[215] It is clear that there are a significant number of legally complex and politically explosive questions regarding what entities should be considered a 'state' under Article 17(1)(a) and (b) and under the Rome Statute in general.

Supranational or regional courts can also test the boundaries of what constitutes a 'state with jurisdiction' for the purposes of Article 17 (particularly (1)(a) and (b)). A kind of 'authorisation from the State' argument has been made to bring such courts within the scope of complementarity. For example, it is suggested that the Criminal Chamber of the African Court of Justice and Human and Peoples Rights, when it becomes operational, "will be empowered with the collectivity of national jurisdictions, thereby indirectly falling within the scope of Article 17 and qualifying as a relevant (active) jurisdiction".[216] This will be all the more evident in situations in which the African Court is exercising jurisdiction on the basis of a deferral by a state that would otherwise have jurisdiction to prosecute the crime itself. This kind of example further supports the view that some kind of empowerment or authorisation by "a State with jurisdiction" is required to bring a prosecution or trial within the scope of Article 17 (1)(a) and (b). It bears noting that the same questions regarding complementarity arise for the African Court itself under the Malabo Protocol, in which Article 17 of the Rome Statute was nearly reproduced as Article 46H.[217] Thus, the African Court may be called to determine whether the activities of courts of armed opposition groups can constitute a bar to its own jurisdiction. The discussion becomes ever more complex under the Malabo Protocol because it envisages that the African Court may not have jurisdiction on a case if it is the subject of proceedings not only by the courts of a state but also by the courts of regional economic communities (Art. 46H(1)).[218] Despite the fact that, arrestingly, the Malabo Protocol makes not mention of the ICC, it is clear that these provisions are derived from the Rome Statute. At this point, prior to the coming into operation of the African Court as amended by the Malabo Protocol, there is little to glean for the

215 See: Report of the Secretary-General on the Situation Concerning Western Sahara, UN Doc S/2019/787 (2019); Claire M Metelits, 'Bourdieu's Capital and Insurgent Group Resilience: A Field-Theoretic Approach to the Polisario Front' (2018) 29 Small Wars & Insurgencies 680; Juan Soroeta Liceras, *International Law and the Western Sahara Conflict* (Wolf Legal Publishers 2014).

216 Alix Janssens, 'A New Star on the Stage: The African Criminal Court: How Will the Court Fit into the Jurisdiction of the ICC?' (University of Amsterdam 2013) 27.

217 Margaret M deGuzman, 'Complementarity at the African Court' in Charles C Jalloh, Kamari M Clarke, and Vincent O Nmehielle (eds), *The African Court of Justice and Human and Peoples' Rights in Context: Development and Challenges* (Cambridge University Press 2019).

218 To make matters even more confusing, while Article 46H(1) proclaims a principle of complementarity of the African Court vis-à-vis states and regional economic communities, Article 46H(2) articulates the principle by referring only to the actions of states, omitting any mention of regional economic communities.

developments at the African level that adds to the analysis of complementarity with respect to insurgent courts.[219]

This initial consideration of the text of Article 17(1)(a) and (b) of the Rome Statute indicates that the concept of 'a state with jurisdiction' does not correspond to an entity easily defined according to well-identified legal criteria. While it seems undeniable that this concept is narrower than the norm contained in Article 17(1)(c), to which I will now turn, it is an open-textured norm that may correspond, in some circumstances, to an insurgent movement in an armed conflict.

ii. Article 17(1)(c): *Ne Bis In Idem*

The formulation used in Article 17(1)(c) is quite different from that of the first two paragraphs of that same article: whereas, as discussed in the preceding, the latter use the expression 'a State which has jurisdiction', paragraph (c) provides that a case is inadmissible if the "person concerned has already been tried for conduct which is the subject of the complaint, and a trial by the Court is not permitted under article 20, paragraph 3". On the face of it, the fact that there is no mention of a state in the third paragraph eliminates a significant barrier to the possible recognition by the ICC of a decision by a rebel court. Paragraph (c) closes with a reference to Article 20(3), which codifies a version of the protection against double jeopardy or *ne bis in idem*. Specifically, Article 20(3) declares that the ICC does not have competence over a crime committed by a person previously tried by "another court". Fundamentally, Article 17(1)(c) is a *renvoi* to the *ne bis in idem* principle as articulated in Article 20. As noted by the ICC Appeals Chamber in the *Al-Senussi* case, the identical wording of the two provisions indicates that they were meant to have the same meaning.[220] The scope of prior proceedings covered by Articles 17(1)(c) and 20(3) is narrower than that to which Article 17(1)(a) and (b) relate, in that they must have resulted in a final decision convicting or acquitting the person for the same conduct.[221] The ICC Appeals Chamber in the *Gaddafi* case interpreted the finality requirement

[219] As of February 2021, the African Union reports no ratification of the Malabo Protocol. In 2015, Kenya proposed to amend the preamble of the Rome Statute to ensure that complementarity was understood to reflect the role of regional criminal mechanisms, but that proposal was not followed up: ICC Assembly of States Parties, 'Report of the Working Group on Amendments', 14th Session, 16 November 2015, UN Doc ICC-ASP/14/34 (2015) 3.

[220] ICC Appeals Chamber, *Prosecutor v Al-Senussi*, Judgment on the Appeal of Mr Abdullah Al-Senussi against the Decision of Pre-Trial Chamber I of 11 October 2013 Entitled 'Decision on the admissibility of the case against Abdullah Al-Senussi', 24 July 2014, ICC-01/11-01/11-565, para 222.

[221] Diane Bernard, 'Article 20 Ne Bis in Idem' in Julian Fernandez and Xavier Pacreau (eds), *Statut de Rome de la Cour pénale internationale: commentaire article par article*, vol 1 (2d edn, Éditions Pedone 2019) 945. The relevance of double jeopardy to the jurisdiction of rebel courts is discussed in Chapter 3, Section III.C.iv(d).

very strictly, to deny that a conviction *in absentia* by a Libyan court was final because it could be subject to a retrial.[222]

There is no element in either Article 17(1)(c) or Article 20(3) explicitly linking the previous trial to a state. The only element that can be taken as filling out the concept of 'another court' in these provisions is the exception to *ne bis in idem* included in Article 20(3), whereby the case may be admissible at the ICC despite an earlier trial if the prior proceedings "were not conducted independently or impartially in accordance with the norms of due process recognised in international law". On the face of it, the requirement of independence and impartiality in this context refers to the quality of the proceedings in the instant case rather than to the institutional features of the previous court. That said, it can be argued that if a court is structured in a manner that appears inconsistent with independence and impartiality, then all its proceedings would fail the test of Article 20(3)(b).[223]

In consideration of this, Kleffner concludes that trials in organised armed group courts "could constitute a bar to admissibility, provided the proceedings were not conducted for the purpose of shielding and were also otherwise conducted independently or impartially".[224] For his part, Jan Willms notes that the participants in the negotiations in Rome that lead to the adoption of the ICC Statute never considered the possibility that *ne bis in idem* could be applied to courts of non-state armed groups.[225] Given that there are considerable variations in the way in which this principle is applied in domestic legal systems around the world, it seems difficult to accept that there could have been an unstated consensus to extent it or not to rebel courts.[226] Ultimately, Willms sidesteps the issue to conclude only that if there were a trial before the court of a non-state armed group aiming to shield an individual from the possible jurisdiction of the ICC, then Article 20(3) of the Rome Statute would not bar a new trial before the ICC.[227] This in fact adds nothing new to the question of the possible recognition

222 ICC Appeals Chamber, *Prosecutor v Gaddafi*, Judgment on the Appeal of Mr Saif Al-Islam Gaddafi against the Decision of Pre-Trial Chamber I entitled 'Admissibility Challenge by Dr Saif Al-Islam Gadafi Pursuant to Articles 17(1)(c), 19 and 20(3) of the Rome Statute of 5 April 2019', 9 March 2020, ICC-01/11-01/11, para 53.

223 The structural dimension of independence and impartiality for rebel courts is discussed in Chapter 2, Section IV.C.iii, while the more procedural aspects are analysed in Chapter 3, Section III.C.i.

224 Kleffner (n 206) 718; Alessandro Mario Amoroso, 'Should the ICC Assess Complementarity with Respect to Non-State Armed Groups? Hidden Questions in the Second Al-Werfalli Arrest Warrant' (2018) 16 Journal of International Criminal Justice 1063, 1085.

225 Jan Willms, 'Courts of Armed Groups—A Tool for Inducing Higher Compliance with International Humanitarian Law?' in Heike Krieger (ed), *Inducing Compliance with International Humanitarian Law: Lessons from the African Great Lakes Region* (Cambridge University Press 2015) 161.

226 Bernard (n 221) 942.

227 Willms (n 225) 165–166.

of insurgent judicial decision-making, as the same would obtain for a decision rendered in similar circumstances by the courts of a recognised state. For their part, Schabas and El Zeidy take the position that[228]

> [t]he situation might be different in case of the application of article 20(3), where the person would have gone through a proper trial for the same conduct shaping the case of the ICC Prosecutor. In a scenario as such, it may be argued that the element of lack of State involvement in the trial proceeding might not be the decisive factor. Rather the decisive factor might rest on the fact that the person should not be tried twice for the same conduct even if his trial was not conducted by a State-like entity.

The emphasis here is on the nature of the interests more centrally protected by *ne bis in idem*, that is the right of the accused not to be punished twice for the same act, regardless of the nature of the tribunal having issued the decision.

None of these analyses adds very much to the text of Article 17(1)(a)(b) and (c) itself. Not surprisingly perhaps, both legs of the bifurcated standard adopted in this provision leave open many questions when they are applied to a decision of the court of a non-state armed group. Fundamentally, the test laid out in Article 17(1)(a) and (b) raises the question of what is a "state which has jurisdiction", while the test laid in Article 17(1)(c) raises the question of what is "another court". To answer these questions more fully in relation to insurgent tribunal, the analysis needs to call on the broader concept of complementarity.

C. Insurgent Complementarity: Conceptual Approach

The questions identified in the previous discussions may appear somewhat esoteric, but their reality has been confirmed by the fact that the ICC already has been confronted with them in the Georgia situation and the *Al-Werfalli* case evoked earlier.[229] These two decisions of the ICC Pre-Trial Chamber are illuminating, not only in that they confirm the immediacy of the concerns explored in this section but also in the limited depth of the analysis that is offered by the Prosecutor and judges (likely fuelled by the ex parte nature of the proceedings, without the benefit of arguments from opposing counsel). No doubt, the recognition of a state can have a significant legal impact in this context, given that a newly formed state would have the same rights and privileges as any other non-party states under the Rome Statute. This relates to a number of potentially

[228] Schabas and El Zeidy (n 211) 795.
[229] ICC, Situation in Georgia (n 188); ICC, *Al-Werfalli* (n 191).

important situations, including Palestine, Taiwan, and Western Sahara, but most likely not the majority of situations that are the focus of this study: non-state armed groups exercising legal governance in zones of armed conflicts. In cases like the Kurdish entities in Iraq, Syria, and Turkey, and indeed perhaps also South Ossetia and Libya, the operation of complementarity will turn on a number of other legal questions touching on the delineation of what constitutes a state and the determination of what constitutes a court.

Turning to the concept of the state, in the situation in Georgia as well as for the KRI in Iraq and the YPG in Syria, there are circumstances under which these entities might properly be characterised as a state pursuant to Article 17 of the Rome Statute even if they are not recognised as states under public international law more generally. One possibility is that a recognised state is exercising a sufficient degree of control over the non-state armed group wielding authority over a territory and population such that the acts of that rebel group are to be considered that of the state. The specific formulation of the legal standard of control has been the subject of divided judicial opinions and enormous doctrinal attention, as to whether it should correspond to a test of 'overall control' as initially devised by the ICJ in the *Nicaragua* case and sharpened in the *Bosnian Genocide* case, a test of 'effective control' as proposed instead by the ICTY in the *Tadic* case, or one of 'overall effective control' devised by the European Court of Human Rights.[230]

Under the ICJ's approach, a non-state armed group will be considered a *de facto* organ of the third state if it is in a situation of complete dependence in all fields to an extent that has allowed that state to actually exert control over the rebels.[231] If this obtains, the armed group is considered an organ of the state, and, as codified in Article 4 of the UN Articles on State Responsibility, its actions are considered to be those of the state itself. Short of such a situation of complete dependence, the acts of a non-state actor may still be attributed to the third state if, as provided for in Article 8 of the Articles on State Responsibility, the non-state actor "is in fact acting on the instructions of, or under the direction or control" of that state. For the ICJ, there will be attribution to the state only if it wields effective control of the non-state group, including in relation to the specific acts under scrutiny. For the administration of justice, that would imply that the third state is exercising effective control of the rebel court system, although perhaps not of the specific trial.

230 See Stefan Talmon, 'The Responsibility of Outside Powers for Acts of Secessionist Entities' (2009) 58 International & Comparative Law Quarterly 493.

231 *Application of the Convention on the Prevention and Punishment of the Crime of Genocide (Bosnia and Herzegovina v Serbia and Montenegro)*, [2007] ICJ Rep 43 at paras 391–397; *Military and Paramilitary Activities in and against Nicaragua (Nicaragua v United States of America)*, Merits, Judgment, [1986] ICJ Rep 14 at paras 109–110, 167.

The ICTY Appeals Chamber in the *Tadic* case found that the approach devised by the ICJ to define *de facto* state organs was not persuasive when applied to external state control over an armed opposition group in the context of an armed conflict; it adopted instead a looser test of 'overall control' whereby if the third state generally exerts significant influence on the armed group at the logistic and operational levels, then the group may be considered a *de facto* organ of that state.[232] There is perhaps some fuzziness as to which leg of the ICJ's test the 'overall control' approach is meant to supplant, whether corresponding to Article 4 or 8 of the Articles on State Responsibility, but in any case it implies a significant loosening of the requirements for attribution to a state of the acts of a non-state armed groups.[233] On the face of it, the ICTY test was meant to apply for the purpose of classifying conflicts under international humanitarian law, and it subsequently has been applied in that context by the ICC, but the *Tadic* judgment did include a claim that this was a standard valid more widely in the law of state responsibility.[234]

The European Court of Human Rights adopted what seems yet a different approach, requiring that the third state have 'overall effective control' over a territory in which a non-state actor operates, or that the state enables the non-state actor to survive and exert authority in a territory.[235] This is a distinct approach that reflects the extraterritorial application of the European Convention in such situations as well as the state's obligation not only to respect but also to secure the rights entrenched in the Convention, resulting in an even lower threshold for attribution.[236] For example, in a series of cases, the European Court determined that Russia's effective control and decisive influence over the 'Moldovan Transdniestrian Republic' meant that individuals in Moldova affected by decisions of this non-state entity were under the jurisdiction of Russia.[237] It is not easy to differentiate in the European Court's decisions the facets of the analysis that concern jurisdiction from those that concern attribution, in principle

[232] ICTY, *Prosecutor v Tadic*, ICTY-94-1-A (1999), Appeals Judgment, paras 131–138.

[233] Talmon (n 230) 507.

[234] ICJ, *Application of the Convention on the Prevention and Punishment of the Crime of Genocide* (n 231) paras 404–405, rejecting that broader claim. For an example of the ICC reliance on the overall control test, see ICC Pre-Trial Chamber, *Prosecutor v Lubanga Dyilo*, 29 January 2007, ICC-01/04-01/06, Decision on the Confirmation of Charges, paras 210–211.

[235] ECtHR, *Cyprus v Turkey*, Judgment, Grand Chamber, Appl. No 25781/94, 10 May 2001, para 77.

[236] See Marko Milanović and Tatjana Papić, 'As Bad as It Gets: The European Court of Human Rights's Behrami and Saramati Decision and General International Law' (2009) 58 International & Comparative Law Quarterly 267.

[237] ECtHR, *Sandu v Moldova and Russia*, Judgment, Appl. No 21034/05, 17 July 2018, paras 36, 89; *Catan and Others v Moldova and Russia*, Judgment, Appl. No 43370/04 18454/06 8252/05, [2012] ECHR 1827, 57 EHRR 4; *Chiragov and Others v Armenia*, Judgment, Appl. No 13216/05, [2015] ECHR 587; *Mozer v the Republic of Moldova and Russia*, Judgment, Appl. No 11138/10, 23 February 2016, para 147.

distinct legal questions.[238] Both strands could be applied to the administration of justice by a non-state armed group, raising the possibility that a rebel investigation or judicial decision could be imputed to 'a state with jurisdiction'.

This is a summary survey of what are extremely complex legal issues that would warrant a considerably more detailed and nuanced analysis. The point here is not to offer a basis on which to apply one or several of these tests in a context such as the administration of justice by the authorities of South Ossetia, but rather more modestly to indicate that the cursory approach adopted by both the Prosecutor and the Pre-Trial Chamber of the ICC in the Georgia situation cannot be defended in light of the significant legal issues at stake. Even taking the most stringent test, developed by the ICJ, whereby a totally dependent non-state entity should be considered a *de facto* agent of another state, it is far from obvious that South Ossetia cannot be considered as an organ of Russia; all the more so if we consider the less demanding tests developed by the ICJ corresponding to Article 8 of the Article on State Responsibility or those articulated by the ICTY and European Court of Human Rights. At the very least, these are questions that warrant a thorough legal and factual analysis of the kind that is entirely absent from the decision of the Pre-Trial Chamber. The lack of discussion at the ICC is all the more unedifying given the conclusion reached by the European Court of Human Rights in *Georgia v Russia (II)* that Russia did exert overall control of South Ossetian authorities.[239] If, applying one of the various tests for attribution identified earlier, the ICC were to consider the actions of South Ossetia to be imputable to Russia, then the door would be flung wide open to arguments that complementarity rules under Article 17(1)(a) and (b) should be applied in relation to the insurgent courts of South Ossetia. In this fashion, the Georgia situation at the ICC stands as an important illustration of the fact that the operation of courts of non-state armed groups may well have an impact on the application of Article 17(1)(a) and (b) of the Rome Statute.[240]

Apart from the possibility that courts of a non-state armed group be considered as organs of another state, as examined earlier, it is still possible that in some circumstances the rebel administration of justice would be attributed to the territorial state, again opening a door to arguments under Articles 17(1)(a) and (b) of the Rome Statute. Article 5 of the UN Articles on State Responsibility provides for the attribution to the state of the acts of a "person or entity which is not an organ of the State under article 4 but which is empowered by the law of that State

[238] ECtHR, *Georgia v Russia (II)*, Judgment (Grand Chamber), Appl. No 38263/08, 21 January 2021, para 162. This is cogently and critically analysed by Marko Milanović, 'Special Rules of Attribution of Conduct in International Law' (2020) 96 International Law Studies 295, 342–349.

[239] ECtHR, *Georgia v Russia (II)*, ibid, para 174.

[240] A reminder, however, that in the specifics of the case brought by the ICC Prosecutor in relation to Georgia, there was no factual evidence of relevant investigations or prosecutions by South Ossetian authorities.

to exercise elements of the governmental authority".[241] The prospective authorisation from the state envisaged under Article 5 is completed by the possibility of an endorsement ex post facto by the state of the actions of non-state actors. As codified in Article 11 of the Articles on State Responsibility, and as exemplified by the ICJ *Tehran Hostages* case, there must be a formal decision by the government to clearly and unequivocally adopt the actions of a non-state actor.[242] The European Court of Human Rights has suggested that an endorsement could have jurisdictional implications for the state, an aspect that not only triggers the imposition of human rights obligations for the state but also that may have an impact on the application of Article 17(1) of the Rome Statute.[243]

The case of the Kurdish entities in Iraq and Syria offers interesting illustrations of how this might be relevant to the establishment of courts by non-state armed groups. In Iraq, the Kurdish Regional Government was entirely disconnected from the state constitutional order between 1992 and 2004, a period during which were established an array of Kurdish courts that answered only to the KRG as part of its resistance to the Saddam Hussein regime. Clearly, for that period in Iraqi history, KRG courts could not be considered to be "empowered by the law of that State" to administer justice in the KRI. In 2004, however, the Coalition Provisional Authority 'recognised' the KRG, and in 2005 the new Federal Constitution of Iraq recognised the KRI as a federated region with power to exercise, inter alia, judicial functions.[244] Even more startlingly, Article 141 of the 2005 Constitution declares that court decisions issued by KRG since 1992 are considered valid unless they contravene another part of the Constitution. As noted in the earlier description of the administration of justice in the KRI, despite a theoretical claim to incorporate them within the fold of Iraqi law, Kurdish courts in fact have remained entirely autonomous from the legal system in the rest of Iraq. The constitutional determination that Kurdish courts are Iraqi courts remains in place to this day, despite the fact that the relationship between the KRG and the central government of Iraq has deteriorated severely in recent time, with episodes of armed confrontation between Kurdish and Iraqi forces. As things stand, for example, if the KRG were to proceed to prosecute some of the Islamic State fighters it holds for acts of genocide and crimes against humanity against the Yazidis, as it announced it would in

[241] See generally: Djamchid Momtaz, 'Attribution of Conduct to the State: State Organs and Entities Empowered to Exercise Elements of Governmental Authority' in James Crawford and others (eds), *The Law of International Responsibility* (Oxford University Press 2010).

[242] ICJ, *Case Concerning United States Diplomatic and Consular Staff in Tehran (United States v Iran)*, [1980] ICJ Rep. 3, 35–36.

[243] The fiendishly complex interweaving of attribution and jurisdiction in relation to acquiescence is evident in ECtHR, *Makuchyan and Minasyan v Azerbaijan and Hungary*, Judgment, Appl. No 17247/13, 26 May 2020, paras 47–52.

[244] See Section I.C, supra, for fuller discussion and references.

May 2020, then that would quite possibly prevent an eventual jurisdiction by the ICC under Article 17(1)(a) or (b).[245]

The case of the Kurdish administration in Rojava, Syria, is even murkier. As noted in the description of the administration of justice in Rojava, the PYD in 2014 declared a subnational autonomous region, with the aim not to break away from Syria but rather to establish a province within a federal system in that country. This move was resoundingly rejected by the central Syrian government, although a certain degree of coexistence obtains on the ground in Rojava, with a presence of institutions of both the central government and the autonomous Rojava administration. According to the International Law Commission, the rule codified in Article 5 of the Articles on State Responsibility is meant to correspond to a narrow category of situations in which the internal law of the state specifically authorises the exercise of public authority.[246] Given that Syria denies that a provincial authority has validly been established in Rojava, it would not appear that the courts of the PYD can be assimilated to the state under public international law. There is a possibility, however, that the situation in Rojava could correspond to the exercise of governmental authority by a non-state actor "in the absence or default of the official authorities and in circumstances such as to call for the exercise of those elements of authority" (Art. 9, UN Articles on State Responsibility). It was previously noted in Chapter 1 that the administration of justice certainly qualifies as 'governmental authority' as envisaged in this provision.[247] The state does not have to be entirely absent, but merely unable to perform the governmental authority in question, for whatever reason, including armed insurgency. Finally, whether it can be said that the administration of justice by a non-state armed group is 'called for' is a looser norm, but arguably the need for legal security in an area wholly or partially under the control of an armed group can give rise to circumstances which could justify rebels establishing their own courts.[248] This would seem all the more so when, as in Rojava, the non-state armed group is not seeking to challenge the sovereignty of the state over the territory in question. Without going so far as to claim that the situation in

[245] Hiwa Shilani, 'Kurdistan Region Announces That First ISIS Trials in Iraq to Start in Mid-2021' *Kurdistan24* (13 May 2020), online: <https://www.kurdistan24.net/en/news/69ef75e5-e47a-4c2f-aff2-194734b7f50b> accessed 12 July 2020.

[246] International Law Commission, Draft Articles on Responsibility of States for Internationally Wrongful Acts, with Commentaries, UN Doc A/56/10 at 43.

[247] See the discussion in Chapter 1, Section III.B.

[248] Gérard Cahin, 'The Responsibility of Other Entities: Armed Bands and Criminal Groups' in James Crawford, Alain Pellet, and Simon Olleson (eds), *The Law of International Responsibility* (Oxford University Press 2010) 225–226; Katharine Fortin, *The Accountability of Armed Groups Under Human Rights Law* (Oxford University Press 2017) 251–252; Katharine Fortin, 'The Relevance of Article 9 of the Articles on State Responsibility for the Internationally Wrongful Acts of Armed Groups' in James Summers and Alex Gough (eds), *Non-State Actors and International Obligations* (Brill 2018).

Rojava clearly fulfils the conditions codified in Article 9 of the Articles on State Responsibility, there is room to argue that an argument plausibly can be made to that effect. This is one more scenario under which the rebel administration of justice could conceivably correspond to an investigation or prosecution by a state pursuant to Article 17(1)(a) and (b) of the Rome Statute.

The third segment of the complementarity tryptic under Article 17(1)(c) of the Rome Statute, whereby the ICC will not have jurisdiction if the accused "has already been tried" for the same conduct, raises the distinct question of the kind of process that will correspond to this criterion. As noted previously, there is no reference here to the state. The subsection links the norm to the protection against double jeopardy in Article 20(3) of the Rome Statute, shielding a "person who has been tried by another court" unless those proceedings "were not conducted independently or impartially in accordance with the norms of due process recognized by international law". The concept of what can count as a 'court' is not entirely disconnected from the ideas of independence and impartiality. As I have suggested in the elaboration of elements of the rebel rule of law in Chapter 1, the very suggestion that an institution or a practice corresponds to the administration of justice imports to some degree intimations of independence and impartiality. As noted by the ICC Trial Chamber in the *Bemba* case, if 'judges' merely are conduits for the execution of orders from a rebel commander based on political or strategic expediency, then there is really no court to speak of.[249] That said, the concept of a court cannot be reduced to merely independence and impartiality, nor can these qualities be presumed once an institution is properly defined as a court. Each must therefore be defined to some extent on its own terms. As for independence and impartiality, these are facets of the rule of law and due process that were discussed respectively in Chapters 2 and 3, and there is no need here to return to explore them further. Likewise, the discussion of the rule of law in Chapter 1 challenged the exclusive association of the administration of justice with the state, opening a door to institutions and practices that are not necessarily emanations of the state. The proposed establishment of a criminal chamber in the African Court of Justice and Human and Peoples' Rights under the Malabo Protocol, it was noted previously, already suggested that courts other than state courts could be viewed as such under the Rome Statute, in that case the African Court but also the courts of the regional economic communities.[250]

The question of the interplay of ICC complementarity and alternative justice mechanisms challenges in a more frontal manner the preconceptions of what type of justice practices can prevent the Court from assuming jurisdiction over

[249] ICC, *Prosecutor v Jean-Pierre Bemba Gombo*, Trial Judgment, 21 March 2016, ICC-01/05-01/08, at 299–300 note 1861. This specific aspect is not discussed in the Appeals Judgment in the same case: 8 June 2018, ICC-01/05-01/08 A.

[250] See the discussion in Section II.B.i, supra.

a case. The role played by *gacaca* in addressing international crimes on a massive scale in Rwanda after the 1994 genocide in that country is a key example. By a sort of state-enforced informality, the traditional practice of local dispute-resolution was co-opted by the government to process the nearly two million individuals who stood accused of participating in the genocide in one way or another.[251] While this was done under the aegis of the state, with the *gacaca* sometimes described as 'courts' and placed under the authority of the Supreme Court of Rwanda, the practice itself diverged in very significant ways from a traditional judicial model: *gacaca* were presided by respected members of the community that generally did not have any legal training, there was no legal counsel, applicable law was not entirely clear, they were competent only for crimes that were considered part of the genocide, and so on.[252] At the same time, the presumption of innocence obtained, the accused were allowed to mount as full a defence as they could manage, and the decision-makers were generally impartial.[253] Ultimately, *gacaca* did not condone impunity, but resulted in findings of personal responsibility and the imposition of sanctions that could include prison terms.[254] Although it does not match a very traditional Western-inspired vision of what a court is, and despite the fact that it likely fell short of due process standards in some ways, the *gacaca* does not seem to depart so radically from the idea of the administration of justice that it couldn't be considered a 'court' for the purposes of Articles 17(1)(c) and 20(3) of the Rome Statute.[255] Indeed, this justice will often be faster, less expensive, and more accessible than that promised by international criminal law.[256] This is consistent with a decision reached on review by the Divisional Court of England and Wales in *Rwanda v. Nteziryayo*, in which a previous prosecution before a *gacaca* court was invoked as a basis for the application of double jeopardy.[257] The Divisional Court concluded that despite the

[251] Paul Christoph Bornkamm, *Rwanda's Gacaca Courts: Between Retribution and Reparation* (Oxford University Press 2012) 35–48; Pacifique Manirakiza, 'Complementing the ICC Efforts to Curb the Impunity of International Crimes in Africa—The Role and Contribution of Community Based Justice Mechanisms' in Charles Jalloh and Ilias Bantekas (eds), *The International Criminal Court and Africa* (Oxford University Press 2017) 345–346.

[252] Bornkamm (n 251) 50–61; Anuradha Chakravarty, *Investing in Authoritarian Rule: Punishment and Patronage in Rwanda's Gacaca Courts for Genocide Crimes* (Cambridge University Press 2016) 135–163; Mark A Drumbl, 'Law and Atrocity: Settling Accounts in Rwanda' (2005) 31 Ohio Northern University Law Review 41, 58–59.

[253] While *gacaca* decision-makers were generally independent and impartial, there were nevertheless serious issues affecting a portion of these proceedings: Pietro Sullo, *Beyond Genocide: Transitional Justice and Gacaca Courts in Rwanda* (Springer 2018) 176, 184.

[254] Chakravarty (n 252).

[255] The *gacaca* are of course taken here only as a model of community-based justice, given that the ICC could not have jurisdiction over the 1994 genocide because of the non-retroactive nature of the 1998 Rome Statute.

[256] Barbara Oomen, 'From Gacaca to Mato Oput—Pragmatism and Principles in Employing Traditional Dispute Resolution Mechanisms' in PAM Malcontent (ed), *Facing the Past: Amending Historical Injustices through Instruments of Transitional Justice* (Intersentia 2016).

[257] *Rwanda v Nteziryayo*, [2017] EWHC 1912.

fact that *gacaca* courts do not meet the requirement of a fair trial under Article 6 of the European Convention of Human Rights, they can be considered as courts with jurisdiction for the purposes of double jeopardy.[258]

A second example of an alternative justice mechanism invoked in the aftermath of the commission of international crimes, *mato oput* in Uganda, poses a considerably greater challenge to the elasticity of the notion of justice embodied in the Rome Statute. *Mato oput* is a traditional Acholi practice whereby an offender returns to the community that he has harmed to literally 'drink the bitter root'. The process aims to cleanse the evil-doer, who admits responsibility, asks for forgiveness, and offers compensation if appropriate, to restore the fabric of community relations.[259] Although this and other community justice mechanisms were mentioned in the 2007 Juba Agreement between the Government of Uganda and the Lord's Resistance Army, these practices were not co-opted by the state to an extent similar to the *gacaca* in Rwanda.[260] Given that there is really no trial of any sort before an independent decision-maker that would result in the individualised sanctioning of the offender, it is extremely difficult to claim that the conception of justice that is written into the Rome Statute and required to trigger complementarity is present in *mato oput*. Some international human rights NGOs in fact suggested that the Acholi should make their practice more oriented towards individual punishment in order to make it more court-like.[261] Even more starkly, Daniel Nsereko, a Ugandan judge on the ICC Appeals Chamber, opined during a visit to his home country that "crimes against humanity, genocide, aggression against other states and war crimes are internationally condemned and cannot be tried by traditional courts but by the ICC".[262] The Rome Statute speaks most clearly to a certain vision of the administration of justice that corresponds to a certain notion of what is a court, and not all justice practices can be fit within that bounded notion.

The examples of *gacaca* and *mato oput* provide a wider context in which to situate the rebel administration of justice in the framework of the ICC and international criminal law generally. As we can derive from these two examples, neither

[258] ibid para 478.

[259] See Tim Allen, *Trial Justice: The International Criminal Court and the Lord's Resistance Army* (Zed Books Ltd 2013) ch 6.

[260] According to Phil Clark, there was a measure of capture of some *mato oput* ceremonies by a mix of local government, international organisations, development agencies, and NGOs, but this represented only a small segment, albeit highly mediatised, of the practice: Phil Clark, *Distant Justice: The Impact of the International Criminal Court on African Politics* (Cambridge University Press 2018) 236.

[261] Sarah MH Nouwen and Wouter G Werner, 'Monopolizing Global Justice: International Criminal Law as Challenge to Human Diversity' (2014) 13 Journal of International Criminal Justice 157, 166–167.

[262] 'Traditional Justice Not Applicable to War Suspects' *New Vision* (Uganda) (30 June 2009), online: <https://www.newvision.co.ug/new_vision/news/1210379/traditional-justice-applicable-war-suspects> accessed 8 July 2018.

the fact that a practice fails to conform in every respect to expectation of what a 'proper court' should look like nor the fact that justice practices are not carried out by state institutions brings an immediate conclusion that complementarity cannot operate. As suggested by Martha Minow, the Rome Statute seeks to encourage the local reckoning with atrocities but does not necessarily foreclose the possibility that individuals might be brought to justice by way of practices that do not completely reflect formal state courts.[263] In every case, further questions must be asked and an investigation carried out into the specifics of what might be a 'court' under Articles 17(1)(c) and 20(3) of the Rome Statute. Seeing the descriptions of the administration of justice carried out by the KRG in Iraq, the PYD in Syria, and even the PKK in Turkey, there is certainly a plausible argument to make that at least some of these institutions are 'courts' able to carry out justice, as that term in understood in these provisions. It is important to keep in mind that, even if this view is adopted, complementarity can operate only if the rebel proceedings were not intended to shield the accused from criminal responsibility and if these proceedings were conducted "independently and impartially in accordance with the norms of due process recognized by international law" (Art. 20(3)(b), Rome Statute).

A final contextual element to the operation of complementarity vis-à-vis the rebel administration of justice is provided by Article 53 of the Rome Statute. That provision proclaims that the Prosecutor may refrain from initiating an investigation or prosecution by the ICC if doing so "would not serve the interests of justice". This is an intentionally nebulous expression that is meant to confer upon the Prosecutor a degree of discretion, to be guided broadly by the object and purpose of the Rome Statute.[264] The vagueness of the expression and resulting prosecutorial discretion are offset by the oversight role of the Pre-Trial Chamber, which can refuse to confirm a decision not to prosecute based on the interests of justice.[265] The question is whether it is conceivable that in some circumstances the Prosecutor may determine that respecting the operation of rebel courts does indeed serve in the interests of justice. The significant academic discussion of

[263] Martha Minow, 'Do Alternative Justice Mechanisms Deserve Recognition in International Criminal Law: Truth Commissions, Amnesties, and Complementarity at the International Criminal Court' (2019) 60 Harvard International Law Journal 1, 3–7.

[264] Office of the Prosecutor, Policy Paper on the Interest of Justice, 1 September 2007, online: <https://www.icc-cpi.int//Pages/item.aspx?name=otp-policy-int-just>, at 4 accessed 9 July 2018; Gabriel Bitti, 'Article 53—Ouverture d'une enquête' in Julian Fernandez and Xavier Pacreau (eds), *Statut de Rome de la Cour pénale internationale: commentaire article par article*, vol 2 (2d edn, Éditions Pedone 2019) 1475–1476.

[265] This power was the focus of a highly contested decision of the Appeals Chamber in the Afghanistan situation, centred on the procedural rather than substantive aspect of Article 53: ICC Appeals Chamber, Situation in Afghanistan, Judgment on the Appeal Against the Decision on the Authorisation of an investigation in the Situation in the Islamic Republic of Afghanistan, ICC-02/17 OA4, 5 March 2020.

the impact of this discretionary power has mostly centred on the possibility that the Prosecutor might decide to abstain from investigating or prosecuting a situation if doing so would impede the achievement of peace in the affected region. This has been most keenly discussed in the context of Uganda, and the perspective that outstanding ICC arrest warrants against LRA leaders made any national peace agreement all the more elusive.[266] Another focus of the discussion has been the suggestion that a national process leading to impunity, such as the South African Truth and Reconciliation Commission, would possibly qualify as warranting non-intervention by the ICC 'in the interests of justice'. In both cases, serious doubt has been expressed that outright amnesties in the name of peace or truth could be reconciled with the object and purpose of the Rome Statute, being the denial of impunity for those most responsible for international crimes.[267]

Closer to the concerns embodied in the rebel administration of justice, Article 53 has also been mentioned as one possible basis for a decision to recognise and respect the contribution of alternative justice mechanisms to post-conflict reconstruction. Scholars have argued that if such mechanisms meet certain criteria such as necessity, legitimacy, and good faith, then a degree of deference appears justified on the part of the ICC.[268] In particular, Phil Clark has persuasively argued that whereas the ICC reflects the Nuremberg tradition of accountability for national leaders in large-scale, industrial international armed conflicts, alternative justice mechanisms better capture the intimacy of violence in most modern armed conflicts.[269] From the perspective of victims in such conflicts, the criminal prosecution of faraway leaders who gave orders often matters less than a frank engagement with the broader social dynamics of conflict and the challenges of reconciliation and reconstruction. The point is not to claim an absolute supremacy of alternative justice mechanisms in every situation, but rather to open a door to a case-by-case assessment of their nature, function, and legitimacy, to determine whether they represent justice in ways that may ultimately prove more meaningful.[270] If we bring these considerations back to the subject at

[266] William Schabas, *The International Criminal Court: A Commentary on the Rome Statute* (2d edn, Oxford University Press 2016) 837–838.

[267] Darryl Robinson, 'Serving the Interests of Justice: Amnesties, Truth Commissions and the International Criminal Court' (2003) 14 European Journal of International Law 481.

[268] Linda M Keller, 'Achieving Peace with Justice: The International Criminal Court and Ugandan Alternative Justice Mechanisms' (2007) 23 Connecticut Journal of International Law 209; Mark A Drumbl, *Atrocity, Punishment, and International Law* (Cambridge University Press 2007) 188–194 (discussing gacaca); Alexander KA Greenawalt, 'Complementarity in Crisis: Uganda, Alternative Justice, and the International Criminal Court' (2009) 50 Virginia Journal of International Law 107, 138–139.

[269] Clark (n 260) 230–231.

[270] Minow (n 263) 43; Michael Newton, 'A Synthesis of Community Based Justice and Complementarity' in Christian De Vos, Sara Kendall, and Carsten Stahn (eds), *Contested Justice: The Politics and Practice of International Criminal Court Interventions* (Cambridge University Press 2015) 138.

hand, a convincing argument can be made that if a rebel court meets the criteria that have been identified up to this point as necessary to fulfill the requirement of the administration of justice, then all the factors identified as consonant with the protection of the interests of justice under Article 53 seem to encourage some degree of international deference towards insurgent justice.

D. International Recognition in the ICC and Beyond

The jurisdiction of the ICC is normatively tied to situations of armed conflicts, even if not exclusively, because the crimes within the competence of the Court are either substantively linked to armed hostilities (for war crimes) or simply more likely to occur in such a context (for genocide and crimes against humanity). As a result, the ICC emerges as a particular fertile environment for claims of recognition of rebel administration of justice. The discussion in the preceding section focussed on the possible operation of complementarity vis-à-vis rebel courts, but there are other ways in which the ICC may be confronted with the rebel administration of justice: as in the *Sakhanh* case before Swedish courts, a person accused of the grave breach of murder or mistreatment of a non-combatant before the ICC could invoke functional immunity related to her position as judge, legal counsel, or executioner participating in the operation of insurgent justice; conversely someone may be accused of the war crime of passing a sentence or carrying out an execution "without previous judgment pronounced by a regularly constituted court" (Art. 8(2)(c)(iv), Rome Statute), again forcing a decision on the issue of whether rebel courts can be considered as 'regularly constituted'. These are indeed part of the indictment in the *al-Hassan* case before the Pre-Trial Chamber of the ICC, in relation to the operation of the courts established in Timbuktu by Ansar Dine/al-Qaeda in the Islamic Maghreb. Unlike complementarity, there are fewer norms that are specific to the ICC in these examples, which are likely to turn on the application of general rules of international humanitarian law that were analysed in greater details in Chapters 2 and 3.

All these questions more broadly send us back to the general discussion of the stranglehold of states and state-created institutions like the ICC on the administration of justice, explored in Chapter 1. It's been said that international criminal law is an 'agent-dependent enterprise', in that it matters not only how well justice is done but also who is doing it: the expressive and communicative act of condemnation of a practice as an international crime can only be done effectively by an organ of the international community like the ICC.[271] While this 'robust

[271] Miriam Gur-Arye and Alon Harel, 'Taking Internationalism Seriously: Why International Criminal Law Matters' in Jens David Ohlin and Frédéric Mégret (eds), *Oxford Handbook of International Criminal Law* (Oxford University Press 2018).

internationalism' can be taken as a call to resist complementarity as synonymous with unconditional and systematic deference to any operational domestic legal system in the repression of international crimes, it also carries with it the seeds of a totalising vision of the rule of law.[272] It does so in two distinct ways: first, it focalises attention on the ICC as the centrepiece of the international effort to end impunity for international crimes, thus fuelling monopolistic discourses on global justice and marginalising alternative conceptions of justice;[273] second, even in presenting the ICC as a principled rather than functional alternative to states, it proclaims the state as the privileged agent to administer justice, from whom small concessions might be obtained in the name of internationalism. In this vision, robust internationalism creates a small opening for the pluralisation of criminal jurisdictions sanctioning international crimes—the ICC and states—while at the same time foreclosing the possible pluralisation of conceptions of justice in the response to mass atrocities.[274] Sarah Nouwen and Wouter Werner persuasively argue that there is a degree of synchronicity between international criminal law and the diversity of discourses on conceptions of justice: they invoke Hannah Arendt, who read the global movement to condemn crimes against humanity as a reflection of the assault on human diversity that such crimes represent.[275] The social construction of justice is a fundamental attribute of any political community, such that the diversity of discourses on justice is a facet of human diversity in general. As a result, the international criminal law regime should be taken not only to embrace the pluralisation of sites in which justice is done, including those beyond the state and international organisations, but also to sustain discourses on justice that are alternatives to that embodied in the approaches of states and international courts and tribunals. This opens a space not only for the recognition of alternative justice mechanisms but also, in some circumstances, to the rebel administration of justice.

The organic link between situations of armed conflict in which may occur the rebel administration of justice and the operation of international criminal tribunals may well result in a greater likelihood that issues of recognition of insurgent justice will arise in a court like the ICC, but it is not the only international

[272] For an argument in favour of a degree of ICC supremacy along those lines, see Frédéric Mégret, 'The Case Against Complementarity' in Jens David Ohlin and Frédéric Mégret (eds), *Oxford Handbook of International Criminal Law* (Oxford University Press 2018).

[273] Nouwen and Werner (n 261) 158–165.

[274] Drumbl (n 268) 143 ("Complementarity, therefore, may encourage heterogeneity in terms of the number of institutions adjudicating international crimes, but homogeneity in terms of the process they follow and the punishment they mete out. In the end, the content of local practices may be excluded regardless of the legitimacy with which these practices are perceived").

[275] Nouwen and Werner (n 261) 159; Hannah Arendt, *Eichmann in Jerusalem: A Report on the Banality of Evil* (Penguin Books 2006) 268–269 ("genocide [. . .] is an attack upon human diversity as such, that is, upon a characteristic of the 'human status' without which the very words 'mankind' or 'humanity' would be devoid of meaning").

legal forum in which that might happen. International bodies entrusted with the application of international human rights law may also be called to pass judgment on the legal nature of insurgent justice. On the whole, bodies established pursuant to human rights treaties have a competence that is directed at the compliance by states with their human rights obligations. Duties of states will directly connect to rebel courts if the acts of these courts or individuals active in them can be attributed to the state, a possibility that is real but limited, as exemplified by the earlier discussion of the courts of the KRG in Iraq and the PYD in Syria and confirmed by the decisions of the European Court of Human Rights mentioned above. A treaty human rights body may also engage with the responsibility of the state if the latter fails to take appropriate and available measure to protect individuals against violations of human rights at the hand of rebel courts. State duty not only to respect but also to ensure or secure human rights, proclaimed in the major human rights treaties, has been taken by a growing number of bodies to imply an obligation to take affirmative steps to guarantee fundamental rights against violations by non-state actors.[276] Situations similar to that of Russia in South Ossetia might conceivably give rise to an argument that the state has an obligation to ensure that rebel courts over which it has influence comply with international human rights standards.

Non-treaty mechanisms established by intergovernmental organisations and civil society organisations are not so constrained by the state-focus of human rights treaties, and could discuss more frankly and in greater details the rebel administration of justice. Initially, there was no willingness to address this issue squarely, as illustrated in a 2006 comment by a UN Special Rapporteur about the Taliban: "The administration of justice is a function that clearly belongs to the State of Afghanistan. It is entirely unacceptable for a non-state entity, such as the Taliban, to exercise a State function by trying and punishing an alleged criminal".[277] The evolution that has taken place is well captured in the 2015 Report by a different UN Special Rapporteur, noting that the Islamic State in Iraq and Syria "has declared itself a 'State', and runs both a civil and a military administration, including the establishment of a 'court' system. The threshold for [Islamic State] to be bound by human rights obligations has clearly been met. This means, at a

[276] See: *Case of Velasquez Rodriguez v Honduras* (1988), Inter-Am Ct HR (ser C) No 4 at para 166 (Inter-American Court of Human Rights); *Storck v Germany*, No 61603/00, [2005] ECHR 406, at para 74 (European Court of Human Rights); *Decision Regarding Communication 155/96 (Social and Economic Rights Action Center/Center for Economic and Social Rights v Nigeria)* Case No ACHPR/COMM/A044/1 (African Commission on Human and Peoples' Rights); Dimitris Xenos, *The Positive Obligations of the State under the European Convention of Human Rights* (Routledge 2012).

[277] UN Special Rapporteur on independence of judiciary condemns public execution following illegal trial in Afghanistan, statement by Leandro Despouy, the Special Rapporteur on the independence of judges and lawyers, 8 June 2006, online: <https://reliefweb.int/report/afghanistan/un-special-rapporteur-independence-judiciary-condemns-public-execution-following> accessed 10 July 2018. See Kleffner (n 206) 715.

minimum, that [the Islamic State] is bound under international law to respect core human rights obligations [. . .] The right to a fair trial should also be guaranteed".[278] There is thus an acknowledgment that non-state armed groups do exercise justice governance in some situations of armed conflicts, and that this fact in itself isn't necessarily a violation of human rights. That said, in both the work of non-treaty bodies and in the reporting by the main human rights organisations like Human Rights Watch and Amnesty International, there is little beyond quite general statements of the binding nature of human rights standards for armed opposition groups.[279] Perhaps because the details of the operation of the rebel administration of justice have been extremely scant so far, we are missing a richer engagement with substantive norms of human rights that would articulate the ways in which some of the rebel courts negate fundamental rights but also, ineluctably, the ways in which they don't. Clearly, a richer engagement of the type attempted in Chapter 3 seems necessary on the part of international bodies if we wish to initiate a meaningful dialogue that can induce armed groups to alter some of their practices.

A final example of the *rayonnement* of the rebel administration of justice within the sphere of international human rights law concerns the condition that local remedies be exhausted prior to a case becoming admissible before an international human rights body like the European Court of Human Rights or the UN Human Rights Committee.[280] If a claim originates from a territory under the control of a non-state armed group that has established a functioning system of courts which otherwise comply with international law, must the claim be first presented to the rebel court? Again, situations of long-term control of national territory by an insurgent group, such as occurred in Sri Lanka with the LTTE or in Iraq with the KRG, suggest that this scenario is far from purely academic. The European Court of Human Rights was confronted with this question in *Chiragov v. Armenia*, a decision concerning the taking of property without compensation by forces linked to Armenia.[281] The takings occurred in the territory of Azerbaijan, and the claimants were nationals of that state as well. The authorities that were said to have interfered with property rights guaranteed under the European Convention on Human Rights were either agents of the state

[278] Ben Emmerson, Report of the Special Rapporteur on the promotion and protection of human rights and fundamental freedoms while countering terrorism, UN Doc A/HRC/29/51, 16 June 2015, paras 30–31.

[279] E.g., Agnes Callamard, Report of the Special Rapporteur on extrajudicial, summary or arbitrary executions on armed non-State actors: the protection of the right to life, A/HRC/38/44, 5 June 2018, para 73.

[280] E.g., Art. 35(1) of the European Convention on Human Rights ("The Court may only deal with the matter after all domestic remedies have been exhausted, according to the generally recognised rules of international law").

[281] ECHR, *Chiragov and Others v Armenia*, Grand Chamber, Judgment, Application No 13216/05, 16 June 2015, para 186.

of Armenia or of the so-called 'Nagorno-Karabakh Republic' (later renamed 'Republic of Artsakh'), an entity that claims statehood but that is not recognised internationally as such. Under these circumstances, the Nagorno-Karabakh Republic can be described as a non-state armed group controlling a portion of Azerbaijani territory for more than two decades. During that time, it is said that the Nagorno-Karabakh Republic adopted over 600 laws, including basic laws establishing a Supreme Court and lower courts.[282] In defence, Armenia claimed that the petition should be rejected because the claimants had failed to use the courts of the Nagorno-Karabakh Republic to enforce their property rights, adducing some decisions of these courts to illustrate their effectiveness.[283] In its judgment, the European Court of Human Rights found that Armenia had failed to show that an effective local remedy existed, on the basis that none of the court decisions adduced as evidence matched the situation of the petition before the European Court.[284] This is a very narrow holding, but it does not close the door to a conclusion that the courts established by the insurgents could in some cases offer an effective local remedy that would have to be exhausted before bringing a case to Strasbourg.

Generally, the relationship between international human rights bodies and national jurisdictions is one of subsidiarity, whereby the international bodies will neither become a court of final appeal nor, a fortiori, a court of first instance for human rights violation on a given territory.[285] If there is a remedy that is available, effective, and sufficient, normally in the form of an independent and impartial tribunal, then it must be relied upon prior to a petition becoming admissible at the international level.[286] In a widely discussed proposal to establish a 'World Court of Human Rights', it was envisaged that 'entities' such as non-state armed groups could establish their own procedures that would have to be exhausted before the proposed World Court could be seized.[287] The rationale for this rule is that an opportunity must be afforded to the author of the alleged violation of human rights to effectively correct its own behaviour.[288] Under the so-called

282 ibid para 79.
283 ibid paras 107–109.
284 ibid paras 117–118.
285 Cesare PR Romano, 'The Rule of Prior Exhaustion of Domestic Remedies: Theory and Practice in International Human Rights Procedures' in Nerina Boschiero and others (eds), *International Courts and the Development of International Law: Essays in Honour of Tullio Treves* (TMC Asser Press; Springer 2013) 563.
286 Dinah Shelton, *Remedies in International Human Rights Law* (3d edn, Oxford University Press 2015) 94–100.
287 See Julia Kozma, Manfred Nowak, and Martin Scheinin, *A World Court of Human Rights: Consolidated Statute and Commentary* (Neuer Wissenschaftlicher Verlag 2010); for a critique of the extension of exhaustion of remedies to non-state actors, see Philip Alston, 'Against a World Court for Human Rights' (2014) 28 Ethics & International Affairs 197, 207–208.
288 European Court of Human Rights, *Practical Guide on Admissibility Criteria*, (2020) 24–25, online: <https://www.echr.coe.int/Documents/Admissibility_guide_ENG.pdf> accessed 12 July 2020.

'Namibia principle' previously invoked by the European Court in relation to Northern Cyprus, the illegality of the broader context does not justify sidestepping existing and effective local remedies.[289] Given the emerging consensus that international human rights law imposes binding obligations on non-state armed groups when they wield power over a population, as explored in Chapter 2, then it follows logically that the insurgents ought to be extended the same invitation to correct their own behaviour.[290] In the context of jurisdiction of human rights courts and bodies, this obtains only if the rebels have regularly established courts that meet the requirement of independence and impartiality.[291] In the example of Nagorno-Karabakh, it would seem wholly self-defeating to abstain from requiring that individuals attempt to use local rebel remedies if these are available, effective, and sufficient, as it would discourage a direct engagement of non-state armed groups with human rights law.

In conclusion, the administration of justice by non-state armed groups in zones of armed conflicts is a legal fact that produces repercussions on the international legal plane that must be carefully examined and, if they meet the required elements of legality, acknowledged.[292] Failure to do so, far from strengthening the international legal order, risks triggering dissonances within that regime and ultimately weaken humanitarian protection for the victims of war.

III. Transnational Recognition by Third States

The recognition of rebel administration of justice by international courts and tribunals is not the only instance where the question of the legal *rayonnement* of the operation of rebel courts will arise. States other than the one on whose territory the armed conflict is taking place may likewise be called upon to determine, for their own purposes, the legal significance of the establishment and operation of courts by non-state armed groups. This transnational recognition of insurgent justice operates in a much thinner normative environment than the possible international recognition of this practice by international courts and tribunals, analysed in the preceding section. Instead of specific legal standards such as complementarity and the exhaustion of local remedies, the legal analysis must on the whole rely on more general norms such as state sovereignty and the

[289] ECtHR, *Demopoulos v Turkey*, Admissibility, Appl. Nos 46113/99, 3843/02,13751/02,13466/03, 14163/04,10200/04,19993/ 04, & 21819/04, 1 March 2010, paras 93–98.

[290] See the implication for non-state armed groups of the duty to respect and ensure human rights in Chapter 2, Section IV.B.i.

[291] See Chapter 2, Section IV.C.ii–iii.

[292] This may occur beyond the fields of international criminal law and international human rights law, as exemplified in the decisions of the Allied-Italian claims commissions discussing the laws of the 'Republic of Salo'. See Chapter 1, Section III.A.

principle of *ex injuria jus non oritur*. That being said, the transnational recognition of insurgent justice corresponds to a reality in the practice of states, which is briefly sketched (A), before it is analysed in light of applicable rules of international law (B).

A. Third State Recognition of Rebel Justice

Although it remains infrequent, there are instances in which states have been called upon to pronounce on the legal status of insurgent legal regimes. A few illustrative cases are presented here, first in the broad area of criminal responsibility, and second in the area of private rights.

In relation to individual criminal responsibility, the most interesting and arresting example is the 2017 case of Haisam Omar Sakhanh in Sweden.[293] As was mentioned previously, Sakhanh was arrested in Sweden in 2016 and charged with murder after he was recognised on a video showing him participating in the execution of seven prisoners during the war in Syria. Sakhanh did not deny that he had indeed executed the men, but pleaded that he had done so as part of an execution squad ordered to implement the capital sentence imposed by a tribunal of the Free Syrian Army, a non-state armed group. As a result of this unique set of circumstances, the courts of Sweden were required to pronounce upon the legality of the establishment of a court by an armed opposition group in the context of a non-international armed conflict. The legal analysis of the legality of rebel courts under public international law offered by the Stockholm District Court and the Svea Court of Appeal was examined in Chapter 2.[294] The conclusion adopted by Swedish courts that the establishment of courts by insurgents does not violate international law then led it to scrutinise the way in which this rebel court exercised its jurisdiction in the case, which resulted in the death penalty executed by Sakhanh. Upon a close examination of the evidence presented on the operation of the rebel court in Syria, the court concluded that "the trial-like procedures held did not meet the basic requirements of the rule of law under international humanitarian law".[295] Sakhanh was found guilty and sentence to life imprisonment. The point to underscore in relation to the recognition of rebel

[293] *Prosecutor v Haisam Omar Sakhanh*, Stockholms tingsrätt (Stockholm District Court), B 3787-16, Judgment of 16 February 2017, online: <http://www.ejiltalk.org/wp-content/uploads/2017/03/Stockholms-TR-B-3787-16-Dom-2017-02-16.pdf> accessed 18 July 2018, with a partial translation in (2018) 16 *Journal of International Criminal Justice* 403–424; confirmed by Prosecutor v Haisam Omar Sakhanh, Svea hovrätt (Svea Court of Appeal), B 2259-17, Judgment of 31 May 2017 (hereinafter 'Sakhanh, Svea Appeal Court'); leave to appeal was denied by the Supreme Court of Sweden, B 3157-17, 20 July 2017.

[294] See Chapter 2, Section IV.C.i. See also Mark Klamberg, 'The Legality of Rebel Courts during Non-International Armed Conflicts' (2018) 16 Journal of International Criminal Justice 235.

[295] Stockholm District Court, *Sakhanh* (n 293) para 50.

administration of justice is the fact that this very exercise by the trial and appellate courts of Sweden did not seem to have raised any objection from the Swedish Ministry for Foreign Affairs. From the description of the proceedings provided in the trial judgment, the prosecution in the case did not appear to directly challenge the accused's argument that an insurgent court had been established; instead, the prosecution appears to have focused mostly on demonstrating that the accused had indeed participated in the execution of seven men in Syria. In a subsidiary manner, the prosecution appears to have contributed to the court's analysis of the evidence to buttress the conclusion that the trial before the rebel court failed to meet the requirements of a fair trial. Indeed, once having cleared the initial hurdle of the legality of rebel justice under international law, the courts of Sweden seem to have approached the examination of the insurgent court as it would have that of another state. The rebel court that issued the death penalty that Sakhanh carried out apparently acquitted two other captured government soldiers accused of war crimes; one could imagine that if one of these acquitted soldiers were later indicted for the same crime in Sweden or another third state, an argument of double jeopardy would be advanced by the defence, triggering an analysis similar to the one found in the Sakhanh decisions.

A different and yet equally remarkable example of the interplay of rebel justice and third states concerns the attitude of the government of France vis-à-vis courts of the PYD in Kurdish Syria. Over the duration of the civil war in that country, several hundred French nationals travelled to Syria to join the forces of the Islamic State. The waning fortunes of the Islamic State in that conflict resulted in reportedly more than 100 French Islamic State supporters being made prisoners by the PYD in Rojava, most of them women who had become spouses of Islamic State fighters. In January and February 2018, the French government speaker and the foreign minister declared that France did not intend to repatriate its nationals but rather preferred to have them judged by the courts of the Kurdish rebels in Rojava, Syria.[296] This is so despite the fact that France does not recognise Rojava as a state or government, but merely as a non-state armed group alongside whom it is fighting in the Syrian conflict. The French government indicated that it would monitor any eventual trial to ensure that due process standards are respected, including the right to a full defence, and that it would oppose the imposition of the death penalty as it always does when a French national is tried abroad.[297] The representative of the PYD in France responded that

[296] Le Point Magazine, 'Le gouvernement souhaite que les djihadistes françaises soient jugées en Syrie' *Le Point* (4 January 2018), online: <http://www.lepoint.fr/monde/le-gouvernement-souhaite-que-les-djihadistes-francaises-soient-jugees-en-syrie-04-01-2018-2183934_24.php> accessed 18 July 2018.

[297] Charles Evrard, 'Faut-il juger en France les djihadistes français partis combattre auprès de Daech ?' *Accueil—Observatoire de la justice pénale* (18 February 2018), online: <https://www.justicepenale.

the Kurds were willing to prosecute foreign Islamic State members locally, or to render them to French authorities if that were the preference of France. In reaction to this position, Human Rights Watch expressed doubt that a fair trial is possible before the People's courts of the PYD, and that it was preferable to transfer any accused to their state of nationality so that they can be tried by a recognised legal system offering guarantees of fairness.[298] Lawyers for some of the French Islamic State members in Syria petitioned French courts seeking a judicial declaration that the position of the French government was an abuse of authority and that the detention of French nationals by armed opposition groups was arbitrary.[299] The petition was blocked by the French Attorney-General, invoking the fact that this is a war zone and France has no diplomatic relations with Syria.[300] This is another example of a state recognising the existence and jurisdiction of the courts of a non-state armed group engaged in an armed conflict in another country. Indeed, the legitimation exceeds mere recognition, in that France here more or less seeks to actively support the exercise of jurisdiction by the courts of a Kurdish rebel group in Syria.[301]

The relations between the Karen National Union/Liberation Army and Thailand offer yet another case of explicit interface of state and rebel

net/single-post/2018/02/18/Faut-il-juger-en-France-les-djihadistes-fran%C3%A7ais-partis-combattre-aupr%C3%A8s-de-Daech-> accessed 18 July 2018.

298 Human Rights Watch, 'Ensure Fair Trials of Syria ISIS Suspects' *Human Rights Watch* (13 February 2018), online: <https://www.hrw.org/news/2018/02/13/ensure-fair-trials-syria-isis-suspects> accessed 18 July 2018.

299 'Des avocats de familles de djihadistes détenus en Syrie portent plainte contre les autorités françaises' *Le Monde.fr* (17 January 2018), online: <https://www.lemonde.fr/societe/article/2018/01/17/des-avocats-de-djihadistes-detenus-en-syrie-portent-plainte-contre-les-autorites-francaises_5242742_3224.html> accessed 18 July 2018 ("Le Kurdistan syrien n'ayant aucune existence légale et ne disposant par là-même d'aucune institution souveraine, ces femmes et ces enfants sont tous détenus sans droit ni titre").

300 'Les plaintes des parents de françaises détenues en Syrie classées sans suite' *Le Monde.fr* (16 March 2018), online: <https://www.lemonde.fr/police-justice/article/2018/03/16/des-plaintes-de-francaises-detenues-en-syrie-classees-sans-suite_5272226_1653578.html> accessed 18 July 2018. Another petition using a variant procedural form was later introduced, using the same arguments: 'Familles de jihadistes au Kurdistan syrien: "L'État français doit prendre ses responsabilités"' *Franceinfo* (14 May 2018), online: <https://www.francetvinfo.fr/replay-radio/info-medias/familles-de-jihadistes-au-kurdistan-syrien-l-etat-francais-doit-prendre-ses-responsabilites_2751985.html> accessed 18 July 2018 ("le Kurdistan syrien n'existe pas, il n'a pas d'existence légale"). As of March 2020, the French government still refused to repatriate its nationals detained by the YPG.

301 France was reported to be considering as an alternative the transfer of its nationals detained in Rojava to Iraq so that they could be tried in that country, but the severe shortcomings of Iraqi justice would likely mean that this would violate France's human rights obligations: Inès Daif, 'L'ONU critique le traitement des djihadistes français' *Le Figaro* (12 August 2019), online: <https://www.lefigaro.fr/international/l-onu-critique-le-traitement-des-djihadistes-francais-20190812> accessed 15 July 2020. See Commission nationale consultative des droits de l'homme—République française, Opinion on French Nationals Sentenced to Death or Facing the Death Penalty in Iraq (2020), online: <https://www.cncdh.fr/sites/default/files/opinion_french_death_penalty_iraq.pdf>.

administration of justice. The KNU/LA is a non-state armed group that operates in a vast section of the territory of Myanmar/Burma alongside the Thai border. It has a separate and independent judiciary whose functions are stipulated in the constitution of the group and further elaborated in a number of legal codes. There is a rebel Supreme Court, district courts, and township courts, supplemented by more informal community justice practices at the village level.[302] It is reported that, on occasion, individuals linked to the KNU/LA who committed offences in Thailand have been handed over by Thai authorities to the KNU/LA for prosecution before the armed group's courts. One case concerned KNU/LA officials beating suspected drug users in the Tham Him refugee camp in Thailand, captured on a video that circulated widely.[303] These KNU/LA officials were arrested by the Thai police and transferred to the KNU/LA justice system for prosecution. Conversely, Thai authorities are said to have requested that the Karen armed group transfer to Thailand individuals wanted for crimes in that jurisdiction.[304]

A final example is slightly different, in that it does not directly engage with the operation of insurgent courts, but it does provide a model of what such an engagement could be. In May 1982, frustrated by its inability to provide humanitarian protection to Soviet soldiers detained by armed opposition groups in Afghanistan, the ICRC managed to arrive at an agreement between the parties to that conflict, the USSR and 'Afghan opposition movements', as well as Switzerland.[305] Under the terms of that agreement, the ICRC visited Soviet soldiers detained by insurgents in Afghanistan to offer that they be transferred to Switzerland to serve a two-year detention or until the end of the conflict, whichever occurred first.[306] The transfer to Switzerland was entirely dependent on the written individual consent of Soviet detainees, and it is reported that only a small fraction of them—11 out of 200–300 held—were willing to be held by Switzerland on behalf of Afghan armed opposition groups. The transferred detainees were held in a military prison in Zugerberg, where they were visited regularly by the ICRC and once a month by Soviet diplomatic representatives.[307]

[302] Brian McCartan and Kim Jolliffe, 'Ethnic Armed Actors and Justice Provision in Myanmar' (Asia Foundation 2016) 20.

[303] 'Video Shows Burmese Militia's Brutal Interrogations' *The France 24 Observers* (8 August 2016), online: <https://observers.france24.com/en/20160808-video-burma-karen-police-army> accessed 14 October 2019.

[304] McCartan and Jolliffe (n 302) 26.

[305] Christiane Shields Delessert, *Release and Repatriation of Prisoners of War at the End of Active Hostilities: A Study of Article 118, Paragraph 1 of the 3rd Geneva Convention Relative to the Treatment of Prisoners of War* (Schulthess Polygraphischer Verlag 1977) 183; Charlotte Carr-Gregg, 'An Extension of Humanitarian International Law: The Case of Soviet Soldiers Captured by Afghan Liberation Movements, 1982–1986' (1989) 7 War & Society 95, 97.

[306] ICRC, 'External Activities May–June 1984' (1984) 24 International Review of the Red Cross 230, 239–240; see also: Carr-Gregg (n 305); Mary Ellen O'Connell, 'Soviet Prisoners in the Afghan Conflict' (1984) 23 Columbia Journal of Transnational Law 497.

[307] Carr-Gregg (n 305) 95.

One soldier managed to escape the prison and reach the Federal Republic of Germany, where he sought asylum. Upon completing the two years in Swiss prison, the detainees were asked whether they wished to return to the USSR, and apparently several opted not to be returned. Under the terms of the agreement, the ICRC was in return to be given access to prisons in Kabul where were detained members of armed opposition groups captured by the government, something that had been denied up to that point. Although inspired by Article 12 of the Third Geneva Convention, which provides for the possibility that prisoners of war be transferred to another state, the agreement in this case related to a non-international armed conflict to which this rule is not directly applicable. Accordingly, the Swiss government indicated that it was applying the Geneva Convention 'by analogy'.[308] The deal seems to have unravelled when ICRC access to Kabul prisons was terminated, after which no more Soviet soldiers were transferred to Switzerland.

The Soviet soldiers in this case were not detained pursuant to convictions imposed by insurgent courts, but the willingness of the Swiss government to hold individuals on behalf of a non-state armed group offers the intriguing suggestion that perhaps a third state might be willing to do so in just such a situation. A parallel may be drawn with a case in Colombia in which the government agreed to 'lend' part of a prison to an Indigenous community whose autonomous court had sentenced some FARC fighters to seventy and forty years in jail for murder.[309] Neither example is a direct instance of a third state recognising the rebel administration of justice, but both are indications that there may be some opening by states to find creative solutions to the inability of most armed opposition groups to operate long-term detention facilities.

Turning to the *rayonnement* of insurgent courts beyond the field of criminal law, the informality usually marking the rebel administration of justice means that it has more rarely crossed borders to intersect with the civil jurisdiction of other states. In a few, rare cases, the legal order of a non-state armed group has become part of a civil case discussed in a foreign jurisdiction. In July 2014, the Iraqi federal government petitioned a US Federal District Court in Texas for an order to seize crude oil produced by the KRG and destined for Galveston, Texas.[310] The cargo in question was aboard the 'United Kalavryta', consisting of

[308] John Darntons, 'Swiss Ponder Future Status of 8 Russians' *New York Times* (26 June 1983) 13.

[309] Notimerica, 'Colombia respeta la sentencia indígena contra miembros de las FARC' *notimerica.com* (11 November 2014), online: <http://www.notimerica.com/politica/noticia-colombia-fiscalia-respeta-sentencia-indigena-contra-miembros-farc-muerte-dos-miembros-tribu-20141111033402.html> accessed 19 July 2018. An important difference is that the 1991 Colombian Constitution formally recognises Indigenous jurisdictions: Daniel Bonilla Maldonado, *La Constitución Multicultural* (Siglo del Hombre Editores 2006).

[310] *Ministry of Oil of the Republic of Iraq v 1,032,212 Barrels of Crude Oil Aboard the United Kalavryta and the Ministry of Natural Resources of the Kurdistan Regional Governate of Iraq*, AMC (Tex 2014), online: <http://www.americanmaritimecases.com/assets/Texas/iraq.pdf>.

about one million barrels of crude oil worth $100 million, pumped from fields in the KRI into an Iraqi-Turkish pipeline.[311] Essentially, the Iraqi central government claimed that the oil belonged to the Baghdad Ministry of Oil and that it was never the property of the KRG. Conversely, the Kurds argued that the US court didn't have jurisdiction, and filed a motion to lift the restrictions on the oil. In a letter to the Federal Court, the KRG's lawyer sought to explain what their rights and status were pursuant to the Iraqi Constitution and the Oil and Gas Law of the Kurdistan Region:

> The oil cargo in question belonged to the KRG before it was legally shipped and sold pursuant to the KRG's authority under the 2005 federal Iraqi Constitution and subsequent Kurdistan law. That constitution reserves the authority over oil produced in the Kurdistan Region exclusively to the KRG. [. . .] The Ministry of Oil's request for the seizure of the oil cargo aboard the United Kalavryta should never have been brought in any U.S. court. The oil cargo is not in U.S. territory, and even if it were, the Ministry of Oil's claims raise fundamentally important issues of Iraqi constitutional law that cannot be argued in foreign courts without the KRG's consent. These issues implicate fundamental aspects of the KRG's sovereignty over its natural resources, essential for its development and its ability to provide for the basic needs of its people.[312]

The KRG then proceeded to highlight that the Iraqi Supreme Federal Court had already rejected the Iraqi Ministry of Oil's request, refusing to issue an injunction until the underlying Iraqi constitutional dispute had been resolved. The KRG added that that they themselves have substantial counter-claims against the federal government of Iraq under both the Constitution and international law. The oil was never delivered to Texas after the KRG declined to risk a judgment in court, but the KRG's motion to vacate was finally granted by the District Court in August 2014. It was found that Kurdistan's unauthorised export of oil over land—and later overseas—may violate Iraqi law, but that it does not violate US maritime law. After that judgment, the KRG reportedly took further measures towards establishing a steady stream of independent oil sales, although that became less significant after the loss of oil fields near Kirkuk in 2017.[313] The case

[311] Anjli Raval, 'US Judgment Due on Iraq-KRG Oil Dispute' *Financial Times* (22 August 2014), online: <https://www.ft.com/content/76825174-29d2-11e4-914f-00144feabdc0 >.

[312] Ministry of Natural Resources of Kurdistan Regional Government, News Release, 'Texas Court Advised of KRG rights and Massive Counterclaims Against Federal Government' (30 July 2014), online: <http://mnr.krg.org/index.php/en/press-releases/400-texas-court-advised-of-krg-rights-and-massive-counterclaims-against-federal-government>.

[313] Anjli Raval and David Sheppard, 'Kurds Defy Iraq to Establish Own Oil Sales' *Financial Times* (23 August 2015), online: <https://www.ft.com/content/aeae33e4-45ae-11e5-af2f-4d6e0e5eda22 >.

mixes elements of Iraqi state law and the laws of the KRI, whose ambiguous status was described earlier in this chapter.

A somewhat similar case concerns the legal regime of the Polisario Front in Western Sahara. In reaction to the Moroccan exploitation of natural resources in the territory of Western Sahara, especially phosphate, the Polisario Front sought to challenge the ownership of cargoes aboard ships as they passed through the waters or docked in ports of selected foreign jurisdictions. On 13 April 2017, the Marshall Islands–flagged bulk carrier 'NM Cherry Blossom' departed Western Sahara with 55,000 tonnes of phosphate rock in its hold, as authorised by the Moroccan government. Stopping in Port Elizabeth, South Africa, on May 1, its cargo was detained by an admiralty order of the High Court pursuant to an application filed by the Polisario Front and its political alter ego, the Saharawi Arab Democratic Republic. The South African High Court directed that the merits of its May 1 ex parte order be revisited, inviting all parties to argue the merits of the detention and therefore whether an ensuing proceeding to address ownership would result. After a hearing on May 18, in which only the two Moroccan state companies defended the proceeding—the vessel's owner, time charterer, and importing (purchasing) company not participating—a three-judge panel of the High Court issued a lengthy judgment on June 15.[314] The Court determined that the detention could be maintained and that the Polisario Front had a *prima facie* claim to ownership of the cargo. On 22 February 2018, the High Court of South Africa issued a further order in the 'NM Cherry Blossom' case, declaring that "ownership in the phosphate [aboard the vessel] has never lawfully vested" in Morocco's state-owned companies responsible for its mining and export "and they were, and are, not entitled to sell the phosphate" to the New Zealand purchasing company.[315] The cargo was later sold at auction for the benefit of the Polisario Front. The case was complex, involving issues related to the immunities of foreign states and the right of peoples to self-determination in relation to the exploitation of natural resources. What is striking here is that the courts of South Africa, referring to a number of recent decisions about Western Sahara issued by UK courts and the European Court of Justice, chose to give preference to the legal regime of a non-state armed group that did not control the territory where the activities were taking place, in lieu of the laws of the occupying state, Morocco, whose effective control of the mining area is not in dispute. The claim centres on property rights in the shipment of phosphate, normally a matter to be determined under the private law of either Morocco or the Polisario

[314] *Saharawi Arab Democratic Republic and another v The owner and charterer of the motor vessel NM Cherry Blossom and others*, 2017 ZAECPHC 31, [2018] 1 All SA 593 (ECP), online: <http://www.saflii.org/za/cases/ZAECPEHC/2017/31.htm> accessed 22 July 2018.

[315] This is a short order that does not seem to have been published. A copy is available at <http://wsrw.org/files/dated/2018-02-23/20180223_south_africa_ruling.pdf> accessed 22 July 2018.

Front in accordance with private international law rules on conflict of laws. In relying more significantly on public international law, South African courts seem to have issued decisions that speak more directly to the Saharawi right to self-determination as a people than to the recognition of the Polisario legal order beyond the borders of Western Sahara.[316]

Private international law does offer elements that are directly relevant to the recognition of insurgent courts by third states. There have been, in many countries, legal actions brought by private parties seeking to enforce locally acts of a regime or government that was not recognised by the executive branch of the local government. Until the beginning of the twentieth century, the position usually adopted by national courts was to reflect the position of the executive branch, to deny any recognition to the decisions of the courts of a regime not recognised by the government. A large number of governments refused for many years to recognise the Soviet regime following the October Revolution in 1917, a stance later repeated in relation to the authorities of the People's Republic of China, resulting in an awkward dissonance between this traditional position and the reality on the ground. Swiss courts were the first to adopt a principle of 'effective law', finding that the non-recognition of the Soviet regime meant that it would not be taken to represent Russia in international relations, but that this did not stop Soviet law from existing and producing legal effects.[317] The same approach later was adopted by Japanese courts that were confronted with the need to apply 'Chinese law', for instance in family law, forcing a choice between the law of the unrecognised People's Republic of China or those of the recognised Republic of China (Taiwan). The Kyoto tribunal concluded that "foreign law applied under private international law principles should not be limited to the law only of a recognised State or Government; effectiveness of foreign law should not depend upon recognition. Non-recognition does not constitute a basis for denying the validity of a particular law which is enforced in a certain society".[318] This is consistent with the jurisprudence of the courts of France, Italy, Belgium, and many others states.[319] The rationale offered by Horacia Muir Watt is that "the protection of private interests demands that the law that is really applicable in

[316] See Tom Ruys, 'The Role of State Immunity and Act of State in the NM Cherry Blossom Case and the Western Sahara Dispute' (2019) 68 International & Comparative Law Quarterly 67.

[317] Joe Verhoeven, 'Relations internationales de droit privé en l'absence de reconnaissance d'un État, d'un gouvernement ou d'une situation' (1985) 192 Recueil des cours 9, 108–111, referring to *Banque internationale de Petrograd v Hausner*, (1925) Revue de droit international privé 118 (Trib. féd.).

[318] Kyoto District Court, *Huang Wen-Ping v Huang Ming-Wen*, 7 July 1956 (1958–1959) 2 Japanese Annual of International Law 149, 151.

[319] WH Balekjian, *Die Effektivität und die Stellung nichtanerkannter Staaten im Völkerrecht* (Springer 1970) 49–109; Verhoeven (n 317) 112–123; Florian Couveinhes-Matsumoto, *L'Effectivité en droit international* (Bruylant 2014) 274–281; Horatia Muir Watt, 'La Fonction de la règle de conflit de lois' (Université de droit, d'économie et de sciences sociales de Paris 1985) 317–324.

a place be given effect, regardless of the status of the law-making authority".[320] In the United States, the courts have upheld the need to acknowledge when the laws of an unrecognised authority are effectively applied in a given territory, for example, concluding that "[t]o refuse to recognize that Soviet Russia is a government regulating the internal affairs of the country, is to give to fictions an air of reality which they do not deserve".[321] This position is reflected in the Third Restatement of the Foreign Relations Law of the United States.[322] Lord Denning in *Hesperides Hotels* summarised the choice between a position that give effect to the recognition of the executive branch and one that assesses the effectiveness of the law applied in a given territory:

> If it were necessary to make a choice between these conflicting doctrines, I would unhesitatingly hold that the courts of this country can recognise the laws or acts of a body which is in effective control of a territory even though it has not been recognised by Her Majesty's Government *de jure* or *de facto*: at any rate, in regard to the laws which regulate the day to day affairs of the people, such as their marriages, their divorces, their leases, their occupations, and so forth: and furthermore that the courts can receive evidence of the state of affairs so as to see whether the body is in effective control or not.[323]

On that basis, the court gave effect to the laws of Turkish Northern Cyprus, an entity not recognised by the British government.[324]

There is significant and no doubt intentional vagueness in the manner in which the courts of various countries have described the entities whose laws are being applied, the nature of that law's effectiveness, and the way in which the entities fail to be recognised.[325] While it would be an exaggeration to claim that there is absolute coherence in the approaches adopted, there is a consensus to decouple at least some of the legal effects of political recognition of a foreign authority and the judicial recognition of an effective legal regime in a contested territory. There is little in this line of cases to suggest that this decoupling of legal and political

[320] Muir Watt (n 319) 322 ("l'intérêt des justiciables exige que soit prise en considération la loi réellement applicable sur le territoire où ils déploient leurs activités, abstraction faite du statut de l'autorité légiférante").

[321] *Salimoff v Standard Oil Co. of New York and Vacuum Oil Co.*, (1933) 186 N.E. 679 (NY Court of Appeals, Pound CJ). For a fuller review of US law on the matter, see Verhoeven (n 317) 124–134.

[322] American Law institute, *Restatement, Third, Foreign Relations Law of the United States* (1987) 91–93 § 205(3).

[323] *Hesperides Hotels Ltd v Aegean Turkish Holidays*, [1978] Q.B. 205, 218. James Crawford, *Brownlie's Principles of Public International Law* (9th edn, Oxford University Press 2019) 147–155.

[324] See RD Leslie, 'Unrecognised Governments in the Conflict of Laws: Lord Denning's Contribution' (1981) 14 The Comparative and International Law Journal of Southern Africa 165.

[325] Balekjian (n 319) 182–183.

recognition could not equally be applied to non-state armed groups effectively imposing its administration of justice on a territory and population.

B. Legal Parameters of Recognition by Third States

The recognition by the organs of a state of the administration of justice carried out by a non-state armed group in another state is, to a large extent, a matter determined by the domestic law of the recognising state. A state could thus adopt a policy, legislated or otherwise, that provides for the non-recognition of insurgent legal orders or, inversely, the conditions under which recognition might be granted. I am not aware of any state with such an explicit policy, whether to recognise or not. This leaves open the question of whether there are norms in international law that would prohibit, authorise, or require a state to recognise the rebel administration of justice in another state. In the following pages, I argue that the recognition of rebel jurisdiction by third states contravenes neither the sovereignty of the territorial state nor the principle *ex injuria jus non oritur.* On the opposite, such recognition may correspond to the fulfilment of the duty to "ensure respect" international humanitarian law and to "ensure" or "secure" human rights.

To begin with, the recognition by another state of the application of insurgent law or the operation of rebel courts does not constitute a violation of the sovereignty of the state on whose territory the conflict is taking place. In order for an action to amount to a violation of the sovereignty of another state, it must trench upon a facet of sovereignty to which attaches the exclusive authority of that state. Thus, as noted by the ICJ in the *Nicaragua* case, the prohibition against intervention in the so-called 'reserved domain', "matters which are essentially within the domestic jurisdiction of any state" (Art. 2(7), UN Charter) includes actions such as the financing, training, and logistical support of an armed opposition group on the territory of another state.[326] The mere provision of humanitarian assistance, even to rebels, as well as economic measures and the reduction in development assistance, do not constitute forms of intervention in the internal affairs of another state, and as such are not a violation of its sovereignty.[327] The emergence of what can properly be described as the rebel administration of justice requires a degree of governance that already corresponds to the *de facto* limitation of a state's sovereignty over its territory.[328] A third state that recognises to

[326] ICJ, *Military and Paramilitary Activities in and against Nicaragua (Nicaragua v United States)*, Merits, [1986] ICJ Rep 14, 114 para 242.

[327] ibid 125–126 paras 244–245. See Crawford (n 323) 453–455; Christina Nowak, *Das Interventionsverbot im Bürgerkrieg Darstellung eines Wandels durch die Bürgerkriege in Libyen, Syrien, Irak, Jemen und Ukraine seit 2011* (Peter Lang 2018).

[328] See Chapter 1, Section III.

some degree the rebel administration of justice is merely acknowledging this factual situation on the territory of another state. In itself, the recognition of rebel justice does not imply that the third state views that exercise of authority by the insurgents as legitimate. The conflict of laws rules on the application of the laws or judgments of an unrecognised authority instead suggest that claims touching on individual rights can be dissociated from the political legitimacy of the authority in question.

As mentioned earlier, the recognition of insurgent justice also reflects the principle of *ex unjuria jus non oritur*. Thus the ICJ in the *South West Africa Advisory Opinion* insisted on the duty of states not to recognise acts flowing from the illegal occupation of Namibia by South Africa, but also noted that this did not necessarily imply that all acts affecting the private rights of people living in that territory should likewise be regarded as without legal effect.[329] The European Court of Human Rights invoked this 'Namibia principle' in its decision in *Cyprus v. Turkey*, to conclude that from a human rights perspective:

> [T]he obligation to disregard acts of *de facto* entities is far from absolute. Life goes on in the territory concerned for its inhabitants. That life must be made tolerable and be protected by the *de facto* authorities, including their courts; and, in the very interest of the inhabitants, the acts of these authorities related thereto cannot be simply ignored by third States or by international institutions, especially courts, including this one. To hold otherwise would amount to stripping the inhabitants of the territory of all their rights whenever they are discussed in an international context, which would amount to depriving them even of the minimum standard of rights to which they are entitled.[330]

The European Court insisted that the limited recognition of the jurisdiction of *de facto* courts did not legitimise in any way the authority of an unrecognised entity. In the *Cyprus* case as in the *Namibia* advisory opinion, the basis of the duty of non-recognition for third states was the illegality under International law of the presence of Turkey and South Africa; in most non-international armed conflicts in which rebels administer justice, there is no original violation of international

[329] ICJ, *Legal Consequences for States of the Continued Presence of South Africa in Namibia (South West Africa) notwithstanding Security Council Resolution 276 (1970)*, Advisory Opinion, [1971] ICJ Rep 16, 56 para 125 ("In general, the non-recognition of South Africa's administration of the Territory should not result in depriving the people of Namibia of any advantages derived from international co-operation. In particular, while official acts performed by the Government of South Africa on behalf of or concerning Namibia after the termination of the Mandate are illegal and invalid, this invalidity cannot be extended to those acts, such as, for instance, the registration of births, deaths and marriages, the effects of which can be ignored only to the detriment of the inhabitants of the Territory"). See Yaël Ronen, *Transition from Illegal Regimes under International Law* (Cambridge University Press 2011) 81–88.

[330] ECHR, *Cyprus v Turkey*, Appl. No 25781/94, ECHR 2001-IV, paras 92, 96.

law, as there is no rule prohibiting the internal use of force by a non-state group. Given that difference, *ex unjuria jus non oritur* does not mandate a broad principle of non-recognition of the rebel administration of justice by third states. On the opposite, if an armed group administers justice in a territory unlawfully occupied by another state, as illustrated by the situation in Western Sahara, the principle mandates refusing to recognise at least some decisions of occupation courts.[331] In an earlier time, Hersch Lauterpacht argued that the principle of non-interference led to a duty for third states to grant recognition of belligerency when the conflict had reached a point where rebels controlled a portion of territory and had a form of government.[332] When a state did recognise belligerency, it claimed a neutral position as between the government and the insurgents, prevented equally from lending assistance to one as to the other. Recognition of belligerency has fallen out of practice, but it nevertheless provides a useful context to measure how limited an interference the recognition of the legal order of a non-state armed group would be.

The duty to "respect and ensure respect" of international humanitarian law under Common Article 1 of the Geneva Conventions provides further support for the legality of the recognition of insurgent justice by third states. The duty is general in nature, imposing obligations that are relevant in times of peace as well as war, for parties to an armed conflict and for those who are not, in the context of international armed conflicts as well as non-international armed conflicts. Common Article 1, by its very wording, only imposes duties on High Contracting Parties to the Geneva Conventions, but the norm has ripened into customary law, which is deemed applicable to both state and non-state actors.[333] The duty to 'respect' speaks to the compliance with humanitarian law by a state and its agents, in addition to acts that can be attributed to that state under the principles of state responsibility examined as part of the analysis of complementarity under the Rome Statute.[334] It is thus possible that the administration of justice by a non-state armed group whose conduct may be attributed to a state will be included in the ambit of that state's duty to respect international humanitarian law.

The duty to 'ensure respect' of international humanitarian law necessarily covers a broader spectrum of agents and actions. The ICJ in its *Advisory Opinion on the Construction of a Wall in Palestine* noted that the obligation to ensure respect in the Geneva Conventions implies that "every State party to that

331 Stefan Lorenzmeier, 'The Duty of Non-Recognition and EU Free Trade Agreements: Lessons for Investment Law from the Case of Front Polisario' in Tobias Ackermann and Sebastian Wuschka (eds), *Investments in Conflict Zones* (Brill Nijhoff 2021).

332 Hersch Lauterpacht, *Recognition in International Law* (Cambridge University Press 1947) 227.

333 Rule 139, ICRC Customary Law Database, online: <https://ihl-databases.icrc.org/customary-ihl/eng/docs/v1_rul_rule139> accessed 24 July 2018.

334 See Section II.C, supra.

Convention, whether or not it is a party to a specific conflict, is under an obligation to ensure that the requirements of the instrument in question are complied with".[335] Does that imply that every state has a duty to take action in relation to any breach of applicable humanitarian law anywhere, at any times, by anyone? While the duty to ensure respect reflects the *erga omnes* nature of obligations under international humanitarian law, meaning that any state has a legal interest in compliance with these norms, that does not necessarily imply an obligation to do so.[336] If the rebel administration of justice can be said to contribute to compliance with international humanitarian law (and other *erga omnes* norms under international law, which include human rights norms), then a third state has a legal interest that can provide a legal umbrella for the recognition of insurgent justice if that state chooses to do so. The extent to which a third state has a duty to take positive steps to ensure respect depends on the circumstances, including the means reasonably available to prevent, stop, or repress a violation of international humanitarian law, and the degree to which the state is in a position to influence a non-state armed group.[337] In the context of the administration of justice by an insurgent group, the obligation to ensure respect can translate into the provision of legislative assistance to help draft rebel laws that are consistent with international law, legal training in human rights and humanitarian law for officers of the rebel courts, or even the provision of direct assistance to that court, possibly remotely using web-based tools. This also seems consistent with the obligation to disseminate international humanitarian law "as widely as possible" in the context of internal and international armed conflicts.[338]

The 2010 decision of the US Supreme Court in *Holder v. Humanitarian Law Project* provides an interesting illustration of the duty to ensure respect of international humanitarian law in relation to armed groups.[339] The petitioners had challenged a statute that seemed to prohibit them from, inter alia, providing training in international humanitarian law to the PKK and LTTE, because that

[335] ICJ, *Legal Consequences of the Construction of a Wall in the Occupied Palestinian Territory*, Advisory Opinion, [2004] ICJ Rep. 136, 199–200 para 158.

[336] Robin Geiß, 'The Obligations to Respect and Ensure Respect' in Andrew Clapham, Paola Gaeta, and Marco Sassòli (eds), *The 1949 Geneva Conventions: A Commentary* (Oxford University Press 2015) 124; Andreas Frutig, *Die Pflicht von Drittstaaten zur Durchsetzung des humanitären Völkerrechts nach Art. 1 der Genfer Konventionen von 1949: auf dem schmalen Grat zwischen Recht und Moral* (Helbing Lichtenhahn 2009).

[337] ICRC, *Commentary on the Second Geneva Convention* (Cambridge University Press 2017) para 187. This corresponds to the external dimension of the duty to ensure respect, which has been the subject of much debate: Théo Boutruche and Marco Sassòli, 'Third States' Obligations Vis-à-Vis IHL Violations under International Law' (Norwegian Refugee Council 2016); Michael N Schmitt and Sean Watts, 'Common Article 1 and the Duty to "Ensure Respect"' (2020) 96 International Law Studies 22.

[338] Art. 19, Additional Protocol II; Rule 142, ICRC Customary Law Database, online: <https://ihl-databases.icrc.org/customary-ihl/eng/docs/v1_rul_rule142> accessed 25 July 2018.

[339] 561 U.S. 1 (2010).

would be taken as material support for groups that had been designated as terrorist organisations by the US government. While the case was of course decided under US and not international law, it offers a picture of the way in which support by a third state to the rebel administration of justice could be represented. The majority of the Supreme Court accepted the government's argument that the PKK and LTTE were so tainted by the terrorist acts that they had committed that any contribution to any facet of these groups would facilitate terrorism on their part.[340] Dealing specifically with the proposed training in international humanitarian law, the Court found that the PKK "might use the information to threaten, manipulate and disrupt" by "buying time [. . .], lulling opponents into complacency, and ultimately preparing for renewed attacks".[341] The Court anticipated that, in that example, Turkey "would react sharply to Americans furnishing material support to foreign troops like the PKK, and would hardly be mollified by the explanation that the support was meant only to further those groups' "legitimate" activities".[342] The picture of groups like the PKK and LTTE that emerges from the reasons of the US Supreme Court in *Holder* is one of entities that are wholly outlaws, whose existence and every actions are marked by illegality. There is no denying that these two groups have indeed committed acts that meet even the narrowest definition of terrorism. The Court may be right that, under US law, they can be characterised as terrorist groups and no more, but international humanitarian law represents the forceful and unambiguous rejection of such reduction of non-state armed groups to acts of terrorism they committed.[343] If armed groups otherwise meet the requirements that justify the application of international humanitarian law to a situation, including responsible command enabling sustained and concerted military operations, then they are actors with a measure of international legal personality that are under an obligation to implement international humanitarian law. As a consequence, legal assistance to insurgent courts in the field of international humanitarian law and human rights may possible draw a sharp political reaction from the state party to the conflict, but it would not be a violation of international law. On the contrary, depending on the circumstances, it may be the filling of an obligation to ensure respect by the third state. This position, amounting to a repudiation of the approach taken in *Holder*, is reflected in a 2020 amendment to the Swiss Penal Code which creates an exception to the crime of providing

[340] ibid 24 (Roberts CJ for the Court).
[341] ibid 32.
[342] ibid 28.
[343] On whether the US statute is incompatible with US obligations under international law, see Justin A Fraterman, 'Criminalizing Humanitarian Relief: Are U.S. Material Support for Terrorism Laws Compatible with International Humanitarian Law' (2013) 46 New York University Journal of International Law and Politics 399.

support to a terrorist organisation in order to exclude humanitarian assistance from its ambit.[344]

Beyond the duty to ensure respect of international humanitarian law, the recognition of insurgent justice by third states can also relate to the duty to ensure human rights. Under International human rights treaties, states have an obligation not only to 'respect' human rights but also to 'ensure' or 'secure' them.[345] Like its equivalent in humanitarian law, the obligation to ensure or secure human rights covers a wider ambit of actions than the obligation to respect, extending in some circumstances to those of actors whose actions cannot be imputed to the state.[346] In both treaty and customary human rights law, the scope of the state's duty to ensure rights is limited to those falling under its jurisdiction, a question that is related in part to territory and in part to the relation between the state and the immediate author of the human rights violation. The expanding interpretation of the extraterritorial application of human rights obligations, led by the European Court of Human Rights, means that there is an increasing possibility that a state may be found responsible for the administration of justice by non-state armed groups in zones of armed conflicts. As far as third states are concerned, a series of decisions of the European Court found that states that did not occupy the territory or have a control relationship that amounted to agency with the non-state armed group could still be found in violation for the actions of the latter. Thus, as discussed in the previous section, the Court found that Russia was responsible for the denial of rights by the 'Moldavian Republic of Transdniestria', an entity it helped establish and over which it held 'decisive influence'.[347] The Court's reasoning could be clearer on the specific basis of Russian responsibility, but it appears that it was in part the state's failure to take steps to prevent or remedy violations under its positive duty to secure human rights.[348]

[344] Art. 260ter(2), Code pénal suisse ("L'al. 1 let. b ne s'applique pas aux services humanitaires fournis par un organisme umanitaire impartial, tel que le Commité international de la Croix-Rouge, conformément à l'article 3 commun aux Conventions de Genève du 12 août 1949"). This echoes the criticism by Tathiana Flores Acuña of ONUSAL's refusal to advise the FMLN in El Salvador to improve their administration of justice: Tathiana Flores Acuña, *The United Nations Mission in El Salvador: A Humanitarian Law Perspective* (Kluwer Law International 1995) 62. On the other hand, more recently, it reflects MONUC's attempt to send lawyers to assist in proceedings before a court of the Mouvement de libération du Congo: Willms (n 225) 149.

[345] E.g., Art. 2, ICCPR; Art. 1, American Convention on Human Rights; Art. 1, European Convention of Human Rights.

[346] Xenos (n 276); Daragh Murray, *Human Rights Obligations of Non-State Armed Groups* (Hart Publishing 2016) 197–199; Laurens Lavrysen, *Human Rights in a Positive State: Rethinking the Relationship between Positive and Negative Obligations under the European Convention on Human Rights* (Intersentia 2016).

[347] ECtHR, *Ilascu v Moldova and Russia*, Judgment, Appl. No 48787/99, [2004] ECHR 318, para 392.

[348] Marko Milanovic and Tatjana Papić, 'The Applicability of the ECHR in Contested Territories' (2018) 67 International and Comparative Law Quarterly 779. In the more recent decision in the case of *Sandhu v Moldova and Russia*, No 21034/05, 17 July 2018, para 89, the Court relies on its earlier cases including *Ilascu* and seems to state more clearly that Russia is responsible for the violations

As with the duty to 'ensure respect' under international humanitarian law, the duty to ensure human rights does not translate into a positive obligation for every state to intervene in each and every situation in which human rights are denied anywhere. In human rights, the foundation of state obligations is expressed in jurisdictional terms, meaning that there must be some basis to find that the actor falls under some form of authority of the state in question. As affirmed on many occasions by the European and Inter-American Courts of Human Rights, jurisdiction is primarily territorial, so the location of the violation may correspond to jurisdiction for the purpose of triggering human rights obligations.[349] The jurisdiction may also be personal, for instance when state agents deployed abroad commit violations of human rights.[350] Neither basis will normally be relevant to the interaction of third states with the rebel administration of justice in an armed conflict to which they are not a party.

One situation in which a state may acquire jurisdiction within the meaning of human rights treaties is by way of individuals subjected to insurgent justice who later are present on the territory of that state. This is a limited jurisdiction in that it does not extend to the operation of rebel courts per se but rather to the legal consequences of their decisions that are being felt on the territory of the other state. The *Sakhanh* case once again can be invoked as an example, with the accused invoking functional immunity as a member of a judicially mandated execution squad. The European Court of Human Rights was confronted with a different scenario in *Mitrovic v. Serbia*, involving a prison sentence for murder pronounced by a court of the 'Republic of Serbian Krajina', an unrecognised self-proclaimed entity in Croatia.[351] The applicant was held in a jail of this unrecognised entity for two years, after which he was transferred to another jail in Serbia, where he challenged the legality of his detention. The European Court found that the detention was indeed unlawful, because it rested on a "non-domestic decision which had not been recognised domestically".[352] What is striking here is that the European Court of Human Rights does not find that the detention by judgment of an unrecognised entity was in itself a violation of human rights, nor that the recognition of a decision of an unrecognised entity by a state party to the European Convention on Human Rights would be a violation. Instead, the European Court treats the decision of the non-state court in a manner that is not clearly different from a decision of the court of another state. Indeed, in finding

committed by the MRT on the basis of attribution reflecting its effective control of the non-state entity.

[349] ECtHR, *Cyprus v Turkey*, Appl. No 25781/94, ECHR 2001-IV; IACHR, Advisory Opinion on the Environment and Human Rights, OC-23/17, 15 November 2017, 34–35 paras 72–78.

[350] See, e.g., ECtHR, *Medvedyev v France*, Judgment, Appl. No 3394/03, 29 March 2010.

[351] ECtHR, *Mitrovic v Serbia*, Judgment, Appl. No 52142/12, 21 March 2017.

[352] ibid para 43.

that the denial of human rights was in the absence of a vetting process for the decision of an unrecognised entity, the European Court implies that it was possible that this process could validate the conviction pronounced by the court of the 'Republic of Serbian Krajina' if that court proved independent and impartial and due process was observed.

The announcement by France that it wished French Islamic State members detained by the PYD in northern Syria to be tried by the courts of that non-state armed group offers a different jurisdictional trigger for the obligation to ensure human rights. The situation is somewhat similar to the line of cases dealing with extradition, started with *Soering v. UK*, in which the European Court found that states had an obligation to ensure that the basic rights of individuals would not be denied by the country to which they sought to extradite them.[353] One clear difference is of course that, in the extradition cases, the individual whose human rights would be violated is in the territory of the extraditing state, and therefore under its jurisdiction in every sense. The eventual act of torture would be committed abroad by another state, in itself beyond the jurisdiction of the extraditing state, but there is a chain of decisions and events that links directly enough the jurisdiction of the extraditing state to the eventual violation.[354] In *Al-Saadoon v. UK*, the European Court of Human Rights expanded the reach of the non-refoulement principle to cover the transfer of individuals detained by British troops in Iraq to the national government.[355] The Court found that the foreseeable risk or torture and the application of the death penalty triggered a duty for the United Kingdom to abstain from any arrangement or agreement to transfer persons under its jurisdiction, even extraterritorial, without obtaining assurances that their rights would be respected.[356] The Court noted that, under its established jurisprudence, non-refoulement also can apply with respect to a flagrant denial of the right to a fair trial, but that there was no evidence to that effect in this case.[357]

The French Islamic State members detained by Kurdish rebels in Syria do not benefit from a similar jurisdictional connection to French territory. There is a link of nationality that, under the personality principle, would ground some measure of French jurisdiction over these individuals. Under general international law, this implies a sovereign right of France to act rather than an obligation to do so. Recent decisions have hinted that a link of nationality may play a role in establishing human rights jurisdiction and, ultimately, it is the French

353 ECHR, *Soering v UK*, Appl. No 14038/88, 7 July 1989.

354 Miles Jackson, 'Freeing *Soering*: The ECHR, State Complicity in Torture and Jurisdiction' (2016) 27 European Journal of International Law 817, 823–824.

355 ECtHR, *Al-Saadoon and Muftdhi v UK*, Judgment, Appl. No 61498/08, 2 March 2010.

356 ibid paras 137–145.

357 ibid paras 149–150, referring to ECtHR, *Mamatkulov and Askarov v Turkey*, Judgment (Grand Chamber), Appl. No 46827/99, 4 February 2005, paras 90–91.

government's decision to decline the YPG's offer to transfer its nationals to France that enables their trial by rebel courts.[358] The situation is somewhat similar to state participation in extraterritorial counter-terrorism measures by way of sharing information or providing logistical support, but not in the execution of the measures.[359] Under general international law, the responsibility of the state could be engaged as a form of complicity if that state was aware of the violation of international human rights law and if the other actor is bound by the same international legal standards.[360] In this perspective, there could be no responsibility for France under the European Convention on Human Rights, given that the PYD is not bound by that regional human rights treaty. On the other hand, there seems to be no reason why the principle of complicity could not apply in relation to customary human rights norms, which bind equally states and non-state armed groups in circumstances such as obtain in Rojava. Complicity is a state responsibility model that leads to attribution to the complicit state, in this example France, of the direct violation of human rights by the insurgent courts in Syria. In that model, the state fails to 'respect' human rights.[361] A distinct model can be said to be at play, involving the state's duty to 'ensure' human rights as corresponding to an obligation to take positive steps. If a state can be held complicit in the violation of human rights by another actor then, a fortiori, it implies that its broader duty to ensure rights is at play in this scenario. This reasoning is consistent with the development by the Inter-American Court of Human Rights of the concept of human rights jurisdiction in the context of transboundary environmental harm. According to the Inter-American Court, a causal link between an act on the territory of the state and denial of human rights abroad is sufficient to bring that matter under the jurisdiction of that state.[362] Likewise, the UN Human Rights Committee has held in *Munaf v. Romania* that "a State

[358] ECtHR, *M.N. v Belgium*, Decision (Grand Chamber), Appl. No 3599/18, 5 May 2020, paras 112–118; UN Committee on the Rights of the Child, L.H. v France, UN Doc CRC/C/85/D/79/2019—CRC/C/85/D/109/2019 (2020) paras 9.7–10; Commission nationale consultative des droits de l'homme—République française, Opinion on the French Under-Age Nationals Detained in Syrian Camps (2019), online: <https://www.cncdh.fr/fr/publications/avis-sur-les-enfants-francais-retenus-dans-les-camps-syriens>. See Yuval Shany, 'The Extraterritorial Application of International Human Rights Law' (2020) 409 Recueil des cours 21, 30 ("a state should be required to uphold the human rights located outside its territory in relation to which they have developed a special legal relationship, or where it becomes known that such individuals find themselves *de facto* dependent upon the foreign state for their protection").

[359] For example, the Canadian government provided inaccurate information to the US government that led to the rendition of a Canadian citizen, Maher Arar, to Syria, where he was tortured. The arrest, rendition, and torture of Arar were all carried out abroad by states other than Canada. See the Report of the Commission of Inquiry into the Actions of Canadian Officials in Relation to Maher Arar, online: <http://publications.gc.ca/site/eng/295791/publication.html> accessed 27 July 2018.

[360] Art. 16, UN Articles on State Responsibility.

[361] Marko Milanovic, *Extraterritorial Application of Human Rights Treaties: Law, Principles, and Policy* (Oxford University Press 2011) 124–126.

[362] IACHR, *Advisory Opinion on the Environment and Human Rights*, OC-23/17, 15 November 2017, paras 101–102.

party may be responsible for extraterritorial violations of the Covenant, if it is a link in the causal chain that would make possible violations in another jurisdiction".[363] It goes without saying that France's duty to 'ensure respect' of international humanitarian law, which is not framed in narrow jurisdictional terms like the corresponding human rights norms, would likewise translate into an obligation to take positive steps. Concretely, reasonable steps that France could take to fulfil its obligations under both international human rights law and international humanitarian law would be monitoring the trials, offering legal assistance to all organs or the court, and interceding with the PYD to correct any aspect of insurgent justice that fails to meet the standards demanded under international law.

In conclusion, the transnational recognition of the rebel administration of justice by a third state is a phenomenon that does occur in a variety of contexts. Far from representing a violation of international law, this practice of recognition is permitted and, in some circumstances, demanded by applicable norms of international human rights and humanitarian law.

IV. National Recognition by the Territorial State

There is a whiff of absurdity to the very suggestion that a government might recognise the legal validity of the administration of justice carried out by a non-state armed group against which it is engaged in armed hostilities. Even if a right to regularly constitute courts is granted to non-state armed groups under international humanitarian law, this does not necessarily imply a corresponding duty for the territorial state to recognise the decisions of rebel courts.[364] A survey of the practice in this regard in fact reveals that states have adopted a range of attitudes towards insurgent justice, from absolute denial to measured recognition. There are indeed a number of norms in public international law that impose some restraints on states' ability to freely determine whether and to what extent they will refuse to recognise the actions of insurgent courts.

[363] UN Human Rights Committee, *Munaf v Romania*, UN Doc CCPR/C/96/D/1539/2006 para 14.2. In dissent, Walter Kälin offered an even broader principle: "A refusal to act on behalf of a person being abroad may be a relevant exercise of jurisdiction, provided there is a genuine link between the state and the person concerned. In the present case, the author has claimed that according to applicable Iraqi law the State party had to authorize the trial of and the imposition of the death penalty on the author because the victims were its own nationals, and thus was supposed to play a direct role in his trial. Such a legal possibility to prevent the imposition of the death penalty in a trial that allegedly violated article 14 would, in my view, be sufficient to create a genuine link between the State party and the author". More recently, the Human Rights Committee held that a state's extraterritorial responsibility for rescue at sea can trigger human rights jurisdiction: UN Human Rights Committee, *A.S.v Italy*, UN Doc. CCPR/C/130/3042/2017 (2021) paras 7.4–7.8; UN Human Rights Committee, *A.S. v Malta*, UN Doc. CCPR/C/130/3043/2017 (2021) para 6.7.

[364] ICRC, *Commentary on the Third Geneva Convention* (Cambridge University Press 2020) para 731.

Not rarely, government officials will issue statements that any form of administration of justice by a non-state armed group in the context of an armed conflict is marked by absolute nullity. For example, the Afghan government categorically denies any recognition to the Taliban shadow judiciary. Mohammad Sarwar Osmani Farahi, co-chair of the judiciary committee of the Afghan parliament, has repeatedly told the media that Taliban judicial rulings enjoy no legitimacy in Afghanistan's legal system.[365] Likewise, Chief Justice Sarath de Silva of the Sri Lankan Supreme Court offered in a media interview an unambiguous rejection of any possible recognition of the administration of justice by the LTTE in the territory it controlled:

> These courts are not consistent with our constitution and they cannot exist under our hierarchy. Our courts are fully functional in those areas and we do not recognise any other courts. The people too should not go there [. . .] We must maintain our courts because that is what holds for governance. Legal systems, courts, police are all incidence of governance. If there is an erosion then there is no state. This is the danger of it.[366]

The Chief Justice specified that if the courts of Sri Lanka were to hear of anyone jailed by order of an LTTE court, that person would immediately be freed by way of a habeas corpus motion. The absolute rejection of any legal validity to insurgent justice has at times been affirmed by state courts further to specific arguments raised in the context of a case being heard. For example, the Colombian Supreme Court convicted Arteta Davila, Commander of FARC Front 29, as the superior responsible for the execution of a man condemned to death for the sexual abuse of an eight-year-old girl in a remote part of the country controlled by the insurgents. For the Colombian Supreme Court, the fact that author of the crime had been 'tried' by a rebel 'court' was immaterial:

> This was a case of private justice, carried out by an outlawed armed group in clear violation of constitutional norms guaranteeing due process and proscribing the death penalty (and any other cruel, inhuman or degrading treatment), which amounts to a grave breach of public order and public security with a view to instill fear or terror among the public.[367]

[365] Hasib Danish Alikozai, 'Corruption Encourages Parallel Judiciary in Afghanistan' *VOA* (12 January 2016), online: <https://www.voanews.com/a/corruption-encourages-parallel-judiciary-afghanistan/3142316.html>.

[366] Laila Nasry, 'LTTE Has No Judicial Authority—CJ' *Sunday Times (Sri Lanka)* (14 November 2004), online: <http://sundaytimes.lk/021208/news/courts.html>.

[367] Case No 23438, Yesid Arteta Davila, 2 July 2008 (Penal Chamber, Supreme Court of Colombia) at 33 ("se trató de un acto de justicia privada, realizado por un grupo armado al margen de la ley en franca contravía de las normas constitucionales que consagran el debido proceso y prohíben la pena de muerte (al igual de cualquier trato cruel, inhumano o degradante), y que lleva necesariamente

There are still further examples of situations in which governments adopted legislation or regulations that provided for the absolute nullity of acts of domestic authorities which they considered to be illegal. The British government thus adopted a statute and issued orders denying any validity to purported official acts of the self-proclaimed government of Rhodesia, further to the unilateral declaration of independence issued by that regime.[368] In a somewhat similar situation, albeit with much less legitimacy and much more vindictiveness, the nationalist government of General Franco in Spain declared upon seizing power that none of the marriages celebrated pursuant to legislation adopted by the Republican government was valid.[369]

Modern state practice also offers examples of some degree of recognition of the rebel administration of justice by organs of the state. In some cases, the official administration of justice was co-opted by non-state armed groups, such that it was not possible to distinguish between decisions that were taken independently by the state judiciary and those that reflected insurgent power. The FARC offers many examples of such instrumentalisation of official courts by armed rebels.[370] More radically, some decisions that were taken entirely by FARC cadres, without any participation or presence of official justice, were on occasion entered into the registers of decisions of local authorities, thus inserting the outcome of rebel decision-making into the official legal process.[371] Another variation was observed in the contemporary working of the courts of Sri Lanka. In the north-east, in areas that were for many years under the control of the LTTE, decisions of LTTE tribunals sometimes are accepted as factual evidence by Sri Lankan courts. For instance, in a 2017 case dealing with a property dispute, the plaintiff adduced as evidence judgments of the Tamil Eelam Mediation Board, the Tamil Eelam Trial Court, and the Tamil Eelam District Court, all organs of the LTTE; the defendant in that case acknowledged that all these decisions favoured the plaintiff, and the Chavakachcheri District Court admitted them into the record as evidence.[372] It bears noting that the District Court, although

tanto a una grave perturbación del orden público y de la seguridad pública como, en consecuencia, a la efectiva provocación o mantenimiento de un estado de zozobra o terror en la población").

368 Verhoeven (n 317) 147. See *Madzimbamuto v Ladner-Burke*, [1968] A.C. 645 (Privy Council).

369 See Jacques Maury, 'Des mariages civils d'Espagnols célébrés en Espagne (zone non nationale) après la loi franquiste du 12 mars 1938 et de leur valeur en France', *Festschrift für Leo Raape zu seinem siebzigsten Geburtstag 14. Juni 1948* (Rechtsund Staatswissenschaftlicher Verlag 1948).

370 See Chapter 1, Section I.B.iii.

371 See Nicolás Espinosa Menéndez, 'La Justicia guerrillera en Colombia. Elementos de análisis para los retos de la transición política en una zona de control insurgente (el caso del Piedemonte amazónico)' [2016] Estudios Latinoamericanos 87, 101. See more broadly the discussion of FARC justice in Chapter 1.

372 Chavakachcheri District Court (Sri Lanka), Case L/7159/2003, 18 September 2017, at 14. Lawyers interviewed at the Chavakachcheri courthouse in 2017 indicated that such a practice was not rare in the region.

an official state court of Sri Lanka, operates in the Tamil language in a region that seems administratively very disconnected from the central judicial authorities in the capital Colombo. The barriers of language and geography may well mean that central judicial and executive organs of government are not aware of this practice, which does not lead to conclude that it is not legally significant. It is reported that there is a degree of coordination between the courts of the government of Myanmar/Burma and the New Mon Liberation Army, a non-state armed group active in that country, such that courts of one will not agree to hear a case that has already been decided by the courts of the other.[373]

The US Civil War provided the most wide-ranging occasion for the rebel administration of justice, leading to an extensive post-war judicial consideration of the possible recognition of the decisions of rebel courts. In the early months of 1861, seven Southern states, later joined by four more, unilaterally declared that they were leaving the United States to form an independent federated state named the Confederate States of America. The seceding states immediately took control of government institutions located on their territories, including federal courts. In March 1861, the Confederate Congress enacted the Judiciary Act, establishing Confederate District Courts with a jurisdiction similar to the previous US District Courts.[374] Under that statute, the Confederate District Courts considered themselves as successors to the US District Courts that they had replaced, sitting in the same courtrooms, not rarely presided by the same judges having switched allegiance from the United States to the Confederacy, using the same dockets and finishing trials that had been ongoing on the day the Southern states seceded and US courts stopped functioning. For example, in one case, a man was convicted of the theft of a slave ship by a Confederate District Court, pursuant to an indictment issued by a US District Court applying US law.[375] The state courts, for their part, continued to operate in an even more seamless manner throughout the Southern states during the same period. The government of the United States never recognised the belligerency of the Confederate States nor, more broadly, the legitimacy of their claim to secession or any act taken in furtherance thereof. During the four years of the Civil War, the Confederate Congress and the legislatures of the Southern states adopted a variety of statutes, and the Confederate and state courts sat continuously, applying a mixture of pre-existing law and new statutes adopted by the rebellion.[376] As a result, when

[373] McCartan and Jolliffe (n 302) 31–32.

[374] Warren Grice, 'A Half Forgotten Chapter in the Judicial History of Georgia' (1930) 1 The Georgia Lawyer 68.

[375] ibid; William Robinson, *Justice in Grey; A History of the Judicial System of the Confederate States of America* (Harvard University Press 1941).

[376] See Warren Moise, *Rebellion in the Temple of Justice: The Federal and State Courts in South Carolina During the War Between the States* (iUniverse 2003); G Edward White, 'Recovering the Legal History of the Confederacy' (2011) 68 Washington & Lee Law Review 467.

the Civil War finally came to an end in 1865, courts of what was now a defeated insurgency had issued thousands of orders, judgments, and convictions on the full range of ordinary legal issues from divorce to murder to contracts. Many decisions produced ongoing effects, such as the sequestration of the property of 'enemy aliens' or a long prison sentence. What legal effect, if any, was given to these judicial decisions by the victorious US government?

The answer, it turns out, is complex and variable. At the institutional level, it can be said that there was a greater degree of continuity at the end of the Civil War in state courts than in Confederate District Courts. In *Sprott v. United States*, a case dealing with the purchase of cotton from the Confederate government, the US Supreme Court declared that the government of the Confederate States of America was in a legal position fundamentally different from that of the governments of the individual rebellious states.[377] This of course reflects the fact that the US Constitution provides for the lawful existence and authority of state governments but is wholly inimical to the creation of a competing federal government. For the Supreme Court, state governments had remained largely unchanged, with largely the same laws being applied by largely the same officers, even if in service to a false cause.[378] As a result, acts of these state governments not in pursuit of the rebellion could be held valid. The same could not be said of the government of the Confederate States of America, founded as a treasonous project to overthrow the legitimate authority of the United States. The nature of the Confederate government as "an enormous evil" implied that none of its acts could be recognised as valid:

> When it was overthrown, it perished totally. It left no laws, no statutes, no decrees, no authority which can give support to any contract or any act done in its service or in aid of its purpose or which contributed to protract its existence. So far as the actual exercise of its physical power was brought to bear upon individuals, that may, under some circumstances, constitute a justification or excuse for acts otherwise indefensible, but no validity can be given in the courts of this country to acts voluntarily performed in direct aid and support of its unlawful purpose.[379]

Thus, we can understand that state courts in Georgia, Mississippi, and South Carolina continued to operate at the end of the war, nearly without interruption and often with the same judges. Sometimes, cases that had been dismissed in 1861 because one party had become an 'enemy alien' were reinstated in 1865, the

377 United States Supreme Court, *Sprott v United States*, 87 U.S. 459 (1874).
378 ibid at 464.
379 ibid.

war a simple parenthesis in the life of the law.[380] Military governments initially took over from the Confederate regimes in the South, with the power to dismiss anyone in civil or military office; as a result, many judges were removed from state courts in the South. The military commander could permit state courts to operate, but had the right to remove any case from a civilian state court in favour of a US military court. When civilian rule resumed in the South, the legislative attitude adopted vis-à-vis judicial decisions issued during the war varied widely, from Georgia validating all judgments to Arkansas annulling all judicial acts save for a few exceptions; not all these approaches were later considered consistent with the US Constitution or the Law of Nations.[381]

The operation of the Confederate District Courts was considered a more direct usurpation by the Confederacy of the legitimate authority of the United States, and therefore were immediately terminated and their decisions viewed with considerably greater suspicion. When the question of the validity of Confederate Courts came to the US Supreme Court, it adopted positions that varied between rigid rejection of the validity of the courts of the rebellious South and some measured acceptance. In *Hickman v. Jones*, decided in 1869, Hickman sued Jones for unlawful imprisonment for having presided as a judge of the Confederate District Court for Southern Alabama over a trial for treason against the Confederate States. Also sued were the court clerk, district attorney, marshal, and members of the jury. The US Supreme Court found that

> [t]he rebellion out of which the war grew was without any legal sanction [. . .]. The proportions and duration of the struggle did not affect its character. Nor was there a rebel government de facto in such a sense as to give any legal efficacy to its acts. It was not recognized by the National, nor by any foreign government. It was not at any time in possession of the capital of the nation. It did not for a moment displace the rightful government. That government was always in existence, always in the regular discharge of its functions [. . .]. For the sake of humanity, certain belligerent rights were conceded to the insurgents in arms. But the recognition did not extend to the pretended government of the Confederacy. The intercourse was confined to its military authorities. In no instance was there intercourse otherwise than of this character. The rebellion was simply an armed resistance to the rightful authority of the sovereign. Such was its character in its rise, progress, and downfall. The act of the Confederate Congress creating the tribunal in question was void. It was as if it were not. The court was a nullity, and could exercise no rightful jurisdiction. The forms of

[380] Erwin C Surrency, 'The Legal Effects of the Civil War' (1961) 5 The American Journal of Legal History 145, 146.

[381] ibid 153.

> law with which it clothed its proceedings gave no protection to those who, assuming to be its officers, were the instruments by which it acted.[382]

This amounts to the absolute rejection of any legality to any facet of the administration of justice by rebels, a position that echoes the official views quoted in the preceding in the recent conflicts in Sri Lanka, Colombia, and Afghanistan. Some state supreme courts in the South followed this line of analysis to conclude that the governments in the Confederacy had been neither *de jure* nor *de facto* governments, and that their actions were null and void, while others refrained from imposing widespread legal uncertainty that would result from denying that statutes and judgments that had been considered valid for years suddenly were without legal effect.[383]

The US Supreme Court adopted an approach more nuanced than in *Hickman* in relation to decision of state courts. Thus in *Texas v. White*, the Supreme Court framed a principle whereby "acts necessary to peace and good order among citizens [. . .] must be regarded in general as valid when proceeding from an actual, though unlawful, government, and that acts in furtherance or support of rebellion against the United States, or intended to defeat the just rights of citizens, and other acts of like nature, must, in general, be regarded as invalid and void".[384] Likewise, in *Horn v. Lockhart*, the Court concluded:

> We admit that the acts of the several States in their individual capacities, and of their different departments of government, executive, judicial, and legislative, during the war, so far as they did not impair or tend to impair the supremacy of the National authority, or the just rights of citizens under the Constitution, are, in general, to be treated as valid and binding. The existence of a state of insurrection and war did not loosen the bonds of society, or do away with civil government, or the regular administration of the laws. Order was to be preserved, police regulations maintained, crime prosecuted, property protected, contracts enforced, marriages celebrated, estates settled, and the transfer and descent of property regulated precisely as in time of peace. No one that we are aware of seriously questions the validity of judicial or legislative acts in the insurrectionary States touching these and kindred subjects, where they were not hostile in their purpose or mode of enforcement to the authority of the national government, and did not impair the rights of citizens under the Constitution.[385]

382 United States Supreme Court, *Hickman v Jones*, 76 U.S. 197, 200–201 (1869).
383 See, e.g., Mississippi High Court of Errors and Appeals, *Sassell v Backrack*, 42 Miss. 56 (1868). See generally Surrency (n 380) 151–155.
384 United States Supreme Court, *Texas v White*, 74 U.S. 700, 733 (1869).
385 United States Supreme Court, *Horn v Lockhart*, 84 U.S. 570, 580 (1873).

The Supreme Court's jurisprudence eventually solidified in a series of decisions that acknowledged that the authorities in the Southern states had constituted *de facto* governments whose courts could indeed issue decisions the validity of which could not be challenged merely on the basis that they emanated from an insurgency. Only for cases effectively contributing to the insurgency, such as the selling of weapons to Confederate forces or the seizing of property on the basis of treason, would the validity of the decisions of rebel courts be revisited.[386] It is interesting to note that the Supreme Court adopted this position by invoking principles of the law of nations, finding that the situation of citizens under insurgent governance was in this respect similar to that of civilians under belligerent occupation by a foreign state.[387] The modulated approach devised by the US Supreme Court was later echoed in decisions of the Mexico/USA General Claims Commission applying principles of public international law. In particular, in *Hopkins v. Mexico*, the Claims Commission found that acts of ordinary administration by an illegitimate regime should be given effect.[388]

Contemporary international humanitarian law on belligerent occupation still adheres to the position that the administration of justice by occupation authority broadly retains its validity even after occupation has ended and the sovereign government has regained control.[389] This is so regardless of the legal validity of the use of force under *jus ad bellum* that led to the presence of a foreign occupier, under the general principle of the equality of belligerents under *jus ad bello*.[390] There is no basis in international law for the returning sovereign to nullify acts of the occupying power that were consistent with applicable norms of international humanitarian law and human rights. On the opposite, in principle legal issues determined by lawful administrative and judicial acts during the period of occupation must be recognised by the returning national government.[391] In the

[386] Surrency (n 380) 164–165; see generally Robert Bruce Murray, *Legal Cases of the Civil War* (Stackpole Books 2003).

[387] See, e.g., United States Supreme Court, *Thorington v Smith*, 75 U.S. 1, 11 (1868) ('It seems to follow as a necessary consequence from this actual supremacy of the insurgent government as a belligerent within the territory where it circulated, and from the necessity of civil obedience on the part of all who remained in it, that this [Confederate] currency must be considered in courts of law in the same light as if it had been issued by a foreign government, temporarily occupying a part of the territory of the United States').

[388] Mexico/USA General Claims Commission, *Hopkins v Mexico*, (1926) 4 Rep. In'l Arb. Awards 41, 44 ("Such acts as the registration of births, deaths, and marriages were practically undisturbed, because they were performed in the orderly functioning of the Government quite independent of the recognition or nonrecognition of the individuals exercising authority. These were unpersonal acts of the Government itself as an abstract entity"). See Haig Silvanie, *Responsibility of States for Acts of Unsuccessful Insurgent Governments* (Columbia University Press 1939) 84–95.

[389] Eyal Benvenisti, *The International Law of Occupation* (2d edn, Oxford University Press 2012) 299–317.

[390] Henri Meyrowitz, *Le Principe de l'égalité des belligérants devant le droit de la guerre* (Pedone 1970).

[391] Yoram Dinstein, *The International Law of Belligerent Occupation* (2d edn, Cambridge University Press 2019) 308; Yutaka Arai-Takahashi, *The Law of Occupation: Continuity and Change*

modern practice of states, even acts of the occupier that violated international law have not necessarily been found null; in general, returning governments have balanced various considerations in determining whether to undo the illegal acts of the occupant, including the nature of the norm violated, the good faith of the civilian population, the length of occupation, and the impact on post-conflict reconciliation.[392] There may be situations of international armed conflicts in which a foreign non-state armed group exercises authority over a territory and population in such a manner that it corresponds to belligerent occupation, in wars of national liberations or perhaps if the group acts in conjunction or collaboration with another state belligerent. Admittedly, most armed conflicts in which non-state armed groups have come to administer justice are not international but non-international armed conflicts. The point to draw from this discussion isn't an argument that the doctrine of belligerent occupation ought to be extended to covers situations of civil wars, although other have made compelling arguments in that direction;[393] rather, it is to signal that the bundle of interests that underpins the rules limiting a returning government's power to undo the administration of justice of a belligerent occupant are equally present in a situation of civil war in which a government regains control of a territory that had been for some time under the authority of insurgents. As a consequence, such restraints should also obtain in non-international armed conflict vis-à-vis rebel administration of justice.

More fundamentally, recognition of rebel justice by the national state has been transformed by the emergence of human rights obligations into positive international law since the Reconstruction-era decisions of the US Supreme Court and the codification of humanitarian norms on belligerent occupation in the 1907 Hague Conventions and 1949 Geneva Conventions. The human rights regime in international law, often mirrored in constitutionally entrenched human rights standards in municipal law, shifts the normative centre of gravity to the protection of individual interests, as contrasted with the more collective interests protected in international humanitarian law.[394] Two situations raise distinct legal issues with respect to recognition by the national state, and must be analysed separately: *in bello* recognition of rebel administration of justice, in areas fully or partially beyond the control of the state, and *post bellum*

of International Humanitarian Law, and Its Interaction with International Human Rights Law (Brill 2009) 25.

392 Benvenisti (n 389) 317.

393 See Chapter 1, Section II.B.ii.

394 René Provost, *International Human Rights and Humanitarian Law* (Cambridge University Press 2002) 16–41.

recognition, after the government has regained control over the relevant territory and population.[395]

Regarding recognition by the national state of the rebel administration of justice while the conflict is still ongoing, the fact that the exercise of insurgent authority is taking place within the territory of the state is of central importance. As mentioned in the previous subsection, in the discussion of the extraterritorial application of human rights treaties, states have human rights obligations towards individuals under their jurisdiction. As noted repeatedly by human rights bodies, jurisdiction in this sense has a particular meaning, and it is understood primarily in territorial terms.[396] Jurisdiction on national territory is presumed to be exercised normally, a presumption that can be rebutted in exceptional circumstances such as foreign occupation or armed insurgency. On several occasions, the European Court of Human Rights found that the territory of a state occupied by another state fell within the human rights jurisdiction of the occupier, but in the same breath it denied that this implied that this territory no longer fell within the occupied state's jurisdiction.[397] Thus, in *Ilascu v. Moldova and Russia*, the Court held that Moldova was the sole legitimate sovereign but that the so-called 'Moldavian Republic of Transdniestria' fell within the jurisdiction of Russia; at the same time, it found that "where a Contracting State is prevented from exercising its authority over the whole of its territory by a constraining *de facto* situation, such as obtains when a separatist regime is set up [. . .], it does not hereby cease to have jurisdiction within the meaning of Article 1 of the Convention over that part of its territory temporarily subject to a local authority sustained by rebel forces".[398] That said, the loss of effective control over that part of national territory does reduce the scope of the state's human rights jurisdiction, limiting its positive obligation to take whatever political, diplomatic, economic, judicial, and other measures that are reasonably available.[399] In a somewhat similar setting, the Venice Commission of the Council of Europe found that there were limits to Georgia's sovereign right to adopt legislation deeming null and void the legal acts of the *de facto* authorities in the contested Georgian territories in South Ossetia and Abkhazia:

> Generally speaking, each State is free to recognize or not to recognize acts of state issued by other States or by de facto authorities (for example, the

[395] The scenario in which the rebels emerge victorious and form the new government is discarded, as their acts are thereafter imputed to the state without any discretion to disavow them, under Art. 10 of the UN Articles on States Responsibility.

[396] ECtHR, *Cyprus v Turkey*, Appl. No 25781/94, ECHR 2001-IV; IACHR, Advisory Opinion on the Environment and Human Rights, OC-23/17, 15 November 2017, 34–35 paras 72–78.

[397] Murray (n 346) 197–199.

[398] ECtHR, *Ilascu v Moldova and Russia*, Appl. No 48787/99, [2004] ECHR 318, para 333.

[399] ECtHR, *Sandhu v Moldova and Russia*, Appl. No 21034/05, 17 July 2018, para 34.

> recognition of these acts can be refused on the basis of considerations of *ordre public*). On the basis of international customary law there is no obligation to recognize such acts. Nevertheless, this freedom ends where basic human rights would be violated. If Georgia refuses to accept e.g. basic documents concerning the personal status such as birth or death certificates, that would violate Article 8 of the ECHR.[400]

In a recent case, the European Court of Human Rights held that Cyprus had an obligation to cooperate with police and judicial authorities of the so-called 'Turkish Republic of Northern Cyprus' to resolve a serious crime, and that such cooperation could not be said to be tantamount to recognition of the latter by the former.[401] More specifically, the Grand Chamber held that "the decisions taken by the courts of unrecognised entities, including by their criminal courts, may be considered 'lawful' for the purposes of the Convention provided that these courts form part of a judicial system operating on a 'constitutional and legal basis' reflecting a judicial tradition compatible with the Convention, in order to enable individuals to enjoy the Convention guarantees".[402]

We see in these holdings echoes of the concerns that moved the US Supreme Court after the Civil War and animate humanitarian rules on belligerent occupation. If a non-state armed group exerts authority over a population and territory for a significant amount of time and administers justice in a fashion that does not on its face violate international law, then a government cannot deny fundamental rights to individuals under its jurisdiction on the basis that they turned to what was in effect the only system of justice available to them at that given time and place. The state does have a legitimate interest in combating the insurgency, and that can justify some limitations of insurgent justice, but not the wholesale rejection that is expressed in some of the official statements quoted at the start of this subsection. International human rights law imposes a duty on states to give recognition *in bello* to the rebel administration of justice at least inasmuch as it is not directly contributing to the insurgency. A wide range of rebel court decisions touching on private claims, property rights, family issues, and even criminal law could be covered by this principle.[403] The alternative is to condemn the civilian

[400] European Commission for Democracy Through Law (Venice Commission), *Opinion on the Law on Occupied Territories of Georgia*, No 516/2009, 17 March 2009, para 43.

[401] ECHR, *Güzelyurtlu v Cyprus and Turkey*, Judgment (Grand Chamber), Appl. No 36925/07, 29 January 2019.

[402] ibid para 249. The Grand Chamber did find (para 253) that the territorial state could refuse to waive criminal jurisdiction in favour of a non-state actor. A duty of recognition is procedural in nature and reflects a limited human rights jurisdiction that does not entail full state jurisdiction over the substantive acts that a rebel court decision relates to: ECtHR, *Hanan v Germany*, Judgment (Grand Chamber), Appl. No 4871/16, 16 February 2021, para 143.

[403] In relation to criminal law, it is worth recalling the conclusion reached in Chapter 3, Section III.C.iv.d that the prohibition of *ne bis in idem* generally does not obtain as between state and rebel jurisdictions. This is an is issue, for example, in relation to Islamic State fighters captured by

population under the authority of non-state armed groups to live in a legal black hole, a possibility that cannot amount to the fulfilment by the state of its obligation to ensure human rights to individuals under its jurisdiction.

Turning to recognition *post bellum* by the national state, the principles that have just been sketched will apply, only with greater effect and certainty. Whereas during the conflict the state had only a limited human rights jurisdiction over territory beyond its control, corresponding to mitigated obligations under human rights law, the restoration of full control over national territory at the close of hostilities means a return to a full-fledged duty to respect and ensure human rights. The end of the conflict also signals that the state's sovereign right to take measure to repress the insurgency will have abated significantly, removing an important foundation for the possible limitation of the recognition of rebel justice. This does not correspond to a requirement that the rebel administration of justice be given wholesale recognition by the government. No doubt, there are aspects of the operation of rebel justice that aimed first and foremost at advancing the insurgency. For example, the very common practice of non-state armed groups of making it a crime to collaborate with the government, not rarely punished with extreme prejudice, seems too closely tied to the pursuit of the insurgency to allow for any plausible argument in favour of recognition. On the other hand, the sanction of an ordinary crime like the punishment of sexual abuse of a child in a village far removed from active military operations seems, in itself, not so tied to the insurgency as to warrant non-recognition (leaving open further questions regarding the fairness of the proceedings and punishment).[404] At a minimum, a victorious state must establish guidelines or a procedure whereby acts of rebel courts can be assessed to determine which ought to be recognised and which ought to be labelled acts of rebellion. The Iraqi government has established the building blocks of such a process upon the liberation of areas that had previously been under the control of the Islamic State for long periods of time, sending mobile courts to camps for displaced persons to assess and validate legal documents issued by the Islamic State. Available reports suggest that mobile courts in Iraq are chiefly concerned with birth, death, and marriage certificates and divorces.[405]

the KRG and convicted under the Kurdish anti-terrorism statute: some have been released after completing their sentence and, upon returning to the zone of Iraq under government control, are being prosecuted again, this time under the Iraqi anti-terrorism statute. See Human Rights Watch, 'Iraq/Kurdistan Region: Risk of Double Trials for ISIS Ties—Lack of Coordination Between 2 Justice Systems' (2018) 9 ("I told them [Iraqi Officials] I had served a sentence in Erbil and had a paper ordering my release. They said they don't care, they don't recognize the Kurdistan Regional Government").

404 *Arteta* Case (n 367).

405 Isabel Coles, 'Iraq Slowly Untangles Islamic State's Bureaucratic Legacy' *Reuters* (20 January 2017), online: <https://www.reuters.com/article/mideast-crisis-iraq-islamic-state/iraq-slowly-untangles-islamic-states-bureaucratic-legacy-idUSKBN154218> accessed 14 August 2018; Claire Thomas, 'Mobile Courts Give Hope to Displaced Iraqis' *Al-Jazeera* (12 March 2017), online: <https://

On the other hand, the Iraqi government earlier had sought to halt all real estate transactions in Mosul and other zones formerly held by the Islamic State, reportedly as a reflection of the invalidity of all relevant Islamic State decisions: as "falsehood cannot be built on falsehood", the aim would be to restore the *status quo ante*.[406] Once more, a blanket approach denying that rebel courts existed or were pure banditry cannot be reconciled with states' obligations under international human rights and humanitarian law.[407]

V. Transversal Recognition by Other Armed Opposition Groups

The reality of contemporary armed conflicts is that they often involve many non-state armed groups, sometimes fighting alongside one another, other times fighting amongst themselves. If one or several of these groups engages in justice governance, there may be issues of transversal recognition of legal acts between armed groups. Two distinct patterns can be identified, one more proactive and collaborative amongst several non-state armed groups, the other ex post recognition by one group upon the defeat or disappearance of another non-state group.

In some situations of armed conflict in which no dominant rebel group has emerged to unify the insurgency, it has occurred that several different non-state armed groups have come together to establish judicial institutions to administer justice in an entire area. This has been especially prevalent in the conflict in Syria, in which there has been extreme fragmentation of the insurgency fighting the established government. Leaving aside the Islamic State, which has tended to operate on its own, many groups have formed collective governance agreements to set up courts and administer justice in a given area.

www.aljazeera.com/indepth/inpictures/2017/03/mobile-courts-give-hope-displaced-iraqis-170306123105478.html> accessed 14 August 2018.

406 Council of Representatives of Iraq, Resolution, 'Preventing All Property Transactions in Areas Under the Control of Terrorists', 8th Session, 1st Legislative Term, 1st Year, 21 August 2014. Information provided to the author by: Professor Ayad Yasin Husein, Salahaddin University-Erbil; Dr. Zahir Majeed Qadir, Legal advisor of the Prime Minister's Office, Kurdish Regional Government; Mrs. Ahlam Assad Muhammed, Jurist and Former members of the Council of Representatives (Parliament) of Iraq; Mr. Ayad Ismaeel Kakayee, Head of Bar Association of Kurdistan—Erbil Branch (16 August 2018).

407 There is some overlap with situations in which a government takes over from an illegal regime, as in Rhodesia or Namibia. In her insightful study of the issue, Yaël Ronen notes that, perhaps surprisingly, "by and large, post-transition regimes have opted for continuity in the law that had previously been enforced by the illegal regime (. . .), implicitly giving effect to acts carried out under that law": Ronen (n 329) 163. On the limitations, flowing from human rights law, to the new government's right to alter property rights granted by the prior illegal regime, see ibid 254–264.

In Eastern Ghouta, an opposition enclave near Damascus, seventeen distinct rebel factions came together in June 2014 to establish the Judiciary Council to help bring security and stability to this chaotic zone. The groups jointly appointed a panel of religious scholars, assisted by a number of practicing lawyers, to handle the day-to-day legal affairs of the community.[408] The Judiciary Council was part and parcel of the power relations among the groups, and there were some complaints that one group sought to dominate the Council and instrumentalise it. One unit of the Nusra Front that had initially supported the establishment of the Council withdrew after only one month to set up its own court; the head of the coalition behind the Council declared that no new court would be permitted in Eastern Ghouta, but the Nusra Front court was tolerated. For two years, the Judiciary Council provided stable and effective administration of justice in Eastern Ghouta, until infighting among participating groups eventually provoked its demise in 2016.[409] In Idlib province, also in 2014, six different non-state armed groups came together to establish an Islamic Court seated in the town of Binnish, sharing the responsibility for operating and staffing the court. Here again, the Nursa Front played troublemaker, starting to establish its own courts a few months after the creation of the Binnish Islamic Court. These courts had overlapping jurisdiction, leading to confusion among the civilian population, until the Binnish Islamic Court collapsed in 2016 further to a military takeover by one armed group.[410] Likewise in Aleppo, all groups save for the Nusra Front joined in the creation of a United Judicial Council that eventually operated twenty-four courts, each presided by one lawyer and two Islamic scholars. The Nusra Front objected to the fact that the United Judicial Council applied the Unified Arab Code, a codification of *Sharīʿa* adopted by the Arab League, and once more established its own competing system of *Sharīʿa* courts.[411] Increasing confrontations amongst the different non-state armed groups in Aleppo translated into competition in the administration of justice, eventually resulting in a multitude of competing courts vying for judicial authority.[412]

A final example comes from the region of Daraa, in southern Syria, where nearly 100 rebel factions came together to establish a House of Justice in 2014. Reportedly, basically all armed opposition groups in the area joined in, including

[408] Ekman (n 61) 100–102; Regine Schwab, 'Insurgent Courts in Civil Wars: The Three Pathways of (Trans) Formation in Today's Syria (2012–2017)' (2018) 29 Small Wars & Insurgencies 801, 808–809.

[409] Schwab (n 408) 802.

[410] Tirwada Abd al-Haqq, 'The Islamist Factions' Judicial System in Idlib' *Atlantic Council*, online: <http://www.atlanticcouncil.org/blogs/syriasource/the-islamist-factions-judicial-system-in-idlib> accessed 15 August 2018; Ekman (n 61) 91–100; Schwab (n 408) 810–811.

[411] Neil MacFarquhar, 'A Battle for Syria, One Court at a Time' *New York Times* (13 March 2013); Ivan Watson and Raja Razek, 'Rebel Court Fills Void amid Syrian Civil War' *CNN* (26 January 2013), online: <https://www.cnn.com/2013/01/25/world/meast/syria-rebel-court/index.html> accessed 15 August 2018.

[412] Ekman (n 61) 82–85; Schwab (n 408) 814.

the Nusra Front, save for small factions affiliated with the Islamic State which were excluded.[413] The court is staffed by a mix of jurists and religious scholars, totalling more than fifty judges, applying the Unified Arab Code, sitting in different trial chambers, an appellate court, and a court of cassation.[414] The House of Justice has a broad jurisdiction, covering civil, criminal, and administrative issues, as well as claims by civilians against members of non-state armed groups and disputes between different armed groups. The various armed groups handed over their detainees to the House of Justice so they could be tried and eventually jailed, using a procedure that was quite similar to that of the courts of the Syrian state.[415] Although there are significant challenges related to funding and security, participating non-state armed groups are said to honour the House of Justice's decisions, even for criminal allegations against their own members.[416]

In a different part of the world, in Myanmar/Burma, a significant number of non-state armed groups wield authority over portions of national territory. Not rarely, more than one group will be present in the same area, especially if the groups have a specific ethnic identity (as most have in that country) and there are nearby villages with distinct ethnic affiliations. Thus, the Karen National Union/Liberation Army and the Mon National Liberation Army recognise each other's jurisdiction over Karen and Mon villages respectively, and have rules to deal with cases from villages with mixed populations as well as inter-community proceedings.[417]

Although these examples do not reach the level of the direct recognition of judgments of the court of another armed opposition group, they do speak to the transversal engagement of armed groups in the rebel administration of justice.

[413] Marika Sosnowski, 'The Syrian Southern Front: Why It Offers Better Justice and Hope than Northern Front' *Syria Comment* (9 July 2015), online: <https://www.joshualandis.com/blog/the-syrian-southern-front-why-it-offers-better-justice-and-hope-than-northern-front-by-marika-sosnowski/> accessed 15 August 2018. Following the usual pattern, the Nusra Front later backed away from the House of Justice.

[414] Ekman (n 61) 87–88. See 'Southern Front—The Structure of the House of Justice in Houran's Court', Geneva Call, Their Words, online: <http://theirwords.org/media/transfer/doc/the_structure_of_house_of_justice_in_houran_s_courts-452d546fae88ede811b8396ad6d05f9a.docx> accessed 15 August 2018.

[415] Suha Maayeh and Phil Sands, 'Rebels' Court in Southern Syria an Alliance of Convenience against Assad' *The National* (13 December 2014), online: <https://www.thenational.ae/world/rebels-court-in-southern-syria-an-alliance-of-convenience-against-assad-1.268534> accessed 15 August 2018; Ekman (n 61) 88. See 'Southern Front—Rules of Procedures in the Courts of the House of Justice in Houran', Geneva Call, Their Words, online: <http://theirwords.org/media/transfer/doc/rules_of_procedures_in_the_courts_of_the_house_of_justice_in_houran-db71495264e650b4b326c4cc01f26131.pdf> accessed 15 August 2018.

[416] Sosnowski (n 413); Waleed a-Noufal and Tariq Adely, 'After Jailbreak and IED Attack, Opposition Court in Daraa Calls on Rebel Groups for More Security' *Syria Direct* (1 November 2017), online: <https://syriadirect.org/news/after-jailbreak-and-ied-attack-opposition-court-in-daraa-calls-on-rebel-groups-for-more-security-and-support/> accessed 15 August 2018.

[417] McCartan and Jolliffe (n 302) 32, 53.

A scenario that is closer to the recognition of the decision of a rebel court by the courts of a different non-state armed groups is the process established by the KRG to address legal issues of internally displaced persons on its territory. As the forces combating the Islamic State in northern Iraq gained ground, hundreds of thousands of civilians fled the hostilities and sought refuge in the KRI. Many of these displaced persons held legal documents that had been issued by Islamic State authorities, from 'repentance cards' that had to be shown at Islamic State checkpoints to certificates for births, deaths, marriages, or divorce. In a manner similar to the mobile courts established by the government of Iraq in some camps for displaced persons near Mosul, discussed in the previous subsection, the KRG provides for a judicial mechanism whereby legal documents emanating from the Islamic State can be recognised and used as a basis to issue corresponding documents under KRG law.[418] Thus a marriage, a divorce, or a will attested to by an Islamic State document may be recognised by KRG courts if the petition is supported by two witnesses. Kurdish authorities in the KRI are of course not a non-state armed group in the most common sense of the expression, but neither are they obviously a regular subnational entity, engaged as they are in an armed stalemate with the Iraqi government. Be that as it may, it suggests that once an armed opposition group administers justice in an area, it may be confronted with the need to consider the decisions issued by other non-state armed groups. The situation in Syria in which a multitude of courts linked to various factions active in the conflict operate in parallel may well have given rise to such situations. More field research is needed to explore this facet of the recognition of insurgent justice.

The question that then arises is whether non-state armed groups have an obligation under public international law to give transversal recognition to the administration of justice by other armed groups. As explored earlier in relation to state obligations, international humanitarian law and human rights suggest distinct approaches to answer that question. Turning to humanitarian law, the fact that the regime regulating belligerent occupation is inapplicable to situations of non-international armed conflict once again comes to limit the range of duties directly imposed on all parties to the conflict. An argument can be made that the obligation to respect humanitarian law recognised as binding on armed opposition groups implies a duty to ensure some degree of order and security in the areas they control. Once it is agreed that armed groups have a range of humanitarian obligations towards civilians, the remarks made in relation to the

[418] KRG courts apply the Iraqi Personal Status Law No 188 (1958). Birth and Death certificates can likewise be 'converted' by Kurdish courts under the Iraqi Birth and Death Registration Act No 148 (1971) and Art. 18 of the Iraqi Evidence Law No 107 (1979). Information provided to the author by Professor Ayad Yasin Husein, Salahaddin University-Erbil, and Dr. Zahir Majeed Qadir, Legal advisor of the Prime Minister's Office, Kurdish Regional Government.

protection of their interests embraced in the post–Civil War jurisprudence of the US Supreme Court and embodied in the legal rules applicable to belligerent occupation become equally applicable in relation to non-state armed groups. According to this approach, an authority cannot impose a blanket nullity on all acts of an actor on the basis of the illegitimacy of the latter's power. This seems all the more so in the case of an insurgent whose own power is equally without recognised foundation in international law. It would be, as the saying goes, the pot calling the kettle black. In seizing the language of justice and the rule of law, a rebel group implicitly make a general claim that it is legitimate for a non-state entity to do the same in a manner that cannot be dependent on how other actors will view the assertion of authority.

The admittedly thin normative basis of obligation to recognise at least some aspects of another armed opposition group's administration of justice under international humanitarian law is buttressed by complementary obligations under international human rights law. Even if we accept the general claim that non-state armed groups wielding power over a territory and population incur obligations under human rights law, it is not easy to map out the implications with regard to the recognition of another group's administration of justice.[419] As we saw in the previous subsection dealing with recognition by the territorial state, obligations under human rights treaties are owed to anyone under the jurisdiction of a state, with jurisdiction having a primarily territorial dimension. Because of their sovereign title over the entire national territory, states have been found to retain at least partial human rights jurisdiction even over national territory controlled by a non-state armed group. Full human rights jurisdiction is recovered as soon as the state regains control over national territory at the end of an armed conflict.

It is difficult to transpose this reasoning to human rights obligations of armed opposition groups, for two reasons. First, no compelling argument can be framed to justify that human rights treaties directly bind non-state actors, as the texts of the treaties themselves formulate a series of injunctions directed only at states.[420] Second, there isn't for non-state armed groups an equivalent to what is national territory for states, that is a geographic area tied to the very existence of the state. Unlike states, armed groups do not have any right to exercise authority over any given territory. International law merely reflects the *de facto* authority that the group has gained over a territory. As a result, human rights obligations for armed opposition groups are tied directly and exclusively to the individuals

[419] On the human rights obligations of non-state armed groups, see Chapter 3, Section III.A.

[420] For an attempt at such an argument, see Murray (n 346); and the critique by Marco Sassòli, 'Two Fascinating Questions: Are All Subjects of a Legal Order Bound by the Same Customary Law and Can Armed Groups Exist in the Absence of Armed Conflict?' *EJIL: Talk!* (4 November 2016), online: <https://www.ejiltalk.org/book-discussion-daragh-murrays-human-rights-obligations-of-non-state-armed-groups-3/> accessed 16 August 2018.

over which they are in a factual position to exert authority. As a result, it seems quite difficult to argue that an armed group has a duty under human rights to recognise the rebel administration of justice of other armed non-state actors in relation to individuals that are not under the authority of the group. If, however, the individual in question does come to be under the authority of that armed group, either because that person has travelled to the territory controlled by the group or because the latter took over an area that had previously been under the governance of another group, then human rights law does impose obligations on rebels vis-à-vis this individual. Whether these obligations are understood as corresponding to a duty to respect or protect human rights, the blanket refusal by a non-state armed group that does engage in the administration of justice to assess the validity of another group's justice practices or decisions would be a violation of international human rights law. Once again, the conflict in Syria provides a useful example: seeing the highly fluctuating situation on the ground in that country, in which a great many factions established their own courts independently or jointly, an understanding of the human rights obligations of a state as rigidly limited to its own doing would be tantamount to permanent legal insecurity for the civilian population. No doubt, there will be considerable legal insecurity in such a conflict to begin with, but it logically flows from a finding that non-state armed groups are bound by human rights law that they have a duty to mitigate legal insecurity to the extent possible in the circumstances. Thus, there seems to be no reason to refrain from imposing upon the institutions of the KRG in Iraq a duty to carefully consider legal documents issued by the Islamic State carried onto its territory by displaced persons. Even in a bloody civil war as in Syria, life is not chaos for all people in all places at all times; life does go on, and if armed opposition groups exercise public governance, it is reasonable to demand that they do so in ways that comply as much as possible with human rights.

******

Armed insurgency evokes images of fleeting guerrillas in remote locations, intermittently appearing in unexpected places to inflict violence and terror upon defenceless civilians, to then disappear again. In this image, recognition of the insurgency speaks to a fuzzy acknowledgment of the legitimacy of their fight. The Kurdish entities in Iraq, Syria, and Turkey have been, on the contrary, quite sedentary, with even the PKK seated in Mount Quandil for many years. That has allowed Kurdish groups to build governance institutions, including courts, that have had a degree of permanence and visibility. In this respect, Kurdish groups are similar to many other non-state armed groups examined elsewhere in this book. With permanence and visibility come the possibility of interaction with a fuller range of actors, including actors beyond the sphere of influence of the armed group to which the rebel courts belong. As it emerges from the analysis in this chapter, armed groups do not engage with outsiders only through their political or military leadership; instead, like states, armed groups that develop governance institutions become in that process disaggregated, with various constituent parts of a group able to engage outsiders. That engagement can take place with international institutions like the ICC, with the legal systems of other states, with legal institutions of the national state, and even with parallel components of other non-state armed groups. The combination of obligations imposed on all these actors under international humanitarian law and human rights, not to mention international criminal law, and the claims to justice advanced by individuals, suggest the ineluctability of engagement with, and in some cases recognition of, the rebel administration of justice. As many examples drawn from past cases studied in the chapter have shown, far from an esoteric curiosity, these questions are likely to become a more fully recognised aspect of any insurgency in which armed opposition groups engage in legal governance.

Conclusion

> [T]he dissolution of a state makes it possible to see everything that is implicit and taken for granted in the functioning of a state.
>
> — Pierre Bourdieu, *On the State* (Polity 2014) 359

Haisam Omar Sakhanh has been in detention in Sweden since 2016 for his brief but brutal brush with insurgent justice in the Syrian war, and he may remain behind bars for many more years. Whether or not one feels that this punishment is deserved and justified, Sakhanh does stand as the embodiment of how real, current, and important the question of the administration of justice by non-state armed groups in conflict zones is. Far from being a unique case, Sakhanh is a stand-in for thousands, if not tens of thousands, of individuals caught up in the rebel administration of justice, whether as judges, counsels, court administrators, enforcers, parties, convicts, or, more generally, persons affected by decisions of insurgent courts. This book is not, need it be said, an argument in favour of courts of armed groups on the supposed ground that rebel courts would be 'better' than state courts. As the case studies in this book have illustrated, the fairness and effectiveness of rebel courts, like that of state courts, is subject to enormous variation, depending on the context of the conflict in which they operate and on the aims pursued by a non-state armed group in becoming involved in the administration of justice. Rather, two central claims have been defended in this book: First, that the rebel administration of justice is not in essence a social evil, that in some circumstances it can correspond to a social good provided by armed insurgents, in situations in which the alternative is a degree of lawlessness. This is reflected in legal standards applicable to situations of armed conflict, whether international or non-international. Both international humanitarian law and international human rights law fairly can be interpreted as providing a legal foundation for the establishment of courts by non-state armed groups. This interpretation reflects an emphasis on the humanitarian protection of the fundamental interests of victims of war, whether civilians or persons hors-de-combat, rather than giving necessary primacy to the sovereignty of the state. Second is the corollary claim that the rebel administration of justice is a common practice that has been left largely unexamined and, as a result, unregulated, in an

Rebel Courts. René Provost, Oxford University Press. © Oxford University Press 2021.
DOI: 10.1093/oso/9780190912222.003.0006

unjustifiable manner. The analysis of the conditions for the regular constitution of courts, for their independence and impartiality, for the valid exercise of their jurisdiction, and for the conduct of a fair trial, all combine to unambiguously attest to the possibility of regulating the rebel administration of justice with existing and applicable standards of international law. Whether one applauds or laments the work of rebel courts, they are a reality of war that produces significant and enduring effects in fact and in law, in the theatre of war and well beyond, during conflicts and well after, among belligerents and for others too. Recognised and applicable standards of public international law must be used to nudge this practice towards as close an approximation of justice as can be achieved in such challenging circumstances.

Adam Baczko refers to the passage from Pierre Bourdieu cited previously to suggest that wars are moments in which are unveiled some of the implicit assumptions that underpin the functioning of the state.[1] A sustained analysis of the rebel administration of justice in the context of armed conflicts speaks to the idea of sovereignty and the necessity of an exclusive link posited between the state and order and justice. Rebel governance in the field of justice is another significant way in which state and non-state powers compete to claim legitimate authority over a population and territory. It draws attention away from the dominant legal focus on the conduct of hostilities and its impact on combatants and civilians to underscore the importance of the regulation of everyday social relations, even in conflict zones. The partial or total dissolution of the state in times of war and the emergence of rebel courts also speak to the nature of law and suggest a different kind of legal pluralism. Most often, an insistence on the reality of multiple, overlapping, and interacting legal regimes carries an acknowledgment, however reluctant, that the state and its normativity remain an influential and often dominant reality.[2] In this view, informal legal normativity operates in the shadow of state law, as a reflection of the monopoly on the use of violence claimed by the state. In times of war, that monopoly stands contested and even denied in places in which the rebel administration of justice emerges. The interplay of insurgent justice and state justice in conflict zones thus appears as a unique laboratory in which to study the interaction of legal normativity that has broken free of the hold of state law. One aspect of normative dynamics of law revealed in this book is that official and rebel laws do clash and compete but also can complement and even mutually support each other. It would be seriously misleading to suggest that a map of military dominance corresponds to a map of juridical effectiveness, with lines neatly drawn.

[1] Adam Baczko, 'Judging in the Midst of Civil War' (2013) 104 Politix 25, 26.

[2] See, e.g., Jeremy Webber, 'Legal Pluralism and Human Agency' (2006) 44 Osgoode Hall Law Journal 167, 189–190.

If the dissolution of the state during war makes visible the implicit foundations of state authority, then the reconstitution of the state at the end of war is a moment of concealment. The post-conflict practice of states in relation to the rebel administration of justice mirrors the general inattention to the phenomenon during conflicts. It is assumed by governments that the disappearance of the non-state armed group and the reassertion of full legal sovereignty on the part of the state will simply wash away any remnants of rebel justice. The more attentive analysis of this form of insurgent governance offered in this book indicates that this is, in many situations, an arbitrary stance that results in injustice. Any sophisticated approach to transitional justice should take into consideration the lingering effects of the rebel administration of justice, if it was present in a given conflict.[3] Part of the challenge is that armed groups tend to be successful in establishing their own court system in places in which the state was previously absent or at least ineffective. This is echoed in repeated comments in many conflicts that people often see rebel courts as faster, cheaper, less corrupt, and more effective than state courts. When the rebel courts disappear at the end of conflict, there is a good chance that no state court will step into the breach, or that if it does, it will suffer from the same defects that made rebel justice seem comparatively effective in the first place. Colombian poet William Ospina wrote in 2016, when peace seemed to be at hand in that country, that "wars are usually presented as temporary suspensions of normality . . . perhaps in Colombia it is not quite a question of returning to a lost normality but of finally inventing an unknown normality".[4] The onset of peace is always a constitutional moment, whether formally so or not, and legal security in post-conflict transition can only be achieved by taking rebel justice as a social fact that obtained in a given place for a period of time. Post-conflict justice can only be achieved by braiding together the wartime reality of insurgent and state justice with the aspiration of building a better society.

Lon Fuller once described lawyers as 'architects of social structures'.[5] What he meant by that was that jurists have a significant role to play in constructing the framework of social relations, which is not to claim that they have some sort of stranglehold over the process whereby social structures are created. Going beyond Fuller, what is striking in the metaphor is how the role of the architect marries an attentiveness to functionality with an aspiration to beauty. Law

[3] Laura Grenfell, *Promoting the Rule of Law in Post-Conflict States* (Cambridge University Press 2013) 7–8.

[4] William Ospina, 'El gran relato' *El Espectador* (9 July 2016), online: <https://www.elespectador.com/noticias/cultura/el-gran-relato/> accessed 5 October 2020 ('Las guerras suelen ser suspensiones transitorias de la normalidad . . . Tal vez en Colombia no se trata ya de volver a una normalidad perdida sino de inventar por fin una normalidad desconocida').

[5] Lon Fuller, 'The Lawyer as an Architect of Social Structures' in Kenneth Winston (ed), *The Principles of Social Order* (Hart Publishing 2001).

stands not only as a system of rules but also as a register of meanings, a claim of identities, and a manifesto of aspirations. In failing to grapple hands-on with the phenomenon of the rebel administration of justice, international lawyers have gravely failed communities affected by war. This book is a call to arms for lawyers to attend to the role of law in understanding and regulating such a practice, to address insurgent justice in all that it stands for, as a system of rules, a register of meanings, a claim of identities, and a manifesto of aspirations. There is much to do.

Index

Tables and figures are indicated by *t* and *f* following the page number

Achutan v. Malawi, 324
Act for the Protection of Tamil Eelam Children (Tamileelam Child Protection Act 2006), 243–44, 255
Additional Protocol I (Protocol I), 350, 351
  Article 1(1), 156
  Article 1(4), 74–75, 143, 155, 174n383
  Article 43(2), 147, 288, 335
  Article 75, 144, 339
  Article 75(1), 170
  Article 75(4), 150, 152, 196, 203, 210, 289, 290, 299, 301–2, 317, 321, 323, 347, 350
    "regularly constituted courts" and, 150, 152, 196, 203, 207, 310
  Article 75(4)(b), 341
  Article 75(4)(d), 318
  Article 75(4)(g), 329
  Article 75(4)(h), 338, 339
  Article 75(4)(i), 337
  Article 86(1), 155
  Article 96(3), 143, 250
  due process and, 289
  human rights treaties and, 293
  self-incrimination and, 347
Additional Protocol II (Protocol II), 350, 351
  Article 1, 7
  Article 3, 79, 152n302
  Article 4, 293
  Article 4(2), 341
  Article 4(3)(a), 275
  Article 6, 169–71, 178, 179, 213, 309, 310
    Common Article 3 and, 169–71, 177, 179
    due process guarantees in, 290, 294, 299, 301, 318, 323
    ICCPR and, 302, 310
    and judicial independence and impartiality, 213, 310
    "regularly constituted courts" and, 215–16
    and the right and means of defence, 315, 322–24, 327–28
    and right to appeal, 350
    and right to be informed promptly of charges, 315, 316
  Article 6(1), 169, 177–78
  Article 6(2), 169, 189–90, 192, 203, 249, 309, 315, 321, 322
    ICCPR and, 301, 317, 343
    and judicial independence and impartiality, 150, 181, 202–3, 206–7, 310
    nullum crimen sine lege and, 274
    principle of legality and, 340, 343
    "regularly constituted courts" and, 153, 167, 180–81, 202–3, 310
  Article 6(2)(b), individual penal responsibility, and, 341
  Article 6(2)(d), 318
  Article 6(2)(f), 347
  Article 6(3), 350
  Article 6(5), 270
  de facto authority and, 275, 282
  due process and, 289
  human rights treaties and, 293
  "regularly constituted courts" and, 203, 204, 215, 216
  self-incrimination and, 347
Afghan judges, 133. *See also* Taliban judges
Afghanistan. *See also* Kabul; Taliban
  corruption, 119–20, 125–27, 135, 138–40, 313–14
  US invasion of, 121, 235
African Charter of Human and Peoples' Rights, 301n384, 326
  Article 7, 321n470, 332, 338, 341, 351
African Commission on Human and Peoples' Rights, 161, 301n384, 324, 326, 338, 351
African Court of Justice and Human Rights, 285, 386, 395, 404
agents of justice, 96–97
Aguilera Peña, Mario, 40–41, 45–46, 49
Ahorugeze v. Sweden, 306
Al-Hassan, Prosecutor v, 176–78, 205, 213, 312
Al-Saadoon v. UK, 431
Al-Senussi, Prosecutor v, 305, 306, 396

Al-Skeini v. UK, 160
Al-Werfalli, Prosecutor v, 387–88, 398
Aleppo, Syria, 111, 115n104, 446
aliocracy vs. rebelocracy, 8
Allott, Philip, 58
alternative justice mechanisms, 186, 404, 406–8, 410. *See also gacaca* courts; restorative justice model
American Civil War, 436–37
American Convention on Human Rights, 69, 326, 332
  Article 8, 309, 328, 330n511, 338, 350
  Article 27, 67, 298, 300, 341
amnesty, 270
Amnesty International, 165, 201
Annan, Kofi, 85
anonymous judges, 335. *See also* judges: faceless
anti-terrorism, 63, 350, 380–81, 432
"Anti-Terrorism courts," 369–70
appellate courts/courts of appeal, 47, 128–30, 233–34, 350–53, 369. *See also specific courts*
  LTTE, 231, 233–35, 238
Arai-Takahashi, Yukata, 317, 352
Arar, Maher, 432n359
Arendt, Hannah, 4–5, 410
Arjona, Ana, 7–8, 35–36, 39, 346
armed conflicts, legal categories of, 141–44
armed groups. *See* rebels
armed non-state actors. *See* rebels
armed opposition groups. *See* rebels
Armenia, 412, 413
Articles of War, 197
Articles on State Responsibility (Draft Articles on the Responsibility of States for Internationally Wrongful Acts), 98, 292, 399–403
Artsakh. *See* Nagorno-Karabakh Republic
Assad, Bashar al-, 1
Atala Riffo v Chile, 312
audi alteram partem ("listen to the other side"), 84, 323
authority, 8–9
Autodefensa agraria, 41
Autodefensas campesinas, 32, 41
Autodefensas unidas de Colombia (AUC), 31, 34, 286
Autonomous Administration of North and East Syria. *See* Rojava

Baczko, Adam, 123n154, 133n226, 454
Baghdad, 376–79
Baghdadi, Abu Bakr al-, 104–5, 109
Balekjian, W. H., 94
Bandaranaike, Sirimavo, 220, 221
Bank of Tamileelam, 285
Barakat, Kanan, 371
Barzani, Masoud, 374, 375n112, 380, 381n158
Battle of Kirkuk (2017), 375, 376, 420
Belgium v Senegal, 97
Bemba, Jean-Pierre, 312
Bemba, Prosecutor v, 83, 165, 166, 201, 207, 282
Bentham, Jeremy, 333
Benvenisti, Eyal, 71, 258
Beuze v Belgium, 308–9
Bingham, Tom (Baron Bingham of Cornhill), 59
Binnish Islamic Court, 446
Black July, 222
Blackstone, William, 184, 185
Bond, James, 180
Bosnia and Herzegovina v Serbia and Montenegro (*Bosnian Genocide* case), 399
Bourdieu, Pierre, 453, 454
Britain, 195, 423, 431, 435. *See also* English common law; United Kingdom
Bureau of Justice and Grievances (ISIS), 107–8

capital punishment. *See* executions
Ceasefire Agreement of 2002 (Sri Lanka), 224
centralism, 11, 62
Chanock, Martin, 62
Charter of the Social Contract. *See* Social Contract
Charter of the United Nations, 424
Chavakachcheri District Court, 248, 436
Child Protection Act (LTTE), 243–44. *See also* Children Protection Act
child rights abuses, 243. *See also* education of children
child sexual abuse, 255–56, 293
  trials and punishments for, 54–55, 109, 173–74, 294, 434
child soldiers, 173, 243, 244
Children Protection Act (LTTE Children Act), 255–56, 277. *See also* Child Protection Act
China, 394, 422
Chiragov v. Armenia, 412–13
chronotopes of law, 194
civil cases, 294, 309, 379–80. *See also* civil courts
  judges for, 132, 234
  LTTE and, 230, 231, 238, 327
  right to present a full defence in, 329
  in Taliban courts, 125, 129, 132
  types of, 247

Civil Code of Colombia, 49
civil courts, 108, 200, 201, 230, 234, 368. *See also* civil cases
civil law jurisdiction, 234, 274–81
civil war, 4, 7, 12, 75, 347, 441
Clark, Phil, 408
Coalition Provisional Authority (Iraq), 259n233, 375, 402
Code of Conduct for the Mujahedin, 349
Colombia, rebel justice in, 30. *See also* *Autodefensas unidas de Colombia*; FARC
Colombian Communist Party, 32, 40
Colombian conflict (civil war), 31–33, 79
  1990s, 33
  FARC governance during, 37, 40, 53 (*see also* FARC governance)
  origins, 31
  paramilitary groups in, 33–34
  rebel governance during, 346
Colombian Constitution of 1991, 33, 50
Colombian Supreme Court, 434–35
combatant, concept of, 147
comités de conciliación (conciliation committees, Colombia), 37, 50, 54
Committee Against Torture (UN), 348
Common Article 1 (Geneva Conventions), 156, 158, 273, 282, 426
Common Article 3 relating to non-international armed conflict (Geneva Conventions), 153, 157, 167–70, 177, 181, 182, 202, 203, 275, 347
  Article 3(1)(d), 149–50, 152
  Elements of Crimes under Rome Statute and, 204, 206, 309–10, 322
  equality of belligerents and, 145–47, 149
  Hamdan v Rumsfeld and, 181, 301
  ICRC and, 168, 173, 192, 198, 203
  judicial guarantees under, 181, 206, 299, 301, 322, 344, 347
  overview, 167
  and the principle of legality, 344
  procedural guarantees and, 289–93
  Protocol I and, 152, 301, 310, 341
  Protocol II and, 146, 147, 149, 153, 157, 167–71, 177, 179, 202–7, 213, 215–16, 275, 291, 293, 299, 301, 309–10, 322, 341
  "regularly constituted courts" and, 149–50, 152, 153, 167–69, 180–83, 195, 196, 198, 199, 202–5, 215–16, 270, 289, 291, 310
  rightness as fairness and, 203–6
  Rome Statute and, 204, 206, 291
  treaty obligations and, 157
  violations of, 2, 322
common law of war, 197, 198
Communist Party of Nepal-Maoist (CPN-M), 281–82
  Public Legal Code 2060 (CPN-M Penal Code), 261–66, 269
complementarity, 409–10, 413. *See also* insurgent complementarity
  Al-Werfalli case and, 387
  ICC and, 307, 385, 387, 388, 390, 391, 404, 409
  principle of, 186, 354, 388, 390–92, 395n218 (*see also* Rome Statute of ICC: complementarity and)
    due process requirements and, 305
  Rome Statute and, 186, 306–7, 354, 385, 392, 395, 396, 398, 401, 404, 406, 407, 426
conciliation committees (*comités de conciliación*, Colombia), 37, 50, 54
conciliation/mediation boards (*inakkai sabha*, Sri Lanka), 229
Confederate Congress, 436
Confederate District Courts, 436–38
Confederate States of America, 436
  de facto authority and, 438–40
Constitution of Iraq. *See* Federal Constitution of Iraq
Constitution of Sri Lanka, 228. *See also* Sri Lankan Constitution of 1972
  minority rights and, 230
Constitution of the Autonomous Administration of North and East Syria. *See* Social Contract
control of territory. *See* territorial control
Convention on the Rights of Persons with Disabilities (UN), 277
cooperation, levels of, 5
corporations, 284–86
corruption, 32, 378–79
  in Afghanistan, 119–20, 125–27, 135, 138–40, 313–14
  efforts to combat, 49, 139, 384
  Islamic State and, 108–9, 112n76, 117
  prevalence, 108, 247, 313–14, 455
counter-terrorism. *See* anti-terrorism
Court of Appeal of Sri Lanka, 233, 234, 352
court(s). *See also specific topics*
  compared with cathedrals, 192–95
  idea of a, 181–84 (*see also* "regularly constituted courts")
  what constitutes a, 180–83, 202
courts-martial, 1–2, 174, 201, 207, 212, 302, 303, 312. *See also Bemba, Prosecutor v*
  FARC and, 44–46, 319–20

courts-martial (*cont.*)
of FARC fighters, 43, 44, 46, 55, 266, 353
independence, 208
PKK, 360
presumption of innocence and, 320
Taliban justice and, 213
Cover, Robert M., 14, 16, 84, 250, 257
Criddle, Evan, 64, 69
crimes. *See also hudūd* crimes; sex crimes; *specific topics*
categories of punishable, 112n76, 369
against international law, 271–74
punishable by execution, 41, 45–46, 111, 112, 235, 265–69, 361, 381 (*see also* rape)
customs of war. *See* international humanitarian law (IHL)/law of armed conflict; Islamic laws of war; *layeha*
Cyprus v Turkey, 425, 443

Da'esh. *See* Islamic State
Damšaka, Mirjan, 307
Daraa, 446
Darcy, Shane, 258–59, 265–67
Davila, Arteta, 434–35
de facto authority, 89, 282, 292, 295, 423, 424
and the Confederacy, 438–40
vs. *de jure* authority, 94, 165
European Court of Human Rights and, 160, 161, 425
Georgia, South Ossetia, and, 386, 387, 442–43
International Court of Justice (ICJ) and, 399–401
international law and, 449
Protocol II and, 275, 282
de facto autonomy of KRI, 374–76, 378, 382
de facto control, 174–75, 292
de facto government, 93, 94, 100
FARC as, 36, 53
death penalty. *See* executions
death squads. *See Muerte a secuestradores*
democratic autonomy, 366
democratic confederalism, 366, 373
democratic federal law, 261, 362, 363, 366
Democratic Republic of Congo (DRC), 158, 194. *See also Mouvement de libération du Congo*
Democratic Union Party. *See* PYD
Denning, Tom (Baron Denning), 423
derecho al juez natural (right to the natural judge), 211
derogability, 67–69, 76. *See also* non-derogable rights
of due process guarantees, 67, 298–301, 317, 333, 347, 352
derogation, 69, 70
constraints on, 68, 69
justifications for, 68–69, 298 (*see also* emergency)
derogation clause, 67
discretionary punishments (*ta'zir*), 112
Divisional Court of England and Wales, 186, 405–6
Diwan al- Hisba, 108
Doswald-Beck, Louise, 316
double jeopardy. *See ne bis in idem*
Draft Articles on the Responsibility of States for Internationally Wrongful Acts (Articles on State Responsibility), 98, 292, 399–403
Drumbl, Mark A., 410n274
due process
in conflict zones, 297–308
before non-state courts, 303–8
in rebel court, 289–90
sources of applicable procedural obligations for non-state armed groups, 290–97
in war and peace, 298–303
due process guarantees, 305
in Article 6 of Protocol II, 290, 294, 299, 301, 318, 323
derogability, 67, 298–301, 317, 333, 347, 352
states of emergency and, 67, 210, 299, 317, 318, 322, 332, 347
Duff, Robin Antony, 95–96

East Germany/German Democratic Republic, 189
Eastern Ghouta (Syria), 446
education of children, 275–77
Eelam War I (Sri Lanka), 222
Eelam War II (Sri Lanka), 223–24
Eelam War III (Sri Lanka), 224
Eelam War IV (Sri Lanka), 224
effectivité, principle of, 92–94, 250–51, 292, 296
Ejército de Liberación Nacional (ELN), 31, 41, 82
El Salvador. *See* Salvadoran Civil War
El Zeidy, Mohamed M., 393, 398
ELN (*Ejército de Liberación Nacional*), 31, 41, 82
emergency, states of
derogation and, 67–70, 298, 347, 352
due process guarantees and, 67, 210, 299, 317, 318, 322, 332, 347
and human rights conventions and treaties, 67, 68, 70, 298, 317, 322, 341

Emmerson, Ben, 296–97
empiricism vs. legal formalism, 23
enforcement discretion. *See* prosecutorial discretion
England. *See* Britain; Divisional Court of England and Wales; United Kingdom
English common law, 237–38
equality
  of belligerents, 144–49
  gender, 148, 236, 366 (*see also* women)
Erbil (Iraq), 16, 18, 373, 378–79
espionage, 266–67. *See also sapos*
  capital punishment for, 139, 266–68
État de droit, 58, 60, 87
European Convention on Human Rights, 67, 73, 202, 298, 430, 432
  Article 6, 306, 308–9, 329, 332, 406
  Article 7(2), 345
  extradition and, 306
  gacaca courts and, 406
  legal assistance and, 326
  property rights guarantee, 412
  Protocol 7, 351
  "regularly constituted courts" and, 202
  right against self-incrimination and, 347
  right to public judgment and, 337–38
European Court of Human Rights (ECHR/ ECtHR), 67, 250, 311, 320, 346, 401, 412
  Al-Senussi and, 306
  Article 8, 443
  Chiragov v. Armenia, 412–13
  Cyprus v Turkey, 425, 443
  de facto authority and, 160, 161, 425
  doctrine of margin of appreciation and, 69–70
  extradition and, 431
  Güzelyurtlu v Cyprus and Turkey, 443
  Ilascu v. Moldova and Russia, 202
  International Criminal Court (ICC) and, 306
  jurisdiction and, 160, 161, 402, 425, 429–31, 442
  Mitrovic v. Serbia, 430
  "Namibia principle" invoked by, 414, 425
  "overall effective control" and, 399, 400
  right against self-incrimination and, 347
  right to a fair trial and, 308
  Soering v UK, 282, 305, 431
  and widening of extraterritorial application of human rights, 73
European Union (EU) law, 363
execution squads, participation in, 415, 430
executions, 82, 381, 434. *See also under* Sakhanh, Haisam Omar
  Common Article 3 and, 149, 167–68, 202
  crimes punishable by execution, 41, 45–46, 111, 112, 235, 265–69, 361, 381 (*see also under* rape)
  by ELN, 41, 82
  by FARC, 41, 42, 45–46, 54, 56, 78, 82, 286
  in France during liberation, 142
  International Criminal Court (ICC) and, 409
  by Islamic State, 17, 109–12, 115, 269
  LTTE and, 235, 247, 263, 265
  PKK and, 361
  public, 17, 134
  reprisal, 181
  Sharīʿa and, 110, 115, 134
  of spies, 139, 265–68
  by Taliban, 134, 139, 151, 265–68
  without due process, 204 (*see also* summary executions)
  World War II and, 142, 168, 181
exemplary justice, 40–41
exile, 56

faceless judges (*'jueces sin rostro'*), 334–35
fair trial
  military justice and, 302
  right to a, 305, 307, 352, 372–73 (*see also* fair trial guarantees before rebel courts)
    derogability in wartime, 299–301
    European Convention on Human Rights and, 306
    gacaca courts and, 406
    Islamic State and, 412
    legal pluralism and, 307n413
    PYD justice system and, 372
  what constitutes a, 308
    markers of, 308–9
fair trial guarantees before rebel courts, 308–10. *See also* fair trial
  judicial independence and impartiality, 310–14
  necessary rights and means of defence, 321–23 (*see also nullum crimen sine lege*)
    individual criminal responsibility, 341–42
    ne bis in idem, 338–41
    right to a public trial, 332–38
    right to counsel, 323–29
    right to judicial and other remedies, 350–53
    right to present a full defence, 329–32
    self-incrimination, 347–50
  presumption of innocence, 318–21
  right to be informed promptly of the charges, 315–18

Fall, Bernard, 1, 355
FARC (Revolutionary Armed Forces of Colombia), 21–23, 56, 79, 82, 277, 325
  Colombian government and, 22, 34, 36, 42, 71
    peace talks and negotiations, 33, 34
  corruption, 32
  courts-martial and, 44–46, 55, 266, 319–20, 353
  economics, 32, 38, 55–56
  High Command (*Estado Mayor*), 34, 45, 47
  history, 32–40 (*see also* FARC justice: evolution of)
  Indigenous people and, 39–40, 50
  Juntas Acción Comunal (JAC) and, 37–38, 42, 48, 50, 52, 53
  membership, 29, 33
  militias, 33, 35
  overview and nature of, 29–30
  politics and, 32
  popular/civilian resistance to, 32–33, 39, 71
  popular/civilian support for, 32, 56, 71
  rape and, 40, 41, 54, 56
  rules and discipline, 38, 40, 48–50, 56, 315 (*see also* FARC justice)
    Manual de convivencia ciudadana (manual for living together), 48, 264, 278, 280, 346
  Statute and Regulations, 43–47, 85
    Disciplinary Regulations, 43, 162, 353
FARC cadres, 435
FARC commanders, 38, 50, 84, 185, 266, 326
FARC courts, 30, 55, 56, 79n227, 187, 314, 435. *See also under* courts-martial
  trials, 46, 54
FARC fighters, 314
  courts-martial of, 43, 44, 46, 55, 266, 353
  criminal sentences imposed on, 44–45, 419 (*see also* FARC justice: executions)
  number of, 33
FARC governance (structure), 34–40, 77–78, 94
  during Colombian conflict (civil war), 37, 40, 53
FARC justice, 81–84, 90, 99–100, 180, 260, 261, 265–66, 313. *See also* FARC; FARC courts
  civilian justice, 47–56
  diversity of approaches, 50
  evolution of, 40–41
    exemplary justice (1964–1976), 41
    retaliatory justice (1976–1985), 41–42
    local empowerment justice (1985–2003), 42
  executions, 41, 42, 45–46, 54, 56, 78, 82, 286
  Human Rights Watch's critique of, 54–55
  military justice, 43–47 (*see also under* courts-martial)
fatwahs, 111, 114
Federal Constitution of Iraq, 375–76, 378, 380
  Kurdish Region of Iraq (KRI) and, 375–78, 402
  Kurdish Regional Government (KRG) and, 380, 384, 420
Federal Supreme Court of Iraq, 378, 420
financial penalties, 55–56
fiqh
  defined, 110n64
  Sharīʿa and, 110n64, 112n77
First Eelam War (Sri Lanka), 222
FMLN (Farabundo Martí National Liberation Front), 307, 326, 327
  code of document, 188, 271
  ONUSAL and, 184, 191
  Salvadoran Civil War and, 144, 191, 271–72, 325
FMLN courts, 325, 344–45
forced confessions, 349–50
forced labour, 41–43
formalism, 22, 23, 224
Fortin, Katharine, 178, 295
Fourth Eelam War (Sri Lanka), 224
Fourth Geneva Convention, 258
  Article 54, 176
  Article 64, 73, 176, 259, 267
  Article 66, 176, 196, 209
  Article 68, 267
  Article 74, 332
  Article 105, 324
Fox-Decent, Evan, 64, 69
fragmented rule of law, 12, 57–66
France, 387, 416, 417, 432, 433. *See also* French government
  liberation of, 142
  PYD and, 416–17, 431–33
Franco-Italian Conciliation Commission, 92, 93
Free Syrian Army (FSA), 1, 108
  courts and tribunals, 1, 102, 260, 272, 287, 288, 344, 415
Free Syrian Army Judicial Council, 1
freedoms, Islamic State (ISIL) and, 297
French courts, 417, 422
French government, 142, 286, 416, 417, 431–32. *See also* France
French Islamic State members, 286–87, 417, 431
French law, 61, 371, 379

French military, 252
"fruit of the poisonous tree" doctrine, 348–49
Fuerzas Armadas Revolucionarias de Colombia-Ejército del Pueblo. See FARC
Fuller, Lon, 12–13, 59, 455
functional immunity, 409, 430. *See also under* Sakhanh, Haisam Omar

gacaca courts, 186, 303n397, 324, 405–6
gacaca judges, 186, 214, 313
Gaddafi, Prosecutor v, 396–97
Gaggioli, Gloria, 336
Garcia v. Peru, 342
Geertz, Clifford, 13, 19, 20
gender equality, 148, 236, 366. *See also* women
Geneva Call Deeds of Commitment, 100, 360, 382
Geneva Convention III. *See* Third Geneva Convention
Geneva Convention IV. *See* Fourth Geneva Convention
Geneva Conventions. *See also* Common Article 3 relating to non-international armed conflict
  Common Article 1, 156, 158, 273, 282, 426
  High Contracting Parties to, 143, 155, 156, 426
  Polisario Front and, 75, 143, 155, 291
  positive law (*qawanīn wad'īyya*) and, 289, 291
  prisoners of war and, 168, 209, 290, 303, 321, 324, 328, 332, 341–42, 350–51, 369, 419
genocide, 399
  defined, 410n275
  Rwandan, 313, 405
Georgia, 386, 398, 399, 401, 442–43
German Democratic Republic/East Germany, 189
Germany, 93, 181, 182, 196–97
governmentality, 9
Green, Les, 91, 92
Grenfell, Laura, 60, 65
guerilla justice, phases in the history of, 40–42
Guggenheim, Paul, 93
Guidice, Michael, 96
Guruparan, Kumaravadivel, 279

hadith
  Islamic State (ISIS) and, 110, 112
  Taliban courts and, 132, 133
Hague Convention IV of 1907, 258
Hague Regulation (Laws and Customs of War on Land, Annex to the Hague Convention IV of 1907)
  Article 30, 267
  Article 42, 72
  Article 43, 72, 175, 176, 258–59, 276, 281
Hamdan v Rumsfeld, 197, 199, 301
  "regularly constituted courts" and, 181, 197, 199
Hanafi jurisprudence, 120, 132–33, 139
Hand, Learned, 252
Havana Accord, 34
Herbert, Henry (4th Earl of Carnarvon), 195
Hessler, Kristen, 96–97
Hickman v. Jones, 438–39
High Command Case, 182
High Contracting Parties to the Geneva Conventions, 143, 155, 156, 426
High Court of South Africa, 421
Hirkuki, Husam, 372
Hobbes, Thomas, 89
Hobbesian state of nature, 90
Holder v. Humanitarian Law, 427–28
Hopkins v. Mexico, 440
Horn v. Lockhart, 439–40
Houran House of Justice, 208, 446–47
House of Lords (UK), 94, 185
Huang, Reyko, 7
hudūd crimes, 112, 134, 345
  punishable by death, 112
  punishments for, 110–12
Human Rights Watch, 54–55, 367–73
hybrid governance, 80
hybrid model of justice, 66

ICC. *See* International Criminal Court
ignorance of the law is no excuse (*ignorantia juris non excusat*), 346
Ilascu v. Moldova and Russia, 160, 161, 202, 442
immunity, state. *See* "NM Cherry Blossom" case
immunity from prosecution. *See also* functional immunity
  combatants and, 147
  of foreign states, 421
  paramilitaries and, 34
impartiality, 313
India, 223
Indian Peacekeeping Force (in Sri Lanka), 223, 226
Indigenous people, 39–40, 50, 279, 307n413
insurgent complementarity. *See also* complementarity
  conceptual approach, 398–409
  contextual approach, 388–91
  textual approach, 392
    Article 17(1)(a) and (b)--"A State which Has Jurisdiction over It," 392–96
    Article 17(1)(c): *ne bis in idem*, 396–98

insurgents. *See* rebels
Inter-American Court of Human Rights, 299, 311, 312, 331, 342, 430, 432. *See also Mapuche Case*; *Velasquez Rodriguez v Honduras*
on evidence obtained by coercion, 348
on faceless judges, 334
on jurisdiction, 430
on presumption of innocence, 318
on principle of correlation, 316–17
and the right to appeal, 351
on torture and inhumane treatments, 347–48
interlegality, 13, 14
International Committee of the Red Cross (ICRC), 157, 165, 168, 174–75, 272, 283, 295, 317, 318, 336
access to Kabul prisons, 419
Commentary to Geneva Conventions, 143, 170, 173, 181, 191, 196, 198, 204, 209, 282, 328n507, 350–51
Common Article 1 and, 156
Common Article 3 and, 168, 173, 181, 192, 198, 203, 204
draft of Article 6(2)(c), 189
initial draft of Geneva Conventions, 168
Protocol II and, 146, 192, 202, 282, 309, 332n528, 338, 350
"regularly constituted courts" and, 152–53, 196, 198, 203–5
and right to a public trial, 332–33
and right to appeal, 350–52
and Soviet soldiers detained in Afghanistan, 418–19
study of customary humanitarian law, 309, 332–33, 338, 341, 352
Rule 100, 152–53, 204, 309, 338
war crimes (prosecution) and, 155, 283
International Court of Justice (ICJ), 67, 158, 251, 399–402, 424
Advisory Opinion on the Construction of a Wall in the Palestinian Territory, 158, 426–27
de facto authority and, 399–401
Geneva Conventions and, 426–27
South West Africa Advisory Opinion, 425
international courts. *See* international tribunals and rebel courts
International Covenant on Civil and Political Rights (ICCPR), 67, 69, 200, 298, 300, 323, 326
Article 2, 68
Article 4, 67, 68
Article 14, 199, 207, 289, 301, 302, 309, 310, 315, 317, 323, 329, 330, 332, 337, 338, 347
Article 15, 189, 289, 302, 343, 345
International Criminal Court (ICC), 408. *See also Al-Hassan*; *Bemba*; Rome Statute of ICC
Appeals Chamber, 305, 396–97, 407n265
complementarity and, 307, 385, 387, 388, 390, 391, 404, 409
due process guarantees and, 305
Georgia and, 386, 401
ICTY "effective control" test and, 400
Islamic State and, 403
Jann Kleffner and, 392, 393, 397
jurisdiction, 385–94, 409, 410
ne bis in idem (double jeopardy) and, 252n206, 396–98
Pre-Trial Chamber, 165, 176–78, 205, 213, 312, 386–88, 394, 398, 399, 401, 407
Prosecutor v Al-Senussi and, 305, 306, 396
Prosecutor v Al-Werfalli and, 387–88, 398
Prosecutor v Ntaganda and, 173, 176
questions related to the interface between rebel courts and, 389
recognition of rebel administration of justice, 409–10
"regularly constituted courts" and, 409
and the rule of law, 385–89
state sovereignty and, 388–91
Trial Chamber, 173, 176, 201, 404
Trial Chamber II, 390–91
UN Security Council deferring cases to, 273
war crimes and, 293
International Criminal Tribunal for the former Yugoslavia (ICTY), 250, 305
Appeals Chamber, 170–73, 201, 400
"effective control" test, 399–401
international humanitarian law (IHL)/law of armed conflict, 3
equality and, 145–48 (*see also* equality)
jus in bello vs. *jus ad bellum*, 144, 145, 176
norms of, 152
International Law Commission Articles on State Responsibility. *See* Draft Articles on the Responsibility of States for Internationally Wrongful Acts
international tribunals and rebel courts, 199, 385–88. *See also specific courts*
Invasion of Kuwait, 72
Iraq, 420, 444–45. *See also* Islamic State
"green line" between KRI and the rest of, 374
1991 uprisings in, 374

Iraqi Code of Criminal Procedure, 379–81
Iraqi Constitution. *See* Federal Constitution of Iraq
Iraqi federal judiciary, 376–77
Iraqi Kurdistan, 142, 214–15, 285, 314, 377. *See also* KRG; Kurdish Region of Iraq
Iraqi Penal Code, 260, 381
Irish National League, 195
irregular armed groups (irregulars). *See* rebels
Islamic courts, 108. *See also Sharī'a* courts; Taliban courts
  Binnish, 446
  Timbuktu Islamic Court, 312, 314
Islamic laws of war, 113–14, 136. *See also layeha*
Islamic State (ISIL/ISIS/Da'esh)
  Bureau of Justice and Grievances, 107–8
  corruption and, 108–9, 112n76, 117
  FARC and, 82–84
  French Islamic State members, 286–87, 417, 431
  hadith and, 110, 112
  human rights violations, 296–97
  Islamic State governance, 105–7
  Kurdish Regional Government (KRG) and, 271, 286, 402, 443n403, 448, 450
  origins, 103–4
  overview, 103
  and the rule of law, 57
  Sharī'a and, 105–10, 261, 278, 315, 345
  sources of norms for, 115
Islamic State justice, 107–18. *See also* Islamic State
  courts, 82, 217, 261
  executions, 17, 109–11, 115, 269
  judges, 116
  a penchant for paperwork, 103–18
Israeli military courts, 328, 331
Israeli-occupied territories. *See* Palestinian territories
Italian–US Conciliation Commission, 92, 93

Jaffna, Sri Lanka, 222–24, 230, 242. *See also Thesawalamai*
Jaffna Peninsula, 225, 227, 229, 242, 263, 279. *See also Thesawalamai*
Jazeera Canton, 371
judges, 83n249, 455. *See also* faceless judges; LTTE courts; Taliban judges
  Afghan, 133
  direct targeting of, 335–37
  executions of, 115
  faceless, 334–35
  FARC, 50–51
  gacaca, 186, 214, 313
  KRG, 378, 383
  "mobile," 194 (*see also* mobile courts)
  as oracles of the law, 184–88
Judicial Power Law of 2007 (KRG), 377, 382
Judiciary Act of 1861 (Confederacy), 436
Judiciary Council, 362, 446
juges sans frontière, 194
Juntas Acción Comunal (JAC), 37–38
  comités de conciliación (conciliation committees), 37, 50, 54
  FARC and, 37–38, 42, 48, 50, 52, 53
jurisdiction
  nature of, 253–54
  personal jurisdiction of armed groups, 281–88
  of rebel courts, 248–49 (*see also* subject-matter jurisdiction of armed groups)
    idea of rebel jurisdiction, 250–52
    territorial jurisdiction of armed groups, 253–57
  state sovereignty and, 91, 249, 250–51, 340, 389–91, 394
jurispathic function of courts, 14
jus ad bellum, 144–45, 258, 440
  vs. *jus in bello*, 72, 92, 144, 145, 176
jus in bello (conduct of war). *See* international humanitarian law (IHL)/law of armed conflict; *jus ad bellum*
Justice and Grievances, Bureau of, 107–8
Justice and Peace Law of Colombia, 34
justicia revolucionaria, 40

Kabul, Afghanistan
  prisons, 419
  Taliban in, 119–22, 126, 127
Kälin, Walter, 433n363
Kalyvas, Stathis N., 4, 20
Karen National Liberation Army (KNLA), 194, 417–18, 447
Karen National Union (KNU), 417–18, 447
Katanga, Prosecutor v, 390–91
Kato mountain, 363
Katsieris, Paul, 193
KCK (Koma Ciwakên Kürdistan)
  Executive Committee, 358–59
  formation, 358
  governance, 358, 359, 362
  overview, 358–64, 367
  PKK and, 261, 358–64, 367
KCK Charter, 261, 358, 361–63, 367–68
KCK justice, 364. *See also* KCK
  challenges to the implementation of, 364
  courts, 363, 364

Kemp, Gerhard, 97
Kennedy, Anthony, 198, 199
kidnapping, FARC's practice of, 32, 33
Kilinochchi, Sri Lanka, 229, 230, 235, 239
Kilinochchi District Court, 235
Kirkuk, Iraq
  Battle of Kirkuk (2017), 375, 376, 420
  Northern Iraq offensive (June 2014) and, 376
  oil-rich region in and around, 375–76, 420
KJB (Koma Jînên Bilind), 362
Kleffner, Jann K., 392, 393, 397
Koma Ciwakên Kürdistan. *See* KCK
Koma Jînên Bilind (KJB), 362
Kongra Gele Kurdistan (Kongra Gel), 359, 362
Koskenniemi, Martti, 87
Kovács, Péter, 386–87
Kreß, Claus, 344
KRG (Kurdish Regional Government), 271, 278, 344, 373–85
  Constitution of Iraq and, 380, 384, 420
  courts, 286, 352, 377, 378–84, 402, 411, 447–48
  Iraqi government and, 374, 384, 402, 448
  Islamic State and, 271, 286, 402, 443n403, 448, 450
  judges, 378, 383
  Kurdish Region of Iraq (KRI) and, 261, 285, 373–77
  oil produced by, 419–20
  overview and nature of, 374
KRG Shura Council, 380–81
KRI. *See* Kurdish Region of Iraq
Kunarac, Prosecutor v, 171–72
Kurdish counter-terrorism law, 380
Kurdish Judicial Council, 377
Kurdish non-state courts, 356. *See also* KCK; KRG: courts; PKK
  PYD/YPG, 364–73
Kurdish Region of Iraq (KRI), 285, 373–74, 379–80, 402. *See also* Iraqi Kurdistan
  Constitution of Iraq and, 375–78, 402
  courts, 261, 314, 376–79
  history, 374
  Iraqi government and, 374, 384, 402, 448
  Islamic State and, 374, 448
  Kurdish Regional Government (KRG) and, 260, 284, 285, 373–77
  legal status under Iraqi law, 375–76, 379, 382, 384, 402
  oil production and, 375, 376, 420
  overview and nature of, 373–74
  political parties and, 382
  politics, 374–75
Kurdish Regional Government. *See* KRG
Kurdistan Integrity Commission, 384
Kurdistan Workers' Party. *See* PKK
Kuwait, invasion of, 72
Kyoto tribunal, 422

La Violencia, 31, 32
La Violencia (Colombia), 53
Laghman Province, Afghanistan, 130, 212
land disputes, 247
Lauterpacht, Hersch, 266, 426
law. *See also* rule of law
  concept of, 188–92
    limits to our conception of law, 12
  as contingent, 12
  as decentralised, 12
  as deliberative, 12
  as a semi-autonomous social field, 13
  and the state, 60, 61
  types of, 363
Law of Administration for the State of Iraq for the Transitional Period, 375
law of armed conflict. *See* international humanitarian law (IHL)/law of armed conflict; *layeha*
Law of War Manual (US Defense Department), 75, 181
laws of war. *See* international humanitarian law (IHL)/law of armed conflict; Islamic laws of war; *layeha*
lawyers (and the legal profession)
  as architects of social structures, 455
  as sinful, 111
layeha (Taliban manual of rules/laws of warfare), 135–36, 139, 213, 269
  forced confessions and, 349
  implementation, 136
  nature of, 133n223, 135–36, 349
Leeb, Wilhelm Ritter von. *See High Command Case*
legal formalism, 23. *See also* formalism
legality, principle of. *See nullum crimen sine lege*
Legg, Andrew, 70
Lévi-Strauss, Claude, 19
liberated area (*zonas liberadas*), 37
Liberation Tigers of Tamil Eelam. *See* LTTE
Libyan National Army (LNA), 387–88
local empowerment justice, 41, 42
Lord's Resistance Army (LRA), 80, 406, 408
Lotus Case, The, 251, 252
LTTE (Liberation Tigers of Tamil Eelam)
  cadres, 223, 225, 231, 232, 236, 239, 245–46, 314
  civil administration, 26, 225*f*, 225–26, 232

governance, 224–27, 225*f*
legislation
Act No 4 for the Protection of Tamil Eelam Children (Children Protection Act), 243–44, 255, 277
Code of Civil Procedure, 237, 242, 278
Code of Criminal Procedure, 237, 242, 263–64, 278
Penal Code, 263–64, 278, 345, 346
"legislative branch"/secretariat, 241–42
origins and revolution, 220–24
LTTE courts. *See also* civil cases: LTTE and
Court of Appeals, 231, 233–35, 238
District Courts, 231, 233–35, 238
High Courts, 233–35, 238
judges, 233*f*, 234–39, 245–46, 256
as "kangaroo courts," 193, 228
Special Court, 233–35, 238
LTTE justice system, 227–28
applicable law, 241–44
assessment of, 245–48
evolution, 229–32
executions and, 235, 247, 263, 265
judicial process, 237–38
legal practice, 239–41
reasons it is difficult to understand, 227–28
structure, 229, 233*f*, 233–37
Luban, David, 96
Lubanga Dyilo, Prosecutor v, 391

M-19 rebel group, 41
Macdonald, Roderick ("Rod") A., 85, 304, 353
Magna Carta, 248
Mahdi, Ahmad al-Faqi al-, 175n385
Malabo Protocol, 285, 395
Article 46H, 395
Mampilly, Zachariah Cherian, 5, 227, 230, 256
Manual de convivencia ciudadana, 48, 264, 278, 280, 346
Mapuche Case (*Leaders of the Mapuche Indigenous People v Chile*), 351–52
margin of appreciation, doctrine of, 69–70
objections to, 70–71
Márquez, Iván, 34
Marulanda Vélez, Manuel ("Tirofijo"), 34, 35
Massoud, Mark Fathi, 57–58
mato oput, 186, 406
Merry, Sally Engle, 16, 354
Military Commissions Act of 2006 (United States), 198
Military Commissions Act of 2009 (United States), 198–99
Mitrovic v. Serbia, 430
MLC (*Mouvement de libération du Congo*), 83, 158, 165, 207, 312
mobile courts, 130, 140, 194, 444, 448
"Moldavian Republic of Transdniestria," 202, 400, 429, 442. *See also Ilascu v. Moldova and Russia*
monism, 11
Moore, Sally Falk, 13
Morocco and the Polisario Front, 75, 143, 421–22
Mosul, Iraq, 16, 108, 323, 330, 334, 445
Mouvement de libération du Congo (MLC), 83, 158, 165, 207, 312
Movement for a Democratic Society (TEV-DEM), 364
Muerte a secuestradores (Death to Kidnappers), 33
mujahedin, 269, 349
Munaf v. Romania, 432–33
Murray, Daragh, 268

Nagorno-Karabakh Republic, 344, 413, 414
"Namibia principle," 413–14, 425
national liberation, wars of, 143
National Liberation Army. *See Ejército de Liberación Nacional*; ELN
nations, law of, 145, 440
natural judge, right to the, 211
Nazi war crimes, 181–82
ne bis in idem (double jeopardy), 338–41
gacaca and, 186
International Criminal Court (ICC) and, 252n206, 396–98
Rome Statute and, 390, 396–98
scope of, 252n206
Nepalese Civil War, 281
Ngudjojo Chui, Prosecutor v, 390–91
Nicaragua v United States, 399, 424
Nigeria, 161, 189–90
9/11 terrorist attacks, 63, 197
"NM Cherry Blossom" case, 421
non-derogable rights, 67, 318, 334, 347–48. *See also* derogability
treaties and, 298–301, 317, 318, 333–34, 338, 341, 344
non-derogable standard, principle of legality as a, 343–44
non-refoulement principle, 431
non-state actors. *See* rebels
non-state armed groups. *See* rebels
North East Secretariat on Human Rights (NESOHR), LTTE, 232
Charter, 244

Northern Cyprus, 414, 423, 443. *See also Cyprus v Turkey*
Northern Iraq offensive (June 2014), 376
Nouwen, Sarah M. H., 19, 410
Nsereko, Daniel, 406
Ntaganda, Prosecutor v, 173, 176
nullum crimen sine lege (principle of legality), 274, 298, 299, 340, 345
  interpretation of, 261
  overview and nature of, 342–46
  and the rule of law, 81, 188, 342–43
  violations of the, 346, 383
Nuremberg trials, 182
Nuri, Shah Jahan, 137–38
Nusra Front, 446

occupation, military
  belligerent, 257, 258, 443, 448
  evolution of the concept of, 74–76
  Eyal Benvenisti on, 71, 258
  fiduciary dimension, 72
  as hostile relations, 71–76
  law of, 71–75, 257–58
  nature of, 71–73
  sovereignty and, 71–72
  "transformative occupation," 73, 259
Occupation of Iraq (2003–2011), 72, 73
Official Language Act No. 33 of 1956 (Sinhala Only Act), 220–21
Oil and Gas Law of the Kurdistan Region, 420
oil production
  Kurdish Region of Iraq (KRI) and, 375, 376, 420
  by Kurdish Regional Government (KRG), 419–20
oil revenues, 104, 375, 419–20
Olson, Mancur, 8
Omar, Mullah Mohammad, 120, 133
O'Neill, Onora, 96–97, 273
ONUSAL (UN Mission in El Salvador), 184, 191
Ospina, William, 455

pacta sunt servanda, 250
Palestinian territories, 74, 158, 303, 328, 331, 394, 426
  Rome Statute and, 394
Pararajasingham, 235
Partiya Karkerên Kurdistan (Kurdistan Workers' Party). *See* PKK
Partiya Yekîtiya Demokrat (Democratic Union Party). *See* PYD
Pashtuns, 133, 138. *See also* Taliban
Patriotic Union of Kurdistan (PUK), 374, 375
Patriotic Union/*Union Patriotica* (Colombia), 32
Peace and Consensus Committees, 368–69
Penal Code of Sri Lanka, 263
Penal Code of Tamileelam, 263, 265. *See also* Tamil Eelam Penal Code
People's Congress of Kurdistan/Kongra-Gel (KGK), 359, 362
People's Protection Units. *See* YPG
PKK (Partiya Karkerên Kurdistan), 21, 90, 159, 261, 356
  codes of conduct, 360
  courts, 360, 361, 363, 384
    Supreme Court of Justice, 352
  executions and, 361
  KCK and, 261, 358–64, 367
  KCK Charter and, 361, 363
  overview, 357–64
  PYD and, 367
  Rojava and, 367
  Syria and, 367
  as terrorist organisation, 367
  in Turkey, 356–59, 361, 363n41, 407, 428
  Turkey and, 367
  United States and, 367, 428
Plan Colombia, 33, 42
Plattner, Denise, 102
pluralisation, 14, 410
pluralism, legal, 11–16, 183, 304, 307n413
  centralism and, 11, 12, 62
  interlegality and, 13–14
  positivism and, 11–13, 62
  rebel courts and, 454
Polisario Front, 144, 421, 422
  characterizations of, 394–95
  Geneva Conventions and, 75, 143, 155, 291
  Morocco and, 75, 143, 421–22
polygamy, 254, 371, 380
portable courts, 193, 302
positive law (*qawanīn wad'īyya*), 93, 155, 162, 429–30, 432, 433, 441, 442
  Geneva Conventions and, 289, 291
  and independence as non-interference, 312, 313
  Islamic State and, 57, 111
  jihadist critique of, 111n67
positivism, 11–13, 62
postmodern view of law, 13
power, 8
Prabhakaran, Velupillai, 245
  criminal punishments and, 235
  death, 224

judges and, 234, 246
law college and, 239
legislation, applicable law, and, 241–42
powers, 224, 234, 235, 242, 245, 246
Tamil youth and, 222, 223
prescriptivism, 11
Prevention of Terrorism Act (Sri Lanka), 350
prisoners of war (POWs)
Geneva Conventions and, 168, 209, 290, 303, 321, 324, 328, 332, 341–42, 350–51, 369, 419
Islamic State and, 114
transferred to another state, 419
YPG and, 369
proletarian-military, 43
prosecutorial discretion, 407–8
Protocol I. *See* Additional Protocol I
Protocol II. *See* Additional Protocol II
public life, 175
public order, 175
PYD (Partiya Yekîtiya Demokrat), 364–67, 371–73
armed wing, 365
courts, 370–73, 403, 416, 417
declared a subnational autonomous region, 403
France and, 416–17, 431–33
Islamic State prisoners detained by, 369–70
KCK and, 367
origin, 367
persecution of political opponents, 372
PKK and, 367
Rojava and, 90, 364–67, 369–70, 403
state penal code applied by, 260
Syrian regime, Assad administration, and, 366, 370
as terrorist organisation, 367
PYD justice system
shortcomings and due process violations, 372–73
Social Contract and, 367–69, 371–73

Qamishli courts, 369, 371
Qandil Mountains, 357, 359
qawanīn wad'iyya. *See* positive law
Quetta, Pakistan, 123, 127
Quirin, Ex Parte, 197
Qur'an, 110–11, 115, 132. *See also hudūd* crimes

Raible, Lea, 8
Ranger, Terence ("Terry"), 279
rape, 174
FARC and, 40, 41, 54, 56
LTTE and, 229, 247, 349–50
punishments for, 2, 56, 189, 247 (*see also under* sexual assault)
executions, 78, 115n104, 229, 235
rape convictions, 2, 189, 288
ratione materia of rebel jurisdiction, 263, 264, 270–72, 274, 281
ratione personae of rebel jurisdiction, 272, 282–84, 286–88
rayonnement, 354, 355, 412, 414, 419. *See also* PKK
Raz, Joseph, 59, 84
rebel court recognition
international recognition in ICC and beyond, 409–15
national recognition by the territorial state, 433–45
transnational recognition by third states, 414–15
legal parameters of recognition by third states, 424–33
third state recognition of rebel justice, 415–24
transversal recognition by other armed opposition groups, 445–50
rebel courts. *See also specific topics*
constitution of, 180–215 (*see also* "regularly constituted courts")
countries with, 2
idea of, 3
legality under international law, 140–41
categories of conflicts and equality of belligerents, 141–49
rebel courts in legal context, 149–50
focus on crimes and a nexus with the conflict, 167–80
a spectrum of obligations, 150–51
command responsibility, 164–67
duty for rebels to administer justice, 153–54
duty to prosecute war crimes, 154–56
a prohibition for rebels to administer justice, 151–53
respect and ensure respect of international humanitarian law, 156–59
respect and secure human rights, 159–64
a right for rebels to administer justice, 153
rebel governance and insurgent rule, 4–11. *See also specific topics*
rebel governance literature, 9, 10–11, 19–20
rebel justice and sovereignty, 86–89
basis of state jurisdiction, 89–94
exercise of jurisdiction by others than the territorial state, 95–99

rebel rule of law, 56–57. *See also* fragmented rule of law; rule of law
elements of a, 76
broader system of governance, 77–80
minimal fairness, 82–84
narrative of social justice, 84–86
stability and predictability, 81–82
rebel territory, the fluid nature of, 254
rebelocracy vs. aliocracy, 8
rebels. *See also specific topics*
talking to, 16–24
terminology and synonyms for, 24
reconciliation. *See mato oput*
Red Cross. *See* International Committee of the Red Cross
"regularly constituted courts," 195, 215–17. *See also* court(s)
aim of the requirement of, 291–92
courts established by law in human rights law, 200–202
in humanitarian law, 195–200
and judicial guarantees of independence and impartiality, 202–3, 207, 216, 310–11
fairness as rightness, 203–6
institutional requirements of independence and impartiality, 206–15
religion, state, 221
reprisals, 181
Republic of Serbian Krajina, 431
restorative justice model, 55
retaliatory justice, 41–42
Revkin, Mara, 111–12nn73–77
Revolutionary Armed Forces of Colombia. *See* FARC
revolutionary court-martial (*consejo revolucionario de guerra*), 44. *See also* courts-martial
Revolutionary United Front. *See RUF Trial*
Rhodesia, 435
Rojava, Syria, 286–87, 363–65, 369–71, 373, 403–4
France and, 416, 417n301, 432
KCK and, 367
PKK and, 367
PYD and, 90, 364–67, 369–70, 403
YPG in, 180, 277, 286, 364
Rojava courts, 370, 371, 373
civil, 368
Rome Statute of ICC
Article 1, 390, 391
Article 8(2)(c)(iv), 204–7, 409
Article 17(1), 186, 305, 386–88, 390–97, 399, 401–4
Article 20(3), 396–98, 404
Article 20(3)(b), 397, 404, 407–8
Article 25, 342
Article 28, 165, 201, 282
Article 53, 407–9
complementarity and, 186, 306–7, 354, 385, 392, 395, 396, 398, 401, 404, 406, 407, 426
Elements of Crimes under, 204, 206, 216, 322
Common Article 3 and, 204, 206, 309–10, 322
"regularly constituted courts" and, 96, 204, 216
ne bis in idem (double jeopardy) and, 390, 396–98
"regularly constituted courts" and, 204, 206, 291
state sovereignty and, 388, 390–92, 394
Roosevelt, Franklin D., 182, 197
RUF Trial (*Prosecutor v Sesay, Kallon and Gbao*), 74, 85n256, 173n377
rule of law, 84, 85. *See also* rebel rule of law
in armed conflict, 66 (*see also* margin of appreciation)
human rights (*see* derogation)
humanitarian law (*see* occupation)
assumptions underlying the modern concept of, 60
fragmented, 12, 57–66
International Criminal Court (ICC) and, 385–89
nature of, 57–58
nullum crimen sine lege (principle of legality) and, 81, 188, 342–43
reasons for the rhetorical popularity of, 57–58
state sovereignty and, 10–11, 29, 60, 71–73, 76, 86–88, 101, 102, 257–58, 303, 389
"thick" version of the, 58, 59, 76, 303
"thin" version of the, 58–60, 76, 82
Russia, 401, 422. *See also Ilascu v. Moldova and Russia*; South Ossetia
European Court of Human Rights and, 400
International Criminal Court (ICC) and, 386, 401
South Ossetia and, 386, 393, 401, 411
Rutledge, Wiley Blount, Jr., 197, 199
Rwanda, 405
Rwanda courts, 306. *See also gacaca* courts
Rwanda v. Nteziryayo, 306, 405–6
Rwandan genocide, 313, 405
Rwandan Patriotic Front, 75, 85

Saharawi Arab Democratic Republic, 395, 421, 422
Sakhanh, Haisam Omar, 1, 186–88, 416, 453
  death penalty executed by, 2, 186, 189, 272, 287, 317, 328, 344, 355, 356, 415, 416, 430
  life history and overview, 1–2
  trial in Sweden (*Prosecutor v Omar Haisam Sakhanh*), 2, 102, 153, 189, 191–92, 261, 272, 288, 340, 352, 415
    defence (functional immunity), 287, 409, 415, 430
Salò Republic, 92–94
Salvadoran Civil War, 144, 191, 334
  FMLN and, 144, 191, 271–72, 325
Santos, Boaventura de Sousa, 13
sapos (government spies/informants), 41, 55, 266
Schabas, William ("Bill") A., 175n385, 393, 398
Schaeffer, Matthew, 96
Second Eelam War (Sri Lanka), 223–24
self-determination, 87
  right to, 74, 279n306, 421, 422
self-incrimination, 347–50
Senegal, 95, 97
SERAC v. Nigeria, 161
Serbia, 399, 430, 431
sex crimes, 272, 280. *See also* rape
  punishments for, 263, 272, 361
  trials, 238 (*see also under* child sexual abuse)
sexual assault. *See also* rape
  punishment for, 46
sexual slavery, 174
Sharīʿa, 185, 261, 329. *See also* Unified Arab Code
  fiqh and, 110n64, 112n77
  forced confessions and, 349
  governance and, 112
  hadith and, 132
  interpretations of, 132, 139, 261
  Islamic State (ISIS) and, 105–10, 261, 278, 315, 345
  Kabul and, 122, 127
  Taliban and, 122, 129–30, 132, 134, 136–39, 315, 345, 349
  Taliban judges and, 120, 128, 129–30, 132, 329
  writing down the rules of, 111n73
Sharīʿa Council, 109
Sharīʿa courts, 112n77, 115, 124, 129–30, 137, 261, 327, 446. *See also* Taliban courts: *Sharīʿa* and
Sharīʿa punishments, 134, 136, 345
  executions, 109–10, 115, 134
Shi'ites and the Taliban, 138–39
Shura Council (Islamic State), 105, 108
Shura (Consultative) Council (KRG), 380–81
Shuras, 123n151
Sierra Leone, Special Court for, 74, 85
Silva, Sarath N., 228, 434
Sinhala language, 220–21, 238
Sinhala nationalism, 220, 221
Sinhala Only Act (Official Language Act, Sri Lanka), 220–21
Sinhalese, 220–23, 246
Sivakumaran, Sandesh, 54n130, 76, 193, 322
Slaughter, Anne-Marie, 15
social contract, 9, 90, 106, 107
Social Contract (Rojava), 90, 365–68, 371–73
Soering v United Kingdom, 282, 305, 431
Somaliland, 285
Somer, Jonathan, 193, 205, 269
South African courts, 421, 422
South Ossetia, 386, 387, 401
  Russia and, 386, 393, 401, 411
sovereign equality of states, 145, 149
sovereignty. *See* state sovereignty
Soviet occupation of Afghanistan, 119
Soviet POWs in Afghanistan, 418–19
Soviet Union (USSR), 422, 423
Spain, 94, 435
Spanish Civil War, 94
Special Court for Sierra Leone, 74, 85
spies. *See also* espionage
  executions of, 139, 265–68
Sprott v. United States, 437
Sri Lanka Penal Code, 263
Sri Lankan Civil War, 220, 228
  ending, 227–28, 247
Sri Lankan Constitution of 1972. *See also* Constitution of Sri Lanka
  and Tamil political separatism, 221
Staniland, Paul, 5
state (with jurisdiction), what constitutes a, 292, 393, 395, 399
state sovereignty, 90, 99, 159, 164, 329
  Colombia and, 87
  concept of, 71, 87, 111, 251, 454
  defining, 71, 87
  doctrine of, 86
  effectivité and, 94
  insurgent justice and, 152, 208, 214, 268, 270–71, 273–74, 424, 444, 453–55 (*see also* rebel justice and sovereignty)
  International Criminal Court (ICC) and, 388–91
  Islamic State and, 105, 111

state sovereignty (*cont.*)
- judges and, 187
- jurisdiction and, 91, 249, 250–51, 340, 389–91, 394
- limited vs. full, 6
- occupation and, 29, 71–73, 257–58, 268
- overview and nature of, 86–88, 152
- principle of, 152
- Rome Statute and, 388, 390–92, 394
- rule of law and, 10–11, 29, 60, 71–73, 76, 86–88, 101, 102, 257–58, 303, 389
- state authority detached from, 175
- war and, 174

Stigen, Jo, 391
Stockholm District Court, 415. *See also* Sakhanh, Haisam Omar
- *Sakhanh* and, 2, 102, 153, 186, 189, 191, 340, 352

subject-matter jurisdiction of armed groups, 257–59. *See also* civil law jurisdiction
- criminal law jurisdiction, 260
  - applicable law, 260–64
  - crimes against international law, 271–74
  - treason and participation in the conflict, 264–71

subpoena, powers of, 130, 330
summary executions, 41, 168, 181, 182, 201n496, 266, 269, 286, 361. *See also* executions
summary justice, 41, 129, 140, 168, 361
Supreme Constitutional Court of Syria, 367–69
Supreme Court of Justice (KCK), 362, 363
Supreme Court of Justice (PKK), 352
Supreme Court of Justice of Colombia, 434–35
Supreme Court of Tamil Eelam ("Special Bench"), 233–35, 238, 352
Svea Court of Appeal (Sweden), 2, 153
Sweden, Ahorugeze v., 306
Swedish courts, 288, 415–16. *See also* Sakhanh, Haisam Omar
Swenson, Geoffrey, 65
Swiss courts, 422
Swiss government, 419
Swiss law, 371
Switzerland, 143, 418
Syrian civil war, 416, 450. *See also* Free Syrian Army
- civil uprising phase, 366
- Islamic State and, 414

Syrian Penal Code, 2, 260, 272, 344

Tadic, Prosecutor v, 75, 170, 201, 399, 400
Taiwan, 386, 393, 394
Taliban
- history, 118–20
- manual of rules/laws of warfare (*see layeha*)
- origins, 119–20
- overview and nature of, 118–19
- *Sharī'a* and, 122, 315, 345, 349

Taliban Commission for Prevention of Civilians Casualties and Complaints, 137
Taliban courts, 123–34, 136–40, 335
- appeals, 128–30
- civil cases, 125, 129, 132
- *Sharī'a* and, 124, 127, 129–30, 132, 134, 136–39, 261
- violence and, 151

Taliban judges, 126, 130, 194, 215, 278, 314
- cases/workload, 132
- dangers facing and measures taken to protect, 335–37
- ethnicity, discrimination, and, 138–39
- monitoring of, 135
- punishments assigned by, 134 (*see also* executions: by Taliban; *Sharī'a* punishments)
- qualifications, 120–21
- reference documents consulted by, 132–33, 329
- salaries, 128
- *Sharī'a* and, 120, 128, 129–30, 132, 329
- US strategy of targeting, 335–37

Taliban justice, 123–40. *See also* Taliban courts; Taliban judges
Taliban motorcycle justice, 118–21
- Taliban shadow governance post-2001, 122–23

Tamanaha, Brian Z., 183
Tamil Eelam Civil Code, 242–43
Tamil Eelam Criminal Procedure Act 14 of 2004, 255
Tamil Eelam Law College, 184, 236, 239–40
- curriculum, 240, 240*t*

Tamil Eelam legislation, 242
Tamil Eelam Liberation Organization, 222
Tamil Eelam Penal Code, 242, 247, 265
Tamil Eelam Secretariat, 225
Tamil Eelam State, 226
Tamil Tigers. *See* LTTE
Tamil United Liberation Front, 221–22
Tamileelam Child Protection Act 2006. *See* Act for the Protection of Tamil Eelam Children
Tehran Hostages case, 402
territorial control, 5, 8–9, 78–79, 216, 254
- nature of, 8–10
- terminology, 8

territorial jurisdiction of armed groups, 253–57. *See also* jurisdiction: of rebel courts
territorial permanence, 79
territory
  concept of, 78
  governance preceding the capture of, 79
terrorism, 3, 4, 6, 369–70, 428–29. *See also* anti-terrorism
TEV-DEM (Movement for a Democratic Society, Syria), 364
Thailand, 417, 418
Thamilchelvam, S.P., 226, 245
Thesawalamai, 242–43, 279–80
Thimpu Principles, 223
Third Eelam War (Sri Lanka), 224
Third Geneva Convention, 209
  Article 1, 442
  Article 105, 321, 324, 328, 332
  Article 125, 393
Thorington v Smith, 440n387
Tigers. *See* LTTE
Timbuktu, 177, 178
Timbuktu Islamic Court, 312, 314
torture
  European Court of Human Rights and, 431
  evidence and confessions obtained under, 347–48, 383
  in Islamic State, 17, 114–18, 349
  in Kurdistan, 372, 383
  LTTE and, 349–50
  prohibitions against, 136, 347–48
"transformative occupation" (military occupation), 73, 259
travaux préparatoires, 190, 203, 249, 295, 298–99
treason, 263–65, 269, 437, 438. *See also* espionage
Trechsel, Stefan, 309
trial/judgment *in absentia*, 45, 329, 397
Turkey, 252, 361–63, 365–67. *See also* European Court of Human Rights
  courts in, 356, 361, 384
  KCK in, 358, 359, 362, 367
  PKK in, 356–59, 361, 363n41, 407, 428 (*see also* PKK)
Turkish Republic of Northern Cyprus, 414, 423, 443. *See also Cyprus v Turkey*

Uganda, 80, 406, 408
UNAMA (UN Assistance Mission in Afghanistan), 151–52
Unified Arab Code, 261, 446–47
Union Patriotica/Patriotic Union (Colombia), 32
unitary state law, 363
United Judicial Council (Syria), 446
United Kalavryta (oil tanker), 419–20
United Kingdom (UK), 190–91, 196–97, 285, 286, 431. *See also* Britain; Divisional Court of England and Wales; English common law; *Soering v United Kingdom*
  House of Lords, 94, 185
United Nations (UN), 64
  Articles on State Responsibility, 98, 292, 399–403
  Basic Principles on the Independence of the Judiciary, 310
  Charter, 424
  Committee Against Torture, 348
  Convention on the Rights of Persons with Disabilities, 277
  Mission in El Salvador (ONUSAL), 184, 191
United Nations Assistance Mission in Afghanistan (UNAMA), 151–52
United Nations Development Programme (UNDP), 66
United Nations Human Rights Council (UNHRC), 114
United Nations Security Council (UNSC), 63, 65, 201, 273
United Self-Defense Forces of Colombia. *See Autodefensas unidas de Colombia*
United States Constitution, 93n303
United States Department of Defense Law of War Manual, The, 75, 181
United States District Courts, 436. *See also* Confederate District Courts
United States Supreme Court, 197–99, 437–41. *See also specific cases*
Universal Declaration of Human Rights (UDHR), 244, 365, 368
University of Jaffna, 236, 239

Vaddukoddai Resolution, 221–22
Vanni, Sri Lanka, 226, 239
Velasquez Rodriguez v Honduras, 163, 277
vigilance committees (LTTE), 229, 232
vigilantism, 88, 90, 205
Violencia, La (Colombia), 31, 32, 53

war crimes, 292–93. *See also under* World War II
  Nazi, 181–82
  prosecution of, 154–56, 283
wathīqat al-madīnah, 106–7

Wellman, Christopher Heath, 389n199
Werner, Wouter G., 410
Western Sahara, 394, 421, 422
  Polisario Front and, 143, 144, 421 (*see also* Polisario Front)
Westphalian sovereignty. *See* state sovereignty
White, Texas v., 439
Wickham-Crowley, Timothy, 35
Willms, Jan, 397
women
  equality for, 148, 236, 366
  legislation and the status of, 243, 366, 368, 371
  Taliban justice and, 139
Women's Communal-Confederal Community system (Koma Jînên Bilind-KJB, KCK), 362
Women's Protection Unit (YPJ), 365
World War II, 142
  aftermath of, 92, 168
  collective punishment imposed by belligerents during, 343
  crimes committed during, 168, 181–82, 196–97, 292–93, 345
  executions and, 142, 168, 181–82
  human rights law and, 292–93, 345, 346
  resistance courts, 142
Worrall, James, 86

Yamashita, In Re, 197–99
Yazidis, crimes against the, 271, 381, 402
Yeager v. Iran, 99
YPG (People's Protection Units, Syria), 180, 356, 365, 399
  French government and, 431–32
  Islamic State and, 286, 365
  prisoners of war and, 369
  in Rojava, 180, 277, 286, 364
  Rules of Procedure, 369
  Syrian government and, 366
  Syrian law applied by, 277

zonas liberadas (liberated areas), 37